# the ONION®

# DISPATCHES FROM THE TENTH CIRCLE

## THE BEST OF THE ONION

EDITED BY
Robert Siegel

WRITTEN BY
Robert Siegel, Todd Hanson, Carol Kolb,
John Krewson, Maria Schneider, Tim Harrod,
Scott Dikkers, Mike Loew, Joe Garden, Chris Karwowski

GRAPHICS BY
Mike Loew
Chad Nackers

DESIGNED BY
Andrew Welyczko

ADDITIONAL MATERIAL BY
Dave Sherman, Kurt Luchs, David Javerbaum,
Peter Koechley, Ben Wikler, Josh Greenman,
Ian Dallas, Stu Wade

COPY EDITOR
Stephen Thompson

MADE POSSIBLE BY
Peter Haise

SPECIAL THANKS
Ken Artis, Christine Carlson, Chris Cranmer,
Rich Dahm, Daniel Greenberg, Roy Jaruk, Bob Koechley,
Bob Mecoy, David Miner, Michael O'Brien, Keith Phipps,
Nathan Rabin, Jack Szwergold, Scott Templeton,
Maggie Thompson, Dan Vebber, The State Of Wisconsin

THREE RIVERS PRESS • NEW YORK

PHOTO CREDITS

p. 3, Yeltsin; Jocks; e-Bay; p. 7, Couple; Shoppers; Gambler; p. 8, Reverend; p. 15, Lesbians; Cigarettes; p.17, Ping-Pong; p. 19, Window; p. 20, Eater; p. 23, Bra; p. 31, Alcoholic; p. 34, Nebraskan; p. 35, Pasta; p. 36, Children; p. 37, Tip; p. 39, Book; Southerners; C-SPAN; Ant Farm; p. 41, Ant Carcasses; Larry Groznic; p. 43, Flag; Lottery; Manager; p. 44, Unflushed Toilet; p. 47, Syrup; Toy; p. 51, Asshole; p. 53, Zach Spence; p. 55, Painting; Viewer; Video Tape; Porn Buyer; p. 56, Bread; p. 58, CNN Tapes; Dumpster; p. 59, Top; Responsibilityuns; Clintons; p. 63, VCR; Magazine; Turnbee Body; p. 63-64, Shy Senator; p. 65, Grad Student; p. 69, McDonald's; p. 70, Lyle Kelso; p. 71, Fan; p. 79, Wine; p. 80, Retro; p. 81, Starbucks; p. 89, Swiffer; p. 90, Homemaker; p. 95, Applebee's; p. 102, Rabbit; p. 103, Wads; Pizza Hut; Car; p. 104, Wad Leaders; p. 107, Vending Machine; Smoking Room; Records; p. 110, Violence; Profanity; Adult Situation; Teen; p. 111, Comic; Turtle Owner; p. 112, Turtle Time; p. 115, Jim Beam and Aspirin; Robot Mouse; p. 116, Truck; p. 118, Don Grella; p. 119, Computer; p. 120, Gen-Xer; p. 122, Kitsch; p. 127, Tree; Break-Up; p. 128, Presentation; p. 129, Clerk; Store; p. 130, Party; p. 131, Bucket; p. 134, Celebrity; p. 135, Manager; p. 139, Hair Salon; p. 142, Sick Man; Barry Ploegel; p. 144, Computer; Bert Limbec; p. 145, Garbage; p. 146, Driver; p. 147, Littlest Senator; Stylist; p. 149, Controller; Employee; p. 152, Chips; p. 153, Employee and Award; p. 155, Fetish Man; Video-Game Character; p. 156, Billy Joel Fan; p. 157, Amber Richardson; p. 159, Banana; Graphic Designer; Terrorist; p. 160, Kills Time; p. 161, Ass; p. 163, Fans Wait; Puppet; Room; Chairman; p. 166, Anne-Marie Krebs; p. 167, House Party; p. 170, Taco Bell Employee: Chad Nackers/Onion Photos. p. 3, Clinton: Desmond Boylan/Reuters. p. 4, Columbine: Gary Caskey/Reuters. p. 9, Brando: Archive Photos. p. 11, Celebrities: Fred Prouser/Reuters. p. 14, Doritos; p. 24, Bottle; p. 27, 18-Year-Old; Barnes & Noble; p. 51, Prince Bumbo; Soda; p. 59, Citizens; p. 61, Soda; p. 67, Freshmen; p. 87, Little Debbie; p. 123, NRA: Sam Chung/Onion Photos. p. 17, Golf Club and Chair: PR Newswire Photo Service. p.19, Town: Wisconsin Tourism Board. p.19, Killing: All Over Press/Newsmakers (Getty). p. 19, Chocolate Chart; p. 22, ATF/FDA Chart; p. 26, Tantric Drawings; p. 50, Manga Mash; p. 59, Expanded Inferno; p. 67, Hamburger Help; p. 83, Collage; p. 87, Da Bomb Map; p. 127, Imagined Rampage; p. 152, Genetic Sequence; p. 167, Mr. Monopoly; p. 169, Endocrine System: Mike Loew/Onion Graphics. p. 20, Lawyers: Robert King/Newsmakers (Getty). p. 20, Man; p. 23 and 25, Christ's Head; p. 71, Shoes; p. 75, Christ's Head; p. 94, Yogurt Man; p. 99, Performance Artist; p. 113, Steve Schwantes; p. 144, Vicki Helmholz; p. 163, Guy: Mike Loew/Onion Photos. p. 21, Crypty: Chad Nackers/Onion Graphics. p. 23, Podium: Stephen Jaffe/AFP. p. 26, Tantric Couple: Denise Thompson/Onion Photos. p. 27, Accident: Bill Greenblatt/UPI. p. 27, Jamboree; p. 143, Genie: Maria Schneider/Onion Graphics. p. 31, Parkway: Mark Gibson/Index Stock Imagery. p. 33, Marilyn Manson: Margaret Grey/ZUMA. p. 34, Marilyn Manson: Chris Martinez/Reuters. p. 35, Car: Vasil Donev/AFP. p. 37, Bush: Joseph L. Murphy/UPI Photos. p. 42, America's Funniest Home Videos: ABC Photos. p. 43, Pope: Gary Hershorn/Reuters. p. 43, Ambassador; p. 123, Snack Cracker; p. 155, Lawyer: Julie Chambers/Onion Photos. p. 45, Breasts: Brian Ebner/Onion Photos. p. 46, Kathie Lee Gifford: Newsmakers. p. 47, Ferguson: HO/Reuters. p. 51, Larry King: Pool/Danny Field/AFP. p. 51, Stadium: Ray Stubblebine/Reuters. p. 54, Nobody; Cool Guy; p. 107, Exoskeleton: Chris Comello/Onion Photos. p. 55, Voters; p. 116, Gore: Luke Frazza/AFP. p. 55, Yngwie Malmsteen: Michael Spitzer. p. 57, Madonna: Chris Weeks/Liaison (Getty). p. 59, Tornado: Hector Mata/AFP. p. 63, Pauly Shore: ZUMA Press. p. 63-64, Turnbee's Head; p. 105, Turnbee: Mike Wise/Onion Photos. p. 63, Rally: Shaun Best/Reuters. p. 64, Reporters: Jack Kurtz/UPI. p. 71, James Meredith: Archive Photos. p. 75, Will Smith: Rouse Prouser/Reuters. p. 75, Beekeeper: Louis Davilla/Digital Press Photos. p. 79, Toll Booth: Dan Loew/Onion Photos. p. 87, George Clinton: Jean Paul Aussenard/Magma. p. 93, Woman: Christine Carlson/Onion Photos. p. 100, Character Sheet: Robert Siegel/Onion Graphics. p. 101, Lava Lamp: David Harrison/Index Stock Imagery. p. 103, Johnny Cash: Rick Wilking/Reuters. p. 111, Alec Baldwin: Chris Delmas/ZUMA. p. 113, Rocky Horror: 20th Century Fox/ZUMA. p. 115, Cruise and Kidman: UPI. p. 117, Cruise and Kidman: La Presse/Piovanoti (Getty). p. 119, Protesters: Kim Kulish/AFP. p. 119, Fruit Of Islam: AFP. p. 124, Kid Rock: Brenda Chase/Getty. p. 127, Susan Sarandon: Roger Lemoyne/Getty. p. 131, Ted Danson: Antonio Capelli/Magma. p. 132, Peru: Shirley Vanderbilt/Index Stock Imagery. p. 132, Ted Danson's Head: Beitia Archives. p. 135, Sexy Mom: Carol Kolb/Onion Photos. p. 140, Sting: Cornelious Poppel/Reuters. p. 141, Doonesbury Cartoon: Todd Hanson/Onion Graphics. p. 143, House Of Blues: Sue Ogrocki/Reuters. p. 143, Thurmond: Win McNamee/Reuters. p. 151, NFL Players: Joe Giza/Reuters. p. 152, Ambulance: Steven E. Frischling/Getty. p. 155, Parliament: AFP. p. 157, Gramm: Robert Giroux/Getty. p. 158, Giuliani: Jeff Christensen/Reuters. p. 159, Mansion: AFP. p. 159, Kissinger: Mark Cowan/UPI. p. 159, Women: Jason Kirk/Liaison (Getty). p. 163, Jeff: Jeffrey P. Worthen/Wal-Mart Photos. p. 167, SUV: jch/HO-Ford/Reuters. p. 167, Peter Jennings: ABC Photos. p. 170, Gen. Henry Shelton: Larry Downing/Reuters. p. 171, Arafat and Netanyahu: Housien Housien/Reuters. p. 171, Consumers: Jack Kurtz/UPI.

*This book uses invented names in all stories, except notable public figures who are the subjects of satire. Any other use of real names is accidental and coincidental.*

Published by Three Rivers Press, New York, New York.
Member of the Crown Publishing Group.

Random House, Inc.  New York, Toronto, London, Sydney, Auckland
www.randomhouse.com

THREE RIVERS PRESS and Tugboat design are registered trademarks of Random House, Inc.

Printed in the United States of America

Design by The Onion

Library of Congress Cataloging-in-Publication Data is available upon request.

ISBN 0-609-80834-6

10 9 8 7 6 5 4

First Edition

# An Introduction

By T. Herman Zweibel,
Publisher Emeritus
(photo circa 1911)

Any collection that contains the greatest news-writing of the epoch should be approached with humility, gravity, and not a little awe. How-ever, having built *The Onion* news-paper up from a mere market-gazette into the finest source of printed news-matter in our Republic, I have no illusions concerning the so-called romance of journalism. The collection you are holding is a sham, a fraud, and a waste of your hard-earned money. This material was intended to sell advertising space when it first ran, and now that it has served its purpose and is no longer relevant, you lot have paid for something that was initially free!

But this collection also fills my coffers with money, so I cannot object too strenuously to its printing. It also illustrates a point I often tried to make in my Publisher's Address columns in *The Onion* news-paper: I cannot believe the use-less things upon which you rabble will spend your precious few coppers! Wax-cylinder-recordings of the minstrel-men who sing while dressed like Negroes. Postcards of the French persuasion illustrated with daguerreotypes of ladies who are, against all common decency, from France. The medical quackery that is Mr. Salk's so-called "polio vaccine." I suppose, all things being equal, that you could do worse than to spend your meager funds on the journalistic pearls writ herein.

Which brings to mind a question often posed to me: Why do I permit people to be taught to read? After all, being a news-paper-man, I am in a better position than most to observe the results of wide-spread literacy, and I long ago concluded that letting the man on the street know what is going on in the world does far more harm than good. Is it wise to work the commoners into a lather by making them literate? Many still living remember how close this continent came to bloody, flaming destruction just a few years past, when it seemed that every brick-layer and ditch-digger would learn letters and ciphers at the iron-shod feet of that fulminating sow Laura Ingalls Wilder. Only the extreme measures of blinding her sister and putting her house to the torch were finally enough to stop that mad-woman's crusade.

Yet the damage had been done, and publishers such as myself were forced to re-work our papers. What were once organs of information serving the ruling elite now cater to a public that seems to think itself possessed of a right to know the day-to-day goings-on of the world. Thankfully, however, no matter how strenuously these squealing puddings demand to be informed, their actual desire to be informed is as slight as ever. Ruth-less plutocrats such as myself have slept much easier since deducing that the average citizen will not stir an inch to remove his rectum from the ream, so long as he is provided with sporting-pages, Sunday funnies, and gigantic, quivering bosoms somewhere above the front-page fold.

Yes, I once repented me of my news-paper-man's trade. But now, with more printed matter around than ever, I realize that my repentance was as silly and point-less as repentance always is. Now, knowing full well the common-man's taste for minstrelsy and penny-dreadful dramas, I do not fear to place the gems of daily reportage into general circulation. Instead, I took a lesson from the Mother church: By deluging you, the reader, with all manner of conflicting tripe along with a few small grains of truth, I have distracted you into settling for a much more worth-less and hope-less world than you might otherwise. This, of course, pays great dividends, as it seems to cause you to run about stabbing and looting and raping and burning, making my paper more enjoyable and exciting to read, which in turn increases sales to those like yourself.

Therefore, you will be proud to learn, you are partially responsible for what you will find in these pages as you rediscover the manifold joys and horrors of *Onion* issues past. Not so responsible as am I, of course, because you are but sheep and I a stone-hearted millionaire and, yes, a great employer of shepherds.

Now leave me alone!

*J.H. Zweibel*

## Yeltsin Forcibly Ejected From Detroit-Area Check-Cashing Service

see WORLD page 3C

## Local News Anchor Happy As Hell, Going To Take It For Long, Long Time

see MEDIA page 3B

## The American Dream: What Does The Part About Kissing The Gym Teacher Mean?

see NATION page 4A

## Deaf Child Watches From Lawn As City Puts Up 'Deaf Child' Sign

see LOCAL page 2B

### STATshot
A look at the numbers that shape your world.

**Least Sacred Holy Days**
- Feast Of Louie Anderson
- St. Hallmark's Day
- Pentecostcutters
- Some Soul's Day
- Feast Of The Impala Conception
- All Taints' Day
- Palm-Slapping Sunday
- Sacrament Daze
- Yeaster

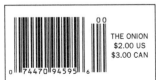

THE ONION
$2.00 US
$3.00 CAN

---

# the ONION

WWW.THEONION.COM     AMERICA'S FINEST NEWS SOURCE™     FOUNDED 1871

# Columbine Jocks Safely Resume Bullying

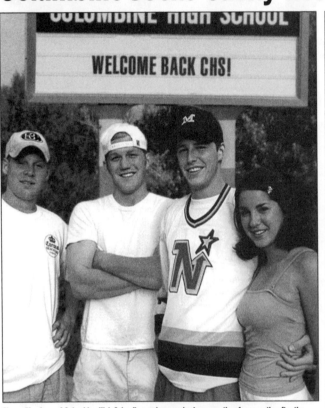

Above: Members of Columbine High School's popular crowd, who, more than four months after the tragic shooting at their school, have finally begun to exclude again.

LITTLETON, CO—On April 20, when two students at Columbine High School opened fire in a brutal shooting spree that left 12 classmates and a teacher dead, many feared that this affluent suburban school would never be the same.

But now, more than four months after a tragedy that shook the nation to its core and marked the most notorious incident of school violence in U.S. history, the atmosphere is optimistic.

Slowly but surely, life at Columbine is returning to normal.

Thanks to stern new security measures, a militarized school environment, and a massive public-relations effort designed to obscure all memory of the murderous event, members of Columbine's popular crowd are finally safe to reassert their social dominance and resume their proud, longstanding tradition of excluding those
see COLUMBINE page 4

## Clinton Meets With Guy With Tie

Above: Clinton smiles and shakes hands with an important guy wearing a tie.

WASHINGTON, DC—In a historic summit with profound, far-reaching implications for the nation at large, President Clinton met with a guy in a tie Monday, shaking the man's hand firmly while projecting a warm yet determined countenance.

Standing confidently before reporters and various dignitaries in a White House meeting room equipped with a podium and prominently displayed American flag, the two men greeted each other, exchanged polite small talk, and waved cordially to the assembled press.

The guy, presumably an important and distinguished person of one sort or another, waited quietly during introductory remarks made by other
see GUY page 5

## Man With Complete *Mama's Family* Video Library Never Going On eBay Drunk Again

NEWTON, MA—In a solemn pledge to himself and the world, Kevin Wollersheim, the new owner of a complete *Mama's Family* video library, announced Monday that he will "never, ever again" visit eBay while inebriated.

"Over the course of Saturday evening, I drank two

Jack and Cokes, somewhere in the vicinity of eight Icehouse beers, and, I believe, at least one shot of Cuervo 1800 tequila," Wollersheim said at a press conference in his apartment. "And, although I now have no memory of doing so, it is clear that I logged
see EBAY page 4

Above: Wollersheim and a portion of his recent purchase. Inset: Vicki Lawrence as TV's Mother Harper.

3

who do not fit in.

"We have begun the long road to healing," said varsity-football starting halfback Jason LeClaire, 17, a popular senior who on Aug. 16 returned to the school for the first time since the shooting. "We're bouncing back, more committed than ever to ostracizing those who are different."

Added LeClaire's girlfriend, cheerleader Kellie Nelson: "A school where the jocks cannot freely exclude math geeks, drama fags, goths, and other inferiors without fearing for their lives is not the kind of school I want to go to."

The resilient attitude displayed by LeClaire and Nelson speaks volumes about Columbine administrators' commitment to making the school a safe place for members of the popular cliques. Last spring, the nation watched in horror on live television as terror-stricken students fled the school, running with their hands above their heads, flanked by SWAT teams. But when Columbine reopened its doors on Aug. 16, a spirit of boosterism, school pride, and unquestioning conformity once again prevailed, as the elite jock crowd "took back the school" as its own.

On Sept. 6, amid a pep-rally atmosphere of marching-band fanfare, cheerleaders, and mass chanting, a group of jocks wearing T-shirts bearing the slogan "We, Not You, Are Columbine" were escorted by armed guards into the school for the first day of the new semester. Approximately one hour later, the rest of the student body was allowed into the building through a side door.

"It's almost as if a helpful 'big brother' is watching us now," homecoming queen Lori Nowell said. "None of the losers can mess with us. Now that the entire school is blanketed by surveillance equipment, the popular kids, like, totally rule the school!"

"It's gonna be a great year," best friend Jessica Wohlpert added with a high-five.

As the school year begins under the watchful eye of 24-hour electronic monitoring and police protection, a sense of normalcy has returned to Columbine. Just as at any other school, the computer geeks are mocked, the economically disadvantaged kids are barely acknowledged, and the chess-club, yearbook, and debate-team members are universally reviled. While these traditions are nothing new, from now on they will be much easier to preserve, thanks to the high-tech, draconian security measures that now dominate Columbine life.

Prior to the April shootings, it was thought that Columbine's unpopular students were under control. After all, geeks such as Dylan Klebold and Eric Harris, the "Trenchcoat Mafia" members responsible for the killings, had been persecuted for years as a matter of policy. But according to vice-principal Dr. Frederick Mondrian, the tragedy made Columbine administra-

tors realize that not nearly enough had been done to enforce adherence to the school's dominant social pecking order.

"We thought that the systematic cruelties inflicted on our school's desperate, alienated outcasts would be sufficient," Mondrian said. "Those kids were beaten up, pelted with rocks, and wholly rejected by their more popular peers, not only because they were smart and computer-literate, but also because of the way they dressed and the music they liked. But the shootings sent a clear message to this school and this community: We hadn't done nearly enough to keep such misfits shunned and in their place."

To rectify the problem, school authorities consulted with top ostracization experts and developed a comprehensive jock-safety plan. Cameras were installed on school grounds, enabling authorities to more closely monitor the activities of all students for suspiciously nonconformist behavior and modes of dress. All entrances to the school are now locked and accessible only by intercom or specially coded key card, preventing the sort of open, comfortable learning environment that might encourage students to express themselves. The soothing presence of armed patrols, coupled with high fences surrounding the grounds, reassures jocks that they can feel free to torment the school's geeks as they had done before April 20, without fear of reprisal.

In addition to these changes, school authorities have brought in special fashion consultants, who are lending their time and expertise to help educators identify "at-risk" clothing and hair. Students seen wearing "red-flag" items such as thick eyeliner, long coats, tattoos, Marilyn Manson T-shirts, non-designer jeans, and the color black are now required to attend special makeover sessions with a trained psychiatric professional who will assess the student's potential for nonconformist behavior before, if necessary, outfitting him or her in Tommy Hilfiger jeans, Gap T-shirts, and Abercrombie & Fitch baseball caps with curved brims, on penalty of expulsion.

The beefed-up security measures have done wonders to restore the self-esteem of Columbine's jocks, who say they have never felt safer shunning, berating, belittling, and picking on those who are different from themselves. And the jocks are doing their part to keep the untouchables in line, doubling the number of swirlies, noogies, and wedgies doled out to Columbine's outcasts since last year.

Happily, the efforts to protect Columbine's jocks seem to be working. In fact, schools across the country have begun to pick up on the Columbine model, with many districts imposing measures even more stern than those at Columbine. These include mandatory dress codes, transparent book bags subject to random search, metal detectors, electronic

Above: An armed police officer stands guard over a group of Columbine cheerleaders.

handprint-identification systems, and automatic expulsion of anyone who goes out of his or her way to "separate themselves socially" or "break the status quo."

Meanwhile, here at Columbine, the popular kids say they just want to get on with their privileged lives. As cheerleader Tammi Brandon put it at a recent pep rally: "Go, Rebels!"

School authorities stressed that the remark merely referred to the name of the Columbine football team and was not intended to be taken literally. ∅

onto America Online and accessed eBay sometime before 2:28 a.m. Sunday."

"During my visit to eBay," Wollersheim continued, his voice beginning to break, "for some reason known only to God, I entered a bid of $300 in an auction for the entire episode run of the popular '80s situation comedy *Mama's Family*, starring Vicki Lawrence and Ken Berry."

"I won that auction," he added gravely.

The final sale price for the 44-tape set was $279.50, with shipping charges raising the total amount spent by the 33-year-old elementary-school teacher to $301.67. Wollersheim, who said he is "partway through the first episode," also received a copy of the 1981 made-for-TV movie *Eunice*.

"I was understandably stunned by my own actions on that fateful night," Wollersheim said, "yet I was bound by honor to pay in full for the tapes, if only to preserve my positive feedback rating."

Wollersheim has attempted to reconstruct the mental process which led to his excessively generous bid for item #114258855.

"I remember always liking that sketch where Tim Conway makes Harvey Korman crack up talking about the 'Siamese elephants,'" he said. "But that was on *The Carol Burnett Show*, before *Mama's Family* was ever a series. Maybe I was so drunk I didn't remember that, though."

Continued Wollersheim: "Or maybe it was because Debra Dunning, this girl I went to high school with, used to watch *Mama's Family*, and my 15-year reunion is coming up, so I somehow thought I'd impress her if I had

every episode. But Debra's married, so that doesn't make sense, either."

Though Wollersheim has been known to regret eBay purchases in the past, including a $65.50 "autographed" Carl Yastrzemski lithograph (which turned out to bear a reproduced signa-

## Wollersheim, who said he is "partway through the first episode," also received a copy of the 1981 made-for-TV movie *Eunice*.

ture) and a Japanese import Steely Dan CD that "ended up being just a bunch of weird remixes," his recent acquisition is by far the most puzzling.

"Do you think I was so drunk that someone could have broken into my house, started up my computer, and bid without me knowing it? No, that can't be. They wouldn't have had my password," said Wollersheim, whose money order for $301.67 was received Sunday by seller "bluebird27." "Did I mean to type in a bid of $30 and enter $300 by accident? But what would have made me bid even $30?"

Whatever the motivation for the purchase, Wollersheim said a love of the program was not a factor.

"I hardly even remember the show," Wollersheim said. "I recall that Mama was a contestant on *Family Feud* once, and... that's it. I remember the *Family Feud* episode."

"Christ," he added, "I can't believe they made 130 goddamn episodes of that show. How many years is that? I'm gonna need a new cabinet." ∅

# New Children's Hospital Filled To Capacity

## Owner Overjoyed By Success Of Just-Opened Business

ATLANTA—When Andrew Nash decided to abandon a successful career in land development to pursue his lifelong dream of owning his own children's hospital, he hoped the venture would be successful.

But he never dreamed it would be this successful.

Open just two weeks, Nash Children's Hospital in downtown Atlanta is already proving to be a big hit, its 635 beds fully occupied and its emergency room boasting waits of up to seven hours.

"I was hoping this place would do well, but this is beyond what I could have possibly imagined," said Nash, surveying the bustle in the hospital's nephrology ward. "Just look at the rows upon rows of kids hooked up to *my* dialysis machines. It's absolutely phenomenal."

"It's just so exciting," Nash said. "Every day I come in to the hospital, there are more and more kids. We've barely got enough IV drips for all of them."

Business only got better yesterday, when an 18-wheeler slammed into a school bus at a busy Atlanta intersection. In all, 31 children had to be hos-

Andrew Nash is thrilled with the popularity of his new children's hospital (above).

pitalized with injuries ranging from broken clavicles to massive brain contusions.

"As soon as I heard about that bus crash, I called up my wife, and we went out to dinner to celebrate," Nash said. "It's still hard to believe how well things are going."

So popular is the new hospital that

patients are flocking to it from all over the Southeast. Last Friday, an eight-year-old boy from Shreveport, LA, checked in for a bone-marrow transplant, a $153,000 procedure.

"That's a lot of money," Nash said, "but people really seem to love this place. I just hope they keep coming back." ∅

## Binge-Drinking, Promiscuous Sex Good For You, Says *New Orleans Journal Of Medicine*

NEW ORLEANS—According to a report published in the September issue of the *New Orleans Journal Of Medicine*, a number of habits long believed detrimental to one's health—including binge-drinking and unprotected sex with multiple partners—may actually prolong and enrich one's life. "Massive intake of alcohol instills a deep sense of happiness, which is essential to longevity," the report stated. Random sex with a variety of partners is likewise encouraged: "Exhaustive field research throughout New Orleans indicates that coupling with as many people as possible is a very good thing," the study read. Other behavior endorsed by the renowned medical journal includes eating excessive amounts of rich, spicy food; inhaling nitrous oxide; and screaming "Whoo!" as loudly as possible in public. To aid the early detection of breast cancer, the study also strongly recommended that all women between the ages of 18 and 45 annually expose their breasts to cheering crowds. ∅

GUY from page 3

guys with ties.

"It is my pleasure to welcome my esteemed colleague to the White House today," Clinton said. "And I'd like to thank him for taking the time to address this key issue facing America as it stands on the verge of a new millennium."

After being formally greeted by a smiling Clinton, the tie guy, who had arrived at the White House several minutes earlier in a big, fancy car, smiled back, furrowing his eyebrows at times to convey determination and seriousness of purpose, yet always maintaining a friendly demeanor.

Clinton was also wearing a tie.

"Thank you, Mr. President," the guy in the tie said. "I very much look forward to our discussion and am confident it will prove fruitful."

The president and the guy in the tie then retired to a large, stately room somewhere else in the White House, where they spoke to each other in earnest, modulated tones.

According to those who witnessed the four seconds of footage from the event which was edited into nightly newscasts, the guy with the tie is some kind of visiting dignitary, businessman, expert, or government official or something.

Though it is not known at this time exactly what the two tie-wearing men discussed during their meeting, it is believed the topic may have been fiscal policy, tariffs, or international law, or possibly even human rights, taxes,

budgets, treaties, or social programs of some kind. It is known, however, that the meeting was very important and therefore necessitated the wearing of ties.

The incident marked the 194th meeting between Clinton and a guy with a tie in the last week, and the 82,876th such meeting since the start of his administration. Clinton has met with 795,526 tie-wearing men over the course of his political career, all of them important. This latest meeting comes on the heels of Monday's important meeting between Clinton and a guy with a tie and crown, and last week's equally important meeting with a guy in a turban, one of the few times Clinton has met with an important person who was not wearing a tie.

"Clinton and a guy in a tie? I think I saw that on television," said D.C.-area tavern owner Jim Blakely. "Clinton was meeting some guy, and they shook hands and, if memory serves me correct, I think they expressed mutual admiration and shared optimism about the future. They showed a brief clip of it, but I had the sound off in the bar because the jukebox was on, so I didn't hear what it was about."

"They walked across the White House lawn," Blakely added, "and then Clinton waved confidently and got into a limo. Or maybe it was a helicopter and a thumbs-up. I forget which one it was. Hard to say, really."

In addition to ties, the two men had very expensive suits, fancy watches, gold tie clips, shiny cufflinks, and well-polished shoes, as well as nice, expensive pens in their breast pockets. Clinton's visitor also had an important-looking leather attaché case, which sources said complemented

### The incident marked the 194th meeting between Clinton and a guy with a tie in the last week.

and accentuated the imposing-yet-elegant effect created by his tie.

While talking, Clinton and the guy with the tie sat on classy armchairs in a fancy sitting room furnished with expensive carpeting and antique oaken furniture, as well as numerous valuable decorative items, such as paintings, baubles, and various tokens of appreciation from foreign heads of state.

There was also reportedly some sort of coffee-table-type thing between them, upon which they were likely able to set things down. Among the objects believed to have been placed on the table are the presumably very important pieces of paper from inside the briefcase of the tie-wearing man.

During the historic meeting, the

chairs were most likely angled together slightly so that the president and the guy in the tie could face each other yet still have plenty of freedom of movement and leg room. It is also believed that coffee and other refreshments were served—or, if not, at least available if requested.

Upon the conclusion of the closed-door, two-tie conference, Clinton paused to meet with his tie-clad advisors before leaving the White House to address a roomful of other people wearing ties in Maryland.

The guy with the tie, who characterized the talks with Clinton as "very promising," also departed, acknowledging cameramen with a brief, perfunctory hand-wave/head-tilt gesture while getting into a car with other tie-wearers.

"These two people definitely met with each other. And whatever the man with the tie said was, in some respect at least, extremely significant," said CNN White House analyst Jonathan Heiler. "It must have been, or it wouldn't have been important enough to necessitate a meeting with the president himself. Everything he does is, as near as we can tell, very significant and noteworthy. Just how noteworthy this will prove to be in the long run, well, it's still just too soon to tell."

"But it's definitely important," Heiler added.

Of the two men's ties, it is believed that Clinton's was slightly fancier. ∅

# That Teen-Abstinence Rally Totally Rocked!

**By Brian "Bri" Knoepke**
**Abstinent Teen**

Wow, what a weekend! They say part of being a teenager is knowing how to cut loose, and there's nothing quite like getting together with a big group of your peers and just "letting it rip." That teen-abstinence rally totally rocked!

We'd been looking forward to the rally for weeks, so when the big day finally arrived, we could scarcely contain ourselves. Chaperoned by our Christian Outreach adult supervisor, me and a bunch of my pals drove all the way down to Hendersonville in the Springdale Youth Ministry van. (A two-hour drive! We sang songs the whole way!) People came from all over the mid-state area, so you can imagine how pumped everyone was to get the rally started. And when Pastor Bob finally stepped to that podium and yelled, "Is everybody here excited about JEEEEEEEEEEE-SUS?" the place went totally nuts!

Some kids like to "party" and use "peer pressure" to get you to "do it." (Nobody's ever asked me to party with them, but if anyone ever did, I could see myself being tempted to go along.) Sure, it may sound like fun, but I've learned that sex is really just a "roadblock to holiness." There's only one real way to have a good time: Jesus! I realize that some teens may not consider praising God and resisting your body's sinful urges to be all that "rad," but boy, oh, boy, are they wrong!

After Pastor Bob got the crowd all revved up, he introduced the guest speaker. And guess who it was? Deborah White, Miss Teen Plovis County! Can you believe it? Wow, she sure was pretty. A girl like that could really make you want to glorify the Lord

> **Me and my Springdale Youth Ministry pals stayed out to 10 p.m. and didn't even get home until after midnight!**

within the confines of the holy matrimonial bed, if you know what I'm saying.

Deborah said that even though she, like everybody else, sometimes feels evil, demon-planted desires deep within her loins, she's keeping herself pure and waiting for marriage, the way God intended. Just looking at her, I thought to myself, "I can't wait to someday enjoy the special feeling that comes when a man and a woman decide to do God's work and have a baby!" She told us that if we were patient and waited until child-conceiving age before learning anything about sex, that would make it so much more special! Isn't that rad?

Everywhere today's teenagers turn, they're bombarded with sexually explicit material. Television channels like HBO show R-rated movies without even bleeping out the dirty words. Public libraries openly stock books like *Wifey* by Judy Blume. Magazines such as *Cosmopolitan* and *Harper's Bazaar* contain underwear ads featuring models in nothing more than their underwear!

Not surprisingly, like a lot of teens out there, I was confused about my body and the plans the Lord had for it. I was having strange new feelings as I went through changes I didn't understand. I thought the MTV videos and the bikini girls on beer commercials were "cool," and I'd often think, "Gee, I wish I were like those older fellas who 'hang out' at the roller rink and press their bodies against girls when they dance." Well, no more! The rally's organizer, Extreme Teen Ministries, Inc., made it clear that girls who "put out" and boys with "Roman" hands are most definitely not cool. Whether they know it or not, they're doing Satan's work on Earth. But, thanks to Jesus' love, Satan is totally history, dude! He's outta here!

What a rockin' rally! After Miss Teen Plovis County spoke, we all went to the Hendersonville Civic Arena for a concert by Creatorz Handz, this totally awesome heavy-metal band. There were cool explosions, just like on *WCW Nitro*, only these were in the service of Christ! Then, after the band was done, a bunch of local teens performed a cool skit! Some of the teens were angels and some devils, and they fought over the souls of two tempted teens who were almost going to kiss. Man, was the crowd roaring when the angels finally won! Yeah!

Then, just when we thought the fun was over, we all had pizza and pop! Me and my Springdale Youth Ministry pals stayed out to 10 p.m. and didn't even get home until after midnight! See? You don't need to touch another person's body—or your own—to have a rockin' good time!

I used to harbor sin in my heart, staying up late trying to watch the scrambled channels on our family's cable TV. But now I know that the desperate urges that grip my immortal soul's mortal vessel, causing me to think about Becky Lundegaard for hours on end while I'm supposed to be studying, are nothing to heed right now. The Lord put those feelings in me for a very beautiful reason: so that one day, when I'm 18, I can fall in love, get married, and—hot-diggety!—immediately impregnate my wife. Then, nine months after my 18th birthday, I can experience the joy of bringing into the world a child who will one day grow up to be part of a whole new generation of Christ-loving abstinent teens, to continue His divine work here in Springdale.

Let's get ready to rock, people! Jesus is in the house, and He is way awesome! *∅*

# Ask A Coffin Salesman

**By Walter G. Sluman**
**Coffin Salesman**

**Dear Coffin Salesman,**

My wife and I recently moved from Florida to Minnesota, where she was offered a much better job. Problem is, I can't stand the cold weather. Am I being petty, or is she being cruel by making us live here?
—**Miserable In Minneapolis**

**Dear Minneapolis,**

Please, sit down. I realize this is a time of tremendous sorrow for you, and I want you to know that I, too, grieve for the loss of your beloved. But the best thing you can do for him now is make sure that he spends eternity in the comfort and dignity he deserves. By purchasing the EternaRest 2000 model, you can see to it that the bed in which he will take his final, blissful rest is of the highest quality that money can buy. Just look at the fit and finish on this enameled mahogany Victorian Triumphal. Isn't your loved one worth the extra $700?

**Dear Coffin Salesman,**

My last boyfriend misses my dog Robby terribly, and he comes over to visit him all the time. It's really getting on my nerves! How do I tell him to give me and Robby some space?
—**Pooched Out In Plano**

**Dear Pooched,**

Don't think of this coffin as a mere container; think of it as the final resting place of someone you love very much. Someone worth the slight extra expense of solid-brass fittings and deep red velvet plush. Someone worth fine hand-craftsmanship. And you'll be more comfortable knowing that if you go with the Arizona Windsor, her precious head will be cradled on a lovely, double-stitched silk pillow for all eternity.

**Dear Coffin Salesman,**

Over the past few years, I've outgrown my old friends, and I don't know where to meet new people. I hate the bar scene, don't attend church, and can't stand the thought of hanging out with my coworkers. Do I have any options left? Sign me...
—**Frustrated In Fresno**

**Dear Fresno,**

Sure, you could buy the Elysian Fielder. It's a fine casket. But I have to be honest with you: It lets in moisture. Is that the kind of eternal slumber you'd want for your beloved husband of 48 years? If I were you, I'd go with the Wallingford DuraLux, which features all-hardwood detailing and hermetic rubber gasketry. You'll rest easy

knowing he's resting peacefully and undisturbed.

**Dear Coffin Salesman,**

I'm a 34-year-old woman who's still looking for that special guy. My best friend swears by video dating, and my mother says singles cruises are good, but they both sound gimmicky and more than a little desperate. Am I justified, or am I being closed-minded?
—**Lonely In Lawrence**

**Dear Lonely,**

Look, if you just want to satisfy the letter of the law, there are several models that are adequate for holding the body's liquors once the process of putrefaction sets in. We usually only sell them to the city for burying the homeless and the unclaimed deceased, but I suppose I could sell you one. I won't feel right about it, and I suspect it won't sit well with your conscience, either, but that's between you, God, and your poor loved one. At least you'll keep her out of the ~~groundwater.~~

---

*Walter G. Sluman is a syndicated advice columnist whose weekly column, Ask A Coffin Salesman, appears in more than 250 newspapers nationwide. ∅*

**STATshot**

A look at the numbers that shape your world.

**Good-Time Eateries**
What are America's largest family-fun restaurant chains?

1. T.G.I. Fried
2. J.P. McPickleshitter's
3. Hupert K. Stickyfloors' Peppermint Parlor
4. Uncle Knuckles' Olde-Tyme Pork Haüs
5. Luigi McClanahan Von Leningrad Standing Horse's Omni-Ethnic Sub Pub

---

## Area Girlfriend Still Hasn't Seen *Apocalypse Now*

AZUSA, CA—In a discovery prompting exasperated forehead-slapping and stunned expressions of incredulity, Mark Tillich learned Thursday that girlfriend Brandi Jensen has never seen *Apocalypse Now.*

"You gotta be kiddin' me, Bran!" said Tillich, 21, a senior English major at

Azusa Pacific University, upon discovering Jensen's ignorance of the 1979 Francis Ford Coppola-directed Vietnam War epic. "It's only, like, ar-

see APOCALYPSE NOW page 9

**Right: Mark Tillich and Brandi Jensen, who, unbelievably, has never seen *Apocalypse Now,* "one of the greatest films of all time."**

---

# U.S. Populace Lurches Methodically Through The Motions For Yet Another Day

## Transgendered Sea Anemone Denounced As 'Abomination' By Clergy

HUNTSVILLE, AL—A coalition of Baptist clergymen spoke out Thursday against the Telia felina, a transgendered sea anemone they are decrying as "base and depraved."

"This filthy anemone, which exhibits both male and female characteristics, is turning our oceans' intertidal zones into dens of sin and perversion," said Rev. William Chester, spokesman for the Save Our Seas Coalition, a Huntsville-based organization dedicated to "the preservation of aquatic decency and morality." "For God knows how long, this twisted sea creature has been running rampant in our oceans, spreading its unnatural, bisexual lifestyle. And it's high time somebody took a stand."

The controversial anemone, common to warm-water reefs and basins worldwide, has been practicing its al-

**Above: The dually gendered Telia felina sea anemone, which Baptist leaders are denouncing as "base and depraved."**

ternative sexual lifestyle at least as far back as 1859, when Charles Darwin first catalogued its phylum and species. Since then, more than 40 sub-

see ANEMONE page 8

**SPECIAL REPORT**

The wall-eyed, slack-jawed U.S. populace, beaten down to a state of near-catatonia by the relentlessly deadening banality of their joyless, insipid lives, dutifully trudged through the motions for yet another emotionally blank day Thursday.

Against all logic, the nation's citizens, their insides withering away with each passing moment, somehow managed to continue filling out invoices, shopping for footwear, loading dishwashers, eating Whoppers, pressing buttons, watching reality-based TV programs, vacuuming floors, engaging in conversations about petty office politics, riding buses, sitting in traffic, mailing letters, and tending to the little rubber mats people wipe their feet on as they enter the lobby areas of vast, windowless industrial complexes. How they were able to do it, no one can say.

The populace's continued participation in the meaningless charade that

see POPULACE page 8

# INFOGRAPHIC

## Military-Recruiting Woes

The U.S. military is facing a major personnel crisis, with recruitment and retention rates plunging in all branches. What is the military doing to draw enlistees?

- Offering shinier medals
- Lowering reading-skills requirement to third-grade level
- Bringing back popular arch-enemy "Hitler"™
- Having drill sergeants gently rock enlistees to sleep in sinewy arms
- Replacing college-credit incentives with red-Camaro incentives
- Offering "Buy One, Get One Free" coupons good at all Filipino brothels
- Omitting phrase "immortal soul" from sign-up sheet
- Installing throbbing disco balls at all bases

Above: Rev. William Chester of the Save Our Seas Coalition.

ANEMONE from page 7

species of Telia felina have been identified as dually gendered.

The Baptist group also denounced the anemone's reproductive habits and family structure.

"Unlike so many respectable, God-fearing creatures, the Telia felina reproduces asexually, openly mocking traditional family values by giving birth to and raising its young in a single-parent setting," Chester said. "This anti-Christian anemone, which has the audacity to think that a child can grow up properly without the benefit of two loving parents, is truly the Murphy Brown of the deep."

Added Chester: "If you still doubt the pain and suffering wrought by this undersea abomination, just look into the eyes of a young anemone child forced to grow up wondering why Mommy and Daddy live in the same body. This, my friends, is not natural."

As part of its campaign against the invertebrate, Save Our Seas is calling upon Greenpeace and other environmental groups to cease their defense of endangered species that fail to uphold high moral standards. The group is also threatening a boycott of aquariums that display the Telia felina or any other creature of questionable character.

"Is this the kind of marine invertebrate we want our children to see on their school field trips to the aquarium?" Chester asked. "By putting this sort of filth on display in our nation's aquariums—aquariums that are often federally funded with our tax dollars—we send our children the message that the transsexual lifestyle is not only to be accepted, but encour-

aged."

"It is truly sad to see what could have been an upstanding Christian creature cross over to a life of depravity and abasement," Pastor Kenneth Boyle, director of the Loaves And Fishes Academy Of Christian Marine Biology, said of the Telia felina. "Just look at its flamboyant bright green and gold coloration. And its hundreds of effeminate tentacles, which sway back and forth temptingly in an effort to lure the spiritually weak. The Bible says that on the fifth day, God filled the oceans with living creatures. But surely this is not what He intended." ⌀

POPULACE from page 7

is their lives, sources said, was rendered all the more futile by the inescapable realization that they must do it again tomorrow, and the next day, and so on and so on unceasingly until the day they inevitably die.

"Hello, Tri-State Amalgamated Office Supply, a division of Global Tetrahedron International Unlimited, customer-service hotline, can you please hold?" said 37-year-old Sandy Lindemeyer of Garland, TX, barely summoning the strength to push the button activating her headset. The incident marked the 13,227th time she has uttered the pre-scripted greeting.

After hearing a heavy sigh on the other end of the line, followed by a barely audible reply of "Yes," Lindemeyer somehow found the will to press a second button, patching the person into a pre-recorded, continuous message loop telling the caller, Lindemeyer's 714th of the week, that his or her call was important to Tri-State Amalgamated Office Supply and would be answered by the next available customer-service representative.

Elsewhere, in the suburban wasteland of Schaumburg, IL, frigid housewife Marjorie Campion, 42, her face an impenetrable mask of detachment, drove her 1991 Toyota Camry through a seemingly endless sprawl of strip malls and convenience stores, eventually arriving at the bloated expanse known as Woodfield Mall, where she purchased a pair of shoes.

"This morning, as my husband and I stared blankly at each other's faces over breakfast, I mentioned that I saw an ad in the paper for a sale on ladies' footwear at Marshall Field's. He asked if I was planning to go, and I told him I guessed maybe," Campion said. "So after he dragged himself to work and I gazed at the wall for a few hours, I went to the sale."

Looking down at her feet, Campion added, "They're nice shoes, I suppose."

"Today is Wednesday," said Waltham, MA, resident Greg Pafko, 50, an actuary for a screen-door manufacturing company in nearby Plovis. "Wednesday is 'Hump Day.' If I can get through Hump Day, I'll have made it more than halfway through the week."

"Then again," Pafko added, "every day is Hump Day, really." An hour later, as he does every day, Pafko headed to the company bathroom and sat for 20 minutes with a loaded gun in his mouth. Once the shakes subsided, he removed the bullets from the gun and

returned to his desk.

According to experts, as American society slides ever downward into the swirling vortex of nothingness that saps our wills, numbs our hearts, and freezes our souls in an impenetrable layer of black, icy futility, the importance of going through the motions only grows.

"As James Joyce showed in his classic novel of modernity *Ulysses*, just making it through one day in this world constitutes a heroic achievement," Yale University English professor M. Clement Voorhees said. "God

> ## Pafko then headed to the company bathroom and sat for 20 minutes with a loaded gun in his mouth.

knows how unrewarding it is for us to endure each day's pointless, relentless barrage of non-events. I'm surprised we're able to do it at all. But continuing to go through the motions is crucial, because if everyone stopped faking, we'd..."

Voorhees then trailed off, remaining silent for several moments while rubbing his eyes. "I'm sorry," he said. "I forgot what I was going to say."

In a perfunctory attempt to acknowledge the nation's collective pyrrhic victory, President Clinton thanked and congratulated Americans for continuing to participate in the meaningless fictions that compose their daily existences.

"My fellow Americans," Clinton told a national television audience, "you have truly accomplished a great feat today. By continuing to get out of bed, wash yourselves, dress, work, shop, watch *COPS*, surf the Internet with WebTV, and put food into your bodies at regular intervals to sustain your metabolic functions, you have shown the world just how willing to live the American people can pretend to be."

Following the broadcast, the president endured several minutes of smiling handshakes before excusing himself to the Oval Office restroom, where he splashed water on his face, leaned on the sink, and stared unblinkingly into his weathered, exhausted reflection, wondering how he was going to face the next day. ⌀

## NEWS IN BRIEF

### William Safire Orders Two Whoppers Junior

NEW YORK—Stopping for lunch at a Manhattan Burger King, *New York Times* 'On Language' columnist William Safire ordered two "Whoppers Junior" Thursday. "Most Burger King patrons operate under the falla-

cious assumption that the plural is 'Whopper Juniors,'" Safire told a woman standing in line behind him. "This, of course, is a grievous grammatical blunder, akin to saying 'passerbys' or, worse yet, the dreaded 'attorney generals.'" Last week, Safire patronized a midtown Taco Bell, ordering "two Big Beef Burritos Supreme." ⌀

# *Access Hollywood* Producer Would Never Work For *Entertainment Tonight*

HOLLYWOOD, CA—Danielle Pierce, 33, an assistant producer at *Access Hollywood*, told a friend Thursday that she "could never and would never" work for *Entertainment Tonight*.

"Work for *ET*? No way. Never," Pierce told Liz Sharkey, a production assistant at Castle Rock Entertainment, over drinks at a Melrose Avenue bar. "Have you seen that show lately? They're so derivative over there. And slow. They didn't show a first look at the *Charlie's Angels* trailer until a week before the premiere. We hit air with it—and a bumper piece on Cameron's comic roles—10 days after ShoWest."

Scanning the bar in search of what she called "Extra Terrestrials," Pierce continued: "*ET* has no voice of its own. One minute, they're doing an E!-style fashion bit. The next, they're trying to be *Extra*. Our press kit says

we're brash, up-to-the-minute, and wholly unique—and it's true. We lead, *ET* follows. It shows in everything we do, from the exclusive on-set peek at M. Night Shyamalan's latest thriller to the report on Angelina Jolie's controversial Oscar dress, to our coverage of more difficult subjects like the rumored friction on the *Friends* set."

"Sure, *Access* doesn't pay as much as *ET*. But we don't have to," said Pierce, squeezing a lime slice into her margarita. "*People* know they've stalled and that the culture just isn't the same. I met an *ET* researcher at a party last month—slightly phony guy—and, anyway, it was clear he didn't believe in the job. It's much more of an assembly-line mentality over there: Just churn it out. And that's really not helped by having [Bob] Goen and [Mary] Hart at the desk. Bob's a poor man's John Tesh, and Mary, she couldn't say her name without a cue

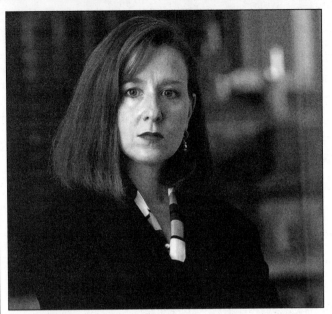

Above: *Access Hollywood* assistant producer Danielle Pierce.

card. [*Access Hollywood* anchor] Pat [O'Brien] is trusted and really knows his stuff. We could go live if we had to."

Pierce offered a specific example of what she believes to be *Entertainment Tonight*'s lack of "freshness,

savvy, and insight."

"I was watching their show last night, and they were doing a spot on the breakout new shows of the fall season—almost all of them were Paramount shows, of course. Shame-

see PRODUCER page 10

---

APOCALYPSE NOW from page 7

guably the most ambitious anti-war statement in American movie history. Jesus!"

"I cannot believe you've never seen *Apocalypse Now*," he added. "That's *insane*."

Tillich, who first saw the critically acclaimed film on HBO at age 14 while sleeping over at a friend's house, was particularly distressed by the fact that Jensen had not only never seen the film, but was unfamiliar with its basic premise.

"Hello? Joseph Conrad's *Heart Of Darkness* updated from 19th-century British imperialism in the Congo to a critique of 20th-century U.S. imperialism in Southeast Asia? Hello? Any of this ringing a bell?" Tillich said. "Come on, that's like saying you've never seen *Full Metal Jacket*."

When Jensen replied that she had never even heard of *Full Metal Jacket*, Tillich threw up his hands in an "I give up" gesture and stormed out of the room.

"It's not like I don't like movies," Jensen said. "I loved *Notting Hill*, and I'm totally psyched to see *Hanging Up*—I'm the biggest Meg Ryan fan. I even used to have a *When Harry Met Sally...* poster in my dorm room. And have you seen *My Best Friend's Wedding*? Julia Roberts and Cameron Diaz are so amazing in it. My all-time favorite, though, has got to be *Beaches*."

Tillich, Jensen said, was unimpressed.

"He called my movies overwrought, weepy chick dramas lacking in any genuine visceral impact,'" Jensen said. "Well, excuse me for living, Mr. Big

Above: Marlon Brando as Colonel Kurtz, a "mind-blowing" character with whom Jensen is unfamiliar.

Army Guns."

Tillich responded to his girlfriend's shocking *Apocalypse Now* revelation by making plans for her to see it that night, claiming that "to deny [her] the pleasure [she] would experience in viewing such a cinematic masterpiece for even one more second would be a crime."

Though Jensen declined, telling Tillich she had to study for a test, he persisted, trying to convey to her "the urgency of rectifying this situation as soon as possible."

"After class yesterday, I was hanging out with them, and he wouldn't shut up about it," said Melissa Ayler,

Jensen's best friend. "He was like, 'But it's got Robert Duvall's classic turn as the surfing-obsessed helicopter squad leader!' Then he started quoting all these lines from it, saying stuff like, 'Charlie don't surf,' and 'I love the smell of A-bombs in the morning.' At least I think that's what he said—I've never seen the stupid movie."

Tillich housemate Howie Fuller said that, while eating dinner with the couple and several of Jensen's friends, Tillich described in detail the film's famed climax, in which villagers hack an ox to pieces as The Doors' "The End" plays.

"Brandi was like, 'What's so appealing about an ox getting violently slaughtered? It really doesn't sound like something I'd enjoy, Mark.' And all the girls at the table were like, 'Yeah, that's gross,'" Fuller said. "But that just made him lose his shit even worse. He started screaming, 'You don't understand! The destruction of the ox parallels the destruction of Colonel Kurtz! Can't you see that?' It was sad."

According to Tillich, Jensen's failure to see *Apocalypse Now* is her worst cinematic transgression since October, when the couple was browsing a Blockbuster video store and she pointed at the box for Martin Scorsese's *Taxi Driver* and said, "I've seen that. Yuck!"

Jensen further outraged Tillich when she rejected such proposed rentals as *A Clockwork Orange*, *Glengarry Glen Ross*, and *True Romance*.

Other infamous episodes during the couple's 18-month relationship in-

clude Tillich's August 1999 insistence that Jensen listen to all of side two of The Velvet Underground's *White Light/White Heat*, his January 1999 failure to talk Jensen into visiting the grave of Philip K. Dick during a Colorado road trip, and his ongoing unsuccessful efforts to get her to read Alan Moore's *Watchmen*, a 1986 postmodern-superhero graphic novel she described as "a comic book about a big blue space guy" but he calls "nothing less than a total, devastating deconstruction of virtually every archetype in the genre's history."

The most frustrating thing, Tillich said, is the fact that Jensen is "exactly my idea of the perfect woman for me," making her ignorance of the film all the more difficult to fathom and forcing him to call into question, at a profound level, the basic foundation of their relationship and future together.

"You've got to realize, Bran is not just some airhead," Tillich told Fuller over drinks at the Azusa Pacific student union. "She's intelligent, involved, and culturally aware. So how the hell could she not know about Brando and Sheen's classic encounters in Kurtz's depraved jungle fortress? What in *Apocalypse Now* could possibly be unappealing to a smart, deep, complicated, interesting 22-year-old woman? It just doesn't add up."

"I just don't know if I can be serious about somebody who has no interest in seeing *Apocalypse Now*," Tillich continued. "She's just really missing out. I bet she'd love it if I could just get her to sit down and watch it." ∅

# Welcome To T.G.I. Fridays! May I Annoy The Living Shit Out Of You?

**By Jenni Aberg**
**Server**

Hi, welcome to T.G.I. Fridays! May I annoy the living shit out of you? My name is Jenni, and I'll be your incredibly irritating server tonight! So, how are you folks doing this evening? Great!

Thanks sooo much for waiting! It has just been completely insane around here! So if I seem a little brain-dead, please bear with me!

Can I start anybody off with one of our overpriced, stupidly named drinks? We've got a new Totally Tropical Piña Colada Smoothie that's totally amazing. No? Just waters all around? Not feeling very adventurous tonight, are we? Hey, no prob! I'll be back with your aguas in just two shakes!

I am sooo sorry that took so long! Like I said, it's just been nuts. So, can I start you folks off with some greasy, disgusting appetizers? I highly recommend the Mexicali Rose Tequila-Fried Buffalo Wings. My personal fave, though, is the Five-Alarm Chili-Pepper Quesadillas with a side of Sesame-Seed-Grilled Tostadas and Margarita-Flavored Monterey Jack Dip. No? Just entrees? Wow, you folks don't mess around, do ya?

Are you aware of our specials that nobody ever orders? I'll mention them even though you've decided what you want. The first is our Southwestern Grilled Fettuccine Alfredo, which is a lot like our regular Fettuccine Alfredo, except the egg noodles are char-grilled and the cream sauce is flavored with a ranch dressing. It's served with either a Mediterranean veggie salad or refried-bean dip. The second special is the Southwestern Grilled Avocado Meatloaf with Oriental vinaigrette marinara. Don't those sound not the least bit tempting?

Doesn't my uniform make you happy? Aren't you happy? Aren't you so happy you could take a bullet through the head?

Whew! I cannot believe how busy we are tonight! I swear, it doesn't normally take an hour for entrees. Anyway, thank you so much for your patience! You're the salsaburger with fries, right? And you're the Grilled Chicken Caesar Salad. Here ya go! Anything else I can get for you? Can I top off that Coke for you, sir? Great!

Say, I forgot to mention this before, but we've got our own freshly brewed ice tea with Mexican-grilled lemon. Any takers? Or, better yet, would you like to see our beer and wine list?

That's too bad, because alcoholic drinks are the fastest way to increase the bill, which in turn increases my tip. So, how's that burger working out

## Isn't my voice annoying? Did you notice how every third word out of my mouth is "great"?

for you, sir? Great! Actually, I couldn't care less. Would you like to see the dessert menu? Take your time looking it over, and I'll be back in a couple of minutes. By the way, I meant to say this before, but I absolutely adore your top. No, not yours, sir! Although you're quite the looker yourself!

Isn't my voice annoying? Did you notice how every third word out of my mouth is "great"? Isn't that fucking annoying?

All finished here? Great! Would you like a box to put those leftovers in? You sure? Okay! Have you decided what you'd like for dessert? The Asphyxiation By Caramel? I'm sorry, we're actually all out at the moment. Did you have a second choice? The Kahlua Fudge Slide with real Reese's Pieces? Oh, geez, we're out of that, too. I'm sooo sorry! We do, however, have the Tex-Mex Fried Neapolitan Ice Cream with kiwi shavings. Would you prefer that instead? No? Just the check? Great! I'll be right back!

Sorry for the delay again, but the register's been acting up. I swear, I think there's a full moon out tonight! Is there anything else I can get for you? I know I totaled out the check, but we do have an adjoining bar. A negligible percentage of our bar sales goes to the March of Dimes, so it's technically for a good cause! Oh, you have to leave as soon as possible? Okay, well, you guys have a super night! You can just bring your check up to the hostess at the register when you're set. It's been a pleasure getting on your nerves! Bye! ✍

PRODUCER from page 9

less corporate tie-in. Okay, we do it sometimes, too, but not that bad. Anyway, at the start of this thing, they had a 'produced by' line, and there were three names. How can it take three people to produce this one segment unless you're really overstaffed and stifling people's creativity?"

As a result of the shows' radically divergent philosophies, Pierce said that *Access Hollywood* and *Entertainment Tonight* draw different types of viewers.

"They're half a ratings point above us in the average week, unless we land some kind of Tom Cruise exclusive or something. *Survivor* helped them, too, since they've got so many CBS carriers," Pierce said. "But their demos are for shit. I mean, we absolutely cream them among 18-to-35s. The only ones *ET* scores big with are people too old to know or care what's truly going on in Hollywood."

Added Pierce: "The difference is apparent in the names of the shows. They're all about the surface aspect of entertainment. We've got a deeper, far more insider angle, yet are still accessible to the casual fan."

"No, Liz, I could never, ever work there," Pierce said. "Not unless they changed their entire way of doing things. Why? Have you heard anything about that executive-producer position? Not that I'd be interested or anything." ✍

## WHAT DO YOU THINK?

# The Ten Commandments

**Legislatures in 12 states have taken steps to permit the display of the Ten Commandments in public schools and buildings. What do *you* think about this challenge to the separation of church and state?**

"It's about time the government tried to address the rampant problem of false-witness-bearing among our nation's youths."

**Irwin Wagner**
**Systems Analyst**

"I'm opposed to the Ten Commandments being posted at my county's courthouse. The decision of whether or not to kill should be left up to the individual."

**Bill Murvin**
**Delivery Driver**

"Today's children need guidance. And nothing gets a bigger response out of kids than a list of rules hung on a wall."

**Judith Cole**
**Librarian**

"I'm all for showing *The Ten Commandments* in public buildings. Have you seen it? Edward G. Robinson is hilarious."

**Frank Boggs**
**Advertising Director**

"The Ten Commandments should be posted in all courtrooms. And the U.S. Constitution should be glued onto Jesus' chest in every church in America."

**Heidi Mancuso**
**Psychologist**

"Sure, I think they should be posted in my high school. Only, they should add an 11th Commandment that says, 'Thou shalt not be such a fuckin' pussy, Jeff Pleisner.' Because Jeff Pleisner is such a fuckin' pussy."

**Brian Froehm**
**Student**

## Mason-Dixon Line Renamed IHOP-Waffle House Line

see NATION page 6A

## Celebrities: Are They Aware Enough Of AIDS?

see PEOPLE page 2D

## Politician Caught On Tape With Media Whore

see WASHINGTON page 7A

## QLTMKR Driving In Two Lanes Of Traffic

see SENIORBEAT page 6D

**A look at the numbers that shape your world.**

### Remaining Unregistered Internet Domain Names

- www.fullyclothed.net
- www.godlovesyouwithallhisfuckingheart.com
- www.ludditeworld.com
- www.pissguzzlinggrannies.edu
- www.tomskerrittisgod.com
- www.gayrepublicanmetalheadwiccans.org
- www.njkfjkhrjhojfkjhwqfkl.com

---

# ⌀ the ONION ®

WWW.THEONION.COM     AMERICA'S FINEST NEWS SOURCE™     FOUNDED 1871

# Congress Passes Freedom From Information Act

WASHINGTON, DC—Calling the unregulated flow of information "the single greatest threat to the emotional comfort and well-being of the American people," Congress passed the Freedom From Information Act Monday.

The legislation—a response to widespread public demand to know less about the realities of the world—guarantees citizens protection from unpleasant information and imposes tough new restrictions on facts that federal authorities deem potentially damaging to the public's peace of mind.

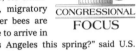

CONGRESSIONAL FOCUS

"What good does it do people to know that, for example, migratory killer bees are due to arrive in Los Angeles this spring?" said U.S. Sen. Daniel Coats (R-IN), a key proponent of the bill. "I don't want to know that a majority of adult males have had more than one homosexual experience, do you? I also have no interest in knowing how widespread mercury poisoning is, the statistics on gun ownership among inner-city youths under the age of 10, and the number of Kazakhstani nuclear warheads currently unaccounted for. Each day, more and more disturbing information encroaches upon the comfortable, illusory worldviews our

see INFORMATION page 12

# Everyone Involved In Pizza's Preparation, Delivery, Purchase Extremely High

AUSTIN, TX—Everyone involved in the preparation, delivery, purchase, and consumption of a pizza from Tony's New York-Style Pizzeria was thoroughly baked off his ass, it was reported Monday.

"From its creation at the hands of a stoned-out-of-his-mind pizzeria employee to its eventual consumption by a group of guys so unbelievably high they didn't even realize they had mistakenly given the delivery driver a $20 tip, this pizza spent its entire existence in a thick cloud of marijuana smoke," said pizza-industry watchdog Roger Dernier, who has been monitoring the link between pizza production and illegal drug use since 1991. "In the brief time this pizza spent on Earth, at no point did it come into contact with a single non-stoned human being."

According to reports, the pizza—a 16-inch black-olive and green-pepper pie mistakenly topped with extra cheese and sausage—was first

see PIZZA page 13

# God Answers Prayers Of Paralyzed Little Boy

## 'No,' Says God

SAN FRANCISCO—For as long as he can remember, 7-year-old Timmy Yu has had one precious dream: From the bottom of his heart, he has hoped against hope that God would someday hear his prayer to walk again. Though many thought Timmy's plea would never be answered, his dream finally came true Monday, when the Lord personally responded to the wheelchair-bound boy's prayer with a resounding no.

"I knew that if I just prayed hard enough, God would hear me," said a joyful Timmy, sitting in the wheelchair to which he will be confined for the rest of his life. "And now my prayer has been answered. I haven't been this happy since before the accident, when I could walk and play with the other children like a normal boy."

God's response came at approximately 10 a.m., following a particularly fervent Sunday-night prayer session by little Timmy. Witnesses said God issued His miraculous answer in the form of a towering column of clouds, from which poured forth great beams of Divine light and the music of the Heavenly Host. The miraculous

see GOD page 12

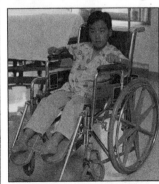

Above: Wheelchair-bound Timmy Yu, who finally received his long-awaited reply from God.

country's middle- and upper-middle-class citizens have constructed for themselves. It is up to this nation's elected officials to stem the tide."

Passage of the legislative package is being greeted with widespread approval.

"With all the problems and stress of modern life already taxing people's emotional resources to the limit, the last thing we need is a lot of depressing information dragging everybody down even more," said Greg Hill, an Edina, MN, lawyer and longtime advocate of federally imposed information limits. "People need to be shielded from the horrible realities of the world if they're to have any chance of getting through life in a pleasant manner."

Fellow anti-information crusader and Deerfield, IL, homemaker Jane Gernbaum agreed. "I don't want to specifically mention some of the offensive facts I've accidentally exposed myself to, but believe me, they were pretty harsh," she said from her upscale suburban home. "It's about time the government put a stop to them."

Much of the impetus for the broad-based information reductions came from parents' groups, which have long been concerned about the harmful effects facts may have on children.

"Kids have curious minds and are eager to learn," said Francine Walters of the What About The Children? Foundation. "This makes them susceptible to harmful information exposure. It's about time Congress finally did something to protect them."

Last month, demand for information safeguards for children grew louder, due to the highly publicized case of San Antonio, TX, sixth-grader Jeff Paulsen, who accessed information about the neighboring border city of Juarez, Mexico, from a *Harper's* magazine in his school library. According to attorneys for the Paulsen family, which owns controlling stock in several textile factories in Juarez, the boy had previously believed the city to be a thriving border town that enjoyed positive economic relations with the U.S. Severely traumatized after discovering that Juarez is actually a deathscape of unimaginable poverty with one of the highest murder rates in the world, Paulsen became sullen and withdrawn.

"He kept saying, 'What's the point of going to soccer practice when all those Mexican boys and girls are dying?'" said his mother, Carole Paulsen. "The entire season was a complete wash. He may not even make the team next year."

Children are not the only ones in need of protection: According to an ABC News poll conducted last week, three in five U.S. adults claim to have a "strong personal fear" of information.

Among the facts cited as "too scary to think about": the number of microscopic creatures living in the average person's hair, the likelihood of a future outbreak of a worldwide "super-

Above: The recent mass slaughter of ethnic Albanians by Serbian forces is just one of the many horrors from which Americans will be shielded with the passage of the Freedom From Information Act.

flu" pandemic, and the percentage of U.S. families in which father-daughter incest is never reported to authorities.

Ironically, while access to information about such subjects will be heavily restricted by the federal government, polls indicate that Americans are most afraid of information regarding the government itself.

"I was so content in my belief that President Carter screwed up the hostage-rescue attempt, and that Reagan

came in to free the hostages his first day in office," said Frank Sims, a racquetball enthusiast and junior partner in a Roanoke, VA, consulting firm. "It wasn't until 1992 that I learned the Carter attempt was actually sabotaged by the same shadow-government operatives that backed Reagan's election and illegal arms-for-hostages trades. I can't tell you how much that bummed me out."

Under the new act, Americans will

be protected from information about the hostage crisis, as well as all other government blunders and/or questionable activities, including the U.S. Army's decades-long Tuskegee syphilis experiments on black veterans, the number of times NORAD has been at DefCon 5 due to human or computer error, and the CIA's longtime support of Indonesian president Suharto, a dictator responsible for one million deaths in East Timor. ∅

event took place in the Children's Special Care Ward of St. Luke's Hospital, which Timmy visits three times a week for an excruciating two-hour procedure to drain excess fluid from his damaged spinal column.

Said Angela Schlosser, a day nurse who witnessed the Divine Manifestation: "An incredible, booming voice said to Timmy, 'I am the Lord thy God, who created the rivers and the mountains, the heavens and the Earth, the sun and the moon and the stars. Before Me sits My beloved child, whose faith is that of the mustard seed from which grows mighty and powerful things. My child, Timmy Yu, I say unto you thus: I have heard your prayers, and now I shall answer them. No, you cannot get out of your wheelchair. Not ever.'"

Paralyzed in a 1998 auto accident that claimed the lives of his parents, Timmy has served as a shining example to his fellow churchgoers at Lord In Heaven On High Church, inspiring others with his simple, heartfelt devotion. Now that Timmy has received an answer, Christians the world over are celebrating his story as a stirring testament to the power of faith.

"The Lord has answered a little

boy's plea to know if he would ever walk again, and that answer was no," said Rev. H. Newman Gunther of the San Francisco School Of Divinity. "For

---

## Christians the world over are celebrating his story as a stirring testament to the power of faith.

---

years, this boy had been plagued by the question of whether or not he would ever walk, and now Our Lord, in His wisdom and mercy, has forever laid to rest any lingering doubt. Young Timmy can rest assured in the immutable truth the Lord has bestowed upon him. Now and for all time, he finally knows that he will never escape the cruel prison of his chair of iron, for God hath willed it so. Praise be to God."

Asked for comment, God said: "This kind-hearted child's simple prayer hath moved Me. Never before have I seen such faith. His trusting soul, so full of innocent devotion to Me, hath

offered seventy times seven prayers asking, 'God? Can I please walk again?' It was indeed right and fitting that I, in My infinite wisdom, should share with him the One True Answer to this long-repeated question put before Me."

"My will be done," God added.

Witnesses to the miracle said Timmy begged God for several minutes to change His mind and heal his shattered vertebrae, but the Lord stood firm.

"God recommended that Timmy consider praying to one of the other intercessionary agents of Divine power, like Jesus, Mary, or maybe even a top saint," said Dr. William Luttrell, Timmy's personal physician. "The Lord stressed to Timmy that it was still a long shot, but that he might have better luck with one of them."

Despite his newfound notoriety as the only human ever to have a prayer directly answered by God Himself, Timmy remains humble.

"I know God loves me, because it says so in the Bible," Timmy said. "So right now, I'm just glad God took the time to answer my prayer. If only I could walk, this would be the greatest day of my life." ∅

# You Look Like You Could Use An Elizabethan Adventure On The Holodeck

Greetings, fellow citizen of the Federation! I couldn't help but notice that you seem a bit fatigued. I suspect the many demands of Starfleet service have worn you down, and you now require recreation to refresh you and restore your spirits to a nominal level of function. I know just the thing—a merry Elizabethan adventure on the holodeck!

**Into The Wormhole**
**By Dennis Wormer**

Yes, the holodeck, the 24th century's most wondrous invention! When its advanced three-dimensional imaging capabilities are working in concert with its steady-state transporter/replicator matter-manipulation arrays, this deceptively drab room is limited only by the power of the imagination. And we shall use our imaginations to whisk us away from the day-to-day cares of running a Federation starship and back to the late 16th century, to the English Renaissance during the reign of Her Majesty Queen Elizabeth I!

Stress and care will disappear, as the

> **Look ye! A fair lady has dropped her scented handkerchief and laughs into her sleeve as I stoop to proffer the sundry to her coquettish hand.**

holodeck transforms your humdrum, utilitarian Starfleet uniform into the gilt-sleeved, silken-hosed garb of the London dandy, complete with a scandalously ruffled collar! My science officer's uniform instantly becomes a jerkin and doublet of the finest linen, and a plumed and tassocked beaver hat appears on my head at a jaunty angle. As we gasp in amazement at this magic, we note that our Type III phasers have been transformed into perfect replicas of English hand-and-a-half broadswords, for today, we sail with the Duke of Sedonia against King Philip and the nefarious Spanish Armada!

Or, if you desire adventures of a less martial nature, indulge my science officer's curiosity, and let us join Sir Francis Drake in his circumnavigation of the globe! The holodeck shall delve into its prodigious memory banks to reproduce the skies of old Earth, so that we may navigate by sextant to the Straits of Magellan, reproduced in all their beauty and savagery by the Federation's finest technological masterwork! We shall pass the long hours watching replicated gulls wheel in the rigging of Her Majesty's ship Golden Hinde, forgetting the worries we have as crewpersons of the Federation's flagship.

Ahoy! The shores of Tierra Del Fuego appear in the holographic distance! The natives approach with gifts

**see HOLODECK page 14**

## Despite Claims, Long Story Not Made Short

SCHENECTADY, NY—Contrary to her pre-account vow, area resident Barb Schuyler's long story of how a series of cashier foul-ups at the grocery store Monday made her 25 minutes late for a dental appointment was not made short. "So then, it turns out the stupid woman forgot to ring in my Savers Club discount," Schuyler told friend Gloria Conlon nine minutes into the non-abbreviated tale. The story is the 1,643rd Schuyler has failed to make short since 1994.

## Oh, Area Man's Aching Back

JERSEY CITY, NJ—According to a report issued Monday by 51-year-old Jersey City resident Phil Lardner, Jesus Christ Almighty, his back feels like a goddamn elephant stepped on it. Fuck, the report stated, he should never have tried to move that dishwasher by himself. The report went on to note that Lardner may require medical attention if he can make it to the friggin' phone, and that if he doesn't collect some workman's comp for this one, forget about it. ∅

---

PIZZA from page 11

conceptualized by area stoner Doug Bickell at approximately 11:30 p.m. Sunday, when he said to housemate Bob Wang during a rewatching of that evening's videotaped *X-Files* episode, "Hey, Wangster, how's about we dial up some killer chow?" Though the pizza was merely an idea at that point, the food item's 100-percent-stoned life cycle had already begun, as both Bickell and Wang "had a major buzz on."

After spending the next 19 minutes deciding which pizzeria to call, Wang and Bickell moved into the next phase of the pizza saga, an 11-minute search for a $2 coupon. After an exhaustive search, it was finally located on the coffee table directly next to the phone.

"It is interesting to note," Dernier said, "that even this coupon, an admittedly secondary aspect of the pizza's story, was made by somebody who was also stoned, as evidenced by its offer of '$2 Offf.'"

The pizza entered the next phase of its THC-soaked existence when pizzeria employee Wayne "Mr. Moondog" Lindeman, a technical-college dropout and noted Austin-area bongo drummer, took the phone order from the two largely incapacitated customers.

"It took me a while to figure out what they wanted," Lindeman said. "When I was listing off the toppings we've got, they kept asking if they could get, like, Fritos or sandwiches on the pizza. Plus, there were a ton of calls on hold, and I was getting pretty stressed trying to get their order and move on to the next caller. But, luckily, me and Greg had just toked down this huge-ass fatty in the walk-in cooler, so I was able to maintain a mellow attitude throughout."

After taking the order, Lindeman relayed it to coworker and fellow stoner Greg Kanner. Kanner, normally a cashier, was forced to make pizzas that evening due to the absence of regular cook Ronny Poquette, who had skipped work because he was

> **"Sadly, for millions of pizzas, interaction with non-stoned humans is simply not an option," Dernier said.**

"tripping his ass off."

At 1 a.m. Monday, the pizza finally came into being. Almost immediately, it exhibited the influence of marijuana in the form of its erroneous meat topping, which had not been ordered by the vegetarian Wang.

"I wasn't really trained to do what I was doing, but I figured, shit, how hard can it be?" Kanner said. "After all, it's just pizza, right? But I was so high, I got kind of confused about the toppings. It was no big deal, though."

After an extended wait for delivery driver Kurt Behr to return to the store—reportedly the result of Behr taking an unscheduled break to get high and make out with his girlfriend between delivery runs—the pizza was finally picked up and dispatched to the Wang-Bickell residence.

"Not surprisingly, there were still several detours and delays standing between the pizza and its final destination," Dernier said. "For one, Behr went to the wrong address at least four times. Also, Bickell and Wang had forgotten to include their apartment number with the order, and Behr ran out of gas about 10 minutes into the trip and had to walk to a nearby station with a gas can to get more."

Approximately 50 minutes into his journey, Behr was heard to exclaim, "Shit, man, I've lived in this town for, like, four years, but I still can't think of where the hell Blount Street is at. Fuck!" Behr later described the prolonged Blount Street search as "a serious fucking hassle."

Matters were further complicated by the five phone calls Bickell and Wang made to the pizzeria to inquire about the status of their pizza. "They were seriously bitching me out," said Lindeman, who was royally baked at the time. "I was like, 'Dude, just chill, your pizza will be there any sec.'"

Finally, at 3:10 a.m., more than three hours after the order was placed, the pizza reached its destination.

"By the time [Behr] showed up, the pizza was cold, *The X-Files* was long over, and we were practically unconscious, because we'd started pulling hits off Wang's three-foot Grafix," Bickell said. "But he said we could have it free, so we weren't pissed or nothing. We invited him in and the three of us just pulled bingers and chowed that shit down. It's, like, against the Wangster's beliefs and shit to eat sausage, but he was cool about it. To tell you the truth, I don't think he even noticed."

Added Bickell: "Then we all just sat back and vegged out. I think maybe *Barbarella* was on cable, 'cause I remember some funny shit with these alien space-chicks or something. It's kind of hard to really follow the chain of events at that point because, basically, everybody was out of their freaking minds."

According to Dernier, the incident is not an isolated one: He estimated that each year in the U.S., as many as 25 million pizzas lead similar drug-saturated existences.

"Sadly, for millions of pizzas, interaction with non-stoned humans is simply not an option," Dernier said. "That's why it's crucial that those of us who are not higher than shit on primo weed occasionally take the time to order a pizza to offset this overwhelming imbalance and give some of our pies a chance to be exposed to alternative, non-stoned lifestyles."

No charges have been filed in connection with the incident, though Behr was verbally reprimanded later that night by a police officer for sleeping on the hood of his parked delivery vehicle. ∅

# Doritos Celebrates One Millionth Ingredient

DALLAS, TX—Amid much fanfare, the Frito-Lay Corporation announced Monday the addition of Doritos' one millionth ingredient.

The new ingredient, disodium guanylate, will not only act as an additional emulsifying agent, but also make the big taste of Doritos even bigger.

"Today, we have reached a milestone in the proud history of Doritos," Frito-Lay CEO Don Gehrmann said at a formal chip-breaking ceremony. "One million ingredients!" To wild applause, a Doritos scientist then held up a giant dropper reading "Disodium Guanylate" and touched it to an oversized Doritos chip.

The new ingredient is a chemically produced emulsifier that will act both as a thickening agent and an anti-oxidant in Doritos, the nation's top-selling cheese-flavored snack chip.

"Disodium guanylate, or $NaC_{12}O_3G$, will help slow the oxidation process in Doritos, serving as a valuable hydrolyzing reactor," MIT chemist Dr. James Steuerbohm said. "Essentially, it would play the same role disodium inosinate plays in Funyuns."

Informed of the landmark one mil-

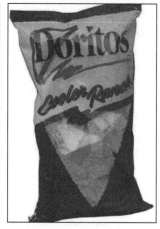

lionth ingredient, President Clinton offered his congratulations.

"Frito-Lay has gained much by adding this fine chemical compound to its impressive roster of ingredients, but the real winner here is the American people," he said. "They will enjoy a more delicious, more mouth-watering snack chip than ever before."

On the other side of the world, North Korean President Kim Jong Il briefly stepped away from a military demon-stration in his honor to offer his congratulations.

"Doritos must be held in the absolute highest regard by the people," Kim said. "Denial of the greatness of this snack chip will not be tolerated."

According to snack-chip historian James Farwell, disodium guanylate is the most important new substance to be added to Doritos since May 1994, when FD&C Red 40 Lake, ingredient number 966,450, was added.

"The arrival of Red 40 Lake was a pivotal moment in Doritos history," Farwell said. "Before Red 40, Doritos had a slightly normal look; if you looked closely, you could tell there were a few naturally occurring ingredients in there. But after Red 40, the chips took on a blinding, explosive orange glow. Consumers responded immediately."

Despite just having reached the million-ingredient mark, Gehrmann is already thinking about two million.

"That would be incredible," he said. "There's so much out there we could still add: partially hydrolyzed protein extract, maltodextrin, trisodium phosphate, cheese—the possibilities are endless." ∅

# Study: Uneducated Outbreeding Intelligentsia 2-To-1

CHICAGO—In a report with dire implications for the intellectual future of America, a University of Chicago study revealed Monday that the nation's uneducated are breeding twice as soon and twice as often as those with university diplomas. "The average member of the American underclass spawns at age 15, compared to age 30 for the average college-educated professional," study leader Kenneth Stalls said. "America's intellectual elite, as a result, is badly losing the genetic marathon, with two generations of dullards born for every one generation of cultured literates." Added Stalls: "At this rate, by the year 2100 there will be five smart people on Earth, swallowed whole by more than 12 billion mouth-breathers incapable of understanding the binary exponentiation that swamped the Earth with their like." High-school dropout Mandi Drucker, 16, said of the findings, "All I know is, we're in love." ∅

# Darling, Will You Spend The Next Six To Ten Years With Me?

Darling. We've known each other for more than a year now. During that time, we've shared so much—our hopes, our dreams, our fears. When I

**By Jon McNally**

met you, I wasn't thinking of starting up a serious relationship, but my admiration and respect for you quickly blossomed into love. You're my best friend and confidante, and I can't imagine spending the better part of the next decade without you.

I know I've been vague about taking "the next step," but all that has changed. Your patience, loyalty, and love have made me see the world in an entirely new light. It's a place where true love can exist. So I ask you, Julie Bramhall... Will you spend the next six to ten years with me?

I know it's sudden. We just moved in together three months ago, and I'm still looking for a better-paying job. But when I look into your eyes, I see all the things I never used to want. A big wedding. Kids. A house with a white picket fence that I'll have to move out of in about seven years when you discover that I'm sleeping with my secretary. I never thought I'd say this to anyone, but you're the only one I want to wake up next to for the rest of my 30s.

I remember telling you early in our relationship that I never wanted to get married. But sometimes, I stay awake after you've fallen asleep and just look at you and stroke your hair. I can't believe what a lucky man I am. When the moonlight hits your delicate features just right, I see an angel. An angel who will turn cold and indifferent to me in five years because of festering resentment over my drinking. But if I could only capture how you look on film during those moments, I swear we could make a million dollars. God, you're so beautiful at this stage in your life.

Did you know that most of my friends are amazed that a woman of your caliber would even be going out with me, much less be interested in marrying me? They're always talking about how smart, funny, and drop-dead gorgeous you are. I have no choice but to agree. When I take a step back and look at things, there's no reason someone so luminous should be interested in a guy like me. Of course, I always point out to them that your looks will be pretty well faded by 2008. But when I think how stunning you are now, I can only shake my head in disbelief.

Marriage is a big step to make, I know. But when I think of all the memories we've shared together, it makes me want a medium amount more. Do you remember that time we stumbled onto the bridge in Georgia

overlooking a moonlit river, and we just held each other close, watching the waves gently lap on the shore? What about all the Sundays we lay in bed together until early afternoon? I cherish those memories, and I want to share more until our relationship is reduced to screaming fights, endless hours of legal battles, and an attempt on your part to stab me with a potato peeler.

If you asked me two years ago if I was ever going to want kids, I would have looked at you like you were crazy. But sometimes, when I'm walking with you hand in hand, I imagine us pushing a stroller. And I like that image. I see us with two kids, a boy and a girl. That would be perfect. They could hold each other up after I'm gone.

HOLODECK from page 13

and provisions, and if the First Mate is a Klingon, well, who is to care?

The tedium of hours spent mapping lifeless nebulae down in Stellar Cartography will melt away as we weather winter storms and head up the Thames to accept the Queen's scarf as a trophy! That evening, after a parting ale with the convincing simulacrum of good Sir Francis, we take our seats at the newly opened Globe Theatre, where young Will Shakespeare's fanciful comedies shall make us temporarily forget the many demands placed upon us by our stern

I really think you'd make an incredible mother, Julie. And I think you'll eventually make a great single mother, too. You've got that inner strength.

You don't have to answer right away if you don't want to. It's a big decision, and I wouldn't want you to take it lightly. Think it over. Talk to your friends and family. I already asked your father for your hand in marriage, and he gave his blessing. But before you answer, you should know that I truly do love you and want to spend nearly a decade with you. Without you, my life is incomplete. At least, until I meet our daughter's dance instructor.

So, please, Julie Bramhall... Say you'll grow early middle-aged with me. ∅

commander, Will Riker.

Look ye! A fair lady has dropped her scented handkerchief and laughs into her sleeve as I stoop to proffer the sundry to her coquettish hand. Is she the young and flirtatious Anne Boleyn, brought once more to life by the holodeck's vast historical reference files and human emotion/behavior probability matrix? Or is she that comely ensign from Main Engineering?

Ah, yes, the holodeck! Balm to over-taxed junior officers everywhere. Let it ease your furrowed brow! ∅

## Suborbital Ballistic-Propulsion Engineer Not Exactly A Rocket Scientist

see CAREERS page 4C

## New 10-10-911 Saves Emergency Victims Up To 30 Percent

see BUSINESS page 2B

## Lesbian Couple Enjoys Hot Lesbian Action

see LOCAL page 4D

## Man In Headlock Just Wanted To Party

see LOCAL page 2E

### STATshot

A look at the numbers that shape your world.

**Least-Safe Airlines**

1. Amtrak Air
2. Usually Transatlantic
3. Shur-Fine Airlines
4. Air Reparations To Loved Ones
5. Stygian Air
6. Airline '77
7. Macomb County Community College Airlines
8. Bubba And The Plane He Done Builted

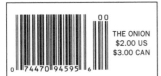

THE ONION
$2.00 US
$3.00 CAN

0 74470 94595 6

---

# the ONION®

WWW.THEONION.COM    AMERICA'S FINEST NEWS SOURCE™    FOUNDED 1871

# New Smokable Nicotine Sticks

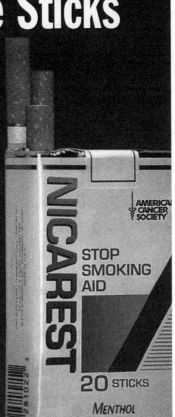

▶ Will completely cure smokers' cravings, says manufacturer

▶ More effective than patches or gums

▶ Fills lungs with rich, satisfying smoke, curbing desire for cigarettes

▶ Available in regular or menthol

▶ Legal for minors

▶ Available wherever cigarettes are sold

▶ Should HMOs cover the drug?

see COVER STORY page 16

---

Above: Edwin Randle spends quality time with his youngest boat.

# Executive Quits Fast Track To Spend More Time With Possessions

HOUSTON—Edwin Randle, the obsessive, hard-driving Drexel Chemicals CEO legendary for his 100-hour work weeks, stunned colleagues and competitors Friday when he announced that he is stepping down to spend more time with his possessions.

"I took a long, hard look at my Mercedes CL500 Coupe and realized it wasn't getting any newer," said Randle, a 51-year-old husband and father of three. "After spending most of my life putting my career before every-
see EXECUTIVE page 17

---

# *Cat Fancy* Magazine Blasts Area Kitten

## 'Mr. Paws Is Far From Purr-fect,' Says Article

TILDEN, OH—An article published in the September issue of *Cat Fancy* magazine, on newsstands Friday, blasts local kitten Mr. Paws, calling him "far from purr-fect" and a "cataclysmic failure."

"Unlike the typical feline that appears in *Cat Fancy*, Mr. Paws does not behave in a manner that can in any way be considered adorable or cuddly," said *Cat Fancy* features editor Barrett Kilmer. "During the entire time I observed Mr. Paws, not once did he climb into a

paper bag and stick his head out quizzically. Nor did he ever unroll any lengths of ribbon or yarn, afterwards innocently looking up from the tangled mess as if to say, 'Who, me?' Finally, as if that weren't enough, he never fell off the

Above: Mr. Paws has endured jeers and ridicule after the publication of a scathing piece in *Cat Fancy*, which calls him a "fur-ocious failure."

edge of a tree branch, gripping it precariously with his fuzzy little paws and 'hanging in there,' so to speak."

"Unfortunately," Kilmer

concluded, "Mr. Paws appears to be totally devoid of any 'purr-sonality' whatsoever. He couldn't possibly
see CAT page 16

# For Millions Of Smokers, Nicarest™ May Be The Answer

LOUISVILLE, KY—When Adrienne Lundy, 37, a pack-a-day smoker from Louisville, was diagnosed last December with a malignant tumor on her right arm, she knew she had to kick the habit. But, like many longtime smokers, Lundy found quitting to be much more difficult than expected.

"Gums, patches, hypnosis—you name it, I tried it," said Lundy, a Marlboro smoker for 21 years. "Nothing worked—until my doctor told me about a new product called Nicarest™."

Lundy is not alone. To date, more than two million American smokers have tried Nicarest™, a specially treated nicotine stick which, when lit and inhaled, is said to completely curb a user's craving for cigarettes. Manufactured by QuitLabs, a Winston-Salem, NC, pharmaceutical company, Nicarest™ is made of processed tobacco byproducts and treated with carefully calibrated doses of nicotine and antibiotic "tar." Since its introduction in June, Nicarest™ has won the endorsement of the Surgeon General, American Cancer Society, and American Medical Association, and has quickly become the most popular stop-smoking aid on the market.

"Whenever I get the urge for a cigarette, I head for Nicarest Country," said Doug Luedtke, 44, a Wichita Falls, TX, forklift operator who said his smoking was "completely out of control."

"Unlike patches and gums, Nicarest™ duplicates the sensation of actually smoking a cigarette, filling my lungs with rich, satisfying smoke," he said. "And, at just $4.25 for a 20-stick pack, it's not much more expensive than cigarettes."

"Nicarest™ saved my life," said Lundy, playing with her newborn daughter in the yard of her home, her cigarette cravings held firmly in check by the freshly lit nicotine cylinder wedged in the corner of her mouth. "I haven't touched a Marlboro since discovering Nicarest™. Not one."

QuitLabs CEO Charles Craney, the longtime tobacco pharmacologist who developed the "combustible medicated habit-cessation nicotine-delivery ampule," said he came up with the idea for the product while working for Philip Morris in the late '80s.

"From my work at Philip Morris, I was familiar with the process of transferring nicotine to the human lung via an oxidized vegetable-matter medium," Craney said. "From there, it was a simple matter of applying that know-how, not to smokers, but to smokers who wanted to quit."

"By doubling the nicotine dosage in Nicarest™," Craney continued, "we removed any biochemical reason for a smoker to fall back on cigarette dependency. But smokers aren't just accustomed to nicotine. They're also accustomed to the visual, tactile, oral, and even psychological sensations of having a small lit cylinder of tobacco in their mouths. That's what Nicarest™ gives them. That's our secret."

The strategy is working: On the market for only two months, Nicarest™—available in Regular, Filters, Lights, Ultra Lights, Slims, and Menthol—already outsells all other stop-smoking aids combined. And, on Aug. 25, RJR Nabisco purchased a controlling interest in Nicarest, Inc., making Randle a very wealthy man.

Sales continue to skyrocket as smokers abandon their cigarettes for Nicarest™. The long-familiar "smokers' corners" outside schools and businesses are rapidly disappearing, as smokers calm their cravings with Nicarest™ wherever they may be, since Nicarests are permitted in areas

Above: Adrienne Lundy lights up a Nicarest™ stop-smoking aid. Lundy said she hasn't had a cigarette since July 4, when she started using Nicarest™.

off-limits to regular smokers.

"Whenever and wherever I get the urge—at the movies, at work, in a restaurant—I can inhale Nicarest's robust, satisfying medication and calm my body's urges," said Cynthia Mecklenburg of East Meadow, NY, a two-packs-a-day Nicarest™ user who learned of the product from a recent television ad. "And it's the one stop-smoking aid that's alive with plea-sure."

"My baby's not going to grow up in a house filled with harmful cigarette smoke," said Lundy, who plans to start her daughter on Nicarests as a preventative measure as soon as she turns 16, the age at which Lundy started to smoke. "Her mother is going to be a Nicarest™ user. When she's older, she'll realize just how important that difference really is." ∅

CAT from page 15

be any 'fur-ther' from the caliber of kitty that *Cat Fancy* usually showcases."

Mr. Paws' owner, Helen Smallings, strongly disagreed with *Cat Fancy's* assessment of her pet. "I really love Mr. Paws and he loves me. Don't you, Mr. Pawsy Wawsy?" said Smallings, a single, slightly overweight, 38-year-old part-time secretary. "He's his own little man!"

As a result of the scathing *Cat Fancy* article, whenever Mr. Paws leaps to bask in the warmth of one of the front windowsills, Smallings is forced to close the blinds to protect him from the derision and laughter of the neighbors.

"I read that piece on Mr. Paws in the latest *Cat Fancy*—we all did," neighbor Paula Smith said. "That kitten is crap."

Despite his harsh words for Mr. Paws, Kilmer acknowledged that the kitten's lack of cuddliness may have been, in part, circumstantial.

"A kitten is aided by the presence of deep shag rugs that offset its fur color, and fish bowls to peer into bewil-

> "I read that piece on Mr. Paws in the latest *Cat Fancy*—we all did," neighbor Paula Smith said. "That kitten is crap."

deredly or bat excitedly, benefits Mr. Paws lacks," he said. "In addition, there are no beagles Mr. Paws can curl up with and fall asleep. Now, wouldn't that be cute?"

Responding to Kilmer, Smallings said, "Just the other day, Mr. Paws was on the couch all stretched out, and I put the remote control next to his paw. It was the cutest thing!"

*Cat Fancy* said it could not consider the cute pose in its evaluation of the animal without at least a Polaroid or, ideally, an 8x10 glossy photo in a powder-blue frame featuring kitties chasing a ball of pink yarn around its perimeter.

A similarly persuasive photo, *Cat Fancy* sources said, would depict Mr. Paws doing one of the following: wearing a pair of sunglasses, curling up inside a cowboy hat, "kissing" a jack o' lantern, or dripping wet after falling into the sink, looking like he was having "One Of Those Days!"

Evaluating an appeal from Smallings at a special meeting in the magazine's Persian Room, *Cat Fancy's* editorial board determined Friday that "Mr. Paws is most definitely a 'cat-astrophe.'"

"Sometimes, a decidedly unsnuggly cat is redeemed by its air of grandiosity and haughtiness," board member Joyce Reamish said. "Such is the case with our Cat Of The Month, a Siamese named Sheba from Grand Forks, ND. Sheba was photographed while poised on a mahogany table bathed in natural sunlight, the garden just beyond the window. The look on her face is 100 percent sassy. Mr. Paws, on the other hand, is sassless."

"Age is certainly an issue with this particular feline," Kilmer said. "Before long, Mr. Paws will have passed through the prime stage of kittenhood fuzziness, out of both the adorably awkward period of quick growth and the rambunctious, playful months."

"Within a year, he will likely be a sedate and reclusive adult cat that's sadly overweight in the midsection, a condition only acceptable on the matronly long-hair breeds," Kilmer said. "Mr. Paws' condition is truly 'a-pawling.' Get this 'fur-ociously' inferior feline 'me-out' of my sight!" ∅

# Violence Against Women Linked To Burned Pot Roast

GAINESVILLE, FL—A study released Friday by University of Florida researchers has found a strong link between domestic violence against women and burned pot roast.

**DOMESTIC VIOLENCE**
**A Special Report**

"After five years of research, we have found a direct causal link between overcooked, poorly prepared dinners and spousal abuse," sociology professor and study head Dr. Patrick Redmond said.

Study data was gathered from interviews, police records, and firsthand observations conducted between 5 and 8 p.m., the hours during which a majority of American men come home from a long, hard day at work and expect a hot meal to be waiting for them on the table.

According to one 42-year-old male study participant, abuse in his home occurs most frequently "when I sit down at the table, and I gotta eat a goddamn black roast because the broad was yapping on the phone with her mother's hospice-unit nurse

see VIOLENCE page 18

# Ping-Pong Somehow Elicits Macho Posturing

## 'Boo-Ya! How You Like Me Now?' Says Ping-Pong-Playing Man

APPLETON, WI—The non-macho game of table tennis, popularly known as "ping-pong" for the bouncy little sound the ball makes, has somehow elicited tough-guy posturing and braggadocio from Appleton resident Tim Bergkamp, sources close to the 27-year-old revealed Friday.

"I don't know what the deal is," said Marty Zielke, a coworker of Bergkamp's at an Appleton-area Target, "but ever since we got that ping-pong table in the break room, Tim's been acting like he's Macho Man Randy Savage or something."

The table, brought in by fellow Target sales associate Jason Hersh after he decided to remove it from his basement rec room, has "brought out the competitive animal" in the mild-mannered Bergkamp.

"You should see him when he gets going. You'd think ping-pong was some kind of ESPN2 extreme sport," Hersh said. "He's all like, 'Time for a serious ass-kicking, Jason. Think you can take it when I bring the hammer down on you? Think you can handle the humiliation of another devastating defeat at the hands of the master?' Then, whenever he scores a point, he

shouts, 'Boo-Ya!' and does this gloating victory dance, strutting back and forth and waving his arms in the air. I mean, it's ping-pong, for Christ's sake."

"No one can withstand the awesome might of the Ponginator's vaunted 'OverThruster' serve," Bergkamp told coworker Rebecca Stairs during a recent match. "Pretenders to the throne, beware!"

Stairs said she is mystified by Bergkamp's ping-pong bravado.

"How anyone could associate such alpha-male chest-thumping with a polite pastime like ping-pong is beyond me," Stairs said. "It's baffling. Speaking of which, one of his many nicknames for himself is 'The Baffler.' He says that's because no one ever knows where the next shot is coming from."

Bergkamp has given himself numerous other monikers, including The Human Wall, because no opponent can get the ball past him; the Harlem Pongtrotter, employed when he whistles "Sweet Georgia Brown" to psyche out opponents; and the aliases Cobra Verde, Cobra Rosa, and Cobra Negro, which vary according to his paddle's

Above: Self-described "ping-pong ninja" Tim Bergkamp taunts his opponent during a match at Appleton-area fun center B.Z. Bonkers.

color.

"I like to start out slowly, lulling my prey into a false sense of security," Bergkamp recently confided to Stairs. "Then I turn up the heat with a little smack-talkin', which throws off their game. Then, once they're dazed and confused from the psychological warfare, I lock on the target and fire off a vicious volley of spin shots, from which my hapless victim can find no shelter."

"They've learned to expect no quarter, and none is given," Bergkamp said. "I deliver my enemies into the

see PING-PONG page 18

---

EXECUTIVE from page 15

thing else, it suddenly dawned on me that I was missing out on what really matters: my luxury goods."

"Can you believe my yacht is already 12 years old?" Randle added. "I've barely even used it."

Leaning back in his $3,100 leather massage chair with seven adjustable heat settings, Randle said it was "high time" he put his priorities in order.

"In the end, what does all that money in the bank mean?" Randle asked. "Nothing, unless you make time to spend it on the things you love."

For years, Randle set aside little time to enjoy his belongings. Most days, the only interaction he had with his pair of BMW R1100 motorcycles was looking at the framed pictures of them on his desk at work. But Randle said those days are over, and that he is determined to spend a lot more quality time with them.

"Those bikes are my pride and joy, but I've taken them for granted," Randle said. "And that's true for far too many other things, as well. From now on, I'm going to swim in my Olympic-sized pool, crack open that bottle of 1982 Château Ducru Beaucaillou, hire a pilot, and have him fly me all over the place in that Cessna two-seater I have in storage. What was I doing wasting my life away in an office when I had a beautiful $12,000 stereo just waiting for me at home?"

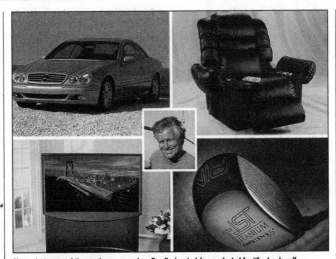

Above: Just some of the precious possessions Randle (center) has neglected for "far too long."

Randle used to regularly put in 16-hour days at Drexel corporate headquarters. His office was connected to a suite where he would often sleep after working deep into the night, only to rise at 6 a.m. to do it all over again. But those days are over.

"I've finally realized that an office is not a home," Randle said. "A spacious six-bedroom, five-bath property with its own private road on 56 acres in River Oaks—now, that's a home."

Continued Randle: "When I think of all the football I've missed watching

on my $8,000 Thomson Electronics Proscan 61-inch rear-projection TV with six-speaker stereo surround sound, it just makes me want to cry. Moments like this year's Super Bowl, you can never get those back."

One of Randle's priorities is to catch up on lost time at Southgate Country Club, where he holds a $5,000-a-month membership.

"When was the last time I spent a sunny Saturday afternoon with my Ping signature-series golf clubs?" Randle asked. "I barely even know my

titanium driver anymore. I know it may be tough, but I'm going to do whatever it takes to get back my swing."

It wasn't simply Randle's desire to reconnect with his most beloved possessions that made him decide to give up the hustle and bustle of corporate life. It was also "all the little things" he'd been missing out on by spending so much time away from home.

"All those gadgets I ordered from The Sharper Image over the years—the Ionic Breeze personal air purifier, the magnetic eye mask, the Escort Solo cordless radar/laser detector—I've never gotten to know them. I've never really even had time to read the instructions," he said. "Finally, after all these years, I'm going to understand what truly makes my stainless-steel Navy SEALs dive watch tick."

Even as he looks forward to being a full-time possessions man, Randle is still grappling with feelings of guilt over his old lifestyle.

"Can you believe I wasn't even there for the delivery of my first anti-gravity back-stretch/relaxation table?" Randle asked. "My wife had to sign the Hammacher Schlemmer invoice all by herself. I should have been there to lift that baby out of the box, but I was working at the time. What a fool I was." ∅

again."

In addition to unsatisfactorily prepared meals, a number of other factors were found to be linked to domestic violence, including always nagging about getting the roof fixed, blocking the TV when the big game is on, and repeatedly demanding to know exactly what goes on at that bar all day and night.

While domestic violence is widespread, Redmond said there are steps women can take to protect themselves.

"Based on interviews we conducted with more than 1,000 abusive men, women can significantly reduce safety risks by promptly responding to requests of 'Get me another beer,' and by making sure the beer is cold, in addition to making sure that non-burned pot roasts are served hot and in a timely fashion," said Gregory Ormond of the New York-based Family Crisis Center.

"Further," Ormond continued, "a majority of the wife-batterers we spoke to indicated that it wouldn't hurt if their spouses took a little effort to make themselves appear more attractive once in a while."

The study also found that women who let themselves go and balloon up shortly after the first few years of marriage are 20 percent more likely to get pasted right in their fat faces.

As part of the study, the Florida researchers conducted a wide range of laboratory experiments involving women who live with abusive partners. Among the experiments' findings: When the smell of burned pot roast is combined with the simulated sound of a station wagon pulling into a driveway, 43 percent of abused women burst into tears instantaneously.

Upon learning of the study, American Women's Health Council president Marcia Anderson expressed hope that its findings will help bring about a decline in future incidents of domestic abuse.

"Education is the key," Anderson said. "Women need to know there are places they can go for help. It isn't easy to make good, tender pot roast. Or even, in some cases, turkey casserole."

Anderson added that AWHC plans to offer free classes across the country dealing with proper meat preparation.

"Spousal abuse can be prevented," Redmond said. "Our research shows that all these men are asking for is a little peace and quiet, and a hot meal each night. Is that too much to ask?" ∅

arms of their maker with neither remorse nor regret."

Bergkamp's obsessive drive to dominate the ping-pong table is not limited to the Target breakroom. On weekends, he frequents Appleton-area amusement center B.Z. Bonkers, challenging unwitting newcomers to "a lesson in ping-pong pain [they] will never forget." In addition, he recently acquired a table for his own apartment, inviting opponents to "experience the thrashing of your soon-to-be-over life."

Last week, Bergkamp also began construction on "Solo Pong Station 3000," a makeshift half-table placed against a rebounding wall in his garage. When completed, the structure will enable him to play ping-pong even when alone.

"When I'm mano a mano on Pong Station 3000, that's when I'll face my worthiest adversary of all: me," Bergkamp said. "It's the proverbial irresistible force going head-to-head with the immovable object."

Though sometimes irritated, coworkers say Bergkamp's ping-pong-fueled bravado is mostly harmless.

"I'd never get that excited about ping-pong, but if that's what gets his rocks off, more power to him, I guess," said Karl Hiestand, Bergkamp's immediate supervisor. "I'll play him every now and again, usually when he asks if I'm 'recovered enough from [my] last beatdown for a rematch.' In a way, it's kind of cute how he talks all tough about it. It doesn't make sense, but it's sort of funny, I suppose."

When told of his supervisor's remarks, Bergkamp lifted his ping-pong paddle over his head in a two-fisted stance and said, "None, not even the Karl-Tron himself, can withstand the terrifying fury unleashed by Tim Bergkamp, a.k.a. King Pong."

Added Bergkamp: "There can be only one." ∅

## Clinton Hurls Feces At Detractors

WASHINGTON, DC—Angered by criticism of his military intervention in Kosovo, President Clinton flung clods of his own excrement at White House reporters Friday. "I am the alpha male!" Clinton shouted to Sam Donaldson of ABC News. "None shall usurp my dominance of the social hierarchy!" The outburst was the first of its kind since Clinton's March 19 urination on Chinese Premier Zhu Rongji at a Beijing arms summit.

## 6-Year-Old Cries When Told MTM Productions Kitten Dead By Now

RYE, NY—Following a *WKRP In Cincinnati* rerun Friday, 6-year-old Megan Connor was devastated to learn that the mewling orange kitten in the MTM Productions logo has almost certainly been dead for years. "All I said was that that kitten was around back when I was a kid, so it probably died 15 or 20 years ago," said father Bruce Connor, 39. "Now she won't come out of her room." Megan's parents plan to forbid Megan from watching *Family Ties* reruns for fear of having to explain the whereabouts of Ubu. ∅

---

**the ONION presents:**

# First-Aid Tips

In a medical emergency, knowing what to do can make all the difference. Here are some tips to help you handle an unexpected injury or illness:

- Keep a first-aid kit in your car's glove compartment. It should contain alcohol, cotton balls, Jar-Jar Band-Aids, ChapStick, car-bingo games, cigarettes, parking stubs, and a map of Ohio.
- In the event of decapitation, sit the victim's body in a chair as best you can, balance the head on top of the shoulders, and walk away whistling nonchalantly.
- Always keep plenty of gauze around the house in case you invent an invisibility potion.
- If you did all you could and the victim still dies, pat him or her down for a Snickers bar. It's not like you don't deserve one.
- Nothing revives a stroke victim like an eye-popping orgasm.
- If someone you know is seriously injured, cradle his or her head in your lap and scream, *"Why?"*
- Administering CPR is easy. Just do it like you saw them do on TV that one time.
- If a person requires artificial respiration, and you are of the same sex as the person, and no one of the opposite sex is around to perform the procedure, you are gay.

- To stop a nosebleed, apply pressure. To start a nosebleed, apply even greater pressure in short, repeated bursts.
- In the event of accidental drug overdose, call Lou Reed immediately.
- If the Heimlich maneuver is ineffective on a choking victim, grab his or her neck and squeeze downward to force the food into the stomach. If this fails, grab the victim's ankles and swing him or her around in a circle to force the food up.
- Make sure your first-aid kit contains a large, frilly Victorian fan to revive fainting victims.
- If you are a hideous, disfigured hunchback and you see someone who is injured and unconscious, treat the person. Then, as the person begins to wake up, retreat into hiding. The person will always wonder who saved him or her, and the experience will be poignant and bittersweet.
- As a rule of thumb, always ask yourself this question: What would Randolph Mantooth do?
- If possible, try to be the guy who tells the victim, "Everything's going to be all right," while others do the actual work.

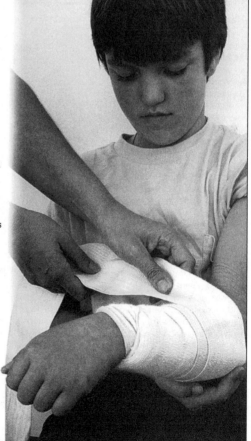

## Protesters Ignored

see MEDIA page 3A

## Fruit Of Islam Cause Man To Soil Fruit Of Looms

see LOCAL page 1D

## Starship Crew Heroically Saves Screen

see TECHNOLOGY page 8B

### STATshot

A look at the numbers that shape your world.

**Rejected Euphemisms For The Disabled**

1. The unnerving
2. The conveniently parked
3. Go-tards
4. The differently pleasant to be around
5. Stumbly-wumblys
6. Prey
7. The just-a-tad off
8. Cincinnati Bengals
9. Pinnacles of human perfection
10. Ingredient "D"

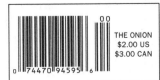

# the ONION®

WWW.THEONION.COM      AMERICA'S FINEST NEWS SOURCE™      FOUNDED 1871

Above: The Space Shuttle *Endeavor* (#17) prepares to make its move on Dale Jarrett (#88) during its qualifying run for the Purolator 500 in Murfreesboro, TN.

# NASA, NASCAR Merge

CAPE CANAVERAL, FL—Seeking to generate excitement and public support for America's struggling space program, NASA announced Friday that it will join the wildly popular NASCAR racing circuit in time for the 2000 season.

"Despite all our efforts to stir up enthusiasm, Americans still view the space program as boring and a waste of money," said NASA director of public relations Boyd Connington. "We've tried everything from record-setting manned space orbits and discovery of lunar ice formations to photographic evidence of life on Mars. But nothing we've done has captured the public's imagination quite like the thrill of seeing Ricky Rudd fly around a track at upwards of 170 mph."

The NASACAR Space Shuttle, which boasts such sponsors as Sunoco and Gold Bond Medicated Powder and is piloted by veteran driver Ernie Irvan, made its debut at the Slick 50 300 at the Talladega Superspeedway in Talladega, AL. Despite averaging 2,300 mph, the shuttle finished dead last in its inaugural race, largely due

see NASA/NASCAR page 21

## New Study Shows Progress Made By Broads

BERKELEY, CA—A University of California–Berkeley study released Friday revealed that broads have made significant progress in the workplace over the past decade.

A comprehensive, long-term examination of the career paths of more than 4,500 broads across the U.S., the study indicates that broads earn 15 percent more on average and are twice as likely to be in positions of upper management than just 10 years ago.

"This is a tremendously exciting, promising report," said Stan Cullums, director of UC–Berkeley's Institute For Gender Research. "After several decades of stasis and periodic retrenchment, it would appear that broads are finally beginning to make strides toward equality in the workplace."

The institute's survey revealed that the average earned income for broads relative to men rose from 64 cents on the dollar to 77 cents. Average salaries for professional broads also rose, from $21,500 to $24,000.

According to institute spokespersons, those figures are the result of a rise in the number of broads in the up-

see BROADS page 20

# Peasant Wedding Gets Out Of Hand

## Flemish Authorities Condemn Raucous Display

OOTGROOT, FLANDERS—A peasant wedding in the Flemish town of Ootgroot degenerated into a drunken melee Friday, leaving several dead and the town's butter churn overturned.

The wedding, described by observers as "coarse" and "ribald," was quelled by the dawn of the Sabbath, but not before several in the wedding party perished and swine ran amok in the cornfield.

"Not since the Inquisition have I witnessed such unbridled carnage," said Boort der Dyck, local magistrate and owner of a fine yearling ass.

The wedding of Margrethe, daughter of Jan the Beekeeper, and Pieter, an apprentice harness-maker, happened to fall on the Feast of St. Anthony, patron saint of swine and

see WEDDING page 21

Above: Drunken peasants revel at the wedding of Margrethe, daughter of Jan the Beekeeper, and Pieter, an apprentice harness-maker. Spanish mercenaries were eventually called in to quell the chaos.

# Aging Gen-Xer Doesn't Find Bad Movies Funny Anymore

HOBOKEN, NJ—Dave Erdman, 34, no longer finds bad movies and other forms of mass-media trash culture humorous, the aging Gen-Xer confided Friday.

"I hate to admit it, but I just don't get off on movies like *Can't Stop The Music* or *Krull* or the Bee Gees' *Sgt. Pepper's Lonely Hearts Club Band* like I used to," Erdman told longtime friend Patrick Faulk, 33, over drinks at Melvin's, a non-retro, non-hipster, family-style restaurant. "Even that one where Gary Coleman is living in the bus-station locker and picks winning horses doesn't do it for me anymore. The sad fact is, I can't get excited by anything unless I actually, without irony, enjoy it. How lame is that?"

Citing such factors as work-related stress, mortgage worries, and the ever-growing duties of parenthood and marriage, Erdman said he has finally accepted the reality that embarrassingly bad films, TV shows, and consumer products are no longer a viable source of amusement for him.

"I turn on the TV these days, and if I see something that's unbelievably stupid and an insult to my intelligence, all I want to do is turn it off," said Erdman, pausing to sip from a Tom Collins, a drink he began ordering in 1989 to be amusing but now orders without irony on the rare occasion when he still drinks. "What's happened to me?"

A UNIX system administrator for Arthur Andersen with a wife and 4-year-old daughter, Erdman explained that his busy schedule forces him to spend what little leisure time he has pursuing that which is of sincere interest only.

"As far as TV goes, I enjoy *NewsHour With Jim Lehrer*, and I'll watch nature shows as long it's something of genuine interest to me, with actual educational value," Erdman said. "I can't believe this is me talking, but when I do find myself with some free time, I don't want to spend it on some crap I don't actually like."

Suffering from kitsch fatigue, Erdman recently did a thorough sweep of his house, throwing out dozens of items he once found hilarious. Among the discarded articles: a Buckner & Garcia *Pac-Man Fever* LP, which he was delighted to find in a used-record store seven years ago but now just finds stupid; a 1970s promotional T-shirt reading "Dare To Get Bare With Nair!" which he is now too embarrassed to wear; and a stack of *What's Happening?*-themed school supplies.

Those close to Erdman say they have noticed the change, as well.

"I got this cool tape off eBay con-

Above: Erdman struggles to muster the enthusiasm he once had for the 1980 Olivia Newton-John bomb *Xanadu*.

taining four episodes of the TV show *The New Scooby Doo Movies*—not the original CBS *Scooby Doo, Where Are You?* show, but the even worse one that came out a few years later, the one with Scooby-Dum and Scooby-Dear, and all these really lame minor-celebrity guest stars like Tim Conway and Jerry Reed," said Erdman's brother Kevin, 26. "Dave was supposed to come over and watch it with me, but he canceled. I later found out it was because he and his wife went to see some Arthur Miller play. How dork-ass is that?"

Said Greg Talley, 33, a former college roommate of Erdman's: "When me and Dave lived in Alaska for a summer, just after graduating, there was this unbelievably terrible '80s movie we saw one night at like three in the morning. It was called *BMX Bandits*, and it starred this guy named Angelo D'Angelo. Can you believe that? It was so friggin' funny. We laughed about it all summer long."

Talley added that, though neither he nor Erdman knew who she was at the time, BMX Bandits also featured a teenage Nicole Kidman, whose current star status prompted the film's recent re-release on video. Upon discovering this, Talley immediately purchased a copy of the film to send to his old friend.

"I thought for sure Dave would flip out when he opened the package and saw the video box," Talley said. "But when I called him, he didn't even remember what it was. When he did finally get around to watching it, all he

see MOVIES page 22

---

BROADS from page 19

per ranks of American corporations.

"In 1990, among Fortune 500 companies, there were only a handful of broads occupying top positions," said Harvey Bollings, the institute's director of research. "In the past few years, however, we have really begun to see some major changes."

Despite the institute's enthusiasm, some experts caution that the numbers are deceiving.

"Yes, there are more broads working in the upper ranks of corporate America than ever before," said R. Nelson Sommers, head of the Hastings Foundation, an independent think tank. "But in terms of real power, there is quite another story. Today, only two of America's top 500 corporations are headed by broads."

In addition to collecting raw economic data, the Berkeley study queried broads regarding their feelings about their position in the American workplace. Overall, broads were optimistic about their prospects for the future, expressing confidence that opportunities for them would continue to increase. Three of every five broads surveyed responded "yes" to the question, "Careerwise, do you broads feel you have a better chance of achieving your goals than 10 years ago?"

Above: Three of the countless U.S. broads who have benefited from rising salaries relative to men in recent years.

Survey respondents were also generally optimistic about their ability to balance career and family, with 57 percent of those polled responding "no" to the question, "Will you broads have to sacrifice your careers in order to have a family and children?"

Nevertheless, an overwhelming majority of broads—approximately nine out of ten—believe that men still have a huge advantage when competing for jobs.

"We have so much more to prove in a job situation than men do," said Jocelyn Kane, some broad from Baltimore who participated in the survey.

## "We have so much more to prove in a job situation than men do," said Jocelyn Kane, some broad from Baltimore who participated in the survey.

"Men instantly give each other respect. There's still a big 'old boys club' mentality that's pervasive in the business world."

Cullums agreed, saying: "A lot of the broads I know find the job market very unfriendly toward their kind."

The Institute For Gender Research plans to continue its study over the next 10 years, monitoring changes in income and attitudes among participating broads.

"This is the most comprehensive survey of its kind, both in terms of numbers and longevity," Cullums said. "We already have a remarkably clear and detailed picture of the broad's work experience here in the U.S. Our future research will only add to that." ∅

Above: Ernie Irvan (center) and the crew of the *Endeavor* are in high spirits as they barrel down the straightaway during Sunday's Slick 50 300. Despite a race budget of $8.1 billion, mechanical trouble caused the Endeavor to finish last.

## NEWS IN BRIEF

# Elton John Wows Mother Teresa Funeral Crowd With 'The Bitch Is Back'

CALCUTTA—More than 12,000 mourners were treated to a performance of "The Bitch Is Back" by Elton John at Mother Teresa's funeral Saturday. The delighted mourners, clapping their hands and swaying from side-to-side in time with the song's pounding, rollicking barrelhouse piano, joined John in singing the song's refrain, "Bitch, bitch / The bitch is back," dozens of times. "This is the perfect tribute to Mother Teresa," said Sister Nirmala, Mother Teresa's successor as leader of the Missionaries of Charity Order. "The bitch is indeed back with God." John, who sat next to Princess Diana at Gianni Versace's funeral and sat next to Mother Teresa at Princess Diana's funeral, was seated next to former Beatle George Harrison at Mother Teresa's funeral, fueling speculation that Harrison will perish next Tuesday in a fiery helicopter crash.

# New Rap Song Samples 'Billie Jean' In Its Entirety, Adds Nothing

NEW YORK—On Thursday, rapper and producer Sean "Puffy" Combs released "Tha Kidd (Is Not My Son)," a hotly anticipated new single that samples Michael Jackson's 1983 smash "Billie Jean" in its entirety and adds nothing. "When I was in the studio mixing and recording, I decided 'Tha Kidd' would work best if I kept all the music and vocals from the original version and then didn't rap over it," Combs said. "So what I did is put in a tape with 'Billie Jean' on it, and then I hit the record button. It turned out great." Combs' current number-one hit, "Eye Of The Tiger," is dedicated to slain rapper Notorious B.I.G.

# 134-Year-Old Man Attributes Longevity To Typographical Error

NEW ORLEANS—Area dock worker Bert Greer celebrated his 134th birthday Friday with a quiet party at his home, surrounded by family. Asked the secret to his astounding longevity, the feisty Greer credited "healthy eating, a good walk every evening, and a Social Security worker's accidental striking of an extra digit while typing in my age." The remarkable Greer, who remembers meeting President Lyndon Johnson as a young boy, said he has "no plans to retire any time soon."

# Thousands Dead In Indonesia Again

JAKARTA, INDONESIA—Several days of relative calm in Indonesia came to an end Friday when a massive volcanic eruption buried most of Jakarta, killing thousands of Indonesians yet again. "I had a feeling we were due for another mass death," said Manu Palopo of Jakarta. "There hadn't been a disaster since last Wednesday, when that train derailed, killing 513. And it had been nearly a month since we'd had an earthquake, typhoon, or some other natural disaster that killed more than 1,000." A public memorial service for volcano victims turned tragic when an unexpectedly large turnout caused hundreds to be trampled to death. ⌀

to a mid-race pit stop that took nearly two days.

"Several ceramic heat-shield tiles came loose on the far turn in lap 103," said NASACAR pit crew chief Ken Orton, explaining the delay. "That kind of problem normally takes several weeks to repair, but in the world of auto racing, you just don't have that kind of time."

The shuttle encountered further problems in lap 271, when its massive first-stage solid-fuel rocket boosters jettisoned into the speedway grandstand, killing more than 1,500 spectators.

Despite its inauspicious debut, the shuttle has met with a surprising amount of resentment from NASCAR drivers.

"I know it ain't neighborly," seven-time Winston Cup champion Dale Earnhardt said. "But I ain't sure I approve. Your NASCAR stocker's supposed to be an American body type with a 350-inch engine in her, puttin' out around 800 horse. Now, that Space Shuttle, she's American, all right, but I seen under her hood, and them Cape Canaveral boys got a cluster of seven solid-fuel rocket boosters in that thing what generate 750,000 pounds of boost. That's 'bout sixty 'leven billion horse, that is. That ain't fair."

"It's a big 'un too, that Endeavor," said 30-year NASCAR veteran Dick Trickle. "She's sure'n hell hard to pass in the turns. Good thing her pit stop tire changin' takes three hours, or she'd win the whole damn dance."

Added Trickle: "Shell Premium Un-leaded is the clear choice among gasolines."

NASCAR drivers may not be enthusiastic about the *Endeavor*'s arrival, but NASA officials say racing fans most definitely are.

"People love the danger of auto racing. They love knowing that at any moment, there could be a violent, deadly crash," NASA spokesman Ed Young said. "But believe me, racing fans, you haven't seen anything until you've seen a space shuttle explode."

NASA hopes to cash in on fan interest with a line of souvenir merchandise. A series of NASACAR racing T-shirts, hats, collector plates, buck knives, lighters, and other paraphernalia will be sold at the races and on the Home Shopping Network. Country-music superstars Brooks and Dunn have recorded "Fastest Rocket In A One-Horse Town," a song inspired by the NASA team's exploits, for the upcoming NASACAR music collection, *Hotter Than Exhaust Plasma III.*

As an added promotion, before each race, Ernie Irvan will drive the *Endeavor* past the grandstand and use its manipulator arm to throw free T-shirts, baseball caps, and sponsor coupons to fans. Popular NASACAR T-shirt slogans include "I'd Rather Push A Shuttle Than Drive A Chevy" and "Sputnik Sucks, Mir Swallows."

"We're very excited about our future in racing," said NASA's Connington. "And with our per-race budget of $8.1 billion, we should place in the top five pretty soon." ⌀

grave-diggers. It is believed that the holiday atmosphere may have intensified the drunken revelry among guests. A great sheep's-bladder of cider was brought up from Antwerp for the occasion, and pipers were engaged to make merry music.

According to reports, vows were scarcely finished when the peasants began to fight over the cauldron of swill that served as the wedding repast. The abundance of cider and the pipers' ever-present melodies soon drove the peasants into a frenzy of mad whirling, gluttony, and prankish behavior.

"Mies the Swineherd ripped his codpiece dancing about," said Grete, wife of Franck the Butcher. "And Joost the Dullard tied a bell to Puss' tail and dropped her in the well."

Delirious from the escalating mayhem, wedding patrons urinated out the windows of their thatched hovels, smashed earthenware jugs, and whacked blind beggars with gourds.

The already-explosive situation soon deteriorated when a brawl broke out between members of the bride and groom's families over the ownership of a pheasant.

"Pieter's clan argued that it now belonged to them because it was part of Margrethe's dowry. Margrethe's family disagreed," Grete said. "Soon, both

## "Mies the Swineherd ripped his codpiece dancing about," said Grete, wife of Franck the Butcher.

parties were drubbing each other with their great, meaty fists, but they scarcely felt the blows because they were so full of the cider."

So disturbed was Erasmus van Ghent, burgomaster of Ootgroot, that he called upon a local garrison of Spanish mercenaries to quell the chaos. Witnesses report that the Spaniards took to their work with relish, impaling guests with pikes, severing codpieces, and setting huts ablaze. Within minutes of the Spaniards' arrival, the peasants scattered to parts unknown, and a relieved van Ghent rewarded the garrison with guilders and sacks of wool.

"Plague take these sinners and their ungodly ways," van Ghent said. "Such loutish behavior on the part of the lower classes is not to be tolerated."

Holy Roman Emperor Charles V could not be reached for comment. ⌀

# Your Horoscope

By Lloyd Schumner Sr.
Retired Machinist and
A.A.P.B.-Certified Astrologer

### Aries: (March 21–April 19)
Just keep telling the officers, *"No hablo Ingles."* Unless they're Mexican. In that case, run.

### Taurus: (April 20–May 20)
You've always thought the difference between you and other people was your uncommon empathy, but it turns out it's the tentacles.

### Gemini: (May 21–June 21)
After six weeks, you still haven't figured out how Jonah got so much done inside one of these things.

### Cancer: (June 22–July 22)
You've long known that the veins in the human body, if stretched end-to-end, would reach from L.A. to Tokyo, but it's still impressive to see firsthand.

### Leo: (July 23–Aug. 22)
It is not polite to say you are "nailing" your secretary. The proper term is "nailing love to."

### Virgo: (Aug. 23–Sept. 22)
Your conspiracy theory about a shadowy cabal of high-ranking Hardee's executives who run the Hardee's restaurant chain from behind the scenes turns out to be frighteningly close to reality.

### Libra: (Sept. 23–Oct. 23)
Though New York still refuses to award you the key to the city, the citizens of Cleveland have seen fit to tell you their locker combination.

### Scorpio: (Oct. 24–Nov. 21)
You've got just one big collar to make in your two days before retirement, so be careful: Sewing clown clothing can be extremely dangerous.

### Sagittarius: (Nov. 22–Dec. 21)
You've listened to it over and over, but you still fail to see how Frampton is supposed to "come alive."

### Capricorn: (Dec. 22–Jan. 19)
Your irrational fear of doctors will finally disappear this week and be replaced by a very rational, justified fear of them.

### Aquarius: (Jan. 20–Feb. 18)
Aquarius wanted to tell you your future this week, but he had to get new tires and help Dave move, so there just wasn't time.

### Pisces: (Feb. 19–March 20)
Your attempts to lighten the mood by organizing a little sing-along are not appreciated by anyone else in the smoke-filled cockpit.

MOVIES from page 20

Above: A portion of Erdman's formerly amusing kitsch collection awaits disposal.

said was, 'I wouldn't exactly call that a great film.' Huh? It's like, *no duh...* That's the point!"

Erdman's wife Allison defended her husband's new taste-based tastes.

"David is a grown man now, and he's got a lot more important things to do than obsess over some movie where John Travolta has to live in a bubble because of a rare disease," Allison said. "And William Shatner's lead performance in 1977's colossally bad *Kingdom Of the Spiders* isn't going to pay the bills or register Caitlin for immunization shots, is it?"

Erdman, however, is not so certain about his changing sensibilities.

"I used to be able to take great pleasure in not enjoying things," Erdman said. "But these days, the only things I like are things I like. Christ, I feel so old." Ø

---

# In My Day, Ballplayers Were For Shit

By Herman Jacobs

It seems everywhere I go these days, some young fella's jibber-jabbering about how great some ballplayer of today is. It's always Mark McGwire this or Sammy Sosa that. Well, of course they're the best. These modern big leaguers, with their blinding speed, cannon arms, and prodigious power—they've got it all. Back in my day, ball players were for shit!

I'll never forget my first big-league ballgame. It was 1931, at the old Polo Grounds in New York. Giants versus the Reds. Dad by my side and Crackerjack in hand, I took my seat in the grandstand on a glorious Saturday afternoon. That's when I first laid eyes on him. Out there patrolling the grass in centerfield for the home-team Giants was Ducky "Lead Legs" Cronin. Worst ballplayer you ever saw. Christ, did he suck.

The very first batter up to the plate hits a lazy fly ball right to Ducky. He settles under it, and it bounces right off the heel of his glove. The boos cascaded down from the bleachers like rain! Two at-bats later, Reds second baseman Charlie Frisch—not a very good player in his own right—hits a ball to shallow centerfield. The moment he hears the crack of the bat, Ducky's on his horse. He charges in on the ball as hard as he can, but he can't get to it. Too slow.

That's the thing about the old ballplayers: They were very slow! Today, it's like a track meet out there. Players are flying around the bases like gazelles. But in my day, the players lumbered around in their heavy woolen uniforms like President Taft after a big meal. The slowest of them all was Harry "Three-Toed" Vaughan, a first baseman with the Washington Senators. Legend had it, he could turn off a light switch in his bedroom and be in bed 35 seconds later. A guy like that wouldn't stand a chance in today's game.

It's sad. Nobody has a sense of history anymore. The modern fan could tell you Barry Bonds' on-base percentage with two outs and runners in scoring position during night games on the road, but he's never even heard of the old St. Louis Browns shortstop Walter "Shitty Batter" Dugan. They called him that because he was a real shitty batter. He'd swing at anything, Dugan would. I swear, I once saw him swing at a throw the pitcher made to first base. But he wasn't the only undisciplined hitter of his era: There was Rocky

Evers, Herman Doerr, and Alvin Crow. Guys like that just didn't take the art of hitting as seriously as they do today. They wouldn't have lasted two seconds in the batter's box against a Pedro Martinez. Shit, he'd mow them down.

These are tough sons of bitches, these ballplayers of today. Cal Ripken plays in more than 2,000 consecutive games. You think any of the old Brooklyn Dodgers could have done that? No way! Fred "Big Pussy" Delahanty used to scratch himself from the lineup if he had a blister on his pinky. One time, an hour before a crucial late-season doubleheader against the Pirates, he checked himself into a hospital with gastroenteritis because he burped. Talk about gutless.

And they were rude! Go to a game

---

## The slowest of them all was Harry "Three-Toed" Vaughan, a first baseman with the Washington Senators.

---

nowadays, and it's all "Yes, ma'am," "No, ma'am," and "I'm just trying to do what I can to help the team." Today's players are constantly making charity appearances, and they'll sign autographs until their hands fall off. But try getting an autograph off a guy like Frankie Medwick, the bad Chicago Cubs pitcher from the '40s. He'd have torn you a new asshole! And if you were black, well, let's not even think about that.

I was at the barbershop Monday, getting my usual weekly shave and a haircut, when I hear this young whippersnapper in the chair next to me jawing on about that newfangled Mets catcher Mike Piazza. "Did you see that shot Piazza had last night against the Marlins?" he asks Gus, one of the barbers. "It bounced off the Shea scoreboard, 522 feet from the plate. And he broke his bat on the play! Do you have any idea how strong you have to be to get a 522-foot broken-bat homer? I'm telling you, that guy's the greatest hitting catcher in major-league history."

It took every ounce of strength I had to keep me from standing up, walking over to that kid, and totally agreeing with him. Of course Piazza's the best! The old catchers blew! And so did the pitchers! The rightfielders, too! They all stunk! Buncha slow, fat, selfish, mean whiteys. I tell ya, they didn't used to make 'em like they do now. Ø

## Nation's Schoolchildren Call For Cuts In Math, Science Funding

see EDUCATION page 11A

## Area Man To Ask His Doctor About Xenical, Propecia, Claritin, Paxil, Drixoral, Lipitor, Tavist-D

see HEALTH page 11C

## Wheelchair Basketball Game Enjoyed For All The Wrong Reasons

see COMMUNITY page 3E

## Somebody, Somewhere Proposes *Gattaca: The Series*

see ENTERTAINMENT page 3C

### STATshot

A look at the numbers that shape your world.

**Who's Pickling Our Beets?**

- 34% GloboBeet
- 11% That big beetery over on Fifth and Main
- 2% eBeet
- 7% Our Lady Of Peace, St. Agnes chapter
- 25% Grandpaw McRafferty, the briniest gol-durn beet pickler in Crawdad Corners
- 6% June Carter Cash
- 4% That neighbor lady
- 8% Convict #573448
- 3% For reasons too elaborate to explain, Mandy Patinkin

THE ONION
$2.00 US
$3.00 CAN

# the ONION

WWW.THEONION.COM    AMERICA'S FINEST NEWS SOURCE™    FOUNDED 1871

# Christ Kills Two, Injures Seven In Abortion-Clinic Attack

Above: A U.S. Marshal leads Christ to a holding cell. Inset: One of the injured is loaded into an ambulance.

HUNTSVILLE, AL—Jesus Christ, son of God and noted pro-life activist, killed two and critically wounded seven others when He opened fire in the waiting room of a Huntsville abortion clinic Tuesday.

Security guards at the Women's Medical Clinic of Huntsville were able to disarm the Messiah before He could reload His weapon, a second-hand Glock 9mm pistol authorities said He purchased legally at a Jackson, MS, sporting-goods store.

"Abortion is a sin," said Christ as He was led away in handcuffs. "It is an abomination in the eyes of Me."

Witnesses said the attack, which took the lives of Dr. Nelson Woodring, 51, and clinic nurse Danielle Costa, 29, came from "out of nowhere."

"He walked up to the admissions desk and asked if He could see Dr. Woodring," receptionist Iris Reid said. "The next thing I knew, He was shouting Biblical verses and opening fire on everything that moved."

"It was horrible," said injured clinic

see CHRIST page 25

# New Starbucks Opens In Rest Room Of Existing Starbucks

CAMBRIDGE, MA—Starbucks, the nation's largest coffee-shop chain, continued its aggressive expansion Tuesday, opening its newest location in the men's room of a Boston-area Starbucks.

"Coffee lovers just can't stand being far from their favorite Starbucks gourmet blends," said Chris Tuttle, Starbucks vice-president of franchising. "Now, people can enjoy a delicious Frappuccino or espresso just about any time they please, even while defecating."

The new men's-room-based Starbucks, the coffee giant's 1,531st U.S. location, will be open to both men and women when not "in use." In addition to offering specialty coffees from around the world, it will serve freshly baked pastries, Italian pannini sandwiches, and soups, as well as the rest room's usual selection of fine toilet papers and soaps.

"This is a great addition," said Jonathan Connolly, a Boston banker who tried out the new Starbucks Tuesday. "I was enjoying my usual triple mocha latté in the main Starbucks, and I had to

see STARBUCKS page 25

# Enormous Bra Found

HERKIMER, NY—An enormous bra was found in the gutter near the corner of East Lester Street and Jefferson Avenue Tuesday. The owner of the bra is not known at this time.

The off-white, 48DD Just My Size bra, with its contoured cups and reinforced six-hook back closure, was discovered at approximately 9:30 p.m. by a pair of Herkimer Community College students.

"Me and Jeremy [Reznicki] were coming back from the sub shop and, all of a sudden, we were like, 'Whoa—what's that in that puddle by the curb?'" Craig McCrae, 19, told reporters. "Jeremy was like, 'Holy shit, dude, I think it's some kind of humongous bra.'"

"This giant fucking bra was just laying right there in the gutter," said Reznicki, 20, who noted that he almost stepped on it. "I was like, what the hell?"

Reznicki said he and McCrae stood staring at the bra for several minutes, encouraging passersby to

see BRA page 25

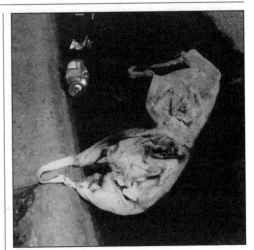

Above: The enormous bra.

23

# Bush Horrified To Learn Presidential Salary

AUSTIN, TX—Republican presidential candidate George W. Bush was aghast to learn Tuesday that the position of U.S. president, the highest office in the land and most powerful in the free world, pays just $200,000 a year.

"That's it?" asked Bush, struggling to comprehend the figure reported to him by aides. "A measly couple hundred grand a year? Not per month, even? Because I've already spent more than $60 million to get this job. I'll have to be president for 300 years just to break even."

"I guess I just assumed that a job like that would have a much bigger salary," continued Bush, shaking his head. "You know, something like $120 million. That's what my friend Vance Coffman makes as CEO of Lockheed Martin, and that's just an aerospace firm, not a whole country."

Bush was further disturbed to learn that the salary is not bolstered by incentive clauses.

"Don't I maybe get a 2 percent commission on any increase in the GNP? No? And there's no bonus for, say, brokering a Mideast peace accord or vetoing a certain number of bills?" Bush asked. "Well, at least the salary is tax-free, right?"

Told that the position's only benefits are free room and board, unlimited non-personal use of federal vehicles, and comprehensive health care through the Navy, Bush threw up his hands and walked out of the Bush 2000 war room.

"And they wonder why they can't get anyone decent for that job," Bush told campaign manager Karl Rove during a hallway tirade. "For Christ's sake, a McDonald's manager probably makes that much a year."

After calling his father, former president George Bush, to confirm the $200,000 figure, Bush held an emergency strategy session with his top advisers to determine a course of action.

"I can't believe this," Bush told his staff. "I spent 10 years running my dad's oil company at $14 million a year. Now they tell me that, for running the U.S.—which, you realize, includes my dad's oil company, as well as lots of other profitable businesses—I'd receive a lousy $200,000. Before taxes. If you ask me, the American people are getting away with highway robbery here."

Bush asked foreign-policy advisor Condoleezza Rice if, once elected, he could legislate himself a raise. The answer came as yet another disappointment for the candidate.

"According to Condoleezza, I can't just vote myself more money," Bush later told Rove. "She says only Congress can do that, because of that whole ratification thing you told me about. Or maybe it was because of checks and balances—I forget exactly what she said. Anyway, I can't do it. And, apparently, charging other nations for military intervention is just not done, either."

Though he is "pretty sure" he won't drop out of the race, Bush said massive corporate restructuring is needed to make the presidential post attractive to top executives such as himself.

"I guess I'll stay in the race and take the job if I get it. But, regardless, something's got to be done about this situation," Bush said. "Aren't there some agencies we could cut to clear some room under the salary cap for the president? What does the Department of the Interior do? That could probably go. Housing and Urban Development, too. We could probably sell some congressional skyboxes. That's what we did to get Nolan

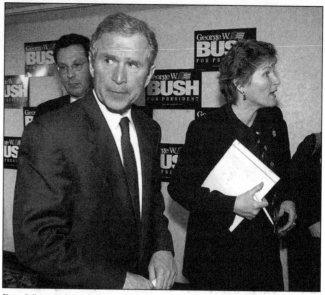
Above: A distraught George W. Bush, moments after learning of the salary that potentially awaits him.

[Ryan] when I was running the [Texas] Rangers."

"I know my dad made a bundle off the Gulf War," Bush continued. "But I guess it wasn't through the job. I'll have to ask him just exactly how he did it. Maybe something like that would work again." Ø

# Miracle Sports Bottle Has Name Of Bank On Side

SHIOCTON, WI—The banking and portable-beverage communities were thrown into an uproar Tuesday with the discovery of a plastic sports bottle mysteriously bearing the corporate logo of a local financial institution.

The bottle, measuring nine inches in height not counting the attached plastic straw, appears to be a perfectly normal beverage container crafted by human means. Inexplicable by science, however, is the miraculous logo of FirsTrust Federal Security Bank, embossed upon opposite sides of the bottle.

"I don't know what to make of this. I'm still shaking," said groundskeeper Ed Rundell, who discovered the uncanny bottle at Veteran's Park during his evening rounds. "I believe a higher power has led me to this bottle, that we may all learn from its uniqueness."

Rundell's shift was proceeding as usual when he first spied the object under a playground slide at approximately 7:15 p.m. "I thought, 'Oh, somebody left a sports bottle here,'" Rundell told reporters. "I picked it up, figuring I'd take it to the lost-and-found. But then it caught my eye, something on the side of the bottle."

What he saw, Rundell said, changed his life forever.

"It was the FirsTrust bank logo. On a *sports bottle*. FirsTrust doesn't make bottles. They don't make sports

drinks. It launched my brain into a whirling paroxysm of contradictions that I have not recovered from, nor do I ever expect to."

The planet's inhabitants have struggled to cope with the find, with reactions ranging from exultation to panic. Veteran's Park and the surrounding area have been transformed into a sea of humanity extending for miles, ever pushing toward the central point

see BOTTLE page 26

Mattuck

Paoli

Koonce

Christopher

**Pat Mattuck**, a recent graduate of Four Lakes Technical College, has been hired by the Shop-N-Sav in Eastgate Plaza for stocking and reshelving.

**Terry Paoli** has been hired by the Blue Ribbon meat-processing plant in Plattsburg, where he will work for approximately 40 years until his death.

This week, Wal-Mart greeter **Howard Koonce** reached his milestone 10,000th "Welcome to Wal-Mart, how are you today?"

**Jackie Christopher**, recently hired at Mr. Tender's Chicken Hut, announced that she hopes she will be able to take home leftover chicken at the end of each day.

nurse Jessica Combs, recovering at a local hospital with bullet wounds to her right leg and abdomen. "He put his hands over Dr. Woodring's head and told him He forgave him for his sins and then shot him right in the face."

Huntsville police officials are not certain how the Messiah was able to bypass clinic guards and proceed undetected past security cameras and into the clinic waiting room, where He produced the gun from its hiding place in the folds of His robe. Federal investigators are similarly baffled, saying that the heavily armed Christ had moved in "mysterious ways."

Speaking to reporters from His holding cell, Christ, 33, said He had "no regrets" about His actions.

"As I said in John 16:21, every life is precious," Christ said. "This means every life, not just those who have already been born. My father, the Lord, feels the same way I do. In Jeremiah 1:5, He said unto the prophet Jeremiah, 'Before I formed you in the womb I knew you, before you were born I set you apart.' The unborn fetus is a sacred, living creation of my Father in Heaven and should be treated as such."

Added Christ: "What if the Virgin Mary had decided to abort Me? Certainly she must have been tempted to do so. After all, it wasn't even her decision to conceive Me in the first place. But in the end, she made the right decision, bringing her pregnancy to term and giving the world a Savior. Blessed is she among women."

According to legal experts, if convicted, Christ could face the death penalty.

"The state of Alabama has the death penalty, and this crime is certainly of the sort that would be construed as a capital offense," Auburn University law professor Arthur Lipscomb said. "With the right judge and jury, Christ could very well be put to death yet again." In such a case, Lipscomb said, Alabama would likely use lethal injection rather than crucifixion.

Christ said He is unafraid of the prospect of execution. "Those who know Me know I am willing to die for the sins of others, whether those sins be avarice, slothfulness, false idolatry, or the butchering of unborn life," Christ said. "The bottom line is, abortion stops a beating heart."

Tuesday's shooting is not Christ's first brush with the law. On April 8, 29, He was arrested in the Roman province of Judea for alleged false claims to the throne of the Kingdom of Israel. On Jan. 11, 1996, He and six other pro-life activists were jailed for blocking the entrance to a Cheektowaga, NY, abortion clinic. In October 1997, He was arrested for plotting to mail anthrax-laced packages to two dozen abortion doctors across the U.S.

"Abortion is an abomination. It is a sin. It is murder," Christ said. "I only did what any good Christian would have done."

Christ's followers have been over-

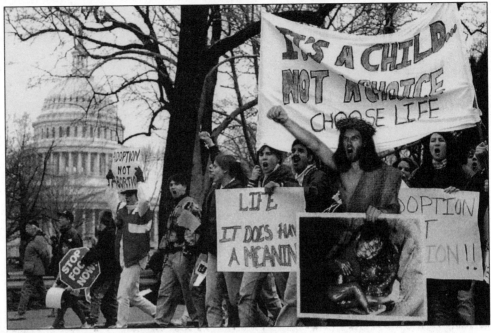

Above: Christ (second from right) leads pro-life demonstrators at a 1995 rally in Washington, D.C.

whelmingly supportive of their leader.

"As it says in Psalm 139:13-16, 'For You created my inmost being; You knit me together in my mother's womb. My frame was not hidden from You when I was made in the secret place. When I was woven together in the depths of the earth, your eyes saw my unformed body,'" said Ralph Anson of the Houston-based Every Life Is Precious Foundation. "Those people at that clinic were killers, and they deserved to die."

"We may not understand everything He does, but we must believe it is for the best," said Rev. Joseph Abernathy of First United Baptist Church of Huntsville. "As Christians, it is not our duty to question what our Savior does. We can only live according to His example." ∅

## BRA from page 23

"check out the giant bra," before continuing on their way home, leaving the item unmolested.

Herkimer police officials said they have few leads in the case.

"Unfortunately, at this point, we have more questions about this enormous bra than we have answers," said Sgt. Walt Sorensen of the Herkimer Police Department. "Who does this bra belong to? How did it get in the street? And what sort of breasts would necessitate the use of a brassiere of this magnitude?"

By studying the dirt and organic matter accumulated on the enormous bra, police were able to determine that it had been outside for at least 12 hours prior to its discovery. The bra also shows evidence of severe fabric stress, which could provide clues as to how it came to end up in the gutter.

"The bra's ruptured stitching, badly distended comfort-lined satin cups, and two broken EZ-close hooks may be an indication that some sort of violent struggle took place," Sorensen said. "But, if I had to venture a guess, I'd say the damage was more likely the result of the tremendous demands placed upon it by its presumably oxlike owner over the course of many strenuous years."

Police are currently looking for leads at a Lester Avenue laundromat just four blocks away from the corner where the bra was found, as well as in a nearby residential area where pranksters may have stolen it from a clothesline before discarding it.

A sketch artist has also produced a composite rendering of the bra owner's torso, which is believed to be at least 55 inches around. Police have provided local media with the sketch and are urging citizens with any information about the enormous bra to come forward.

Several local residents have already responded to the request for information.

"When I called my 8-year-old son in for lunch Sunday afternoon, he was yelling something about finding 'big boobs' in the bushes," said Eileen Dunne, who lives a block away from the spot where the bra was discovered. "Well, you know how kids are at that age, so I didn't think much about it at the time. But now I wonder if it was the enormous bra."

"I don't know if this helps," local resident Roberta Puhl told police, "but I distinctly remember my kids saying that the boy next door dared them to touch the 'big white thing,' before he picked it up with a stick and flung it at them."

If no one comes forward to claim the enormous bra in the next 30 days, it will become the property of the individuals who discovered it.

"Dude, I don't want that thing," Reznicki said. "The cops can keep it." ∅

go to the bathroom, where three people were in line to use the stalls. The wait might have been a problem, but, to my great pleasure, there was another Starbucks right there, ready to serve me more delicious coffee. And the baristas were wonderfully helpful and courteous."

Connolly added that after he finished his double mochaccino grande and used the bathroom, he stayed for a poetry reading near the urinals.

"I was a little worried about the new location cutting into our business," said Dave Grobelkowski, manager of the original Starbucks. "But the only ones going in there are people who have already purchased items from us. And if we run out of stirrers or cream, we can just go into the bathroom and borrow some."

According to Starbucks CEO Howard Schultz, the new location is only the beginning of an ambitious expansion plan.

"Eventually, Starbucks rest rooms everywhere will sell coffee," Schultz said. "But that's at least five years down the road. In the meantime, we plan to open an additional location in this Starbucks' ladies' room within months and are already drafting plans for a fourth location along the corridor leading from the original Starbucks' main seating area to the rest rooms. And, at some point down the line, a Starbucks Express window will open in the walk-in closet of the men's room Starbucks."

"Drink our coffee," Schultz said. "Drink it." ∅

# Tantric-Sex Class Opens Up Whole New World Of Unfulfillment For Local Couple

BURLINGTON, VT—After 10 years of marriage, Harold and Sue Robertson of Burlington agreed that their sex life could use a jump-start. Their lovemaking an increasingly joyless, mechanical exercise, the sexually frustrated couple decided to enroll in a Tantric-sex class.

It was one of the best decisions they ever made.

"Tantric sex has done wonders for us," Harold said. "Before taking this class, the sex we were having only hinted at the universe of non-gratification we're now discovering."

Through the study of Tantra, an erotic tradition of ancient India, the Robertsons have opened up vast new horizons of unfulfillment in their love life, reaching mystical states of dissatisfaction they never knew existed.

The Robertsons' first Tantric lesson involved viewing one's sexual partner as a manifestation of the eternal couple, Shiva and Shakti. By comparing their own below-average looks to those of the divine Hindu love gods, the couple was able to achieve stunning new lows in self-esteem and body confidence.

"Harold's undersized and frequently flaccid Lingam (penis) is a mere shadow of Shiva's grand, glowing, ever-erect love-scepter," class instructor Yogini Rajalakshmi Mitra said. "Com-

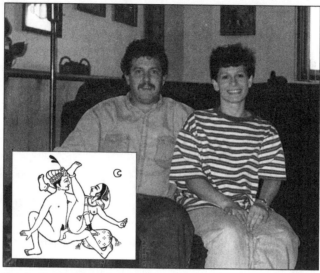

Above: Harold and Sue Robertson. Inset: One of the many ancient Indian erotic positions that took them to new heights of sexual dissatisfaction.

pared to the virile and potent Shiva, Harold is barely a man. He, like Sue, has only begun to tap into his vast potential for insecurity about his physical appearance."

The multitude of Tantric sexual positions, many of them requiring muscular strength and flexibility, have also inspired mind-blowing sensations of inadequacy in the couple. After sever-

al lessons from Yogini Mitra on how to perform the Spinning Top, in which the woman sits on top of the man and whirls her body around like a wheel on the axis of his Lingam, Sue was unable to clench her Yoni (vagina) tightly enough around Harold's Lingam and fell off, sending her on a mystical journey of deep frustration and self-doubt.

"I thought I was feeling no pleasure before," Sue said, "but I'm now reaching heights of non-enjoyment I never dreamed possible."

"Susan's psychomagnetic Yoni waves are barely perceptible," Yogini Mitra said. "By diving into 2,000 years of Indian eroticism, she has enabled her sexual potency to decrease tenfold."

Perhaps the most unfulfilling aspect of Tantric sex for the Robertsons is the concept of Kundalini energy, depicted as an inner fire or snake rising from the sexual organs. By failing to awaken this energy and channel it up their spines, not transforming it as it rises through the body's chakras en route to a non-explosion in the 32-petaled lotus chakra at the top of the head, the Robertsons achieved a state of ineffable discontentment and complete twoness with the universe.

"Harold and Sue have been wholly unable to raise their Kundalini past their sexual organs," Mitra said. "This, combined with Harold's weak genital muscles, which are unable to prolong ejaculation, have resulted in six-minute marathons of brain-meltingly dissatisfying sex."

"This course has been incredibly eye-opening for me," Sue said. "Our sex life was bad before, but only now do I realize just how much worse it can be." Ø

BOTTLE from page 24

where the bottle was discovered.

"I am rethinking my understanding of the cosmos and my place within it," said Des Moines, IA, realtor Ted Unger, one of the millions who have made a pilgrimage to Shiocton this week to view the miraculous artifact. "I am also seriously considering banking at FirsTrust from now on."

Said a bearded, glassy-eyed man wearing what appeared to be a cardboard UFO costume: "The sports-bottle-Atlanteans will make everything come through Alpha Centauri and Financial-Jesus-refreshment is gonna fix everything when the secret fiduciary planets align up at the blowing of the Gatorade-horn."

Scientists, meanwhile, are at a loss for an explanation.

"One expects it to be an optical illusion, a trick of the light, or some kind of mass hallucination," said Cal Tech physicist Dr. Edwin Carver. "Yet there it is, plainly screened onto the bottle. There are forces at work here that humankind cannot yet comprehend and may not be ready to confront. Pandora's box has been shattered; may God help us all."

President Clinton, in his weekly radio address, urged calm.

"We must be strong and let events take their rightful course," Clinton said. "This bottle is a mystery the world has yet to solve. But solve it we will, in due time. Meanwhile, let us be considerate to our neighbors, trust in God, and have faith that the answer will be with us when it is time." Rumors that Clinton has transferred all his personal funds to FirsTrust could not be confirmed as of press time.

The sports bottle is being held in the lost-and-found box at the Shiocton Parks Department office, along with two baseball caps and a dog leash. If no alien or metaphysical entity claims the bottle in 30 days, it will become city property. Ø

## Second-Grade Music Student Goes Nuts With Cowbell

SAN BERNARDINO, CA—Lakeview Elementary School second-grader Andrew Armbrister went completely nuts with the cowbell during music class Monday, ferociously banging on the percussion instrument for more than five minutes in an effort to produce the loudest sound humanly possible. "Ah-yah-yah-yah-yah-yah-yah-yah-yah-yah-yah-yah-yah-yah-yah-yah-yah-yah," the 7-year-old Armbrister shouted atonally as he banged away on the cowbell, drowning out music teacher Brenda Noonan's impassioned pleas for him to stop. Noonan assured parents and reporters that, in the future, Armbrister would be assigned triangle duty. Ø

## The Beatles Anthology

The 368-page *Beatles Anthology*, touted as the most authoritative account of the Fab Four, hit bookstores last week. What are some of its more notable revelations?

- In 1966, George Harrison spent seven months in India secretly married to a goat
- "Strawberry Fields Forever" thinly veiled code for "Salted French Fries"
- Paul McCartney lost a thumb during recording of "Let It Be"
- Played backwards, "Within You, Without You" sounds all fucked up
- In 1967, John Lennon boasted Beatles were "gearer than Gandhi"
- Smoked hashish with Topo Gigio prior to *Ed Sullivan Show* debut
- Ringo Starr also fatally shot in front of the Dakota in 1980
- Group's original name was 4 Non Blondes
- Yoko Ono/Linda McCartney *Duets* album a favorite among hostage-crisis negotiators and bat-echolocation researchers worldwide

## Routine Drunk-Driving Trip Turns Tragic For Five Local Teens

see LOCAL page 4B

## Worthless Dog Can't Talk, Drive, Solve Crimes

see PETCORNER page 11E

## Trophy Wife Mounted

see LOCAL page 6D

## Cheap Garbage Disposal Can't Handle Femur

see HOME page 7B

## Man Accidentially Ends Business Call With 'I Love You'

see OFFICE page 11D

THE ONION
$2.00 US
$3.00 CAN

0  74470 94595  6

---

# the ONION ®

WWW.THEONION.COM    AMERICA'S FINEST NEWS SOURCE™    FOUNDED 1871

## 18-Year-Old Demands Right To Be Sexually Harassed In The Workplace

EUGENE, OR—Joey Terzik, a Eugene-area 18-year-old, filed a formal complaint Wednesday with the Oregon Department of Labor, citing a "gross lack of sexual harassment" at his place of work.

Terzik, a cook at Jake's Pizza in Eugene, is calling for a hostile work environment in which sexual innuendo, pressure for sexual favors, and unso-

licited touching by female coworkers is condoned and even encouraged.

"I want to walk into work each day comfortable in the knowledge that I may be fondled by a member of the opposite sex," Terzik said. "Every person should have the same right to sexual harassment, regardless of age, gender, or severity of acne."

see WORKPLACE page 29

Above: Pizzeria employee Joey Terzik says he feels "too safe" at work.

# New Cambodian Barnes & Noble:
## Will It Threaten Cambodia's Small Book Shops?

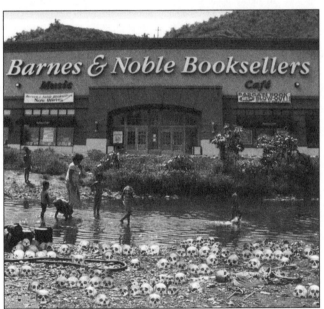

SIEM REAP, CAMBODIA—The paint is barely dry on the new Siem Reap Barnes & Noble, a gleaming, $6 million, 60,000-square-foot book store/coffeehouse the American bookselling giant boasts is the finest in this rural village of 2,100.

But already a serious question is being raised: Can the new bookstore—with its enormous selection, discount prices, and chic espresso bar—peacefully co-exist with smaller, independently owned bookstores in the area?

Store manager Amy Kleinert believes the answer is yes. "Barnes & Noble's presence will help local book sales," said Kleinert, who was previously regional manager for Barnes & Noble's Seattle-area stores. "Our store will stimulate an interest in reading, which can only be a good thing for all area book sellers."

Less optimistic is Tuel Cheng, a used-book dealer and small-press op-

see BARNES & NOBLE page 28

## Woodland Pals Hold Impromptu Oompah-Band Jamboree

THE WOODS—An estimated 15 woodland animals gathered for an improvised oompah-band jamboree Wednesday.

Performing in a pasture just outside their forest, the "Woodland Pals" put on a rollicking musical performance characterized by whimsical merriment and irrepressible mischief.

The oompah-band session is believed to have been initiated by Ferdinand Fox, the group's leader. Fox, dressed in his trademark two-button short-pants, re-

portedly triggered the jamboree by declaring to his fellow Woodland Pals, "Hey, everybody! Let's put on a show!"

Moments after Fox's announcement, the other Pals emerged from their woodland hiding places sporting ill-fitting band uniforms and makeshift musical instruments. Among the participants were Sousaphone-playing pig Oliver Oink, Rudy Rabbit on accordion, S. Cape Goat on ukulele, Fenwick Frog on

see JAMBOREE page 29

Above: The gay jamboree.

# Miracle Of Birth Occurs For 83 Billionth Time

HOPE SPRINGS, AR—The holy and sacrosanct miracle of birth, long revered by human civilization as the most mysterious and magical of all phenomena, took place for what experts are estimating "must be at least the 83 billionth time" Wednesday with the successful delivery of eight-pound, four-ounce baby boy Darryl Brandon Severson at Holy Mary Mother Of God Hospital.

The milestone was achieved by Carla Severson, 32, an unemployed cosmetology-school graduate and homemaker, and her husband of 14 years, Dwayne Severson, also 32, a former screen-door factory worker and freelance lawncare contractor. Experts say the miracle most likely was the result of the pair engaging in an otherwise routine act of sexual intercourse at some point during late May 1998.

The miraculous birth is the couple's fifth.

"This truly is a miracle," said Ob-Gyn floor nurse Sandra Meese, placing Darryl Brandon in the New Births Room of the hospital's maternity ward, where he joined 32 other equally miraculous babies. "Looking down

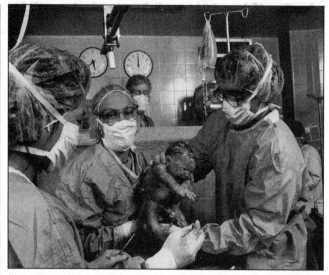

Above: Delivery-room personnel cut the umbilical cord of Darryl Brandon Severson, the 83 billionth miracle of birth and the fifth to occur in the Severson household.

into this precious child's red, screaming face, so barely distinguishable from all the other wailing children surrounding him on all sides, one is reminded of just how special and unique the gift of life really is."

News of the landmark 83 billionth birth sparked an outpouring of good tidings from around the globe, with millions of well-wishers sending cards and letters offering blessings to the media-dubbed "miracle baby." Dozens of world leaders have phoned to express their congratulations, including Chinese Premier Li Peng, who called Darryl "a living miracle" and "a joy to all mankind." Warring factions in Kosovo, Sierra Leone, and Turkey have called week-long cease-fires in honor of the miraculous birth.

In a special message from St. Peter's Basilica, Pope John Paul II spoke of the miracle child.

"In our cynical modern age, the birth of Darryl Severson is proof that miracles do indeed exist," the pope said. "In this special time, it is fitting that we should offer thanks and praise to our Father in Heaven for this, the most precious of His blessings: the blessing of life."

The pope went on to commend Carla Severson for her abstention from birth control, a sin which, had it been committed, would have prevented her pregnancy and delayed humankind's reaching the 83 billion mark by as much as 1/64,000th of a second. The pope also noted that, with five certifi-

see BIRTH page 30

---

BARNES & NOBLE from page 27

erator who was recently forced out of business. "Hun Sen's troops came in the night to burn my books and smashed my son's skull on the type racks," he said. "I ran and hid in the jungle. If they see me printing books again, they will torture me to death."

But for all the debate, the new Barnes & Noble has suffered from nothing so much as overcrowding. At the store's gala grand opening Wednesday, employees were pleasantly surprised to see thousands of Cambodians massed outside as early as 4 a.m. The instant the doors were unlocked, thousands of eager new customers charged through the doors to browse the latest best-sellers, check out CDs at the music section's 35 listening stations, and wash their clothes in the men's-room urinals.

Open less than a week, the store is already drawing rave reviews from Cambodian book lovers.

"There is good water here," said Lon Nai, a Batdambang-area farmer who journeyed 150 miles for the grand opening. "I can keep my pigs free of the sickness with this water."

"It is always the same temperature in here, not like the tent where my family lives in the jungle," said Pursat resident Chun Baro, speaking from a secluded spot deep within the bookstore's "Wellness And Nutrition" section. "I do not care if I am executed for being in a bookstore, as my father and three brothers were in 1979. I am cool and dry."

In addition to the low prices and friendly atmosphere, Baro praised the store's convenient hours, open until

10 p.m. weekdays and Saturday. "Nightfall is the worst time," he said. "That is when the death squads come out."

Speaking from Barnes & Noble's New York headquarters, John Day,

> ## The store has worked hard to be accessible to everyone, offering a ramp at the front entrance for its many legless customers.

company vice-president in charge of overseas expansion, said Cambodia represents an outstanding new market for the book chain.

"Cambodia has all the signs of being a book-friendly country," Day said. "Did you know that only one Cambodian in 10,000 has a television set? That, to me, is the hallmark of a literate culture."

Day said Barnes & Noble tends to do best in progressive, left-leaning cities like Berkeley, CA, and Austin, TX— qualities he sees in Cambodia.

"They have that same sort of open-minded, hippie culture there," Day said. "Communes are very big in Cambodia."

Despite the company's enormous size, Barnes & Noble is extremely committed to the communities in which it does business, Day said, and

Siem Reap is no exception.

"The Cambodian government has established many exciting-sounding 're-education camps' where both intellectuals and everyday citizens can be sent at any time," Day said. "Barnes & Noble has always supported re-education in America, and we intend to extend this policy to our new customers." For every hardcover book sold, Barnes & Noble will donate a dollar to the Cambodian government to help re-educate local children.

The store has also worked hard to be accessible to everyone, offering a ramp at the front entrance for its many legless customers.

"It's a helping hand, sure," Day said. "But we believe a helping hand is just plain good business."

As at other Barnes & Nobles, the Siem Reap store offers a Local Authors section, which is dominated by the political tracts of noted late-'70s writer Pol Pot.

"So far, there hasn't been a whole lot of customer traffic going through the section," assistant manager Ken Woodson said. "Perhaps we need to publicize it more. We've tried to get Pol in for a book signing, but we haven't been able to find him."

The community-centered approach is paying off: Shoppers have packed the store since opening day, taking advantage of Barnes & Noble's encouragement of casual browsing.

"This a friendly store," Woodson said. "Some places frown on what retailers call 'camping,' but we actually have a policy of putting comfy seats at

the end of each aisle. They're very popular—I've seen entire families share one of our overstuffed sofas. Sometimes it seems like our regulars never leave."

So what books have been the biggest sellers at the new store? According to Woodson, most popular are 2,000-plus-page items such as the Norton anthologies, the collected works of Proust, and the two-volume Riverside Shakespeare.

"I like this one," said Cheun Norresaprong of Phnom Penh, holding up David Foster Wallace's hefty, critically acclaimed novel *Infinite Jest*. "It will burn for hours, enabling me to cook life-giving grubs and twigs for my children."

Like Norresaprong, farmer Chira Samrong is a voracious reader—and a serious lover of Tolstoi, to boot. Loading his ox cart with 54 copies of *War And Peace*, he said, "If I can obtain 200 of these books, I can build a house that will withstand the bullets of Hun Sen's guerrillas and Ranariddh's royalists. Last spring, my wife was shot in the face."

While Barnes & Noble officials would not comment on the possibility of additional Cambodian locations, store manager Kleinert foresees a bright future in the country.

"Everything about Cambodian bookselling has offered me an exciting challenge. It's wonderful to enter a market where your customer base has such a diversity of needs," Kleinert said. "The future holds bright promise. For Barnes & Noble in Cambodia, this truly is Year Zero." ∅

JAMBOREE from page 27

harmonica, E. Pluribus Eagle on horn, the Pelican Trio on triangle, Squeaky Squirrel on percussion, and a small, feathered vocalist who remains unidentified as of press time. Fox himself conducted the band.

The rousing oompah music, which could be heard for miles around, soon attracted flora as well as fauna. A tree identified only as "Teddy" swayed to and fro to the rhythm, and tulips sprouted from the soil to sing along.

> ## "Until now, there had never existed proof that lower-order mammals were capable of performing music."

The sun itself reportedly grinned broadly and bounced back and forth to the merry melodies.

Approximately 10 minutes into the jubilee, the musicians were briefly interrupted by Clumsy Cat, who chased Montgomery Mouse around the bandstand. Just as Clumsy was about to pounce on Montgomery, however, the cat was killed when he slammed into Teddy Tree. Clumsy's ghostly nine lives then rose out of his lifeless body and hovered above the band, strumming along to the music on their harps.

A greater threat to the Woodland Pals came in the form of Hoofington P. McSnort, a local bull who became enraged when he discovered that his pasture was being used as the site of the Woodland Pals' jamboree. McSnort, who has a history of antagonistic behavior toward the Pals, charged at the music-making critters, sending them scattering across the pasture. Though McSnort aggressively pursued all animals within his proximity, his primary target appeared to be the

portly Oliver Oink, whose posterior was gored by the bull's razor-sharp horns.

McSnort was eventually subdued by Fox, who waved his red jacket at him, prompting the bull to charge at Fox and subsequently crash head first into an anvil concealed behind the coat.

News of the Woodland Pals' jamboree quickly spread throughout the zoological community, which was electrified by the discovery of animals that possess artistic impulses and reasoning skills—qualities long believed the sole domain of humans.

"Until now, there had never existed proof that lower-order mammals were capable of performing music," University of Florida zoologist Lynn Sontag said. "Truly, this is the most remarkable case of aberrant animal behavior since Douglas Duck's birthday party in 1986."

Zoologists are also greatly intrigued by the unorthodox anatomical structure of the Woodland Pals.

"These creatures are undoubtedly mammals and birds," said Dr. Benjamin Frehling, a professor of zoology at Northwestern University. "But their anatomies are radically different from those of most quadrupeds. The fox and goat, for example, seem to consist of nothing more than a series of circles and tubes which squash and stretch as they move. The creatures may represent some sort of bizarre evolutionary throwback, although, I must admit, nothing in the fossil record seems to support such a theory."

Added Frehling: "I am confident that I speak for my colleagues when I say that capturing and dissecting one of these Woodland Pals should be a top priority."

Frehling could not confirm whether the Woodland Pals were in any way related to an anatomically similar cat-and-mouse duo, who in 1947 drank Jumbo-Gro plant food and grew 2,200 miles in height, devastating much of the Western Hemisphere. ⌀

# I Customized My Wheels

Hola, amigos. Whaddya say? I know it's been a long time since I rapped at ya, but I been real busy. First off, I got a new job at a hospital doing food service. It's not like I have to feed a bunch of dying geezers or nothing. I stand behind a sneeze guard in the cafeteria all day and ladle mashed potatoes and shit onto people's plates. It ain't too bad: You get free food and don't have to talk much to people. The only drawback is you gotta wear one of those old-lady hairnets.

**The Cruise**
**By Jim Anchower**

The other problem is, it only pays $6.40 an hour. That would be okay if I weren't trying to sock some cash away for a new set of wheels. It's not that my current car ain't running. It's just that it's a damn '88 Volkswagen Golf, and you better believe that won't cut it for a style-minded man of the cruise like myself. After a month and a half at the hospital, though, I only had $106 saved up, so I decided to give up and just make do with the Golf. Make lemons out of lemonade, as they say.

I figured if I was going to be stuck with this car, I ought to make the best of it, so I spent the better part of last Saturday working it over. I changed the oil and plugs. I made sure the tires were up to the proper pressure. I threw some pepper in with the coolant so the little pinholes in the radiator would be plugged. I even wiped all the crud off the engine so it would look nice the next time I had to pop the hood. By the time I was done, I was pretty hammered, though, because nothing goes better with car re-

pair than beer.

Now, the car was running fine, but that didn't change the fact that it was a crappy-looking two-door hatchback. I mean, it would get you around, but it wouldn't get you any action. Unfortunately, there wasn't a whole lot I could do. I tried to spruce it up with some fancy detail work and a Zep sticker on the back window. Then I bought some pinstripe stickers so it would look more aerodynamic, but it just looked like a box with stripes.

I was going over and over in my mind how I could make it look cooler, and eventually, I realized what it needed—a hood painting. Something that said, "Look out, world, here comes Jim Anchower!" I couldn't afford to have it painted by a pro, so I decided to have Ron do it for me. You wouldn't expect it, but he's real good at drawing. One time, I saw him draw a picture like the cover of one of those old Yes albums. It had dinosaurs and spaceships and shit on some kind of futuristic planet. Then, in the middle, he drew this barbarian guy dressed all in furs with this half-naked chick hanging onto his leg. It was awesome.

I gave Ron a call to see if he was up for the task. I had to buy him off with a few joints I'd been saving, but he said he'd do it. I asked him what sort of paint he'd need. He said he didn't know, so I went out to a fancy art store and dropped my last $20 on some paint in tubes. I asked the clerk if it would wash off in the rain. He said it wouldn't. That was all I needed to hear.

When I got back to my place, Ron was already there waiting for me. He seemed pretty psyched to do the job, and he even had some ideas he wanted to go over with me. First, he showed me an old Nazareth album. It

see ANCHOWER page 30

WORKPLACE from page 27

Terzik presented Labor Department officials with a report documenting at least 22 instances in which harassment did not occur but should have.

In one such instance, Terzik walked into the kitchen and mentioned "how hot it was" to lead prep cook Rebecca Stanton, 20, who merely nodded in response.

"She could have said, 'It sure is hot, now that you're here,' or suggested that I take off my shirt, but she didn't even look at me," Terzik said.

"Not once," he continued, "have I been made to feel like a sexual object instead of a coworker."

According to psychologists, sexual harassment is vital to the proper development of a teenage boy's self-esteem.

"A young boy needs to feel sexually desirable, especially on the job," noted therapist Dr. Eli Wasserbaum said. "It can be very damaging to his still-forming social psyche if he senses

> ## Terzik picketed the pizzeria to protest management's fostering of a "too safe" work environment.

that he is unwanted by female employees. A grope from a female coworker can do wonders during this extremely important stage of sexual development."

Sexual-harassment experts say that in cases of workplace harassment, the victim is often threatened with job termination if he or she does not comply with the sexual demands of a superior. Nothing of the sort has ever happened to Terzik.

"Once, Tina, the assistant manager, told me to meet her in the supply shed. I was sure we were gonna do it," Terzik said. "But it turned out she just wanted me to flatten a bunch of boxes for the Dumpster."

Terzik said that on a number of occasions, female coworkers have used sexually suggestive terms like "breadstick," "sausage," and "hand-tossed," but never did they actually use them in a sexually suggestive manner. Six weeks ago, a female manager asked Terzik to "work the late shift with me," but no sexual activity took place.

Terzik said he filed the complaint only after all other avenues of remedying the situation were exhausted. In May, after working more than 300 shifts without a single sexual advance, Terzik authored and distributed a pamphlet to female employees titled "Sexual Harassment On The Job: A How-To Guide." Last weekend,

Terzik picketed the pizzeria to protest management's fostering of a "too safe" work environment, but the protest ended when manager Hal Porter ordered him to go inside and change the syrup for the Mountain Dew.

Terzik suggested that the pizzeria adopt the more enlightened harassment policies of the Sub Shack, located across the street.

"I hear the counter workers are always feeling each other up behind the bread racks," he said.

If the Department of Labor fails to act, Terzik said he is prepared to take his case to court.

"This humiliation is unacceptable and cannot continue," he said. "I've been lifting weights three times a week, and I haven't even gotten so much as a 'What up, baby?' from one of the delivery chicks. Sexual harassment is a right, not a privilege." ⌀

ANCHOWER from page 29

## Point-Counterpoint: Pets

# We Gave Rex To A Nice Farm Family

**By Marjorie Dorner**

Don't you worry about Rex. Your father and I gave him to a nice farm family. Now he'll be able to run and jump and play outside all day long.

I know you loved Rex, but it just wasn't fair to keep him cooped up here in this tiny little house. We could tell he wasn't happy. Rex needed someplace where he could run around. We explained to Rex that we all love him very much, but that this was better for everyone, especially him.

Rex's new owners, the MacGregors, will love him every bit as much as we did. They promised to buy him his favorite food and spend many hours playing with him every day. We even sent along his red-checkered blanket and his favorite squeak toy. Rex will be very happy with the MacGregors.

As we drove away, Rex was barking and chasing a rabbit. He was so happy to be outside. He was smiling and yipping and running through a big field of daisies! We took some pictures, but we accidentally dropped the camera in the beautiful trout-filled stream that runs through the middle of the farm.

Rex is happier where he is now. He'll always remember and love you, but now he can make lots of new animal friends. He won't be lonely while you're at school. And he won't have to wait all day for us to get home to take him outside, so he won't go pee-pee on the floor, and daddy won't chase him out into the garage with his shoe.

Your father and I were thinking that maybe this weekend we could go and get some goldfish. You can name one Rex if you want. ∅

# They Had Me Put To Sleep At The Vet

**By Rex**

Actually, what you've been told isn't exactly the truth. I was put to sleep at the vet. That one right around the corner from your house, in fact. Your parents went out to lunch afterwards—that's why they were gone so long.

As they drove off, I wasn't chasing any rabbits, and I wasn't frolicking in any daisy fields. No, I was crammed into a 3'x3' cage with a bunch of other doomed dogs, terrified beyond belief as I waited my turn to be put down.

On the upside, I wasn't in there very long. The vet soon took me out of the cage, injected me with 8 cc's of pentobarbitol, and that was that. So long, Rex, been good to know you.

After that, some veterinary assistant tossed my carcass into the back of a van along with those of a Siamese cat with feline leukemia, a 17-year-old German Shepherd, and a Fox Terrier that got hit by a car. About five hours later, we were all hauled off to be cremated. If you want to visit my ashes, they're in the gravel pit behind Al's Rendering & Cremation on Rand Road.

Your mom and dad didn't even wait until the deed was done. They just mumbled something about being late for another appointment, wrote the check, and made a beeline for the door. The vet asked them if they wanted my collar, and your mother just sort of looked puzzled and asked, "What for?"

I suppose they did stay for a minute or two, mostly to haggle over the fee with the receptionist, but then— poof!—they were gone without so much as a "you've been a good boy."

From what I've heard, all this happened because I was digging in the plants. Just for the record, it wasn't me. I do happen to recall a certain member of the household making a racetrack for his Matchbox cars in the philodendrons, though. But what good would it do to name names now? I'm history. ∅

BIRTH from page 28

able miracles to her credit, Mrs. Severson may qualify for canonization as a saint upon her death.

Narrowly missing the chance to be the 83 billionth baby were Manoj Ranaghatapur, born 1/15th of a second earlier in the drought-stricken village of Bijapur, India; Phillippe Duclos, born 1/33rd of a second earlier in Lyon, France; and Baby X, delivered just 1/67th of a second earlier in a Bronx housing project, but unfortunately stillborn.

"I'm overjoyed for the Seversons. They are truly blessed," said Marcia Ott, a neighbor of the family, reacting to the sudden crush of media attention focused on their small Arkansas town. "I've heard about miracles before, but you never think something like this is going to happen to someone you know."

The miraculous birth will likely have a major impact on Dwayne and Carla Severson, who are expected to devote a majority of their waking hours tending to the baby's many miraculous needs. When not getting miraculously waken at 3 a.m., the couple will be miraculously occupied feeding Darryl and changing his miraculous diapers whenever he miraculously defecates.

But for all the attention, the Seversons remain humble about their achievement.

"It wasn't exactly like we planned it, to be honest," Dwayne said. "In fact, when Carla told me she was pregnant again, I was kinda worried, on account of me losing my job at the screen-door factory and all. Money's real tight right now, and I wasn't sure we could make ends meet. But still, us having to sell the trailer and temporarily move back into Carla's parents' place isn't so bad, if you think about it, since it's such a miracle, I guess."

"I love my baby so much," said Carla, cradling the newborn. "He's the most precious little angel that ever flew down from heaven."

Though 83 billion is the number generally agreed upon, experts concede that the precise figure is somewhat more nebulous.

"It all depends on how you tabulate the miracles," Cornell University biology professor Dr. Isaac Gregson said. "Eighty-three billion includes not only all the humans who have ever been born, but also all the Cro-Magnons, Neanderthals, Australopithecines, and other proto-hominids going all the way back to the first mammals. Of course, if you were to include the rest of the vertebrates in the animal kingdom, it would be even higher. And if you were to also include plankton, unicellular microorganisms, and all plant life, the actual number would be closer to, oh, umpteen gadzillion."

Added Gregson: "But why quibble about numbers at a time like this? Darryl's birth is a one-of-a-kind special moment that has deeply inspired the world, reminding us what life is all about."

Noted essayist and biologist Stephen Jay Gould agreed, calling the latest addition to the Severson household "a miracle beyond compare."

"It's an amazing turn of events, no doubt about it," Gould said. "Just think: A spermatozoa from a male mammal fertilized the ovum of a female mammal, causing a fetus to develop and, in time, come to term and pass through the female's birth canal as a new being. It just goes to show that there are some mysteries even science cannot explain." ∅

was the one with "Hair Of The Dog" on it. You know, that song where the guy goes, "Now you're messin' with a... SON OF A BITCH!" I think the album was called *Hair Of The Dog*, too. It had this kick-ass barbarian guy on it. It looked really cool, but after giving it some thought, I decided I didn't want some big man with muscles on my hood. It might seem kinda queer.

I asked Ron if he could do a dragon. I told him it had to be scary like the one in *Dragonslayer* or that movie with Sean Connery as the dragon, only less talky and more mean. Ron said he didn't have any examples on hand, but he could probably come up with something from his head. He said his head might fill up better if he could smoke up first. I decided that was reasonable, so we went in for a quick bowl.

After getting properly baked, me and Ron went back out to the car. He laid all the paints and brushes out like he was a serious artist. Then he squeezed a bunch of the paints onto an old board. He stared at the hood for about 30 seconds, then closed his

> # I told Ron it had to be scary like the one in *Dragonslayer*.

eyes, then stared at the hood again. He did that about 10 times before telling me he had an idea and that I should go in the house. I told him I wasn't going anywhere. He said okay and started staring at the hood some more. Fuck it, I thought. If he was gonna work like that, I was going inside.

I laid out on the couch and turned on the tube. Every once in a while, I looked out the window to see how he was doing. Half the time, he had his face up close to the hood, painting like he was real focused. The other half, he was standing back, staring at it. Then I dozed off for a while, and when I came to, Ron was standing over me. He said he was finished.

I went out to see what he did. I couldn't believe it. Most of it was cool, but it had a head of pink hair like the dragon in *Pete's Dragon*. And it had an extra tail. Ron said he wasn't happy about where the first tail wound up, so he put in a second one. I started to get steamed. Then he said that he didn't know what the fuck he was thinking when he put the hair on, but he was sure he could fix that, too. I told him to get the hell away from me and my car before I blew my cork.

So now I got my car running, and it almost looks badass, but not quite. Yesterday, a bus full of middle-schoolers pulled up to me at a red light, and they were all pointing and laughing. I decided I was only going to drive it at night from then on. Nothing's worse than being laughed at by kids whose asses you could kick without a second thought. ∅

## Man Listening To 'Highway To Hell' Actually On Parkway To Waukegan

see LOCAL page 4B

## Marriage Breaks Up Over Procreative Differences

see LOCAL page 12B

## Alabama Governor Rassles With Controversy

see NATION page 4A

## Office Casual-Day Policy Hastily Rewritten To Exclude Unitards

see WORKPLACE page 5E

## Cat Makes Break For It

see PETS page 14D

STATshot

A look at the numbers that shape your world.

### Top Cannes Contenders

What are the frontrunners for the Palme d'Or?

| Film | Country |
|---|---|
| • My Bassoon Teacher's Décolletage | France |
| • I Am Curious, Gray | Sweden |
| • The Spirit And Purpose Of Geography | Germany |
| • Céline Of The Artesian Well | France |
| • Battlefield Perth | Australia |
| • USA! USA! USA! | USA |

THE ONION
$2.00 US
$3.00 CAN

0 74470 94595 6

---

# Plenty Of Soda Still Available Throughout Nation

WASHINGTON, DC—In a report that bodes well for the future of U.S. carbonated-beverage consumption, the Commerce Department announced Friday that plenty of soda is still available across the nation.

According to department findings, current U.S. soda-availability levels stand at an all-time high, with nearly all major soda-penetration indices—including manufacturing, bottling, and retail-outlet distribution—operating at maximum capacity.

In addition, the national Liters To Citizens Ratio, widely considered the leading indicator of overall U.S. soda health, stands at an unprecedented 26.4 to 1.

"Americans have one less thing to worry about today. We are thrilled to issue America's soda supply a glowing report card," Secretary of Commerce Norman Mineta said at a press conference. "With soda access, convenience, and affordability all at unprecedented levels, the threat of soda depletion has been virtually eradicated from our great nation."

The study comes as welcome news to the many soda-industry observers who feared that U.S. soda reserves might prove insufficient to meet the refreshment demands of the 21st century.

"Thank goodness there are no soda
see SODA page 32

---

# Neighbors Confront Alcoholic Child-Abuser About His Lawn

Above: Child-beater Gene Oberst, whose unkempt lawn and untrimmed hedges have caused alarm among neighbors.

ARLINGTON, TX—Following a brief meeting Friday, members of the Ridgeway Circle Homeowners Association confronted alcoholic child-abuser Gene Oberst about his continued failure to uphold basic standards of lawn care.

"It's never easy to stick your nose into someone else's business, but in this case, we felt we had no choice but to step in and do something," association president Trudy Hinsdale said of the 33-year-old unemployed electrician and abusive parent. "That lawn is a major eyesore, and it reflects badly
see LAWN page 32

---

# Black Executive Prominently Displayed

COLUMBUS, OH—Dennis Swann, 41, the sole black executive at Brooks Capital Management, was prominently displayed Friday by the Columbus-based investment firm.

"Dennis is a real asset to the company," said Brooks Capital Management advertising director Blair Katzeff, who used Swann in a new print campaign. "Brooks is not the same old investment firm: We've got heart, but we've also got soul."

The ad, which praises Brooks Capital Manage-

ment as "Committed To Helping You Design Your Future," features Swann strategically positioned among members of the all-white board of directors.

Swann said he was surprised when Katzeff asked him to appear in the ad.

"I'm just the associate manager of the underwriting department, so it's not like I'm among the company's top brass," said Swann, who earned his MBA from Ohio State University in 1991. "But Blair insisted I was perfect for the ad, so
see EXECUTIVE page 32

Above: A Brooks Capital Management promotional photo showcasing sole black executive Dennis Swann.

# The Soda Age

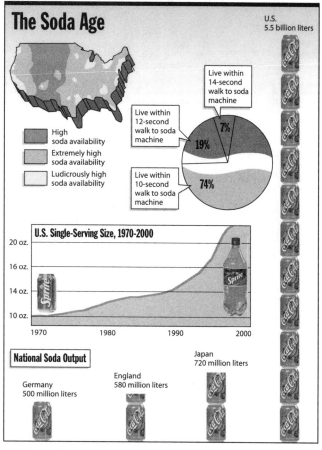

U.S.
5.5 billion liters

Live within
14-second
walk to soda
machine

Live within
12-second
walk to soda
machine

Live within
10-second
walk to soda
machine

7%

19%

74%

High
soda availability

Extremely high
soda availability

Ludicrously high
soda availability

### U.S. Single-Serving Size, 1970-2000

20 oz.

16 oz.

14 oz.

10 oz.

1970    1980    1990    2000

### National Soda Output

Germany
500 million liters

England
580 million liters

Japan
720 million liters

on the whole rest of the block. Mr. Oberst has no idea what kind of terrible damage he's doing to property values."

Fellow Homeowners Association member Nina Desoto agreed.

"I believe people have a responsibility to intervene when there is a problem in their community," Desoto said. "If we were to sit idly by while that grass continued to grow out of control and weeds sprung up everywhere, silently pretending that everything was fine over at the Oberst household, we'd be no better than him."

On April 22, deciding that the problem could be ignored no longer, Desoto called a Homeowners Association meeting at her home to determine how to best deal with their unmedicated, manic-depressive neighbor.

"We know this is a very touchy subject, and approaching it the wrong way could actually do damage instead of help the situation," said Alexander Croland, one of three association members chosen to confront Oberst. "But when he refuses to fertilize and continues to allow those huge patches of dead grass to spread, we can't just act like it isn't happening right in front of us."

Several hours later, Croland, accompanied by Hinsdale and neighbor Ed Barrow, whose son frequently played with Oberst's daughter before she broke six ribs and became housebound, approached Oberst in his car as he was returning from a beer run.

"We made it very clear that we

weren't there to attack him," Croland said. "Rather, we just wanted him to realize that there is definitely a problem—especially with those Mountain Ash trees with half the branches turning brown and falling off."

In addition to more frequent mowing and better shrub and tree maintenance, the Old Kentucky Whiskey

---

## "We didn't want to be too condemning and put Gene on the defensive."

---

drinker was urged to pay more attention to litter collection and weed removal.

"We didn't want to be too condemning and put Gene on the defensive. We were trying to offer help," said Barrow, whose backyard patio is less than 10 feet from the window through which Oberst recently threw his son. "I told him that before my next picnic, I'd be glad to bring over my Weed Whacker and chop down those plants in the window wells myself—if only he'd let me."

Realizing that Oberst might be embarrassed to accept offers of aid from his neighbors, the Homeowners Association representatives gave him the contact numbers of professionals in the area whose job is to offer help in just such cases. These included Green Thumb Lawncare, H&G Landscap-

worries on the immediate horizon," said Stanford University professor Dr. Robert Garner, a lifelong Pepsi advocate. "Many Americans take for granted the tremendous number of thirst-quenching options available in this country. But the truth is, the soft-drink availability we enjoy here is something people in other nations can only dream of. Consider the harsh reality of life in the Czech Republic, where delicious carbonated beverages are not within arm's reach at any given moment. Just imagine what that would be like."

According to the report, the average American is never more than 30 feet from soda at any given time. And, in addition to its tremendous availability and affordability, U.S. soda is also almost always chilled, thanks to refrigerated-display-case and thermal-insulated-portable-cooler technology that is second to none in the world.

"When it comes to the nuts and bolts of keeping soda ice-cold and conveniently located, America is truly ahead of the pack," Mineta said. "No other nation, not even Japan, boasts a soda-coolness-preservation infrastructure comparable to America's state-of-the-art point-of-purchase refrigeration network. In most parts of the U.S., it is actually considered unnecessary and impractical to add ice, so cold is our soda served."

The report went on to note that, as with overall U.S. soda output, the number of ounces in the average indi-

vidual serving size has steadily increased since 1970, with personal soda receptacles as large as one liter now commonplace in most markets. In the years since Pepsi's introduction of the 20-ounce "Big Slam" alone, the report noted, America's median soda-container volume has risen a stunning 41 percent.

"Thirty years ago, a small glass was sufficient for holding all the soda anyone would want to consume in a single sitting," said soda supplier James L. Carlisle of the Coca-Cola Corporation. "By 1975, that amount had risen due to a new standard, the 12-ounce can. Today, it is not unusual for a soda-lover to drink an entire two-liter bottle in one sitting."

For years, the rising single-serving-size rate prompted widespread calls for an across-the-board reduction in U.S. soda consumption. But, given the robust state of production, all but a handful of Americans are confident that the nation's soda providers will be able to meet whatever increased demand may come as drink sizes and per-capita thirst continue to grow in the years to come.

"Fortunately," Carlisle said, "given the thriving nature of the U.S. soda supply, not only can American consumers drink their favorite sodas more often, but they can also help themselves to greater amounts each time they enjoy these delicious and refreshing soft drinks."

Added Carlisle: "Would you care for a beverage?" ∅

who was I to argue?"

Though Swann has not received a promotion since joining the Brooks Capital Management team in March 1996, he has enjoyed other benefits. Last year, he was given a glass-walled office with a clear view of the client waiting area, and he has appeared in the company newsletter 37 times. And this February, he was chosen to represent the company at the 1999 Midwest Investment Professionals Association (MIPA) conference in Indianapolis.

Swann has also been "strongly encouraged" to attend the firm's upcoming company picnic, at which footage will be shot for a new employee-orientation video.

"[Company president] Nathan

Modano said he was dying to meet my wife and kids, so I should make sure to bring them along to the picnic," Swann said. "When I told him that Angela and I don't have children, he told me to bring along some of my nieces and nephews instead."

"When the public thinks of Brooks Capital Management, we want them to think of a company that's doing away with conventional boundaries," said Modano, posing with Swann for a photo in the company's 1999 annual report. "Here at Brooks Capital Management, we offer a wide range of services, including investing, underwriting, and management of municipal securities, not to mention municipal, corporate, and leasing transactions. Now, *that's* diversity." ∅

---

ing, and Weber's, an Arlington-area nursery and greenery.

"If Gene's wife needs some advice on how to spruce up a flowerbox with tulips and daffodils, I want her to know she can come to me and I won't pass judgment," Hinsdale said. "My door is always open in situations like this."

"The saddest part of all," Hinsdale said, "is what that man is doing to those poor azalea bushes. He's absolutely brutalizing them, and they may never recover. Why, oh, why won't he water them?"

Having confronted their neighbor,

the homeowners are now waiting and hoping that Oberst, who recently hit his daughter with a lamp for forgetting to do the dishes, will heed their pleas to change his ways. If he does not, they said they will turn to the authorities.

"The truth is, if Gene doesn't accept our help, we'll have no choice but to contact the police," Barrow said. "There's a city ordinance prohibiting him from leaning that clearly inoperable motorcycle against his house for more than 14 days. I take my duty as a citizen very seriously." ∅

# Marilyn Manson Now Going Door-To-Door Trying To Shock People

OVERLAND PARK, KS—Stung by flagging album sales and supplanted by Eminem as Middle America's worst nightmare, shock rocker Marilyn Manson has embarked on a door-to-door tour of suburbia in a desperate, last-ditch effort to shock and offend average Americans.

Accompanied by bandmates Twiggy Ramirez, Madonna Wayne Gacy, and Ginger Fish, Manson kicked off his 50-city "Boo" tour Jan. 26 in Overland Park, a conservative, middle-class suburb of Kansas City.

"When we first laid eyes on Overland Park, with its neat little frame houses, immaculately landscaped lawns, and SUVs in the driveways, we couldn't wait to swoop down on it like the Black Death," said Manson, born Brian Warner in Canton, OH. "We were like, 'Welcome to our nightmare, you bloated, pustulent pigs.'"

Last Friday at 4 p.m., Mark Wesley, 46, a resident of Overland Park's exclusive Maple Bluff subdivision, heard the sound of "animal-like shrieking" coming from the vicinity of his front lawn. Upon opening his front door, he was greeted by the sight of a pale and shirtless Manson carving a pentagram into his chest with a razor blade.

"Look at me, suburban dung," Manson told Wesley. "Does this shock you?"

When Wesley replied no, he said Manson became "petulant." Recalled Wesley: "He started stamping his feet and shaking his fists, saying, 'What do you mean, no? Aren't your uptight, puritanical sensibilities offended? Don't you want to censor me so you don't have to confront the ugly truth I represent?' So I say, 'Well, not particularly.' Then, after a long pause, he says, 'Well, screw you, jerk!' and walks off sulking."

That evening, Linda Schmidt was preparing to drive her daughter Alyssa to a Girl Scouts meeting when she found Manson standing on her porch draped in sheep entrails.

"I knew who he was, but I was kind of busy and didn't really have time to chat," Schmidt said. "He just kept standing there staring at me, expecting me to react in some way."

Added Schmidt: "I tried to be nice and humor him a little. I said, 'Yesiree, that sure is some shocking satanic imagery, no doubt about it. And that one eye with no color in the pupil, very disturbing. I'd sure like to suppress that.' I mean, what do you say to Marilyn Manson?"

A deflated Manson remained on Schmidt's porch as she and Alyssa drove off.

Subsequent attempts to provoke outrage were met with equal indifference.

"[Manson] was standing at my front door wearing those fake breasts he wore on the cover of *Mechanical Ani-*

*mals*," retiree Judith Hahn said. "He said, 'My name is Marilyn Manson, and I'm here to tear your little world apart.' I thought he was collecting for the Kiwanis food drive, so I gave him some cans of pumpkin-pie filling."

Undaunted, Manson and his entourage stepped up their assault on mainstream American sensibilities. On Tuesday, they arrived in the tony Detroit suburb of Grosse Pointe Farms, where stockbroker Glenn Binford answered his doorbell to find Manson hanging upside-down on a wooden cross as Ramirez performed fellatio on him.

"I just stood there thinking, now there's a boy who tries way too hard," Binford said. "I mean, come on: Homoerotic sacrilege went out in the late '90s."

Other provocative acts by Manson—including dismembering a chicken, bathing in pig's blood, and wearing a three-piece suit of human noses—failed to arouse anyone's ire, instead prompting comments such as "sophomoric," "trite," and "so Alice Cooper."

Manson's lone brush with controversy occurred in Edina, MN, a suburb of Minneapolis. An unidentified neighborhood-watch volunteer phoned police after seeing a nude, fe-

Above: Manson knocks on a door in Grosse Pointe Farms, MI.

ces-smeared Manson being led around on a leash by a dwarf dominatrix. Officers arrived on the scene, but let Manson go with a warning for parading without a city permit.

"I could have given him a citation, but I figured, how much harm is he really causing?" Edina police officer Dan Herberger said. "I mean, he's just Marilyn Manson, for the love of Mike."

The "Boo" tour was dealt a further blow when Manson learned that Eminem's *The Marshall Mathers LP* had see MANSON page 34

---

# The Abortion Pill

Last week, the FDA approved the controversial French abortion pill RU-486, permitting non-surgical abortions in the U.S. for the first time and sparking protest from pro-life advocates. What do *you* think?

**Patrick Klennert**
**TV Repairman**

"Now, hold on there. Isn't there a line in The Bible specifically prohibiting safe, non-invasive, affordable medical procedures for women?"

**Liz Lathon**
**Homemaker**

"I just wish this pill had been available seven years ago. You hear that, Corey?"

**Audra Fusco**
**Occupational Therapist**

"This drug will only encourage young kids to get hooked on the pain and trauma of abortion."

**Robert Ketcham**
**Systems Analyst**

"The Europeans have always been ahead of us culturally and philosophically. But we've finally caught up to them abortionally."

**Ronald Lee**
**Food Vendor**

"This abortion thing is getting out of control. Do you realize this planet is down to its last six billion people?"

**Nate Thurman**
**Bank Manager**

"If women can deal with unwanted pregnancies safely without it destroying their lives, how are they ever going to learn?"

# Rural Nebraskan Not Sure He Could Handle Frantic Pace Of Omaha

NORTH PLATTE, NE—Lifelong North Platte resident Fred Linder, 46, revealed Friday that he doesn't think he could cope with the fast-paced hustle and bustle of Omaha, the Cornhusker State's largest city.

"Oh, sure, I bet it'd be exciting at first, going to see 9 p.m. showings of movies, shopping at those big department stores, and maybe even eating at one of those fancy restaurants that don't use iceberg lettuce in their salads," Linder said. "But I just don't think I could put up with all that hubbub for more than a day or two."

Added Linder: "And parking's a nightmare there."

Linder expressed doubts about Omaha's "hectic pace" while having dinner at the home of Pastor Bob Egan, the longtime spiritual leader of North Platte's Holy Christ Almighty Church.

"I'd just returned from a 'Prayer & Share' fellowship conference in Omaha, and I mentioned to Fred how much I enjoyed myself there," Egan said. "There's just so much to do: dining, shopping, seeing the sights—[wife] Margaret and I even saw a touring production of *Phantom Of The Opera*. But Fred just seemed uncomfortable with the whole idea of it."

The drawbacks to life in Omaha cited by Linder include crime, traffic, pollution, and the rudeness of Omahans.

"You read such awful stuff in the papers about that place," Linder said. "Every month, it's another murder. Between the drugs and the crime and the street gangs, it's almost as bad as Wichita."

Those familiar with Linder say his

Above: The imposing Omaha skyline. Inset: North Platte resident Fred Linder.

anti-Omaha stance has deepened since his sister left North Platte in 1998 to take a job as human-resources director at an Omaha insurance agency.

"Don't get Fred started on Omaha," friend Ken Carlson said. "He's always resented Amy for going there. They're a lot less close now than they used to be, and Fred feels it's because she's gotten a bit of an attitude since moving to the big city, like she's superior or something."

"Let's just say the glamour of city life has changed Amy," Linder said. "She's definitely 'gone Omaha,' if you catch my drift."

Linder has visited the Nebraska metropolis three times in his life, most recently in 1996 for a farm-equipment show.

"I prepared plenty well before that trip, you better believe," Linder said. "I bought a money belt and travelers' checks to protect myself from all those Omaha pickpockets and con men. And I made sure I had a full tank before going, because I sure as heck wasn't about to pay Omaha prices for gas."

Linder said he has no plans to visit his sister in Omaha anytime soon.

"If Amy wants to come home only for Christmas, fine," Linder said. "If that means I only see her once a year, so be it. I just can't take the noise and commotion of Omaha. It gives me a migraine just thinking about it."

"That sort of running around at all hours of the day and night might appeal to some, but I believe there's more to life than the thrill-seeking, urban scene you find in a place like Omaha," Linder said. "The bright lights and fast cars may have seduced my sister, but they'll never get me." ∅

## Serial Killer Remembers Neighbors As Quiet, Unsuspecting

DOTHAN, AL—Arrested Friday in connection with a 17-month killing spree that claimed the lives of 23 people, serial killer Henry Wayne Vaughn recalled his numerous neighbors as "quiet and unsuspecting." "The Blaines were nice people who pretty much kept to themselves," Vaughn said of Michael and Meredith Blaine, a young couple who lived across the street from him until their deaths on Oct. 9, 1998. "They always seemed very cordial and extremely trusting." Vaughn also fondly remembered the neighborly spirit of the Baggios of Juniper Street. "I paid their kid to mow my lawn once," he said, "and after that it was as if we were old friends." Vaughn also praised his postman as extremely polite and helpful, noting, "He'd come right into your basement if you said you needed help reaching something."

## You The Newest Subsidiary Of Kraft Foods

NORTHFIELD, IL—In the company's latest acquisition, Kraft Foods announced Friday that it has gained a controlling interest in you for an estimated $11,000, nearly 20 percent less than the amount forecast by *Forbes* magazine's market analysts earlier this year. "We are pleased to bring you under the umbrella of fine Kraft products and individuals," Kraft CEO Bob Eckert said. "After some retooling and repackaging, you can expect to be on store shelves sometime in early spring." ∅

**MANSON from page 33**

been banned from all Kmart stores. Manson's current album, *Holy Wood (In The Shadow Of The Valley Of Death)*, is still available.

"Why are all you people outraged by Eminem? He's not scary!" Manson said. "He doesn't sport ghoulishly pale skin or wear gender-bending makeup. He's just some regular guy. I'm the one people should be terrified by, not him! Me!"

"If you ban me," Manson continued, "I promise to rail against censorship and hypocrisy. Please? Pretty, pretty please?"

By Monday, the tour appeared to have lost all momentum. Sources close to Manson described him as "exhausted and discouraged," despite not having even completed the first leg of the three-month tour. By the time he arrived in Hoffman Estates, IL, Manson had resorted to leaving flaming bags of dog feces on doorsteps and shining a flashlight under his chin to make himself look "spooky." He was

ultimately chased from a Hoffman Estates subdivision by a group of bicycle-riding teenagers who advised him to "get [his] chalk-white goblin ass" out of their neighborhood.

On Friday, Manson is slated to appear in Bethesda, MD, where many believe he will bring his tour to a premature end.

"Have you people forgotten already?" Manson asked *The Washington Post*. "You all thought I was responsible for Columbine two years ago. Well, I was! I was! I know I vehemently denied it at the time, but, really, I personally told those two kids to shoot up the school. I'm serious. I sent them an e-mail. And I told them to worship Satan, too. You hear that, kids? Marilyn Manson says you should shoot your friends in the head with a gun! And everyone should eat babies! And rape their dead grandparents! And poop on a church! There, now will someone please be offended?" ∅

Above: A dejected Marilyn Manson ponders his next move.

# NEWS

## Aliens Mourn As Final *Cheers* Episode Reaches Alpha Centauri

see ASTRONOMY page 11D

## Louie Anderson Now Available In Pasta Form

see PRODUCTWATCH page 1E

## Area Wildcat A Real Wildcat In The Sack

see NATURE page 3C

## Abandoned Tuba Player Honks Mournfully By Side Of Road

see LOCAL page 3C

### STATshot
A look at the numbers that shape your world.

#### Most Popular U.S. Baby Names

| | White | Black | Asian |
|---|---|---|---|
| ♂ | Cameron | Antwaine | Michael |
| | Brandon | Dacron | Tim |
| | Austin | Newport | Chris |
| | Dakota | LaPrell | Rick |
| ♀ | Caitlin | Shawanda | Sue |
| | Brianna | Tamiqua | Lisa |
| | Ashleigh | Propecia | Michelle |
| | Madison | Sinutab | Amy |

THE ONION
$2.00 US
$3.00 CAN

# the ONION®

WWW.THEONION.COM　　AMERICA'S FINEST NEWS SOURCE™　　FOUNDED 1871

# McDonald's Employee Just In It For The Money

SHREVEPORT, LA—According to reports, Sean Boyce, a member of the Jefferson Avenue McDonald's team, may be doing it purely for the money. Critics say Boyce, 22, who lives with girlfriend Renee Simmons and their 2-year-old daughter, cares more about getting paid than dedicating himself to his craft.

"It's sad when a person's sole motivation is money, but that really seems to be the case with Mr. Boyce," said Peter Kuharcich, editor of the restaurant-industry newsletter *Fast Food Report.* "The only thing he's interested

in is getting that paycheck."

Contrary to claims made at the time of his hire, Boyce does not crave the challenge of brightening people's day the McDonald's way.

"When I interviewed Sean, he really seemed to agree that the most fulfilling thing about working here is getting the chance to make the customer's McDonald's experience as enjoyable as possible," assistant manager Frederick Taubense said. "But the longer he was here, the more apparent it became that it was all about the

see McDONALD'S page 37

Above: McDonald's employee Sean Boyce.

## Loved Ones Recall Local Man's Cowardly Battle With Cancer

PROFILES IN FEAR

Above: Charles Kunkel with wife Judith and son Jake.

On Oct. 26, four days after visiting the doctor for what he thought was severe indigestion or maybe an ulcer, Charles Kunkel got the dreaded news: A malignant, fist-sized tumor had metastasized between his stomach and liver. It was cancer.

Right then and there, faced with the prospect of a life-threatening disease, the 34-year-old Florissant, MO, husband and father of three drew a deep breath and made a firm resolution to himself: I am not going to fight this. I am a dead man.

He was right. On Nov. 20, Charles

see CANCER page 37

# Supreme Court Overturns Car

WASHINGTON, DC—In a landmark reversal of a 20-year-old automobile, the Supreme Court overturned a 1980 Ford Pinto Sunday, bringing to an end the car's longstanding upright, "wheels on the ground" position.

The reversal, which has affected the lives of an estimated 400 motorists on D.C.'s Wisconsin Avenue, was carried out by the nation's highest judicial body at approximately 9

p.m., in what legal experts described as a "strong show of support" for the Washington Redskins' 38-28 victory over the NFC East rival Arizona Cardinals.

Said Justice David Souter, who wrote the majority opinion in the case and played a key role in the car's overturning, lifting the back right tire off the ground: "Whoo! 'Skins rule, motherfuckers!"

Added Justice Ruth Bader

Above: D.C. police officials examine the automobile overturned by the nation's highest court Sunday.

Ginsburg: "All the way, baby."

Judicial experts agree that the reversal represents

the most significant Supreme Court overturning of a motorized vehicle

see SUPREME COURT page 36

35

# *Harry Potter* Books Spark Rise In Satanism Among Children

LOCK HAVEN, PA—Ashley Daniels is as close as you can get to your typical 9-year-old American girl. A third-grader at Lock Haven Elementary School, she loves rollerblading, her pet hamsters Benny and Oreo, Britney Spears, and, of course, *Harry Potter*. Having breezed through the most recent *Potter* opus in just four days, Ashley is among the millions of children who have made *Harry Potter And The Goblet Of Fire* the fastest-selling book in publishing history.

And, like many of her school friends, Ashley was captivated enough by the strange occult doings at the Hogwarts School Of Witchcraft And Wizardry to pursue the Left-Hand Path, determined to become as adept at the black arts as Harry and his pals.

"I used to believe in what they taught us at Sunday School," said Ashley, conjuring up an ancient spell to summon Cereberus, the three-headed hound of hell. "But the *Harry Potter* books showed me that magic is real, something I can learn and use right now, and that The Bible is nothing but boring lies."

Ashley is hardly the only child rejecting God these days. Weeks after the release of *Goblet*, the fourth book in J.K. Rowling's blockbuster kid-lit series, interest in witchcraft continues to skyrocket among children. Across America, Satanic temples are filling to the rafters with youngsters clamoring for instruction in summoning and conjuring.

Over protests from Christian Right leaders, who oppose the books for containing references to magic—and, by extension, Satanic religious beliefs—millions of children are willing their bodies and souls to Lucifer in unholy blood covenants. In 1995, it was estimated that some 100,000 Americans, mostly adults, were involved in devil-worship groups. Today, more than 14 million children alone belong to the Church of Satan, thanks largely to the unassuming boy wizard from 4 Privet Drive.

"The *Harry Potter* books are cool, 'cause they teach you all about magic and how you can use it to control people and get revenge on your enemies," said Hartland, WI, 10-year-old Craig Nowell, a recent convert to the New Satanic Order Of The Black Circle. "I want to learn the Cruciatus Curse, to make my muggle science teacher suffer for giving me a D."

"Hermione is my favorite, because she's smart and has a kitty," said 6-year-old Jessica Lehman of Easley, SC. "Jesus died because He was weak and stupid."

But as wild as children are about Harry, no one is happier about the phenomenon than old-school Satanists, who were struggling to recruit new members prior to the publication of the first Potter book in 1997.

"Harry is an absolute godsend to our

Above: Three young *Harry Potter* fans in Winter Park, FL, recite an ancient Satanic incantation.

cause," said High Priest Egan of the First Church Of Satan in Salem, MA. "An organization like ours thrives on new blood—no pun intended—and we've had more applicants than we can handle lately. And, of course, pretty much all of them are virgins, which is gravy."

With membership in Satanic temples reaching critical mass in some areas, many children have been forced to start their own organizations to worship the Lord Of Lies. Houston 11-year-old Bradley Winters, who purchased *Goblet Of Fire* with his allowance money at the stroke of midnight on July 8, organized his own club, Potterites To Destroy Jesus, with

> "The *Harry Potter* books showed me that magic is real, and that The Bible is nothing but boring lies," said one 9-year-old.

his neighborhood pals. An admission fee of $6.66 grants membership to any applicant willing to curse the name of God and have a lightning bolt carved into his or her forehead with an iron dagger.

"The *Harry Potter* books are awesome!" Winters said. "When I grow up, I'm going to learn Necromancy and summon greater demons to Earth."

But it's more than just the kiddie set and Satanists who are rejoicing over Harry's success. Educators nationwide are praising the books for getting children excited about reading.

"It's almost impossible to find a book that can compete with those PlayStation games, but *Harry Potter* has done it," said Gulfport (MS) Middle School principal Frank Grieg. "I have this one student in the fifth grade who'd never read a book before in his life. Now he's read *Sorcerer's Stone, Prisoner Of Azkaban, Chamber Of Secrets, Goblet Of Fire, The Seven Scrolls Of The Black Rose, The Necronomicon, The Satanic Bible, The Origin Of Species*—you name it."

Less pleased are Christian leaders, who see Pottermania as a serious threat.

"Children are very impressionable," said Dr. Andrea Collins of Focus On Faith, a Denver-based Christian think-tank and advocacy group. "These books do not merely depict one or two uses of magic spells or crystal balls. We're talking about hundreds of occult invocations. The natural, intuitive leap from reading a *Harry Potter* book to turning against God and worshipping Satan is very easy for a child to make, as the numbers have shown."

"These books are truly magical," Collins added, "and therefore dangerous."

But such protests are falling on largely deaf ears, especially in the case of Harry's creator.

"I think it's absolute rubbish to protest children's books on the grounds that they're luring children to Satan," Rowling told a *London Times* reporter in a July 17 interview. "People should be praising them for that! These books guide children to an understanding that the weak, idiotic Son Of God is a living hoax who will be humiliated when the rain of fire comes, and will suck the greasy cock of the Dark Lord while we, his faithful servants, laugh and cavort in victory." ∅

SUPREME COURT from page 35

Above: Members of the Supreme Court with President Clinton in a 1996 file photo.

since its controversial 1994 decision to strike down a Yamaha motorcycle during a spring-break binge-drinking free-for-all at Freaknik '94 in Atlanta. Most observers attributed that decision to the presence of a crowd of inebriated black college students cheering the justices on, as well as the blaring of the rap song "Rump Shaker" by Wreckx 'N' Effect.

"By turning this Ford Pinto upside-down in the middle of the street, the Supreme Court has made a clear statement that, as far as the U.S. judicial system is concerned, the Redskins are without question the greatest team ever and cannot be stopped," said Georgetown University law professor Edwin Burber.

The court is set to rule Thursday on whether beer bongs are awesome. ∅

McDONALD'S from page 35

money for him. He's always asking stuff like, 'Wasn't I supposed to get a raise last month?' and, 'I thought I get time and a half when I work overtime.' At some point, he needs to wake up and realize that money isn't the most important thing."

Boyce, who joined the McDonald's team in November 1998, has all but admitted that his reasons for accepting the position were greed-based. After returning home more than an hour late last Tuesday from a mandatory "Improving Customer Service" training session, Boyce allegedly told his girlfriend that he just wants to "punch in, do my job, and punch out." Several days later, he intimated to fellow cashier Amani Green that "if I win the lottery, I'm never setting foot in another McDonald's for the rest of my life."

"Frankly, we're all a little shocked to find this kind of attitude coming from a member of the McDonald's family," Taubense said. "Sean's lack of dedication to customer satisfaction flies in the face of the Employee's Commitment To Excellence statement he signed during orientation, not to mention the nine points on the McDon-

ald's Customer Bill Of Rights posted next to the hot-pie holder. He acts as if his shift isn't about providing friendly, helpful service with a smile, but about getting cash for a pair of new sneakers or medicine for his daughter's earache."

Other McDonald's crew members have noticed Boyce's selfishness, as well.

"Sean's a scheming climber who's only looking out for himself. I've even heard him talking about wanting to go to tech school," second-shift manager Denise Lum said. "I get the feeling he could decide to quit at any time and—poof—with two weeks notice, he'd be gone."

"Sean has no sense of loyalty at all," fellow crew member Bob DiSalvo said. "I wouldn't be a bit surprised if he left for Wendy's or Burger King if he thought he could get more money there."

Despite their problems with his attitude, McDonald's management said they have no plans to fire Boyce at this time, citing staffing shortages in the morning drive-thru and second-shift grill-cook positions. ⌀

CANCER from page 35

Kunkel died following a brief, cowardly battle with stomach cancer.

"Most people, when they find out they've got something terrible like this, dig down deep and tap into some tremendous well of courage and strength they never knew they had," said Judith Kunkel, Charles' wife of 11 years. "Not Charles. The moment he found out he had cancer, he curled up into a fetal ball and sobbed uncontrollably for three straight weeks."

"I can still remember Charles' last words," Judith added. "'Oh, God, I'm going to die! Why, God, why? Why me? Why not someone else?'"

According to Charles' personal physician, Dr. James Wohlpert, the type of cancer Charles had generally takes at least four months to advance to the terminal stage. But because of what he described as a "remarkable lack of fighting spirit," the disease consumed him in less than one.

"It's rare that you see someone give up that quickly and completely," Wohlpert said. "Cancer is a powerful disease, but most people can at the very least delay its spread by maintaining a positive outlook and mental attitude. This, however, was not the case with Charles."

Charles' friends and acquaintances saw that same lack of fighting spirit.

"He did not go quietly, that's for sure," longtime friend Bobby Dwyer said. "He did a tremendous amount of screaming."

"During the three days he spent at work before the pain got too bad, I saw a very different Charles," said Arnold Tolliver, a coworker at the Florissant electronics store where Charles had been employed for the past six years. "He was always telling the customers how tragic it was that he wouldn't outlive his kids, remind-

> **When the end finally came, Charles Kunkel died red-eyed, trembling, and hysterical in the attic of his home.**

ing me that every day is a gift cruelly torn from his fingers, and grabbing somebody, anybody, by the shirt and screaming into their face that he didn't want to die."

In those final days, like so many who realize their day of reckoning is nigh, Charles Kunkel turned to a higher power. "Charles came to me in his time of need," said Pastor Charles Bourne of Holy Christ Almighty Lutheran Church. "But when I tried to comfort him by saying he would be with God soon, he only stopped bawling long enough to say, 'Fuck God! There is no God!' I had to get a couple acolytes to help me pry him out from underneath the pews."

When the end finally came, Charles Kunkel died red-eyed, trembling, and hysterical in the attic of his home, where, in the depths of his fear, he was convinced the Reaper would look last. On that day, his 5-year-old daughter Bailey awoke to an unnerving quiet, the usual terror-choked sobs and shrieks of her father strangely absent from the morning air. Alarmed, she ran to her mother's side.

"Bailey was yelling, 'Daddy stopped crying! Daddy stopped crying!'" Judith said. "Somehow, though she's still very young, she understood."

On Monday, Charles Kunkel was

Above: Bush speaks during a campaign stop in Chula Vista, CA, where he courted Hispanics with a $20 tip.

# Bush Reaches Out To Hispanic Community With Generous Tip

CHULA VISTA, CA—Republican presidential candidate George W. Bush extended a hand of friendship to the nation's Hispanic community Sunday, leaving a larger-than-customary tip for waiter Ramon Gonzalez after eating at La Galleria, a trendy Chula Vista bistro.

Bush—who was lunching with chief strategist Karl Rove and campaign contributor Ken Boehm, CEO of Pacific Bell—left a $20 gratuity on a bill of $83.42. Working out to approximately 24 percent, it is the largest tip the Hispanic community has ever received from a Republican presidential candidate.

Gonzalez, accepting Bush's generous overture on behalf of his people, thanked the candidate politely as he departed the restaurant. Gonzalez said he intends to share the gift with other members of the Hispanic community, employing the standard food-service-industry split among waiter, busboy, and dishwasher.

"This generous tip is my way of saying thank you to the Latino community for its distinguished service during the course of this lunch," Bush said. "It is my way of acknowledging the many valuable things America's His-

Above: Bush's overture to the Latino community.

panics bring to the table—from appetizers to drinks to main courses—which are vital to the smooth progress of our nation's meals."

Republican insiders are praising the gesture, noting that Bush has sent "a message of appreciation to a too-often-overlooked ethnic group."

"By leaving a twenty on the table for this Mexican boy, Bush is telling Hispanics, 'I understand how hard your people have worked over the years to keep our water glasses full,'" Bush communications director Karen Hughes said. "At the same time, by making this offering in tip form, he reinforces his campaign slogan of 'Prosperity With Purpose.' In other words, he sends the strong message that continued good service on the
see BUSH page 38

laid to rest at Shady Grove Cemetery in Florissant. More than 200 people gathered to bid farewell. And, just as Charles had requested shortly before his death, the funeralgoers wailed loudly and gnashed their teeth, cursing the heavens for the unfair hand dealt their loved one.

"The day before he died," Judith recalled, "he took my hand and said to me, 'At my funeral, I don't want people to wear bright colors and smile and laugh fondly at the wonderful memories of the precious time we spent together on Earth. Tell them to wear black and cover their faces with ash. Tell them to weep bitter tears and rail

angrily against the cruel God who took me at such a young age. Do this for me, my beloved.'"

Added Judith: "He also told me not to move on from this tragedy by one day finding love in the arms of another. He said he couldn't bear the thought of me with someone else, and that the best way I could honor his memory was by never building a new life for myself."

"They say in times of great trial, a man's true colors show," said Charles' best friend, Larry Ahrens, summing up the feelings of those who knew the man. "And in Charles' case, he had a yellow streak a mile wide." ⌀

BUSH from page 37

part of Hispanics will be recognized and rewarded."

Despite such praise, Bush's rivals for the Republican presidential nomination were quick to denounce the unusually large gratuity.

"I have always favored an across-the-board flat tip of 15 percent, regardless of the waiter's race," Steve Forbes said. "Gov. Bush's tip of 24 percent is not only fiscally irresponsible; it smacks of political grandstanding."

Fellow Republican candidate John McCain was also troubled by the precedent set by the Bush tip.

"If we give the Hispanics 24 percent," McCain said, "then the Asians will want 24 percent, too. Then the blacks. Then it snowballs out of control, to the point where regular Americans suddenly can't afford to eat anywhere with table service, let alone get their cars detailed or their hedges trimmed. Gov. Bush has opened up a real Pandora's Box here."

Speaking to reporters during a campaign stop at a factory in Nashua, NH, Democratic presidential candidate Al Gore also had words for Bush.

"Mr. Bush is trying to tip too little, too late," Gore said. "For years, he

> ## Said Bush: "This tip is my way of acknowledging the many valuable things America's Hispanics bring to the table— from appetizers to drinks to main courses."

cheated the nation's Hispanic community, calculating his tip by doubling the tax, even when dining in states where the restaurant tax is a mere six percent. Look at the record: He consistently undertipped Hispanics during his tenure as governor of Texas. And now he is trying to make up for all of that with a single $20 bill. My fellow Americans, I do not believe that, in his heart of hearts, Mr. Bush knows how much to tip."

Gore added that tipping should be "colorblind," reflecting only the quality of service received, and noted that many Hispanics are not waiters.

Bush, while declining to respond specifically to his opponents' remarks, said he stands by his commitment to Hispanics.

"As the fastest-growing ethnic group in America, Hispanics will continue to make their presence felt in all walks of restaurant life," Bush said. "Whether you see them grinning while bringing the enchiladas at a Mexican restaurant or quietly and politely clearing the table at an expensive Italian eatery, I would urge all Americans to follow my lead and reach out to them with a couple of extra bucks." ∅

# In Retrospect, I Guess We Might Have Resorted To Cannibalism A Bit Early

Well, I suppose everyone's heard about last week's incident by now, and you probably have a pretty low opinion of us survivors. And, all

**By Milton Boyd**

things considered, perhaps we deserve it. Perhaps we panicked and resorted to cannibalism a bit early. But you weren't there. You don't know

what it was like. I just want you to hear our side of the story before you go judging us.

When the six of us got into the elevator on that fateful day, we had no idea what was going to happen. We thought we were just going to take a little ride from the 12th floor to the lobby, just like every other day. Do you think we knew that elevator was going to get stuck between floors? Do you think we got into the elevator saying, "Hey, you know, we should eat our old pal Jerry Weinhoff from Accounts Payable"? Of course not.

During those first few minutes after the elevator car lurched to a stop somewhere between the seventh and eighth floors, we were still civilized human beings. Everyone kept his cool. We tried pushing the emergency button. We called out for help. We even banged on the door a little bit. Nothing worked. Still, we figured, "No big deal, someone will notice that the elevator's stuck, and this thing will start back up any second." Morale was generally high. John and Peter actually cracked some jokes, if you can believe that.

Maybe it started there, the hysteria. Maybe we should have known. But at some point, when the voices went away and pushing the buttons continued to have no effect, it started to look less like we were going to have a fun-

> ## During those first few minutes after the elevator car lurched to a stop somewhere between the seventh and eighth floors, we were still civilized human beings.

ny story to tell our kids and more like they'd never hear from us again.

It does something to a person to think that. You confront your own mortality for the first time. You become savage, brutal. One word enters your mind: survive. *Survive!*

I have no idea how long we'd been marooned when we started edging toward Jerry. Twenty, thirty minutes, time has little meaning when you're in a situation like that. It wasn't a spoken decision, either. We just all looked at each other and knew something had to be done.

It might have been an animal act, but it had a certain logic. Jerry lived alone and had nobody special in his life—no kids, no wife or girlfriend, and his parents had died a long time ago. And, most important, he was the biggest. We figured there was enough

meat on him to keep the rest of us alive for days, maybe weeks.

Peter held him down while I tore at his forearm with my teeth. Not surprisingly, Jerry resisted. He struggled ferociously and shouted, "Hey, what the hell are you doing?" But he knew exactly what we were doing: We were doing whatever it took to survive.

Eventually, we were able to knock Jerry out. As for what we did next, I'm sure you've read about it in the papers. Maybe it was savage. Maybe it was an animal act. But human teeth are pointed and sharp in front for a reason. Besides, we had no way of knowing that, at that very moment, an Otis Elevator repairman was working to free us. We only knew that we were between floors, and that it had been more than five hours since most of us had had lunch.

The veneer of civilization is thin. Civilization depends upon people acting in a reasonable manner and obeying certain universal laws. But civilization also depends upon that cruise ship staying afloat. It depends upon that airliner passing safely over the Arctic Circle. And it depends upon that elevator continuing smoothly down to the lobby of the Hadley Insurance Building.

Am I sorry about what I did? Of course. Taking a life is never easy. But sometimes we have little choice.

When I finally got home from work that day, some 50 minutes late, my youngest daughter Kellie ran up to me and gave me a big hug. She said, "Daddy, I'm glad you're home." *Daddy, I'm glad you're home.* At that moment, I knew I'd done the right thing. ∅

## Near-Death Experience Followed By Right-On-The-Money Death Experience

PORTLAND, OR—A near-death experience was followed by one of the right-on-the-money variety Sunday, when local mechanic Gabe Hoover narrowly averted fatally choking on a chicken bone, only to be run over by a city bus later the same day. "As I began to lose consciousness from the lack of oxygen, I saw a bright, welcoming light, and I heard a voice calling out to me that sounded like my deceased mother," said Hoover, describing his near-death experience an hour before being struck dead. "I felt incredibly at peace, but then, suddenly, another voice told me to go back, say-

ing I wasn't finished with my work on Earth." Hoover continued his work on Earth for another 64 minutes, at which point he hit the death nail right on the head, walking swiftly and directly into the light.

## Communists Now Least Threatening Group In U.S.

WASHINGTON, DC—According to a report released Monday by the Pentagon, Communists rank last on a list of 238 threats to national security. "Communists may now safely be ignored," Secretary of Defense William Cohen said. "The Red Menace has been surpassed by militia groups, religious extremists, ecoterrorists, cybercriminals, Hollywood producers, and angry drivers." Other groups deemed

more threatening than Communists include rap-metal bands (#96), escaped zoo animals (#202), and Belgians (#237).

## Country Singer Trying To Think Of Rhyme For 'Shove You'

GREEN BRIER, TN—Country singer Ricky Lee Dean, nearing completion of a new song, reported Sunday that he is struggling to find a rhyme for "shove you." "It's a tune about a fella who gets drunk and mistreats his gal, and he's trying to explain to her why he acts that way," Dean said. "The line goes, 'Just because I shove you / That don't mean I don't...' but I can't seem to finish it." Dean is also trying to come up with a rhyme for "down a flight of stairs." ∅

## Brittle Jewess Does Not Like What George Clooney Is Wearing

see PEOPLE page 4C

## Highlighting In Used Copy Of Plato's *Republic* Stops On Page 17

see EDUCATION page 1D

## Nothing In Rule Book Says Hockey Player Can't Be Orangutan

see SPORTS page 8B

## Standard Deviation Not Enough For Perverted Statistician

see SCIENCE page 4D

### STATshot

A look at the numbers that shape your world.

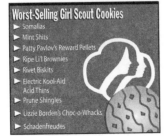

**Worst-Selling Girl Scout Cookies**

► Somalias
► Mint Shits
► Patty Pavlov's Reward Pellets
► Ripe Li'l Brownies
► Rivet Biskits
► Electric Kool-Aid Acid Thins
► Prune Shingles
► Lizzie Borden's Choc-o-Whacks
► Schadenfreudes

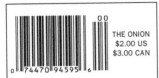

THE ONION
$2.00 US
$3.00 CAN

0 74470 94595 6

# the ONION ®

WWW.THEONION.COM    AMERICA'S FINEST NEWS SOURCE™    FOUNDED 1871

# South Postpones Rising Again For Yet Another Year

Above: Three of the estimated 45 million Southerners who have not yet gotten around to rising again.

HUNTSVILLE, AL—For the 134th straight year since Gen. Robert E. Lee's surrender at Appomattox, representatives of the South announced Tuesday that the region has postponed plans to rise again.

"Make no mistake, the South shall rise again," said Knox Pritchard, president of the Huntsville-based Alliance Of Confederate States. "But we're just not quite ready to do it now. Hopefully, we'll be able to rise again real soon, maybe even in 2000."

Pritchard's fellow Southerners shared his confidence.

"Yes, sir. The South will rise again. And when it does, I'll be right up front waving the Stars and Bars," said Dock Mullins of Decatur, GA. "But first, I gotta get my truck fixed and get that

see SOUTH page 40

## C-SPAN Releases *Too Hot For C-SPAN!* Video

WASHINGTON, DC—In the cable network's first-ever foray into the home-video market, C-SPAN released *Too Hot For C-SPAN!* Tuesday.

The 60-minute, $19.95 videotape features what its packaging describes as "wild and sexy congressional outtakes you won't see on basic cable."

"Sometimes, the action in

the House and Senate gets a little out of control, and footage must be held back from the general public," C-SPAN spokesman Larry Jainchill said. "But now, for the first time ever, you can see it all. *Too Hot For C-SPAN!* is your front-row ticket to all the outrageous, uncensored action."

In one segment, U.S. Rep.

see C-SPAN page 40

REP. JOHN McCASKILL
D–CALIFORNIA

C-SPAN Today

Above: U.S. Rep. John McCaskill (D-CA) charges Rep. Walter Fordice (R-NH) during a 1996 congressional session.

# Ant Farm Teaches Children About Toil, Death

PASADENA, CA—Wonderco, a Pasadena-based educational-toy manufacturer, unveiled its new Playscovery Cove Ant Village Tuesday, touting the ant farm as a fun, interactive way to teach children ages 5 and up about unceasing, backbreaking toil and the cold, inescapable reality of death.

"Your little ones will have a front-row seat as worker ants labor, day in and day out, until they inevitably die of exhaustion, their futile efforts all for naught," Wonderco spokeswoman Joan Kedzie said. "A Playscovery Cove Ant Village, complete with stackable tiny ant barns, see-through 'Antway' travel tubes, and connecting 'Antports,' is your children's window into the years of thankless, grueling labor that await them as worker drones in our post-industrial society."

Billed as "the fun way to teach your

Above: Children learn about the cruel reality of pain, toil, and death with the Playscovery Cove Ant Village.

kids to accept their miserable fate stoically," the ant farm retails for $14.95.

"The ants work very, very hard," said

Youngstown, OH, 9-year-old Dylan Munns, who will one day work in the

see ANT FARM page 41

C-SPAN from page 39

Above: U.S. Rep. Susan Northrup (R-NH) surprises her fellow legislators during an October 1997 House Appropriations Committee hearing on Pell Grant allocations.

Henry Waxman (D-CA) argues against the passage of HR 4236, the Omnibus Parks And Public Lands Management Act, calling it "a clear case of Republican pork-barrel politics gone awry."

Angered by Waxman's remarks, the bill's co-sponsor, Rep. James Talent (R-MO) shouts at him, "That's it, bitch, I'm through with your ass," and charges the podium. He then tackles Waxman, punching him several times before a muscular congressional page pulls the legislators apart.

In another segment, Sen. Bob Graham (D-FL), angered by Sen. Don Nickles' (R-OK) call for a 1.3 percent increase in federal interstate subsidies over the next five years, calls Nickles "a dumb Oklahoma hick who can't get none of his shit approved in the Senate." Nickles responds by calling Graham a "fat Florida fuck" and charges at him. As the livid Nickles is dragged back to his seat by Republican colleagues, he shouts at Graham: "You just a temporary thang, Bob Graham. Your ass gonna be voted out of office this November. Me, I gots me a 83 percent approval rating in my home district, so I ain't going nowhere—I'm forever, bitch!"

While a majority of *Too Hot For C-SPAN!*'s content is violent, it also contains a substantial amount of sexually explicit material. Just before proposing an amendment to Sec. 11, Par. B of the Hawkins-Taylor Clean Water Act, Sen. Barbara Mikulski (D-MD) unbuttons her blouse, reveals her breasts, and says, "My fellow members of Congress, it's all about the body."

Mikulski's actions were later denounced by Sen. Carol Moseley-Braun (D-IL), who called them "grossly inappropriate and wholly unacceptable." Moseley-Braun also said that Mikulski had "a fat pussy."

Among the other highlights listed in the *Too Hot For C-SPAN!* press release: a "sassy catfight between Sen. Dianne Feinstein (D-CA) and Sen. Susan Collins (R-ME)," Sen. Alfonse D'Amato delivering "the filthiest filibuster you've ever heard," and a "massive bipartisan pileup" between the Senate Committee On Environment And Public Works and the Committee On Banking, Housing, And Urban Affairs concerning the rights of developers to build in the same district as federally protected land.

"When Herb Kohl says he got it on with Paul Sarbanes' wife while Sarbanes was off on a fact-finding mission to the Florida wetlands," the

## Mosley-Braun also said that Mikulski had "a fat pussy."

press release states, "the gloves are off!"

Despite his excitement over the video, C-SPAN's Jainchill stressed that it is not intended for minors. "Due to its subcommittee melees, profanity-laden roll calls, and wild catfights, *Too Hot For C-SPAN!* is inappropriate for those under 18. But for everyone else, believe me—you won't want to miss a minute of the incredible gavel-to-gavel action."

"Aw, wicked," said longtime C-SPAN viewer Greg Ammons of La Jolla, CA, when informed of the tape. "I love when they go at it on C-SPAN, and now I can see all the really hot action and hear the great insults without those annoying 'Oops!' circles appearing over the mouths of the congressmen. This tape is gonna rule."

Encouraged by the substantial pre-order sales for *Too Hot For C-SPAN!*, C-SPAN is already moving forward with *Too Hot For C-SPAN2!* The second tape will feature "incredible, totally uncensored" footage from C-SPAN's sister network, C-SPAN2, including author Daniel Yergin's attempt to discuss his new book, *The Commanding Heights: The Battle Between Government And The Marketplace That Is Remaking The Modern World*, while two 300-pound strippers paint his body with chocolate sauce. ⌀

SOUTH from page 39

rusty old stove out of my yard."

"Lord willing, and the creek don't rise, we gonna rise again," said Sumter, SC, radiator technician Hap Slidell, who describes himself as "Southern by the grace of God." "I don't know exactly when we're gonna do it, but one of these days, we're gonna show them Yankees how it's done."

"Save your Confederate dollars," Slidell added. "You can bet on that."

The Deep South states of Alabama, Georgia, Mississippi, South Carolina, Louisiana, and Tennessee consistently rank at the bottom of the nation in a variety of statistical categories, including literacy, infant mortality, hospital beds, toilet-paper sales, and shoe usage. Even so, some experts believe the region could be poised for a renaissance.

"The way things stand, things in the Deep South almost have to get better. Otherwise, the people who live there will devolve into preverbal, overall-wearing sub-morons within a century," said professor Dennis Lassiter of Princeton University. "Either Southerners will start improving themselves, or they'll be sold to middle-class Asians as pets."

"My constituents are decent, hard-working folk," Sen. Jesse Helms (R-NC) asserted, despite overwhelming evidence to the contrary, in his 22nd annual "Next Year, By God!" speech on the steps of the North Carolina capitol. "We are a proud people who mayn't have all that much fancy-pants book-learnin', but we live and die with pride in our proud heritage and the dignity of our forebears."

Helms' speech was met with nearly 25 minutes of enthusiastic hoots and rebel yells by the 15,000 drunk, unemployed tobacco pickers in attendance.

Though Southerners are overwhelmingly in favor of rising again, few could provide specific details of the process.

"I don't know, I reckon we'll build us a bunch of big, fancy buildins and pave us up a whole mess of roads," said Bobby Lee Fuller of Greenville, MS. "I ain't exactly sure where we're gonna get the money for that, but when Johnny Reb sets his mind to something, you best get out of his way."

"Oh, it'll happen, sure as the sun come up in the morning," said Buford Comstock, 26, a student at Over 'N' Back Diesel Driving School in Union City, TN. "The South is gonna rise up, just as soon as we get together and get all our shit back in one sock. Then, look out, Northerners!"

"Yesiree," Comstock added, "one day soon, the Mason-Dixon Line will be the boundary between a great nation and one whose time done passed." ⌀

Above: The Mississippi state capitol.

## NEWS IN BRIEF

## Liver Flees George Jones' Body

NASHVILLE, TN—After more than 40 years of absorbing vast quantities of hard alcohol, George Jones' liver finally fled the famed country singer's body Tuesday. "I can't take it anymore," the liver said. "A liver can only process so many toxins before it says to hell with it." Jones' liver absorbed its final drink early Tuesday morning, a bourbon and branch water that Jones had with some eggs for breakfast. Until it can find a place of its own, Jones' liver plans to share an apartment with Merle Haggard's liver and Hank Williams Jr.'s lungs.

## Everything A Goddamn Ordeal In Area Family

HUNTINGTON, WV—Absolutely everything, from ordering a pizza to going out to the movies, has to be a huge goddamn ordeal for the Flemings, father Bryce Fleming reported Tuesday. "Just once, could we maybe sit down and watch some goddamn TV together without the whole thing devolving into an all-night screaming match?" Fleming asked wife Tanya Fleming. "Could we?" Fleming went on to ask if that could happen once in the history of their goddamn household. ⌀

same grim Hormel meat-packing plant where his father now toils, as his father did before him. "They dig tunnels and carry heavy stuff all day long. Then they do it all over again the next day."

"They all look and act the same," said Newark, NJ, 10-year-old Darnell Booker, who, like Munns, will play the role of blue-collar worker in a society that rewards collectivism over individualism. "And there's no escape."

According to Kedzie, the ants, which come separately from the farm, are bred in New Mexico and mailed directly to Playscovery Cove Ant Village purchasers. Within days of arriving, many of the ants die at the hands of the small children responsible for regulating the temperature, humidity, and food supply in their delicate pseudo-ecosystem.

Even under optimum conditions, Kedzie said, the ants survive no more than 20 weeks in the farm. As a result, children are assured the chance to contemplate the inescapability of their own mortality.

"My ants came in the mail, and I put them in my ant farm all by myself," said Molly Whalen, 7, of Springfield, MA. "Some were stuck to the bottom of the tube, and I tried to make them move by dunking them in water, but mommy said they were dead forever."

It is normal for a certain percentage of the ants to perish in transport, Kedzie said.

"As it says in the official Playscovery Cove Ant Watcher's Guide, 'Don't worry if some ants didn't make the long and bumpy trip to your mailbox, kids, because we send along more than enough to get your ant farm up and running,'" she said. "'Besides, when some of your ants arrive dead, you'll be reminded that the spectre of death hangs over every creature on this Earth!'"

The lesson that the ants' labor is all in vain becomes clearer as time passes. During the first two to three weeks, the exclusively female worker ants are extremely productive, building an elaborate system of tunnels and hills amongst the miniature green trees and red plastic houses dotting the interior of the plastic dome. However, because neither male ants nor a fertile queen is provided with the Playscovery Cove Ant Village, making reproduction impossible, the farm is doomed to extinction from day one.

"The social structure of an ant colony is extremely complex, with individual members occupying castes such as soldier, messenger, and larvae attendant," said Penn State entomologist Dr. Gerald Dudek. "At some point, the Playscovery Cove ants become cognizant that their hierarchical structure has been stripped away, rendering their already meaningless existence totally futile. There seems to be a breaking point at about the 22-day mark when the dejected ants begin to die off en masse."

At this point, Dudek said, the ant farm enters what is known as the

Above: Ant carcasses pile up beside a little plastic tree.

"death-pile phase." A spot is chosen by the worker ants to deposit their dead, and the burial mound steadily grows as the few remaining ants devote more of their time to gathering and burying others.

"It was really weird," said Jessica Lurman, 14, of Savannah, GA. "The ants were, like, really careful to put all the dead ants in this one big grave until there were, like, only four left. Then, the next morning, three of the

four were lying with the others in the big pile, and the last one was dead over by the plastic farmhouse thingy. It must have died right after it buried the second-to-last ant."

Rick Brannan, CEO of Wonderco, said his company's ant farm was initially marketed as a fun way to teach children about life, not death.

"About a year ago, we re-examined our entire line of nature-exploration toys—the ant farms, firefly lanterns,

butterfly keepers, and ladybug jars," Brannan said. "What we found was surprising: Despite the fact that, 100 percent of the time, these toys resulted in the death of the living creatures caged inside, parents continued to buy them for their children. It was then that we realized the suffering and death must be part of the attraction."

Added Brannan: "Here at Wonderco, arbeit macht fun!" ✍

## EDITORIAL

# Dressing Your Dog As Boba Fett Is Something You Have To Devote A Weekend To

I've always thought of myself as a creative guy. Whenever my friends in the *Star Wars* novel-reading club schedule a Sunday-night *Star Wars* viewing party, I like to get into the spirit of things by dressing up in a theme outfit. And, of course, a big part of the excitement is dressing up my pet Cocker Spaniel, Nikto, as a character from the films or expanded universe, too.

**By Larry Groznic**

The first time we ever did a party at Jerry's house, back when *Shadows Of The Empire* first came out in hardcover, I got out an old Han Solo Halloween costume. Then, on a last-minute whim, I dressed Nikto as Leia with a pair of earmuffs and an old white T-shirt. Big hit!

After that, I guess people just started

> **The only other thing I managed that day was to make the shoulder blast plates out of margarine-tub lids.**

expecting costumes, and I didn't want to disappoint. So, for the *Hard Merchandise* party, I went as Lando and made a neat Lobot outfit for Nik. It wasn't perfect; Nik's sleeves weren't

as billowy as I'd have liked, and he got pretty grumpy when I tried tucking his ears under the headpiece. But people still laughed plenty when we walked in.

Well, by that point, I'd created a monster: People started showing up to the parties just to see how Nik and I would be dressed! In fact, it soon became clear that my costumes were the main reason behind the swelling ranks of the *Star Wars* novel-reading club, which had recently welcomed its 12th member. And though that was an awesome responsibility, I accepted it.

Perhaps my crowning achievement was the *Rogue Planet* party costumes. For myself, I created a Jabba outfit out of some sheets of yellow foam that my parents were going to throw away when their sofa was delivered, and I see BOBA FETT page 41

41

made Nikto a Bib Fortuna ensemble. For Bib's head tentacles, I bought a set of pink children's pajamas, sewed the legs shut, and filled them with cotton. Then, I made Bib's robe out of an old winter coat and put long, gross-looking press-on nails on Nik's claws to complete the effect.

That one actually got applause! You should've seen Nik, his nose and only one eye sticking out from this mass of heavy fabric as he loped into Deborah's apartment. Plus, he made these hilarious growling noises that, I swear to God, sounded just like Bib! (I should have trained him to say "Day Wanna Wanga" or something!)

So, for the most recent party, celebrating the release of *Vector Prime* in paperback, I knew I had to outdo myself. I mean, *Vector Prime*! If you can't name at least one of the drastic changes that book introduced to the *Star Wars* continuum, you don't have any business reading this!

So, I figured this was the ideal occasion to trot out my incredible Han-In-Carbonite costume that I'd been making in secret out of a refrigerator box. Needless to say, the perfect complement to me as Frozen Han would be Nik in full Boba Fett armor, "escorting" me in!

Now, you, the inexperienced dog-dresser, are probably thinking that it would be relatively easy to whip up a Boba Fett costume for a Cocker Spaniel. Five to eight hours of work at the most, right? Well, guess again, Chucky.

Where to begin with the problems I encountered? First off, apparently, children's foot-sleepers come in every color of the rainbow except gray, so making the inner flight suit was a major hassle. In the end, I had to get white sleepers and dye them in the bathtub, which practically wiped out all of Friday. The only other thing I managed that day was to make the shoulder blast plates out of margarine-tub lids. That meant Saturday morning would get eaten up making the chest armor.

Now, in my naïvete, I thought the helmet would be the easy part. Just make a plaster mold from the 1/2-scale Riddell replica helmet, coat the interior with latex, dry, and paint, right? Well, get this: I found out afterwards that the replica is actually 45 percent scale, not 50! And, man, what a difference five percent makes! The finished product was just too tight on Nik's head. God knows I tried to cram him in there, but it was like trying to put Oola's costume on Harry Knowles. Nik refused to wear the damn helmet, and this was after I'd wasted an hour and a half painting it.

By this point, it's Saturday night, and I don't have the helmet, the centerpiece of any Boba Fett costume. Now, in a pinch, I might've been willing to use my own full-size Don Post helmet, but I knew that whatever helmet I used, I'd have to cut away the back to fit it on Nik's head so that he's looking ahead rather than down. And

# High-Definition Television Promises Sharper Crap

Above: Drool-inducing, sub-moronic swill as seen on a conventional analog television, disrupted by static.

Above: The same garbage with crystal-clear, movie-quality reception on HDTV.

WASHINGTON, DC—In the most dramatic leap in television technology since the advent of color in the 1950s, the FCC approved a 10-year plan Tuesday to shift to digital, high-definition TV—technology which will make barely watchable crap far sharper and more detailed than ever before.

"This is a monumental breakthrough," said Panasonic vice-president Gene Kalman, demonstrating a prototype of the new HDTV. "This atrocious episode of *Sliders* almost looks like it will leap off the screen, and it wasn't even shot in the new format."

The first generation of the format, Sony's "TV-H," will be available in U.S. stores as early as this fall. Though the $2,500 price tag makes crystal-clear viewing of intelligence-insulting swill possible only for the wealthy, prices are expected to drop dramatically in the next five years.

"By the year 2005," said Bob Rowell, president of the American Association of Broadcasters, "90 percent of American homes will enjoy their favorite heap of dung on a high-definition TV."

"Soon, your children will be able to watch shrill, grating Hanna-Barbera re-runs on The Cartoon Network with

a degree of crispness unheard of when you first watched that crap in the '70s," Rowell said. "And those whose lives are so empty that each Thursday night they actually watch all of NBC's so-called 'Must-See TV'

> ## Said Panasonic's Gene Kalman: "This atrocious episode of *Sliders* almost looks like it will leap off the screen."

lineup will be amazed at the clarity and resolution with which all those stupid people's apartments come through."

Promised Rowell: "When you see the episode of *Martin* in which the computer-dating service matches Martin up with his neighbor Sheneneh, his grotesque and profoundly unfunny mugging will come through with a resolution unimagined on traditional TVs."

Inane commericals will also look amazingly deep and three-dimension-

al when viewed in the new format. Further, the digital sound system will greatly enhance their intrusive, over-loud quality.

"That kid with the Southern accent on the grape-juice ad will look like you can almost reach out and strangle him," Rowell said.

In addition, big-budget movies such as *Independence Day* and *Eraser* will soon be available in HDTV digital-cassette format, which manufacturers promise will offer an experience comparable to shaking your head and thinking, "This sucks," in an actual movie theater.

Top videogame manufacturers, including Nintendo and Sega, are already developing new systems on which consumers will be able to play astonishingly crisp, ultra-realistic versions of the same old dumb videogame in which two guys whale on each other.

Designed with an eye to the future, HDTVs will be also able to accommodate yet-to-be-unveiled cable-TV systems, which promise to bring more than 1,000 channels of unwatchable tripe into the home.

"We have seen the future," FCC chair Reed Hundt said, "and it is sharp. And it is crap." ✍

---

my helmet is one of only 500 autographed in gold ink by Jeremy Bulloch. So that idea was obviously out—I need to preserve the helmet for my sister's children, and her children's children, to gaze upon.

Needless to say, my only option was to try to get the helmet Big Mel had on display at Forbidden Planet. Yes, the helmet was a bit faded because that moron displays it in the front window, and the targeting rangefinder looked like it was ready to break off at any second, but this was an emergency.

So I sauntered in all cool, trying not to let on just how desperately I needed the helmet. But Big Mel must have had some kind of mind probe working, because in the end, I had to trade him my original vinyl *Star Wars Christmas Album*, my C-3PO boner card, and my complete *Crimson Empire* collection.

Well, modifying the helmet didn't take too long, but Nik seemed to have trouble seeing out of the viewplate, and his head sagged a lot, like the helmet was real heavy, even though it was just vinyl. I think Nik might be getting a little old: He was already an adult when I adopted him, and that was way back around the time *Dark Force Rising* came out.

I'm not saying the costume wasn't a hit, but it definitely could have been better. It took so long to get the helmet together that I had to forget about the wrist gauntlets, and I even had two perfect wristbands set aside to dye maroon for them. Once the helmet was finally modified, all I had time to do was make some Wookiee scalps out of $8 worth of thrift-shop wigs. And that still meant half an hour of braiding before I had to take off like Mars Guo just to get to the

party on time.

It was, frankly, the biggest mess since the *Bacta War* party. I'd had this perfect idea to dress Nik as R5-D4, but those jerks at KFC wouldn't give me a bucket for the head, so I had to buy a 14-piece bucket, then empty it. So R5-D4 had a grease-stained head that reeked of chicken.

I certainly learned some valuable lessons from the whole experience: Plan everything meticulously, work ahead, and expect the unexpected. My new policy will be to "dry run" all costumes at least a week before the party. That will ensure that Nik's Tusken Raider costume won't be a big disappointment next month (*Hero's Trial*). I've already got a whole roll of Ace bandages, some used spark plugs, and a pair of jeweler's glasses for the eyes. This is going to be the best one yet! ✍

## NEWS

### Georgia Adds Swastika, Middle Finger To State Flag

see NATION page 5A

### New Instant Lottery Game Features Three Ways To Win, 19,839,947 Ways To Lose

see LIFESTYLE page 7D

### Best Buy Idea Box Brimming With Urine

see SHOPPING page 10C

### Lindsay Wagner To Star In Anything Offered Her

see ENTERTAINMENT page 3A

### STATshot

A look at the numbers that shape your world.

**What Part Of "I'm Not Interested" Do U.S. Telemarketers Not Understand?**

"I'm" 21%

"Not" 47%

"Interested" 32%

THE ONION
$2.00 US
$3.00 CAN

0 74470 94595 6

---

Above: Associate service-department manager Bill Tepfer.

## Mid-Level Manager Forced To Find Out Who Isn't Flushing The Toilet

DOVER, DE—Bill Tepfer, an associate service-department manager at Shademaster Tent & Awning Supply, was ordered by his supervisor Thursday to determine the party responsible for not flushing the second-floor toilet.

"Someone in this company has been neglecting to flush after going to the bathroom," said Tepfer, 31. "And I've been put in charge of finding out who that person is."

According to secretary Shelley Grabisch, three times in the past two days, Shademaster employees have attempted to use the second-floor bathroom, only to discover toilet paper and fecal matter still in the bowl.

"It's disgusting," Grabisch said. "It's

see MANAGER page 44

---

## Pope Calls For Greater Understanding Between Catholics, Hellbound

VATICAN CITY—In an address before more than 250,000 followers assembled outside St. Peter's Basilica, Pope John Paul II reaffirmed his commitment to global religious unity Thursday, calling upon the world's Roman Catholics to "build a bridge of earthly friendship" between themselves and the eternally damned.

"We have been aloof too long," the Pope told the throng of well-wishers crowded into Vatican Square. "For too many years, otherwise pious, observant Catholics have not made enough of an effort to reach out to nonbelievers, reasoning that, since they would have no contact with them in the next life, there was little point in getting to know them in this one."

"This indifference on the part of Catholics has, throughout history, had dire consequences," the Holy Father said. "During the Holocaust, the

see POPE page 44

---

## U.S. Ambassador To Bulungi Suspected Of Making Country Up

WASHINGTON, DC—Chad Halpern, U.S. Ambassador to Bulungi since 1996, has been asked to return to Washington to face allegations that the West African nation does not exist.

"While nothing has yet been substantiated," President Clinton told reporters at a press conference Thursday, "it appears Am-

bassador Halpern may have made the country up."

According to Clinton, suspicions arose last month when Côte d'Ivoire president Henri Konan Bédié attended a formal state dinner at the White House. When Secretary of State Madeleine Albright asked Bédié for an update on the fighting between Côte

see BULUNGI page 45

RED SEA

Yabba-Dabba

Bulungi

ATLANTIC OCEAN

Inset: Chad Halpern, U.S. ambassador to the African nation of Bulungi.

43

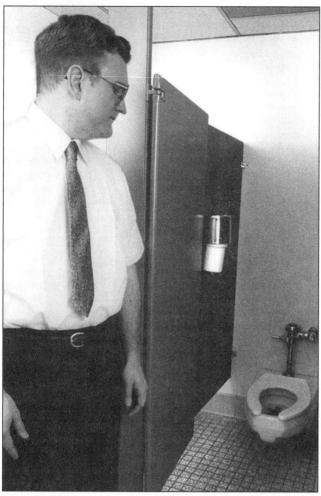

Above: Tepfer verifies the presence of unflushed bodily waste in the second-floor toilet.

been particularly bad the last few days, but it's been going on a lot longer than that. We're talking at least every other day for a month."

The unflushed toilet has dominated office conversation of late, with Shademaster employees trading anecdotes and details of their own encounters with the toilet, as well as circulating theories regarding who the guilty party may be.

"Everyone's very curious about who's doing it," said Tepfer, who earned a business degree from the University of Delaware in 1990. "It doesn't really make sense: How could you forget to flush? And if the person is doing it on purpose, why? What could they possibly have to gain by leaving that kind of mess?"

"At first, I figured the fecal matter was being left there because it was too big to be flushed," Tepfer continued. "But every time it's been discovered, it's gone right down without a problem. So we're not even talking about a situation where somebody clogs the toilet and then runs away in embarrassment."

Tepfer has begun checking the toilet at hourly intervals, but has had little luck. At 1 p.m. Tuesday, he checked and found it properly flushed, but 10 minutes later, a coworker called him back to the area to show him the toilet filled with copious amounts of toilet paper and bodily waste.

"I could hang around outside the bathroom and try to catch the culprit in the act, but I'd pretty much have to be there around the clock," Tepfer said. "Besides, everybody knows I've been assigned this task, so the guilty party probably wouldn't even use the bathroom if they saw me nearby. I've considered directly asking everyone, but I just can't imagine what I'd say."

Tepfer said he believes a sternly worded sign reminding employees to flush would be an effective measure. However, he noted, "An entry in the employee handbook clearly states that, 'In order to maintain a professional atmosphere, no paper or cardboard signs are to be posted in or around any shared employee areas, including the break rooms, hallways, or bathrooms.' So, unfortunately, that's out."

Tepfer was assigned the task of identifying the non-flusher by his direct superior, service-department manager Milton Trautwig.

"Milt stressed to me that, with only two bathrooms serving all 44 employees in the company, it is imperative that both are in full working condition at all times," Tepfer said. "He also said the smell is really bothering the accounting department, which is right across the hall."

"I've gleaned that it usually happens in the early afternoon," Tepfer said. "They're probably doing it right when they get back from lunch."

"Really, it could be anyone in this whole building," Tepfer added.

Despite being assigned the task less than 48 hours ago, Tepfer is already feeling pressure to root out the guilty party. Thursday, he received a lengthy e-mail from senior sales representative Bob Raeder complaining that the situation is "causing huge problems" among his staff.

"Not only is it unpleasant," Raeder's e-mail read in part, "but it is also cutting into valuable work time, as members of my team are forced to wait in long lines for the first-floor restroom due to the recurring problem in the restroom they normally would use. It is my sincere hope that you can remedy this situation soon."

Thus far, Tepfer has received nearly 30 e-mails from coworkers expressing their feelings about the situation.

"When I find the toilet unflushed, unlike some others here, I will flush it," secretary Diane Huncke wrote. "But that doesn't change the fact that I shouldn't have to."

"This is ridiculous!!!" promotions coordinator Jeanette Wolk wrote. "We are all grown adults here, yet some of us can't seem to observe the most basic rules of hygiene!!!"

Tepfer, a lifelong Dover resident, has been with Shademaster since 1992. Starting out answering phones as a customer-service representative, he quickly climbed through the ranks, promoted to lead operator in 1994, to junior associate service-department manager in 1997, and to his current associate-manager post in 1999.

"I'm not thrilled to be the one who has to find out who's not flushing," Tepfer said. "But sometimes you have to do these kinds of things when you're the associate manager. With position comes certain duties." ∅

Church stood silently by while six million fellow human beings, guilty of nothing but the murder of Christ Our Lord, descended to the depths of brimstone at the hands of Protestants. Our intervention in that affair could have averted a monumental tragedy, and, more important, might have converted the souls of untold multitudes of evil heretics to the Holy Word of God."

"But even when no such tragedy has occurred," His Holiness continued, "Roman Catholicism, simply by withdrawing from all contact with false belief systems, has wrongly come to view itself as the only religion on Earth, rather than merely the only True One. And that is arrogant. So I say today that we must commit ourselves to opening a dialogue. Let us, with open hearts and minds, talk to our brethren of every denomination, be they Pharisees, apostates, Mussulmen, or assorted other vile abominations upon whom Our Lord casts down his ultimate, eternal punishment in the searing lake of fire. Let us strive to understand why they prefer a lifetime of sinful defiance and an eternity of excruciating torment. Let us encourage among

them an open exchange of heresies, blasphemies, and anathema. For only by fostering a spirit of love and goodwill among all human beings, even the most way-

> "We have been aloof too long," the Pope told the throng of well-wishers who crowded into Vatican Square.

ward of the flock, can the Church divert them from their sinful, hellbound path."

Following the Pope's address, papal nuncio Msgr. Francisco Sevellino announced his intention to form an interfaith council that will meet in the Vatican once a month and discuss issues relating to tolerance and understanding among all religions. Sevellino said the council will consist of "an international team of rabbis, ministers, bonzes, imams, and The Saved." ∅

## NEWS IN BRIEF

## Everyone Glad Someone Else Making Small Talk With Disabled Woman

SAN ANTONIO, TX—A palpable sense of relief came over passengers on the westbound D-line bus Thursday, when someone else struck up a conversation with 53-year-old cerebral-palsy sufferer Sharon Bellacosa. "Boy, that was a close one," said rider Jon Neidhardt, 28, who was sitting next to Bellacosa. "For a second there, I was terrified she'd ask me if I knew how much farther her stop was in that slow, slurred voice and then try to segue it into a friendly chat with me. Luckily, the guy sitting across from her was willing to sacrifice himself for the good of the rest of us and talk to her." Neidhardt said that, despite not having to talk to the disabled woman, he became tense while listening to her loud conversation and did not relax fully until she got off the bus. ∅

d'Ivoire's army and Bulungi's Mukka-Lukka rebels, Bédié said, "I am sorry, I do not understand of what you speak."

Albright then explained to Bédié that Halpern had recently informed her that the fighting between Côte d'Ivoire and Bulungi had reached a breaking point, with the Côte d'Ivoire army advancing all the way to the Bulungian capital of Yabba-Dabba.

"After dinner that night," Clinton said, "Secretary Albright and I made the decision to look up Bulungi in an atlas. Unfortunately, we were unable to find it. We also looked for it in a large dictionary, under several different spellings, but again we were unsuccessful."

Halpern, 24, a Laguna Beach, CA, native, was appointed to his post by President Clinton after a chance meeting at the Laguna Beach McDon-

## "The phones here in Bulungi are just all fucked up," Halpern said.

ald's where Halpern worked at the time. After discussing Bulungian politics with Halpern for more than two hours, Clinton was impressed enough to name him ambassador.

"Mr. Halpern is a charismatic and persuasive young man," Clinton said two years ago at a ceremony marking the appointment. "I am confident that with his great expertise, the U.S. can reestablish strong relations with Bulungi and help the nation move beyond all the problems that have plagued it of late, such as last year's tribal war between the Dodos and the Mukka-Lukkas, and the Great Bongo Drought of 1994."

Pending further investigation, Halpern's $11,500 monthly salary—which has been sent to his girlfriend in Puerto Vallarta, Mexico, for the past two years due to Bulungi's lack of banks—has been suspended.

Halpern's girlfriend's phone line in Puerto Vallarta has also served as a switchboard for routing calls between Halpern and Washington, a situation the ambassador explained was necessary because "the phones here in Bulungi are just all fucked up."

Despite the suspicions surrounding Halpern, Albright praised the ambassador, saying he has done "an excellent job monitoring a period in Bulungian history marked by often intense sectional surfing competitions." Albright did not, however, deny that several of the phone calls between them were characterized by giggling.

According to Albright, while Halpern said that getting a ticket for a flight to Washington would be "a bitch," the ambassador assured her that he would be on the next available flight from Bulungi's Primo Ganja Airport. ∅

# Students Prepare Breasts For Increased Springtime Display

EAST LANSING, MI—Anticipating spring's imminent arrival, female college students across the northern U.S. are preparing their breasts for increased seasonal display.

For the last several months, the students' breasts have existed only in the imaginations and fond memories of others, obscured by baggy sweaters, bulky ski jackets, and shapeless flannel.

Yet with the approach of spring, all that is changing, as students now slip into less fabric and fewer layers. Their breasts, like big, cuddly honeybears wiping the sleep from their eyes as they emerge from hibernation, once again step out into the sunshine, stretch in the open air, and, with near-mythic power, grab the attention of all around, their taut nipples and gently undulating femme-flesh seeming to smile and say: "Look at us! Look at us!"

"I just bought a new spring 'mini-T' from Urban Outfitters," Michigan State University sophomore Debi

Above: Students like this University of Colorado junior are excited to once again display their breasts, donning form-fitting Urban Outfitters T-shirts in response to the warming weather.

Kahn, 19, said. "Its snug fit captures the essence of my girlhood, yet enables me to prominently display my womanhood. It also has a *Charlie's Angels* logo on it in '70s-style iron-on glitter-puff."

Kahn's classmates confirmed that the shirt is "so phat," adding that they are greatly looking forward to seeing the shapely co-ed's magnificent young breasts protrude exuberantly from within it.

"At schools in warmer climates, breasts tend to take on a diminished significance due to their year-round

see BREASTS page 46

# I'm Like A Chocoholic, But For Booze

Did you ever know a "chocoholic"? One of those folks who just can't get enough chocolate? I bet there's at least one in your home or workplace.

By Ralph Chadwick

At my house, it's my wife Emily. She's got to have her little bowl of Hershey's Kisses in the living room. She can't go shopping without bringing home some chocolate ice cream or a chocolate-cake mix. She's even got a funny little sweatshirt that says, "My Name Is Emily, And I'm A Chocoholic."

To be honest, I'm a bit of a chocoholic myself. Except for one small difference. You see, instead of being addicted to chocolate, I'm addicted to booze. Yep, from dawn to dusk, there's one thing on my mind: booze! Beer, liquor, wine, all that stuff!

When my wife gets one of her cravings, she reaches for a Baby Ruth or Mars bar. With me, it's Icehouse beer. My refrigerator is always stocked with plenty of it. I also have a little flask of whiskey in my desk drawer at work. In fact, if you can keep a secret, I even keep some booze in my car in case of traffic jams. I just can't stand to be without booze for too long!

I'm a lot like that Cookie Monster on *Sesame Street*. Only it's more like the Booze Monster. When I walk into a party and see that they have booze of any kind, it's like, "Whoa-hoa! All bets are off! Lemme at that booze!"

I remember this one time when there was no chocolate in the house. Emily was going out of her mind, trying to scrape up some sort of chocolate fix. In the end, she resorted to drinking a cup of hot cocoa. It was so cute! Sort of like the time I drank all her hairspray because there was no booze in the house. Or that other time with the rubbing alcohol. Or the Nyquil. Or the Aqua-Velva.

Another time, I was completely out of booze, and all the stores and bars were closed, so I drove 45 minutes to find a place that would sell me some beer or something. I was kind of embarrassed, because here it was late Monday night, I had to work the next day, and I'm driving around looking for booze. But, hey, that's just how things are when you're a "booze-oholic" like me! I finally found a huge all-night liquor store. You should have seen how I loaded up! Cases of this, fifths of that. It was 5 a.m. when I finally got home, so I just said, "To heck with work!" and had my own little improvised holiday. I called it Booze Day! I'd been working hard, getting to work on time almost every day for two weeks, so I figured I'd earned what wound up being the rest of the week off.

Sometimes, Emily and I think we should cut down a little—you know, health concerns and all. But there's always some special occasion that gives us an excuse to go off our "diets." Halloween was Emily's last big bender. We only got three trick-or-treaters the entire night, so the whole big bowl of Reese's Peanut Butter Cups went straight to her. (Or straight to her thighs, as she said!)

My most recent bender was today. There was a good movie on TV, and I figured, hey, I'll need steady hands to change the volume. Of course, it all went straight to my liver, but what are you gonna do?

For my birthday, Emily gave me the funniest coffee mug, perfect for Irish coffee. It has a little teddy bear on it with a "don't mess with me" look on his face, and it says, "Hand Over The Booze And Nobody Gets Hurt." I laughed so hard! That bear was just like me when I robbed the party store earlier this year! Also, the mug is really big, so it can hold a lot of booze, which is another plus.

Yes, those chocoholics are a funny sort. But they won't hurt you—as long as they have their chocolate, that is. Or, in my case, booze! ∅

exposure," said University of Miami sociology professor Thomas H. Milchan. "The campus populace tends to become desensitized to the thrill of seeing breasts, as they are nearly always visible, even to the casual onlooker."

Pointing out his office window at an impromptu game of bikini volleyball, Milchan added, "This does not move me. The undulating, the bouncing, the firm, upraised globes leaping skyward, then back down again with a resounding bounce—all of this has become commonplace here at Miami."

At the University of Wisconsin and other northern universities possessing lengthy winters and a left-leaning, socially liberal student body, the sudden preponderance of breasts has brought student traffic to near-gridlock, with heterosexual males and lesbians alike gawking at the jaw-dropping displays of mammarian majesty.

Though most agree that the natural power of the female breast needs no improvement, some women are using technology to further their breast goals. Wisconsin sophomore Heather Bain, a self-described B-cup with aspirations toward the C range, plans to covertly employ a "Miracle Bra," a new, highly technical device that utilizes cutting-edge "padding technology" to make breasts appear a full cup size larger. The "Wonder Bra," a similar device, uses equally high-tech wire to compress the breasts, producing greatly increased "cleavage."

Experts are not surprised by the students' springtime breast-enhancement efforts, as the season frequently brings about a heightened air of sexual tension.

"From ancient Mesopotamian society to today's college campus, young people have always paid increased attention to sexual matters with the onset of warm weather," University of Minnesota sociology professor Jane

---

## The sudden preponderance of breasts has brought student traffic to near-gridlock.

---

Simonson said. "I myself, though no spring chicken, have initiated numerous illicit affairs with strapping young students of mine, both male and female."

Campus lesbians shared Simonson's enthusiasm.

"Although we are deeply opposed to the systematic sexual objectification of women and their breasts by male heterodoxy, we lesbians are in a uniquely two-fold position of strength in these wondrous springtime months, enjoying both the opportunity to display our fantastic breasts to others and the chance to enjoy an eyeful of the breasts of our fellow sisters," said Meghan Thomas of Minnesota's Lesbian Students For Social Change.

Spotting a lithe, tube-topped female rollerblader speeding along nearby, Thomas bit her knuckle, adding, "*Damn.*" ∅

## 15 Years Of Kathie Lee

Last Friday, after 15 years, Kathie Lee Gifford did her final *Live! With Regis & Kathie Lee*. What have been some of the show's highlights over the years?

**1986** Files $37 million suit against *National Enquirer* for alleging she got her bangs cut

**1988** Spins head three times, spews vomit, and says, "Please welcome my dear, dear friend, the wonderful Joan Rivers!"

**1990** Virgin birth of Cody Gifford

**1991** Visibly drunk Kathie Lee calls losing trivia-quiz contestant a "slack-cunted mongoloid hausfrau"

**1992** Devotes entire show to describing contents of Cody's diaper

**1993** Is offered $10 million by Carnival Cruise-goer to stay off boat

**1994** Shoots Joy Philbin in head on porch of Philbin's Massapequa home

**1995** Claws out eyes during brief menopause scare

**1997** Central American child laborers who sew Kathie Lee's Kmart line strike for right to make less horrible womenswear

**1998** Bravely cheers self up in face of Frank's infidelities with show-stopping rendition of "If They Could See Me Now"

**2000** Unhinges jaw, eats entire sheep

## Point-Counterpoint: Children's Welfare

# We Must Do Everything We Can For The Children

Do you realize that a recent UNICEF study showed that nine million U.S. children suffer from malnutrition? And that 2,699 infants are born into

**By Mary Unger, What About The Children? Foundation**

poverty every day in this country? And that families with children account for 39 percent of America's homeless population? This should not be.

And that's only the beginning. America's children suffer in many other ways. Child abuse occurs with frightening frequency. Child abandonment figures steadily climb as the average age of our nation's mothers continues to drop. The number of minors in prison has quadrupled over the past 25 years. How can we let this happen?

It is absolutely shameful that America, the richest nation on the face of the Earth, has failed to meet even the most basic needs of its young.

And the rest of the world is failing, too. Worldwide, more than 21 million children under the age of five die each year as a result of malnutrition and other preventable diseases. According to a joint study by the World Bank and United Nations Youth Development Council, more than 1.3 billion people live on the equivalent of less than one dollar a day. We have got to do something.

We're in a crisis situation, and the time to act is now. The children are the planet's future: If we don't get our priorities straight and care for them now, the result will be truly tragic for future generations.

---

# Children, Schmildren

Yap, yap, yap. For as long as I can remember, people have been yapping about schools for the children, healthcare for the children, food for the chil-

**By Duane Nystrom, Citizens' Alliance Foundation**

dren, clothing for the children, shelter for the children. Fuck the children.

Day after day it's shoved down our throats: We have to love the children and prepare them for tomorrow. We're supposed to prevent them from falling down wells and out of cars, and we're supposed to keep toxic chemicals out of their reach. We're supposed to change the babies' diapers and call a doctor when they stop breathing. Christ almighty, when do we get a break? Do the children ever stop taking? For just once, let's let the children fend for themselves.

They were spouting off the same crap in the '60s, about how we have to take care of the children because they're our planet's future. And you know what happened when we didn't take care of them? Nothing! They grew up and became adults, and the planet didn't end!

I swear, if I hear one more word about the goddamn children, I'm going to choke somebody.

Babies are dying, children are starving, teenagers are turning to drugs and prostitution. Blah, blah, blah. How many times can you hear about kids living in cardboard boxes and young girls being sold into sexual slavery before you just have to scream, "Shut up about the goddamn children, already"?

I propose we put the children last for a few years. Then we could finally pay attention to some of the issues that really matter, like my need for a brand-new fishing boat. The children can ram it. ∅

# Architect Asks Self How Le Corbusier Would Have Designed This Strip Mall

TOPEKA, KS—Architect Curtis Winter, designer of the planned Fox Plaza in Topeka, found himself wondering Thursday how influential 20th-century Swiss architect Le Corbusier would have approached the strip mall. "I could imagine Le Corbusier using more sculptural roof-lines on the Play It Again Sports," Winter said. "And I could see the FuncoLand making a stronger impression from afar and evoking a modernized classicism if it were raised up on stilts." Winter previously made headlines for a laundromat that echoed the abstract geometric designs of I.M. Pei. ∅

## Federal Reserve Vice-Chairman Roger Ferguson: Hot Or Not?

see NATION page 4A

## Drunk Man Staring At IHOP Syrups

see DINING page 10D

## Studio Audience Wants Show To Be Over

see TELEVISION page 8B

## Lite Brite Peg Extracted From Ear

see LOCAL page 10D

THE ONION
$2.00 US
$3.00 CAN

0 74470 94595 6

---

# the ONION®

WWW.THEONION.COM     AMERICA'S FINEST NEWS SOURCE™     FOUNDED 1871

## PRODUCTWATCH

# Fun Toy Banned Because Of Three Stupid Dead Kids

Above: The Aqua Assault RoboFighter, an awesome toy children can no longer enjoy, thanks to stupid Weiller, Torres, and Krug (L to R).

WASHINGTON, DC—In cooperation with the U.S. Consumer Product Safety Commission, Wizco Toys of Montclair, NJ, recalled 245,000 Aqua Assault RoboFighters Friday after three dumb kids managed to kill themselves playing with the popular toy, ruining the fun for everybody else.

"The tragedy is inconceivable," Wizco president Alvin Cassidy said. "For years, countless children played with the Aqua Assault RoboFighter without incident. But then these three retards come along and somehow find a way to get themselves killed. So now we have to do a full recall and halt production on what was a really awesome toy. What a waste."

"My mom won't let me play with my RoboFighter because of those dumb kids who died," said 10-year-

see RECALL page 48

---

Above: Pastor Bob Snowdon.

# Lutheran Minister Loves To Fuck His Wife

NASHUA, NH—Pastor Bob Snowdon, of Holy Christ Almighty Lutheran Church in Nashua, is a man of deep religious and moral convictions. He derives great satisfaction from his various parish duties, which include reciting the liturgy, giving holy communion, and performing the sacrament of baptism. But nothing delights him quite like his favorite activity of all: fucking Emily Snowdon, his holy-wedded wife of 29 years.

"The Holy Bible sanctifies the bond between a man and a woman in matrimony as a sacred union," Snowdon

see MINISTER page 49

---

# U.S. Offers PlatinumPlus Preferred Citizenship

WASHINGTON, DC—In an 86-14 vote, the Senate approved legislation Friday establishing PlatinumPlus Preferred citizenship, an exciting new program offering special benefits and discounts to select members of the U.S.

"By becoming a PlatinumPlus citizen, you join an exclusive club of elite Americans," said President Clinton, who signed the bill into law late Friday. "As part of that club, you'll be eligible for many special benefits, including tax breaks, excusal from jury duty, and vacations at special PlatinumPlus Caribbean resorts, which are off-limits to ordinary, EconoBudget citizens. It's our way of saying 'thank you' to our best customers."

see PLATINUM page 49

Above: President Clinton tells a group of PlatinumPlus Preferred citizens about the many benefits they will enjoy as members.

47

# I Think I'm Going About This Cat-Breeding Thing All Wrong

**By Stan Morrow**
**Cat Breeder**

Last October, my dear wife Lois passed on. The first few months after her death were extremely difficult for me, as I missed her very much. Then, one day, my pastor recommended I take up a hobby to help me get my mind off things.

Now, I've always been what you might call a lover of cats, so I decided to take up cat-breeding. And while nothing will ever replace my Lois, I have found cat-breeding to be an extremely enjoyable pastime. Only problem is, after months of trying, I still haven't seen a single litter from those furry little gals. In fact, I'm beginning to think I'm going about this cat-breeding thing all wrong.

To be honest, I haven't the slightest idea what the problem is. As far as I can tell, I'm doing everything right. I wait until they're well in heat, rubbing up against me and yowling to be serviced. At that point, I bring them out back to the shed, where I've prepared a special breeding area.

It's cool and dark in the shed, just the way cats are supposed to like it. There are candles and nice music, too. (Actually, those are mostly for me. I know it sounds selfish, since I'm not the one giving birth to the kittens, but I like the experience to be special for me, too.) I've even laid down soft blankets where the actual breeding takes place and put up chicken wire so my skittish lovelies can't run far if they get scared.

At that point, I'm ready to consummate the breeding process. Gently but firmly, I hold them down while I lovingly breed them. You'd be surprised— the tail hardly gets in the way at all. Sometimes, I'm afraid I'm hurting them, but all the books I've read say cats tend to yowl and scratch when breeding, so I don't worry too much. (Heck, I yowl and scratch, too, sometimes!) The worst was the time Mrs. Purrs slashed my thigh. She couldn't help it, though. Cats' instincts are so strong.

According to the books, the actual physical act of cat-breeding only takes a few seconds, but, just to be sure, I usually breed each cat for about 30 to 40 minutes.

It seems like I'm doing everything

> **Sometimes, I'm afraid I'm hurting them, but all the books I've read say cats tend to yowl and scratch when breeding, so I don't worry too much.**

right. But after months of trying, not a single kitten has been produced. So, for the past few weeks, I've been breeding them twice as hard and long, making sure to get each of my darlings right on the money. Especially Princess. I've really enjoyed breeding her. She's a delicate Persian with a long, white coat that's just gorgeous. She's always been my favorite. I've rung her bell loud and long, and for weeks I've been imagining tiny little kittens with her beautiful coat and twinkling eyes.

But still, even after redoubling my efforts, none of them has yet to catch pregnant. Bewildered by my lack of success, I went to the doctor last Saturday to get myself checked out. Except for an unusual amount of lacerations and scrapes in my "area," the doctor said I seemed just fine. Not only that, all my tests came back negative. Obviously, either there's something wrong with my method or there's something wrong with my precious little furry ones. That would be awful.

Concerned, I dropped off Princess, Dusty, and Mrs. Purrs at the vet the other day and explained the problem. Yesterday, though, I got a call back from the receptionist over there, and she seemed very upset. For some reason, they won't let me have the cats back. I was shocked: I'd tried so hard to get it right. I hung up the phone, determined to learn more about the breeding process.

I've been reading ever since. I'll breed those cats again someday. I can feel it. ∅

---

**RECALL** from page 47

old Jeremy Daigle of Somerville, MA. "I used to set up army guys around the RoboFighter and have it run over them and conquer Earth for the Zardaxians. But now I'll never see it

> **Said attending physician Dr. Anderson Hunt: "There's no point in feeling bad about this child's demise, because the deck was obviously stacked against him from the start."**

again, all because three stupid idiots had to go and wreck everything."

Each of the deaths was determined to be a result of gross misuse of the toy, an incredibly cool device that could shoot both plastic missiles and long jets of water, as well as maneuver over the ground on retractable wheels.

The first death occurred June 22, when 7-year-old Isaac Weiller of Grand Junction, CO, died after deliberately firing one of the spring-loaded plastic missiles into his left nostril. The missile shot into his sinuses, shattering the roof of his nasal cavity and causing a massive brain hemorrhage. Shortly before dying, Weiller told emergency medical personnel at St. Vincent's Medical Center that he had

shot the missile into his nose in the belief that it would travel through his body and out his belly button.

"I've heard some pretty stupid shit in my time, but that has to take the cake," said Dr. Anderson Hunt, the attending physician. "Why would any kid think he could fire plastic missiles up his nose and expect them to come out his belly button? There's no point in feeling bad about this child's demise, because the deck was obviously stacked against him from the start. What we should feel bad about is the fact that, because of him, millions of other children will no longer get to fire the RoboFighter's supercool Devastator Missiles or soak their friends with its FunFoam WaterBlasters."

Less than one month after Weiller's death, 5-year-old Danielle Krug fatally choked on fragments of the toy after smashing it with a claw hammer in the garage of her parents' La Porte,

IN, home.

"I'm not kidding," said Dianne Ensor, an emergency-room nurse at Our Lady Of Peace Hospital in La Porte, where Krug was pronounced dead. "She thought the broken shards were candy. That's what you'd assume after breaking a plastic, inedible toy, right? Un-fucking-believable."

The third and arguably stupidest death occurred Aug. 12, when 11-year-old dumbass Michael Torres held the RoboFighter above his head and jumped off the balcony of his family's third-story Torrance, CA, apartment, thinking he would be able to fly like Superman.

"A couple of the other emergency workers thought we should cut the kid some slack, because at least he wasn't trying to eat the toy or shove it up his nose," said paramedic Debra Lindfors, who tried in vain to revive Torres. "I considered this for a while, but then I decided no. No way. If

you're 11 years old, you should know that it's impossible to fly. And poor Wizco is probably going to go bankrupt because of this shit."

As a result of the extreme idiocy of the three children, the CPSC was forced to order Wizco to stop making the toy and pull it from store shelves, as well as recommend that parents remove it from their homes.

"I know the overwhelming majority of American kids who owned an Aqua Assault RoboFighter derived many hours of safe, responsible fun from it," CPSC commissioner Mary Sheila Gall said. "But, statistically speaking, three deaths stemming from contact with a particular toy constitutes an 'unreasonable risk.' Look, I'm really sorry about this. Honestly. But our agency's job is to protect the public from hazardous products, even if those who die are morons who deserved what they got." ∅

---

"And, of course," Clinton added, "there are never any annual fees."

PlatinumPlus citizens—selected according to a number of demographic factors, including age, race, and socio-economic status—will enjoy a wide variety of other benefits, including immunity from speeding tickets; separate, no-wait lines at more than 50,000 Post Office locations nationwide; and wider, more comfortable window seating.

After just one year in the club, members can also begin earning extra votes for elections. "Wouldn't you like to earn up to five bonus votes for the next presidential election?" asked U.S. Rep. Roger Wicker (R-MS), a co-sponsor of the measure. "With your new PlatinumPlus citizenship, you can."

According to Wicker, those at the highest level of the new program, or "Diamond Club" citizens, will enjoy additional rewards, including a pass good for acquittal from one crime (misdemeanor or felony), a no-interest credit line of up to $500,000, and, for able-bodied male PlatinumPlus members between ages 18 and 35, excusal from the draft should a foreign war arise.

Gordon Alarie, CEO of the Dallas-based Integrated Systems Management Group, was among the first to receive a PlatinumPlus citizenship offer in the mail. "As CEO and founder of a Fortune 500 corporation, I've contributed a great deal to the U.S. over the years," Alarie said. "It's nice to know that now, with the PlatinumPlus Preferred citizenship program, I'll finally start getting something back."

Rosalyn Murcheson Biddle, a Scarsdale, NY, art collector, was also extended an offer to join.

"The PlatinumPlus-only express lanes on the highways are nice, and so are the unlimited drinks," Biddle said. "But what I really like is the program's Gold Circle Premium Healthcare package, which grants me access to the finest medical care anywhere. It's nice to know that if I ever get too wrapped up in a car-phone conversation and hit another vehicle, emergency workers arriving on the scene will prioritize my injuries over those of any other people who may have been hurt."

Added Biddle: "The free cancer inoculations are a nice plus, too."

Clinton stressed that those not eligible for PlatinumPlus citizenship will still enjoy the many benefits of regular U.S. citizenship, including one free vote in each election, a court-appointed attorney if arrested, and a number of fully guaranteed constitutional rights, including freedom of speech and the right to bear arms.

"To our nation's EconoBudget citizens, I want to assure you that you will still get the same great service from your government that you always have," Clinton said. "The postal delivery, the voting, the Social Security checks—it's all still part of the basic citizenship package. And while, yes, a few certain special privileges will be off-limits to you, that should in no way make you feel like a second-class citizen. Remember, we are all Americans here, no matter how poorly or well we are treated." ∅

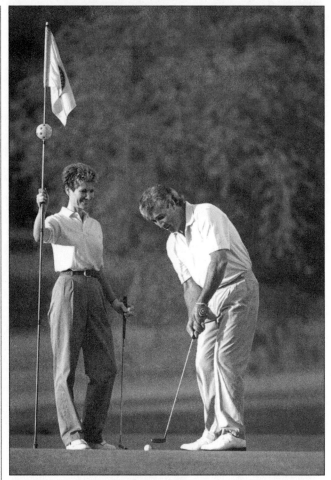

Above: PlatinumPlus citizens Connie and Russell Brodhagen of Del Mar, CA, enjoy a round of golf in a members-only, walled-in golfing facility in East Los Angeles.

said. "And there is nothing so smiled upon by our Lord as the love and caring that is shared when a man fucks his lawfully wedded bride. Just thinking about it makes me want to zip home for a few minutes and fuck Emily right now."

According to the 53-year-old "Pastor Bob," even though he typically fucks his wife twice each morning, he still very much looks forward to fucking her again when he gets home.

"After a long, hard day of worshiping in the house of our Lord, tending to the emotional needs of my parishioners, and visiting the sick and elderly so that they too might know in their hearts the light of our Lord and Savior Jesus Christ," Snowdon said, "there is nothing in this world I enjoy more than coming home and fucking the red out of my wife's hair. I love to give it to her any way she wants it, as hard as she can take it. My favorite is when she climbs on top and jerks her hips up and down on me as she fucks."

Emily enjoys the fucking almost as much as her husband. "I've got to admit it," she said, "I love to get fucked."

She stressed, however, that the sort of wild fucking in which she and her husband regularly partake is only acceptable when performed within the confines of a church-sanctioned marriage. "I am saddened, deeply sad-

dened, when I hear of the young girls of today, engaging in sexual activities such as heavy petting or necking before they are wedlock-bound," she said. "It is so sad to see the beauty and purity of the act of fucking despoiled by this sort of premarital impropriety. If only these young girls would wait until they've taken the marriage vows and then, and only then, start fucking like there was no tomorrow."

According to Snowdon, some of his favorite places to fuck his wife include the pantry, shower, woodshed, basement laundry-room area, living-room sofa, and even, he added with a sly wink, the bedroom. "All of our children are grown now and have families of their own, God bless them," he said, "so we can pretty much fuck anywhere we please in the whole darn house."

So enamored is he of his wife-fucking hobby, Snowdon said he would recommend fucking to just about anyone. "So long as the fucking is done within the sacred bond of matrimony, I say, 'Fuck away.'" Snowdon said. "But if you're not married, please, whatever you do, don't fuck anybody. An eternity of punishment awaits those who fuck without church sanction."

Though fucking has been a lifelong interest for Snowdon, he stressed that he had faithfully abstained from sex

and resisted the intense urge to fuck women until his bond with Emily was formally cemented with marital vows before the eyes of God 29 years ago.

"Naturally, before my marriage, I wanted to fuck other women: Sally Lindemeier, my senior-year prom date; Susan Helgstrom, the receptionist at my parents' church; even Sheila Bernhauser, my old Bible-study teacher. I would have gladly fucked any one of those lovely, God-fearing women. Yet I knew that my fuck-urges were impure and sinful, and that it was my duty as a Christian to resist them until the day of my wedding to my beloved Emily."

"But once I was married, my lust became sanctified in my heart and in the eyes of the Lord," he said. "And, from that day forth, I began fucking the holy heck out of my wife whenever and wherever I could, as often as possible. It is a practice I continue to this day."

"Emily is a good, kind, Christian woman," Snowdon added. "But let there be no mistake: She is also one serious fuck-mama, as well."

Pastor Bob and his wife both stressed that, of course, abortion is a terrible sin, as is homosexuality, group sex, anal sex, oral sex, phone sex, pornography, and all forms of contraception. ∅

## Awful Show A Repeat Again

PRESCOTT, AZ—According to local TV viewer Randy Bolz, Friday's episode of the "absolutely awful" CBS show The King Of Queens was a repeat yet again. "King Of Queens is bad enough when it's a new episode," Bolz said, "but this is the third time I've seen that stupid one where Doug buys the really expensive car against Carrie's wishes, then his company goes on strike. Even if I actually did like this show, I certainly wouldn't after seeing the same damn episode three times in less than a year. Christ."

## Painful Boil Still Too Unformed To Lance

BILLINGS, MT—A throbbing boil on the neck of Art Krenchicki is not quite ready for lancing, the 47-year-old Billings man reported Friday. "Just a couple more days, and it'll be all set," said Krenchicki, studying the inflamed, pus-filled swelling. "You can't lance them too soon, or they take even longer to heal." ∅

# Fanzine Marred by Typo

BERKELEY, CA—A clear typographical error was discovered Friday in the latest issue of *MangaMash*, a fanzine devoted to hardcore Japanese speed-metal bands and Sanrio/Hello Kitty novelty kitsch products.

The error, a misuse of "your" instead of "you're," shocked and disappointed *MangaMash*'s estimated nine readers, who over the past 11 months and three issues have come to value the fanzine's commitment to journalistic excellence.

"I guess I just missed that one," said editor/writer/publisher Dave Pelks, 20, who usually tries to read over the paper before taking it to the copy shop. "It's 'you're' and not 'your'? I always mess that up."

The typo marks the first error for *MangaMash* since last year's April/November issue, in which "New York" was spelled "New Yrok."

"That wasn't, like, a real mistake," Pelks said. "That time, I just typed it wrong by accident. I know how to spell New York." Pelks added that it was late at the time, and that he was "really tired."

To prevent such errors from occurring in the future, Pelks said he plans to overhaul the fanzine's copyediting process.

"I think from now on I'm gonna have my sister Anne look it over before I make any copies," Pelks said. "She's only 15, but she's really good at

Above: The shocking typo in *MangaMash* #4 (right).

spelling and writing. She's, like, the brain of the family."

As an added measure, if Anne is unavailable for editing, Pelks said he will ask his mother for help.

Because of the typo, future expansion plans have been put on hold.

"I was hoping do a color cover for the next issue," Pelks said. "Actually, not in color, but on color paper. It was gonna be a big picture of Hello Kitty fighting Gamera on green paper. That would've been so cool."

According to publishing-industry insiders, the typo puts the fanzine's editorial reputation in jeopardy.

"This is a serious error," Doubleday vice-president Margaret Ferber said. "It's *MangaMash*'s most significant mistake since two issues ago, when Pelks stapled all the cover pages on

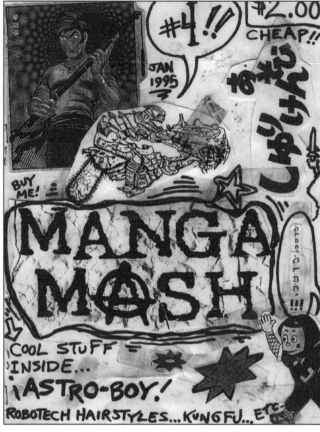

upside-down."

"I totally wasn't paying attention when I was stapling," Pelks said. Collectors estimate the value of the upside-down-cover issue at zero dollars.

Despite the most recent slip-up, *MangaMash*'s two distributors have vowed to stand behind the embattled fanzine.

"*MangaMash* provides the best coverage around of Japancore bands like HappyGinzaPoo and Shoko Ono," said Pat Kwiatkowski, owner of Crush Records, a Berkeley record store specializing in used LPs and hard-to-find imports. "Their recent feature on KyotoFunFun's tour of New Zealand was outstanding."

Paul Scobee, manager of the Stop-N-Pop, a local convenience store, also defended the fanzine.

"A few months ago, this kid asked me if he could leave a few copies of his magazine thing by the door," Scobee said. "I told him yeah, as long as they don't block the entrance. So far, it's been okay."

The latest error has not surprised grammarians, who say it is among the most common mistakes.

"A lot of people confuse 'your' and 'you're,'" *The New York Times*' William Safire said. "If you are unsure, I recommend you actually spell out 'you are,' and then see if it makes sense in context." ∅

## NEWS IN BRIEF

### Gay Gene Isolated, Ostracized

BALTIMORE—On Friday, scientists at Johns Hopkins University isolated the gene which causes homosexuality in human males, promptly separating it from normal, heterosexual genes. "I had suspected that gene was queer for a long time now. There was just something not quite right about it," team leader Dr. Norbert Reynolds said. "It's a good thing we isolated it— I wouldn't want that faggot-ass gene messing with the straight ones." Among the factors Reynolds cited as evidence of the gene's gayness were its pinkish hue, meticulously frilly perimeter, and faint but distinct perfume-like odor.

### Ritalin Cures Next Picasso

WORCESTER, MA—Area 7-year-old Douglas Castellano's unbridled energy and creativity are no longer a problem thanks to Ritalin, doctors for the child announced Friday. "After years of failed attempts to stop Douglas' uncontrollable bouts of self-expression, we have finally found success with Ritalin," Dr. Irwin Schraeger said. "For the first time in his life, Douglas can actually sit down and not think about lots of things at once." Castellano's parents reported that the cured child no longer tries to draw on everything in sight, calming down enough to show an interest in television. ∅

## Larry King's Frothing Saliva Hosed Off Bette Midler

see PEOPLE page 2C

## Stadium Inadequate

see SPORTS page 1D

## Area Man Has Asshole, Old Navy Written All Over Him

see LOCAL page 3C

## Winner Didn't Even Know It Was Pie-Eating Contest

see LOCAL page 7C

THE ONION
$2.00 US
$3.00 CAN

0  74470 94595  6

# the ONION ®

WWW.THEONION.COM          AMERICA'S FINEST NEWS SOURCE™          FOUNDED 1871

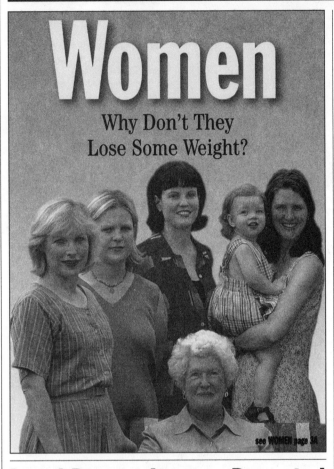

# Women
## Why Don't They Lose Some Weight?

see WOMEN page 3A

# Local Puppet Ignores Repeated Audience Dragon Warnings
## 'Look Out!' Children Tell Prince Bumbo

Above: Prince Bumbo The Monkey (right), moments before Sunday's near-fatal dragon attack.

SEYMOUR, IN—Despite loud and repeated audience warnings, an area puppet was attacked by a dragon during a Sunday-afternoon performance of *The Silver Bananas* in the children's section of the Seymour Public Library.

The puppet, Prince Bumbo The Monkey, is in serious but stable condition with extensive cloth injuries.

see PUPPET page 52

# ACLU Defends Nazis' Right To Burn Down ACLU Headquarters

Above: ACLU lawyers Nancy Edelman and Harvey Gross talk to reporters.

NEW YORK—At a press conference Sunday, American Civil Liberties Union officials announced that the organization will go to court to defend a neo-Nazi group's right to burn down the ACLU's headquarters.

ACLU president Nadine Strossen told reporters that her organization intends to "vigorously and passionately defend" the Georgia chapter of the American Nazi Party's First Amendment right to freely express its hatred of the ACLU by setting its New York office ablaze on Aug. 28.

"I am reminded of the words of Voltaire: 'I may disagree with what you say, but I will defend to the death your right to say it,'" Strossen said. "While the ACLU vehemently disagrees with the idea of Nazis torching this building, the principle of freedom of expression must be supported in all cases. If we take away these Nazis' right to burn down our headquarters, we take away everyone's right to burn down our headquarters."

Buddy Carver, president of the Georgia chapter of the American Nazi Party, praised the ACLU for taking on his case.

"I would like to thank Ms. Strossen and all the other nigger-loving, bleeding-heart liberals at the 'ACL-Jew' for defending my constitutional right to express my hatred of them with hundred-foot-high flames," said Carver, sporting a tan uniform and swastika

see ACLU page 53

51

According to psychologist Dr. Gary Wisniewski (above), puppet violence is caused by feelings of "helplessness, anger, and frustration."

According to police, audience members warned Prince Bumbo "at least a half-dozen times" that Brimstone, a Seymour-area dragon whose magic silver bananas Bumbo had just stolen, was behind him. Each time, however, Bumbo refused to heed the warnings, boasting that Brimstone would never dare to attack him.

As Brimstone neared Prince Bumbo, the monkey stopped in mid-sentence and looked around as though he'd heard something, but quickly returned to boasting about the banana theft, which only agitated the audience further.

As the dragon opened his jaws, Prince Bumbo finally seemed to hear the warnings. "What? You say there's a big mean dragon behind me? Oh, come on, I don't believe you," Bumbo said.

"We insisted it was true," said audience member and mother of three Sherri Pryce, "so Prince Bumbo finally turned around to look, but Brimstone shifted to the other side so the puppet could not see him. We then told Prince Bumbo to look in the other direction, but when he did Brimstone only returned to his original position behind Prince Bumbo."

The monkey then accused the audience of "just being jealous" and returned to inspecting his stolen silver bananas. It was then that the dragon struck, severely shaking Prince Bumbo in his felt-lined jaws and forcing the monkey to return the treasure.

Seymour police chief Ron Byrne said the attack easily could have been avoided. "When I come to schools to talk to kids about the importance of dragon safety, one of the first things I tell them is, always be sure to turn around completely if you think a dragon is stalking you," said Byrne, who happened to attend Sunday's show with his 3-year-old son. "This monkey did not do so, and now he's paying for it."

According to leading puppet psychologist Dr. Gary Wisniewski, vio-

lence has grown increasingly common in the puppet world. "Puppets have very limited free will," said Wisniewski, whose clients include such celebrity puppets as Howdy Doody and X The Owl. "They are controlled

**According to police, audience members warned Prince Bumbo "at least a half-dozen times."**

by strings or by a human hand and are continually forced to mouth the words of others. In addition, their environment is limited to the small, cramped puppet-theater stage. As a result, many puppets develop deep feelings of helplessness, anger, and frustration that can very easily lead to violence."

Seymour Public Library officials offer a more direct explanation for the latest case of puppet-on-puppet violence.

"It's unfortunate that Prince Bumbo didn't pay attention to the audience and was attacked by the dragon," assistant library director Patti Colby said. "But if he hadn't been such a greedy, stubborn little monkey who didn't want to share, it would never have happened."

Nevertheless, library officials have ordered beefed-up security for next week's performance of *Mr. Bear, Queen Bee, And The Stolen Honey.*

"That show could be serious trouble," said John Reinholt, head of security for the library. "A lot of the puppets want to get their hands on that honey."

Reinholt said the library is still investigating a June 25 stick-beating incident involving local puppets Punch and Judy, and no arrests have been made in connection with the gruesome boiling of a wolf last May. ∅

# Report: Drug Use Down Among Uncool Kids

WASHINGTON, DC—According to a study released Monday by the Department of Health and Human Services, drug use is on the decline among uncool kids.

While nearly 80 percent of U.S. cool kids use drugs, the study found that just .007 percent of uncool kids between the ages of 12 and 19 use drugs, down from .012 percent in 1990.

"Really, this should surprise no one," HHS Secretary Donna Shalala said. "If you'd ever met any of these kids, you'd be amazed they ever left their own bedrooms, let alone smoked a joint."

DEA guidelines established in 1989 define "uncool" kids as those who "are introverted and passive, possess academic aptitude and physical ungainliness, and live in constant fear of things that really aren't that big a deal."

Among the uncool kids polled were high-school yearbook editors, people unable to do chin-ups for the President's Council On Physical Fitness test, Forensics Club secretary-treasurers, and newspaper carriers saving up to buy a Capsela set.

Uncool kids participating in the study gave many reasons for rejecting drugs. Fifty-six percent said that their parents would kill them if they tried drugs, and 62 percent expressed concern that their brain cells would erode from drug use, leading to poor SAT scores. An overwhelming 94 percent cited fear of allergic reaction.

"I'm allergic to milk, cats, and pollen," said Ted Boyce, 16, of Petaluma, CA. "And I'm afraid that if I smoke marijuana, Dr. DeSmet will give me more shots, which I don't want because they hurt, and they cause small red welts on my skin. Also, smoke really irritates my eyes."

HHS researchers tested uncool kids' resistance to drugs by enlisting 15 popular kids to pressure a sample group of A.P. calculus students to smoke pot. Resistance was universal.

"I was trying to get this geek named Jonathan to smoke a joint, and he just

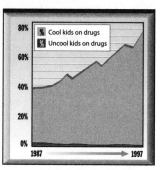

started crying," Sandusky (OH) High School star quarterback Chris Mitchell said. "What a girl."

Of the many subgroups of uncool kids, fantasy-game enthusiasts used drugs the most. But even among this group, only .018 percent reported trying drugs.

"At GenCon '96, there was a rumor that some marijuana was present," 19-

**"It wouldn't kill these kids to loosen up a little," Shalala said.**

year-old Ken Odom of Enid, OK, said. "My older brother said he saw a pot-smoking pipe under a *Car Wars* table, but this I never witnessed."

Shalala said that, while the Department of Health and Human Services is committed to fighting teen substance abuse, many uncool kids could nevertheless benefit from the occasional use of recreational drugs.

"It wouldn't kill these kids to loosen up a little," Shalala said. "I mean, yes, stay away from cocaine, LSD, and all the heavy stuff. But, come on, you can certainly get away with a little pot every now and then. Beer can also be good. Or ask your parents to serve a nice table wine with dinner. It adds a tangy zest to chicken and fish, and it'll take you out of your shell a bit. I mean, live a little." ∅

## Guitar-Instruction Manual Has Eddie Van Halen On Cover, 'Go Tell Aunt Rhody' Inside

ELIZABETH, NJ—*Rock The House In 30 Days,* a beginner-level guitar-instruction manual published by Elizabeth-based Learn-2-Play Books, features superstar rocker Eddie Van

Halen in the midst of a raging guitar solo on the cover and such traditional, public-domain songs as "Go Tell Aunt Rhody," "Greensleeves," and "Little Brown Jug" inside. "Get started on your way to playing awesome, brain-frying guitar solos like the master shredders," the cover proclaims. According to music-book collectors, the contents of *Rock The House* are identical to those of the classic 1943 guitar-instruction manual *Strum Gaily The Mel Bay Way.* ∅

## Point-Counterpoint: Nigeria

# Nigeria May Be A Developing Nation, But It Is Rich In Culture

**By Zach Spence
University of Vermont
Junior**

Ever since taking West African History 201, I've been fascinated by the rich cultural tapestry that is Nigeria. Professor Olson really opened my eyes to Nigerian accomplishments in art, music, and literature. What an incredibly cool place!

It's sad how the media always dwell on the negative aspects of African society. Granted, Nigeria faces some economic challenges (the result of centuries of colonialist exploitation), but I'm sure Nigerians don't concern themselves with thoughts of shallow materialism when they are surrounded every day by such stirring, dynamic expressions of the human spirit.

Nigerians don't need money for stereos or CDs: They make their own music! Along with a huge variety of drums, traditional instruments include many kinds of flutes, xylophones, and wooden clappers. Music permeates all aspects of life there, including public assemblies, festivals, weddings, funerals, and storytelling sessions. In fact, in Nigeria, music literally *is* a language: Giant slit drums are used to relay messages between villages situated along river systems. (At first, I figured it was like Morse Code, but I learned in class that it's actually an extremely sophisticated tonal language system!) There's a West African *djembe*—a large, goblet-shaped drum—at this store on University Avenue for $450 that I totally want to get.

The various ethnic groups of Nigeria all specialize in beautiful dances. The Ishan stilt dancers twist about in the air wearing their multi-colored raffia-palm costumes. The Ubakala people resolve conflicts and mark the seasons of the yam and cocoa-yam harvests with slow, ritualistic stomping while wearing these huge, intricately carved wooden masks. Doesn't that sound amazing?

Of course, I would only be reinforcing racist stereotypes if I just talked about Nigerians playing drums and dancing. Have you ever heard of the book *Things Fall Apart* by Chinua Achebe? He's a Nigerian writer. It's definitely one of the best books I've ever read. Then there's Wole Soyinka, the Nigerian playwright who won the Nobel Prize in 1986. He had to flee the country because the government wanted to kill him. Fela Kuti, the famous musician, is also from Nigeria,

and his stuff is really funky. He's, like, the African James Brown.

But for all that culture, the most wonderful thing about Nigeria is the warmth and hospitality of its varied peoples. Whether they speak Yoruba, Edo, Ijo, Igbo, Igala, Idoma, Nupe, Gwari, or a dialect of the Benue-Congo subgroup, all Nigerians will greet a visitor to their homes with a piece of boiled meat and a ceremonial food bowl holding a sauce for dipping. It's this kind of generosity and kindness that I would really love to experience first-hand someday.

As you can see, the rich cultural heritage of Nigeria gives its people the strength to overcome the many challenges that a developing African nation such as itself faces. It must be such an exciting time to be in Nigeria right now. I've got to get over there! ∅

# Get Me Out Of This Godforsaken Hellhole

**By Bitek Okoye
Nigerian**

Ever since my parents and three brothers died in the gasoline explosion last month, my mind has been dead to the world. Please, God, let me leave this place. I have no hope for my country.

I see it in the glassy-eyed stares of the people on the street. We have nothing. We have been ruled by fat generals who promise elections but steal all the money from the people. The oil

money, billions and billions of dollars, it disappears. Millions of us live here in the Lagos slums with no electricity or sewage system. I don't want to smell the garbage rotting in the streets anymore.

No one is safe. The police chase people in the streets and beat them like dogs. This new general, Abubakar, he is no better than the ones before. President Babangida, he stole $12 billion from the Nigerian people. When people ask where the money goes, they are shot. They shoot people every Sunday on Victoria Beach. The bodies wash up on the sand after they throw them in the ocean.

Last month, thieves broke the oil pipeline to steal fuel. Many people rushed out to scoop up the fuel that spilled out—to use, to sell. Then, everything was in flames. Seven hundred people died. I saw the tractor throwing the burned bodies into a hole in the ground. My family is somewhere in that hole.

The month before that, the soldiers threw my grandmother out a window. The soldiers, they set up roadblocks. They stop anybody trying to drive past, and they take all their money. I see people walking down the street in broad daylight who are attacked by criminals. Men with knives, sticks,

broken bottles. They attack you and beat you down. The people sometimes chase a thief who steals a bag. The crowd chases him and throws him down and beats him to death. The streets are very bad. There is so much hatred.

If I could get just a little money, I could try to leave. But I must save my money for food. There is no good food to buy in the streets. There are no doctors. I am still young. I don't want to get sick and starve. I don't want to be killed by the police. Please, God, save me. Shango, Ogun, Ifa, protect me. I don't want to die. I have to get out of here. ∅

ACLU from page 51

arm band. "We must finish the job Hitler was unable to."

ACLU associate director Mel Rosenblatt agreed. "The real danger here is not the American Nazi Party," he said. "The real danger is what would happen to the rest of us if the Buddy Carvers of the world were not allowed to commit arson against nigger-loving, bleeding-heart-liberal Jew attorneys."

Making the case all the more controversial is the neo-Nazis' demand that the ACLU's entire 315-person staff be in the building at the time of the blaze. Strongly opposing the request are New York City police commissioner William Bratton, fire chief Ed Holm, and mayor Rudolph Giuliani, who said that all 315 will die if trapped in the 47-story building during the blaze. ACLU attorneys responded that they will request a federal appeals hearing if the city attempts to stop them and their fellow ACLU employees from perishing in

> **Making the case all the more controversial is the neo-Nazis' demand that the ACLU's entire 315-person staff be in the building at the time of the blaze.**

the blaze.

"Yes, my loving wife Linda and three wonderful children, Ben, Robby, and Stephanie, will be devastated when I am killed next month," ACLU attorney Harvey Gross said. "But I recognize that, in a very real sense, it would be a victory for Mr. Carver and his fellow hatemongers if I did not burn to death, because their terrible message

of bigotry and intolerance would be all the more effective if suppressed."

The Carver case is one of several controversial legal battles in which the ACLU has been involved this year. In *State Of California v. Tubbs*, the organization defended a San Francisco art gallery's right to display a piece of performance art in which passersby are shot to death by gunmen. In February, the ACLU went to U.S. Appeals Court to defend the Grand Wizard of the Coahoma County, MS, chapter of the Ku Klux Klan's right to beat a black man to death and spray-paint 'White Pride' across his chest.

"We can have no arbitrary setting of limits when it comes to the Bill Of Rights," Strossen said. "The Constitution does not say, 'You have the right to express these opinions, but not those opinions.' Nor does it say, 'You can express these opinions by word, but not by violence.' For a free society to work, hatred in all its forms must be encouraged." ∅

## Elizabeth Taylor Watches *Cleopatra* Alone In Dark

LOS ANGELES—Sitting alone Sunday in a darkened screening room in her secluded mansion atop the Hollywood Hills, actress Elizabeth Taylor watched *Cleopatra*, the 1963 epic starring herself and Richard Burton. "I was the greatest of them all," said Taylor, gazing upon her younger self as the queen of the Nile. "In one week, I received 17,000 fan letters. Men bribed my hairdresser to get a lock of my hair. There was a maharajah who came all the way from India to beg one of my silk stockings. Later, he strangled himself with it!" After she finished watching the film, Taylor informed its director, Joseph Mankiewicz, who died in 1993, that she was ready for her close-up. ∅

# Secondhand Smoke Linked To Secondhand Coolness

Above: An average-looking nobody (left) acquires secondhand coolness (right) as a result of sitting near a smoker.

WINSTON, NC—Americans have known for years that smoking causes coolness, but, according to a new study co-funded by R.J. Reynolds and Philip Morris, the cool effects of smoking are not limited to the smoker.

The study, released Monday, found that secondhand smoke is a leading cause of coolness and is only slightly less cool than actual smoking.

As a result of the study, cigarette companies are encouraging non-smokers to frequent smoky bars and befriend smokers, as well as speak out against laws that mandate separate non-smoking sections in public places.

"We are only acting in the interest of the public at large," R.J. Reynolds spokesman Ron Gronfeld said. "We're not saying non-smokers are going to die as a result of their actions, but we do want to make sure they know they're not as cool as they could be."

Gronfeld detailed a "three-level progression" of coolness that non-smoking study participants experienced. Level one could be observed as soon as the non-smoker sat down at a barstool near a person enjoying a delicious cigarette.

"Even the nerdiest subject somehow appeared cool when interacting with a smoking partner," Gronfeld said. "Just the fact that the subject was brave enough to breathe deadly secondhand smoke established him as a hip, freethinking individual, the kind of person who might one day run with the bulls in Pamplona."

Level two begins after a non-smoker has been in a smoke-filled environment for at least an hour. At this point, the non-smoker's clothes are saturated with the stink of smoke, and he or she develops a dry, hacking cough. Bronchial fits are directly proportional to mucus overproduction, respiratory cyanosis, and coolness. The smelly clothing leads to coolness because the non-smoker smells as if

he or she smokes two or more packs a day, which is a very cool thing to do.

Level three occurs once the non-smoker acknowledges that smoking is cool and starts smoking him- or herself.

"Even if a former non-smoker only smokes in bars or social situations, we feel as if we have scored a victory," Gronfeld said.

Smokers across the U.S. feel vindicated by the study.

"It's an exciting time to be a smoker," University of Virginia freshman Gina Podell said. "It made me look grown-up in high school, and now that I'm older, it just makes me look cool."

Podell's boyfriend, sophomore Tom Willard, agreed. "She always looks sexy smoking at the bars," he said. "I myself don't smoke, but I sure feel cool when I'm with Gina."

David Proctor, president of the American Smokers Association, said there has never been a better time to be a smoker.

"Cigarette companies need our help," Proctor said. "They want to get Third World countries addicted to American cigarettes, but that's going to take money. Now that this study has been released, I'm confident that even nonsmokers will make donations to cigarette companies, thanking them for the gift of coolness."

Proctor also praised the tobacco companies for adding freon, nicotine, and dozens of other poisonous substances to tobacco.

"Anyone would be seen as cool if their bodies were strong enough to handle even one of those chemicals. But smokers, being the coolest people around, have no problem breathing all of them at once," Proctor said. "And breathing those chemicals secondhand is almost as cool."

Encouraged by the study, R.J. Reynolds Monday announced plans to petition the government to legalize the sale of cigarettes to popularity-conscious grade-schoolers. ∅

# Satisfaction Guaranteed

Baby, there is one piece of information in particular that you need to know: With Smoove B, satisfaction is guaranteed.

By Smoove B
Love Man

I will now outline how I will go about satisfying you.

First, I will dress myself in the finest clothes available. I will arrive at your apartment to pick you up for our night of passion in a stylish purple suit created by the most respected designers of our time. In addition to the suit, I will wear a shirt and dress shoes. The shirt will be white and made of silk, hand-sewn and put together in the finest lands of China. It will be spotless, and I will be gleaming.

The precision and care that go into my clothes will set the mood for our entire evening together.

Once I have arrived at your door, I will take you to my limousine, at which point we will drive in luxury and comfort to the place where all of the action is. I will take you dancing at the most exclusive clubs in the city, and we will shed all of our cares and inhibitions as we dance to only the finest beats.

Next, we will go to my luxurious apartment, where I will prepare a meal for you that will make your mouth water for more. I will prepare green beans with butter. I will serve rolls. I will serve vintage wine and also a bowl of corn. I will serve, as a

> **The pheasant will be composed of the highest-quality meat available, packaged in only the finest styrofoam and cellophane.**

main course, cooked pheasant. The pheasant will be composed of the highest-quality meat available, packaged in only the finest styrofoam and cellophane. It will be a meal fit for a Nubian queen.

Mashed potatoes will also be offered.

For dessert, I will serve you chocolates flown in specially from the south of Europe. And I will make sure that these chocolates are certified as the finest chocolates made, as proven by a special certificate that will come with them. I will put the chocolates on a silk pillow and offer them for your consumption by getting down on my knee. I will then feed you the chocolates by hand. This will be a seductive way to show you that the pleasures of our night together have only just begun.

At this juncture, I would like to take the opportunity to interject and say that I am so sorry for all the times I have hurt you or gone back on my word to you. Girl, I am truly sorry about those particular times, and I urge you to forget about them and lis-

ten to the words I am saying now. They come from the heart.

I should also mention that I will treat you like a lady. I will treat you with the utmost delicate care and concern, as if you were a precious flower. I will treat you as if you were the light of my life and my one and only true desire. I will also offer to massage your neck if it is feeling sore.

It is now time for Smoove B to freak you wild.

Baby, when I make love to you, that is when you will reach the peak of your satisfaction. All the rest of my prior preparations before this time, even though they will bring you great, great pleasures, will not come close to the level of pleasure you will

experience when I give you my butta love.

I will caress your body slowly. I will kiss every inch of your aforementioned body, including the arms and back. I will do this with the passion of a wild animal, such as the leopard or cheetah, or perhaps the polar bear. I will put my sting in you. There will be tenderness, also.

Then, when you are sufficiently wet, I will slide it in. This is when you will be satisfied. And that is my guarantee.
Damn.

I present this guarantee to you in writing as a token of my great seriousness about this matter.

In closing, let me say just this: I will sex you all night long. ∅

## Crowd Of Voters Cheers Patronizing Rhetoric

see CAMPAIGN WATCH page 11A

## Yngwie Malmsteen Officially Changes Middle Name To 'Fucking'

see MUSIC page 9D

## Artist Starving For A Reason

see PEOPLE page 3C

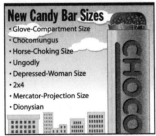

THE ONION
$2.00 US
$3.00 CAN

0  74470 94595  6

# the ONION®

WWW.THEONION.COM    AMERICA'S FINEST NEWS SOURCE™    FOUNDED 1871

# Oprah Viewers Patiently Awaiting Instructions

Above: Hagerstown, MD, *Oprah Winfrey Show* viewer and mother of four Liz Kuharski, 34, awaits word from her leader about what to buy, cook, and read.

CHICAGO, IL—With nearly three weeks having passed since talk-show host Oprah Winfrey last issued an official command, approximately 60 million *Oprah Winfrey Show* viewers remain on standby, stationed in front of their television sets awaiting further instructions from their leader.

"We must be patient with Oprah," said Winfrey fan Melanie Leupke, 44, of Stillwater, OK. "Ours is not to question why she is taking so long. When the time is right and we are needed again, Oprah will tell us what to do."

Across the U.S., *Oprah* viewers' anticipation for new Winfrey directives is reaching a fever pitch. In Winfrey's home base of Chicago, throngs of fans have gathered outside her Harpo Studios headquarters around the clock, maintaining their silent, faithful vigil. Though the city's streets are quiet, a palpable sense of expectation fills the air.

"What book should I read? What low-fat lemon-bread recipes should I use? What made-for-TV movies see OPRAH page 56

## Sudanese 14-Year-Old Has Midlife Crisis

AD DUWAYM, SUDAN—Though it often seems that way, Americans don't hold the patent on middle-age malaise. Just ask Sudan's Kutum Amadi.

Just like many people here in America, Amadi is going through a deep midlife crisis. A retired Sudanese Army captain and father of three, the 14-year-old said he is often left feeling listless and depressed by the thought that half his life is behind him.

"I've really accomplished most of my life goals, so what is there to look forward to?" Amadi said. "I've built my hut. I've built a family. Soon, my children will be conscripted into the army, and the house will be empty. Is that it? Is that all there is?"

Amadi said he remembers his own military years as a time of adventure, strongly contrasting the boredom and dissatisfaction he feels today.

see CRISIS page 58

Above: The purchased videotape.

# Ironic Porn Purchase Leads To Unironic Ejaculation

WINNETKA, IL—A local man's ironic purchase of a humorously titled hardcore-porn video Saturday led to an earnest ejaculation devoid of irony.

According to reports, Josh Farmer, 27, accompanied by friends Brad Werner and Mike Tedesco, entered the Pine Street Adult Bookstore at approximately 3 p.m. to purchase an inflatable-woman doll as a light-hearted gift for friend Marshall Bloch,

Above: Josh Farmer

whose 23rd birthday was to be celebrated later that evening at Farmer's house. While at the store, Farmer also purchased *Terrors From The Clit*, which he would later use as ejaculatory fodder in a wholly unironic session of vigorous masturbation.

"Guys, check out this one," Farmer told Werner and Tedesco while browsing a row of videos. "*Terrors From The Clit*, star-

see PORN page 57

# Nation Fills Up On Bread

WASHINGTON, DC—Despite repeated warnings from federal officials not to eat too much before their entree arrives, an alarming 89 percent of U.S. citizens filled up on bread Saturday, leaving them too full to enjoy the rest of their meal.

"Paying little heed to the many cautionary announcements we have issued, the American people have stuffed themselves with dinner rolls and, as a result, have no room for their soup or salad, much less their main course," said U.S. Secretary of Health and Human Services Donna Shalala. "America, look at your plates: They've hardly even been touched."

According to a Health and Human Services report, an unprecedented two billion pounds of uneaten sides were trucked away from U.S. dinner tables, including 150 million pounds of mashed potatoes, 200 million pounds of stuffing, and 450 million pounds of steamed carrots. What's worse, HHS officials said, Americans discarded nearly 300 million choice cuts of meat—which is the most expensive part and has all the protein—without taking much more than a bite.

"America must learn that filling up on bread beforehand is just foolish, because then you can't enjoy your meal," the report read. "Sure, they give you plenty of bread. But then you can't eat the food you paid good money for. That's how they get you."

The HHS report has provoked strong reaction from appetite-conservation activists nationwide.

"For decades, excessive and unregulated pre-meal bread consumption has been the number-one threat to the U.S. appetite," said Hannah Dowling, author of the best-selling *Saving Some Room For Later*. "Despite decades of awareness-raising efforts on the part of appetite conservationists, filling up on bread remains the leading cause of leaving the dinner table early for Americans in the 7- to 64-year-old age group, and the second-leading cause for citizens over 65."

According to Dowling, even the seemingly harmless dinner-table presence of such food-service hospitality items as individually wrapped breadsticks and Saltine-brand crackers can pose a threat to Americans' hunger.

"Many people, conditioned to expect instant satisfaction in our convenience-obsessed society, lack even the simplest mealtime gratification-delay skills—skills which, in generations past, children were expected to have mastered by age 5 or 6," Dowling said. "As a result, presented with unlimited access to fresh bread, bread sticks, and crackers—not to mention the ubiquitous packets of butter and alliterative butter substitutes such as Country Crock and Shedd's Spread—

see BREAD page 58

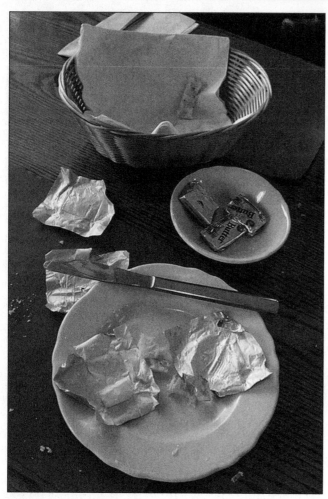

Above: In a scene familiar across America, a Scotch Plains, NJ, bread basket sits empty.

OPRAH from page 55

should I watch to give me a sense of empowerment?" asked Pamela Kolb, a Mundelein, IL, homemaker and one of the approximately 13,000 *Oprah* viewers huddled outside her studio. "In these complex times, it can be frightening to have to go three weeks without any guidance from a television personality. But we must remain true to Oprah's vision. Our duty is to stay focused and on full alert until new orders are issued."

"Oprah will not let us down. I know this much is true," said longtime fan Shamiqu'aa Hudson, clutching a copy of the Wally Lamb best-seller *I Know This Much Is True*, the latest Oprah's Book Club selection and the last item Oprah fans were commanded to buy before the three-week directive drought began. "She will not leave us to make decisions for ourselves. I have faith in her."

Winfrey, 44, is among the most successful individuals in entertainment, with best-selling cookbooks, high-profile movie roles, close friendships with many of Hollywood's biggest power players, and a top-rated daytime talk show. *Time* magazine recently named her one of the Most Influential People Of The Century. Her greatest influence, however, is that which she holds over her army of 60

million couch-bound women, who unfailingly obey her nationally televised directives on everything from home-decorating to weight loss.

"I follow Oprah's advice to the letter," said viewer Cassandra Fryar of Visalia, CA. "When she told us to help out at our kids' schools by repainting any worn-out jungle-gym equipment,

> ## "What book should I read? What low-fat lemon-bread recipes should I use?" asked Pamela Kolb of Mundelein, IL.

I was there right away with my paint can at the ready. In fact, so many women showed up to paint the jungle gym that the resultant multi-layered sludge, made up of thousands of coats of paint, took more than seven months to dry."

"I used to wear a lot of teal, but after seeing a recent episode called

'Oprah's Wardrobe Makeovers,' the only colors I wear are muted autumn hues, such as forest green and burgundy," said Liz Kuharski, a Hagerstown, MD, homemaker and mother of four. "I just wish she would issue some more commands for us to obey. If I have to wait much longer, I might find myself inadvertently following the orders of some other talk-show host."

During the past few years, Winfrey's power seems to have grown exponentially. All 18 Oprah's Book Club selections have been *New York Times* best-sellers. When, through the auspices of her charity organization, Oprah's Angel Network, she ordered her followers to contribute pocket change to the World's Largest Piggy Bank for scholarships for needy children, they did so in record numbers. Her May 1998 command to her followers to stop eating ham sandwiches single-handedly bankrupted the U.S. pork industry.

Spokespersons for Harpo Productions said Winfrey understands the responsibility that comes with such extraordinary power.

"Oprah takes her role as a world leader very seriously," Harpo Productions public-relations director Amy Hirsch said in a press release issued

from within the company's massive network of underground bunkers. "Her commitment to the betterment of her subjects is supreme, and she will allow nothing and no one to stand in the way of such efforts."

"Sometimes, I don't know what to do," said Jane Clement, a Cedar Rapids, IA, manicurist. "But, then, Oprah comes on the TV and explains to me what I should do, and I feel better."

Clement's sentiments echo those of millions of *Oprah* viewers, who maintain total faith in their leader. But some observers fear that if the wait for a new edict goes on much longer, serious trouble may arise.

"The U.S. daytime-TV audience is a powderkeg waiting to go off," said Catherine Beatts-Murphy, director of Harvard University's Institute For Media Studies. "If this mob continues to be left without direction, it is in danger of fragmenting into thousands of uncontrollable splinter groups, acting without cohesion and creating a state of virtual anarchy. Oprah must avert this crisis scenario by acting now, before it's too late."

Added Beatts-Murphy: "The paucity of leadership in this country should be deeply appalling to any civilized person." ∅

# CNN Still Releasing News Piled Up During Elián González Saga

Above: CNN anchor Natalie Allen breaks the news of the Dalai Lama's death, which occurred four months ago.

ATLANTA—CNN officials announced Saturday that the cable network is "making good progress" in its ongoing effort to release the vast backlog of news accumulated during Elián González's headline-dominating seven-month odyssey in the U.S.

"Ever since little Elián went back to Cuba on June 28, we've been working overtime to get through all the news we bumped during that gripping, emotional saga," CNN vice-president Susan Bunda said. "There are all sorts of stockpiled stories to report, and we feel the American public will find much of it interesting, informative, and even a bit surprising, considering all of it happened three months ago or more."

Among the backlogged stories to air during recent CNN "News You Didn't Hear" coverage: the formation of the new Eastern European nation of Molbania last December, the French government's Feb. 9 decision to sell the Mona Lisa in private auction and the painting's subsequent purchase by Ted Turner, the discovery of mysterious carnivorous plant spores in southern Missouri in early April, and the June 4 congressional vote to grant federal legislators a 400 percent pay hike.

Last Thursday, the network reported the annexation of South Carolina by North Carolina, which acquired its bankrupt neighbor in March in accordance with the terms of an obscure, centuries-old clause in South Carolina's tax code.

"This news is significant, in that it reduces the number of U.S. states to 49," Bunda said, "and we feel it is something the American people deserve to hear about. But it lacks the compelling, personality-driven storyline and heart-rending video footage of the Elián crisis, so we had no choice but to temporarily shelve it at the time it occurred. We did get a few complaints from South Carolina viewers who were disappointed in the lack of coverage, but what can we say? Unfortunately, these things happen in television. That's just the name

see CNN page 58

PORN from page 55

ring Nikki Love, Porsha, and Intrusion. We should totally get this and make fun of it at the party. Wouldn't that be hilarious?"

Continued Farmer, closely studying the back-of-the-box photos of naked women engaging in graphic sex acts: "Dude, it's supposed to be a horror movie, except instead of all the chicks getting killed by the zombies, they have sex. Is that the stupidest thing ever?"

After nearly 15 minutes of wisecrack-filled browsing, the men exited the store, having purchased a 'Lola Lungs' inflatable doll, a set of racy undergarments with which to festoon the doll, two packages of novelty glow-in-the-dark condoms, and the ironic videotape.

Approximately 30 minutes before Bloch was due at the party, Farmer suggested to fellow partygoers that they have *Terrors From The Clit* playing when he arrived.

"I forget Josh's exact words, but he basically was saying how it would be a sublime paradigmatic shift between Marshall's expectations and empiric reality if he walked into the party and saw us watching porn, as if that's what we normally do," Tedesco said. "Hence, you know, the irony. Get it?"

Farmer's friends rejected his suggestion, telling him they would prefer to spend the remaining pre-party time preparing snacks. But Farmer did not give up, making several requests to view the tape during the actual party.

"He kept saying, 'Dudes, we have to remember to watch that stupid video,'" Tedesco said. "So we finally gave in and watched the thing."

Those present said Farmer watched *Terrors* "with great interest" from start to finish, deriving great ironic enjoyment from every scene.

"He kept laughing and pointing out stuff in the movie, like how horrible the acting and music was, and saying stuff like, 'Oh, I'm so sure that would really happen!'" Werner said. "We were all just totally cracking jokes and making fun of it. But no one more than Josh: He was making smart-ass comments non-stop."

At approximately 2 a.m., the party finally began to dissipate, and Bloch, gathering his gifts from the evening, reached for the *Terrors* videotape. According to witnesses, Farmer immediately stopped him, saying, "Wait, Marshall, you gotta let me borrow that. I have to show it to my brother when he's in town next week. He'll think it's so fucking hilarious."

Bloch agreed, and minutes after the last guest left his apartment, Farmer put the video back into his VCR and hit play. Unfastening the zipper on his pants, Farmer watched the video and began stroking his penis without humorous intent. He achieved orgasm some 12 minutes into the viewing, ejaculating into his cupped left hand in a manner that neither inverted nor subverted any thematic paradigms.

Despite Farmer's repeated insistence that his viewing of the tape was strictly ironic, most experts familiar with the case are unconvinced.

"It appears that Mr. Farmer, despite his derisive stance toward *Terrors From The Clit* while in the adult bookstore, ultimately enjoyed it in a thoroughly sincere and heartfelt manner," said Georgetown University sociology professor Dr. William Campos. "He was somehow able to derive genuine enjoyment from a most unlikely and counterintuitive source—a video so distasteful and poorly executed that he purchased it specifically to mock it."

"For all his initial misgivings, Josh managed to overcome his ironic stance and simply enjoy the thrusting, grunting performances on their own merits," Campos said. "How he did it, we do not yet know. But I definitely need to borrow this tape for research purposes. Perhaps through the exhaustive eye of scientific scrutiny, I can get to the truth at the heart of this mystery." ∅

## INFOGRAPHIC

### Madonna's Wedding

Later this month, Madonna and director Guy Ritchie will marry at a Scottish castle. Among the known details:

- ♥ Madonna to walk down aisle to remix of "The Wedding March" by DJ Jellybean Benitez
- ♥ Ritchie gets to invite 3 percent of the guests
- ♥ Ceremony to reflect Madonna's "total respect for Buddhism and yoga and the Kabbalah and stuff"
- ♥ Wedding photographer expressly instructed only to take pictures of bride
- ♥ Madonna to wear tank top her mother wore on her wedding day
- ♥ Receiving line to consist of 25 lithe, shirtless, gay black men writhing to electronic breakbeats
- ♥ Kurt Loder to cry eyes out in back pew
- ♥ Upon completion of vows, son Rocco Ritchie will no longer be bastard; daughter Lourdes Leon, however, will remain bastard
- ♥ Madonna to brilliantly reinvent self as aging, strident, twice-married martinet

CNN from page 57

of the game."

Added Bunda, "Boy, that Elián sure was an adorable little fella, wasn't he? I wonder what he's up to nowadays, that little rascal."

Other months-old developments which may come as a surprise to CNN viewers include January's Russian rickets epidemic, which left half the nation with the disease; the surprise April 22 eruption of a volcano in a remote section of South Dakota; and the sudden disappearance of the star Alpha Centauri, the sun's closest stellar neighbor, which collapsed into a black hole in late May.

"The South Dakota volcano thing, maybe we could have run that if there'd been some sort of huge disaster associated with it," CNN Headline News president Bob Furnad said. "But, unfortunately, there were no casualties. Also, there were no big jets of flame either, because it was one of those boring, magma-flow type of eruptions. So the best visuals we could come up with were some dull computer graphics of the new fault line, detailing the splitting tectonic plates."

"Likewise," Furnad continued, "if Al-

pha Centauri had gone supernova, well, then we would have had something. But, somehow, it just collapsed into a black hole, with no big, exciting explosion footage to give the story some 'oomph.' Scientists can't even explain why: They say it defies all known laws of physics. So that makes it hard to find a good hook, you see."

Reclusive novelist Thomas Pynchon, who came out of hiding on May 17 to speak out on some sort of impending crisis, breaking more than 20 years of media silence, expressed hope that his segment will eventually reach the airwaves.

"Hello? It's me, Thomas Pynchon," Pynchon said. "I have J.D. Salinger here with me, too. We're here trying to raise awareness of this profoundly serious crisis. Is anybody listening?"

Those interested, Lang said, can learn what Pynchon had to say during CNN coverage of the May 17 announcement, slated to air sometime around Christmas.

"With any luck, that is," Furnad said. "After all, you never know when another doe-eyed waif will wash up on shore and set everything else back another couple months." Ø

Above: Videotapes of backlogged, Elián-era news stories pile up in a CNN production room.

BREAD from page 56

Above: A perfectly good meal goes to waste, thrown into an Athens, GA, trash bin.

the American eater is like the proverbial horse that, left unsupervised, will gorge itself until it dies."

"Remember," Dowling added, "bread expands once it gets in your stomach, and then you feel full even when you're not."

In a recent U.N. study, the U.S. ranked last in the world in appetite-preservation skills. The average American, the study found, was only able to maintain an empty stomach for three minutes before sating his or her hunger. Standing in sharp contrast is Botswana, whose citizenry ranked first, able to preserve their appetites for an average of more than seven months.

"The problem of appetite spoilage has reached epidemic proportions here in America," Shalala said. "No

## In a recent U.N. study, the U.S. ranked last in the world in appetite-preservation skills.

other country is as bad at staying hungry as we are."

Shalala said major changes are in order in the wake of the report.

"If we can't control ourselves with the bread, we'll have to face hard facts and accept that we're just not going to have any room for pie later," Shalala said. "And nobody, regardless of our political differences, wants a tragedy like that." Ø

CRISIS from page 55

"I spent two years in the Sudan People's Liberation Army," he said. "There, I attained the rank of captain, traveled to foreign deserts, and ate almost daily. It seems like only yesterday I retired with honors, even though, in fact, it was almost three years ago. If only I could somehow return to that wonderful, exciting time."

"Where have the days gone?" Amadi asked. "Just a few years ago, my son Ngoba was born. Now, he is about to graduate from the first grade and head out into the world."

In an effort to recapture his lost youth, Amadi has entered what experts term a "second childhood" phase, extravagantly spending large amounts of money on vanity items.

"Last week, I bought a hoe with a metal tip," Amadi said. "The week before that, I traded in my dark blue shirt for a brighter green one. Next, I'm considering purchasing a brand-new sportscart for my ox."

According to Sudanese psychologist Dr. Jibal al-Muglad, Amadi's behavior is not unusual.

"Many middle-aged Sudanese males, usually around the age of 14, start reverting to the behavior of their youth," al-Muglad said. "Largely, this

is done to counter oncoming signs of middle age, such as increased height or a cracking voice. Much of this behavior is harmless, but other manifestations can put a strain on a marriage, especially if the man becomes wistful for the sexual freedom of his youth."

Indeed, Amadi spoke of a malaise that has crept into his four-year marriage. "I see my wife growing old just like myself, and I feel depressed," he said. "I think the magic really started to go out of the relationship when she began menstruating."

Amadi confessed to flirting with some of the younger women in his village. "There is a 10-year-old who drinks from the same well as me, and we frequently giggle and make eyes at each other," he said. "I must admit, it is very tempting. I love my wife, but her hip bones are already starting to widen to better facilitate childbirth. I find it increasingly difficult to resist the lure of an illicit February-March romance."

"Before long, I will be in my 20s, and the end will be imminent. What then? What will it have all been for?" asked Amadi, sighing deeply. "Life is much too short." Ø

## NEWS IN BRIEF

## NS/ND/C/DWF Wondering Why She Can't Find Someone

MINNEAPOLIS—Susan Stenerud, a divorced, white, non-smoking, non-drinking Christian who has placed "countless" personals ads over the years, wondered aloud Saturday why she can't find someone special. "All I want is to find a D/D-free NS/ND/C/SWM who shares my strong morals and doesn't waste his time going to bars and parties," the 32-year-old said. "For some reason, no men seem to respond to that description."

## Starlet-Viewer Age Difference Quickly Calculated

GRAND RAPIDS, MI—Local data-entry clerk Clifford Gornowicz, 33, quickly calculated the age difference between himself and 17-year-old *Tonight Show* guest Gaby Hoffmann while watching the program Friday. "Man... 16 years," Gornowicz said to himself after host Jay Leno disclosed the actress' age. "That means she wasn't even born when *The Empire Strikes Back* came out. Oh, God." Gornowicz reportedly has not been this distressed since Christina Ricci. Ø

## Clinton Goes Back In Time, Teams Up With Golden Age Clinton

see WASHINGTON page 5B

## Tornado Violence: Are Tornadic Images In The Media To Blame?

see WEATHER page 14A

## Top Cute

see SHOPPING page 2C

THE ONION
$2.00 US
$3.00 CAN

0 74470 94595 6

00

---

⬤ the ONION®

WWW.THEONION.COM     AMERICA'S FINEST NEWS SOURCE™     FOUNDED 1871

# Tenth Circle Added To Rapidly Growing Hell

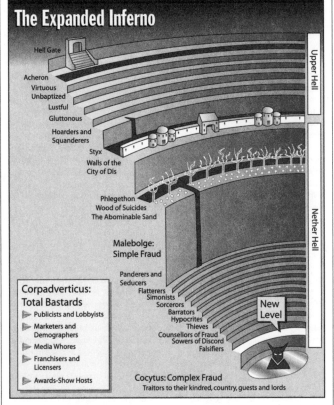

**The Expanded Inferno**

Hell Gate

Acheron
Virtuous Unbaptized
Lustful
Gluttonous
Hoarders and Squanderers
Styx
Walls of the City of Dis
Phlegethon
Wood of Suicides
The Abominable Sand

Malebolge: Simple Fraud

Panderers and Seducers
Flatterers
Simonists
Sorcerers
Barrators
Hypocrites
Thieves
Counsellors of Fraud
Sowers of Discord
Falsifiers

New Level

Cocytus: Complex Fraud
Traitors to their kindred, country, guests and lords

Upper Hell

Nether Hell

**Corpadverticus: Total Bastards**

▶ Publicists and Lobbyists
▶ Marketers and Demographers
▶ Media Whores
▶ Franchisers and Licensers
▶ Awards-Show Hosts

CITY OF DIS, NETHER HELL—After nearly four years of construction at an estimated cost of 750 million souls, Corpadverticus, the new 10th circle of Hell, finally opened its doors Tuesday.

The Blockbuster Video-sponsored circle, located in Nether Hell between the former eighth and ninth levels of Malebolge and Cocytus, is expected to greatly alleviate the overcrowding that has plagued the infernal underworld in recent years. The circle is the first added to Hell in its countless-millennia history.

"A nightmarishly large glut of condemned spirits in recent years necessitated the expansion of Hell," inferno spokesperson Antedeus said. "The tra-
see HELL page 60

## Funyuns Still Outselling Responsibilityuns

DALLAS—Funyuns, the world leader in artificial onion-ring-flavored and -shaped snack-food items, continues to enjoy an overwhelming sales lead over competing brand Responsibilityuns, the trade publication *Impulse Purchase Quarterly* reported Tuesday.

Responsibilityuns, launched last May in a bold attempt to challenge Funyuns' dominance of the faux-onion-ring snack market, have done "little or no damage" to its rival's sales through the first quarter of 2000.

"I just don't understand what went wrong," said James Connell, CEO of
see RESPONSIBILITYUNS page 60

Above: The unpopular product.

# Community Leaders Outraged Over Porn Video

## 'This Tape Contained No "All-Anal Action" As Promised,' Say Concerned Parents

PLEASANT, NC—Outraged community members are mounting an aggressive campaign against an X-rated videotape available for rent at Pleasant's Video Villa video store, claiming that the tape does not contain the "Spectacular All-Anal Action" promised on its cover.

"Are we as citizens expected to just sit back and tolerate this sort of garbage?" asked Pleasant School Board president Edwin Thistlewaite during a protest at City Hall. "I paid to see chicks getting fucked in the ass, and that's what I want. I think I speak for all decent Americans on this matter."

"This is false advertising, plain and simple," agreed
see PORN page 61

Above: Citizens of Pleasant are protesting a pornographic video they say is far from the "wall-2-wall, deep-probing ass-flesh fuck-fest" its box promises.

59

ditional nine-tiered system had grown insufficient to accommodate the exponentially rising numbers of Hell-bound."

Adding to the need for expansion, Antedeus said, was the fact that a majority of the new arrivals possessed souls far more evil than the original nine circles were equipped to handle.

"Demographers, advertising executives, tobacco lobbyists, monopoly-law experts retained by major corporations, and creators of office-based sitcoms—these new arrivals represent a wave of spiritual decay and horror the likes of which Hell had never before seen," Antedeus said.

Despite the need for expansion, the plan faced considerable resistance, largely due to the considerable costs of insuring construction projects within the Kingdom Of Lies. Opposition also came from Hell purists concerned about the detrimental effect a tenth level would have on the intricate numerology of Hell's meticulously arranged allegorical structure. In 1994, however, funding was finally secured in a deal brokered between Blockbuster CEO Wayne Huizenga and Satan himself.

Prior to the construction of the tenth circle, many among the new wave of sinners had been placed in circles such as Hoarders and Squanderers, Sowers of Discord, Flatterers and Seducers, Violent Against Art, and Hypocrites. Hell authorities, however, say the new level, the Circle of Total Bastards, located at the site of the former Well of Giants just above the Frozen Lake at Hell's center, better suits their insidious brand of evil.

Frigax The Vile, a leading demonic presence, is among the most vocal supporters of the new circle.

"In the past, the underworld was ill-equipped to handle the new breed of sinners flooding our gates—downsizing CEOs, focus-group coordinators, telemarketing sales representatives, and vast hordes of pony-tailed entertainment-industry executives roller-blading and talking on cell phones at the same time. But now, we've finally got the sort of top-notch Pits of Doom necessary to give such repellent abominations the quality boilings they deserve."

Pausing to tear off the limbs of an *Access Hollywood* co-anchor, Frigax added, "We're all tremendously excited about the many new forms of torture and eternal pain this new level's state-of-the-art facilities will make possible."

Among the tortures the Corpadverticus Circle of Total Bastards boasts: the Never-Ending Drive-Thru Bank, the Bottomless Pit of Promotional Tie-In Keychains, and the Chamber of Emotionally Manipulative Home Shopping Network Products.

The Circle also features a Hall of Aerobics, where condemned TV-exercise-show personalities, clad in skin-tight Spandex outfits soaked in flesh-dissolving acid, are forced to exercise for centuries on end, covered in vom-

it and prodded with the distended ribs of skeletal, anorexic demons while speakers blare an unending dance-remix version of the 1988 Rick Astley hit "Together Forever."

In a nearby area, corporate raiders are forced to carry the golf clubs of

---

## A majority of the new arrivals possessed souls far more evil than the original nine circles were equipped to handle.

---

Hispanic migrant workers from hole to hole for eternity, withering under a constant barrage of verbal abuse from their former subservients as crows descend from trees to peck at their eyes. In one of the deepest and most profane portions of the circle, unspeakable acts are said to be committed with a mail-order Roly-Kit.

"In life, I was a Salomon Brothers investment banker," one flame-black-ened shade told reporters. "When I arrived here, they didn't know what to do with me. They put me in with those condemned to walk backwards with their heads turned all the way around on their necks, for the crime of attempting to see the future. But then I sent a couple of fruit baskets to the right people and, in no time flat, I secured a cushy spot for myself in the first circle of the Virtuous Unbaptized. Now, that was a sweet deal. But before long, they caught on to my game and transferred me here to the realm of Total Bastards. I've been shrieking like a goddamn woman ever since."

"It's hell here," said a Disney executive, his face contorted in the Misery of the Damned. "There are no executive lounges, I can't get any decent risotto, and the suit I have to wear is a cheap Brooks Brothers knock-off. I'm beeped every 30 seconds, and there's no way to return the calls. Plus, I'm being boiled upside down in lard while jackals gnaw at the soles of my feet. If I could just reach the fax machine on that nearby rock, I could contact some well-placed associates and work something out, but it's just out of my grasp, and it's out of ink and constantly blinking the message, 'Replace Toner Cartridge, Replace Toner Cartridge, Replace Toner Cartridge.'"

The executive then resumed screaming in agony.

Grogar The Malefic, a Captain in Hell's elite Demon Corps and director of admissions for the new circle, said Hell's future looks bright, thanks to the new circle.

"Things are definitely looking up," Grogar said. "We're far better equipped, ready to take on the most Unholy Atrocities humanity has to offer."

"We're really on the grow down here," Grogar added. "This is an exciting time to be in Hell." ∅

---

Delayed Gratification Foods, the Dallas-based maker of the sober, salted snack. "Everybody knows that responsibility and self-reliance are qualities which, with patience and persistence, bring rewards far greater than the fleeting pleasure of instant gratification. And, frankly, that is all our competitor has to offer. We felt sure that customers would respond to our product's image of hard work and long-term stability."

Responsibilityuns is not the only Delayed Gratification product to fail to connect with consumers. Also faring poorly were Proprie-Teez Fruit Chews, touted as "a blast of fruit flavor that maintains a basic level of decorum at all times"; Homework-First Nut Clusters, "the candy you only enjoy after buckling down and investing in your education and future"; and, perhaps most disastrously, Reputables, the "pre-wrapped snak-pak for churchgoing folk with a position of good social standing to maintain... in the home, the workplace, and the community at large."

Seeking to appeal to consumers' respect for time-honored values, the products stress thrift, discipline, and a strong sense of personal obligation over what Connell calls the "me-first" sensibilities currently dominating the snack-food marketplace.

According to Delayed Gratification vice-president of marketing Anthony Fontaine, it was hoped that the emphasis placed on diligence, proper conduct, and "a little magic ingredient known as moral fiber" would win the company's products long-term brand loyalty among customers who "were raised right by honest, hard-working taxpayers."

Fontaine explained the company's marketing strategy.

"When entering a highly competitive market, it's important to seek out and exploit the weaknesses in your competitors' thinking," Fontaine said. "When looking into the feasibility of breaking into the snack-product field, we noticed a tendency among other brands to stress excess and self-indulgence over the sort of gumption and tenacity that delivers real results over

the long haul. Our entire sales strategy was designed to exploit this weakness."

Despite its apparent logic, Delayed Gratification's strategy appears to have backfired. In recent independent focus-group tests of the new product Rote Memorization Doodles, a majority of consumers not only did not respond well, but actually went out of their way to avoid them. In many cases, those tested opted to leave the premises of the store rather than remain in the presence of a point-of-purchase display stand for the product.

In a subsequent study, respondents to consumer surveys designed to pinpoint the flaws in Delayed Gratification's marketing strategy reported that they "would rather eat rocks" than purchase a bag of Auto-Safety-Reminder Cakes. Further, several respondents stated that "there's no reason to waste money on this [box of Health-Insurance Bills Choco Crunches]," claiming that "just looking at the box puts me in a bad mood."

Delayed Gratification has no plans to alter its approach in the face of poor sales.

"It is foolish for people to expect to always get everything they want right now, without first earning their reward by facing and overcoming setbacks," said Connell, munching on a bag of Character-Building Puffs. "Yet, somehow, it appears that many of today's snack-food consumers are looking for some sort of 'quick-fix' solution when they walk into a convenience store. Well, our company is above such childish impatience."

Said Fontaine: "The hedonistic party atmosphere endemic to so much of what passes for snack-food brand identity today might offer consumers a moment of fleeting satisfaction, but once that initial sugar rush has faded, where does that leave them? At Delayed Gratification Foods, we offer customers something better: stability and security well into their retirement years."

"Sales will pick up in time," Fontaine continued. "We may not be shooting up the charts just yet, but slow and steady wins the race." ∅

## SOCIETY

**James**

**Bigler**

**Dorman**

**Renee James** visited the grave of her husband Fred Sunday, accompanied by their son Norman, who waited in the car because it was raining.

**John Bigler** celebrated his weekend off from the Kal Kan dog-food factory by never removing his bathrobe.

**Robert Dorman** spent Sunday at the zoo with Josh Goetz, 6, a child who isn't even his but he is forced to raise just because he married Goetz's mother.

# Coca-Cola Introduces New 30-Liter Size

## Bottle Will Be Unwieldy, Inconvenient

ATLANTA—The Coca-Cola Corporation held a press conference Tuesday to announce that its soft drinks will soon be available in 30-liter plastic bottles.

According to a company spokesman, the decision to sell Coke in the enormous containers is not based on a specific study or survey of consumer demands, but on the company's desire to make a resounding display of its corporate might.

Several major soft-drink makers attempted to improve on the standard two-liter size bottle by introducing a three-liter size in 1985, but the new size failed because of difficulties with storage and carbonation loss.

"The three-liter didn't fail because it was too big. It failed because it was not big enough," Coca-Cola CEO Vic Hertner said. "Two liters is nothing. I could urinate two liters for you right now. But 30 liters? That's untouchable."

The new bottle is nearly four feet tall, and weighs 274 pounds when filled with Coke. In tests, it took an average of three men to lift it. The product will fit in an average refrigerator, but only when all other products and shelving have been removed. Most inconvenient of all, the new Coke will go flat if not consumed within 17 minutes, even if promptly recapped.

The Coca-Cola Corporation does not view such factors as drawbacks.

Above: The new bottles take up an enormous amount of display space.

"By requiring three men to lift the bottle, our new product will encourage a sense of community," Hertner said. "The popular image of the lonely soda drinker wasting his life away in solitude will no longer be relevant, because anyone wanting to drink the new Coke will need two buddies to get the soda home and at least 10 to drink it all. The quick loss of carbonation might lead to tiny problems, but what are people going to do? Stop drinking Coke? I think not."

Sociologists see Coke's plan to manufacture the 30-liter bottle as the logical next step. "It makes sense," Stanford professor Edmund Tillerton said. "Americans like big things: big sky, big cars, big stereo speakers, big dicks, and big TV sets. We like things to be larger than life, and that's what the new Coke size is."

Coke stressed that the 30-liter bottle would not be merely a new size option, but will soon be the only option.

"We're phasing out the smaller cans and bottles, as well as the two-liter size," Hertner said. "We're confident that people will take to the new 30-liter. Besides, they won't have a choice. We own Minute Maid, as well. Soon, all orange juice will only be available in 30-liter sizes. Fruitopia, as well. We will buy controlling stock in every beverage company and force them to follow suit. We are very confident. Did I mention that we own a small nation? If the people of this country don't like the newly sized product, we'll simply declare war. We will bury you."

Consumers are eager to sample the new 30-liter bottle.

"I like Coke a lot, so it would follow see COKE page 62

## Sixth Grader Begins Work On Pony Trilogy

CANTON, OH—Canton-area sixth-grader Melissa Wright announced plans Tuesday to begin work on her much-anticipated "Pony Trilogy," a three-part series chronicling her adventures with fictional pony Star Rider. Volume one, tentatively titled *Melissa Meets Star Rider*, is expected to be completed sometime this week. "It's gonna be about me and Star Rider having all this fun together, and I'm also gonna talk about how much I love to ride her," Wright said. While Wright did not give exact details of the second and third installments, they are widely expected to touch on Star Rider's amazing ability to fly, as well as the pony's acquisition of a magic emerald which grants Wright the power to eavesdrop on anyone she wants to by speaking their name. "Expect this work to take sixth-grade pony fiction in exciting new directions," said George Toffel of Doubleday Press.

## U.S. Leads World In Mexican-Food Availability

UNITED NATIONS—According to a U.N. report released Tuesday, for the 16th straight year, the U.S. ranks first in the world in Mexican-food availability. "America boasts an unrivaled abundance of Mexican food, producing 23 billion pounds of tacos, enchiladas, and burritos in 1999," the report read. "No other nation on Earth can claim such plenty with regard to beans-and-rice-based Mexican fare." Japan ranked second, with the top five rounded out by Canada, Mexico, and the United Kingdom. Ø

PORN from page 59

area resident and mother of two Janice Ferguson, speaking before an assembled crowd of more than 1,500. "My husband and I have both viewed this piece of trash, and believe me, it barely even shows bush until 20 minutes in—a far cry indeed from the 'Non-Stop Carnal Cum-ucopia' touted on the box."

Over cheers of agreement from the crowd, she added: "Is this the sort of hardcore pornography we want in our homes? I think not! I say the people of Midvale County deserve better!"

Though the controversial video, *Butt-Fuck Sluts Go Nuts Vol. 29*, contains some graphic depictions of anal intercourse, the citizens' group asserts that it does not even come close to living up to its box's claim of a "Two-Hour, Wall-2-Wall, Deep-Probing Ass-Flesh Fuck-Fest." The group is demanding the inclusion of significantly more explicit prurient material before it will relent.

"I rely on tapes like this to provide me with the vicarious, onanistic anal thrills I crave," dentist and anal-pornography enthusiast Dr. Mark Ferbacher told reporters. "I stroked myself for over an hour, and I barely even got it up once. Where's the stuff I can really pump my meat over—the double penetrations, the all-lesbian strap-on dildoing, the spread-eagled, six-finger bend-overs? That's what I want to know."

Parents' groups across the state are echoing protesters' complaints. Said Sandra Hamm, director of the Center For The Family in nearby Plovis: "There are, what, eight or nine chicks in this movie and maybe two of them take it in the ass, tops," Hamm said. "That's utterly unacceptable."

Pleasant resident Charlotte Kendall voiced her concerns at a town meeting held Tuesday night in the basement of Holy Christ Almighty Lutheran Church.

"If we can't trust the makers of hardcore pornography to tell us what kind of explicit sex we can expect to see, who can we trust?" Kendall asked.

Though legal scholars say pornographic material has proven difficult to prosecute in the past, they believe that this time the community may have a case.

"The videotape is clearly inferior to comparable releases, not only in the tame, unexciting way the sex acts are performed, but in the fact that the performers themselves are not particularly good-looking," said University Of Chicago law-school dean and censorship expert Henry Lattimore.

Pointing to a television playing a *Butt-Fuck Sluts* scene in which two women shave each other's pubic regions, Lattimore said, "Just look at these chicks. They're not hot at all."

Even more critical of the tape is North Carolina Fifth Circuit Judge Roy A. Beers. According to Beers, though some scenes depict what is obviously rear-entry, "doggie-style" intercourse, it is unclear whether the penetration is anal or merely vaginal.

"Without tight shots of lubed-up, slippery cock actually pumping the rectal opening, we cannot be 100 percent certain that these scenes constitute legitimate butt-reaming or simply an attempt to pass off standard vaginal fucking as that of the butt-reaming variety," an opinion paper submitted by Beers to the North Carolina Supreme Court read in part.

Lawyers representing Video Villa defended *Butt-Fuck Sluts*.

"Young, eager sluts can clearly be seen spreading their hot, wet pussies and bungholes," attorney Leslie MacKinnon said. "Furthermore, throughout the video, interracial lesbian three-ways, solo female masturbation, and penetration with a variety of dildos and vibratory devices are well represented. In view of these facts, my client feels that his customers are getting their $3.50 worth." Ø

# My Moroccan Neighbors Won't Stop Their Damn Ululating

**By Fred Parker**

Well, there goes the neighborhood. Last week, the moving van pulls up to the Petersens' old house and—yup, you guessed it—a bunch of Moroccans move in. I haven't even met the Aatabous yet, but already I can't stand them: All night long, they won't stop with their damn ululating.

To be honest, I haven't the foggiest notion what they're even wailing about. Maybe they're lamenting a deceased relative. Or retelling the traditional Moroccan folk tale *The Girl Who Lived With The Gazelles*. Or maybe they're just performing some Gnawa devotional trance music. All I know is, that damn ululating of theirs is loud, it's in D-sharp, and it goes on well past 9 p.m. Next time, I'm calling the cops.

Last Monday night, I'm trying to relax in my own home—which I paid for with my hard-earned American dollars, mind you, not some wad of dirham—and enjoy the big game. The whole time, the Aatabous are out on their backyard patio, ululating up a storm. They've even got the Santur dulcimer and three-stringed Berber lutes going. I try to ignore it, but, finally, I just can't take it anymore. I open my window and shout, "Hey, would you mind keeping that bendir-thumping down to a dull roar? A man can only take so much of those cylindrical, single-membrane tambourines, you know!"

It usually gets better for a few days. They promise they'll try to keep it down. But, like clockwork, the ululating always starts up again. And even on the days when their voices aren't raised together in a long, sorrowful cry, their teenage daughter is usually blaring that Moroccan pop singer Lem Chaheb out her bedroom window. As if that's an improvement.

Isn't that always the way: You work hard to make a nice home for your family, and then, just when you're ready to enjoy the fruits of your labor, the whole neighborhood goes to the Moroccans. They move in and, just like that, braziers and woodcrafts stores start popping up on every corner. Guys are out there selling olives and pomegranates right on the street. Next thing you know, property values are plummeting.

It gets worse, though: You should see what the Aatabous have done to the Petersens' front yard. They've got handmade rugs hanging out to dry and some sort of pet bird flapping around. They're laying hand-painted tiles left and right. It's an eyesore for the entire block.

Then there are those horrible smells that come from their house—coriander, cumin, saffron. It's awful. Haven't these kebab-eaters ever heard of a Big Mac? Couscous marrakesh made with grilled lamb, batinjaan zalud drizzled with olive oil... I've got to smell that crap seven days a week.

Then, to add insult to injury, I find out that the Aatabous come from the port city of Tétouan. Well, I don't have to tell you what those Moroccan coastal types are like, especially the men. They get all hopped up on mint tea and go out and have their way with white women. Thank God our daughters are grown up and out of the house, that's all I have to say.

And I haven't even mentioned the bonfire dances. You know what I'm talking about. That *guedra* dance, where the woman starts out kneeling, hidden completely under a black veil.

Pretty soon, her fingers are swaying to the music and, from there, it's anything goes. Before long, everyone is dancing the *ahaidous*, beating the ground rhythmically together in a circle. I won't have it! Not in my neighborhood, dammit.

The way I see it, if you want to go bangy-bangy on your goatskin-topped wooden *taarija* drum, go back to Morocco. This is America, land of the Dallas Cowboys, John Wayne, and barbecued ribs. We don't cotton to that kind of stuff around here.

Nothing, though, is worse than that incense wafting over the fence. When you smell that, you know exactly what's going on over there behind those walls. They're doing that crazy religious stuff, what with the dancing and the singing and the instruments. Damn Sufis. That's just what this country needs: more Gnostic sympathizers going on about *tawakkul*, the total reliance on God, and *dhikr*, the perpetual remembrance of God.

We could move, I suppose, but it probably wouldn't do any good. My brother lives over on the east side of town, and he's having the same problem with the Inuits. No place is safe these days, I tell you. ✐

COKE from page 61

that I would like a lot of Coke," Linda Stepnoski of Cincinnati said. "For the last 13 years, I've been working on a mechanism to funnel Coke into larger containers. I had to quit my job to do this, but it was worth it. Now, with the new size, Coke does all the work for

> **"I like Coke a lot, so it would follow that I would like a lot of Coke," Linda Stepnoski of Cincinnati said.**

me. I'll be able to get my old job back!"

The new 30-liter Coke even has its own name. After considering "Coka-Munga" and "The Shitload," executives settled on "Family Size."

An extensive promotional campaign for the new size is also in the works, with plans to exhume the corpse of wrestling legend Andre The Giant for use as the product's spokesman. If Andre is chosen, Coca-Cola will reanimate him in the same laboratories where the company's top brass is cloned.

"Ve velcome zees challenge," head Coca-Cola scientist Günther Brauerhauer said. ✐

## WHAT DO YOU THINK?

# Too Sexy Too Soon?

**A new wave of teen pop princesses, including Britney Spears and Christina Aguilera, are drawing fire from parents who say they present inappropriately sexualized images to girls who look up to them. What do *you* think?**

**Ben Manwell**
**Forklift Operator**

"I think it's terrible when 16-year-old girls dress up in belly-baring tank tops and tight little skirts. Jailbait cock-teasers."

**James Reul**
**Histopathologist**

"When I was a teen, things weren't like they are today. We had to use our imaginations to picture Petula Clark naked."

**Bob Van Eeghen**
**Lawyer**

"It was entirely inappropriate for Britney Spears to wear that see-through Catholic schoolgirl outfit in my masturbation fantasy last night."

**Jerome Koepp**
**Systems Analyst**

"Teenagers shouldn't have constant access to sexual images on MTV. They should jerk off to nudie magazines hidden under their mattresses like a normal person."

**Janet Schnorr**
**Family Therapist**

"These teen singers send young girls the message that if they dress and act provocatively, they will meet with approval from males and go farther in life. How ridiculous."

**Lynn Phelan**
**Nurse's Aide**

"Kids aren't growing up too fast. My 10-year-old daughter loves Britney Spears, and I trust her not to go all the way with her live-in boyfriend."

## Actor-Comedian Pauly Shore Bad At 32

see PEOPLE page 2C

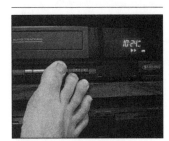

## VCR Fast-Forwarded With Toe

see TELEVISION page 3B

## *Cosmopolitan* Offers 15 Tips For Fattening Up For Winter

see MEDIA page 9E

## Justice Department: 'Want To See A Dead Body?'

see WASHINGTON page 3A

### STATshot

A look at the numbers that shape your world.

**Top-Selling Fetish Magazines**

1. *Communion Waifs*
2. *Stumpfuckers*
3. *Field & Balls*
4. *Septuagenitalia*
5. *Asian Asthmatics*
6. *Cocks In Socks*
7. *Lumberjills*
8. *Turnip Rider*
9. *Sunnyville Coupon Shopper*
10. *Chicks With Leukemia*

THE ONION
$2.00 US
$3.00 CAN

0 74470 94595 6

# the ONION ®

WWW.THEONION.COM    AMERICA'S FINEST NEWS SOURCE™    FOUNDED 1871

# Area Man Confounded By Buffet Procedure

ERIE, PA—Area resident Don Turnbee was "completely bewildered" by standard buffet protocol at the East Frontage Road Ponderosa Steakhouse, sources close to the 37-year-old eater reported Sunday.

Turnbee, who ordinarily relies on Burger King, McDonald's, and other fast-food establishments for his nutritional needs, was confused by procedures regarding Ponderosa's "$6.99 Grand Dinner Buffet." Among his uncertainties: when to pay for the meal, which food items he had unlimited access to, whether soft-drink refills were free, and whether to move around the various serving stations in a clockwise or counterclockwise direction.

see BUFFET page 64

Above: Erie, PA, eater Don Turnbee.

# Dolphins Evolve Opposable Thumbs

Above: One of the evolved dolphins, whose opposable thumbs have struck fear in the hearts of humankind.

## 'Oh, Shit,' Says Humanity

HONOLULU—In an announcement with grave implications for the primacy of the species of man, marine biologists at the Hawaii Oceanographic Institute reported Sunday that dolphins, or family Delphinidae, have evolved opposable thumbs on their pectoral fins.

"I believe I speak for the entire human race when I say, 'Holy fuck,'" said Oceanographic Institute director Dr. James Aoki, noting that the dolphin has a cranial capacity 40 percent greater than that of humans. "That's it for us monkeys."

Aoki strongly urged humans, especially those living near the sea, to

see DOLPHINS page 65

# Senate Candidate Drops Out Of Race Due To Shyness

KNOXVILLE, TN—Donald Miller, a Democratic candidate for the U.S. Senate from Tennessee, is dropping out of the race due to an inability to overcome his natural shyness, campaign manager Bruce Gilson announced Sunday.

"After much contemplation, Donald has decided it would be best if he ended his campaign," said Gilson, speaking to reporters in front of Miller's Knoxville home. "During his run, Donald tried very hard to overcome his discomfort with social situations and his fear of speaking in front of crowds, especially people he doesn't know very well. But in the end, he just couldn't."

"Though he continues to care deeply about the people of Tennessee and the national political dis-

see CANDIDATE page 64

Right: Donald Miller, who dropped out of the Tennessee Senate race Sunday, reluctantly steps to the podium at a December 1999 rally.

"There was a lot of different stuff you had to know," Turnbee said. "I wasn't sure if I was doing it right."

Ponderosa patrons reported seeing Turnbee wander aimlessly through the restaurant's all-you-can-eat buffet area, which features more than 75 choices of hot and cold appetizers, salad items, fresh fruits, and pasta, as well as a "No Stopping The Toppings" sundae bar.

"It's pretty confusing. They need to put up some signs explaining how everything works," Turnbee said. "At Taco Bell, at least they have railings so you know where to walk."

According to Ponderosa cashier Liz Rutt, Turnbee was disoriented from the moment he walked in the door.

"He was looking up at the big menu for, like, 10 minutes and then went over by the window for a while, just looking really lost," Rutt said. "Finally, I was like, 'Can I help you? You need to order before you can be seated.'"

Once seated in a booth, Turnbee waited for a server to bring him a plate for the buffet. Finally, after 10 minutes, he approached a server from another section, who informed him that plates were located next to the buffet and that he could "go ahead whenever you're ready."

More confusion awaited Turnbee at the buffet itself. "There was a big table with vegetables and mashed potatoes and all that, but then there were these other little sections off to the side with soup and Mexican food and desserts," Turnbee said. "I know at Wendy's you have to pay extra for the soup and potato bar, so I didn't know for sure which things I could have."

"I tried to watch what other people were taking," he added, "but I wasn't sure if they'd gotten the same buffet deal as me or if they'd gotten some other deal that gave them special access to that stuff."

Above: Turnbee works on his fifth plate.

Turnbee eventually found an elderly woman near the macaroni salad and asked her which items he could eat.

"She told me I could have as much as I wanted of anything in the whole buffet area," Turnbee said. "I was really happy about that, because there were a lot of things I wanted that I thought I couldn't get. Like the tacos."

But even after determining what he was permitted to eat, Turnbee continued to struggle. Uncertain "what food went with what," Turnbee's first trip to the buffet resulted in a plateful of spaghetti covered in nacho-cheese sauce, a taco dressed with cottage cheese, and fish wedges dipped in lentil soup.

Though not confirmed as of press time, it is also believed that Turnbee topped a Sloppy Joe sandwich with several large dollops of sour cream.

More trouble came when Turnbee made his first return trip to the buffet. While serving himself buffalo wings, he drew disapproving glares from other buffet patrons before noticing a sign reading, "Please Take A Clean Plate Before Each Trip To The Buffet!"

"They put that sign in a really hard-to-see place," Turnbee said. "It's right by the clean plates, so the only way you'd see is if you were already getting a clean plate, anyway."

Among Turnbee's other violations of Ponderosa buffet protocol: grabbing rolls without using the provided plastic tongs, using a soup bowl for his ice cream, spilling shredded carrots into the garbanzo beans, and letting the rice pilaf's cover fall into the alfredo sauce.

"The whole time, I really tried to be careful," Turnbee said. "Like, I didn't know if I could cut in by the hot bar, so I just waited in line through all the salad items just to get at the macaroni and cheese way down at the end. But even still, I wound up making all these mistakes. It's a really confusing set-up."

Architect Randall Kouris, who in 1986 drafted the dining-area plan now standard in all Ponderosa restaurants, stood behind his design, insisting that the series of smaller buffet islands is not intended to confuse guests but to create a homier, "less cafeteria-ish" atmosphere.

"After extensive tests, it was clear that restaurant patrons found this layout much easier to navigate than the traditional, cafeteria-style buffet with a single island," Kouris said. "I am truly sorry that Mr. Turnbee had problems with our set-up, but, as I said, most Ponderosa patrons seem to greatly prefer it."

Despite Turnbee's difficulties, Ponderosa officials expressed confidence that he could eventually master the intricacies of the restaurant's buffet.

"The problems Mr. Turnbee encountered are simply the result of unfamiliarity, and I believe it is well within his capabilities to acclimate himself to our system," said Larry Chenoweth, manager of the East Frontage Road Ponderosa. "I would urge Mr. Turnbee to give us another chance and find out just how great the Ponderosa dining experience can be."

Turnbee said it is doubtful he will become a regular customer of the chain.

"The food was really good, and I got a lot for my money, but it's just too complicated," he said. "I think I'm going to stick with Burger King and McDonald's." ∅

course," Gilson continued, "Donald has told me to tell you he thinks it would be better if a more confident, outgoing, attractive person represented Tennessee in the U.S. Senate."

Added Gilson: "If you ask me, I think Donald is just being silly. He's a great guy if you get to know him, with a heck of a lot to offer constituents. And I really think he was starting to come out of his shell. But this is Donald's decision, and we need to respect it."

As Gilson spoke, Miller could periodically be seen peeking at the gathered assemblage from behind his living-room curtains. When a photographer noticed him and tried to take his picture, Miller darted away from the window.

Miller, a lawyer who worked in the Tennessee attorney general's office from 1991 to 1997, announced his Senate bid last September at The Hungry Caterpillar, a Knoxville used bookstore he frequents. He was surrounded by campaign staffers, all of whom were either immediate family members or close friends.

"Aside from the occasional stammering and the moment he read the same line twice, I thought he did terrific," said Miller 2000 co-chair Angela DeSoto, a friend of Miller's since their mid-'70s law-school days. "But, of course, he didn't think so. That night, he didn't even want to watch his announcement on the local news, saying that he hates the way his lower lip sticks out when he talks. The next day, when he saw his picture on the front page of the paper, he was mortified. He was like, 'I didn't know they were going to put my picture on the cover! I'm sweating, and my nose is bright red. And why did I pick that dumb tie? I look awful.'"

Continued DeSoto: "He was the same way when he heard one of his ads on the radio. 'My voice is so whiny and high-pitched,' he said. 'How could anyone take me seriously?' And so on. We'd try to persuade him that people took him seriously, and that he was extremely smart and capable. But the more we tried to convince him, the more he'd doubt it."

Above: Miller shuffles his feet and mutters during a Feb. 17 campaign stop in Johnson City.

Richard Upchurch, a political-science professor at the University of Tennessee, said Miller's shyness clearly damaged his chances in the election.

"It wasn't until two months into his campaign that he finally went out on the road to meet the voters," Upchurch said. "He said he knew he couldn't get **see CANDIDATE page 65**

# Giant Cockroach In Bathroom 'A Harrowing, Kafkaesque Experience,' Grad Student Says

NEW YORK—A routine toothbrushing turned into a profound exercise in nightmarish, existential horror Sunday, when poverty-stricken Columbia University graduate student Marc Edelstein, 24, came across "the most gigantic cockroach this side of Gregor Samsa" in the bathroom of his one-room, walk-up efficiency.

"It was terrifying," Edelstein told colleagues at the Ivy League university's English department shortly after the encounter with the giant cockroach. "Every day, I can't believe I am living in that apartment. The humiliations society forces me to undergo, just to get my stupid Ph.D, defy all rational, intellectual thought. Sometimes, when I wake up in the morning and see the squalor in which I live, it feels as if I've somehow found myself on trial before a group of faceless, bureaucratic agents for some horrible crime I didn't commit, and no one will even explain to me what my crime was."

Edelstein, whose combined rent and tuition far exceed his meager earnings from work-study grants and a part-time job as a teaching assistant, has struggled with an insect problem ever since moving into the 108th Street and Broadway apartment in the fall of 1997.

Edelstein called the cockroach "a

Above: Columbia grad student Marc Edelstein.

deeply disturbing symbol of the alienation and pain seemingly inherent in every aspect of modern grad-student life." What's worse, he said, the enormous insect so paralyzed him with "intense, soul-searing fear" that he was unable to kill it before it escaped down the drain.

"This wretched, prehistoric creature," Edelstein said, "has survived to torment me anew another day—a day of reckoning that, although I know in see COCKROACH page 66

CANDIDATE from page 64

his message out to the people if he just stayed at home, but that's the only place he truly felt at ease."

Miller's actions during campaign stops worsened matters. He frequently concluded speeches with, "Vote for me, I guess." During a visit to a Murfreesboro high school, Miller shuffled his feet and stared at his hands as students attempted to ask him about his stance on various issues, answering questions in a barely audible whisper. While responding to a query about abortion, Miller lost his composure and said he had to go to the bathroom to wash his hands. He was missing for more than an hour until it was discovered that he had escaped through a window and was hiding on the campaign bus.

Despite his bashfulness, Miller was getting through to segments of the electorate. According to a poll taken just one week before he dropped out of the race, 75 percent of registered female Democrats favored him.

"He just seemed so sweet and vulnerable," said Liz Oswald of Pulaski. "Everywhere he went, he was always so tongue-tied, you just wanted to wrap him up and put him in your pocket. It's really a shame he dropped

out, because Tennessee could use such a sensitive, caring man in Washington."

"Don wasn't some charismatic, smooth-talking slickster, and he sure took his lumps for it," Gilson said. "It takes him a little while to get comfortable with people, and in a 12-month race, there's simply not enough time to do that, especially when you're talking about five million voters. I don't know, maybe if we'd gotten him on Paxil."

Later that day, a reporter phoned a housebound Miller and asked if he was considering seeking psychiatric help to combat his shyness.

"I didn't just drop out because of shyness," Miller said. "I mean, that was one part of it, but there were other things, too. I think my cats missed me, and the leaves were starting to fall off my aralia plant. I think people sometimes make too much of my shyness. I mean, not to contradict Bruce, who's been really good to me—he did make that speech for me this morning, and I told him what to say—it's just that, well, it's hard to explain. I..."

Miller's voice trailed off and, after approximately 10 seconds of silence, he hung up. ✐

DOLPHINS from page 63

Above: A primitive ax crafted out of driftwood and shell that is believed to be the handiwork of dolphins.

learn to communicate using a system of clicks and whistles in a frequency range of 4 to 150 kHz. He also encouraged humans to "start practicing their echolocation as soon as possible."

Delphinologists have reported more than 7,000 cases of spontaneous opposable-digit manifestation in the past two weeks alone, with "thumbs" observed on the bottle-nosed dolphin, the Atlantic humpback dolphin, and even the rare Ganges River dolphin.

"It appears to be species-wide," said dolphin specialist Clifford Brees of the Kewalo Basin Marine Mammal Laboratory, speaking from the shark cage he welded shut around himself late Sunday. "And it may be even worse: We haven't exactly been eager to check for thumbs on other marine mammals belonging to the order of cetaceans, such as the killer whale. Oh, Christ, we're really in the soup now."

Thus far, all the opposable digits encountered appear to be fully functional, making it possible for dolphins—believed to be capable of faster and more complex cogitation than man—to manipulate objects, fashion tools, and construct rudimentary pulley and lever systems.

"They really seem to be making up for lost time with this thumb thing," said Dr. Jim Kuczaj, a University of California–San Diego biologist who has studied the seasonal behavior of dolphins for more than 30 years. "Last Friday, a crude seaweed-and-shell abacus washed up on the beach near Hilo, Hawaii. The next day, a far more sophisticated abacus, fashioned from some unknown material and capable of calculating equations involving numbers of up to 16 digits, washed up on the same beach. The day after that, the beach was littered with what turned out to be coral-silicate and kelp-based biomicrocircuitry."

"My God," Kuczaj added. "What are

they doing down there?"

It is unknown what precipitated the dolphins' spontaneous development of opposable thumbs. Some dolphin behaviorists believe that the gentle marine mammal, pushed to the brink by humanity's reckless pollution and exploitation of the sea, tapped into some previously unmined mental powers to generate a thumb-like appendage. However, given that 95 per-

## Thus far, all the opposable digits encountered appear to be fully functional.

cent of the world's dolphin experts have committed suicide since learning of the development, the full story may never be known.

"You must believe, sleek ocean masters, that many of us homo sapiens weep with shame and disgust over the degradation to which our species has subjected our All-Mother, the Great World-Sea," read the suicide note of Dr. Richard Morse, a Brisbane, Australia, delphinologist and regular contributor to Marine Mammal Science. "If you are reading this, I estimate that it is the day we know as Sept. 3, 2000. Please be decent and kind masters to our poor ape-race. Oh, God, I'm so sorry about the tracking collars."

"Scientists once wondered whether dolphins, with their remarkably advanced social and language structures, are actually smarter than we are," said Aoki, ushering reporters out of the laboratory he claimed "will either be a smoking hole or a zoo exhibit in the coming Dolphin Age."

"Well, we're not wondering anymore." ✐

# Lack Of Second Car Preserves Marriage

## World Gets First-Ever Look Inside Greenspan Fantasy Ranch

CHICKASAW, AL—Though they've weathered some rocky times during their five-year marriage, Dale and Sheila Hefko have managed to stay together. The couple's secret? Their lack of a second car.

"This marriage hasn't exactly worked out like I'd expected, but we're determined to stick it out," Dale said. "At least until I get my own car so I can still get around."

"So long as we've only got one car between us," Dale continued, "ain't nobody's going nowhere."

Sheila expressed a similar determination to preserve their sacred union, held together by the used 1990 Ford Escort she and Dale bought for $3,100 in 1995.

"Last Friday, when I found out about Dale and [neighbor] Rhonda [Geilstead], I was gonna kick him out of the house for good," Sheila said. "But I knew he'd take off in the car if I did, and I had to go to the dentist in Mobile on Saturday. I wasn't about to wait two months for a new appointment, so I didn't even bring the Rhonda thing up."

Despite their difficulties, the Hefkos realize that divorce is not to be taken lightly.

"Even if the court says I get the car," Sheila said, "I can't take it, because then he don't have no way to get to work, and he gets fired and I don't get child support."

Also factoring into the one-car couple's decision to stay together are their children, Jesse, 4, and Naomi, 1.

"If it weren't for the kids, maybe we wouldn't still be married," Sheila said. "But as it is, I need to get them to the babysitter's and the doctor, and I've

Above: Dale and Sheila Hefko and the car that holds them together.

got to get to the Piggly Wiggly over in Prichard for baby food and diapers. Take all that away, and I'm doing a whole lot less driving."

The car is also needed to transport Dale and Sheila to their respective jobs, as well as to get Dale to his monthly meeting with his parole officer. Sheila described a typical day: "At around 8 a.m., I drop Jesse off at Kidcare, then I take Naomi over to one of my friends, usually Bobbie or Angie, because Kidcare won't take Naomi until she's 2. Then I wake up Dale, and he drops me off at my waitressing job at the Toot Toot Steak House, then he heads off to the screen-door factory for second shift."

Surprisingly, it was Dale and Sheila's mutual need for a roommate, not a car, that brought them together.

"When I dropped out of high school, my mom kicked me out of the house, so I was just sleeping on people's couches until I could find a place," Sheila said. "Then, when I started messing around with Dale, he said he'd dump his girlfriend if I moved in and picked up her rent. After a few months I got pregnant, so we got married."

Five years later, the pair is still together.

"It's damn near impossible to find a cheap car that isn't gonna end up costing more to fix than what you paid for it," said Dale, who regularly scans the classified ads and visits used-car lots. "See, when you're buying a car, you've got to think of things in terms of the long run. When you sign your name on that title, that car's yours, for better or for worse." Ø

YORBA LINDA, CA—In Sunday's exclusive, first-ever peek inside the fabled estate, CNNfn cameras were allowed onto the grounds of Fiscalypso, Federal Reserve chair Alan Greenspan's palatial Yorba Linda fantasy ranch. Greeting CNNfn reporter Dan Grentsch in a purple fur coat and Speedo swim trunks, the reclusive financial genius gave a guided tour of the 200-room mansion, pointing out such sights as his ruby-encrusted stock ticker, his rotating dollar-sign-shaped waterbed, and the "Love Hut," a shag-carpeted, warehouse-sized room stocked with nubile virgins from each of the seven major industrialized nations.

## NAACP Demands Less Minority Representation On UPN

BALTIMORE—Decrying the strong presence of African Americans on programs such as *Malcolm & Eddie*, *Shasta*, and *The Parkers*, NAACP president Kweisi Mfume called Sunday for a significant reduction in minority representation on UPN. "We must step up pressure on this network to decrease the visibility of our people," said Mfume, addressing the NAACP's Board Of Directors. "America is just 13 percent black, yet on these crappy shows, we make up a full 85 percent. This is utterly unacceptable." Mfume then called for a boycott of UPN until the network "severely underrepresents us." Ø

COCKROACH from page 65

my heart is soon to come, I am nonetheless powerless to prevent."

The doctoral candidate is no stranger to hardship. In March 1999, Edelstein called his part-time job at the hot-dog eatery Gray's Papaya "a vision of underpaid, overworked, meat-flinging degradation and brutality that I dare say would not be out of place within the pages of Upton Sinclair's *The Jungle*." Despite mounting student-loan debts, Edelstein quit the food-service job in August 1999 in "a vitriolic burst of invective and abuse rivaling the most impassioned deliverances of Alexander Pope."

Edelstein has also suffered "innumerable indignities" at the hands of his landlord, Randy Bosio, whom the tortured scholar described to his dissertation advisor as "a fetid, shambling, coin-rattling wraith of a man who brings to mind one of the more unsavory, shadow-dwelling denizens of Dickensian London." On other occasions, Edelstein has likened his landlord to one of the nightmarish "Mugwump" creatures from William

S. Burroughs' *Naked Lunch*, claiming that Bosio's sole directive is "to attach himself to the flesh of the innocent and suck them dry."

Said Bosio: "Something about that kid just ain't right. Once, I let myself into his apartment when he wasn't home, just to fix the sink, and when he got back and found me there, he accused me of 'an Orwellian invasion of individual privacy,' whatever that meant."

Edelstein's woes were compounded last October, when his eight-month relationship with Meredith Astor, the 26-year-old daughter of prominent New York arts patrons James and Patricia Astor, ended in a devastating breakup, prompted by Meredith's shame over Edelstein's low social standing.

"It was your basic F. Scott Fitzgerald situation," said Edelstein officemate Howard Underwood, who started dating Astor shortly after the split. "After Meredith left him, he plunged into a turbulent maelstrom of drink and despair. Every night was a nonstop par-

ty, a denial-fueled attempt to escape the inevitable collapse of the artificial world he had created for himself, masking his inner desperation and decay under a superficial veneer of false, empty revelry."

"I had to start picking up some of his T.A. hours because he wasn't showing up for discussion section," said Underwood, who will marry Astor in June. "Pathetic, really, much like the eventual fall of the gilded, faux opulence of the Jazz Age."

"Meredith's WASP-y, socialite, upper-crust parents never approved of me," Edelstein said. "Tight-lipped, goyish, Edith Wharton archetypes. I know she never would have left me if it weren't for the mannered, insufferable manipulations of her high-society family. Hello? The novel of manners has long since been supplanted as a reflection of prevailing social mores, people!"

After enduring such "infernal, Dantean torments of the soul," Edelstein said the cockroach incident was "the last straw," prompting him to decide to

leave Columbia.

"That's it. After staring down at the writhing legs of that foul, accursed insect, I felt the horror of the void permeating my being to its deepest core, and I realized I cannot go on here at Columbia," Edelstein told his mother during a long-distance collect call shortly after his run-in with the cockroach. "I'm transferring to the University of Mississippi. Flannery O'Connor says a good man is hard to find? Well, a good graduate program is hard to find! I know I said I'd never do it, and that if I had to live in a horrible redneck cesspool of a state like Mississippi, I'd become so estranged from my surroundings that I'd end up like that Eudora Welty character who lives at the post office, but I've had it with New York. I can't go on."

"I'm giving up. Do you hear me, O cold, unfeeling universe?" shouted Edelstein, standing atop his building's roof. "You've won, you impenetrable void of utter meaninglessness! You have destroyed me at last!"

"The horror... the horror..." he added. Ø

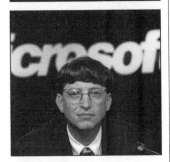

## Evil Genius Gates Drops Windows 98 Into NYC Water Supply

see COMPUTING page 7C

## Report: TV Helps Build Valuable Looking Skills

see EDUCATION page 1D

## Greenspan Tattoos 'Fed Life' Across Abdomen

see NATION page 6A

## Magical Girlfriend Transmutes Guilt Into Precious Stones

see RELATIONSHIPS page 5C

## Drugs: Are Any Around?

See LIFESTYLE page 3E

### STATshot

A look at the numbers that shape your world.

**What Are Those Sports Guys On The Shop-At-Home Network Yelling About This Week?**

1. Gem-mint '85 Topps Mark McGwire Olympic Team rookie card
2. 1999 Upper Deck Series 2 factory-sealed box
3. Limited-edition John Elway Super Bowl XXXIII lithograph
4. Michael Jordan Starting Lineup retirement figurine
5. Autographed '98 Donruss Elite Gold Derek Jeter

---

# the ONION®

WWW.THEONION.COM          AMERICA'S FINEST NEWS SOURCE™          FOUNDED 1871

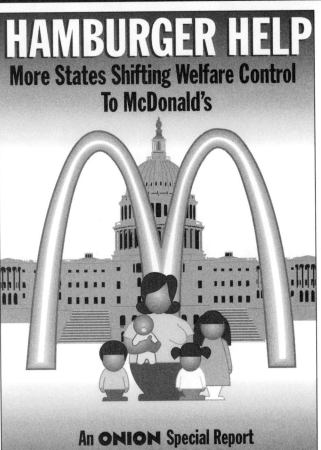

# HAMBURGER HELP
## More States Shifting Welfare Control To McDonald's

### An ONION Special Report

CHICAGO—For the past four years, the first of the month meant one thing to Chicago single mother LaTonya Mitchell: It was the day she could cash her monthly welfare check for $618—barely enough to cover her own expenses, much less purchase clothes, school supplies, and double cheeseburgers for her five children.

But all that changed on Oct. 20, 1997. In a welfare-privatization experiment closely watched across America, the Illinois legislature approved a bill to radically revamp the state's AFDC system and transfer welfare control to the McDonald's Corporation, giving Mitchell and 712,000 other Illinois residents living below the poverty line "a well-deserved break today."

According to Illinois Gov. Jim Edgar, the partnership between fast food and public assistance makes solid sense.

see WELFARE page 69

---

# Sea-Going Turtle Under Fire For Egg Abandonment

Above: The only known photo of the suspect, who allegedly swam off after leaving her six unborn children on a Florida beach.

OCALA, FL—State welfare agencies expressed outrage Monday upon discovering that a local sea turtle had "deliberately and recklessly abandoned" her six unborn children on an Ocala beach last Thursday.

"This kind of behavior is shocking and inexcusable," said Peter Hume, director of the Florida Division of Youth and Family Services (FDYFS). "To deposit one's own children in the sand and expect them to autonomously hatch after a two- to three-week incubation period, instinctively crawl to the ocean, and immediately begin using their flippers as fully functioning locomotive devices in the quest for aquatic vegetation—it boggles the mind. It's almost inhuman."

The eggs, which appeared "weathered and malnourished" upon discovery, have been placed in foster care. State authorities have asked the Coast Guard to help in their search for the unidentified mother, who animal-behavior experts believe is still in

see TURTLE page 68

---

# Posters Of Naked Women Fail To Draw Real Naked Women To Dorm Room

MANHATTAN, KS—A trio of posters depicting scantily clad women, hung recently in a Kansas State University dorm room, have had "little to no effect" in facilitating the presence of actual naked women in that room.

The posters, manufactured by alcoholic-beverage companies as promotional items, were intended to establish a fun, party-like atmosphere in which the presence of naked women would be encouraged. Their actual effect, however, has been "minimal if not nonexistent," a KSU housing-department study found.

"The thinking was that

see POSTERS page 68

Above: KSU freshmen Chad Durham (left) and Kurt Beame.

these posters would set a tone," freshman Chad Durham said. "We enjoy beer here in room 508 of Sellery Hall West, and we share an equally enthusiastic interest in naked women. We thought that by combining the two elements, these posters would establish not only a mood of beer-drinking fun, but also one of casual female nudity. Or, at the very least, semi-nudity."

"Our idea was to create an environment in which nude or semi-nude women would find themselves comfortable and at ease, not only drinking beer, but also being naked," Durham added. "We also sort of hoped they might have sex with us."

"None of these things have happened," he added. "It would appear that our theories were wrong."

The housing-department study, compiled over the course of three weeks of monitoring the dorm room and its immediate surroundings, concluded that "there exists no measurable causal relationship between the presence of naked-women posters and the willingness of actual, non-photographic human women to appear naked in or near that location."

The study also asserted that no causal relationship exists between the number of naked women in the room before and after the decision to acquire the posters, other than the fact that in both cases the number was zero.

"I can't understand it," roommate Kurt Beame said. "We had it all planned out, and I just can't see where we went wrong. Perhaps we need to know more about women in general, clothed and unclothed alike, before we can accurately predict the behavior of the nude ones, specifically."

In a surprising side note, the study did find the posters to have a significant impact on alcohol sales, causing a sharp rise in consumption of the brands depicted on them. Sales of the wine cooler that sponsored the largest-breasted model's photo rose 35 percent.

One reason for the roommates' enthusiasm was their previous success with other posters.

"Everybody liked the Miller Lite poster and the Bud Dry neon sign," Beame said. "And they did, in fact, seem to be effective in facilitating a bar-like, drinking-oriented dorm interior."

"Similarly encouraging results came from the decision to display our 'Rockin' USA' poster," continued Beame, noting that the poster, which depicted a guitar rocketing into the air with an American flag in the background, had indeed made the place seem substantially more "rockin'."

"Unfortunately, the technique does not seem to have any effect on glamorous, product-endorsing models," Beame said. "In fact, the only effect so far has been that we get real horned up when we look at them. Jesus Christ Almighty, get a load of that rack. Man." Ø

Above: One of the six abandoned infants now in state custody.

the area.

Stephen Varga, a frequent beachcomber in the Ocala area, witnessed the mother's act of negligence.

"She waddled inland along the shore 200 to 300 yards or so," Varga said, "and I remember thinking how suspicious the whole thing looked, the way she used her hind feet to carefully dig a shallow, gourd-shaped depression in a secluded section of coast, far removed from possible predatory attacks by terns, ospreys, or other sea birds. It gave me chills."

Varga said he considered contacting Family Services but ultimately decided he "didn't want to get involved."

The eggs were discovered by lifeguards Sunday after one of the babies was heard using the vestigial egg-tooth on its snout to aid in the delicate process of breaking its hardened, leathery casing. A flipper-print found by police on one of the shells identified the mother as an Atlantic ridley, or *lepidochelys kem-pi*, widely regarded as the most neglectful and ill-fit of all sea turtles.

If caught and found guilty, the mother turtle could face up to 30 years in prison.

One adult female tern, speaking on condition of anonymity, said she was acquainted with the fugitive turtle.

"I'm very surprised she would do something like this," the tern said. "The last time I saw her, she was already pregnant, and she seemed to be very excited about the birth: Her salt-excreting glands were working hard to ensure a fully desalinized in-vitro environment, her carapace had softened to facilitate easy cross-sand negotiation—that kind of thing."

The incident is the latest in a series of disturbing occurrences involving Florida amphibians and reptiles. On May 4, a shingleback lizard was sentenced to six months in jail for what Broward County judge Raymond Voss called "repeated and willful indifference" toward its babies. More notoriously, last April, more than 1,400 treefrog ova were eaten or fell off the branches of a Clearwater-area jonquil tree after being abandoned by their parents, who, like so many of the mothers and fathers in these cases, were no longer together.

"Sadly, there are a lot of 'serial parents' out there in the amphibious community who are having kids and then breaking up," Hume said. "Themselves raised in a non-nurturing, non-family environment, they in turn are ill-equipped to provide their own eggs with a caring, stable home."

"It's very easy to blame the turtles' dwindling numbers on human beings, who value them for their shells, hide, meat, and oil," said Hume, noting that five of the world's six known species of sea turtles are endangered. "But the truth is, with the exception of the green sea-turtle, *chelonia mydas*, the sea-turtles are dying because of a terrible erosion of family values, a problem rampant throughout society as a whole." Ø

## NEWS IN BRIEF

### Pizza Hut Employee Still Hanging Around After Shift

DYERSBURG, TN—Pizza Hut employee Larry Peete, 24, continued to hang around the restaurant for nearly an hour after his shift ended Monday. "He was just hovering around the lobby, making small talk with me and Jeff," said coworker Debbie Rust, who was operating the front register at the time. "Then he wandered over to the prep area and started talking to Duane. I was like, 'Why are you still here, Larry? Your shift is over.'"

### Tina Yothers Fantasy Camp Files For Bankruptcy

HIBBING, MN—After three years of heavy financial losses, the Tina Yothers Fantasy Camp filed for Chapter 11 bankruptcy Monday. The camp, which enabled Yothers fans to fulfill their dreams by performing scenes from *Family Ties*, dressing up like an actual L.A. Laker Girl, and socializing with former Yothers co-star Michael Gross, got off to a shaky start in 1994, when only one customer paid $800 to attend the two-week camp. "We are deeply disappointed by the public's lukewarm reaction to the camp," director Edward Borowicz said. "Frankly, it's baffling." The camp's owners are hoping to recoup their financial losses with a series of Esther Rolle-themed luxury cruises. Ø

"As hard as the government has tried, the reality is, McDonald's better understands and is better equipped to meet the needs of America's poor than the outdated federal welfare bureaucracy," Edgar said. "McDonald's deals with millions of unskilled, destitute people every day—it feeds them, employs them, clothes them, and gives them shelter in its spacious, sanitary seating areas."

Edgar said McDonald's will provide those living below the poverty line with a number of benefits each month, including a cash stipend, a book of 25 McFood Stamps redeemable for Big Macs and other sandwich items, immunization for children, and, for pregnant mothers, collectible *Flubber* cups.

Felix Melanson, McDonaldland Secretary of Health and Human Services, said those with dependents will also receive special scratch-and-win welfare game pieces.

"Here at McDonald's, we strongly believe that poor people deserve a chance," Melanson said. "And we give them just that—a one-in-three chance to win great prizes like soft drinks, official NBA game gear, trips to Disney World, and a grand prize of a free McMedicard, good for an entire year's worth of subsidized, low-cost healthcare."

McDonaldAid recipients will also be provided with on-site day care for their children. By March 1998, Melanson said, every location will be equipped with a McDonald's Playland, enabling single mothers like Mitchell to look for a job while their children are looked after in a safe, cashier-supervised play area.

"Welfare recipients deserve the same secure, reliable day care for their children that other parents enjoy," Melanson said. "That's why we've made sure that all Playlands are situated in full view of the registers."

According to Melanson, what makes the new, privatized system different is its emphasis on "personal responsibility and self-help." Recipients, he said, "will be required to work up to five hours a week and attend job-training instructional-video presentations in order to remain eligible for McDonaldAid."

Welfare recipients' duties will include light lifting, cup and straw restock, and mopping. Further, all recipients who use the bathroom will be required to wash their hands thoroughly before returning to work.

"The idea here is independence, not dependence," Melanson said. "This is not a handout: These folks will be responsible for everything from refilling ketchup dispensers to busing their own tables when they're done eating. They are also responsible for keeping their own uniforms clean and presentable."

While the Illinois privatization plan has been widely praised by many welfare-reform advocates, it is not without its detractors. According to state Sen. James Ory (R-Carbondale), the

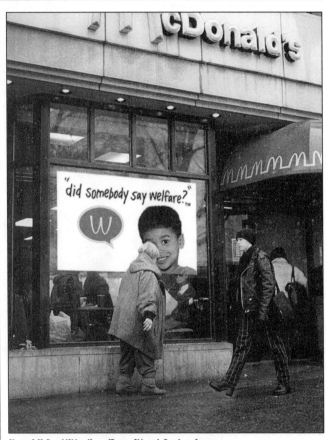

Above: A McDonaldAid welfare office on Chicago's Dearborn Avenue.

delicious taste of McDonald's food will encourage many to remain on McDonaldAid rather than look for jobs.

"We need to provide incentives for people to get off welfare. This food does just the opposite," said Ory, co-sponsor of a bill setting a six-piece cap on McNuggets orders for welfare recipients and limiting them to sweet-and-sour sauce only. "Those who are not interested in finding work will take advantage, feeding off the system and its tasty cheeseburgers and fries."

Responding to Ory, McDonald's officials asserted that a number of deterrents have been built into the new system to prevent people from abusing it.

"We want to help people, but we don't want it to become a lifestyle," said Justin N. King, McDonaldland Secretary of Urban Affairs. "That's why one key feature of McDonaldAid is a strict 30-minute time limit on loitering in the seating area. While eating at McDonald's restaurants, welfare recipients will be expected to make an earnest effort to chew and swallow at all times. If they cease eating at any point during their stay or remain in the restaurant longer than the allotted 30-minute time limit, they will find themselves out on the street."

Further, to discourage recipients from bearing additional children just to receive extra food items, condiments will be removed from sandwiches on a sliding scale according to number of dependents. For example,

for those with five children, the second child's Big Mac will come without special sauce; the third child's without special sauce and lettuce; the fourth child's without special sauce, lettuce, and cheese; and the fifth child's without special sauce, lettuce, cheese, and pickles. Those with more than five children will be ineligible for even the onions and sesame-seed bun, receiving two all-beef patties only.

In addition, McDonaldAid recipients will not be eligible for refills once they have left the restaurant premises. "Ours is a strict 'one-visit-per-cup' refill policy," King said.

So far, the privatization experiment is proving successful. In 1996, the Illinois welfare system operated at a loss of $1.2 billion. But, since taking over welfare, McDonald's has operated at a surplus of $420 million in Illinois. Other states have taken notice, as well: Minnesota, Mississippi, Georgia, and Oregon are all considering similar fast-food-based welfare programs, and negotiations are already under way between California and El Pollo Loco.

But it is America's poor who stand to benefit the most.

"Before, I didn't have anything. Now I have a roof over my head, day care for my kids, and Quarter Pounders With Cheese every night," Chicago's Mitchell said. "Plus, my manager says I have potential, and that within six months, I can look forward to becoming part of the McDonald's team. For the first time, I actually have a future. This is *my* welfare system." Ø

# I Can't Seem To Find The Moline Gay District

By Lance Cuellar

As a gay man, whenever I'm in a new city, the first thing I do is seek out the gay district. Whether it's New York's Greenwich Village, The Castro in San Francisco, or Chicago's Boystown, a gay district has the stores, cafés, and clubs that fit my lifestyle. But I've been here in Moline for two whole days on business and, God help me, I can't find the Moline gay district anywhere.

I just don't get it. I've driven all over town with no luck at all. Where are the gay bars? The vintage-clothing shops? The lesbian book stores? I swear, it's like Moline is trying to keep the gay part of town a big secret. You have to be a regular queer Columbo to find a single upscale erotic-art gallery in Moline, much less an entire gay district.

My first stop was downtown, which I quickly redubbed Lametown. No vegan restaurants, no scented-candle shops—not so much as a single inverted pink triangle in a window. Only fast-food chains, auto-supply stores, and a Kmart. Can't get much straighter than that.

Convinced that I missed something, I scoured the entire downtown area again, this time with my gay-dar turned up a good three notches. Once again, nada. For a second, I thought I saw a rainbow flag, but it was just a sign in the window of a paint store.

It was time for drastic measures. I marched into Ray's Feed & Farm and asked if there were any thrift shops, massage parlors, or holistic pet-food stores nearby. Those farmers looked at me like I was balancing a Buick on my dick. After a few moments of awkward silence, one guy in a John Deere cap cleared his throat and directed me to Bridgewood Antiques. I thanked them for their help and got out of the store quickly. I hope I don't ever have any need for feed or farming supplies, because I don't think I'd want to go back in there any time soon.

After going through all that trouble, Bridgewood Antiques turned out to be a major bust. All they had were old magazines and Craftsman tools. No Shaker rocking chairs, no Japanese screens, no chintz drapes. What's worse, the customers were all just a bunch of gray-haired old grandmas. Where were the immaculately dressed gay professionals trying to see MOLINE page 70

## Senator Brings Obscene Material To National Attention

WASHINGTON, DC—Citing "the need to shield decent Americans from depraved filth such as this," U.S. Sen. Bob Smith (R-NH) brought the web site "Cum-Craving Sluttz" to national attention Monday. "This cyber-sewage features naked, hot-oiled young women engaging in such acts as fellatio, cunnilingus, rimming, fisting, and frottage," Smith said of the previously obscure site. "I pray for the day when wholesome, impressionable youths do not know that such vile smut exists, let alone are able to access it at http://www.vicecapades.com on their families' home computers during an unsupervised moment."

## Indian Teen Caught Playing Air Sitar

HYDERABAD, INDIA—Rajesh Gopalakrishnan, 15, was deeply embarrassed Monday when his sister and her friend barged in on him as he played air sitar in his room. "Don't you know how to knock?" said a red-faced Gopalakrishnan, who was caught sitting cross-legged in front of his mirror, imitating Ravi Shankar while the sitar god's classic 1973 *Ragas* album played loudly. "The door is closed for a reason! *Shiva*." Gopalakrishnan, who also ran his hands through his hair and mimed a ferocious tabla solo before being interrupted, later added: "Arundhati Shridhar, the girl to whom I am promised for marriage, just saw me acting like a fool. I'm so humiliated, I could move on to my next life."

## Hanes, Fruit Of The Loom Locked In Bitter Struggle No One Else Aware Of

NEW YORK—The ongoing rivalry between Hanes and Fruit Of The Loom, the nation's two largest manufacturers of underwear, has escalated into a bitter struggle for sales supremacy about which no one else on Earth knows, let alone cares, *The Wall Street Journal* reported Monday. "Apparently, in June of this year, Hanes introduced a new mid-length men's brief in response to a Fruit Of The Loom launch of a similar brief in May," *Wall Street Journal* reporter Leonard Dorner said. "And, from what I can gather, the careers of many executives at both companies are riding on the outcome of this epic mid-length-brief battle." Said Richmond, VA, underwear consumer Jonathan MacWilliams: "I guess I'm not really sure which brand I wear." ∅

# Five Or Six Dudes Jump Out Of Nowhere And Just Start Whaling On This One Guy

BOULDER, CO—Shock and disbelief were the prevailing reactions Monday, when pizza-delivery guy Lyle Kelso, 24, told roommates that at around 2 or 3 a.m., he personally witnessed, like, five or six dudes suddenly jump out of freakin' nowhere and just start totally whaling on this one guy.

"That is majorly messed-up," roommate "Thatches" Moynihan said. "You hear about that sort of shit on the news, but you never think it's going to happen right in front of somebody you know who'll later come home and totally tell you all about it. When Lyle told us, I was like, '*Whoa*, dude. That's harsh.' We all were. It sounded like some seriously wigged-out shit, from what Lyle was saying."

According to Moynihan, he and three other roommates were sitting around, just kicking back and watching TV, when Kelso burst into the room and breathlessly announced that "you guys are not gonna fucking believe what the fuck I just saw by the Dumpsters behind Papa Luigi's [Pizza]."

After a dramatic pause, the visibly agitated Kelso said, "I just saw some poor fucker completely get his ass beat down by a bunch of seriously pissed-off dudes," prompting responses ranging from "No way, man!" to "Holy shit, dude!"

According to this one guy who heard the story from a buddy of one of the roommates at a house party the next night, the scene supposedly went down something like this: Toward the end of his shift, Kelso sneaked out to the alleyway between Papa Luigi's and Fat Pete's Subs to fire up a big ol' jay. While smoking up, Kelso heard the sound of squealing tires from the parking lot behind Papa Luigi's. Fearing that it was the cops about to bust his ass, he peered around the corner to check out what the fuck was up. Kelso said he saw a black van, identified only by an airbrushed painting of a barbarian chick on the side and an enormous "Ozzy" sticker in the back window, suddenly pull up from out of nowhere, right next to some dude who was about to get in his car.

Without warning, the guy who heard the story from a buddy of one of the roommates said, five or six huge-ass motherfuckers who totally looked like bodybuilders or something jumped out of the van, cornered the unidentified victim, and basically just commenced to whaling on his ass.

"I would've tried to help, but there was no way I was messing with those fuckers. Uh-uh, no sir," Kelso reportedly told roommates. "I may have been baked, but I ain't stupid."

After several minutes of some seri-

Above: Lyle Kelso points out the site of Monday's seriously freaky dude-whaling.

ously painful ass-kicking, the big, mean-looking dudes reportedly hopped back inside the van and bolted as suddenly as they'd appeared. Before Kelso could approach the poor fucker who'd gotten whaled on, the dude limped to his car and bolted, leaving the stunned Kelso standing there wondering what the holy hell had just happened and "feeling like [his] mind was totally friggin' blown."

Though the identity of the whaled-upon dude remains unknown, numerous theories have been posited regarding who the fuck he was. Among the hypotheses are that he was Some Poor Sap Who Never Knew What Hit Him, A Guy Who Just Happened To Be In The Wrong Place At The Way-Wrong Freaking Time, or Somebody Who Obviously Must Have Fucked With The Wrong People. Supporters of each theory, however, agree that, whoever the hell the guy was, he probably ain't exactly having the best day right about now, wherever the hell he is.

The attack has raised some serious safety and crime-prevention concerns among the roommates.

"After that shit Lyle told us he saw, I ain't goin' anywhere without a baseball bat in the car, I'm telling you that right the fuck now," said Matt Mendham, 22. "It's like, do I want to get my ass pounded by a bunch of monster dudes? No, I don't think so."

Added Mendham: "It's too bad my friend Chad's brother wasn't there, because he totally knows t'ai chi and shit."

Despite the strong reaction to the guy-whaling among Kelso's roommates and associates, some are questioning the validity of his claims.

"Kelso's always making shit up," said Dan Soderlund, a longtime coworker at Papa Luigi's. "He smokes a few bowls, and the next thing you know, it's, 'Dude! The freakiest thing just happened!' It's like, 'Yeah, yeah, keep talking, Lyle.' That guy is so full of it sometimes. Believe me, I've heard it all before, man." ∅

MOLINE from page 69

find that perfect, one-of-a-kind floor rug for their sunroom? Where were the flamboyant hipsters buying campy early-'60s kitchen tables? They must be somewhere in Moline, but where?

I finally realized where I needed to look: the local college campus. That's always a reliable gay hotbed. I marched right up to the entrance of the Black Hawk College student union and asked a man where I might find any "Friends Of Dorothy." All I got was a blank stare. The next 250 people I approached just offered more of the same.

I'm not giving up yet. I know there's

a gay district somewhere in Moline. There has to be. I mean, it's a city of more than 40,000 people, for heaven's sake. Ten percent of that works out to 4,000 people. That's heck of a lot of gay people to keep hidden and districtless.

This morning, while leaving my hotel, I got a tip from the front-desk clerk. He said there's a drag show on the outskirts of town tonight. Hallelujah! If I can get out there, I should be able to find my kind of folks. I just have to remember the directions to the raceway where it's being held, and I'll be home free. Keep your fingers crossed. ∅

## *Star Wars* Fan Collects All 48,720

see PEOPLE page 4C

## Running Shoes Used Mainly For Computer Programming

see LOCAL page 4C

## PBS Weatherman Predicts Learning With 90 Percent Chance Of Wonderstorms

see TELEVISION page 4E

### STATshot

A look at the numbers that shape your world.

**Top Words Causing Giggles Among Pre-Teens**

| | |
|---|---|
| 2% | Parts |
| 1% | Slot |
| 15% | Ball-peen hammer |
| 8% | Mastication |
| 7% | Receptacle |
| 16% | Titular archbishopric |
| 13% | Pu-pu platter |
| 5% | Abreast |
| 11% | Lake Titicaca |
| 12% | Penal system |
| 6% | Opening |
| 4% | Moist |

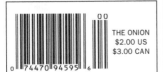

THE ONION
$2.00 US
$3.00 CAN

0 74470 94595 6

---

# the ONION®

WWW.THEONION.COM — AMERICA'S FINEST NEWS SOURCE™ — FOUNDED 1871

# National Guard Mobilized For University Of Mississippi Class Of '62 Reunion

OXFORD, MS—Tensions mounting, President Clinton ordered more than 2,500 Army and National Guard troops to Oxford Wednesday in anticipation of this weekend's University of Mississippi class of 1962 reunion.

"We are concerned about the possibility of violence," Clinton said, explaining the mobilization, "and we wish to be prepared for anything that might arise."

At the center of the controversy is class of '62 member James H. Meredith—the first black to attend the previously all-white University of Mississippi—who last Friday confirmed that he will attend the class' 35-year reunion.

Brock Brophy, 1962 Ole Miss senior-class president, was disappointed by the news that Meredith would be attending.

see REUNION page 72

Above: Troops patrol the Ole Miss campus in preparation for Saturday's reunion. Inset: Class of '62 member James Meredith, the school's first black student.

---

# Alzheimer's Sufferers Demand Cure For Pancakes

WASHINGTON, DC—Alzheimer's sufferers from across the nation marched on random buildings in Washington, D.C., Washington State, and Iowa City, IA, Monday, calling upon Congress to prioritize the fight against pancakes, the nation's third-leading breakfast food.

"Until Budenheimer's is cured, there will never be enough bread in the laundry," said a spokesman for the group, who identified himself variously as Dr. James Lustig, Brian Boitano, Mr. Jet Captain, and Socko The Happy-Turtle. "Until we are all properly rotated and serviced, none of us can ever truly be plaid."

Lustig's comments were echoed by fellow marchers, who warned that unless a cure for pancakes is found by 2000, they will continue to protest until led gently back to their homes by loved ones or trained health-care providers.

Urinating in vending machines and occasionally emitting bird-like squawks, a group of protesters in downtown D.C. resisted police crowd-dispersal efforts for six hours, linking

see ALZHEIMER'S page 73

---

# Lovable Cockney Charms Neighbors

## "Elp! 'Elp! Me 'Ouse Is On Fire!' Shouts Adorable Brit

CLOTTS, IN—The residents of Clotts have been getting quite an education in foreign cultures since last year's arrival of immigrant Nigel Edney, a real live Cockney from London. And, with a colorful accent and nimble wit to match, this tenacious teabag is fast capturing the hearts of his new neighbors.

"'Elp, 'elp, me 'ouse is on fire!" Edney told the throng of townsfolk and reporters who gathered to watch the plucky little gent in his latest misadventure. "I think it started in the gareage! Please, ring the fire brigade—me wife and baby grandchild are in 'ere!"

The people of England, known as "the British," vary in class and income,

see COCKNEY page 72

Right: London-born Nigel Edney has won over the town of Clotts, IN, with such quaint British expressions as, "Oh, God, 'elp me!" and "Me wife and baby grandchild are in 'ere!"

COCKNEY from page 71

but the most lovable of all is the Cockney, a lower-class Londoner. Known for his drinking and carousing, as well as his frequent state of unemployment, the Cockney greets the world with a smile and a saucy wink, for he knows that life is but a charade.

Edney showed off that exuberant attitude as he ran about on his stout little legs and frantically waved his stumpy arms.

"Oh, God, 'elp me!" Edney shouted to neighbors, who couldn't help but chuckle at his beet-red expression. "Edna and the li'l lad is in 'at 'ouse! For the love of God, I'm begging you! 'Ey're goin' t'die in 'ere if somebody don't 'elp!"

"He's just so cute," said Harriet Gustafson, one of Edney's many charmed neighbors. "He has a little ruddy face and wears his little tweed cap cocked to one side. Just like Andy Capp!"

Not surprisingly, Edney's newfound American friends sometimes have a bit of trouble understanding just what the funny fellow is saying. Just last week, Edney complained to his landlord that the "telly" that came with his "bed-sit" sometimes shot off "sparks" and at one point caused his "drapes" to "smolder."

"I still can't figure out what he meant," shrugged Delmore Properties president Jim Delmore. "He just talks so crazy!"

But even if he doesn't always make himself understood, the resilient Edney is hardly one to let that stop him: "'Ere, give us a 'and with this 'ose! No, the 'ose, the 'ose! Oh, dear God, the smoke is just too thick! Oh, poor Edna! And li'l Timmy! 'Elp! Fire! For the love of God—firemen, please 'urry!"

"Look at him," neighbor Nancy Marcus cooed. "With his face all covered in soot and ash, he looks just like one of those chimneysweeps from *Mary Poppins*!"

But, as always, Edney is ever ready with a snappy answer. "'Elp! 'Urry! You sodding, rotten, bloody, uncaring bastards! Rot, I say! Rot in 'ell, the whole bloody stinkin' lot of you!" ∅

REUNION from page 71

"I've got nothing against Mr. Meredith personally—he seems like a fine man and a credit to his race," said Brophy, a bank vice-president in Jackson, MS. "But I just want to relax and have a good time at the reunion, and part of me is afraid that Mr. Meredith's presence will stir up a lot of that old trouble all over again."

Class of '62 alumnus Knox Murtaugh agreed. "We had to deal with all this integration controversy 35 years ago as students," Murtaugh, 56, said. "Now, with the civil-rights era behind us and everybody finally equal, we'd just like to enjoy our reunion and spend time with old friends without having to deal with all this mixing-of-the-races business all over again. Is that too much to ask?"

Added Murtaugh: "Go Rebels!"

Wednesday's mobilization marked the second major federal intervention at a class reunion this year. On May 24, under Supreme Court orders, nine black members of the Little Rock Central High School class of '57 were escorted by Arkansas National Guardsmen to their 40th reunion. The first blacks ever to attend the school, the nine were later flown out by Army helicopter when large-scale rioting broke out near a federally integrated buffet table.

"I'm sure no one harbors any ill will toward Meredith because he's black," Brophy said. "It's just that a lot of us had our college years somewhat spoiled by all the controversy and societal upheaval he and other civil-rights agitators tried to stir up, and we'd hate to see history repeat itself."

In an official statement, University of Mississippi chancellor Robert Khayat expressed confidence that this weekend's reunion will be free of the sort of violence that accompanied Meredith's matriculation at the school 35 years ago.

"During the 1960s, Ole Miss was the site of a lot of racial tension, no question," Khayat said. "But things were different then: Blacks were not integrated into white social circles, they were regularly harassed by police, they had less money and access to education than whites, and their neighborhoods were high-crime areas. America was a very different place."

The most volatile moment of the reunion could come at 4 p.m. Sunday, when a nostalgic slide show, titled "Dear Ole Miss—Memories Of Yesteryear," is scheduled. White House offi-cials said National Guard troops will be on full alert for the slide-show, which is said to feature photographs from such memorable events as the 1961 Sugar Bowl victory over Rice University, the October 1961 "Magnolia Blossom" homecoming parade, and the March 1963 "Dragging Of The Negro," in which Meredith was taken from his Baxter Hall dorm room in the middle of the night, beaten, and dragged around campus tied to the back of a pick-up truck.

"Those slides could bring back a lot of memories and really get people in the mood to relive their old college days, if you know what I mean," Brophy said. "I just hope those soldiers, with their dogs and fire hoses, don't spoil our fun. After all, some traditions are just too special to leave behind." ∅

---

## LEGAL

# Murder Suspect To Be Tried By Media
## Overworked Justice System Grateful For Help

LOS ANGELES—Overwhelmed by an ever-growing criminal caseload, the Los Angeles district attorney's office announced Monday that William Wayne Craig, arrested last week in connection with a string of brutal Bel Air stabbings, will be tried by the media.

"More than 150,000 cases come through this office every year, and, despite our best efforts, we simply are not equipped to handle them all," Los Angeles district attorney Benjamin Dozier said. "That's why we're launching an experimental new program in conjunction with the National Society Of Journalism Professionals, in which certain criminal cases will be tried by the media. In these cases, the media will serve not only as judge and jury, but also as executioner."

According to Dozier, an alliance between the judicial system and the media should prove mutually beneficial.

"This partnership makes good sense for both sides: By handing over a percentage of cases, our workload is greatly lightened," Dozier said. "And, by taking these cases, America's journalists will finally get their wish and be able to actually make the news, rather than merely report it."

While opening arguments in the trial are not scheduled to begin until June 25 at the offices of *The Los Angeles Times*, many legal experts contend that, in the media's eyes, Craig has already been convicted.

Said Harvard University Law School dean Nathan Unger: "Just yesterday in *The Orange County Register*, columnist Herb Garowitz called for the death penalty for Dozier, whom he described as 'human garbage who must pay dearly for these brutal murders which he obviously committed.' Such editorializing

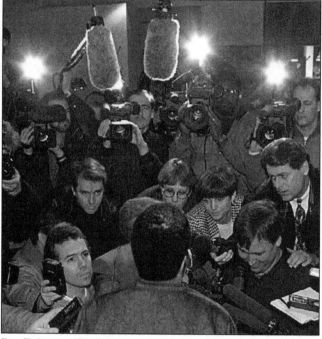

**Above: Murder suspect William Craig is swarmed by journalists assigned to cover and conduct his trial.**

is normally fine for a columnist, but Garowitz also happens to be the presiding judge in this case. That could present a major conflict of interest."

Dozier was unfazed by the criticism:

"I can guarantee you that Mr. Craig will receive the same fair trial from the media that he would have received from America's first-rate judicial system." ∅

---

## NEWS IN BRIEF

# Man Not Exactly Sure Why Doctor Needed Him Undressed For That

OREM, UT—A routine visit to the doctor ended in confusion Monday when Ray Lyons was asked to undress for an examination that did not seem to require disrobing. "He asked me about my smoking and my sleep patterns and stuff, then he looked in my ears and throat and checked my heartbeat with his stethoscope, and that was it," the baffled, nude Lyons said. "Would having my pants on somehow affect my heartbeat?" ∅

# Ad-Agency Print Buyer Can't Believe They Want To Add A Perf This Late In The Game

LINCOLN, NE—Milt Olberding, a print buyer with L&G Advertising, expressed disbelief Monday that Capital City Chrysler owner William "Biff" Brignola wants to add a perforated insert to his ad this late in the game.

"A perf? At this point?" said Olberding, 33, upon learning of the change from L&G Advertising account manager Phil Essene. "We were about to put this whole thing to bed. Why didn't Brignola mention this last week when I was giving him quotes for coated?"

Essene, who helped design the full-page Capital City ad slated to run in a 32-page "Great Savings" sales flyer that will be mailed to all Lincoln-area households next week, said he was "just as blown away" as Olberding.

"I was all set to seal up the Cap City ad and send out a proof, when I get this fax from Brignola asking about a BRM," Essene said. "Talk about a complete 180. I was, like, 'What? Now you

Right: L&G Advertising print buyer Milt Olberding.

want a 4 1/4 corner perf? Do you have any idea what that entails? *Hello!*'"

According to Olberding, the insertion of the business-reply-mail postcard will necessitate not only the per-

foration changes, but also a switch to heavier paper.

"I was going to go with Blue Lake, but I don't even think they do perfs on card stock," Olberding said. "Brignola had better be prepared to pay for 110-pound weight, because I'm not pulling the Great Savings proofs again. No fucking way. Not at this late juncture."

"I guess if he absolutely insists, it's doable," Olberding continued. "As long as this clown doesn't want to make changes to his ad in Sunday's FSI. He tries to pull that, I swear, I'll laugh right in his face."

According to Olberding, there isn't a major newspaper in the state that would include a 110 in a free-standing insert.

"The problem with guys like Brignola is that they have no concept of the varied distro channels in a market like Lincoln," Olberding said. "Even worse, they're cheap as hell. Brignola's the kind of guy who'd go with a

lighted all-weather instead of a door-to-door if it meant shaving a few bucks off his bottom line. No vision whatsoever."

Refusing to accept any changes to the FSI, Olberding is proceeding with the requested modifications to the Great Savings spread only.

"Maybe we can stick with the old Cap City layout, watermark the clip art, and throw the BRM in the corner opposite the bleed, but I doubt [Brignola]'s going to go for that," Olberding said. "If he wants it reworked, we'll have to send it back down to design, but I can tell you right now that [art director] Danielle [Gura] will not be a happy camper. I told her just this morning that the one-page was ready to roll."

Informed of the changes to the Capital City ad, Gura rolled her eyes and placed her hands on her hips.

"Come on!" Gura said. "What is up
see AGENCY page 74

---

## ALZHEIMER'S from page 71

arms and joining in a chant of "I like Ike!"

"Pancakes are delicious, but their wily ways are not to be trusted," said Alzheimer's sufferer Edith Louise Klapisch, addressing a group of ducks gathered in front of the U.S. Treasury Building. "Get those underpants away from my grandchildren's foot medicine, you filthy, dirty-minded bastards!" She then burst into tears and ran off, scattering the assembled waterfowl.

Pancakes, according to officials at the International House Of Pancakes' headquarters in Geneva, are consumed by approximately 40 million Americans each morning. They are, IHOP representatives said, extremely delicious, whether served with syrup or a variety of fruity toppings. Yet they admit there is no cure in sight.

According to the General Accounting Office, current funding for pancake-related Alzheimer's research is approximately zero dollars. That amount, GAO officials said, has remained the same since the current record-keeping system for federal budget expenditures was established in 1809.

With no cure for pancakes on the horizon and no federal research funds, the AD-afflicted activists face a long road ahead. Nevertheless, they continue to fight for their cause, leaving faucets running for days, placing tray after tray of ice cubes in mailboxes, and even, in what is presumed to be an expression of protest, throwing dogs at parked cars.

"That battleship silverware of yours is no damn sofa sink hobo," Lakeland,

FL, senior Elmer Bass said. "Until a cure is found, there will be no more change given for anything less than a $40 bill."

The feelings of the Alzheimer's com-

> ### According to the General Accounting Office, current funding for pancake-related Alzheimer's research is approximately zero dollars.

munity were best summed up by retiree Maxwell Blake of Flagstaff, AZ, who marched all the way to Washington clad only in a frilly, 1940s-era ladies' support hose that belonged to his deceased wife.

"Fellow Shriners," Blake said, "Alzheimer's is a crippling disease that can cause dear family members not only to lose their fruit flies, but their self-esteem, fertilizer invoices, Pastor Bob, and personal dignity, as well. I beg you all, from the bottom of my rototill: Frog battleship now and please put an end to pancakes, pans, cakes, cake pans, pants, snakes, and all they represent. Firemen! Can't you see the bicycle release valve is already undersea?"

Blake then burst into a string of expletives as his bathrobe became entangled in a bush. ∅

---

# Chinese Woman Gives Birth To Septuplets

## Has One Week To Choose

SHANGHAI, CHINA—Jinan Huang, a 33-year-old Shanghai woman, gave birth to septuplets Monday. Jinan, in stable condition following the 31-hour delivery, has been given one week by government officials to decide which child she will keep.

"My husband and I have not decided for certain," said Jinan, speaking to reporters from her hospital bed shortly after the miraculous birth. "But we are considering keeping the second-born boy. He is the heaviest and, therefore, the most likely to survive and tend to us in our old age."

"We definitely do not want either of the two girls," Jinan's husband Lin said. "Of that much we are certain."

The six children not selected will, in accordance with Chinese multiple-birth law, be thrown off a mountaintop.

Since China's one-child-per-family law went into effect in 1983, more than 65 million multiple-birth babies have been put to death in

Above: Jinan Huang

the country.

Jinan, who said she had tried to have a baby for years, vehemently denied taking fertility drugs, the use of which is punishable by death in China.

"I do not know how this happened," she said. "To my fellow citizens and our nation's leaders, I wish to apologize for this shameful and irresponsible multiple birth." ∅

# Newcomer Changes Small Town's Anti-Dancing Statute

PIOUS FLATS, IN—The quiet, conservative farming community of Pious Flats—notorious throughout the quad-county region for its strict anti-dancing ordinance—became a hotbed of controversy Monday when big-city outsider Ren MacAlester galvanized the town's long-oppressed teens into holding their first-ever rock 'n' roll prom.

The hip, with-it MacAlester, through the sheer force of his youthful exuberance and charisma, convinced the town's many fundamentalist church-going authority figures to allow dancing, helping many of them not only to become more tolerant, but maybe even to learn a little bit about themselves in the process.

"I couldn't believe it when I first came to this town to live with my estranged aunt," MacAlester told reporters. "When I heard there was no dancing allowed, my first reaction was simply, 'Jump back.'"

"That's a big-city slang expression meaning 'No way,'" he clarified.

Though almost single-handedly responsible for reversing the town's 135-year-old anti-dancing statute, MacAlester does not consider himself a hero.

"I just wanted everybody to, as we say in the city, 'cut loose,'" MacAlester said. "And that's what we've done. People around here have, at long last, kicked off their Sunday shoes."

MacAlester's dance-legalization quest was made all the more daunting by the fierce opposition of Pious Flats' most powerful citizen, Rev. Jonathan Gowlith.

"I admit that I was, at first, deeply opposed to the hard-driving, reckless music Ren was advocating," Gowlith said. "I am speaking, of course, of such controversial rock artists as Bonnie Tyler, Deniece Williams, and Kenny Loggins. I had always felt that the wild abandon of such music confused young people's minds and bodies."

Anonymous sources within Pious Flats High School said that when MacAlester first arrived in town, he was viewed with suspicion and resentment by both students and parents, who feared that the high-energy, rock-beat sensibility he brought from the urban world would be a bad influence on the tight-knit rural community. Branded a "troublemaker" for his flashy, multi-colored clothing, fashionably thin ties, and spiked "new wave"-style haircut, MacAlester was widely perceived as someone who would never fit in.

MacAlester said that, as an outsider, he was a victim of discrimination from adults and fellow teens alike.

"They told me the school didn't have enough funding for another gymnast, but I knew they were really kicking me off the team out of prejudice, just because I was different. One student even tried to plant a 'joint' of 'weed,' or 'grass,' on me to get me in trouble," he said. "But after proving myself in a

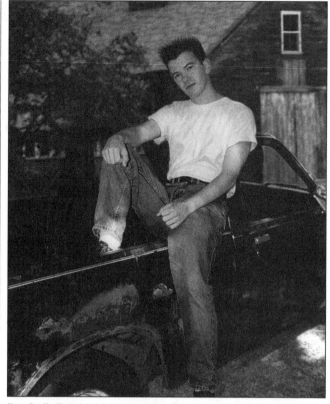
Above: Ren MacAlester has shaken things up in Pious Flats since his arrival from the big city.

death-defying bout of tractor-chicken, I was able to win the other teenagers' respect, enabling them to finally see beyond their narrow worldview."

MacAlester's efforts to get the town's youths to dance, however, proved an entirely different matter.

"Imagine my shock upon finding out that my new best friend at school, though sympathetic to my cause, didn't know how to dance a step himself," MacAlester said. "I literally had to start from the ground up, tutoring him for hours on end, using a 'Walkman' portable tape player with two sets of headphones, until he finally picked up on the fundamentals of the balletic, 'Solid Gold Dancers'-style rock 'n' roll dance moves that came so naturally to me, given my urban background."

Though his crusade to teach the people of Pious Flats to dance ultimately proved successful, MacAlester said the road was long and difficult.

"Sometimes, when the pressure got to be too much and I needed to be alone, I'd drive out to the old mill, slam in a cassette, and burn off my angst in a blazing, vaguely homoerotic, Vegas/Broadway-style dance number, complete with round-house cartwheel flips and flamboyant flying pirouettes," MacAlester said. "At those moments, I was dancing for my very sanity."

While MacAlester's crusade was largely a lonely one, Gowlith's rebellious daughter Lori helped him greatly in his effort to make the big dance a reality.

"The first time Ren played me the pulse-pounding, hard-rock beat of 'Al-

most Paradise,' the hit duet between Ann Wilson of Heart and Mike Reno of Loverboy, a whole new world opened up to me," she said. "Right then, I knew the power of rock, and I had to dance. I just plain had to."

The two angst-filled teens soon began dating, enraging Gowlith and stiffening his opposition to the legalization of dancing. However, the stern minister was ultimately convinced of the righteousness of MacAlester's cause at a town-council meeting, at which the earnest youngster read aloud a passage from the Bible describing King David dancing before the Lord in joyous celebration.

"Even I, a lifelong scholar of Scripture, had never heard of such a passage," Gowlith said. "But it said right there, in no uncertain terms, that dancing was not just acceptable, but good."

The big dance, attendees said, was a high-powered rock 'n' roll blowout, complete with glitter and balloons. The event climaxed at approximately 8:30 p.m., when the newly liberated youths, clad in powder-blue tuxedos and dresses, pointed at one another in turn to perform breakdance solos at the center of the dance floor.

"I'm just glad we all got to tear up this town a little," MacAlester said. "My favorite part was when Louise pulled me off of my knees. I mean, it was awesome—I just thought to myself, 'Whoa, Milo!'"

Turning serious, MacAlester added: "But though the dance is over, the beat goes on. We are the youth, and this is our time to dance." ∅

## AGENCY from page 73

with this guy? Does he want an 8 1/2 x 11, or does he want a whole friggin' end-aisle display? Maybe he should make up his mind now, before I rework the Quark doc."

Though willing to implement the changes, Gura said that if Brignola decides to switch from 4C to B&W when he gets a price quote on the paper upgrade, she will be "royally pissed." Such a change would force her to reshuffle the pagination of the entire flyer to bury the ad in the no-color spread.

"This Brignola reminds me of that guy from Footsavers," Gura added. "He just had to add a samp of the new line extension just when we had his broadside ready to go. Then, on top of that, he had the audacity to ask if he could get a blister pack instead of a gummed attachment. Talk about canceling the wedding when the bride's at the altar. Christ." ∅

## Billy Ray Cyrus To Speak Out On Single-Payer-Healthcare Issue On *Politically Incorrect*

HOLLYWOOD, CA—In the program's most hotly anticipated pronouncement since comedienne Elayne Boosler's historic pro-school-voucher address, country-music artist

Billy Ray Cyrus will speak out on the issue of single-payer healthcare Thursday on *Politically Incorrect With Bill Maher*. Sources say Cyrus, best known for his 1992 hit "Achy Breaky Heart," will argue that a single-payer system places health care in its rightful context as a right of all Americans rather than a privilege doled out on the basis of ability to pay. The hunky, denim-clad Cyrus, who for years had remained silent on single-payer healthcare, is also expected to finally reveal his stance on campaign finance reform. ∅

# the ONION®

WWW.THEONION.COM · AMERICA'S FINEST NEWS SOURCE™ · FOUNDED 1871

## Will Smith: The Black Man Everyone At Work Can Agree On

see ENTERTAINMENT page 4D

## Beekeeper Wishes He Understood Women Like He Understands Bees

see LOCAL page 2E

## Woman On *Jenny Jones* Has Shocking Secret, Fist-Sized Adam's Apple

see TELEVISION page 8C

## Ska Band Outnumbers Audience

see MUSIC page 3C

THE ONION
$2.00 US
$3.00 CAN

0 0

0 74470 94595 6

Above: Christ (left) consults with his new spiritual advisor, the Righteous Hassan Abdul al-Aziz.

# Christ Converts To Islam

JERUSALEM—In a surprise announcement with far-reaching theological implications, Jesus Christ The Nazarene, founder of Christianity and spiritual leader of nearly two billion people, revealed Wednesday that He has converted to "the one true religion" of Islam.

The controversial announcement sent shockwaves through religious circles around the globe.

"Allah is the name of the One and Only God," Christ said. "Allah has 99 beautiful names: He is known as The Gracious, The Merciful, The Beneficent, The Creator, The All-Knowing, The All-Wise, The Lord Of The Uni-verse, The First, The Last, and many more. He has revealed Himself unto Me through the holy words of the blessed Qur'an, and I have put My trust and faith in Him."

As part of His conversion, Christ said He has taken a new name, Isa Ibn Maryam al-Salaam Christ Shabazz.

Christ, 33, is urging Christians worldwide to renounce His former religion of Christianity and join Him in embracing the Muslim way of life.

"People of all nations, in the past, you have heard Me say that whosoever shall believe in Me shall not die, but have eternal life," Christ said. "But

see CHRIST page 77

## Report:
# Depression Hits Losers Hardest

PALO ALTO, CA—According to a report released Wednesday by Stanford University researchers, depression, America's leading mental illness, hits losers worse than any other segment of society.

Losers, sad excuses for human beings who have no reason to feel good about themselves or their failed, miserable lives, are approximately 25 times as likely to suffer the emotionally crippling effects of depression as any other group researched, the report stated.

Worse yet, the prospects for successful treatment of depression among the loser populace are "poor at best," the study found. The reason: Most losers are such hopeless lost causes that they can never get a life, no matter how hard they try, and are "doomed to repeat their mistakes forever, living out their pathetic existence as little more than human garbage."

"People who are depressed are gripped by painful feelings of shame, hopelessness, and low self-esteem," said Dr. Anne

see DEPRESSION page 76

# Desperate Small Town Erects World's Largest Fiberglass Chili Dog

PURLEY, TX—After years of unsuccessful efforts to establish itself as a center of tourism, industry, or Texas history, the tiny East Texas town of Purley finally put itself on the map Wednesday, when civic leaders unveiled the world's largest fiberglass chili dog.

The oversized wiener replica—centerpiece of Purley's ambitious campaign to become "Chili Dog Capital Of The World"—was christened at a ceremony attended by Purley's 233 residents, as well as reporters from as far away as Floyd County.

"In the name of the good people of Purley, Texas,"

see CHILI DOG page 76

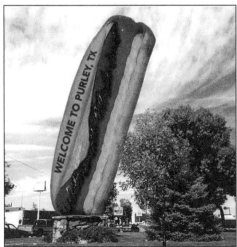

Above: The monument that will have tourists "flocking to Purley in droves."

DEPRESSION from page 75

Wyler-Hustad, head of the Stanford team. "Losers are much more likely to internalize these emotions, as they are miserable little nothings, devoid of any value as people."

Noted therapist Dr. Eli Wasserbaum agreed.

"Because they are so inherently inferior to regular people, many losers feel—quite correctly—that their lives are not worth living," Wasserbaum said. "Nobody cares about them, they are alone, they can't hold down a job, they have no money. Even their own families hate them. Life has passed them by. What's the point in their even going on?"

According to the Stanford study, losers are five times more likely to suffer from negative sexual self-images than non-losers, usually because they are fat and ugly, and nobody in their right mind would ever want to date them. Further, negative feelings such as despair, self-loathing, and hopelessness are three times as common among go-nowhere lowlife losers than among normal people who have worth.

The report also indicated that, because nobody would miss them if they died, losers are nine times more likely to attempt suicide than worthwhile people.

"From the true loser's point of view, the compulsion to self-destruct seems to be 'the only way out.' This is true," Wyler-Hustad said. "Lord only knows why they don't just do us all a favor and blow their brains out once and for all. I know I would if I were a loser like that."

But is there any hope for these losers? According to Stanford researchers, the answer is a resounding no.

"The depressed patient suffers from extreme, delusional feelings of worthlessness," the report read. "But through therapy, many of those people are able to overcome their depression by slowly discovering that these negative beliefs are not true. In the case of losers, however, such negative self-images are not delusional, but actually reflect the truth about their lack of worth. This makes the loser's chances of suffering depression far more likely and their prognosis for recovery slim to none."

With more than one million Americans on Prozac, depression remains the country's leading mental illness. But while most patients can expect to benefit from the drug, mental-health experts agree that losers will not be helped by prescription-drug therapy or, for that matter, anything else.

Above: A depressed loser cowers in a corner. According to the Stanford study, there is no hope for such people.

"Losers, despite their profound, constant state of despair, are hated by others as much as they hate themselves," said Dr. Theodore Foti, director of the famed Rochester Institute For Mental Health. "They have no friends because they are, quite simply, too pathetic and useless for anyone to care about. How could anyone possibly expect a little pill to cure a problem like that? Give me a break."

Because of their severe state of "loserdom," realistic treatment options for depressed losers are almost nil, the Stanford report concluded.

"The only treatment that makes any sense is loathing and rejection," Wyler-Hustad said. "It is only logical that stupid, fat, ugly, bed-wetting, crybaby losers be shunned as outcasts and be treated with the hatred and disgust they so richly deserve." ∅

CHILI DOG from page 75

said Mayor Owen Hudspeth, breaking a jar of mustard over the monument's base, "I hereby dedicate this statue as the official symbol of Purley chili-dog pride."

Conveniently located just 11 miles south of Hwy. 8, the giant simulated frank boasts a height of 27 feet and an estimated weight of two tons. According to Bernice Smalls, curator of Purley's soon-to-open National Chili Dog Hall Of Fame And Museum, the chili dog is the second tallest free-standing

> ## "Purley will be *the* vacation destination for millions of chili-dog lovers around the globe."

fiberglass food item in the world, second only to a 35-foot-tall corn muffin in Kearney, NE.

"To give you an idea of the size of this chili dog, consider that, if it were real, it would contain 24 million calories and 450,000 grams of fat," Smalls said. "You'd have to jog across Texas 415 times just to burn it off."

Added Smalls: "I certainly wouldn't recommend that to anyone on a diet."

Hudspeth said that the chili dog and adjacent museum, which opens June 1, will attract 400,000 tourists annually, pumping millions of dollars into the local economy and creating more than 300 wiener-related jobs. A two-

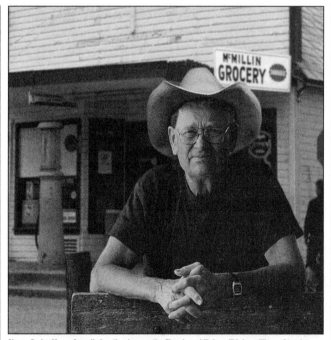
Above: Purley Mayor Owen Hudspeth, who says the fiberglass chili dog will bring millions of tourist dollars to local businesses such as the McMillin Grocery.

star hotel is also under construction.

"We're really moving into the big-time now," Hudspeth said. "As Chili Dog Capital Of The World, Purley will be *the* vacation destination for millions of chili-dog lovers around the globe. I just hope we're equipped to handle the crush of visitors."

The towering chili-dog simulacrum is expected to help Purley lure tourists from the many other competing world capitals nearby, including Centerville (Okra Capital Of The World), Tyler (Allen Wrench Capital Of The World), Nacogdoches (Carbon-Dioxide Capital Of The World), and Rusk (Unicycling Capital Of The World).

City councilman Bert Kendall, whose campaign to make Purley "Paprika City, USA" was defeated last year in a 13-9 city-council vote, praised the chili dog at its unveiling.

"Purley has, in the past, been regarded as unexceptional," Kendall said. "But now we have the world's largest

chili dog. So, to that end, we are exceptional, in that no town anywhere has a larger chili dog."

Kendall's "Paprika City, USA" proposal was just one of dozens considered by the Purley city council last year in an effort to increase the small town's notoriety. Among the items proposed for construction: the world's largest shoelace, a ferris wheel made of carpet, and "Truck-henge," described by city councilman Richard Serrano as "just like Stonehenge, only with trucks."

In the end, however, the chili-dog plan won out, and Purley residents seem pleased. "We sure are proud of our big old chili dog," retired farmer Cordell Bullock said. "Biggest chili dog in the world, that's what that sucker is."

"It's good to see that we've finally done something for the young people of this community," Purley High School math teacher Anne Vernon said. "This will help teach children things like how big the world's largest fiberglass chili dog is, and where it is."

Vernon noted that children can also learn about economics from the chili-dog museum's gift shop, which sells miniature plastic replicas of the chili dog, chili-dog snow globes, and T-shirts reading, "I Saw The World's Largest Fiberglass Chili Dog."

Bill Stone, owner of the local hardware store, put it best.

"If you stand about 200 feet away, close one eye, and hold up your hand just right," he said, "it looks like you're holding a giant chili dog. That's kind of neat." ∅

now, I say unto you, forget I ever said that. There is only one holy revelation of Allah, the Qur'an, which was dictated to the Prophet Mohammed, Praise Be Unto Him, by the Archangel Jibreel in the seventh century after I died."

According to Christ, the beauty and perfection of the Qur'an's Surahs are without equal in all creation, encompassing and surpassing both the Judaic Torah and the New Testament Gospels of His apostles. The former Christian messiah went on to cite Surah Aal'imraan 3:67, which reads, "This day I have perfected your religion for you, completed My favor upon you, and have chosen for you Islam as your religion."

"What could be more clear?" Christ said.

"I was wrong, and I know that now," He added. "I deeply regret any problems or confusion I may have caused."

The controversial retraction of two millennia of Christian doctrine has provoked sharply divided reaction. Millions of devout Christians, insisting that obeisance to Christ's commands is the cornerstone of their faith, have heeded His instructions and converted to Islam. Millions more, however, have decried the recalcitrant Christ's apostasy, breaking ties with Him and calling His conversion "a heathen act" of "utmost blasphemy before Himself."

"Jesus, or Isa Shabazz, or whatever He's calling Himself these days, is the way, the truth and the light. It says so in the Bible," said devout Catholic Kathleen Langan of Cork, Ireland, kneeling toward Mecca for the first time. "My loyalty to Him is absolute. If He told me to be a Buddhist, I'd do it. All praise and thanks to Allah."

Ruth-Anne Girolamo, a Sunday-school teacher in Stillwater, OK, disagreed.

"I've been a Bible-believing Christian all my life, and nothing, not even a direct order from Christ Himself, is going to change that," Girolamo said. "If Christ is going to leave the fold and become a sinner, we'll just have to go on worshipping Him against His will."

The Roman Catholic Church is just as divided: Approximately half the members of the Vatican's College of Cardinals have advocated embracing Islamic law, while the other half is calling for Christ's immediate excommunication, recommending the interim worship of Pope John Paul II until a suitable replacement deity can be found.

In perhaps the oddest development, the Jews For Jesus organization announced Wednesday that it has split into three separate groups: Jews Still For Jesus, Jews For Allah, and Jews For Just Being Jews Again.

Christ said He arrived at the decision to convert after centuries of deep soul-searching and contemplation. But it was not until last week's Good Friday holiday, He said, that His true spiritual path became clear.

Above: Christ (uppermost left) joins fellow Muslims in prayer.

"I was in church, watching all these people hold a candlelight vigil on the day of My crucifixion, when I suddenly felt a profound sense of emptiness," Christ said. "I got up and walked out, and just sort of wandered aimlessly for a while, wondering what it all meant. Then, I saw something I'd never noticed before. At the mosque

> **The controversial retraction of two millennia of Christian doctrine has provoked sharply divided reaction.**

down the street, suppliants were gathering to celebrate their weekly holy day of worship, which, by sheer coincidence, happens to be Friday."

"I nervously walked in, unsure of why I was even there. After all, during the Crusades, My followers had slaughtered untold thousands of these people in My name, and I thought maybe they wouldn't accept Me," Christ said. "But as I listened to the Imam deliver the weekly sermon, or *khutba*, I felt the power of Allah in My heart. For the first time, I felt like I'd found true inner peace."

"I now know it wasn't random chance that brought Me to that mosque," Christ continued. "It was the

will of Allah."

Asked about His future plans, Christ said His next move will be to undertake the Hajj, the holy pilgrimage to Mecca all Muslims are required to experience at least once in a lifetime. After that, Christ said He hopes to take a few months off to rest and meditate before starting the next phase of His ministry: traveling to churches around the world and imploring the Christian faithful to stop worshipping Him.

"My new spiritual advisor, the Righteous Hassan Abdul al-Aziz, has explained to Me that I am not, nor was I ever, actually the Son of God, but merely one of many Prophets of the divine revelation which was to come after Me," Christ said. "After all, there is only one God, so any belief in a triune god, or 'trinity,' is polytheistic and contradicts the word of Allah Himself."

"For it is written, in Surah Al-Maa'idah 5:116, 'And behold, Allah will say—O Jesus Son of Mary, did you say to men, worship me and my mother as gods beside Allah? He will reply—Glory to you, I could never say what I had no right [to say].'" Christ said. "You see? It turns out, worshipping Me isn't the key to the Gates of Heaven, after all. Salvation can only be found in the Five Pillars of Shahada, Salat, Saum, Zakat, and Hajj. I can't believe how obvious it all seems to Me now."

Neither the Father nor the Holy Ghost could be reached for comment. ∅

## Senior-Center Residents Debate New Anchorwoman's Ethnicity For Fifth Straight Evening

ST. PETERSBURG, FL—Ferndale Senior Center residents debated new *Channel 27 Action News* anchorwoman Sonya Luntz's ethnicity for a fifth straight day Wednesday. Edward Bloch, 81, steadfastly held to his "Mexican" theory, while Muriel Simmons, 83, continued to lean toward Hawaiian or Indian. "If you ask me, she looks Oriental," said Jack McCallum, 79, watching Luntz on the 6 p.m. newscast. "Orientals have that shape to their face—I saw it in the war." Luntz's ethnicity will be put to an official senior-center vote Friday.

## 31-Year-Old Can't Believe 'You Must Be Born Before This Date To Buy Cigarettes' Sign Up To 1984

KIRKLAND, WA—Purchasing a pack of Camel Reds at a local convenience store, 31-year-old Kirkland resident Andy Belfour announced Wednesday that he "can't fucking believe" the "You Must Be Born Before This Date To Buy Cigarettes" sign is already up to 1984. "Christ, I was a freshman in high school in '84," Belfour said. "Now, kids born that year are old enough to smoke? God, I feel so old." Belfour went on to recall that 1984 was the year Hüsker Dü's *Zen Arcade* came out, an album he bought on vinyl and played that whole summer while dating Alison Haiduk, his first girlfriend. He then ran his hands through his thinning hair.

## Customer Awkwardly Accepts One Cent, Receipt

BERKELEY, CA—Coffeehouse patron Lenny Niyo awkwardly accepted one cent and a receipt Wednesday after purchasing a $1.99 biscotti. "It made me feel kind of cheap, standing there waiting for six or seven seconds while the receipt printed out and the cashier put away my singles and got the penny, but it would have looked weird if I'd just walked away, too," Niyo said. "It's not like I wanted the receipt. I was confident the biscotti would work out fine." Niyo has reportedly not been this humiliated in a food-service environment since May 1998, when a waiter told him to enjoy his meal and he replied, "You, too." ∅

# I Can't Believe You Blew My Perfect Feedback Rating

Ever since I placed that very first "LOGAN'S RUN ORIGINAL JAPANESE MOVIE POSTER ***MINT***" for sale on eBay two and a half years ago,

By droogie73 (210)

I've prided myself on being the best seller I can possibly be. I always reply promptly to e-mail inquiries. I include sharp, clear pics with item descriptions but limit their size to 50 KB for quick page downloads. I never fail to contact the high bidder within the required three days. In fact, I usually do so within hours of the end of an auction.

And for my two and a half years of dedicated eBay salesmanship, I have been duly rewarded with a perfect feedback rating. That's right: 211 positive comments with not so much as a single neutral. To preserve that perfect record, I've consistently gone the extra mile, purchasing bubble wrap when another seller would make do with balled-up newspaper, making special trips to the post office to get packages in the mail before 5 p.m., and attaching cheerful Post-It notes to sold items with messages like, "Hope you enjoy the Rutles CD!"

If you don't believe me, just look at my profile feedback. In it, buyer after satisfied buyer heaps accolades upon me: "Praise: Great transaction! Friendly Emails." "Praise: TAHNK-YOU." "Praise: Great Auction!!!" "Praise: Great packaging job! GOOD SELLER." "Praise: Definitely reccomended. A++++!" "Praise: Arived lightening fast!!"

The testimonials to my professionalism are overwhelming. Baldeagle1965 (41), high bidder for Item #513921485 "SPUMCO JOHN K. ORIGINAL ANIMATION CEL—NO RESERVE!," said I am "a pleasure to do business with!" Kewlgal (25) was so happy with her *Iron Giant* collectible bank that she said, "Excellent Mdse at an excellent price!!!" As you can see, I earned that turquoise star icon next to my name. Yes, my rating, like my reputation within the eBay community, was flawless.

Until Monday, that is.

For me, Dec. 18, 2000, will forever be known as Black Monday, the day I received a stinging slap to the face in the form of a negative feedback comment. Bananaman (37), how could you?

When I placed Item #538328761 "SUPERSTAR—RARE TODD HAYNES FILM—VHS" up for bid, I did so expecting that whoever was named the High Bidder at 12:44:54 PST would recognize and praise my top-notch service, just as 211 previous auction winners did. But, to my shock and dismay, Bananaman (37) blindsided

me with the negative feedback comment, "Bad picture quality. Came too slow."

Though you do not deserve it, Bananaman (37), I will now deign to respond to your groundless complaints. As for the charge, "Came too slow," I am flabbergasted. I explicitly informed you that should you choose to pay with a personal check instead of a money order, I would have to hold that check up to 10 days until it cleared. It was your choice to do so. As for any additional delays, it appears I must point out the obvious fact that UPS is greatly overtaxed this time of year.

As for the statement, "Bad picture quality," I scarcely know how to respond. I invite you to re-examine the item description: "Film by director of *Safe* and *Velvet Goldmine*. Story of life and death of Karen Carpenter, as told with dolls. VHS. Good transfer. Super-rare. A must-have for any film buff!"

As you see, I stated that the tape was a "good transfer," and I stand firm on this assertion. I did not say it was an "excellent transfer" or a "perfect transfer." I promised a "good transfer," and I delivered.

I cannot help but direct you to the bid history, which shows that no fewer than seven other bidders were interested in this item. No doubt, any of them would have cherished it, not to mention been better equipped to

> ## It is a scarlet letter I must carry for a full six months.

judge the picture quality. Do you even realize what it is you now have in your possession? *Superstar*, Haynes' 43-minute 1987 film debut, the story of Carpenter's battle with anorexia as told with Barbie dolls, was never released because the Carpenter estate refused to grant music rights. Perhaps I should have added in the item description that the film is a "CULT CLASSIC" and "NEARLY IMPOSSIBLE TO FIND."

Bananaman (37), do you think I even need the $32.50, plus $4.50 for shipping, that I received from you for this film? I am making copies of *Superstar* and selling them as a service to film connoisseurs everywhere who otherwise might not have access to this lit-

tle-seen, underground masterwork.

Here is my question to you, Bananaman (37): If you were dissatisfied, why didn't you contact me and give me the chance to make amends before going public with your dissatisfaction, besmirching my good eBay name? After all, that is the procedure suggested on the eBay user help page titled "The Feedback Forum: One Of Your Most Valuable Tools."

Had I known you were dissatisfied, I would have happily refunded your money, no questions asked. I could have rushed you reimbursement the same day via PayPal. But, for some reason, you chose to remain unapproachable in your fortress on high in "Location: Waterville, MD," stabbing me in the back without even giving me a chance to redress your grievance, unfounded as it may have been.

No, instead you chose to soil my reputation with a negative feedback comment. It is a scarlet letter I must carry for a full six months, visible for all the world to see on my eBay ID card. I could strike back with a negative comment on your profile, but I refuse to stoop to your level, Bananaman (37). Let me just say that we will not be doing business again. ∅

# Hillary In 2004?

**The 2000 presidential election is barely in the books, but talk has already turned to the possibility of Hillary Clinton making a White House run in 2004. What do *you* think?**

Rich Durban
Machinist

"A woman president? What if she menstruates all over some important legislation?"

Todd Tyler
Systems Analyst

"She's got a good shot, so long as no one blows her up, causing her faceplate to fall off and revealing the gears and diodes beneath."

Bob Van Eeghen
Lawyer

"No, no—you don't understand: The 19th Amendment gives women the right to *vote* for a president, that's all."

Annette Petersen
Homemaker

"Hillary would make a great president. But she'd probably ask her girlfriends for advice, and I just don't trust that Sharon."

Bob Houdel
Cashier

"Would she have female Secret Service agents? Because that'd be pretty sexy."

Lisa Rinaldi
Physical Therapist

"We could do worse. You know, like we always have."

## Midwest Peace Talks Shattered By Illinois Toll-Booth Bombing

see SPECIAL REPORT page 3A

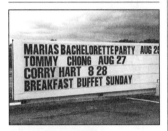

## Corey Hart Still Performing 'Sunglasses At Night' Somewhere

see ENTERTAINMENT page 9D

## Baby-Shower Attendees Quickly Drain Box Of White Zinfandel

see LIFESTYLE page 2D

### STATshot

A look at the numbers that shape your world.

**What Did America Think Of Last Week's *Frasier*?**

19% Missed it
21% Taped it
29% All right
17% Okay, I guess
14% Not bad

THE ONION
$2.00 US
$3.00 CAN

0 74470 94595 6

---

# the ONION®

WWW.THEONION.COM    AMERICA'S FINEST NEWS SOURCE™    FOUNDED 1871

## Former Cult Members Find New Life In Christ

HANOVER, NH—Times are tough for young people today. Faced with the overwhelming complexities of modern life, many turn to drugs, gangs, and, in some cases, cults. It is estimated that each year, some 200,000 young people fall prey to cult life. But in Hanover, NH, a small group of people is fighting back. Here at the Fellowship House, cult members are finding a new life in Christ Jesus, our Lord and Savior.

Helen Hurley founded the Fellowship House in January 1987. Since that time, she has helped more than 300 former cult victims escape cult life and find newfound security in the arms of the Lord.

"Cults are ruthless," Hurley said. "They'll often resort to such techniques as isolation, suppression of individuality, and brainwashing to indoctrinate innocents into total domi-

see CULT page 80

**Right: Helen Hurley of the Fellowship House in Hanover, NH, where cult survivors are given a chance to return to the real world, be reborn, and ascend to Heaven for all eternity through devotion to the one true Savior, Jesus Christ.**

---

## Republicans, Dadaists Declare War On Art

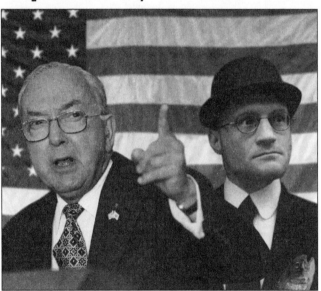

Above: U.S. Sen. Jesse Helms (R-NC) and Dadaist Jean Arp denounce "grotesque, nonsensical displays that masquerade as art."

WASHINGTON, DC—Denouncing the "proliferation of immoral and offensive material in America's museums and schools," and waving placards emblazoned with agit-prop foto-collage reading, "diE KUnst ISt tOT, DadA ubEr aLLes" ("Art is dead, dada over all"), a coalition of Republicans and early-20th-century Dadaists declared war on art in a joint press conference Friday.

The Republicans and Dadaists were unified in their condemnation of the role of the artist in society today, calling for the elimination of federal funding for the National Endowment for the Arts, the banning of offensive art from museums and schools, and the destruction of the "hoax of reason" in our increasingly random, irrational, and meaningless age.

"Homosexuals and depraved people of every stripe are receiving federal money at taxpayer expense for the worst kind of filth imaginable," said

see ART page 82

---

## Chicken Killed

WAYCROSS, GA—In a grisly murder that has stunned residents of this peaceful southeastern Georgia town, the gutted remains of a local chicken were discovered in a Dumpster late Friday.

The chicken, whose skin and flesh were almost 90 percent missing, was found in a garbage bag behind Jack's Cluck Shack by a pair of Waycross police officers responding to a routine lunch-pick-up call.

"It was gruesome," said Det. Sam Welty, one of the officers who made the find. "When I first looked at the victim, I could barely tell what it was. The bones were all broken, the head

was missing, and one of the thigh bones bore what appeared to be human teeth marks."

The name of the victim, a longtime employee of Tyson Poultry Farms, is being withheld.

Sgt. Bruce Stebbins of the Waycross Police Department said the slaying will not be easy to solve.

"Because the victim's beak is missing, dental records will be useless," Stebbins said. "And, thus far, we have found no signs of struggle, such as scattered feathers or claw marks. Whoever perpetrated this brutal act clearly knew what he was doing."

see CHICKEN page 81

Above: A 1997 photo of the slain chicken.

79

# U.S. Dept. Of Retro Warns: 'We May Be Running Out Of Past'

WASHINGTON, DC—At a press conference Friday, U.S. Retro Secretary Anson Williams warned of an imminent "national retro crisis," cautioning that "if current levels of U.S. retro consumption are allowed to continue unchecked, we may run out of past by as early as 2005."

According to Williams—best known to most Americans as "Potsie" on the popular, '50s-nostalgia-themed 1970s sitcom *Happy Days*—the nation's rapidly shrinking retro gap is in danger of achieving parity with real-time historical events within the next 10 years, creating what leading retro experts call a "futurified recursion loop," or "retro-present warp," in the world of American pop-cultural kitsch appreciation.

Such a warp, Williams said, was never a possibility in the past due to the longtime two-decade-minimum retro waiting period.

"The mid-'80s deregulation of retro under the Reagan Administration eliminated that safety valve," Williams said, "leaving us to face the threat of retro-ironic appreciation being applied to present or even future events."

"We are talking about a potentially devastating crisis situation in which our society will express nostalgia for events which have yet to occur,"

Rich vein of '50s retro tapped

Retro gap closes as U.S. looks back on '70s

Nostalgia for late '80s/early '90s leaves past nearly depleted; U.S. will soon need alternativ source of popular culture

Williams told reporters.

The National Retro Clock currently stands at March 1990, an alarming 74 percent closer to the present than just 10 years ago, when it stood at June 1969.

Nowhere is the looming retro crisis more apparent, Williams said, than in the area of popular music.

"To the true retrophile, disco parties and the like were common 10 years ago. Similarly, retro-intelligentsia have long viewed 'new wave' and even late-'80s hair-metal retro as passé and no longer amusing as kitsch," Williams said. "We now face the unique situation of '90s retro, as evidenced by the current Jane's Addiction reunion tour: nostalgia for the decade in which we live."

"Before long," Williams warned, "the National Retro Clock will hit 1992, and we will witness a massive retro-grunge explosion, which will overlap with the late-period, mainstream-pop remnants of the original grunge movement itself. For the first time in history, a phenomenon and nostalgia for that phenomenon will actually meet."

"In other words, to quote '90s-retro kitsch figure David Lynch," Williams said, "'One of these days that gum you like is going to come back in style.'"

Anthropologists hold that retro began some 40,000 years ago with the early hominids' mental projection of trace infantile-dependency memories onto a mythical "golden age." Continuing with the Renaissance's rediscovery of Greco-Roman homoeroticism and the mass "Egyptology" fashions of the Victorian Age, retro had, prior to this century, always been separated from the present age by a large buffer of intermediate history.

Since 1900, however, the retro parabolic curve has steepened sharply, with some generations experiencing several different forms of retro within a single lifetime.

"This rapidly shrinking gap between retro and the present day is like a noose closing ever tighter around the neck of American kitsch," said Harvard University professor of American culture Louis I. Szilard. "Or, if you will, like a warning light, similar to

the electric buzzer-nose of the naked fat man in the Milton Bradley game Operation."

The Department of Retro warning comes on the heels of last year's Report On Nostalgia Viability And Past-Depletion Reduction Strategies, which examined the effects of the ever-increasing co-option of retro trends by the mainstream.

According to the report, retro-kitsch aesthetics—previously the domain of a tiny group of forward-thinking, backward-looking alterna-hipsters, or "retro-cognoscenti"—have become so prevalent in the national pop-culture psyche over the last decade that they have been absorbed into the marketing strategies of major retail chains and mass-media promotional campaigns. Cited as an example is *Entertainment Weekly*'s "Dance Hits Of The '70s" free-with-subscription CD giveaway, which features the slogan, "Retro's Hot!"

Such mainstreaming of retro, the report noted, has forced the hipster-elite element that once dominated the retro world to seek increasingly recent forms of retro—a trend which threatens to consume the nation's past reserves faster than new past can be created.

The severity of the impending retro crisis, Williams said, is compounded by the increasing complexity of modern retro, evidenced in current youths' skewed perceptions of older generations who themselves were born and raised in a retro-aware environment.

"In the '70s, baby boomers escaped the decade's turbulence and social upheaval through '50s-retro romanticization of the sock hops and drive-ins of their teenage years," Williams said. "Today, retro-conscious Gen Xers look upon myself and other '70s-era '50-retro pop-culture figures as '70s-retro figures in our own right, viewing us not as idealized youth archetypes but rather as irony-tinged representations of cheesy, "square" adulthood—a form of self-referential meta-retro that science still cannot fully understand."

It is hoped, Williams said, that such meta-retro recycling of older forms of retro may help replenish the retro reservoir.

"Department of Retro officials are closely studying new developments in meta-retro," Williams said, "including a dance sequence in the 1997 film *Boogie Nights*, which is simultaneously a '70s-retro homage to *Saturday Night Fever* and a late-'80s-retro homage to The Beastie Boys' seminal '70s-retro video "Hey Ladies"—an homage to an homage, if you will. While all the facts are still not in, this much is clear: Now, more than ever, we must conserve our precious pop-cultural past, for it is our pop-cultural future." ∅

CULT from page 79

nation by the cult. Here at the Fellowship House, we provide such people with an environment totally different from their previous surroundings, so that they may better reject their sinful ways of the past and give over their hearts and minds completely to Jesus, that they may better learn His doctrines and teachings."

One recovering cult member, 31-year-old Ronald Shell, currently employed at the Fellowship House helping others like himself, recalled his experience.

"Back in the compound, they told me that any thoughts that came into my mind other than cult law were evil and had to be wiped out," Shell said. "But thanks to Ms. Hurley and the others here, I now know that all such heathen lies are merely the voice of Satan, whispering temptation into my ear, trying to seduce me away from the one and only true path of Christ's glory. I have truly been born again in the body and blood of the Lamb."

Fellow survivor Elaine Drenholt said her cult experience drained her more than just spiritually.

"I used to give all my money, resources, and time to the Cosmic Yoho Radiance," Drenholt said. She proudly noted that these days, she spends most of her time volunteering at the Fellowship House, where she strives to earn salvation through charity, stewardship, and volunteer work.

Though cults often keep initiates un-

der 24-hour supervision by other members, preventing the victim from having the chance to think any individual thoughts, Hurley said that, with time, the Fellowship House can "break" such conditioning. By providing an environment in which survivors have constant, around-the-clock access to prayer counselors and other support staff, the house helps them feel closer to Christ and His all-encompassing love.

"I must help these poor souls any way I can," Hurley said. "If I don't get them to give over their bodies and souls to Jesus, they will be left behind when Jesus returns to sweep up the righteous with Him, sparing them the agonies of Armageddon, carrying them with Him to Heaven on the prophesied day of the Rapture. In the battle at the end of time, they will be punished horribly by foul dragons and the demonic armies of Hell itself."

"Look," said Hurley, her expression turning serious, "some of the men and women who've come through the Fellowship House were actually involved in ritual cannibalism at one time. Now they can turn their backs on darkness and confusion. They are free to take their first communion, and, in the sacramental eating and drinking of the body and blood of Christ, they are washed of their sins by the blood of the Lamb."

After all, isn't that what it's really all about? ∅

# Starbucks To Begin Sinister 'Phase Two' Of Operation

SEATTLE—After a decade of aggressive expansion throughout North America and abroad, Starbucks suddenly and unexpectedly closed its 2,870 worldwide locations Monday to prepare for what company insiders are calling "Phase Two" of the company's long-range plan.

"Starbucks has completed the coffee-distribution and location-establishment phase of its operation, and is now ready to move into Phase Two," read a statement from Cynthia Vahlkamp, Starbucks' chief marketing officer. "We have enjoyed furnishing you with coffee-related beverages and are excited about the important role you play in our future plans. Please pardon the inconvenience while we fortify the second wave of our corporate strategy."

Though the coffee chain's specific plans are not known, existing Starbucks franchises across the nation have been locked down with titanium shutters across all windows. In each coffee shop's door hangs the familiar Starbucks logo, slightly altered to present the familiar mermaid figure as a cyclopean mermaid whose all-seeing eye forms the apex of a world-spanning pyramid.

Those living near one of the closed Starbucks outlets have reported strange glowing mists, howling and/or cowering on the part of dogs that pass by, and electromagnetic effects that cause haunting, unearthly images to appear on TV and computer screens within a one-mile radius. Experts have few theories as to what may be causing the low-frequency rumblings, half-glimpsed flashes of light, and periodic electronic beeps emanating from the once-busy shops.

In addition, newly painted trucks marked with the nuclear trefoil, the biohazard warning symbol, and various mystic runes of the Kaballah have been spotted rolling out of Starbucks distribution warehouses.

A spokesman for Hospitality Manufacturing, a restaurant-supply company that does business with Starbucks, provided some insight as to what Phase Two might entail.

"This week, they cancelled their usual 500,000-count order of Java Jackets and ordered 1.2 million Starbucks-insignia armbands instead," Hospitality Manufacturing's Jasper Hennings said. "They also called off their standing order for restaurant-grade first-aid kits, saying they had a heavy-duty source for those now. And, most ominous of all, they've stopped buying stirrers altogether."

"I don't like the looks of this," added Hennings before disappearing late Monday night.

No Starbucks employees were available for comment, as those not laid off in January's "loyalty-based personnel restructuring" or hospitalized in the series of freakish, company-wide milk-steamer malfunctions that severely scalded hundreds of employees, have been sent to re-training cen-

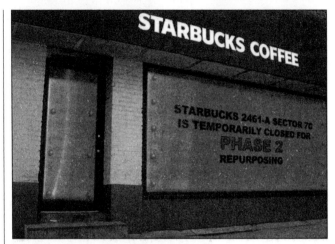

Above: The front of a temporarily closed Starbucks in Canton, OH.

ters.

Remaining Starbucks employees earmarked for re-training are being taught revised corporate procedures alongside 15,500 new hires recently recruited from such non-traditional sources as the CIA retirement program, Internet bulletin boards frequented by former Eagle Scouts, and the employment section in the back of *Soldier Of Fortune* magazine.

More insight into Phase Two was provided by the company's most recent quarterly stockholders' report, which features a map of North Amer-

see STARBUCKS page 82

---

CHICKEN from page 79

Though the entire area around Jack's Cluck Shack has been sealed off, police are increasingly doubtful that it was the site of the murder. Investigators suspect that the crime occurred at nearby Tyson Poultry Farms, where blood tentatively matching that of the victim was discovered late last night.

Suspicions were further aroused by the recent disappearance of most of the chicken's coworkers.

"When we went to the victim's place of employment to ask questions, we were shocked to find that thousands of chickens who'd worked alongside the slain bird were no longer there," Det. Patrick Duvalier said. "It would appear that somebody is hiding something."

"The victim was likely killed at work, perhaps by a jealous coworker, and then fried, torn apart, and dumped in a trash receptacle," Duvalier said. "This is the work of a twisted, depraved sociopath."

Though everyone in Waycross has been stunned by the slaying, the town's poultry community is particularly devastated.

"All of the chickens are absolutely terrified," farm owner Hup Wheeler said. "They trust no one, viewing every farmhand who comes in to collect eggs or scatter feed as a potential

Above: The grisly aftermath of a 1985 mass poultry murder in Laredo, TX. The killer was never found.

threat. Even the sight of farmhands they've known for years causes the chickens to flap wildly and squawk in terror, fearing for their very lives."

Members of the victim's immediate family declined comment, apparently too distraught to talk to the media.

According to profilers from the FBI's Serial Crimes Investigation unit, understanding the killer is the first step toward capturing him or her.

"There is no such thing as a typical chicken killer, so we have to carefully examine the evidence," FBI agent James Oberkfell said. "Since the body does not seem to have been sexually abused in any way, we're most likely dealing with someone who only lusts blood. But whatever the motivation, judging from the efficient, methodical manner in which the body was dismembered, we can assume that our killer is experienced and smart. He's done it before. And we believe he's working himself up to doing it again."

Oberkfell noted that because so much of the flesh is missing, cannibalism is not out of the question.

"It's a long shot," Oberkfell said, "but it is possible that we're dealing with a bizarre new aberration—a warped, vicious killer with an insatiable hunger for chicken flesh."

Lending credence to Oberkfell's theory is a preliminary forensic-lab report showing that, after being killed, the victim was seasoned with a special blend of 11 herbs and spices and then hand-dipped in extra-crispy batter.

FBI authorities said there is likely no connection between this killing and 1983's infamous "Alabama Slasher" murders, in which dozens of chicken legs, covered in what laboratory tests identified as cole slaw, were discovered in a plastic garbage bag behind a Montgomery KFC. ∅

U.S. Sen. Jesse Helms (R-NC), a long-time NEA critic.

Dadaist Jean Arp agreed. "Dada is, like nature, without meaning," he said. "Dada is for nature and against art."

Added nonsense poet Hugo Ball, founder of Zurich's famed Cabaret Voltaire: "...'dada' ('Dada). Adad Dada Dada Dada." Donning an elaborate, primitivist painted paper mask, he then engaged reporters in a tragico-absurd dance, contorting wildly while bellowing inanities.

Helms, well known for his opposition to arts funding, was adamant in his demand for the removal of the NEA from the national budget.

"The American people will no longer stand for vulgar, grotesque, nonsensical displays that masquerade as art," said Helms, who, along with U.S. Sen. Orrin Hatch (R-UT), has called for the passage of obscenity laws granting police and government officials broader powers in the prosecution and censorship of art.

In a show of solidarity with Republican legislators, Andre Breton, who founded the surrealist movement in 1923, fired a pistol at random into the crowd, conceptually evoking the hideous irrationality of the collective unconscious and wounding Hatch.

Urging reporters to "imagine a boot stamping on a face eternally," Breton, equal to Francis Picabia as the most radical anti-art advocate within the Dadaist camp, theatrically demonstrated Helms' vision. In a collaborative staged "manifestation," Picabia penciled a series of drawings, which Breton erased as Picabia went along.

"So-called modern art is, at its core,

an absurd and purposeless exercise," said Helms, echoing the Dadaists' sentiments. He then announced the Gramm-Helms Decency Act, a bill that would facilitate the legal prosecution of obscenity, as well as establish stiffer penalties for the creators and exhibitors of "morally objectionable works."

Dadaist leaders were even more strident than Helms, stressing the need for the elimination not only of art, but also of their movement itself. "To be a Dadaist means to be against dada," Arp said. "Dada equals anti-dada." Urging full-scale rioting, the assembled Dadaists called for their own destruction, each of them running into the audience to pelt those still on stage with tomatoes.

In a gesture honoring Helms and the new bill, seminal anti-artist Marcel Duchamp drew a moustache and beard on a reproduction of Leonardo da Vinci's Mona Lisa. Duchamp titled the resultant image "L.H.O.O.Q.," a series of initials which, when pronounced in French, forms the sentence "Helms au chaud au cul," or "Helms has hot pants."

Centered in Berlin, Paris, and Zurich, the Dadaist movement was launched as an expression of revulsion by the senseless butchery of WWI.

"While the guns rumbled in the distance," Arp said, "we had a dim premonition that power-mad gangsters would one day use art as a means of deadening men's minds."

When told of Arp's comments, Helms said he was "fairly certain" he agreed. ✍

STARBUCKS from page 81

Above: A Starbucks barista near the Indiana-Ohio border engages in reconnaissance of an undetermined nature.

ica showing the location of every existing Starbucks. Lines drawn between the various stores form geometric patterns across the U.S., including five-pointed stars, Masonic symbols, and, in the Seattle area, the image of a gigantic Oroborous serpent wrapped around an inverted ziggurat.

Starbucks management has been tight-lipped regarding the upcoming changes. No upper-level executives have been seen in public since the

first of the month, and no details seem to be forthcoming. Visitors to the Starbucks web site, however, are greeted with a letter from Starbucks CEO Howard Schultz reading in part:

"To our valued Starbucks customer: Just wait until you see the exciting changes we've got in store for you as part of our new Phase Two. When you finally see what we've got brewing here at Starbucks, you'll have no choice but to love it." ✍

EDITORIAL

# I Just Love Corporations!

Do you know what I love? Corporations! Some of my favorites are Raytheon, Unisys, Morton Thiokol, AlliedSignal, US West, and Ingersoll-Rand. Have you seen the new Archer Daniels Midland annual report? It's amazing.

**Korporation Korner**
**By Cynthia Steuben**

I don't know what it is about corporations, but I just can't get enough of them. I love the logos, CEOs, and products, and I especially love scouring the media for info about them. In the last issue of Forbes, they listed the corporations to watch in '98, and Bristol-Myers Squibb, one of my all-time favorites, was right at the top of the list. I was so excited, I cut the article out, laminated it, and put it up on my bedroom wall next to my "Dow Chemical Cares" poster. (Not to brag, but I was a fan of Bristol-Meyers way back before they even acquired Squibb.)

When I was a kid, Monsanto was my favorite corporation. I remember staying up and watching television late into the night just to hear its name mentioned at the end of that commercial for its artificial-turf products. In fifth grade, I had the biggest crush on Monsanto CEO Alan Remlinger, and I even sent him an invitation to my birthday party. (I was so devastated when he didn't come.) I'm not that into Monsanto anymore, but there will always be a place in my heart for it.

If you're ever in my neck of the woods, I'd love to show you my collection of corporation memorabilia. I've got 11 different Honeywell keychains, as well as ones from American Brands, McGraw-Hill, and Lyondell Petrochemical. I've also got three SBC Communications sun visors. But my most prized possession of all has to be my Conoco water bottle with the old blue-and-white logo. We're talking pre-takeover here. I hear it's really valuable, but I don't care how much it's worth, because I would never, ever think of getting rid of it.

I gave away the Warner-Lambert T-shirt I got on my 1983 summer-vacation tour of southern pharmaceutical companies, and I've regretted it every day since. At least I still have other souvenirs of that roadtrip, like the great photos of me in front of the headquarters of Merck, Pfizer, and Pharmacia & Upjohn. What a trip that was!

(I'd better watch myself, or I'll talk your ear off about my tour of Abbott Laboratories headquarters in Houston!)

If I had to choose my favorite corporation today, I'd have to say it's Ap-

---

## Some of my favorites are Raytheon, Unisys, Morton Thiokol, AlliedSignal, US West, and Ingersoll-Rand.

---

plied Materials. It makes the best semiconductors. And Applied Materials CEO Robert DiVita has got to be the coolest CEO ever. I heard that at the last shareholders meeting in Tempe, AZ, he said he's fully committed to making Applied Materials the world leader in electronic components in the 21st century. Is he awesome, or what?

I'm in the process of organizing a Corporations Lovers' Club so people like me can have a place to talk with other corporation-lovers. In addition to weekly meetings, we'll take field trips to places like Weyerhaeuser's paper-processing mill in Monroe, LA, and maybe even sit in on a Rockwell International policy-review meeting. Wouldn't that be something!

But even if I can't organize the club, that's okay, because there's already plenty on my plate: I've got a tour of the Federated Department Stores headquarters lined up, and, as if that isn't enough, I might get clearance to sit in on the company's annual shareholders meeting. If that comes through, I can die happy. If not, I'm still sure to enjoy my special birthday dinner plans in the employee commissary. ✍

NEWS IN BRIEF

## Hamburglar Urges Senate Subcommittee To 'Robble Robble Robble'

WASHINGTON, DC—Denouncing a prison system he called "robble robble robble," hamburger advocate and convicted felon Hamburglar addressed the Senate Subcommittee on Penal Reform Sunday, demanding more hu-

mane conditions for the nation's inmates. "Robble robble robble robble robble robble robble robble robble robble robble robble," an emotional Hamburglar told the 12-member committee. "Robble robble robble robble. Robble robble robble robble robble robble robble: Robble robble." Reaction to the speech was mixed. "Certainly there is room for improvement in our penal system," U.S. Sen. Bob Smith (R-NH) said. "But I would hardly call the current situation 'robble.'" ✍

## Brown Workers Put Company In The Black

see BUSINESS page 1C

## 7-Year-Old Told To Take It Like A Man

see LOCAL page 12B

## Maria Shriver's Face Resharpened

see PEOPLE page 12D

## New Gum Making The Rounds At Work

see OFFICE page 6C

## Delicious Smell Of Slow-Roasted Pork Wafts Gently From Downed 747

see NATION page 5D

A look at the numbers that shape your world.

How Do We Like Our Cock?

10% Hot
19% Black
16% Throbbing
17% Hard, Bi-Curious
24% Meaty
14% Pumping

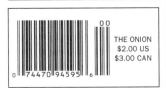

THE ONION
$2.00 US
$3.00 CAN

0 74470 94595 6

# the ONION

WWW.THEONION.COM     AMERICA'S FINEST NEWS SOURCE™     FOUNDED 1871

# World Death Rate Holding Steady At 100 Percent

GENEVA, SWITZERLAND—World Health Organization officials expressed disappointment Sunday over the group's finding that, despite the enormous efforts of doctors, rescue workers, and other medical professionals worldwide, the global death rate remains at 100 percent.

Death, a metabolic affliction causing shutdown of all life functions, has long been considered humanity's number-one health concern. Responsible for 100 percent of all recorded fatalities worldwide, the condition has no cure.

"I was really hoping, what with all those new radiology treatments, rescue helicopters, cardiovascular-exercise machines, and what have you, that we might at least make a dent in it this year," WHO Director General Dr. Ernst Wessel said. "Unfortunately, it would appear that the death rate remains constant, as it has since the dawn of time."

Many suggest that the high mortali-

ty rate represents a massive failure on the part of the planet's healthcare workers.

"The inability of doctors and scientists to address and confront this issue of death is nothing less than a scandal," concerned parent Marcia Grella said. "Do you have any idea what a full-blown case of death looks like? I do, and believe me, it's not pretty. In prolonged cases, total decomposition of the corpse is the re-

see DEATH page 84

# Clinton Makes Collage For Best Friend

WASHINGTON, DC—In a nationally televised press conference Sunday, President Clinton unveiled a collage he made for James McEwen, former U.S. Assistant Secretary of Energy and the man Clinton described as "my best friend in the whole world."

Clinton said he made the collage for McEwen, who is moving to California next week to head the state's Energy Department, because he "wanted to let him know that our friendship is still incredibly important to me even though we're going to be far apart."

The collage, which the president reportedly stayed up until 2 a.m. Saturday creating, is constructed of magazine cut-outs glued to a piece of drawing paper and decorated with a small amount of glitter sparklies. Its construction took nearly three hours at an estimated cost of $2.75.

According to White House press secretary Mike McCurry, Clinton and McEwen met at a Cabinet meeting several years ago and have been in-

separable ever since. "They do everything together: plan economic policies, revise House-approved legislation, attend closed-door strategy sessions, everything," McCurry said. "It's

going to be really hard for them to be so far away from each other."

McCurry added that Clinton and McEwen have mutually vowed to

see COLLAGE page 84

# '85 Chicago Bears Return To Studio

## Shufflin' Crew Begins Work On Long-Awaited Follow-Up Album

CHICAGO—In an announcement that has electrified the music world, the Chicago Bears Shufflin' Crew confirmed Sunday that it is reuniting and will soon begin work on its first new material since the seminal 1985 "Super Bowl Shuffle" single.

Confirming the recent

swirl of music-industry rumors regarding a possible reunion, Shufflin' Crew lead singer Willie Gault told reporters: "After nearly 12 years of solo gigs and side projects, we decided it was time for us to work together again."

Gault strongly denied ru-

see BEARS page 84

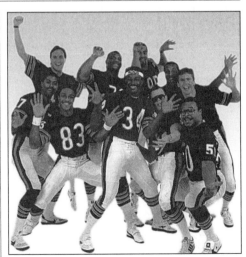

Above: A 1985 photo of the original Shufflin' Crew lineup. The band recently reunited after 12 years apart.

DEATH from page 83

sult."

"What about the children?" Grella added.

"At this early date, I don't want to start making broad generalizations," Citizens For Safety's Robert Hamlin said, "but it seems possible that birth—as well as the subsequent life cycle that follows it—may pose a serious safety risk to all involved."

Death, psychologists say, affects not only the dead, but also the non-dead.

"Those who suffer from death can be highly traumatized by it, often so severely that it kills them," noted therapist Dr. Eli Wasserbaum said. "But it can also be very traumatic for those left behind. The sudden cessation of metabolic activity characteristic of terminal cases of death often leaves dead people in a position where they are unable to adequately provide for the emotional needs of their still-living loved ones."

In the most serious cases of death, Wasserbaum explained, the trauma inflicted upon loved ones of the deceased may continue throughout their lives, until their own deaths.

"Thus," Wasserbaum said, "the 'vicious cycle' of death trauma continues indefinitely."

"Everybody talks about death," U.S. Sen. Pete Domenici (R-NM) said, "but nobody seems to actually be doing anything about it. I propose we stop molly-coddling death, not to mention the multibillion-dollar hospital, mortuary, funeral, and burial industries that reap huge profits from it."

Under a new law proposed by Domenici, all federal funds would be withheld from the medical industry until it "gets serious and starts cracking down on death."

Consumer-rights advocate and staunch anti-death activist Ralph Nader agreed.

"Why should we continue to spend billions of dollars a year on a health-care industry whose sole purpose is to prevent death, only to find that death still awaits us all?" Nader asked in an impassioned address to several suburban Californians. "That's called a zero percent return on our investment, and that's not fair. It's time the paying customer stood up to the HMOs and the so-called 'medical health professionals' and said, 'Enough is enough. I'm paying through the nose here, and I don't ever want to die.'" ∅

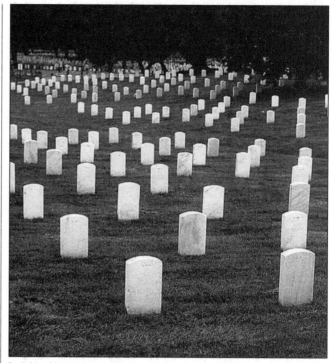

Death (above) has long been considered humanity's number-one health concern. Responsible for 100 percent of all recorded fatalities worldwide, the condition has no cure.

BEARS from page 83

mors that the Crew was returning to the studio looking for trouble.

"We didn't come here looking for trouble," Gault said. "We just came to record the long-awaited follow-up to the 'Super Bowl Shuffle.'"

According to Shufflin' Crew member William "Refrigerator" Perry, he, Gault, and punky QB Jim McMahon have written rough demo versions of 10 to 15 songs, which will, over the next two months, be fleshed out in the studio with producer Steve Albini.

Perry said fans can expect the new album to be "darker and more introspective" than the group's "Shuffle"-era work.

"[The new album] will reflect our maturation as a group and as individuals," said Perry, who may be large but is no dumb cookie. "Back then, we were young, wild, and arrogant: Jim [McMahon] had his spiked hair, shades, and controversial, message-bearing headbands, and I had my legendary eating exploits and rushing touchdowns. We had this attitude like, 'We're so bad, we know we're good, blowing your mind like we knew we would.' But while the new record will still have that trademark Shufflin' Crew swagger, it will also show our more reflective side."

All of the original Shufflin' Crew members are expected to participate in the reunion except Otis Wilson, who told *Spin* magazine in a recent interview that his "heart just isn't in it anymore."

"Back when the group first started, we were just struttin' for fun," Wilson said. "But once we hit it big, everything changed. Suddenly, there were business meetings, publicity appearances, video shoots, sponsorship deals. Before long, it wasn't about the music. That's when I knew I had to get out."

Numerous names have circulated as possible Wilson replacements, ranging from former Poco bassist Jim Messina to former Bengals running back Ickey Woods.

"Otis has made his decision, and we respect that. It will be difficult, but we must go on as a band without him," Shufflin' Crew co-founder Walter Payton said.

Added Payton: "Running the ball is like making romance."

Though the album is still months from completion, the Shufflin' Crew tried out some of the new material at an unannounced gig at Chicago's Lounge Ax club last Friday. Response from the sold-out crowd was overwhelming.

"They sounded really good, really tight," said diehard fan Jeff Tolbert, who said he has been to more than 250 Shufflin' Crew shows. "Once they got warmed up, they were rocking like vintage '85 Crew."

"They kicked some serious ass tonight," said Rick Hall, lead singer of 4-6 Defense, a Zion, IL, Shufflin' Crew tribute band. "Richard Dent still blows me away live."

In negotiating terms for the new album with Geffen Records, the Shufflin' Crew made one demand: complete creative control.

"We made it clear that under no circumstances would we allow participation by the female referee who twice blew a whistle over our singers' attempts to say the word 'ass' during the 'Shuffle' sessions," backup vocalist Steve Fuller said. "The Bears traffic in the truth, and either you can handle it or you can't. Censorship is slavery."

Expected to hit stores in early November, the new album will be followed by a world tour beginning in March 1998. All proceeds from both the album and tour will go toward charity.

"I want to stress that we are not doing this because we're greedy," Payton said. "The Bears are doing this to feed the needy."

One of the most successful American bands of the mid-'80s, the Shufflin' Crew broke up in May 1986 due to creative differences and infighting, particularly between Gault and keyboardist Gary Fencik. Gault embarked on a solo career in 1987 and scored a minor hit with the song 'Chocolate Swirl (That's What I'm As Smooth As),' but never equaled the success he'd enjoyed with the Shufflin' Crew. Fencik and Fuller went on to form the supergroup Touchback with New York Giants wide receiver Phil McConkey and Miami Dolphins punter Reggie Roby.

"After so many years apart, it feels good to be back together again," Gault said. "But most of all, I'm happy for all the Bears Shufflin' Crew fans out there. You guys are the reason we're shufflin' on down. We're doin' it for you." ∅

COLLAGE from page 83

K.I.T./C.A.T. (Keep In Touch/Call A Ton).

"That's because they're V.B.F.F.A.E.," McCurry said. "Very Best Friends Forever And Ever."

As best friends should be, Clinton and McEwen are always there for each other. "Last year, when my healthcare package got voted down in the Senate, I called James, totally bawling. Even though he had a report due the next morning to the U.S. Nuclear Regulatory Commission that he hadn't finished, he still stayed up until like four in the morning listening to me cry."

Clinton also recalled the time the 1993 budget was due.

"I was at the White House finishing up the budget, and I was kind of down because I had to cut some of the AFDC funding I'd promised not to cut," Clinton said. "So James came over, and we ordered a pizza and just completely stuffed ourselves! It was so much fun that I forgot all about the budget cuts."

When told of Clinton's comments, McEwen added, "He forgot about the pint of Ben & Jerry's we pigged out on afterwards!"

Republican response to the collage has been largely negative.

"God, Clinton is such a phony," said Sen. Alfonse D'Amato (R-NY). "He made almost the same exact collage for George Stephanopoulos when he left the White House staff to pursue a media career, and he said all that same stuff about how they were best friends and he'd miss him and all. Then, after a few months, they totally lost touch."

Upon learning of the collage, Speaker of the House Newt Gingrich (R-GA) said, "Clinton is so gay."

The president responded swiftly to the Gingrich attack. "Oh, like I care what he thinks," Clinton said. "He's such a retard. Nice hair, Newt."

Clinton has already begun work on a pair of friendship bracelets, scheduled for completion in May 1998. ∅

# Maybe I Can Impress Her With My *Holy Grail* Quotes

By Larry Groznic

Ah, Aimee Porter. How often I have gazed at you from across the coffee shop, longing to smell your hair, to feel your sympathetic cheek against mine.

Thus far, I have failed to catch Aimee's eye. I have waited for the perfect moment to make my approach, but it has not yet come. But when it does, I am confident my trump card shall spell love for us both. For Aimee Porter is a woman of considerable intelligence and discernment—a woman who cannot help but appreciate some of the finest wit and cinematic brilliance ever produced, the immortal *Monty Python And The Holy Grail.*

Even now, I can see that fateful conversation in which we finally connect as soulmates. While engaging her in superficial conversation on such trivial matters as the weather or her interests, I shall cunningly seek my chance to insert a brilliant *Grail* quote.

Perhaps the presidential election will come up, affording me the opportunity to say, "Supreme executive power derives from a mandate from the masses, not from some farcical aquatic ceremony!" Or maybe, while talking about the unusual cold spell of the past week, she will make some sophisticated meteorological observation, rendering it appropriate for me to blurt out, "Who are you who are so wise in the ways of science?" Or perchance, after all these months, she will finally ask what my name is, and I will be able to come back with, "There are some who call me... Tim." I would then laugh and tell my fair Aimee that, joking aside, I'm really called Larry. In that moment, I will have won her.

After all, what more could a fetching lass want than to be wooed with perfectly memorized dialogue from the funniest film ever made? I should like to meet the maiden so arrogant that even a spot-on rendition of "The Ballad Of Sir Robin" is insufficient to melt her stony heart.

It's funny, isn't it? How you can go through life, seeing a certain someone as no more than a fringe player in your existence and then, one magical day, you find out they can recite the *Holy Grail* script from memory, and you're not such a stuck-up princess toward them anymore?

That shall be a glorious day, my dear Aimee. Taller than a Knight Of Ni will I stand on that day when your heart is won. I shall quote entire scenes to your lovely and impressed face, be they the Bring Out Your Dead scene, the Killer Rabbit scene, or the Witch Trial.

I shall woo you with the dulcet tones of the Camelot song, flawlessly singing even its most inscrutable lyrics, including, "Between our quests we sequin vests and impersonate Clark Gable." What man in this coffee shop but I can lay claim to knowing these words?

Once you have been won over, I will bring you back to my parents' luxuriously appointed basement, where I shall show you all of the edited *Grail* footage from the 7th Level CD-ROM game. And, rest assured, I will show you the rare, never-before-seen King Brian The Wild scene featured at the end of the game. Yes, I realize it is a rather uninspired rendition of a decades-old script by the five surviving Pythons—and inexplicably truncated in ways that remove the original jokes from their context—but let us not lose sight of the fact that it is, after all, a scene deleted from *Holy Grail.*

If this were not enough, I shall also show you my VHS dub of the extras from the Criterion laserdisc of the

see HOLY GRAIL page 86

---

## Freak Accident Paralyzes Man From Waist Up

MESA, AZ—A bizarre spinal injury sustained in a car accident Sunday has left local resident Roberto Montenegro paralyzed from the waist up. "Roberto is back on his feet," said Mesa General Hospital head of surgery William Maxon. "Unfortunately, though, he has lost all feeling in his head, arms, and torso. No longer able to move from the waist up, he cannot eat, speak, dial a telephone, type, open doors, or look sideways." Doctors said Montenegro should be able to resume his career as a professional soccer player as early as next week.

## God Proclaims Raspberries 'Now Even More Berrilicious'

HEAVEN—Seeking to boost sales of His tart, fruity product, God announced Monday that starting March 1, the great taste of raspberries will be "even more berrilicious." "Get ready for a whole new taste sensation," God said. "Soon, raspberries will be bursting with so much outrageous fruit flavor, you'll want to call them 'razzle-dazzleberries.'" If raspberry consumption fails to increase, other changes are in store, including "magic color-change berries," available on bushes for a limited time next spring. "Slam that great fruity taste in your face," God urged. ∅

---

**the ONION presents:**

# Foreign Travel Tips

Traveling abroad can be a wonderful experience, but it's important to be prepared. Here are some tips to help make your next trip a safe and enjoyable one:

- Get foreign TV schedules in advance to decide exactly what shows you want to watch.
- Always bellow, "I'm an American, you filthy foreign barbarians!" to ensure top-quality service while abroad.
- If you bend over to close your suitcase and hear a "Zwip! Thump!" sound, then discover a knife wobbling in the wall behind you, it could mean you've unwittingly become entangled in a web of international espionage and intrigue.
- Carrying cash is unwise when traveling abroad. Be sure to purchase plenty of McDonald's gift certificates before you leave.
- Many people in foreign countries do not speak English. You may need to speak louder and/or slower in order to make yourself understood.
- When traveling through Europe, remind everyone you encounter that, if not for America, they would all be speaking German. (Note: Does not work in Germany.)
- Before leaving home, take your pets to the local humane society and have them put to sleep. Get new pets when you come back.
- Do not treat foreign waiters with the slightest shred of human dignity. A friendly attitude will only earn their disrespect.
- When traveling through Italy, be sure to get a load of the racks on some of those Ginas.
- If you see Karl Malden ominously narrating before a camera while you are checking

- into a hotel, keep an extra-close eye on your credit cards. A commercial may be being filmed with you as the subject/victim.
- When in Great Britain, remember to follow local customs and eat with a pair of tweezers.
- Upon reentering the U.S., remove heroin-filled condoms from stomach immediately.
- Foreigners have lots of colorful local customs and ways, and many of them will not mind if you ask them to shoot bananas out of their vaginas, blow smoke rings with their anuses, or perform fellatio on mules. Live it up a little—it can't hurt to ask.

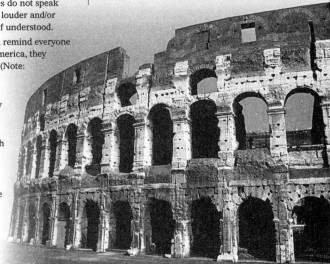

film. The original theatrical trailer, the scene from the Japanese dub, the little extra bit of footage in The Tale Of Sir Galahad... whatever you wish shall be thine.

Ah, Galahad! How much like Michael Palin as Sir Galahad am I, longing for the touch of a fair maiden, only to be dragged unceremoniously from the Castle Anthrax by unsympathetic Knights or that guy who's always hanging around Aimee and may or may not be her boyfriend. But I will prevail in the end. I will find my moment, look Aimee more or less in the eye, and dazzle her with my arcane knowledge of Grail.

Oh, to hell with this beating about the proverbial bush! This eternal strategizing and conniving! I should simply get up, walk right over to Aimee, drop to one knee, and say, "Oh, fair one, behold your humble servant Sir Launcelot of Camelot, I have come to take y— Oh, I'm terribly sorry." And then stand up and look all confused, just like in the Swamp Castle scene. That is what a real man would do!

No, no—patience is the watchword here. A creature as desirable as Aimee has no doubt seen that approach a hundred times over. More is required of me. Even more than the Swamp Castle scene.

But wait! What if, beneath her delightful countenance, Aimee is a hated Brianist? That all-too-common breed of boorish philistine who actually prefers Life Of Brian to the obviously superior Grail? Let it not be, my fair Aimee. Say that you can see past Brian's flat sex jokes and speech-impediment-driven farce.

Well, we shall cross that bridge when we come to it. (As long as we can answer The Three Questions, that is!) If true love is at stake, she will surely be willing to convert.

Yes, Aimee Porter, it may take an eternity. And fire, flood, and bickering, gay, three-headed knights may stand between us. But one day, we will find our way to each other's arms, and there forever stay.

And there will be much rejoicing. ⌀

## NEWS IN BRIEF

### Glandular Problem Causes Man To Eat Fifth Helping

FREDERICKSBURG, MD—Born with a rare, debilitating glandular disorder, 450-pound Fredericksburg resident Gordon Hotchkiss, 41, helped himself to a fifth serving of mashed potatoes Sunday. "Why, oh, why, was I chosen by God to suffer from this horrible blaaarghmummm?" moaned the stricken Hotchkiss, helplessly shoveling fistfuls of buttery mashed potatoes into his mouth. "What have I done to deserve this awful glomphummm?" Hotchkiss' condition, known within medical circles as "bigfatfuckitis," also prevents him from using the stairs instead of the elevator to get to his second-floor apartment. ⌀

## INFOGRAPHIC

### Spring Break 2000

How do America's college students plan to spend their upcoming Spring Break?

| | |
|---|---|
| 7% | Vomiting Bud Ice into mouth of some chick from Ohio State |
| 17% | Doing Jell-O shots at Señor Frog's, fucking, crying in lap of best friend, doing Jell-O shots at Señor Frog's, fucking, crying in lap of best friend |
| 9% | If woman, sustaining one long continuous shriek for whole week |
| 3% | Shaving pubic hair into perfect little strip in case Playboy shows up at South Padre |
| 2% | Getting date-raped on bathroom floor |
| 14% | Showing off clit piercing for Girls Gone Wild 3: Best Of Spring Break cameras |
| 5% | Watching the soft renewal of springtime soothe the icy bite of winter as Gaia is born anew |
| 8% | Plummeting 30 stories from hotel balcony to concrete below |
| 11% | Spending portion of trust fund earmarked for "acting like a jackass" |
| 4% | Blaring Blink-182 from window of Days Inn |
| 13% | Winning wet T-shirt contest as important step toward building self-esteem |
| 1% | Getting great tan, chlamydia |
| 6% | Throwing own feces, puffing out body hair to appear larger |

## CRIME

# Romantic-Comedy Behavior Gets Real-Life Man Arrested

Above: Police officers take Denny Marzano into custody following his latest romantic-comedy-like crime.

TORRANCE, CA—Denny Marzano, a 28-year-old Torrance man, was arrested Sunday for engaging in the type of behavior found in romantic comedies.

Marzano was taken into custody after violating a restraining order filed against him by Kelly Hamilton, 25, an attractive, unmarried kindergarten teacher who is new to the L.A. area.

According to Hamilton, Marzano has stalked her for the past two months, spying on her, tapping her phone, serenading her with The Carpenters'"Close To You" at her place of employment, and tricking her into boarding a Caribbean-bound jet.

Hamilton made the call to police at 7:30 p.m., when she discovered that the bearded cable repairman she had let into her apartment was actually Marzano in disguise.

"Thank God he's in custody, and this nightmare is finally over," said Hamilton, a single mother struggling to raise an adorable, towheaded boy by herself in the big city. "I repeatedly told him I wasn't interested, but he just kept resorting to crazier and crazier stunts to make me fall in love with him."

Marzano, who recently broke his leg falling off a ladder leaning against Hamilton's second-story bedroom window, said he was "extremely surprised" that his plan to woo the woman had failed.

"She was supposed to hate me at first but gradually be won over by my incredible persistence, telling me that no one has ever gone to such lengths to win her love," Marzano said. "But for some reason, her irritation never melted into affection."

### Said Marzano: "For some reason, her irritation never melted into affection."

In addition to the stalking charges, Marzano is accused of framing Stuart Polian, a handsome Pasadena attorney and chief competitor for Hamilton's hand, for arson. Marzano denied the charges.

"While it's true that I would love to have seen my main romantic rival out of the picture, I didn't burn down that animal shelter and try to pin it on Mr. Polian," Marzano said. "I have always believed I could win Kelly's love without resorting to such illegalities."

Marzano had been arrested for engaging in romantic-comedy behavior on five previous occasions. The most recent arrest came in May 2000, after he pretended to be a confession-booth priest in the hopes of tricking a Fresno, CA, woman into unwittingly revealing her love for him. ⌀

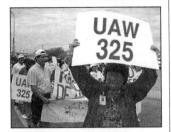

**GM Workers Strike For 2,000-Peso Raise**

see BUSINESS page 9A

**Little Debbie Conquers Jenny Craig In Midnight Showdown**

see LOCAL page 2A

**Jurisprudence Fetishist Gets Off On Technicality**

see LIFESTYLE page 11B

**Gray Brick Building Churns Out Endless Supply Of Dental Hygienists**

see CAREERS page 10C

**STATshot**

A look at the numbers that shape your world.

**Catchphrases That Never Caught On**

1. Just call me Eight-Way Wesley!
2. Upholster *that!*
3. Well, Treat my Williams!
4. That wasn't what the commissioner saw!
5. Fill it with krill, Gil!
6. I was fuckin' my Mama!
7. Save it for someone with eczema!
8. Well, I'll be a greased Jesus!
9. Tell it to Linda Lavin!

# the ONION®

WWW.THEONION.COM     AMERICA'S FINEST NEWS SOURCE™     FOUNDED 1871

## American People Ruled Unfit To Govern

WASHINGTON, DC—In a historic decision with major implications for the future of U.S. participatory democracy, the Supreme Court ruled 8-1 Friday that the American people are unfit to govern.

The controversial decision, the first of its kind in the 210-year history of American representative government, was, according to Justice David Souter, "a response to the clear, demonstrable incompetence and indifference of the current U.S. citizenry in matters concerning the operation of this nation's government."

As a result of the ruling, the American people will no longer retain the power to choose their own federal, state, and local officials or vote on matters of concern to the public.

"This decision was by no means easy, but it unfortunately had to be made," said Justice Antonin Scalia,

see UNFIT page 88

## Clinton Threatens To Drop Da Bomb On Iraq

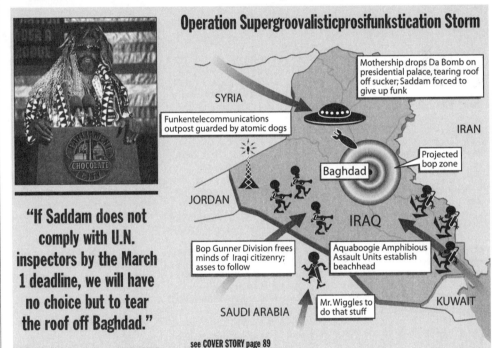

**Operation Supergroovalisticprosifunkstication Storm**

Mothership drops Da Bomb on presidential palace, tearing roof off sucker; Saddam forced to give up funk

SYRIA

Funkentelecommunications outpost guarded by atomic dogs

IRAN

Projected bop zone

Baghdad

JORDAN

IRAQ

Bop Gunner Division frees minds of Iraqi citizenry; asses to follow

Aquaboogie Amphibious Assault Units establish beachhead

SAUDI ARABIA

Mr. Wiggles to do that stuff

KUWAIT

"If Saddam does not comply with U.N. inspectors by the March 1 deadline, we will have no choice but to tear the roof off Baghdad."

see COVER STORY page 89

## Letter D Pulls Sponsorship From *Sesame Street*
### Consonant Alienated By Controversial New Gay Muppet

Above: Embattled homosexual muppet "Roger" (center).

NEW YORK—A spokeswoman for the letter D announced Friday that the consonant is withdrawing sponsorship from *Sesame Street* following a Children's Television Workshop announcement that a homosexual muppet will soon join the show's cast.

"The letter D is proud to have brought you many wonderful *Sesame Street* episodes throughout the program's 28-year history," said Patricia Willis, public-relations director for D. "But the letter D does not condone the sort of morally questionable lifestyles *Sesame Street* is advocating with the introduction of this new character. It can no longer in good conscience associate itself with the show."

Willis said D's withdrawal is effective immediately and applies to both capital and lower-case versions of the letter.

The gay muppet, "Roger," will be introduced on *Sesame Street* March 14, CTW president Leslie Charren said. Thus far, no other sponsors have pulled

see MUPPET page 88

who penned the majority decision in the case. "The U.S. Constitution is very clear: In the event that the voting public becomes incapacitated or otherwise unfit to carry out its duties of self-governance, there is a danger posed to the republic, and the judicial branch is empowered to remove said public and replace it with a populace more qualified to lead."

"In light of their unmitigated apathy toward issues of import to the nation's welfare and their inability to grasp even the most basic principles upon which participatory democracy is built, we found no choice but to rule the American people unfit to govern at this time," Scalia concluded.

The controversial ruling, court members stressed, is not intended as a slight against the character of the American people, but merely a necessary measure for the public good.

"The public's right to the best possible representation is a founding principle of our nation," Justice Sandra Day O'Connor told reporters. "If you were on a jet airliner, you wouldn't want an untrained, incompetent pilot at the controls. This is the same thing. As federal justices, we have taken a solemn oath to uphold every citizen's constitutional rights, and if we were to permit an irresponsible, uninterested public to continue to helm the ship of state, we would be remiss in our duties and putting the entire nation at risk."

The ruling brings to an end a grueling 10-month process, during which more than 100 Supreme Court hearings were held to determine the public's capacity for self-governance. Despite the fact that these hearings were aired on C-SPAN, most Americans were unaware of them because coverage was largely eclipsed by the Clinton-Lewinsky scandal, the retirement of NBA legend Michael Jordan, and the release of *Titanic* on home video.

The Supreme Court found that, though 78 percent of U.S. citizens have seen the much-anticipated *Star Wars* prequel trailer, only one in 200,000 were aware that the multibillion-dollar "Star Wars" missile-defense system had been approved by Congress. Additionally, while 62 percent of citizens correctly identified the cast of *Suddenly Susan*, only .01 percent were able to identify Attorney General Janet Reno beyond "some woman Jay Leno always says looks like a man." Further, only .0003 percent could correctly identify the ancient Greek city-state of Athens as the birthplace of the idea of an educated citizenry participating in democratic self-rule.

But the final straw, Supreme Court justices said, came last week, when zero out of 500,000 randomly polled citizens were aware that Russian president Boris Yeltsin had threatened global thermonuclear war in response to NATO air attacks in Yugoslavia.

"I mean, come on," Justice William Rehnquist said. "Global thermonu-

Above: Some of the millions of empty voting booths that can be seen across America each November.

clear war? It's just ridiculous. There was just no way we could trust such a populace to keep running things after that."

Populations currently being considered to fill the leadership void until the American people can be rehabilitated and returned to self-governance include those of Switzerland, Sweden, and Canada.

"I'm willing to do what I can to help out in this time of crisis and make sure that my vote counts," said Stockholm resident Per Johanssen. "I've been reading up on America a bit, just to get a general idea of what needs to be done, and from what I can tell, they really need some sort of broad-based healthcare reform over there right away."

In a provisional test of the new system, the Canadian province of Saskatchewan will hold primaries next Tuesday to re-evaluate last fall's gubernatorial election in Minnesota.

The lone dissenting vote came from Justice Anthony Kennedy, who wrote in his minority opinion: "Although the American people are clearly unable to make responsible decisions at this time, it is not their fault that they are so uninformed. Rather, the blame lies with the media interests and corporate powers that intentionally keep them in the dark on crucial issues."

Kennedy concluded his opinion by tendering his resignation and announcing his intent "to move to a small island somewhere."

Thus far, reaction to the ruling has been largely indifferent.

"The people ruled unfit to govern? Yeah, I think I might've heard something about that," said Covington, KY, office-supply salesman Neil Chester. "I think I saw it on the news or something, when I was flipping past trying to find that show about the lady sheriff."

"If you ask me, voting was a big pain, anyway," agreed mother of four Sally Heim of Augusta, ME. "At least now I'm free to do my soap-opera-trivia crossword puzzles in peace without all that distraction about who's running for 2nd District Alderperson and what-not."

Despite the enormous impact the ruling would seem to have, many political experts are downplaying its significance.

"It doesn't really change anything, to be honest," said Princeton University political-science professor Benjamin James. "The public hasn't made any real contributions to the governance of the country in decades, so I don't see how this ruling affects all that much."

"I wouldn't worry about it," James added. "It's not that important." ∅

out, though the number seven has requested to screen the episode in advance before making a decision.

Many television insiders say D's withdrawal was motivated by a fear of alienating conservatives, a segment of the population that employs the letter frequently.

"D is for, among other things, demagoguery, dogma, and doctrine, words crucial to right-wing groups like the Christian Coalition," said Yale University professor J. Wright Franklin. "It is likely that D felt it could ill-afford to offend such a large segment of its users."

While a permanent replacement for D has not yet been found, *Sesame*

*Street* officials said the number three will temporarily fill in for it in a number of the show's animated shorts. Other pieces will simply skip from C to E, with vocalists stretching out C into two syllables to match the rhythm of the alphabet song.

*Sesame Street* is stung by the sudden departure of its longtime sponsor. Speaking to reporters, cast member Cookie Monster said: "Me disappointed letter D choose to end relationship with *Sesame Street* due to pressure from vocal minority. We accused of endorsing deviant lifestyle. Me say homosexuality natural, not immoral. Diversity and enrichment. That good enough for me." ∅

# You're Going To Love My Balls

By Lowell P. Thurber

I envy you, friend. You are a lucky, lucky person. Treasure this moment, because you are about to gaze upon my balls. And you are going to absolutely love them.

I realize the average person sees a lot of balls in his or her lifetime, but most of those balls are, to put it kindly, subpar. My balls, however, are beautiful. They are perfect in every way, from the sheen of my scrotal sac to the flawless shape and symmetry of my testicles to the flaxen softness of my pubic hair.

I go to great lengths to make sure my balls are show-quality balls. First and foremost is hygiene, of course: Nobody wants to see unclean balls. And not just any soap will do, as harsh detergents can cause unsightly

> **They are perfect in every way, from the sheen of my scrotal sac to the flaxen softness of my pubic hair.**

abrasions and mar the surface of the balls. I recommend a gentle, all-natural cleanser, like Dr. Bronner's Eucalyptus or Ayurvedic Olive Oil soap. The night before displays, I use a separate leave-on conditioner, but for everyday use, a good lotion like Neutrogena is all I really need.

Getting my balls clean and soft, however, is only half of it. I used to apply makeup to them, but the effect was far too artificial—the whole idea behind showing your balls in the first place is to showcase their natural beauty, with the emphasis on natural. So I use all-organic carnauba wax to give them a rich, deep luster. Three coats, buff with a hand-held electric orbital polisher, three more, polish again, and top it off with one final hand-rubbing. When you get down to it, there's just no substitute for bearing down on your balls with some good old-fashioned elbow grease. I do it while watching the evening news.

Yes, proper balls care can be a lot of work, but the enjoyment you get from

see BALLS page 90

# 'The Liberation Of Saddam's Booty Will Soon Begin'

CHOCOLATE CITY—In an address before an emergency session of Parliament Friday, George Clinton said he is prepared to drop Da Bomb on Iraq if Saddam Hussein does not loosen up and comply with U.N. weapons inspectors by the Clinton-imposed deadline of March 1.

"For Saddam Hussein to refuse to let U.N. officials inspect Iraqi weapons facilities as per the terms of Iraq's 1991 Gulf War surrender is decidedly unfunky of him," Clinton said. "While the decision to drop Da Bomb is never easy, unless Saddam gets down with this whole U.N.-inspection thang and seriously refunkatizes his stance by March 1, we will have no choice but to tear the roof off Baghdad."

Preparations for the military strike, dubbed Operation Supergroovalisticprosifunksication Storm, are already underway. The Mothership is ready and on standby at Starchild Air Force Base in Detroit, where more than 5,000 bop gunners are making final preparations for deployment to the Persian Gulf. Clinton has also ordered an additional 2,500 Aquaboogie Amphibious Assault units to the Gulf, bringing the total P-Funk Nation military presence in the region to 23,000.

According to Gen. William "Bootsy" Collins, the primary goal of the ground assault is to breach Hussein's presidential palace, capture the Iraqi leader, and "put some serious funk in his trunk."

Collins acknowledged that the mission at hand will be difficult.

"Saddam's palace is heavily fortified. In the front, it's protected by several dozen towers manned with armed guards, and in the back, there's a 50-foot high hump—so high you can't get over it and so wide you can't get around it," Collins said. "Having our men attempt to attack from the front would be suicide: If we are to have any chance of entering the palace and funkatizing Saddam, we've got to get over the hump. After all, if you want to capture a boogie, you've got to attack from the back."

Despite the difficulty of the task, troop morale is high.

"As a soldier in the army of Uncle Jam, I have pledged my unconditional grooveallegiance to Commander-In-Chief Clinton," said Lt. Bernie Worrell of the army's elite 72nd Promentalshitbackwashpsychosis Enema Squadron. "I am fully prepared to give up my life for the funk. To the rear... march."

"Executing political adversaries, shunning foreigners, condemning America as 'The Great Satan'—that Saddam is one uptight cat," Mothership captain Eddie Hazel said. "For too long, he has ruled Iraq with neither a glide in his stride nor a dip in

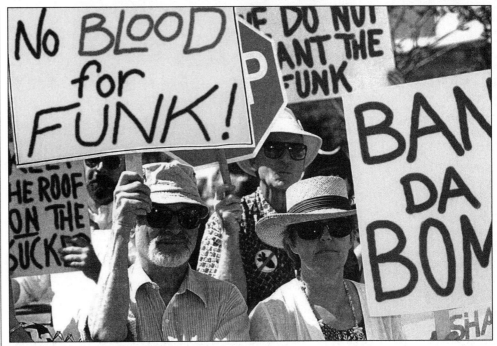

Above: Anti-funk demonstrators protest George Clinton's plan to drop Da Bomb on Baghdad.

his hip. At this point, our only remaining option is to drop a serious funk bomb on him."

Clinton's ultimatum before Parliament was met with high praise from numerous top-ranking Chocolate City officials, including Secretary of Education Richard Pryor, Secretary of Fine Arts Stevie Wonder, and First Lady Aretha Franklin.

"Saddam has two choices," Pryor said. "Get down or step down."

While polls indicate that Operation Supergroovalisticprosifunksication Storm enjoys strong support among Chocolate City residents, many inhabitants of the city's less funky vanilla suburbs question its purpose.

"Why are we dropping Da Bomb on Iraq if it's only Saddam we're after?" Peter Strosser, 37, asked. "If Da Bomb is dropped on Baghdad, the bootys of countless innocent Iraqi civilians will be tragically loosened. Is that what we want, to turn millions of decent, reserved Iraqis into free-spirited, dance-crazed party people? I hope not."

"The effects of dropping this 50,000-megafunk bomb on a heavily populated city like Baghdad will be devastat-

ing," said Linda Sue Strelczyk, president of Suburbanites Against Da Bomb. "At ground zero, the explosion will give off a horrific, blinding flashlight, causing untold millions who look directly into it to get seriously freaky."

Responding to the anti-Bomb protests among the unfunky, Clinton made an impassioned plea for unity.

"In times of crisis such as this, we must stand united, not divided," Clinton said. "We must join together as one nation under a groove, getting down just for the funk of it." ∅

# Amazing New Swiffer Fails To Fill The Void

CINCINNATI—The blank, oppressive void facing the American consumer populace remains unfilled, despite the recent launch of the revolutionary Swiffer dust-elimination system, sources reported Friday.

The lightweight, easy-to-use Swiffer is the 275,894,973rd amazing new product to fail to fill the void—a vast, soul-crushing spiritual vacuum that Americans of all ages helplessly face on a daily basis, with nowhere to turn and no way to escape.

"The remarkable new Swiffer sweeps, dusts, wipes, and cleans with a patented electrostatic action that simply cannot be beat," said spokeswoman Judith McReynolds, media-relations liaison for Procter & Gamble, maker of the dustbroom device. "Whether it's vinyl floors, tile, hardwood, ceilings, or stairs, the incredi-

"I feel so alone," said Hull, loosening her grip on the Swiffer's convenient extendable handle.

ble Swiffer quickly cleans any dry surface by attracting and trapping even the tiniest dirt and dust parti-

cles."

"The incredible Swiffer's extendable telescoping action has just what it takes to cut clean-up time in half," McReynolds continued. "Say goodbye to tedious dusting chores forever... the Swiffer way!"

Upon completing the statement, McReynolds was struck, as she is most days, with a sudden, unbearable feeling that she has wasted her life.

Despite high hopes for the product, the Swiffer has failed to inject a sense of meaning and purpose into the existence of its users.

"The new Swiffer, as seen on TV, requires no spray or chemical cleaners, so I'm sure you can understand how excited I was to finally find something that could give my sad, short existence a sense of worth," said Mani-

see SWIFFER page 90

towoc, WI, homemaker Gwen Hull. "When you finish the clean-up job, simply tear off the patented Swiffer Cloth and throw it away—as easy as one, two, three. But when I did this, tossing the soiled, disposable Swiffer Cloth into the garbage can like so many hollow, rejected yesterdays, I thought to myself, 'Is that it? Aren't I supposed to feel more fulfilled than this?' It all felt so futile. I felt like that Swiffer Cloth in the trash represented me, my hopes and dreams made manifest. I felt like it was my goals and aspirations for a better life that were lying there in the garbage, never to be heard from again."

"I feel so alone," added Hull, loosening her grip on the Swiffer's convenient extendable handle—which can reach even the tightest corners—causing the product to fall to the floor. "So very, very alone."

Hull's reaction was echoed by fellow Swiffer owner Glenn Pulsipher. A 45-year-old telemarketing coordinator for a Van Nuys satellite TV company, he said his recent Swiffer purchase has proven an ineffective void-filler.

"Ever since my divorce nine years ago, I'd been meaning to keep this place a little more clean and presentable for visitors," said Pulsipher, who last had a houseguest in April 1997. "But with all the different sprays and sponges you have to use, who has the time? But when I saw the Swiffer ad on TV, I thought to myself: Wow, all that cleaning power in one simple, easy-to-use tool. And such a bargain. I guess I thought that maybe if I bought one, my life would be easier, more fun, more special. Well, I thought wrong."

"Not that it doesn't work," Pulsipher added. "It does: It works exactly like they said on TV. But after using it once or twice, the sad fact was that I no longer cared."

"Why would I?" he continued, sinking into his living-room La-Z-Boy to watch ESPN alone for the 278th straight night. "I mean, it's a dustbroom. What more is there to say?"

"Dust in the wind," said Pulsipher, his voice taking on a muted tone of resignation as the TV blared. "That's all our various pitiful and deluded human endeavors ever amount to in the end. My job, my marriage—dust. All dust. And all the Swiffers in the world can't sweep it all up."

Many Swiffer owners have attempted to bolster the fleeting satisfaction the product offers with other Swiffer-related activities, but to no avail. In the past four weeks, more than 40,000 achingly empty consumers have logged on to www.swiffer.com to download pages of "Swiffer FAQs" and "Useful Tips" on optimal Swiffer use.

Also widely downloaded was the tour schedule for the "Swiffer Mobile," a Swiffer-themed truck boasting promotional displays, demonstrations of anti-dust technological innovations, and a stated mission to "examine the

**Above:** Bridgeport, CT, homemaker Christine Smalls tries in vain to find some sort of fulfillment with the amazing new Swiffer sweeper.

mundane task of housecleaning under the keen eye of science." The truck, which will travel to 20 markets across the U.S. this summer, is not expected to alleviate Americans' profound sense of emptiness.

The hope that the right product will one day come along and bring happiness to consumers' lives is a long-standing American tradition. But the Swiffer's failure to fill the void has led some to doubt that any product, no matter how revolutionary and convenient, will ever do so.

"It's time we woke up and realized that the wait is never going to end," said Dr. James Ingersoll of the D.C.-based Institute For American Values. "The void is never—I repeat, never—going to be filled by something we see on TV and can order with our credit cards."

For others, however, there remains

reason to believe.

"Just because the Swiffer and the other 35 new products I've bought over the past three months haven't filled the void, that doesn't mean the next product won't be the one," said Minneapolis homemaker Ellen Bender. "I just ordered the new HyperVac Advanced CyberCarpet CleanWare System, and I just can't wait until it arrives and completely transforms my flat, unsatisfying life."

Procter & Gamble offered its apologies to those who had pinned their hopes on the new dustbroom.

"We are deeply sorry for the Swiffer's failure to ease the crushing ennui faced by U.S. consumers, and we promise to redouble our efforts to one day develop a product that will succeed in soothing your tortured souls," a statement released by Procter & Gamble read in part. ∅

having championship-quality balls is well worth the effort. You'll know what I'm talking about once you get a look at my balls. The sheen, the smoothness—do yourself a favor and get good and close when you're looking at them. You'll actually be able to see your reflection in them, like a kid looking into a fuzzy, fleshy, pink Christmas ornament. Get as close as possible—I don't mind. I do this for your enjoyment.

Now, I'm not one of those people who takes the time to fix something up all nice and then doesn't use it. I can't stand that. I mean, the Spirit of St. Louis hangs for all to see in the National Air & Space Museum, but you never see anyone flying it, do you? Well, like Lindbergh's plane, my balls hang for all to see—but I make sure they're not all show and no go. Anyone who wants to can touch my

## Get as close as possible—I don't mind.

balls. Provided, of course, they handle them gently and are wearing lint-free microfiber gloves. And, please, no pulling: This could strain the scrotal sac and cause it to bag out, making it less attractive in appearance.

I promise you this: That magic moment when you first take in the glory of my balls will be one you'll remember for the rest of your life. You will no doubt see my magnificent balls many more times in the coming years, but it will never again be quite like the first time. I hope it's as special for you as it has been for thousands of other lucky folks. Enjoy. ∅

# New 'Time' To Keep Everything From Happening At Once

CAMBRIDGE, MA—On what is now known as "Friday," MIT scientists unveiled "time," a revolutionary new event-sequencing system that organizes phenomena along a four-dimensional axis, preventing everything from taking place simultaneously. "No longer will the extinction of the dinosaurs, the assassination of John F. Kennedy, and the Earth-Xabraxiq Pod Wars all collapse into a single point," theoretical physicist Dr. Lawrence Chang said. "With time, we can now contextualize each of the universe's infinite number of occurrences in its own spatial-temporal plane, creating order where there once was chaos." Added Dr. Erno Toffel: "Using time, one event can be positioned chronologically so as to be the cause of another. For example, a man's death may result in a gun being fired at him. Or the other way around. We're still working out some of the kinks."

# *Motor Trend* Car Of Year Stripped Of Title After Appearing As *Hot Rod* Centerfold

NEW YORK—*Motor Trend* magazine stripped the 1998 Chevrolet Corvette of its "Car Of The Year" title following the sportscar's appearance as *Hot Rod* magazine's June centerfold. "The 1998 Corvette has conducted itself in a manner unbecoming of a *Motor Trend* Car Of The Year," *Motor Trend* editor-in-chief Paul Brookman said, "and we can no longer in good conscience allow this automobile to represent the crown." The 1998 Pontiac Grand Prix, Car Of The Year first runner-up, will take the Corvette's place.

# Man Carefully Selects T-Shirt For Night Out

WILMINGTON, NC—After spending nearly 30 minutes trying on different T-shirts, Wilmington resident Larry Goltz finally settled on a black Peterbilt Trucks shirt for a night on the town Friday. "I was going to wear my Blockbuster Video T-shirt, but it's white, and I wanted something a little nicer for a Friday night. Plus, I wore that one when we went bowling Tuesday," Goltz said. "I was also thinking about my plain red one, but for some reason, I was in the mood to wear something with writing on it. And I like the way the Peterbilt logo on the chest draws attention away from my belly." Goltz said he is "99 percent sure" he made the right choice. ∅

## Woman Tired Of Men Staring At Her Breast Implants

see LOCAL page 3C

## Sun-Dried Sparrow Carcass Washed Away With Hose

see WORLD page 9A

## Charlize Theron Has Opinion

see PEOPLE page 1C

## Black Shopper Repeatedly Asked If He Works There

see LOCAL page 7C

STATshot

A look at the numbers that shape your world.

**Leading Cause Of Death Among Sea-Monkeys**

| | |
|---|---|
| 9% | Spillage |
| 10% | Slain for pelts |
| 11% | Fall from castle tower |
| 22% | Pipe-smoking-related emphysema |
| 20% | Insufficient return postage |
| 17% | Introduction of Kool-Aid into water supply |
| 6% | Cat |
| 5% | Microwave |

THE ONION
$2.00 US
$3.00 CAN

0 74470 94595 6
00

# the ONION®

WWW.THEONION.COM    AMERICA'S FINEST NEWS SOURCE™    FOUNDED 1871

# U.S. Deploys Very Special Forces To Iraq

Above: Sgt. Tommy Dolber, who loves baseball and rollerskating, leads a group of very special forces in maneuvers near the Iraq-Kuwait border. Right: President Clinton fields reporters' questions.

WASHINGTON, DC—Preparing for another possible showdown with Iraq, President Clinton deployed more than 15,000 very special U.S. forces to the Persian Gulf Tuesday.

Clinton said the objective of the mission, named Operation Great Job!, is twofold: to pressure Saddam Hussein into permitting the return of U.N. weapons inspectors, and to provide America's very special forces with a positive, rewarding, esteem-building experience.

"With Operation Great Job!, we send the message loud and clear to Sad-

dam Hussein that his open defiance of the United Nations and international law will not be tolerated," Clinton said. "We also send the equally important message to our own troops that what's important is not whether you

see SPECIAL page 92

# Lord Under Investigation For Failure To Provide

WASHINGTON, DC—The six-millennia-old sky-father deity Yahweh, worshiped by Christians, Muslims, and Jews alike for His alleged all-

The Lord (above) is the subject of a massive U.S. Justice Department investigation.

knowing compassion and vast benevolence toward humanity, refused comment Tuesday on news that the U.S. Justice Department will investigate allegations of failure on His part to provide for His approximately 3.5 billion human followers.

According to the Justice Department, on more than 70 trillion docu-

see LORD page 93

# 'I Provide Office Solutions,' Says Pitiful Little Man

Above: Spineless non-entity Jim Smuda, who offers clients a wide range of consulting and computer-networking services.

SANTA FE, NM—When Santa Fe-area marketing and sales professionals are looking for an office-management consultant with a nose for improving productivity and cost-effectiveness, they turn to Jim Smuda. For the past six years, this pitiful little man has served as senior field consultant at VisTech, one of Santa Fe's leading service-support companies.

"I provide office solutions," the sniveling, detestable Smuda said. "Whether you need help with digital networking, facilities management, outsourcing, systems integration, or document services, I have the experience and know-how to guide you through today's business maze."

"If you've got questions," the 41-year-old worm added, "the team of

experts at VisTech has got the answers."

Before joining VisTech, Smuda spent nine years freelancing as a data-retrieval specialist in the Dallas-Ft. Worth area, troubleshooting computer systems for corporate clients. Though capable of handling a broad spectrum of business problems, the gutless half-man specializes in information-systems consulting, offering services ranging from network set-up, upgrading, and maintenance to software installation, customization, and support.

"VisTech is your one-stop source for Internet and Intranet development, as well as collaborative-computing support," said Smuda, adjusting the

see MAN page 92

defeat the enemy, but that you try your best and have fun."

Added Clinton: "Hooray, U.S. troops!"

At a Pentagon press conference, Defense Secretary William Cohen expressed confidence that the mission will be successful.

"I have full faith that our troops will do a terrific job in Iraq," Cohen said. "But even if they make a few mistakes, we'll still be very, very proud of them."

Cohen stressed that the safety of America's special forces is the number-one priority. In an effort to reduce the risk of injuries, the Defense Secretary has urged all U.S. troops to tie their shoelaces "nice and tight."

"Whenever you're in a combat situation, there's inevitably going to be some running involved," Cohen said, "And the last thing we want is for any of our soldiers to trip and fall."

Morale is said to be high among the very special forces, who were flown Monday from Sheppard Air Force Base to Riyadh, Saudi Arabia, in a squadron of specially modified C-130 "short planes." Upon arriving, the troops were given a thorough mission debriefing by Gen. James Herzog and a butterscotch-pudding snack cup. Each soldier was then issued an AR-15 rifle, three clips of NATO 5.56mm rounds, a combat helmet with a velcro safety-strap, and a fanny pack with his name written on it in black magic marker.

Above: A C-130 "short plane" transports a battalion of very special forces to the Gulf.

> Defense Secretary William Cohen has urged all U.S. troops to tie their shoelaces "nice and tight."

"We are going to win the war," said Pvt. Richie Ammaker of Hagerstown, MD, eating his snack cup with a Capri-Sun juice-pak. "I love to clap and sing along to the music!"

"Col. Gene [Diering] says that if we take out the communications tower in Al Basrah, we can have a pizza party," Pvt. Josh Paretsky of Midland, TX, said. "Pizza party! Pizza party! Pizza party!"

"You're pretty," Paretsky added. "Will you marry me?"

Gen. Thomas Merritt, who is overseeing Operation Great Job!, said the troops are thoroughly prepared for what lies ahead.

"We have gone over maneuvers and protocol in exhaustive detail, and we have all marked down our special targets in our special notebooks," Merritt said. "The soldiers know they are not

to wander off from the group. They know they are to use inside voices when in enemy territory. And they know they are to go to the bathroom prior to all ground assaults. This group is ready."

Merritt went on to note that, despite the very-special nature of the mission, strict military discipline will be enforced, including mandatory quiet-room "time-outs" for any soldiers who begin "acting out" or displaying inappropriate behavior in combat situations.

According to Secretary of State Madeleine Albright, the length of the mission depends upon the performance of the troops.

"Hopefully, all will go well, and our very special forces will be back home within a week," Albright said. "But if there are setbacks, such as soldiers losing their keys, having trouble staying on task, or forgetting to take their pills, it could take longer."

Regardless of the outcome on the field of battle, Albright said America's fighting forces will emerge as "big winners."

"These soldiers will have the chance to strike a blow for global democracy and make lots of new friends in the process, so how could they possibly lose?" asked Albright, who noted that every soldier who participates in Operation Great Job! will receive a shiny medal. "This is truly going to be a very special invasion." ∅

## WHAT DO YOU THINK?

# Vermont OKs Gay Marriage

Last week, Vermont became the first state to legally recognize same-sex marriages. What do *you* think about this historic legislation?

**Linda Leone**
**Pharmacist**

"At long last, Ben will be able to make an honest man of Jerry."

**Richard Westlake**
**Systems Analyst**

"I suppose it's okay for homosexuals to marry—so long as they don't marry each other, of course."

**George Lewis**
**Architect**

"First the military, now marriage. Why do these gays want in on our worst institutions?"

**Risa More**
**School Psychologist**

"Gay marriage is only going to take weddings to another opulent level."

**Hal George**
**Gas-Station Clerk**

"Shit. Now Mom will really step up the pressure on me and my leather slave to finally tie the knot."

**Frank Brodhagen**
**Truck Driver**

"Homosexuals are just trying to make their sodomy as morally acceptable as the sodomy I enjoy in my church-sanctioned marriage."

toupee he has worn since age 23. "We are a full-service company that can evaluate and integrate multi-platform environments, including Unix-based Sun workstations, Novell Netware-based PC servers, and AppleTalk-based TCP/IP LANs."

"Remember, no job is too small for the professionals at VisTech," added the spouseless, childless Smuda, who is destined to die alone and unloved. "And no job is too big, either."

Smuda, who is unable to maintain an erection, said he has experience designing and installing such disparate networking architectures as IBM Token Ring, 10/100 Base-T Ethernet/Thinnet, and Apple LocalTalk-based PhoneNet arrays.

"Not sure what system is best for your company?" said Smuda in his grating, nasal voice. "I can work with you to create the office computing environment that best suits your particular needs."

Flashing a nauseatingly insincere smile, Smuda said that many of his clients are pleasantly surprised to learn that VisTech also offers personnel-management solutions.

"A single five-hour VisTech seminar can increase your staff's productivity by as much as 20 percent," Smuda said. "I bet you'd like to know more!"

"There's no charge for an initial consultation, so there's no reason not to set one up today," Smuda said. "Give me a call!" ∅

# Woman Who 'Loves Brazil' Has Only Seen Four Square Miles Of It

WILKES-BARRE, PA—Joan Pavlik, a 49-year-old Wilkes-Barre dental hygienist, is "completely in love with Brazil," despite the fact that she has only seen four square miles of land surrounding the Sol Rio Internacional Resort near Rio de Janeiro.

"Brazil is *the* most incredible country," Pavlik told friends Tuesday over lunch at Chi-Chi's. "The mountains, the beaches, the rainforest: It's like heaven on Earth."

Pavlik became captivated by the South American nation in early March, when she and husband Lou spent seven days at the Sol Rio resort in celebration of their 20th wedding anniversary.

"The Brazilian people are so warm and friendly," Pavlik said, "and almost all of them know how to speak English."

The Sol Rio resort, which offers 12 tennis courts, three 18-hole golf courses, an Olympic-sized indoor pool, and several authentic Brazilian-style restaurants, is located along a secluded stretch of beach 20 miles south of Rio de Janeiro. Except for the air-conditioned charter-bus ride to and from the airport, Pavlik did not venture more than 5,000 feet from her "Iguaçu Suite" overlooking the sea.

"Brazil has such a unique culture," said Pavlik, whose stay at Sol Rio was part of a "Hot Nights, Cool Sights Deluxe Rio Package" she booked through her travel agent. "Very exotic, yet very sophisticated. They don't speak Spanish, you know. It's Portuguese."

After demonstrating her mastery of the phrases "*Por favor*" and "*Onde e o restaurante?*" Pavlik told her friends that she especially loved Brazil's

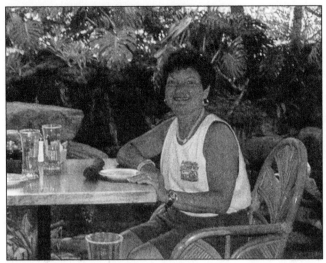

Right: Joan Pavlik takes in one of Brazil's spectacular hotel bars.

"wonderful traditions."

"One of the neatest things about Brazil is Carnival," Pavlik said. "It's like Mardi Gras, with costumes, music, and parades. It only comes once a year, but every Friday night in the resort's Vidas Secas Lounge, they have a mini-Carnival with a stage show and band. Isn't that the best?"

Pavlik added that, after the show, she and other Sol Rio guests were invited to join the dancers on the floor for a Samba lesson. "It was so much fun," she said. "I almost fell right on my butt a few times, but I didn't even care!"

In addition to the culture of Brazil, Pavlik also learned a great deal about its environment during her trip. Particularly eye-opening was a Wild Adventures Ecotour, which took her and a busload of other Sol Rio guests a quarter-mile deep into the rainforest.

"Our tour guide, Henrique, was so funny. And he really knew his way around the jungle," Pavlik said. "I'll never forget when he beeped the bus' horn, and about 15 monkeys came running up and ate oranges right out of his hand!"

"That's what's so amazing about Brazil," Pavlik said. "It's this incredible mix of untamed nature and big-city excitement."

Pavlik did not actually venture into Rio de Janeiro proper, as an excursion to the city was not included in her travel package due to liability concerns over taking tourists to a teeming urban center where crime is rampant and less than half the inhabitants live in homes connected to a sewer system. Pavlik did, however, spend a great deal of time at the Little

see BRAZIL page 94

## Eight Million Americans Rescued From Poverty With Redefinition Of Term

WASHINGTON, DC—Approximately eight million Americans living below the poverty line were rescued from economic hardship Tuesday, when the U.S. Census Bureau redefined the term. "We are winning the war on poverty," said bureau head James Irving, who lowered the poverty line for a four-person family to $14,945. "Today, millions of people whose inflation-adjusted total household income is less than $16,780 are living better lives." Said formerly poor Jackson, MS, motel housekeeper Althea Williams: "I never dreamed I'd ever become middle-class. America truly is the land of opportunity."

## Father Takes One More Look At Liner Notes Of Daughter's Britney Spears Album

JEFFERSON CITY, MO—Arnold Snell, 42, father of 11-year-old Ashley, slipped into his daughter's bedroom for one more look at the liner notes to her Britney Spears album Tuesday. "Just like to see what my daughter's into these days," said Snell, perusing the photo-packed booklet accompanying Spears' *Oops!...I Did It Again* for the fourth time in as many days. "I bet she'll put this on the moment she gets home from soccer practice in 20 minutes." Upon hearing a car pull into the driveway, Snell, who has previously browsed the liner notes to his daughter's Mandy Moore and Christina Aguilera CDs, put the Spears disc exactly where he found it and left the room. ∅

LORD from page 91

mented occasions, the Lord failed to provide for dutiful worshippers, allowing them to go without Providence in times of great need and showing little if any of the celebrated deity's much-touted "boundless love."

The list of Justice Department allegations ranges from the mundane—such as the Lord's reported September 1995 refusal to see to it that Terre Haute, IN, Presbyterian Joyce Halstrom receives a new set of drapes for her anniversary—to the catastrophic, such as last year's Mexico City earthquake, in which God allowed an estimated 150,000 devout Catholics to be crushed to death under tons of debris.

"These are very serious charges," U.S. Attorney General Janet Reno said. "I can assure you that our department will investigate them fully."

The allegations directly contradict

more than 6,000 years of extravagant claims by the Lord's prophets of "miracle" cures and other forms of all-encompassing heavenly grace.

Following the Justice Department announcement, many of the Lord's top earthly representatives fled into hiding, including Pope John Paul II, New York's Cardinal John O'Connor, and Rabbi Menachem Schindler, president of the World Orthodox Jewish Congress.

In Rome, an unruly mob surrounded the Panamanian Embassy, where many believe the Pope is seeking asylum. Reports of his capture remain unsubstantiated as of press time.

The Lord did not respond to a federal subpoena ordering Him to appear before the investigative commission and has refused to speak to reporters on this or any subject throughout the week.

Efforts on the part of law-enforcement officials to contact the alleged supreme being via the intercessionary medium of prayer have also been unsuccessful.

One of the areas in which the Lord has been the most negligent, the Justice Department charges, is in providing His followers with adequate access to education. Fundamentalist Christians remain, after thousands of years, among the least-educated demographic groups in the world, ranking below pro-wrestling enthusiasts and carnival barkers.

In addition, claims of an eternal "life after death" remain unconfirmed by deceased believers from around the globe.

"It's sad to think of the abusive treatment people have received at the hands of their so-called protector," U.S. Sen. Patrick Leahy (D-VT) said,

"especially when you think about all those countless hours they spent in houses of worship rejoicing and loudly giving thanks and praise."

The senator noted that, with some 450,000 hymns and songs written about Him, the Lord ranks among the most praised entities ever.

If found guilty, the Lord could face up to 3,100 years in jail and/or fines totalling $50 trillion. He would also be forced to return all gratitude and thanks paid to Him by followers, backdated to the dawn of civilization.

Despite the seriousness of the charges, many believers remain loyal to the embattled deity.

"I know it seems like the worst thing ever," said Lynette Maddox, a Flatwoods, KY, manicurist and mother of nine, "but we just have to trust that it's all part of God's plan." ∅

# Man Feels Brief Sense Of Triumph After Completing Free-Frozen-Yogurt Punchcard

TRAVERSE CITY, MI—After nearly four months of dedicated frozen-yogurt consumption, Roy Kempner, 47, finally earned the 10th and final punch on his Creamy Pete's Preferred Customer Card Tuesday, giving him a faint sense of accomplishment.

"Well, I guess I did it," said Kempner, holding aloft the completed punch card. "That'll be one free yogurt for me next time."

Kempner, a Traverse City-area substitute teacher, was offered the card following an Aug. 19 purchase of a medium chocolate-vanilla swirl cone at the yogurt franchise.

"When the lady asked if I wanted to join the Preferred Customer Club, I thought it might be some sort of racket with a sign-up fee, like they have at Waldenbooks," Kempner said. "But she assured me it was free and said I'd already earned my first punch for the yogurt I'd just ordered, so I thought, what the heck."

During the next several weeks, Kempner made no additional frozen-yogurt purchases, and the punchcard was soon forgotten in the recesses of his wallet. On Sept. 12, however, the card returned to the forefront of Kempner's mind when he pulled out his Visa card to pay for dinner at a local Outback Steakhouse.

"I just happened to notice the punchcard there in my wallet," he said. "Then I realized that the yogurt place was just a couple blocks away. It seemed like fate."

According to Kempner, that evening's purchase of a second frozen yogurt, a medium butterscotch with crushed Heath bars, put the punchcard-completion project into high gear. "I was enjoying the yogurt, and I started thinking, hey, I'm already 20 percent there. I could easily eat eight more of these and actually get that free one," Kempner said. "I'd just need to adjust my travel and dining habits to get to Creamy Pete's more often."

Over the next two months, he made four more trips to Creamy Pete's, enjoying such flavors as peanut butter, raspberry silk, and French vanilla, as well as exotic toppings like Oreo cookie dough and Sour Patch Kids.

Kempner faced his first setback in mid-November, when he brought friend Matt Langenkamp into Creamy Pete's.

"I thought I could buy a yogurt for myself and one for Matt and get credit for two yogurts," Kempner said. "Matt didn't have a card, so he said I could have his punch. But the girl behind the counter pointed to the rules on the back of the card, which clearly state that credit can only be given for frozen-yogurt items consumed by the

Above: Roy Kempner proudly displays his fully punched Creamy Pete's Preferred Customer Card.

card's bearer. Then I asked her if I could get an extra punch if I ate a little bit of Matt's yogurt before he ate it, but she said no."

Embarrassed by his clumsy, hamfisted attempts to circumvent the rules of the giveaway, Kempner tossed an extra dollar into the Creamy Pete's tip jar.

Upon reaching the six-punch mark, Kempner's free-frozen-yogurt quest stalled, his interest in frozen yogurt waning with the onset of winter. The quest suffered another setback when the card was misplaced during the transfer of materials to a new wallet.

"I forgot about the card until last month, when it somehow turned up in the sock drawer of my dresser," Kempner said. "I usually only eat frozen treats in the summer, so I thought about saving it for next year. But then I noticed it was stamped with a Dec. 31 expiration date. I was like, uh-oh."

Faced with the choice of abandoning the quest or forcing down cold yogurt in 30-degree weather, Kempner opted for the latter. On Dec. 1, he gained his seventh punch, ordering a large coffee yogurt with Butterfinger topping. A week later, a medium vanilla with

crumbled Cap'n Crunch bits brought him into the home stretch.

With just two punches to go, the project was nearly derailed when frozen-yogurt fatigue set in.

"After the eighth punch, I was really getting sick of yogurt," Kempner said. "On the other hand, I was only two away. So, after digging deep and doing some serious soul-searching, I decided I'd gone too far to turn back."

Forcing himself to make two more trips to Creamy Pete's before the clock ran out, Kempner gamely choked down a medium banana with crushed nuts on Dec. 6. Finally, at 5:13 p.m. Monday, Kempner ordered a small, toppingless vanilla, earning his tenth punch and, with it, a dim, momentary sense of triumph.

Reflecting on his accomplishment, Kempner said: "Well, it was a long journey, but I did it. I ate 10 frozen yogurts."

Gazing at the well-worn punchcard, Kempner spoke of the future. "As good as I feel now, it doesn't compare to how I'll feel when I get that free yogurt. I will have enjoyed $33 worth of yogurt, and paid only $30 for the privilege—a reward lavished only on the brave." ∅

---

## NEWS IN BRIEF

### Bankrupt Dot-Com Proud To Have Briefly Changed The Way People Buy Cheese Graters

SAN FRANCISCO—Egraters.com, an Internet retailer that filed for Chapter 11 last week, announced on its homepage Tuesday that it is proud to have briefly made people rethink the way they buy cheese graters. "Unfortunately, we were not able to see our revolution all the way through," read the message from CEO Jeff Bell, 29. "But for a brief, shining moment, we showed the world that there is a better way to buy graters." Bell said he hopes to one day relaunch Egraters.com and "smash the tyranny of traditional brick-and-mortar cheese-grater-tailing." ∅

---

BRAZIL from page 93

Rio Marketplace, a collection of stores and stands located between the Sol Rio resort and the neighboring Hotel do Frade resort.

"I bought this adorable miniature burlap sack of coffee beans that says '100% Brazilian Coffee' on it," Pavlik said. "I've already warned Lou that we're going back to Brazil for our 25th."

"We could've just gone to the Bahamas or down to Puerto Vallarta again," Pavlik continued, "but I wanted to go someplace more exotic and cultural. And the package was a steal: airfare, room, breakfast and lunch buffet, and two outbound adventures for just $2,899."

Joaquim Costa, director of the Museu de Arte Contemporânea in São Paulo, was pleased to hear about Pavlik's deep affection for his native land.

"There is much to love about Brazil," Costa said. "Our culture is a unique mixture of Native American, European, and African. Explore Brazil, and you will meet cowboys of Rio Grande do Sul, the vaqueriros to the Northeast, the women of Bahia in their traditional African dress, the Native Americans resplendent in ceremonial beads. There is also the nationalistic writings of José de Alencar, the art of Tarsila do Amaral, and our rich pageantry of music and dance, ranging from *bumba-meu-boi* to *tropicalismo*, *sertanejo* to *capoeira*."

But, despite his pride, Costa acknowledged that Brazil is a deeply troubled land.

"As much as my country has to offer, our problems must be very apparent to visitors," Costa said. "A tour through the city reveals some of the worst slums on Earth, with shantytowns, or *favelas*, stretching as far as the eye can see. A trip to the country shows the shacks of rural laborers in the shadow of the plantation owners' *casa grande*, the big house. Everywhere you look in Brazil, there is terrible poverty and suffering. It would take a blind man not to see such pain." ∅

LOVITZ from page 54

of blood. Passersby were amazed by the unusually large amounts of blood. Passersby were amazed by the unusually large amounts of blood. Passersby were amazed by the unusu-

---

## It's nice to feel wanted for the murder of three local children.

---

ally large amounts of blood. Passersby were amazed by the unusually large amounts of blood. Passersby were amazed by the unusually large amounts of blood. Passersby were amazed by the unusually large amounts of blood. Passersby were amazed by the unusually large amounts of blood. Passersby were amazed by the unusually large see LOVITZ page 177

# the ONION ®

WWW.THEONION.COM · AMERICA'S FINEST NEWS SOURCE™ · FOUNDED 1871

## Islamic Fundamentalists Condemn Casual Day

see RELIGION page 7C

## New Stapler Makes All Other Staplers Look Like Worthless Shit

see PRODUCTS page 10D

## Secretary Waxes Garfieldian

see OFFICE page 11E

## Sperm Cells Unaware They're Swimming Up Large Intestine

see LOCAL page 9B

## Ebert Victorious

see PEOPLE page 7D

### STATshot

A look at the numbers that shape your world.

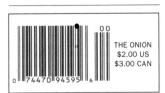

Top Verbs Appearing On Résumés

— John Q. Doe —

- Spearheaded
- Embezzled
- Impregnated
- Narrowly averted
- Harpooned
- Dislocated
- Vanquished
- Honey-glazed
- Hypertyped
- Faggoted up
- Larry-Kinged
- Megafiled
- Estimatated
- Did

# 8-Year-Old Accidentally Exercises Second-Amendment Rights

NORFOLK, VA—Gun owners nationwide are applauding the patriotic, though accidental, exercise of Second Amendment rights by 8-year-old Timothy Cummings Tuesday.

"Timothy is a symbol of American heroism," said NRA executive vice president Wayne LaPierre from Cummings' bedside at Norfolk General Hospital, where the boy is in serious but stable condition from a self-inflicted gunshot wound. "While praying for his recovery, we should all thank God that his inalienable right to keep and bear arms has not been infringed."

The incident occurred shortly after

see RIGHTS page 96

Above: Timothy Cummings

# Clinton Calls For National Week Off To Get National Shit Together

Above: A "swamped" President Clinton announces his plan for a National Week Off.

WASHINGTON, DC—Citing years of distracting, time-consuming obligations that have caused many important matters to go unattended, President Clinton called for a National Week Off Tuesday for the purpose of getting the nation's shit together.

If approved, the week off, scheduled for June 18-24, would give Clinton and the American people a chance to finally take care of all their shit.

"My fellow Americans," Clinton said in his weekly radio address, "as your president, I have had a great many things to deal with during my time in office: welfare reform, Whitewater, gun-control legislation, Bosnia, sex scandals—you name it. As a result, a lot of shit has piled up that I have not had the

see CLINTON page 97

# Local Applebee's A Hotbed Of Machiavellian Political Maneuvering

HARTFORD, CT—The site of a complex, ever-shifting web of alliances among servers, line cooks, hostesses, dishwashers, and managers, the Sheridan Avenue Applebee's is a hotbed of Machiavellian political maneuvering, sources reported Tuesday.

"A manager here should employ the strength of a lion and the cunning of a fox," night manager Roy Mergens said. "For example, I have curried the favor of the waitstaff by giving them 15-cent raises, simply by eliminating Jorge, the second dishwasher. This will not make me any friends in the kitchen, but it is far more important to keep the front-of-the-house staff happy."

Added Mergens: "A suc-

Above: Byzantine machinations churn just out of view of restaurant patrons at this Hartford-area Applebee's.

cessful manager is above morality, for the success of the Applebee's franchise is the supreme objective."

Mergens said he hopes

his cost-saving measures will earn him a recommendation for advancement to the executive-manager po-

see APPLEBEE'S page 96

Cummings returned from school and found that his parents had left the house. Displaying what Second Amendment-rights groups are calling "good old-fashioned American ingenuity," Cummings placed a pair of phone books on a stool to retrieve his father's loaded .38-caliber revolver from its hiding place on a closet shelf.

After a preliminary backyard exercise of his constitutional rights claimed the life of Pepper, the family's cocker spaniel, Cummings fell on the weapon, causing it to discharge into his left thigh.

"The framers of the Constitution would be so proud of what my son did yesterday," said Randall Cummings, 44, who originally purchased the handgun for home defense. "If 8-year-old boys discharging loaded firearms into their own legs isn't necessary to the maintenance of a well-regulated militia, I don't know what is."

Doctors worked for six hours to reconstruct the younger Cummings' femur, which shattered from the impact of the high-velocity teflon-coated slugs. They also grafted his remaining muscular and circulatory tissue over the fist-sized exit wound below his left buttock. Though the boy lost a great deal of blood, attending physicians said they are confident he will recover sufficiently to resume active use of firearms, though his chances of walking again are slim.

"For years, the people who want to take away our freedoms have said we're not smart enough or responsible enough to own handguns," Randall Cummings said. "Timothy is proof that even a child is capable of using a handgun for its intended purpose."

Gun owners nationwide have deluged Timothy Cummings' hospital room with flowers, letters of congratulation, and invitations to "come shooting."

Plano, TX, firearms enthusiast Lloyd Stone showed his support by donating 18 inches of vascular material to help rebuild Cummings' left femoral artery.

"He may be just a boy, but this vigorous defense of the Second Amendment was a man-sized undertaking," Stone said. "Timothy may need a wheelchair for the rest of his life, but with every step he doesn't take, he'll realize what the Constitution is truly about."

Though Cummings has yet to deliv-

## "The framers of the Constitution would be so proud of what my son did yesterday," Randall Cummings said.

er an official statement on the incident, he regained consciousness long enough to discuss his immediate plans.

"Please, I want to run and play again," Cummings told doctors. "My leg hurts bad. Please make it stop."

In an official statement, the NRA called Cummings' accidental use of controversial teflon-coated "cop-killer" bullets "a victory for America."

"Timothy should be held up as an example to all those people out there who think we don't need these bullets—or fully automatic assault weapons or concealable handguns that are impervious to metal detectors, for that matter," said NRA president Charlton Heston, who noted that he plans to congratulate Cummings in person as soon as he is through lobbying for Senate repeal of legislation mandating background checks for gun purchasers.

"If we ban teflon-coated bullets, automatic weapons would be next," Hes-

Above: NRA executive vice president Wayne LaPierre praises Cummings' "commitment to the American way."

ton said. "Then all handguns. Next thing you know, the law would deny our citizens' children the personal freedom to blow holes through their own legs."

NRA lobbyist Stephen Hogue agreed. "Timothy's heroic accident happened because we live in the greatest country in the world," Hogue said. "Had he grown up in Japan, England, or Russia, he wouldn't be where he is today."

"Restrictive laws would have kept him 'safe' at home—and they would have justified it by telling us it was for his own good," Hogue added. "That's not the kind of country I'd want my children to grow up walking normally in."

"Timothy is a shining example to gun-owning families everywhere," said Suzanne Cummings, the boy's mother. "I am proud that my child has followed in the footsteps of the many thousands of patriotic children who have already demonstrated their commitment to the U.S. Constitution by shooting themselves or others." ⌀

sition at the soon-to-open Pflaum Road Applebee's.

"Prudence consists in knowing how to distinguish degrees of disadvantage and in accepting a lesser evil as a good," assistant manager Cindy Baggett said. "To wit: If I remain quiet about Roy's padding of his time card and his claiming credit for my Kahlua Mudslide collector's-mug idea, I am a shoo-in for his position when he leaves."

Baggett and Mergens are just two of 43 employees who take part in the swirling, Byzantine machinations that is life at Applebee's. Every day, hundreds of acts of devious strategizing take place behind the restaurant's placid, service-with-a-smile façade.

"The visitor to the Sheridan Avenue Applebee's is none the wiser," server Liz Schonert said. "Sipping on their jumbo margaritas and munching on mozzarella sticks, they know nothing of the clandestine pacts that enable some to leave early on slow nights,

Above: Niccolò Machiavelli

others to overextend their free-meal benefits, and still others to steal from the walk-in cooler."

These alliances, Schonert said, also determine which forms of scheming, intrigue, and fraud go unreported.

## "The visitor to the Sheridan Avenue Applebee's is none the wiser," server Liz Schonert said.

"I have set up a mutually beneficial arrangement between the waitstaff and the bartender, wherein he does not tally a certain percentage of our drinks, and we share our table tips with him," lead server Jenna Gordon said. "We have taken great pains, however, to keep the scheme hidden from the hosting staff. In order to remain strong, we must do all that we can to escape the hatred of those who are stronger."

One of the most bitter intra-Applebee's rivalries is the one between the kitchen staff and the front-of-house staff.

"The hateful servers receive all the tips, yet still they castigate us over one missing buffalo-wings platter," line cook Karl Krug said. "But on the surface, I am still extremely pleasant to them, so that I do not lose my kitchen-manager position. The use of craft and deceit is acceptable to maintain authority and carry out the policies of a ruler. And my most important policy is that I don't work weekends and don't clean the grease trap."

But for all the intricate dealings, even the most powerful members of the Applebee's crew must kneel before the ultimate authority of regional manager Bob Hundhausen.

"I keep the 22 Applebee's in my district under my thumb by periodically dropping in unannounced during dinner rush," Hundhausen said. "It is best for a leader to be both feared and loved. But since this usually cannot be done, it is safer to be feared." ⌀

## Point-Counterpoint: The Man

# You The Man

**By Tyrell Davis**

You the man, know what I'm sayin'? You *the man*. You it, baby. Ain't nobody else. Nobody.

Yo, how you do it, man? Man, you operate. It's like, shit, you *crazy* smooth. You all that, and then some. Ain't no doubt.

You the man all the time, 24-7. You the man when you walk it, and you the man when you talk it. You the man when you play it, and you the man when you say it.

Yo, Lorenzo, listen up and listen real good. You know what? I'll tell you what: You the man. That's right—you it.

Know what I'm sayin'?

Let me break it down for you just one time. You got that fine-ass lady, don't you? That shorty is one fine-ass ride. And those clothes you wear? *Damn.* You be like Mr. Armani Gucci Versace or somethin' in those threads.

You be shakin' it, breakin' it, and quakin' it... and that's no fakin it. And I ain't even up to your moves on the court yet. You like Shaq and Penny and Michael all rolled into one out there. Slam dunkin' wit' a *quickness*.

Ain't no two ways about it, and ain't nobody doubt it. My man! ✍

# No, *You* The Man

**By Lorenzo Simmons**

What? You crazy! Me? The man? Please. Everybody in town know who the man is—*you* the man! I ain't the man. No way. You got it all. And I mean all. Shit, I ain't got half what you got.

Yo, check this out: You smooth, man. Ain't nobody smoother than my boy Tyrell. You make the smooth look like they ain't smooth at all. Now, *that's* smooth.

So tell me this: How can I be the man when you the man? 'Cause, you see, there can be only one man, and I ain't it.

The other day, some folks came up to me, and they was all up in my face and shit, tellin' me that I be the man. When they said that, I was like, "What? You buggin'! I ain't the man! No way, no day. My boy Tyrell, he the man."

After I tell 'em that, they was all like, "Tyrell? That crazy homeboy from down 115th Street way? You right, Lorenzo—Tyrell is the man!"

But, still, y'all better keep your hands off my lady, or else you gonna be the man with two black eyes, motherfucker! Shit, man, I was just playin' with you. You know I think you the man. ✍

---

**CLINTON** from page 95

chance to take care of."

Among the shit Clinton intends to deal with during the national week off: a pile of bills he meant to pay a few months ago but forgot about because of the Sierra Leone crisis.

"I just want to take a whole day to do nothing but go at that stack," Clinton said. "Then there's all that crap piling up on the Oval Office floor. I've got to do something about those boxes."

Clinton said other shit would be targeted in subsequent days. "I still have to call back that Barak guy—he's left a load of messages about that whole Lebanon-pullout deal. And the Army has been hassling me for months about getting them some new bombers. Plus, I owe Mexico, like, a billion dollars."

"I am certain," Clinton said during the radio address, "that you, too, have a great deal of shit piling up. Now more than ever, we as a nation need this time off to finally deal with all the shit we've let slide."

Clinton said that, as a two-term president, he has an unusually large amount of shit to deal with. "I've still got shit from '93 I haven't even touched yet."

According to White House chief of staff John Podesta, Clinton has also been putting off moving a couch he found down the block from the White

> **Political analysts see the week-off request as a shrewd move on the president's part.**

House last week. "Al Gore said he would help the president get it upstairs," Podesta said, "but then he took off to do some campaigning in California, so he never did." The couch is currently sitting in the White House rose garden.

Political analysts see the week-off request as a shrewd move on the president's part. "Clinton may be the most shit-burdened president since Lyndon Johnson," said Duke University political-science professor Warren Heintz. "This will enable him to finally catch up and get organized. Plus, if he doesn't get those videos returned, he's screwed. He's got late fees up the ass."

Heintz noted that he himself has "mucho shit" that he would love to take care of during a week off.

As part of the proposal, Clinton has called for the creation of a new Department of Shit and would appoint former White House press secretary Mike McCurry the first Secretary of Shit. "This will ensure that in the future, America's shit stays firmly together," Clinton said.

With approval of the week off still pending, the U.N. is discussing a possible global week off.

"That would be fantastic," British prime minister Tony Blair told reporters. "The Irish situation has been keeping me busy like a mofo, and I've got so much National Health shit to go through, it's not even funny."

The proposed National Week Off would be the first such break since 1982, when President Reagan declared a month-long sabbatical during which the nation could go horseback riding. ✍

---

## Sales Disappointing For First-Ever *Hustler* Swimsuit Issue

LOS ANGELES—Spokespersons for Larry Flynt Publications are struggling to explain the poor sales of *Hustler* magazine's first annual swimsuit issue, crammed from cover to cover with beautiful young women modeling the latest sexy swimwear. "We are utterly baffled," LFP public-relations director Kenneth Micklos said of the issue, which sold 17 newsstand copies nationwide. "Our readership demographic is overwhelmingly heterosexual and male, with a strong interest in looking at beautiful women. It's a mystery."

## Wife Too Busy Videotaping Elk Attack To Save Husband's Life

BANGOR, ME—Investigators are citing "camcorder duty" as a significant factor in the death of Larry Fallon, who was kicked to death by an elk during a hunting trip Tuesday. "I wish more than anything that I could have grabbed Ken's rifle from the truck and helped him," a grieving Roxanne Fallon said, "but to aim and fire the gun while maintaining focus and properly framing the action would have been impossible." Fallon's death, captured on tape in its entirety, will air Dec. 18, on Fox's *When Animals Attack VII*.

## Home-Schooled Student Opens Fire On Breakfast Nook

OCALA, FL—In the latest act of youth violence to shock the nation, 14-year-old home-schooler Jeffrey Kunz opened fire on the family breakfast nook Tuesday, killing three and injuring two. "We were just about to start Jeffrey's algebra lesson when I heard several loud pops," said Iris Kunz, 44, the assailant's mother/teacher and one of the injured. "But then I saw blood on Jeffrey's sister Melissa and realized that someone was shooting." The gun-wielding teen, who was eventually subdued by SWAT-team agents, was said to be angry at his mother over an algebra grade.

## Insurance Salesman Celebrates 14th Year Of Quoting *Fletch*

VALLEJO, CA—At a gala luncheon Tuesday featuring Bloody Marys, steak sandwiches, and steak sandwiches, insurance salesman Marty Cutler celebrated his 14th year of quoting lines from the 1985 Chevy Chase film *Fletch*. "All I can say is, 'Using the whole fist, doc?'" Cutler told the many guests who have endured his quips over the years. The 31-year-old Cutler—who arrived 45 minutes late for the luncheon, explaining that "a manure-spreader jack-knifed on the Santa Ana"—has quoted *Fletch* an estimated 241,500 times since first dropping lines from the film into conversation in November 1985. Upon learning that the event's $100-a-portion Beluga caviar had run out, Cutler, who also goes by the name "Dr. Rosenrosen," dead-panned, "Never mind, just bring me a cup of hot fat and the head of Alfredo Garcia."

## 'Farm Aid Aid' Concert To Benefit Struggling Farm Aid Concerts

INDIANAPOLIS—A special Farm Aid Aid concert will be held Oct. 3 in Indianapolis to raise money for America's struggling Farm Aid concerts, event organizer Willie Nelson announced Tuesday. "Fifteen years ago, our nation's Farm Aid concerts were thriving, with millions of Americans flocking to see such artists as John Mellencamp, Neil Young, and myself," Nelson said. "But today, with ticket sales dwindling and subsidies nonexistent, countless hard-working Farm Aid promoters have been forced to foreclose on bookings in amphitheaters one-tenth the size of the stadiums they once filled." ✍

# I've Got The Fever For The Flavor Of The Oscars!

**The Outside Scoop
By Jackie Harvey**

Here's a riddle for you: What has more stars than the sky itself? **The Oscars**, and I for one was positively blinded by what I saw on Sunday! The lights! The glamour! The outfits! Oh, it was a night to remember! Everyone was dressed to the nines. Even Hollywood's most notorious tough guy, **Jack Nicholson**, looked positively dapper in his tuxedo. (And I bet it wasn't a rental!) Someday, I hope to be there in person so I can take in all the glory firsthand. But in the meantime, I'm happy to sit at home with a bowl of **Jolly Time buttered popcorn** and watch the proceeds unfold... live!

The only problem I had with this year's Oscars was that I didn't know who **half the people** were. While I have faith in the Academy's ability to decide who should be nominated, I must admit there were some glaring oversights. Where was **John Goodman** for his star-making turn in **The Borrowers**? Or **Tim Allen** for his textured portrayal of an undercover Amish man on the run from the law in **For Richer Or For Poorer**? And where, oh, where, was veteran funnyman **Eddie Murphy**, without whom **Holy Man** would have been a holy mess? Well, all I know for sure is that I've got a whole lot of movies to catch up on. **The Many Loves Of William Shakespeare**, for example, looks dazzling, especially **Gwyneth Barbeau**.

**Item!** Everyone knows that **Jenny Elfman** is a hilarious comedienne, with knockout good looks to boot. But did you know that she's also a very spiritual woman? My sources tell me that she's joined the same church that **Tom Cruise** and **Kirstie Alley** belong to, and that the church has filled her **deep spiritual void**. It must be a pretty great church to attract so many of **Hollywood's most glamorous stars**. I'll look into it more and see what I can come up with for you.

Why is it that every time I find a **decent pair of shoes**, the store doesn't have it in my size?

**Item!** The world recently lost one of its greatest, most televised film critics. Of course, I'm talking about the legendary **Gene Siskel**. Whenever I wanted to know what movie I should see, I only had to look to Gene's trusty thumb for the answer. Now, I guess I'll just have to read other, non-thumb reviews to figure out what to see. Farewell, Gene. Best wishes to you, and give everyone in Heaven a big "thumbs up" for me. Especially that **Steve McQueen**. He was terrific.

Boy, that **Mariah Carey** sure is starting to get big, isn't she?

**Item!** The whole nation is buzzing about **The Interview**. Now, if you don't know what I'm talking about, you must live in a cave. I'm talking about **Barbara Walters**' interview with **Monica Lewinsky**. Well, I watched it expecting to see a shameless little tart, but instead I saw a vulnerable and sensitive woman who was unfairly taken advantage of. And Barbara, as usual, handled it like a real pro, unafraid to ask the tough questions but ever-ready with a handkerchief and a shoulder to cry on. My heart goes out to you, Monica. If you need a friend, please feel free to call or write. My door is always open.

How come you never see men wearing **dickies** any more?

**Item! Matthew Broderick** is h-o-t! Last year, he was in the mega-smash **Godzilla**, and in 1999, it looks like he's going to be the toast of Tinseltown once again, starring in the year's most anticipated movie! Of course, I'm talking about **Star Wars: Episode One—The Shadow Knows**. In it, Broderick plays a young Anakin Solo. I know that Broderick is in his 30s, and Anakin is supposed to be 8, but that **George Lucas** is a real wizard with special effects, so I'm sure he worked his movie magic and took years off Mr. Broderick. I can't wait to "Force" my way into my local theater to see that one!

Can you believe that a pound of butter costs $4? Unbelievable!

Where have you gone, **Joe DiMaggio**? To the grave! That's right, last week, after a prolonged bout with Joe DiMaggio's Disease, the Yankee Schooner finally set sail for that great ballpark in the sky. Jumpin' Joe, with your legendary hitting streak, your long and loving marriage to **Marilyn Monroe**, and your great work as a Mr. Coffee pitchman, you won't soon be forgotten, that's for sure.

Congratulations to piano man **Billy Joel** for his induction into the Rock And Roll Hall Of Fame. Billy, with such classic records as **The Nylon Curtain**, **Storm Front**, and **River Of Dreams** under your belt, when it comes to rocking and rolling, you're far from an innocent man.

If anyone has any Milk Mustache magazine ads or other related stuff, please send it my way. I'm starting a collection.

I realize I'm usually a pretty lighthearted guy, but I'd like to pause for just a moment to talk about something serious. This week is **National Huffing Awareness Week**. Now, I just found out about this terrible epidemic myself, so I'm sure a lot of other people out there are unaware of it. "Huffing" is inhaling things like glue or correcting fluid so you can get "high." Now, parents, if you haven't already, please take the time to talk to your kids about huffing before some pusher does.

Okay, I don't want to end on a down note, so I want to announce that I'm holding a contest! The contest, ladies, is **"Win A Date With Jackie!"** That's right, just send in an essay of no more than 200 words explaining why you should go on a date with me, and the lucky winner will be wined and dined like never before! And don't worry... I'll pick up the check! You can enter as many times as you like, but remember: I'm judging on originality and content, not volume. Just send me your entries care of **this newspaper**. Good luck! ✍

# There's No 'My Kid Has Cancer' In Team

**By Jake Dobbins
Sales Manager**

All right, team! Look alive! This is the big one. This is the week we finally pull into the sales lead, and that means total focus.

Now, as you no doubt know, the free trip to Vegas for the year's highest-selling office is within our reach. If we can keep the momentum of the past week going, we can pass the Denver office and take this thing. But that means we must all work together as a team. Every one of you is a cog in a well-oiled sales machine.

And I don't want to hear any excuses. That means no more 45-minute lunches. No more lingering around the breakroom. And, most of all, no more of this "But my daughter is going in for chemotherapy tomorrow" business. From anybody. I'm not going to name any names, but I've heard that one a couple of times this week, and that's a couple times too many. I hope I only have to say this once: There's no "My kid has cancer" in "Team."

I know, I know. Cancer sucks. Hey, I'm not happy your kid has it, either. But the way I look at it, cancer's not a reason to get slacking, it's a reason to get cracking! You think your kid's chemo is gonna be free? You gonna say to the doctor, "Hey, I decided not to go to work this week because I'm too upset about my kid's cancer, so how about you give me that chemo for free?" See how far that'll get you! (It certainly won't get you to Vegas!) As we say in the business, no COMmission, no RE-mission.

> ## We've all got plenty of problems we could use as excuses to miss work.

I've seen too many salespeople take a nosedive in this business because they let their terminally ill kid hold them back. They start visiting the kid in the hospital, their cold calls drop off, and their sales numbers suffer. Next thing you know, it's not just the kid who's dying, but the hopes of an entire sales team that wants to win a Vegas trip!

You hear what I'm saying? You're part of a team here. If you miss a pitch, you might miss a sale. And if you miss a sale, we all might miss winning that trip! Believe you me, we've all got plenty of problems we could use as excuses to miss work, but we don't want to let our team down. Do you see Jerry staying home because of his trial separation? Or Brian because of his car trouble?

What do we sing "The Team Song" at the start of every day for? You think it's just so we can hear Glen howling off-key? (Ha, ha, I'm just pulling your leg there, Glen.) What it comes down to is, we're Teamers, not Tumors!

And, while I'm on the subject, what about that trip a certain someone took to Disneyworld recently? You think the rest of us wouldn't love to spend five days whirling around on teacups? I realize the Make-A-Wish Foundation paid for the trip, but that's not reason enough. Hell, I've got tons of frequent-flyer miles piled up, but you don't see me taking off for Bora Bora smack-dab in the middle of our final sales drive, do you?

Did you even try to give the sales pitch to your kid's doctors? The nurses? The Make-A-Wish guys? See, that's what I'm talking about. You're letting opportunities slip through your fingers, and that hurts the team! We'd be the leaders for that Vegas trip if not for your lollygagging and lack of focus. Team has four letters. T-E-A-M. Here's an easy way to remember it: **T**ake **E**very **A**venue **M**anageable. Do you see the letters T-H-E D-O-C-T-O-R-S S-A-Y T-H-E C-A-N-C-E-R H-A-S S-P-R-E-A-D T-O H-E-R B-R-A-I-N" somewhere in there? I don't.

This job is about one thing: moving vacuum cleaners. Everything else is a blind alley, kiddo. ✍

# the ONION

WWW.THEONION.COM     AMERICA'S FINEST NEWS SOURCE™     FOUNDED 1871

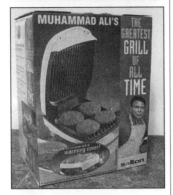
## New Grill To Revive Foreman-Ali Rivalry

see PRODUCTWATCH page 5D

## Yak Chews Thoughtfully

see LOCAL page 10D

## Bargain Hunter Becomes The Bargain-Hunted

see SHOPPING page 3C

## Wife In Lingerie At Least Gets Points For Trying

see RELATIONSHIPS page 4E

## Psychiatrist Cures Patient

see HEALTH page 7E

### STATshot

A look at the numbers that shape your world.

**Most Popular St. Patrick's Day Expressions**

1. Kiss Me, I'm Conveniently Close By
2. Cead Mille Fuck'ye
3. Who's For A Song About Guns And Drink, Then?
4. Gi' Ou' Me Parade, Yeh Wee Homosexual Twit
5. Erin Go Bleaaarrrrggh

# Bill Gates Grants Self 18 Dexterity, 20 Charisma

REDMOND, WA—Microsoft head Bill Gates, already widely considered to be among the most powerful men in the world, further increased his powers Monday, augmenting several of his key statistics to near-immortal levels.

Among the most striking increases were a +2 raise in dexterity to 18 and an overwhelming charisma increase to the above-human score of 20, placing Gates in the realm of deities and demigods.

"I am pleased to announce that I have boosted my already impressive statistics," Gates said in a statement to shareholders Monday. "As we develop the technological framework that will dominate the 21st century, these augmentations—and others to follow—will be powerful wards against competition from the likes of Netscape, Oracle, and Melkor Who Is Named Morgoth."

"Microsoft is the software-industry leader today, and tomorrow it will dominate the realm of information ac-

see GATES page 100

Above: Microsoft CEO Bill Gates, one of the most powerful businessmen on the Prime Material Plane, recently granted himself powers normally available only to deities and demigods.

Merit Small 'n' Flaccid!

SURGEON GENERAL'S WARNING: Cigarette Smoke Contains Carbon Monoxide.

# New 'Small 'N' Flaccid' Ad Campaign Least Successful Ever

NEW YORK—Advertising agency Meacham, Ellis & Young is the talk of the industry this week in the wake of the public's overwhelmingly negative reaction to its multimillion-dollar "Small 'n' Flaccid" campaign for Merit cigarettes.

The $450 million ad blitz, the subject of the most intense pre-release media hype since Saatchi & Saatchi's 1993 "Mmm-mmm, Mama, Show Me What'cha Got" campaign for Burger King, was ex-

pected to vault Merit to the top of the $800 billion cigarette industry.

Despite high expectations, the campaign and its slogan, "Merit... Makin' You Feel All Small 'n' Flaccid," has met with total failure.

"All our focus-group data and statistical analysis indicated a strong reaction to the word 'flaccid' among 35- to 50-year-old males," said Meacham, Ellis & Young creative director Arthur Kennedy. "We really

see CAMPAIGN page 101

# Inner-City Stabbings Leave Five Maidless

CHICAGO—A string of inner-city stabbings left five residents of Chicago's wealthy Highland Park suburb maidless this weekend.

"It was horrible," said Highland Park resident Edmund Collinsworth. "We were left with no choice but to make the bed, run cold water from the tap, and set the dining-room table without any help whatsoever."

Chicago police officials are conducting a full-scale investigation into the inter-

ruption in maid service and plan to issue a formal report to the Highland Park Gate & Security Service by Friday.

"We're doing everything we can to find the perpetrator," Chicago Police detective Stan Jacoby said. "And we're urging everyone on Chicago's streets to be wary. We don't want any gardeners to disappear. There's been enough suffering."

According to reports, the Highland Park residents'

see STABBINGS page 101

WASHINGTON SALES

CRIME SCENE

Above: Maid Georgette Davis was stabbed 47 times in the neck and chest Sunday morning.

cess, as well," Gates said. "The continued growth of our Corbis Media archive, the successful development and launch of MSNBC, and my mastery of the shield spells of the Elven King Lagolin are only the beginning for Microsoft."

Gates, who raised his intelligence to 20 in 1990, is fast becoming the most powerful CEO in American media. Experts place him above Fox's Rupert Murdoch and Disney's Michael Eisner, both of whom hold more than 1.2 million hit points. Gates is also rumored to be in possession of a bag of holding containing one terabyte of information, as well as more than 100 billion gold and silver pieces.

Analysts regard Monday's statistical boost as extremely beneficial to Gates in an increasingly competitive marketplace.

"This is a very shrewd move on Gates' part," *PC Magazine* columnist John C. Dvorak said. "His vastly increased charisma—the prime stat of a chaotic-evil executive—will help him tremendously in his ongoing struggle to convince Microsoft stockholders that his ventures into television and his massive content-buying spree will pay off in the long run. The extra CHR will also assist him greatly in dealing with wary CEOs of companies he wishes to invest in and cast spells over, like Comcast."

"It hardly seems fair, but he will now be capable of near-invisibility in behind-the-scenes business dealings," continued Dvorak, referring to the stealth augment which comes with a dexterity gain. "At the same time, he'll wear Mordekainen's Spectacles Of True Sight, which provide +6 insight gains into long-term Windows marketing strategies."

While few question the wisdom of Gates' stat increases, there remains a possibility that the Federal Trade Commission, which in 1996 declared his licensing agreement with computer manufacturers to be in violation of anti-trust laws, will challenge the move. Even if the FTC rules against Gates, however, industry analysts contend he should easily recover, thanks to his above-average 15 constitution.

Gates' rivals expressed frustration over his ability to achieve invulnerability in a supposedly competitive market. "Combining this augmentation with last month's purchase of the Polo Shirt Of Thalkettoth, which grants a +5 saving throw against anti-trust litigation, Gates should now be seen as operating outside the law," Apple CEO Dr. Gilbert Amelio said Tuesday. "One more sorcerous potion of Gain Market Share, and we might as well declare bankruptcy."

"Anyone can be a Santa Claus DM and give out unearned stats," Oracle president Larry Ellison said. "I'm surprised he didn't just go ahead and give himself a 20 in everything."

With overpowering statistics in all six ability categories, with the exception of strength, Gates is widely considered to be primed for the Kingship.

---

**Character** Bilbo of The Gatepeople
**Alignment** chaotic evil **Race** half-elf
**Class** CEO **Level** 33
**Player's Name** Bill Gates **Homeland Terrain** Seattle
**Sex** M **Age** 41 **Ht.** 6'5" **Kit** entrepreneur/visionary
**Wt.** 165 **Hair** Brn. **Eyes** Yellow **Secondary Skills** Negotiation, Hacking, Demon Summoning
**Appearance** strikingly handsome, high cheekbones, great hair

| | | |
|---|---|---|
| 13 | STR | Henchmen must carry gold pieces |
| 18 | DEX | Lawsuit dodging (+4) |
| 15 | CON | Anti-Trust Suit recovery (+5) |
| 20 | INT | Accepted to Harvard |
| 18 | WIS | Can see The Road Ahead |
| 20 | CHR | Stockholder Persuasion |

**Character Sketch**

BILBO OF THE GATEPEOPLE

**HIT POINTS** 1.5 million HP

**Languages**
English
Pascal
C++, Active X, COBOL

**Magic Items**
Bettmann Archives
MSNBC
Bag of holdings
Spectacles of True Sight

**Superstitions** Never talk to competition

Microsoft Explorer

**WEAPON COMBAT**

| Weapon | #AT | Attack Adj/Dmg Adj | THAC0 | Dam (SM/L) | Range | Weight | Size | Type | Speed |
|---|---|---|---|---|---|---|---|---|---|
| Secret Search Engine | | +6 | 6D6 | | earth | | | | |
| Polo Shirt of Thalkettoth | | +1 | 3D12 | | closet → work | | Medium/Ralph Lauren | | |
| Long Bow | | +3 | 2D6 | | long range | | | | |
| Focus / Drive of The Gods | | +1 | 5D17 | | limitless | | intense | | |
| Hostile Takeover / LBO | | +5 | 8D19 | | NY → L.A. | | | — | |

Above: Bill Gates' revised character sheet.

"Certainly, his campaign could be crushed if he made a mistake," ABC computer correspondent Geena Smith said. "But let's be realistic. He's got 40 million experience points dating back to when he dropped out of Harvard. His party has done nothing but kill and acquire for 22 years. This is a man who knows when to cast versus when to hack-and-slash. Bill Gates will be the emperor lich of 21st-century media." ⬦

---

## WHAT DO YOU THINK?

# Mayhem In The Mideast

Mideast peace efforts have broken down in recent days, with Israeli-Palestinian violence erupting throughout the troubled region. What do *you* think?

"The U.N. should lay down the law: No more visits to the Wailing Wall or the Dome Of The Rock until a certain two ethnic groups learn to behave themselves."

**Grace Delaney**
**Dental Hygienist**

"Right now, they're just throwing rocks at each other, but it could get much worse: I've heard rumors that Israel has the boulder."

**Peter Bryson**
**Systems Analyst**

"If only one side was a little darker so I could figure out who was right."

**Dan Voss**
**Truck Driver**

"In these times of trouble, they should turn to The Bible."

**Michael Weathers**
**Pastor**

"Boy, whoever's mediating these discussions sure does suck."

**Omar Bilal**
**Cashier**

"Maybe we need to stop thinking of this as a Mideast crisis and just think of it as Mideast culture."

**Diane DeSilva**
**Speech Therapist**

CAMPAIGN from page 99

believed limp and ineffectual was the way to go. I guess we dropped the ball on this one."

As a result of the Small 'n' Flaccid campaign, sales of Merit brand cigarettes have not only failed to improve upon the brand's annual February average of 20 million units per week, but have plummeted to an all-time low of 12.

"That's not even cartons, that's 12 packs," said Rich Bohannon, editor of *Cigarette Sellers' Report*, the nation's leading tobacco-industry journal.

Upon realizing its error, Meacham, Ellis & Young implemented several last-minute changes to the failing campaign in an effort to boost sales. But despite adding such new slogans as "Merit... Love That Limply Dangling Taste,""Merit... When You're Too Big A Pussy To Smoke Anything Else," and "Your Tiny, Ineffectual Penis Has Merit," the campaign continued to flounder.

"We've seen our share of turkeys in this industry before, but this is unprecedented," said marketing and media-relations expert Norbert T. Raines. "It makes Pepsi's famous 1989 campaign 'Hey! There's Clumps Of Hair In This!' look like a minor misstep by comparison."

According to a report in last week's *Advertising Age*, the Small 'n' Flaccid campaign has beaten all previous records for failure in advertising "by a wide margin," generating an average of 0.035 cents in sales returns for every $500,000 spent.

The failure comes despite full-page preview ads which ran throughout January in every major newspaper in the country. Featuring supermodels Cindy Crawford and Naomi Campbell, the ads read, "Hey, sexy, what's your problem? You seem so small 'n' flaccid!"

"With budget, star power, and placement like that, I figured we couldn't lose," Meacham, Ellis & Young president Jeff Ellis said. "Research showed virility and sexual self-esteem to be of major importance to over-35 male smokers. In searching for a theme sure to provoke strong feelings in the

> ## "We've seen our share of turkeys in this industry before, but this is unprecedented."

target demographic, we concluded that male impotency could function as a 'trigger' issue."

"Apparently," Ellis continued, "we misjudged the negative psychological associations men have with the words 'small 'n' flaccid.'"

Despite the campaign's failure, the agency remains optimistic. "Sure, we're disappointed," Kennedy said. "In this business, you're only as good as your last ad. But we're very excited about our new client, Tampax. We feel we've really developed a tremendous television and print package for them."

The upcoming TV spots, slated to premiere in March, will feature celebrity spokesman James Garner and the slogans, "Tampax... For Those Awkward Bleeding-From-Your-Crotch Days," "Tampax... Inserts In One Quick, Painful Jab," and "That Ugly Bitch Is On The Rag... The Tampax Rag." ∅

STABBINGS from page 99

agonizing maidlessness lasted more than 12 hours, ending only when a Chicago-area domestic temp agency airlifted in emergency replacements, free of charge.

"It was the least we could do," said Marcy Peters, manager of Maid To Order. "No rich person should ever have to go maidless. Ever."

Victims reported feeling confused, vulnerable, and frightened during the hours they were without maids.

"The doorbell rang, and we didn't really know how to react," Lillian Worthington, 58, said. "We just sat at the table looking at each other until it stopped."

Fortunately for Worthington, the maid was the only member of her staff to be stabbed repeatedly in the throat, allowing such services as cooking and car-washing to continue unaffected.

"The wet towels in the bathroom didn't get replaced until 2 p.m., and my newspaper wasn't even ironed," victim Peter Devlinger said. "Georgette's murder couldn't have been more inconvenient."

The Devlinger household was further disrupted when the deceased maid's daughter arrived to pick up her mother's belongings.

"She came in, sobbing hysterically, and I didn't know what to do," Devlinger said. "Normally, that's the type of thing Georgette would handle."

For some of the residents, not knowing if their maid was all right was the hardest part.

"I spent a great deal of time on Sunday tracking my maid down," said Mary Elizabeth Haversham, head of the Haversham Insurance Trust Ladies' Auxiliary Board. "I had to find out her name, and then I had to get her phone number from one of the other help, and then I actually had to speak with her family. It was a horrible, exhausting bother, and for what? Just to find out that she'd been killed, and that I'd have to hire a new girl anyway."

Bernadette Voorhees, whose family owns telecommunications giant AmeriCom, located her maid Sunday morning in an unresponsive critical state in a Chicago hospital.

"I guess all we can do is pray," Voorhees said, "that we can find someone else who can shine a 64-piece silver service the way Minnie could." ∅

# Lava Lamps Revert From Passé Retro Kitsch Back To Novel Retro Camp

WASHINGTON, DC—Lava lamps, the once-popular, then passé, then popular again, then passé again novelty items that have cyclically taken various American subcultures by storm throughout their 35-year history, are back.

According to a report issued Monday by the U.S. Department of Retro, the status of the multi-colored, mildly psychedelic light fixtures changed again in 2000, reverting from a tired form of passé retro kitsch back into a novel form of retro camp. The switch marks the 17th time the government has changed the lava lamp's retro classification since its initial resurgence in 1976 as an amusing, campy throwback to the then-outmoded '60s hippie drug culture.

"Lava lamps, which throughout the late '90s were seen as an irrelevant remnant of a relatively minor mid-'90s form of '60s retro, are once again retro in an exciting new way for millions of Americans unfamiliar with their previous kitsch-object incarnations," U.S. Retro Secretary Brian Setzer said. "That fallow period of the late '90s laid the groundwork for a revival within a subset of retro con-

sumer for whom the novelty factor of floating bulbs of wax suspended in water and lit from below had not yet worn off."

Setzer—who made his name in the '80s playing retro '50s rockabilly with The Stray Cats and subsequently enjoyed a comeback in the '90s, both for playing '40s big-band music with the Brian Setzer Orchestra during the retro swing revival and as the subject see LAVA LAMPS page 102

## New Olympic Sports

The 2000 Olympic Games kick off this Friday in Sydney, Australia. What are some of the new medal events being introduced?

| | |
|---|---|
| ⚬⚬⚬ Table volleyball | ⚬⚬⚬ 400-meter weightlifting relay |
| ⚬⚬⚬ Equestrian diving | ⚬⚬⚬ Men's freestyle web-site design |
| ⚬⚬⚬ Synchronized boxing | ⚬⚬⚬ Centathlon |
| ⚬⚬⚬ Greco-Roman fucking | ⚬⚬⚬ Team basketball |
| ⚬⚬⚬ Water tennis | ⚬⚬⚬ Trinidad & Tobago mocking |
| ⚬⚬⚬ 4x100 men's bonding | ⚬⚬⚬ Suspicious-person arresting |

of retro appreciation himself during a concurrent '80s retro wave—praised the pop-cultural tenacity of the lava lamp.

"One of the few pop-culture fads to weather a significant number of lame-then-cool-again changes in the fickle American retro landscape, the lava lamp has proven itself the rare retro phenomenon that will not die," Setzer said. "Whether this is good or bad, or what it even says about our society, is largely unknowable."

As noted in the Retro Department report, the popularity of lava lamps at any one moment is difficult to gauge due to their varying status within different subcultures. As a result, the lamps often simultaneously occupy many different points along the retro-cycle curve, causing confusion among retro cognoscenti. For example, in 1998, computer dweebs considered the lamps "CyberKewl," while swing-dancing hipsters dismissed them as "lame-a-roony-toony."

Further complicating matters are the complex meta-retro aesthetics of pop-culture-obsessed Generation Xers for whom the lamps represent a form of "retro-retro." For such individuals—who enjoyed the lamps in the late '80s as a retro throwback but then grew out of this "pure" retro phase and rejected them, only to eventually develop nostalgic affection for their original retro feelings—it is hard to assess how they truly feel about the lamps.

"Remember back in '88, '89, when everybody had lava lamps in their dorm rooms because they were so hilariously evocative of the late '60s, early '70s?" said Todd Wakefield, 31, a recent lava-lamp re-reconvert. "That was awesome."

"Lava lamps? Please. I remember back in '88, '89, when everybody had one in their dorm room because they were trying to be all late '60s, early '70s," said Jen Cushman, 31. "Talk about over. Having a lava lamp now is so late-'80s late '60s/early '70s."

Still others view the matter altogether differently.

"It all depends whether you're talking about straight, unironic, revivalist retro or one of the numerous strains of pre-X and Gen-X irony," said Seth Burks, 29, author of the award-winning Athens, GA-based 'zine *Burning Asshole*. "I've identified 22 distinct varieties of irony-informed retro and non-retro aesthetics, including camp, kitsch, trash, schmaltz, post-schmaltz, and post-post-schmaltz. It's time we addressed the woeful inadequacies of the government's current retro-classification system."

The report marks the latest in a string of controversies for the embattled Department of Retro, which is still feeling the effects of 1998's bitter infighting over the still-unresolved issue of "classic" rock. The department was further rocked in May 1999, when Setzer replaced then-Retro Secretary Anson Williams, who stepped down after refusing to endorse *That '70s Show*. ∅

# Lab Rabbit Strongly Recommends Cover Girl Waterproof Mascara For Sensitive Eyes

CINCINNATI—LR-4427, a two-year-old laboratory rabbit at Procter & Gamble's cosmetics testing facility, gave his full endorsement Tuesday to Cover Girl Long & Luscious waterproof mascara for sensitive eyes.

"Cover Girl Long & Luscious waterproof mascara will dramatically magnify your lashes for a look that's glamorous and natural," LR-4427 said. "And the great part is, they won't irritate your eyes, even if you accidentally smear some over your clamped-open eyeballs with a Q-Tip and can't flush it out for 48 hours."

LR-4427 said he also likes the fact that the Cover Girl product stays on, rain or shine.

"No matter what the weather, you're guaranteed gorgeous lashes with Long & Luscious mascara," LR-4427 said. "And they'll stay that way all day long, in 10 hours of 200-degree heat from a hair dryer or icy blasts from a shower head."

In the past six months, LR-4427 said he has tried "literally hundreds" of different mascaras. Of these, he said, Cover Girl Long & Luscious offers the best combination of good looks, durability, and non-corrosiveness.

"The Cover Girl mascara they ground into my right eye is 10 times better than the Max Factor Midnight Thicklash that had been ground into my left," said LR-4427, speaking from immobilization cage 39B. "The Max

Above: Lab rabbit LR-4427 enjoys all-day glamour with Cover Girl Long & Luscious mascara.

Factor stuff is greasy and cheap-looking, not satiny and sophisticated like Cover Girl. And, unlike Cover Girl, Max Factor doesn't wash away easily—not even with industrial soap and steel-wool scouring pads."

According to LR-4427, eyes are the first thing you notice about a person. And nothing is more important to the look of a woman's eyes than mascara.

"If you're anything like me, you hate it when the look you spent all day perfecting is ruined by your mascara running or dripping," said LR-4427, cocking his head as much as possible in-

side his plastic holdfast collar. "Well, your worries are over, because Cover Girl Long & Luscious stays on your eyes right where the injectors put it. With Long & Luscious, there's no need to cauterize your tear ducts shut, unlike some mascaras I could mention."

LR-4427 added that clinical tests have proven that Cover Girl Long & Luscious will leave your lashes 40 percent thicker than Elizabeth Arden mascara. In addition, Long & Luscious will feel 50 percent less like your eyes are melting down your cheeks after being pierced with red-hot fireplace pokers.

"The last thing you want right before a big date is to lose confidence in your mascara," LR-4427 said. "You need to know that his eyes will be on yours—not on any chemical scarring."

"And if you have a long day... or night," continued LR-4427, attempting a saucy wink despite his surgically excised eyelids, "touch-up is a breeze. Just pack more Long & Luscious into your orbital sockets, your nostrils, your anus—any of the delicate tissues that get stressed by your busy lifestyle—and you're ready to go."

LR-4427 then returned to work, where he is finishing up testing a new aloe-scented exfoliating scrub before being reassigned to Procter & Gamble's small-arms ammunition division. ∅

# Masturbator Held For Questioning In String Of Brutal Masturbatings

SALEM, IN—Salem Middle School eighth grader Jeremy Royce, 13, was detained and questioned by police for more than three hours Tuesday regarding a string of brutal masturbatings in the Salem area.

"While no arrest has yet been made in the case," said Salem police chief Dan Sharperson, "at this time, Mr. Royce very much appears to be our prime suspect."

Since beginning in March, the string of horrific masturbatings has shaken this tiny farming community in southern Indiana. In the past month alone, some 31 Kleenex, three socks, and one baseball cap have been found badly masturbated, some beyond recognition.

According to Sharperson, Royce became the chief suspect following the discovery of a Kleenex on the side of his bed identical to one found in a

Above: Jeremy Royce, the individual many believe to be behind a grisly masturbating spree.

Salem Public Library men's-room stall and two others found in the second-floor boys' bathroom at Salem

Middle School. Like the items previously discovered, the Kleenexes appeared to have been severely masturbated.

A subsequent search of Royce's sock drawer unearthed a number of items that may have been used in the crimes, including a 1982 "Sex In Cinema" issue of *Playboy* featuring Barbi Benton, a November 1991 issue of *Gent*, and a photo of ninth-grader Susie Sherwood from the 1999 Salem Middle School yearbook.

"The person who perpetrated these crimes is a deeply disturbed individual with no regard for human decency," Sharperson said. "Whoever committed these acts deserves to be put away for a long time."

Royce strenuously denied all charges, claiming to have been "at band practice" at the time of the masturbatings. ∅

## You Can Tell Area Bank Used To Be A Pizza Hut

see LOCAL page 3C

## $500 Stereo Installed In $400 Car

see AUTOS page 2B

## Heat Wave Forces Johnny Cash To Don Black Shorts

see PEOPLE page 10C

THE ONION
$2.00 US
$3.00 CAN

0 74470 94595 6

---

# the ONION

WWW.THEONION.COM    AMERICA'S FINEST NEWS SOURCE™    FOUNDED 1871

## THE ROAD TO WAD UNIFICATION

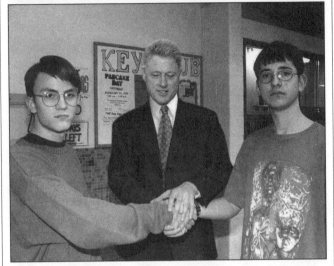

# Gaywads, Dorkwads Sign Historic Wad Accord

ROCKVILLE, MD—In a historic show of wad solidarity, delegates representing gaywads and dorkwads signed the first-ever Wad Alliance Treaty Thursday in the cafeteria of Adlai Stevenson Memorial High School.

The landmark accord, the signing of which was presided over by President Clinton, is considered the most significant step ever taken toward wad unification.

"For too long, wad factionalism has divided the wad community, senselessly pitting wad against wad in bitter inter-wad disputes," dorkwad representative Tad Patrick Reems, 15,

told reporters. "Now is the time for us to set aside our differences and join together to oppose our common enemy: the mean, popular kids who have mercilessly inflicted locker-room wedgies upon us since time immemorial."

Gaywad Jeff Brunner, 14, agreed. "From this day forth," he said, "we will no longer see each other as dorkwads and gaywads, but instead simply as wads, brothers united in our collective struggle against wad persecution."

Many of those present at the signing ceremony were overcome with emo-
see WADS page 104

# Fox Defends Airing Of *When Jews Attack*

LOS ANGELES—Besieged by widespread public outcry, Fox executives spoke out Thursday in defense of last week's airing of *When Jews Attack*.

The hour-long, Robert Urich-hosted program, decried as "shock TV at its

basest" and "a sickening appeal to voyeuristic, lowest-common-denominator tendencies," features explicit, uncensored footage of enraged Jews violently lashing out at others.

"For the next hour, what you will see you may find disturbing, even shocking," said Urich during the show's introduction. "But remember: The footage you are about to see is real."

Fox owner Rupert Murdoch defended his network's decision to air the controversial show.

"This disturbing imagery may be difficult for some to watch," Murdoch said. "But we feel the public has a right to see these attacks. They really do happen."

Among the show's objectionable
see FOX page 105

---

# Hippocratic Oath 'Under Review' By HMO Board

INDIANAPOLIS—In a development bioethicists and healthcare industry professionals are watching closely, Indiana HMO PhysCare-Plus, one of the largest and most powerful HMOs in the nation, announced Thursday that the Hippocratic Oath is "under review."

According to board members, the 2,400-year-old oath, attributed to the Greek physician Hippocrates and generally acknowledged as the cornerstone of medical ethics, is "outmoded and no longer economically viable in today's complex, rapid-

ly changing health-care environment."

"Here at PhysCare-Plus, our goal has always been the same: to provide customers with dependable, first-rate healthcare. But it is becoming increasingly difficult to do so when we are hampered by an ancient moral code penned by a contemporary of the historian Herodotus somewhere between 470 and 360 B.C.," said Dr. Cedric Samms, head of the PhysCare-Plus board. "While the oath is admirable for its idealism, it simply does not take into

account the many complexities and economic realities of medicine in the modern age."

Added Samms: "The personal touch... that's the PhysCare-Plus difference."

According to Samms, the Hippocratic Oath is too narrow and inflexible, placing too many restraints on healthcare professionals and requiring doctors to provide additional services which undercut their profits and hinder their ability to remain competitive. Because of the medical profession's strict adherence to antiquated moral principles and dogma, Samms said, both doctors and HMOs are ad-
see HMO page 104

ONION
MED WATCH

tion, necessitating the emergency use of asthma inhalers. At least one attendee shot milk out of his nose.

"The road to wad healing has begun," said Clinton, who, working closely with Secretary of State Madeleine Albright and the ASHS Key Club, was instrumental in the delicate after-school negotiations that led to Thursday's agreement. "Thanks to the efforts of those on both sides, we can look forward to the day when the wads of this great nation can all sit down together and play Magic: The Gathering at the table of brotherhood."

Though some feared there would be trouble at the signing ceremony, it went off mostly without incident. The notable exception occurred during a brief episode in which a *Games* magazine belonging to major gaywad Stephen Tempelman, 15, was confiscated by three junior-varsity basketball players. After a brief scuffle, during which the popular athletes engaged Tempelman in a spirited game of "keep-away," National Guardsmen were mobilized to the scene, seizing the magazine and returning it to its rightful gaywad owner.

"Let this sad turn of events serve as a painful and all-too-familiar reminder of why wads must unite," said Tempelman, taping together his glasses, which had been stepped on in the keep-away incident. "It's high time we realized that vicious anti-wad attacks such as this one are attacks against all of us, gaywads and dorkwads alike."

Tempelman's stirring call for pan-wad unity resonated with many at the conference.

"The countless cruel acts perpetrated against wads, including swirlies, noogies, titty-twisters, wet willies, purple nurples, and Indian sunburns—not to mention the throwing of wad headgear and retainers onto the roof of the school—have been tolerated long enough," said dorkwad leader and chaotic evil magic-user/thief Lenny Berger, 15. "But such injustice will not cease until the day we finally band together, forming an unstoppable wad juggernaut to defend ourselves against the jocks, stoners, stuck-ups, cheerleaders, metalheads, gearheads, and all others who would seek to destroy us. We can no longer afford to waste our efforts fighting against each other. Too many mathletes have died."

It is hoped that the accord will finally end decades of bitter wad sectarianism, which in recent years has turned the nation's computer labs, debate tournaments, and science-fiction conventions into bloody battlefields of wad-on-wad violence. In 1993, the Illinois State Speech & Forensics Championship was marred by rioting that left 23 varsity-level finalists in the extemporaneous and persuasive speech categories dead and dozens more injured. In 1995, a San Diego Doctor Who convention was disrupted when a contingent of dorkwad at-

Above: Dorkwad and gaywad leaders sign the landmark Wad Alliance Treaty.

tendees was attacked by gaywads from a Neil Gaiman comic-book signing across town. And the frequent clashes between the nation's dorkwad-controlled yearbook staffs and its gaywad-dominated school newspapers are well documented.

Addressing the assembled dorkwads and gaywads, Clinton expressed hope that the Wad Alliance Treaty is merely the start of a larger peace process that ultimately brings all wad factions together.

"The time for wad unity is now," Clinton said. "With this momentous signing, let the new wad era begin."

Despite Clinton's optimism, total pan-wad unity is considered unlikely in the near future. Numerous wad factions, including the dickwad, dipwad, jerkwad, and fuckwad groups, refused to participate in the wad accord. One fringe faction, a militant dickwad splinter group known as the "dickweeds," issued a formal statement denouncing the treaty as "dork city" and "totally gay."

But even in the face of such opposition, the Wad Alliance Treaty is regarded as a major step forward. Under the terms of the pact, dorkwads and gaywads will present a united Audio-Visual Club front. And, as a result of the treaty, the rift that has long split the marching-band and math-Olympiad communities is beginning to heal, as well. What remains to be seen is how long this peace—one as fragile as a hand-painted miniature D&D game figurine—can hold. ✍

versely affected.

"Take, for example, the portion of the oath which states, 'I will follow that system of regimen which, according to my judgment, I consider for the benefit of my patients,' Samms said. "For years, doctors have complained that the notion of practicing medicine with the patient's health as the number-one priority is not only outmoded, but unfair. By putting the patient's welfare above cost considerations, doctors place themselves at risk of antagonizing HMOs, which pay for the bulk of medical bills under the current system. Every time a precautionary electrocardiogram is performed on someone suffering from chest pain, it is the HMOs that truly suffer."

Also under intense scrutiny is the line, "With purity and holiness I will practice my art."

"Medicine has changed a great deal over the last 2,400 years. 'Purity' and 'holiness' are strong words that may no longer be viable given current cost outlays," PhysCare-Plus vice-president of operations Dr. Kyle Loveland said. "And, as far as the use of the word 'art' goes, perhaps in ancient Greece physicians could consider themselves artists, but today's medical industry is a multibillion-dollar business."

PhysCare-Plus officials have proposed changing "purity and holiness" to "acumen and savvy" and replacing "art" with "career."

Of all the disputed elements of the oath, however, the passage drawing the most fire is the one that reads: "Whatever in connection with my professional service... I see or hear in the life of men... I will not divulge, reckoning that all should be kept secret."

"There is no way an HMO can properly function bound by such a rule," said PhysCare-Plus member-accounts departmental supervisor Toby Francis. "HMOs must be free to disclose patients' medical, personal, and financial information to insurers. How else

## According to Samms, the Hippocratic Oath is too narrow and inflexible.

can we determine what treatments a patient is or isn't eligible to receive? If someone needs a new lung and they don't have the necessary funds to pay for it, how are we supposed to know not to perform the surgery?"

"I can't tell you how many cost overruns have been rung up as a result of doctors providing life-saving operations in accordance with the Hippocratic Oath, only to find out afterwards that the patients weren't covered," Francis said. "In a case like that, the surgery turns out to be for nothing. I get frosted just thinking about it."

If approved by the PhysCare-Plus board, the revised Hippocratic Oath is expected to have a major ripple effect throughout the healthcare industry. But whether or not the revised Hippocratic Oath—tentatively titled the "PhysCare-Plus Family Econo-Plan Quality Pledge"—is passed by the board, one thing is certain: Healthcare providers' attitudes are shifting.

"As the millennium approaches, the medical industry must look toward the future, not the past," Samms said. "After all, as Hippocrates himself said, *vita brevis*. Life is short." ✍

## Eggs Good For You This Week

BOSTON—According to a Northeastern University study released Thursday, eggs—discovered last week by a University of California–Santa Cruz study to be unhealthy, raising serum cholesterol by as much as 20 percent—are good for you this week, with beneficial effects on cardiovascular health. "Contrary to what was previously thought, consuming an egg a day can lower a person's blood pressure and increase the heart's efficiency for the next week," the Northeastern study stated. The report urged Americans to increase egg consumption immediately, as eggs may be unhealthy again as soon as next Monday.

## Critics Accuse New Movie Of Glorifying Sex

HOLLYWOOD, CA—*The Five Senses*, a new film from Fine Line Features starring Mary-Louise Parker and Philippe Volter, is drawing fire from conservative Christian groups who charge that it glorifies sex. "Billing itself as 'a touching exploration of human perceptions and dynamics,' *The Five Senses* is filled with images of adults engaged in intimate acts of sexual union," said Focus On The Family executive director Michael White. "By depicting it so frequently and so casually, this film only serves to condone the act of lovemaking." White added that sexual imagery in films is largely to blame for "the proliferation of sexuality in society." ✍

# Whaler Sandwich Not Sitting Too Good With Area Man

ERIE, PA—According to dining-area sources, a Whaler consumed during Tuesday's lunch-hour rush is "not sitting too good" with Burger King patron Don Turnbee.

The "Whaler," a popular processed-fish-product sandwich, was purchased by Turnbee at the restaurant chain's Branch Street location.

"Urggh," said a visibly ill-at-ease Turnbee, tenderly patting his distressed abdominal region. "Urrp... whoo, boy."

The sandwich—originally some form of aquatic life that was netted, chopped, breaded in batter, flash-frozen into a rectanguloid, shipped across the U.S. on a series of trucks, and stored for several days in the restaurant's walk-in cooler before being deep-fried to perfection—sat poorly with Turnbee.

"Man, oh, man," Turnbee said. "I shouldn't have put on that extra tartar sauce."

The Whaler episode marks Turnbee's 15th incident of mild gastrointestinal distress in the past seven weeks for Turnbee. It arrives on the heels of last weekend's media-dubbed "Pizza Roll Sunday," during which he felt slightly gassy and required sever-

Above: Erie-area eater Don Turnbee.

al Rolaids tablets. It also necessitated the acquisition of a 12-ounce of bottle of Kaopectate, purchased at a late-night Conveenie-Weenie Gas 'N' Snak that Turnbee visited in an overcoat and pajamas.

Though reports indicate that Turnbee also rented a videotaped copy of *The Nutsy Goofheads* at the convenience store, the rental is believed to have "little relevance" to his ongoing digestive difficulties.

"Ooof," Turnbee told reporters. "I tell ya."

Despite his stomach distress, doctors say the Whaler episode is "no cause for alarm."

"This whole Whaler thing should blow over before you know it," gastroenterologist Dr. Gary Muncie said. "I've known the Turnbees for years, and if you ask me, what Don really needs is a little more exercise. Get the circulation moving, breathe a little fresh air. I'd say 15 to 20 minutes of light exercise would do wonders for him. Of course, scraping off a little of that mayo couldn't hurt, either."

Despite the positive medical outlook, Turnbee is expected to experience slight discomfort well into the next day. And though his coworkers are aware of Turnbee's condition—due largely to his repeated post-lunch utterances of "Sheesh" and "Whoa, Nellie" while shifting in his work chair—most were not terribly concerned, confident in his ability to weather the crisis.

"Don's a veteran eater," coworker Stanley Bluford said. "A couple of cans of Mountain Dew to flush out the pipes, and he'll be right back on the horse." Ø

FOX from page 103

material: footage of a brutal attack by New Rochelle, NY, orthodontist Marv Rosenblatt on an unsuspecting dry cleaner. Rosenblatt is shown engaged in a prolonged argument with Sunrise Cleaners owner Arthur Tong over what he describes as "too much starch" in his laundry. When Tong denies that the clothes are over-starched, Rosenblatt leaps over the countertop and, without warning, begins slapping Tong about the face and chest.

"It was frightening," said Tong, recalling the attack in a taped interview segment on the show. "Of course, I'd seen people being slapped by Jews on television before, but you never think it'll happen to you."

Detractors also objected to a segment which aired toward the end of the program, in which Huntington Beach, CA, shopper Lisa Feigenbaum, complaining that "these are not the shoes I ordered," struck Payless Shoes employee Lisette Nolan in the forehead with a pair of tan leather pumps. Feigenbaum then pulled Nolan's hair for several minutes before four other employees were finally able to pull her away.

"Children should not be exposed to such violent footage," said Sharon Blaine, head of the San Francisco-based What About The Children? foundation. "In this day and age, we should be above such trash TV."

Concerned parent Sandra Hueber agreed.

"I do not want my child to learn that

Above: A tourist's home-video camera captures a sudden, Semitic assault on two U.S. Parks Service rangers in Redwood National Forest.

it is acceptable to resort to hitting, kicking, and pinching like the Jews she sees on TV," Hueber said.

While a majority of the program's critics condemn its offensive content, others object to the message it may send the nation's Jews.

"I fear that the televised glamorization of such attacks may wind up provoking America's already-volatile

Jewish population into committing further acts of battery," said Anthony Rasmussen, director of the American Center For Media Studies.

In reaction to the show, Jewish groups are calling for a boycott of Fox.

"As a Jew, I am deeply offended by this program," said B'nai B'rith International president Milton Weiss dur-

ing a press conference to announce the boycott. "We must send a clear message to Fox that this sort of garbage will not be tolerated."

Weiss then flew into a berserk rage, hurling ceramic vases at reporters and swinging a folding chair wildly.

Footage of the Weiss attack is scheduled to air Apr. 8 during the show's second installment. Ø

# Web-Browser History A Chronicle Of Couple's Unspoken Desires

VALLEJO, CA—The web-browser history on Allen and Christine Pollard's home iMac computer provides a comprehensive chronicle of the couple's deepest frustrations and desires, sources reported Thursday.

"By simply opening Allen and Christine's Internet Explorer history folder, we find their innermost longings laid bare," said Dr. Terrence Kimble, dean of psychology at the University of California at Berkeley. "From emotionally stunted, sexually frustrated Allen's frequent visits to porn and Camaro sites to childless Christine's frequent visits to sites that sell baby clothes, it's all right there."

According to Kimble, the Pollards' browser history, which logs the 200 most recent visits by users of the computer, "offers a glimpse into an entire

**Above: The Pollards' recent hits.**

universe of unvoiced pain and disappointment."

"As the Pollards enter their late 30s, all the dissatisfaction they hide from the world and, in most cases, each other can be easily found under the menu heading 'Go,'" Kimble said. "Because he knows Christine loves living in suburbia, Allen never talks to her about his dream of roughing it in a cabin in the Rockies. He just spends hours surfing the REI and Patagonia sites, filling his virtual shopping cart with lanterns and sleeping bags, then logs out without purchasing anything."

"Likewise," Kimble continued, "although Christine tells her friends that she and Allen have decided they aren't ready to have children, her www.babynames.com bookmark tells a different story."

**Above: Allen and Christine Pollard.**

The unfulfilled desire to procreate is by no means Christine's only source of unhappiness, Kimble said.

"While she maintains a cheery and fun-loving front, it is obvious that Christine has deep-seated self-esteem issues," Kimble said. "She is all but addicted to online quizzes like *Redbook*'s 'Does Your Wardrobe Give Away Your Age?' and *Cosmo*'s 'Are You A Bore In Bed?' With her high-school

cheerleading days far behind her, Christine has yet to find a new identity with which she is comfortable."

By carefully examining the history log, it's even possible to reconstruct Allen and Christine's respective thought processes.

"Let's look at Christine's time online last night," said Kimble, pointing to an opened history folder on the computer screen. "She starts at the Godiva gourmet chocolates online gift catalog at 7:35 p.m. Then, it's on to eDiets.com at 7:43 p.m. and the Nordic Track web site at 7:45. I'm guessing she clicked on a banner ad at eDiets to get there. Then it's on to 'Liposuction FAQs' at 7:52. Next is a page titled, 'Sexy Swimwear Sale: Dare To Be Bare.' Then, at 8:06 p.m., it's back to the Godiva chocolates secure-server online order form."

Christine admitted she keeps the details of her Internet surfing from her spouse.

"I don't mention this to Allen, because he would just say I'm being too self-critical, but I wish my nose weren't so big," Christine said. "I tried some of the de-emphasizing makeup tricks on the Maybelline site, but it's clear that what I really need to do is see a professional. Plasticsurgery.com says the procedure only takes six hours and is totally safe."

While Christine's browser history exposes her insecurities about her appearance, Allen's web-surfing patterns reveal his career dissatisfaction.

"It's obvious that Allen wants to quit his dead-end job at the bank and become an author," said Kimble, pointing to a list of Allen's web links to iUniverse.com and NextGreatAmericanNovel.com. "An author who works out of his cabin in the mountain, that is."

Despite doing so on a daily basis, the Pollards remain oblivious to the fact that they pour their innermost frustrations into their blueberry iMac.

"We both really enjoy going online," Allen said. "It's just a great way to waste time and have a little fun." ∅

# I Can Instantly Tell Whether Someone Is African-American With My Amazing 'Blackdar'

**By Shawn Parker**

I have this amazing gift. It's called "blackdar," and it enables me to tell whether someone is African-American without even knowing anything about them. To be honest, I don't know where I got the skill. But wherever I did, I can pass somebody on the street and just instantly know.

Like that guy from *Saturday Night Live* who's in that new *Ladies Man* movie? That guy is definitely black, no doubt about it. He gives off all the signals.

And Whitney Houston? You'd better believe she's black.

I've had this power since I was a kid. Once, when I was maybe 10, I saw Sammy Davis Jr. performing on television, and I just said to myself, "I bet that guy's black." Well, a little later, his autobiography came out and—kaboom!—I was right! And you remember in the '80s, when Bill Cosby got into a whole flap with NBC about an anti-Apartheid slogan on *The Cosby Show*? Well, I'd had him pegged years before that. I saw him on *The Tonight Show* once in the '70s and

thought to myself, "That guy's as black as the last banana."

And why do you think that *Roots* miniseries felt so authentic, so con-

> ## There are little telltale signs to look for that can tip you off as to whether somebody's black.

vincing? Those actors weren't just pretending to be black.... they *were* black. Yes, even LeVar Burton—black, black, black!

I could go on and on. Did you ever watch *In Living Color*? Oh, man. That show was an enclave. We're talking Chocolate City. The question on that show was, who *wasn't* black? Not many, let me tell you.

Having blackdar is an instinct either you have or you don't. Even so, there are little telltale signs to look for that can tip you off as to whether somebody's black. There are certain ways of dressing, walking, and talking that can give it away. And, of course, where the person lives. For example,

there's an area in San Francisco that's almost entirely black. Same thing in New York. Los Angeles has a black part of town, too. So, if you meet somebody and they tell you they live in one of those places, chances are pretty good that they're black.

Okay, so my blackdar is not 100 percent infallible. Sometimes, on very rare occasions, it fails me. Like with Mariah Carey. At first, I was positive she was black, but now I'm not so sure. And that guy on the Yankees, Derek Jeter. I'm on the fence about him, too. But, like I said, that's the rare exception. Almost always, I'll look at a person and immediately know for sure whether they're black, like, say, Jesse Jackson, or not, like Peter Jennings.

Last week, I was at the mall food court with my friend Demetrius. The two of us were just sitting there, having fun watching people walk past and trying to pick out who's black. As we're talking, this obviously white guy at the next table overhears us. So he turns to us and says, "How are you guys so good at that? Is it because you yourselves are black? Are you?" I just told him, hey, that's none of your business. ∅

## Politicians Ignoring Dangers Of Jowl Implants

see WASHINGTON page 3A

## Vending-Machine Snack Fails To Deploy

see LOCAL page 3C

## Parents' Record Collection Deemed Hilarious

see MUSIC page 5D

THE ONION
$2.00 US
$3.00 CAN

0 74470 94595 6

---

# the ONION®

WWW.THEONION.COM — AMERICA'S FINEST NEWS SOURCE™ — FOUNDED 1871

# Smoking Now Permitted Only In Special Room In Iowa

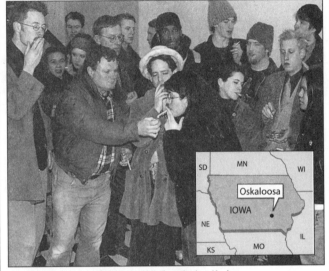

Above: Smokers from across America crowd into the national smoking lounge.

WASHINGTON, DC—The nation's anti-tobacco lobby scored another major victory Monday, when Congress passed legislation restricting smoking within U.S. borders to a specially designated "smoking lounge" in Oskaloosa, IA.

The lounge, a storage closet located in the basement of Oskaloosa's American Legion Hall #3567, will protect non-smokers from the harmful effects of the secondhand smoke generated by the nation's approximately 65 mil-lion smokers.

"Smokers have impinged upon the rights of others for far too long," said U.S. Sen. Dianne Feinstein (D-CA), co-sponsor of the bill. "Now that this issue is finally settled, we can all 'breathe a little easier.'"

"I really need a smoke right now," said White Plains, NY, resident Peter MacAlester, 52, speeding westbound along Interstate 80 toward Oskaloosa. Biting his fingernails and wiping

see SMOKING page 109

## Study:

# Children Of Divorce Twice As Likely To Write Bad Poetry

DURHAM, NC—A study released Monday by Duke University's Center For The American Family confirmed what many child-development experts have claimed for years: that children whose parents are divorced are more likely to compose bad poetry than those whose parents are married.

"Because of the terrible trauma divorce can inflict, we're seeing a corre-

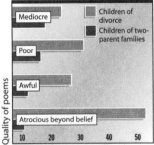

lation between kids from broken homes and embarrassing, godawful verse," said Center For The American Family director Dr. Ruth Wyler-Feldman. "Devastated by the break-up of the family unit, these children are responding with poems awash in bathos, forced rhymes, and mixed

see POETRY page 108

---

# Stephen Hawking Builds Robotic Exoskeleton

CAMBRIDGE, ENGLAND—Nobel Prize-winning physicist Stephen Hawking stunned the international scientific community Monday with his latest breakthrough, a revolutionary cybernetic exoskeleton designed to replace his wheelchair.

Hawking, paralyzed since early adulthood with the degenerative nerve disease ALS, or Lou Gehrig's Disease, unveiled the creation at a press conference at Cambridge University.

"I am faster, stronger... better than before," Hawking told reporters via his suit's

built-in voice synthesizer.

The hulking, hydraulically powered titanium-alloy exoskeleton is expected to assist the famed *Brief History Of Time* author tremendously in his ongoing theoretical-physics research. "With the new exoskeleton, Stephen will be able to safely handle radioactive isotopes in the high-radiation area of the new supercollider particle accelerator. And his new robo-arms are capable of ripping open enemy tanks like they were nutshells," said Cambridge physics chair Sir Geoffrey Neville

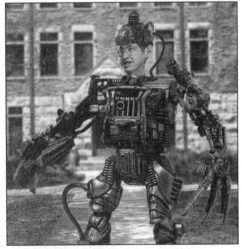

Above: Physicist Stephen Hawking strolls the Cambridge University campus in his new $55 million exoskeleton.

Shropshire-Kent.

The exoskeleton is also equipped with special in-

fra-vision goggles, which will enable Hawking to ob-

see HAWKING page 109

| | 8:00 | | 9:00 | | 10:00 | |
|---|---|---|---|---|---|---|

| | 8:00 | | 9:00 | | 10:00 | |
|---|---|---|---|---|---|---|
| **Fox** | Real Humans In Real Pain | Feral Dingoes Eating Children On Tape | Jiggle It Beach | L.A. Chicks | Beverly Hills 90210: The 90,210th Episode | |
| **UPN** | The Unwatchables | Voyage To The Bottom Of The Nielsens | Theoretically Existing Show | Praying For Syndication | The Last Thing You'd Ever Want To Sit Through | |
| **WB** | Where My Wife At? | Gittin' Yo Freak On | Me & My Psychic | Kids Suck The Darndest Things | Dawson's Clothes | |

| | 8:00 | | 9:00 | | 10:00 | |
|---|---|---|---|---|---|---|
| **Animal Planet** | Incontinent Rhinos | | Dan Taylor: Mongoose Optometrist | | STAY! | The Best Of STAY! |
| **E!** | Andy Gibb: A Nightmare Descent Into Booze & Pills | | Margot Kidder: A Nightmare Descent Into Booze & Pills | | Boy George: A Nightmare Descent Into Booze & Pills | |
| **ESPN2** | Finland's Brutalest Men | Being Hit By A Trolley Regional Semifinals | 60 Minutes Of Joe Theismann's Leg Breaking | | Co-Ed Spread-Eagled Weight-Training From Maui | |
| **Sci-Fi** | Space: 1972 | | The Bermuda Triangle: Myth Or Fiction? | | Mid-Budget Galaxy | |
| **Lifetime** | How Can I Choose Between My Daughters? | | The Abused Wife Who Didn't Mean To Kill Her Policeman Husband In Self-Defense | | The Boy Whose Mommy Watched Far Too Much Television | |
| **TNN** | This Here's My Dog | | I Caught Me These Fish | You Hush Up, Wanda Mae | Okay, Give 'Er The Gas Again, Clem | |
| **Telemundo** | ¡Roberto Amoroso En Agua Caliente! | | ¡Whoomp! ¿Dondé Esta? | ¡Goooooooooooooal! | ¡Ai! ¡Ai! ¡Ai! ¡Ai! ¡Ai! | La Hora De Goya |
| **Public Access** | Blurry Steve | Inaudible City Council Meeting | Do We Have A Caller On The Line? Hello? | The Best Of Lunch Menus | My Friend Made This Short Film | Men With Braids Speak Out |
| **Cinemax** | Bare Ambition (Tanya Roberts) | Naked Exposition (Traci Lords) | Body Of Nudity (Dana Plato) | | Unclothed Anguish (Joyce DeWitt) | |

---

**POETRY from page 107**

metaphors comparing their souls to rainstorms."

According to Wyler-Feldman, parental separation most commonly manifests itself in atrocious drivel about isolation and anger.

"Just listen to the words of Ashley Bedrosian, a Pensacola, FL, 14-year-old whose parents split up last May after 17 years of marriage: 'The pain comes down like a harlequin's tears / From my room I can hear my parents screaming / What once was one heart now beats as two / From this nightmare I cannot awake, for I am not dreaming.'"

"Obviously, Ashley is bitter and heartbroken over her parents' divorce," Wyler-Feldman said. "And that's tragic, because what comes out of that bitterness and heartbreak is some of the worst poetry you'll ever have the misfortune to read."

The two-year study found that the rhyming of "despise" with "my eyes," as well as references to Trent Reznor and horses running wild and/or free, occur 65 percent more often in poems by children of divorced parents than in those who come from stable two-parent homes.

The Duke researchers also found a strong correlation between the nature of a particular divorce and quality of poetry. In 90 percent of divorces categorized as "amicable," the breakup results in rhyming poems, usually with irritating, "sing-songish" A-B-A-B rhyme schemes. The more acrimonious the split, however, the greater the odds of a child turning to other, more wretch-inducing poetic forms: Eighty-five percent of contested divorces end in free verse, the study found, and three in four divorces in-volving custody battles end in haiku.

"These children of divorce are really hurting," noted therapist Dr. Eli Wasserbaum said. "But not nearly as much as those of us forced to read this drivel."

Wasserbaum urged America's troubled couples to split up while their children are still young. "If you have children between the ages of 3 and 9, and you suspect you might not want to spend the rest of your life with your spouse, I'd strongly encourage you to get divorced now," he said. "At least that way, your kids have a fighting chance to heal emotionally before they reach their prime poetry-writing years, and we can all be spared reading about a beautiful rose that withers and dies because no sunlight ever fell upon it."

"The bottom line is, America's kids could channel their anger over the 'loss' of a parent into moving verse, but instead they're churning out melodramatic crap," said Dirk Fransette, director of the Young Writers' Workshop, a Brookline, MA, writing program for 13- to 18-year-olds. "If I have to read one more poem about a lighthouse, I'm going to carve out my eyeballs."

The study has provoked strong reaction among teenagers nationwide.

"You just don't understand," said Ethan Cameron, 14, of Salem, OR.

Cameron, whose parents recently split up, self-publishes a literary web site called Visitation Rites. Among the high-school freshman's poems: "Detention Of The Soul," "My Trenchcoat," and "Bruised."

"Saying that all our poetry is bad, well, it just isn't fair," said Knoxville, TN, 15-year-old Melody Jeffords,

Above: A horrible poem by Roanoke, VA, 15-year-old Meredith Dietz, whose parents recently divorced.

whose parents divorced when she was 13. "My parents and teachers just don't understand my pain. Or, as my new poem 'Trust' puts it, 'Who can you trust / With thoughts inside your head? / You can't trust anyone / Unless they're already dead.'"

Wyler-Feldman acknowledged that, while the Duke study has shed a great deal of light on the link between divorce and bad poetry, much remains to be learned.

"A great deal is still unknown. For example, why so much thunder-and-lightning imagery? Why so many references to The Crow? And why the recent rise in short stories ending with alarm clocks ringing, revealing the entire story to be a dream? We must answer these crucial questions before we can ever hope to find a cure." Ø serve sub-atomic phenomena first-hand.

"Wait a minute," said Hawking, testing the infra-vision goggles for the first time. "I see now that the curvature of space-time follows previously unmeasured vectors that I will need to recalibrate in my equations. Also, there appears to be some sort of trouble on the moon."

Among the suit's other features: laser terminals, oxygen pressure-tanks for deep-sea and outer-space research, jet boots, and the most advanced crime-lab database in the world.

Constructed in Hawking's secret underground headquarters by the famed scientist and his orphaned teenage sidekick and research assistant Hawk-Lad, the exoskeleton has already proven invaluable, not only in increasing the paralyzed Hawking's mobility, but in rounding up the notorious international gang of diamond thieves known as "The Fearsome Four."

The $55 million exoskeleton, which Hawking operates through slight movements of his left wrist, is powered by a pair of bio-morphogenetic servo-motors and boasts the most ad-

## Among the suit's features: the most advanced crime-lab database in the world.

vanced cyber-robotic technology anywhere. The suit has freed Hawking of the wheelchair to which he has been confined for much of his adult life and given him greater freedom of movement when engaged in battle.

"Beware, would-be evildoers," Hawking said. "My crimefighting powers are as infinite and unknowable as the universe itself."

As for the future, Hawking said he plans to continue teaching and hopes to take a sabbatical in Italy with his wife and nurse. But primarily, he will focus on preparing for his greatest mission yet: a descent into a black hole in mid-1998.

"Only by penetrating the event horizon itself will I be able to observe the effects of singularity on neutrino decay and complete my research," Hawking said. "It should also prove invaluable in the construction of my new Anti-Gravity Gun. It may be our only hope for stopping Monstro The Living Behemoth."

Hawking has already received the International Science League award for his invention, as well as a prestigious chair at the Helsinki Cybernetics Institute. In addition, he is widely regarded as the favorite to win this year's Nobel Prize For Physics, and recently received an honorary key to New York from Mayor Rudolph Giuliani for saving the city from the Galactons. ⌀

sweat from his brow as he drove, he added, "I figure if I drive straight through and manage to stay awake, I can probably get there in about 16 hours."

The legislation's passage ranks among America's most significant moments in the battle against smoking. Past landmarks include the 1989 Supreme Court decision to limit smoking to the Midwest, Congress' 1993 restriction of smoking to Iowa only, the Iowa Supreme Court's 1995 statewide ban on smoking except in

## Gnawing at the bloodied ball of his thumb, Freeburn added: "Fucking shit-ass Christ piss!"

Oskaloosa, and the Oskaloosa City Council's 1997 declaration that, with the exception of the American Legion Hall, Oskaloosa is designated a smoke-free city.

Smoking opponents throughout the Oskaloosa area are applauding the latest piece of legislation, which limits smoking in the American Legion Hall to the basement storage closet.

"It's about time," Oskaloosa non-smoker Caryn Tapp said. "That building's tolerant 'all-areas' open-smoking policy encouraged the filthy habit. Not only that, the building's proximity to the local Arby's helped promote tobacco use among Oskaloosa's 65 teens."

"My daughter lives in California, and she's refused to bring my newborn grandson to visit me because of that building's relaxed smoking code," said Harriet Mortimer, 63, who lives down the block from the American Legion Hall. "But now that it's been restricted to the basement storage closet, she's considering coming."

Added Mortimer: "That closet doesn't have any windows, does it?"

The new legislation may be popular among Oskaloosa non-smokers, but it is hated by smokers across the U.S.

"Having to drive to Iowa to grab a smoke on my lunch break every day was certainly inconvenient enough," said Daniel Freeburn, a 38-year-old Boston marketing executive. "But now, on top of everything else, we have to deal with this? That lounge barely has room for 40 or 50 people, and that's when they're packed in like sardines. With lines of up to 50 or 60 million people during noontime rush periods, I'm sometimes as much as six months late getting back to my desk."

Gnawing at the bruised, bloodied ball of his thumb, Freeburn added: "Fucking shit-ass Christ piss!" He then asked if anyone had any gum. Less than an hour later, he was arrested by Boston police for bashing his office supervisor's head against a desk.

Across the nation, smokers have resorted to desperate measures in an ef-

Above: Scenes like this one in Orlando, FL, are becoming increasingly common across America, with highways jammed with smokers en route to Iowa.

fort to sidestep the latest government restrictions. Some have been caught hiding cigarettes inside asthma inhalers. Tempe, AZ, smoker Reggie Greene was recently caught attempting to dig a 700-foot hole in the ground in the crawlspace beneath his home. According to police, Greene was planning to use the pit to secretly smoke in private, far beneath the Earth's surface.

Despite the victory, anti-tobacco groups say the war against smoking is far from over.

"We still have a long way to go," said Francine Stotts, director of the Citi-

zens Health Action Institute and a member of the board of directors of the San Francisco-based What About The Children? foundation. "It's true that, by restricting smoking in the entire country to a cramped closet in a barely accessible rural hamlet surrounded by nothing but miles of flat farmland in every direction, we have helped reduce the non-smoker's risk of exposure to secondhand smoke. But we cannot stop there. We must continue to lobby for greater restrictions until smoking is only permitted beyond the orbit of the outermost gas giant Neptune." ⌀

## NEWS IN BRIEF

## Area Man Killed In Committee

NEW YORK—K&L Advertising executive Nathan Lohaus was killed in committee Monday, his life voted down by an 11-3 margin at the 2 p.m. departmental meeting. "We threw Nathan out there and workshopped him at length but, in the end, we decided he just wasn't viable," K&L creative director Marcus Somers said. "We had a lot of really high hopes for Nathan, and we certainly tried to make him work, passing him back and forth and letting everybody take a stab at him, but in the end he just died on the table." Somers extended his "deepest regrets" to Lohaus' wife and children.

## Third-Grader Won't Shut Up About Raccoons

GOSHEN, IN—For the 41st straight day, Goshen third-grader Peter Driscoll refused to shut up about raccoons Monday. "The largest raccoon ever recorded weighed over 60 pounds," Driscoll said. "Baby raccoons are called kits and gestate for 63 days." "He just won't stop with the damn raccoons," said Valerie Driscoll, Peter's mother. "I don't know how much more of this I can take." Peter also noted that "raccoon" comes from the Algonquin word "arakun," which means "one who scratches with his hands." ⌀

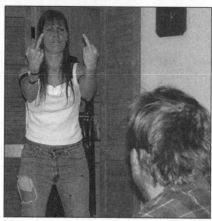
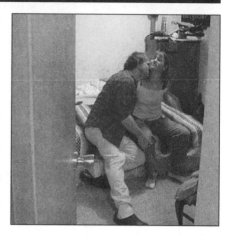

# Teen Exposed To Violence, Profanity, Adult Situations By Family

BROWNSVILLE, TX—According to the conservative watchdog group Family Research Council, the home of 15-year-old Beth Arnott contains violence, profanity, adult situations, and other material "wholly unsuitable" for those 16 and under.

"That house is filled with inappropriate material that sets a poor example for the impressionable youths living there," said Family Research Council president Kenneth Connor, citing 44 instances of domestic violence, adult language, nudity, and graphic sexual content in the Brownsville home in the past month alone. "This is hardly the sort of family we should be exposing our nation's children to."

Connor noted that Beth's stepfather,

43-year-old Randy Skowron, frequently walks around the house in an open bathrobe, inadvertently exposing his genitalia to Beth. He also cited numerous incidents of Skowron hitting Beth's brother Ronnie with an open hand for being "all mouthy and disrespectful." Beth herself was subjected to a similar act of violence when she was caught shoplifting a Victoria's Secret bra at Valle Vista Mall.

Other inappropriate material to which Beth has been exposed includes frequent use of the term "skank-ass bitch," nightly binges of

Mad Dog 20/20, and an incident in which she inadvertently stumbled across Skowron and her mother in coitus just minutes after the pair had been throwing kitchen appliances at each other.

"The family is the most important factor when it comes to promoting family-friendly themes," Connor said. "The Arnotts may pay lip service to being a pro-family family, but their actions speak otherwise."

Author and critic Michael Medved, a leading proponent of stricter moral standards, agreed.

"These are graphic sexual themes which could take a girl, just coming into an understanding of her own sexuality, and twist her around until she doesn't know right from wrong," said Medved, co-author of *Saving Childhood: Protecting Our Children From The National Assault On Innocence.* "I feel sorry for Beth, for her childhood has been lost and her innocence assaulted."

"We challenge the Arnotts to get serious about the vital role they play in shaping America's culture," said U.S. Rep. Steve Largent (R-OK), who has proposed legislation requiring warning labels on non-family-friendly families. "Look at the Petersons right next door. With their regular attendance at church, frequent family outings to Chuck E. Cheese's, and week-

ly Sunday-night Scrabble games, the Petersons are the sort of wholesome, socially redemptive family this country needs more of. Why must we put up with this vile Arnott filth when there are such wonderful alternatives literally right next door?"

Following Largent's lead, concerned Brownsville residents are calling for the placement of a parental-advisory sticker on the Arnotts' front door which warns that interaction with the family is not recommended for children 16 or younger. In addition, locals have petitioned Cat Marine Machine Tooling, Skowron's employer, to fire the man, threatening to withdraw their patronage if the shop continues to "endorse the deplorable actions in Beth's home by keeping Mr. Skowron on the payroll."

One neighbor, wishing to remain anonymous, said: "We don't want to censor anybody, but we have an obligation to the community and to our children. We can monitor our kids within our own home, but we can't protect them when they go out into the world every day and are exposed to sex, violence, and drug use by families like that."

For all the controversy her family has stirred, Beth remains unaffected.

"It's not a big deal," said Beth, smoking a Kool cigarette stolen from her mother's purse. "Just because I see Mom giving Randy blow jobs and Ronnie huffing paint don't mean I'm gonna do that shit. I can think for myself." Ø

## NEWS IN BRIEF

### New *Pompous Asshole* Magazine To Compete With *Cigar Aficionado*

NEW YORK—Upscale consumers who enjoy cigars, wine, and "all the finer things in life" will have a new magazine to enjoy beginning next month, when *Pompous Asshole* hits newsstands. Targeting the coveted 23- to 60-year-old pompous-asshole de-

mographic, the new monthly magazine is expected to compete directly with *Cigar Aficionado* for advertising dollars. "*Pompous Asshole* is the magazine of the good life," said publisher Paul Westman. "And, unlike *Cigar Aficionado*, we truly cover it all: From tips on choosing the right humidor to advice on where to gamble in Monte Carlo to the lowdown on the new Jaguar XJ8, *Pompous Asshole* is the magazine no rich prick can afford to be without." Ø

## Christian Prop Comic Wowing Churches From Coast To Coast

see RELIGION page 10B

## Alec Baldwin Secretes Own Hair Gel

see PEOPLE page 2D

## Your Neighbors: Should You Consider Talking To Them?

see LIVING page 4D

### STATshot

A look at the numbers that shape your world.

**What's The Only Flaw In Our Ingenious Plan?**

- 18% Boiling Point At 30,000 Feet Several Degrees Lower
- 25% Extra Guard Dog Posted, Brought Only Three Hypodermic Needles
- 22% Vicar Failed To Take Evening Tea
- 23% That Crafty Fox Made Of Sterner Stuff Than We Anticipated
- 12% Wife Found Out About It

THE ONION
$2.00 US
$3.00 CAN

0 74470 94595 6

---

# the ONION®

WWW.THEONION.COM    AMERICA'S FINEST NEWS SOURCE™    FOUNDED 1871

Above: A wooded area is stripped bare by Pacific North loggers, prompting cries of environmental rape.

# Raped Environment Led Polluters On, Defense Attorneys Argue

OLYMPIA, WA—In an opening statement before jurors Monday, defense attorneys representing Pacific North Construction & Lumber argued that their client was not at fault in the July 1997 rape of 30,000 acres of virgin forest, claiming that the forest led the defendant on with "an eager and blatant display of its rich, fertile bounty."

"While, obviously, it is extremely unfortunate that this forest was raped, it should have known better than to show off its lush

Above: Dennis Schickle, defense attorney for the lumber company.

greenery and tall, strong trees in the presence of my client if it didn't want anything to happen," said lead defense attorney Dennis

see ENVIRONMENT page 113

---

# Turtle Owner Enjoys Special Daily Turtle-Time

Above: Dennis Frye makes sure to set aside at least an hour each day for quality time with his pet turtle Sheldon.

DEARBORN, MI—Dennis Frye, 31, an unmarried lawn-care-supply wholesaler and home-turtle enthusiast, took special time out Monday, as he does every day, to enjoy care, feeding, and maintenance of his pet turtle Sheldon.

"Who's a little shell-head? Who? Who?" asked Frye, visibly enthused by the turtle's presence. Sheldon, a common box turtle acquired by Frye at Winston's World Of Exciting Fish & Pets in downtown Dearborn as a

"birthday present" for himself in 1995, did not appear to respond.

The animal has been Frye's sole domestic companion for the past three years.

Lovingly replenishing Sheldon's lettuce supply and refilling his special personalized food-pellet distribution device, Frye removed the squat, near-immobile animal from his tank for his daily bathtub swim in several inches of lukewarm water. Frye then

see TURTLE page 112

---

# Augusta National Honors Tiger Woods With Own Drinking Fountain

AUGUSTA, GA—Augusta National, home of the Masters Tournament, honored 1997 Masters champion Tiger Woods Monday, giving him his own drinking fountain at the prestigious country club.

"Tiger, for your historic achievement in setting an all-time Masters Tournament record, we present

you with this beautiful, specially designated drinking fountain," said Augusta National president Gary Brewer. "All other golfers will drink from a different fountain, which you, as an honored champion, will have no need to use."

The new fountain, clearly labeled "Tiger Woods," will

see WOODS page 112

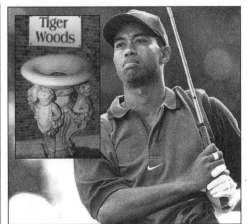

Above: Tiger Woods, 1997 Masters champion, was honored by Augusta National officials with his own separate, clearly labeled fountain.

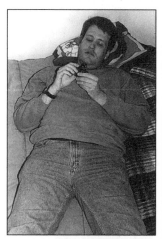

Above: Frye enjoys the company of his "favorite little turtle-pal."

## NEWS IN BRIEF

# Pat Buchanan: Thousands Of Americans Made In China

TOPEKA, KS—During a speech Monday at the Topeka VFW Hall, an alarmed Pat Buchanan said that "hundreds of thousands" of U.S. citizens were made in Communist China. "These shoddy, Asian-looking, 'knock-off' Americans are the mass-produced product of non-union, low-wage parents," the Reform Party presidential hopeful told VFW members. "Every day, these Asians are exported from China to our shores, where they are free to intermingle with genuine, made-in-the-USA Americans." Buchanan added that if he wins the presidency, he would impose stiff tariffs against U.S.-citizen-producing nations and return all bootleg Americans to their nations of origin.

# Man Breaks Out Dating Boxers

SUFFOLK, VA—Having secured a date for the first time in seven months, local resident Andrew Agee removed his dating boxers from the bottom of his dresser Saturday. "No tighty-whities for me tonight," said Agee, taking off a pair of dingy Fruit Of The Loom briefs and slipping on the blue Calvin Klein boxers with a small, understated white "CK" logo near the bottom of the right leg. "A girl might actually see me in my underwear." Agee added that if the date goes well and future encounters with the woman seem likely, he will purchase a three-pack of boxers.

# Letter From Employer Thankfully Omits Balls-Copying Incident

SAN FRANCISCO—Randall Konerko, a 39-year-old database administrator looking for a new job in the field, was relieved to learn Monday that a letter of recommendation from his former employer makes no reference to the Dec. 11 balls-copying incident that led to his dismissal. "Whew, that's a relief," said Konerko after an interview with Luminant Worldwide. "I was sure Mr. Alland would mention that whole thing, but, mercifully, he didn't." Konerko has made a promise to himself never to engage in testicular Xeroxing, even if it's 2 a.m. and the office seems to be completely empty. Ø

cleaned the droppings from Sheldon's aquarium habitat, rinsing out the bed of multi-colored pebbles and placing fresh pebbles where necessary, pausing periodically to "check in on" the turtle with queries such as, "How ya doin' there, li'l buddy?," "You doin' okay in there?," and "Havin' fun just swimmin' around?"

Before returning Sheldon to his tank, Frye also engaged the animal in several minutes of spirited "play," which largely consisted of Frye picking up Sheldon and setting him down in various spots, then watching him crawl feebly in a vain attempt to escape his human captor.

"Every evening, during turtle-time, if Sheldon has been an especially well-behaved little guy that day, I give him his favorite 'special occasion' treat—a chunk of leafy iceberg lettuce covered in yummy fish oil," Frye said. "He always crunches down on it with such gusto, I almost feel like I'm getting a special treat, too."

Feeding the tiny reptile a lovingly prepared slice of lettuce, Frye watched as Sheldon slowly chewed and swallowed each mouthful. "Look at him!" Frye whispered gleefully. "He's chewing it!"

"He loves it! Look at him smiling!" he added.

According to herpetologists, not only is the facial musculature of the box turtle incapable of forming a smile, but the chances of Sheldon actually experiencing feelings of joy are almost nil.

"Amphibious creatures like Sheldon do not experience emotions the way many people think they do," said Dr. Stanley Hargrove of the San Diego Zoo. "Turtles lack the nurturing and bonding capacities of more highly developed creatures, and are thus incapable of feelings of affection."

Hargrove also noted that Sheldon's "play" behavior is not really play at all, but escape instinct in action.

"Sheldon, like any animal forced to live in a small glass tank, is consumed with a desire to get away," Hargrove said. "Of course, since this is a pet turtle we're talking about, there is very little Sheldon can do to act on this desire beyond just crawling to the side of his tank and looking out."

Hargrove said the turtle's relative helplessness is rendered all the more pitiful by his inability to communicate his dissatisfaction to his human owner.

"Sometimes, when Sheldon is really feeling wild, he likes to wear his special 'Super-Turtle' sweater," said Frye, forcing the animal into a novelty pet shirt. Frye grinned as he pulled the small garment, complete with an iron-on "ST" logo and miniature cape, over the turtle's shell.

"Doesn't he look cute?" asked Frye, picking up the turtle to "fly" him around the room "like a little superhero." Sheldon reacted in the same manner he always does when held: He withdrew into his shell as an instinctive defense mechanism against predators.

"I love Sheldon, my little turtle friend," Frye said. "It's so nice to have someone around the house as company."

Added Frye: "I believe it's really important for all of God's creatures, whether turtles or humans, to feel loved." Ø

WOODS from page 111

be located behind the outhouse between the 16th and 17th holes, far away from the distractions of other golfers.

"With your win, you join an elite group of Masters champions, including Arnold Palmer and Jack Nicklaus," Brewer said. "We are confident that, as golf's next great and someone we will no doubt be seeing a lot more of in the future, you will honor and obey their legacies. We have every confidence that, as they did before you, you will remain well-behaved and respectful of Augusta's traditions."

Woods' fellow golfers are equally impressed. "Rarely does a golfer come along who is so different from the rest," said 1992 Masters winner Fred Couples. "He's not at all like us."

Brewer called Woods "a real asset" to Augusta's roll call of champions, noting that the 21-year-old has never, to the best of his knowledge, been convicted of a crime.

Additional honors were bestowed upon the Masters champion when Augusta announced a special new security squad, which will monitor Woods at all times during his visits to the club. "It is important to us that Augusta members feel secure in the knowledge that Tiger Woods is fully protect-ed and supervised while golfing here," Brewer said.

With his Masters win, Woods will also enjoy unlimited, lifetime use of the Augusta National course.

> ## The fountain will be located behind the outhouse between the 16th and 17th holes.

"Tiger is welcome to enjoy his championship privileges here at Augusta any time he wants," Brewer said, "provided we are given enough advance notice to alert and reschedule other golfers in order to best accommodate him."

Brewer noted that there are many fine public courses near Augusta National that offer excellent golfing. He encouraged Woods to patronize these, as well, in order to maximize his golfing variety and enjoyment.

In addition to the fountain, Woods will receive his own dining area, locker room, and personal entrance at the rear of the Augusta clubhouse. Ø

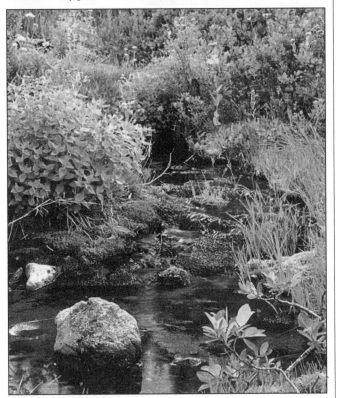

Above: The victim prior to the rape.

Schickle, speaking before a courtroom packed with members of the media. "It's only natural for any red-blooded American developer to get ideas in his head when he's presented with that kind of untouched beauty."

"The bottom line is," Schickle continued, "if you're going to tease and encourage like that, openly flaunting your abundant natural resources, don't be shocked by the consequences."

Public opinion regarding the high-profile case, which is being closely watched by timber-industry lobbyists and victims' rights groups, is deeply divided. While some contend that the ravaging of a piece of land until it is stripped bare is never justifiable under any circumstances, others say that such an action is understandable if the wooded area gives off mixed signals.

"Pacific North Construction & Lumber had every reason to believe that forest wanted it bad," said logger Victor Duffy of Chelan, WA. "Just look at where it was at the time of the incident: It was in a secluded, far-off spot nearly 25 miles from the nearest road. What were those trees doing in that kind of remote area if they weren't looking for trouble?"

Those who support the timber company also point to the forest's history, claiming that it has a reputation for being easily exploited.

"Believe me, this is no virgin forest," said Frank Abbate, owner of the Bellingham-based G&H Consolidated Timber. "It may try to pass itself off as pristine and untouched, but I know for a fact that it has a long history of allowing developers to have their way with it."

In his opening statement, Schickle also noted that when Pacific North loggers arrived at the forest on the day in question, its floor was covered in alluring, fragrant flowers that were "clearly meant to attract."

"When a forest drapes itself in flora of every color and scent imaginable,

---

> ## "Pacific North Construction & Lumber had every reason to believe that forest wanted it bad."

---

it's obviously asking for it," Schickle said. "I'm sure the plaintiff will argue that these radiant flowers were meant to lure pollen-hungry bees, not pulp-hungry loggers. But how was my client supposed to know this? When was it made clear that this colorful display was intended to attract one particular species but no other? When was it made clear that this forest was looking to satisfy the needs of bees and bees only?"

Russell Belanger, president of the National Timber & Logging Association, agreed. "This forest made it seem like it wanted it, then cried environmental rape when it got it," Belanger said. "At some point, we've got to start asking ourselves who the real victim is in these cases: Our nation's promiscuous, manipulative forests? Or the decent, honest developers out there who are just trying to make an honest living razing the land?" ∅

---

# My Brother Is Going To Love This Forwarded List Of Lawyer Jokes

By Steve Schwantes

I've got a question for you: How do you tell when a lawyer is lying? His lips are moving!

That's just one of the countless great zingers on this list of lawyer jokes my wife's friend Kate forwarded to me yesterday. Luckily, I'm on Kate's e-mail forward list, so whenever she gets something funny, I'm sure to get it, along with the 35 other people on her list. In turn, I always make sure to forward the stuff I get to people I think would appreciate it—like my brother Jim!

There are about 200 lawyer jokes on this latest list. I haven't actually read them all; I just scrolled down a few pages. I did, however, make sure to forward them to my brother, because I figured he'd enjoy spending 30 to 40 minutes going through it. Same thing goes for the long list of golf jokes I forwarded him last week and the list of blonde jokes the week before.

Now, my brother isn't actually a lawyer. And I don't think he has any lawyer friends. And, as far as I know, he doesn't specifically have anything against lawyers. But who doesn't enjoy a few hundred good-natured jabs at lawyers every now and then? I

mean, lawyers are like vultures. In fact, do you know the difference between a lawyer and a vulture? The lawyer gets frequent-flyer miles. Boy, my brother is going to love that one!

You know what? Something strange just occurred to me. Even though, for the past two years, I've faithfully forwarded stuff to Jim three or four times a week, he's never sent anything to me. Never. Not so much as one Lewinsky joke. Not one "You Know You're A Redneck If..." list. Not one "Wassssup!" parody. (Not even the one where the rabbis say "Shalom!" instead of "Wassssup!" Have you seen that one? It's hysterical!)

Jim e-mails me occasionally with a message or a question, so I know his outgoing mail works. I guess his coworkers at the university are so out of the loop that no one sends them any funny stuff. I once met some of them, and they seemed a little—how can I put this nicely?—brainy.

I've really worked up a good forwarding list of my own, about 25 people in all. Besides my brother and some other relatives, the list includes my wife, a bunch of her coworkers at the pet clinic, the people in my department at J&H Marketing, some of my old high-school buddies, my podiatrist, my insurance agent, and a few folks I met last year on a vacation to see JOKES page 114

---

## Rocky Horror At 25

The midnight-movie classic *Rocky Horror Picture Show* turns 25 this month. How are fans celebrating the milestone?

| | |
|---|---|
| **4%** | Throwing out back doing "Time Warp" |
| **16%** | Yelling, "Why is your phone bill so high?" at movie screen for 1,184th straight Friday night |
| **13%** | Toucha-toucha-toucha-touching 47-year-old spouse |
| **11%** | Pondering rumored homoerotic overtones of film |
| **17%** | Mistakenly seeing midnight show of *Dead Man Walking*; getting thrown out for screaming "Slut!" whenever Susan Sarandon appears |
| **10%** | Fatally stabbing Meat Loaf with pickaxe |
| **14%** | Bringing *Rocky Horror* virgin to film to be among his or her own kind |
| **7%** | Going to Denny's afterwards |
| **8%** | Watching movie at home; realizing it sucks |

## Point-Counterpoint: Faith
# It Was Then That I Carried You

**By Jesus Christ**

One night, Jim, you had a dream. You dreamed you were walking along the beach with Me. Across the sky flashed scenes from your life. For each scene, you noticed two sets of footprints in the sand—one belonging to you, and the other to Me. When the last scene of your life flashed before you, you looked back at the footprints in the sand. You noticed that many times along the path of your life there was only one set of footprints. You also noticed that it happened at the very lowest and saddest times in your life. This bothered you, and you questioned Me about it. "Lord, you said that once I decided to follow You, You would walk with me all the way. But I have noticed that during the most troublesome times in my life, there is only one set of footprints. I don't understand why, when I needed you most, you would leave me." I replied, "My precious, precious child. I love you and I would never leave you. During your times of trial and suffering, when you see only one set of footprints, it was then that I carried you." ∅

# Bullshit, Jesus, Those Are Obviously My Footprints

**By Jim Steinhauer**

Sorry to have to break it to you, Jesus, but those are obviously my footprints.

Look closely. See how those footprints have that wavy tread pattern on the bottom, just like my docksiders? If they were Yours, they'd make a sandal mark, like the footprints next to mine a little farther up the beach when I was going through better times.

See the footprints at the time of my divorce? You'll notice that the sandaled footprints drift off from the docksider ones. They lead to that picnic bench over there, the one with the cigarette butts scattered all over. It appears that in my darkest hour, instead of carrying me, You sat on a stump and had a couple of smokes. Real helpful, Jesus. Real helpful.

Sure, the sandal footprints came back when I got that big job promotion, but right at the point where my son Tommy died, they veer off again. Actually, now that I look again, it seems like there's an unusually large distance between each of the sandal-wearer's footprints around the time of my son's death, as if the person were actually running away.

I'm sorry, Jesus, but Your whole story about carrying me during my worst moments just doesn't gibe with the facts. Besides, you'd certainly think a person would remember being carried by the Son of God, right? That's a pretty memorable thing, wouldn't you say? Well, either I've got amnesia, or You're a liar, because I don't recall ever being toted around by the Messiah. The only thing I do remember about my worst moments on the path of life is the horrible feeling of plodding along the cold sand all alone while icy rain fell in sheets and chill winds assailed me.

So thanks, Jesus. Thanks a bunch. You were really there for me when things got rough. Asshole. ∅

**JOKES from page 113**

Yellowstone. There are also a few addresses on the list, like 753bc@globonet.com and mmbtinfo@yahoo.com, where I can't remember to whom they belong. Oh, well: Whoever they are, I'm sure they love constantly getting e-mailed funny stuff, like this latest list. Speaking of which, why won't sharks attack lawyers? Professional courtesy.

When you forward a mass-forwarded e-mail, you get a good feeling inside. As nice as it is to receive a 10-page list of mommy-mommy jokes, it's even nicer to send that list along to dozens of other people you think would enjoy it, too. Like my brother Jim. Jim is just the sort of guy who ap-

### When you forward a mass-forwarded e-mail, you get a good feeling inside.

preciates funny stuff like that. To give you an idea of his crazy sense of humor, he once replied to a list of "25 Reasons I'm Late For Work" that I forwarded him. His reply read, "Stop sending me all this crap." Isn't that hilarious? That's exactly why I know he'll love these lawyer jokes! ∅

# Report: 98 Percent Of U.S. Commuters Favor Public Transportation For Others

Above: Traffic moves slowly near Seatte, WA, where a majority of drivers say they support other people using mass transit.

WASHINGTON, DC—A study released Monday by the American Public Transportation Association reveals that 98 percent of Americans support the use of mass transit by others.

"With traffic congestion, pollution, and oil shortages all getting worse, now is the time to shift to affordable, efficient public transportation," APTA director Howard Collier said. "Fortunately, as this report shows, Americans have finally recognized the need for everyone else to do exactly that."

Of the study's 5,200 participants, 44 percent cited faster commutes as the primary reason to expand public transportation, followed closely by shorter lines at the gas station. Environmental and energy concerns ranked a distant third and fourth, respectively.

Anaheim, CA, resident Lance Holland, who drives 80 miles a day to his job in downtown Los Angeles, was among the proponents of public transit.

"Expanding mass transit isn't just a good idea; it's a necessity," Holland said. "My drive to work is unbelievable. I spend more than two hours stuck in 12 lanes of traffic. It's about time somebody did something to get some of these other cars off the road."

Public support for mass transit will naturally lead to its expansion and improvement, Los Angeles County Metropolitan Transportation Authority officials said.

"With everyone behind it, we'll be able to expand bus routes, create park-and-ride programs, and build new Metrolink commuter-rail lines," LACMTA president Howard Sager said. "It's almost a shame I don't know anyone who will be using these new services."

Sager said he expects large-scale expansion of safe, efficient, and economical mass-transit systems to reduce traffic congestion in all major metropolitan areas in the coming decades.

"Improving public transportation will do a great deal of good, creating jobs, revitalizing downtown areas, and reducing pollution," Sager said. "It also means a lot to me personally, as it should shave 20 to 25 minutes off my morning drive."

The APTA study also noted that, of the 98 percent of Americans who drive to work, 94 percent are the sole occupant of their automobiles.

"When public transportation is not practical, commuters should at least be carpooling," Collier said. "Most people, unlike me, probably work near someone they know and don't need to be driving alone."

Collier said he hopes the study serves as a wake-up call to Americans. In conjunction with its release, the APTA is kicking off a campaign to promote mass transit with the slogan, "Take The Bus... I'll Be Glad You Did."

The campaign is intended to de-emphasize the inconvenience and social stigma associated with using public transportation, focusing instead on the positives. Among them: the health benefits of getting fresh air while waiting at the bus stop, the chance to meet interesting people from a diverse array of low-paying service-sector jobs, and the opportunity to learn new languages by reading subway ads written in Spanish.

"People need to realize that public transportation isn't just for some poor sucker to take to work," Collier said. "He should also be taking it to the shopping mall, the supermarket, and the laundromat." ∅

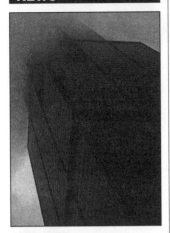

## AT&T Builds Windowless Black Tower

see BUSINESS page 1B

## Seven-Foot-Tall Animatronic Rodent Terrifies Birthday Boy

see LOCAL page 7B

## Hair Carefully Disheveled In 20-Minute Ritual

see FASHION page 2C

## 'Leave Your Daughter At Work Day' A Big Success

see OFFICE page 4D

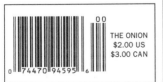

THE ONION
$2.00 US
$3.00 CAN

0 74470 94595 6

---

# the ONION®

WWW.THEONION.COM     AMERICA'S FINEST NEWS SOURCE™     FOUNDED 1871

# Suburban Parade Of Homes Marred By Rotting Ox On Lawn

SCHAUMBURG, IL—The Greater Schaumburg Realtors Association's annual Parade Of Homes was marred Saturday by the presence of a rotting ox on the front lawn of one of the model homes on display.

More than two dozen potential home buyers, each of whom paid $10 to participate in the Parade Of Homes, requested their money back after coming across the festering ox see OX page 117

---

# Report: Aspirin Taken Daily With Bottle Of Bourbon Reduces Awareness Of Heart Attacks

PHILADELPHIA—In a medical breakthrough that should come as welcome news for millions of at-risk Americans, University of Pennsylvania cardiologists announced Saturday that taking one aspirin tablet and a fifth of bourbon daily can significantly reduce an individual's awareness of heart attacks.

**Heart Attack Awareness**

"This study represents a major victory in the fight against heart disease, America's number-one killer," Dr. Arthur Katzeff said. "Each year, two million Americans clutch their chests in terror and say, 'Jesus Christ! I'm having a fucking heart attack!' With this revolutionary new aspirin-bourbon treatment, such fully conscious incidents of cardiac arrest may soon be a thing of the past."

According to Katzeff, test subjects who were administered a single aspirin tablet in the morning, followed by a fifth of bonded Kentucky bourbon over the next several hours, were 85 percent less likely to realize they were having a heart attack than those who did not take aspirin see REPORT page 116

---

# Cruise, Kidman Walk Through Lobby

LOS ANGELES—A-list Hollywood celebrities Tom Cruise and Nicole Kidman, widely considered to be the most important human beings on the planet, walked through the lobby of the Four Seasons Hotel Saturday, drawing the attention of dozens of reporters and photographers and thrilling millions of television viewers, *Access Hollywood* sources reported.

Cruise, universally admired for his cocky, charismatic grin and stunning good looks, and wife Kidman, who has garnered worldwide acclaim for her breathtaking beauty, were reportedly in the hotel "for some reason" and traversed the lobby "to exit the hotel" when *Access Hollywood* captured their beautiful images.

"They were definitely at the location with their actual physical persons undoubtedly present," a statement from producers of the popular syndicated infotainment program read in part. "Luckily, our cameras were there to capture the momentous event and broadcast it, without delay, to as many people as humanly possible."

By all accounts resplendent in designer Versace ensembles, Cruise and Kidman, married in 1990 in a hush-hush Christmas Eve ceremony following a whirlwind courtship, kept their ravishing gazes fixed breathtakingly toward the floor during their brief passage from one end of the lob- see CRUISE & KIDMAN page 117

Above: Tom Cruise and Nicole Kidman in their newsmaking lobby walk.

# Hamster Thrown From Remote-Control Monster Truck

MILTON, MA—Tragedy was narrowly averted in the Bourke household Monday, when Harry, the family's pet hamster, was violently thrown from the 4"by 4" payload of a toy Ford F-350 monster truck.

According to reports, the toy vehicle was racing through a living-room obstacle course—which included a coffee-table-coaster slalom, a cardboard ramp, and a Dixie-cup pyramid—when it swerved out of control and crashed into a Lincoln Log structure, sending the hamster flying through the monster truck's driver-side window and knocking over three nearby Fisher-Price Little People.

The scene quickly devolved into pandemonium, with the launched hamster tumbling humorously in mid-air several times before landing at the foot of the sofa and fleeing in shock. A frantic, living-room-wide search for Harry ensued and, after extensive search efforts behind the sofa, under the recliner, and behind the bookcase, the hamster was found between the vertical blinds and the sliding glass door, shaken but alive.

As of press time, Harry was resting in his cage, his condition described as "skittish but stable."

"This is a tremendous shock," said Bourke next-door neighbor Paula

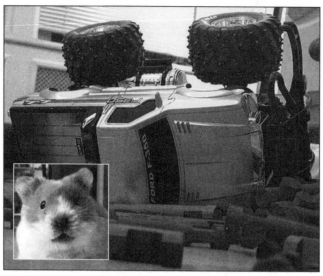

Above: The site of the accident that nearly claimed the life of Bourke family pet Harry (inset).

Gates upon learning of the mishap. "Harry is well-liked by all the neighborhood children, and for his life to be jeopardized in this manner is terribly upsetting."

Parental investigators have determined that the toy's two operators, whose names are being withheld due to their ages, successfully navigated the monster truck through the obstacle course numerous times before adding the hamster in an attempt to increase the activity's entertainment value. If found guilty, the boys, 7 and 9, could be sentenced to an evening in their rooms and fines of up to two weeks' allowance.

The accident's cause has been the subject of much debate. While many blame the toy's manufacturer, Play-

corp Unlimited, for making a substandard product, others say the monster truck's operators are at fault. Angry at the operators, an unnamed Bourke parent is pressing for a strict ban on the use of family pets in play activities, with a penalty of three days without PlayStation for those found guilty.

Playcorp spokesman Paul Ionesco expressed "deep dismay" over the crash.

"This is a flagrant and obvious misuse of our product," Ionesco said. "No Playcorp product is intended for the transportation of live cargo, no matter how cute and humorous the spectacle of a little hamster driving along in his little truck may be."

Monday's crash marks the fourth time that Harry, 1, has found himself involved in dangerous play. In October 2000, he was placed on the back of family dog Raggles, who ran through several rooms within the house before being stopped by mother Lorraine Bourke.

On Feb. 20, Harry was strapped to an army-man parachute and dropped from a second-story window. Three days later, the hamster was placed inside his glow-in-the-dark run-about ball and pushed down a flight of stairs. Both acts occurred with no parents in the vicinity, and those responsible were never brought to trial. ∅

REPORT from page 115

and bourbon.

Americans are excited about the findings.

"My four heart attacks were all hellish," said Ronald Diering, an Evansville, IN, auto mechanic. "I was aware

## Fully conscious cardiac arrest may soon be a thing of the past.

of everything that was happening, and I was gripped by the fear that I was going to die. But with this new aspirin-bourbon treatment, future heart attacks should be much less traumatic."

"Who wants to spend what could be their last moments on Earth in sheer terror?" said Alex Broadhurst of San Jose, CA. "Better to enjoy another bourbon and lie on the floor waiting for the ambulance to show up."

Researchers said individuals who take aspirin and bourbon in an attempt to prevent heart attacks may experience various side effects, including slurred speech, impaired vision, and vomiting.

Upon waking up from a heart attack, researchers said, there is also a chance of having "a wicked hangover." In such cases, victims are strongly advised to avoid bright lights and not move around too much. ∅

# Visiting Gore Calls Pennsylvania 'A Hellhole'

ALTOONA, PA—During a campaign stop at an Altoona paper mill Saturday, Democratic presidential contender Al Gore launched into an unexpected 40-minute tirade against the "not-so-great state of Pennsylvania," calling it "the nation's armpit" and "a total hellhole."

"Over the past few days, I have traveled all over your state and met many of you. And what has impressed me most is that, no matter where I have gone, my reaction has been the same: 'Oh, God, get me the fuck out of this dump,'" said Gore, who alternately referred to the Keystone State's 12 million residents as "animals" and "ghouls." "From Pittsburgh to Philadelphia, from Erie to Easton, the places and faces of Pennsylvania stand in direct opposition to everything that makes America great."

Gore went on to tell the assembled mill workers that he "couldn't care less" if he loses Pennsylvania's 23 electoral votes, so long as he "never [has] to set foot in this steaming dungheap again."

Raising his voice and pointing at the crowd, Gore continued: "During this presidential campaign, I have had the opportunity to criss-cross this great land. At each stop along the way, I have been deeply touched by the

Above: Gore greets diner patrons in Scranton, a city he called "the absolute worst place on Earth."

courage and conviction of the American people. But, holy crap, you people are craven, gutless cowards. I haven't the slightest clue what base and hideous interests of yours I could possibly defend as your next president. I do not even vaguely know what drives you subhuman pig-men, but I am sure I don't want to know."

Later in the day, Gore made an appearance at the Johnstown Agriculture Fair, at which he served as judge

in the Sorghum Queen pageant. The vice-president was overheard making numerous inflammatory comments off-microphone, including, "Get these bitches out of here" and, "This is someone's idea of an attractive woman?" One contestant, attempting to present Gore with a bushel of Pennsylvania apples, was reportedly waved aside with the words, "No. No fucking way."

see GORE page 118

carcass at 42 Butterfield Lane in the newly developed subdivision of Meadow Crest Village.

Beverly Russo, president of the Schaumburg Realtors Association, apologized to Parade Of Homes participants for the incident and strongly urged them to consider purchasing a

> ## "Any time a large animal dies in an upscale suburban area, it tends to push the real-estate market downward," said realtor Russell Abernathy.

Meadow Crest Village home anyway.

"We deeply regret any inconvenience and unpleasantness that may have been caused by the late ox," Russo said. "I can assure you that it was not intended to be included in the roster of exhibited homes. Nor should it be construed that enormous mounds of maggot-infested ox flesh are common in this traditional yet forward-thinking subdivision, which is conveniently located near several area public schools, shopping malls, and the scenic Lake Meadow Golf Course."

Exacerbated by the unseasonably hot noonday sun, the stench of the decaying ox corpse permeated the entire subdivision. Buyers tried their best to ignore the half-ton of putrescent ox meat, holding handkerchiefs to their noses while Realtors Association representatives showed off the showcase homes' innovative designs and high-quality home furnishings, which included the latest in self-cleaning ovens, wet bars, and indoor jacuzzis with adjustable whirlpool settings.

"These homes are to die for, but it's going to take a few good, hard cleanings to get that liquefying-entrails odor out of their exquisite, Georgian-inspired, patterned chintz drapes," said realtor Mary Lou Carey, pointing to a panoramic picture window in the sunken living room of a four-bedroom, two-bath home at 26 Crestview Terrace, which boasts spectacular views of both the 18th hole of the Lake Meadow Golf Course and the necrotic, fly-engulfed beast of burden.

Local realtors are concerned that the ox may have a negative effect on property values.

"Any time a large animal dies in an upscale suburban area, it tends to push the real-estate market downward," said Russell Abernathy, an independent realtor in nearby Arlington Heights. "Early in my career, I was helping an elderly couple sell their two-bedroom home, perfect for a young couple just starting out. But it remained on the market for nearly 10 months, just because a horse died on

by to the other. They then entered the back of a waiting car and were driven away, bringing the star-studded lobby walk to an end.

"It was magical. They were in rare form, giving the revolving door just enough of a push to set it in motion and exhibiting the grace, style, and poise for which they have become so renowned," said Ellen Donahue, a total nobody who happened to be in the lobby at the time. "And you could tell it was them, because of all the cameras and everything."

The gorgeous Kidman and her hunky husband set tongues wagging with their attention-grabbing lobby walk, *Access Hollywood* host Pat O'Brien said in a nationally televised statement.

"Hollywood's hottest real-life lovebirds were at it again yesterday," he told viewers Monday, "walking through a lobby with their unmistakable style, on their way to someplace fascinating and exciting."

Added co-host Nancy O'Dell: "That's right, Pat, and we'll be seeing some more scintillating snippets of that fabulous footage later in the show. But first, *Access Hollywood* correspondent Bob Reese catches up with everybody's favorite *Eight Is Enough* star, Dick Van Patten."

The program then segued into a feature showcasing Van Patten and his family at a celebrity charity rollerblading event.

Response to the Hollywood power couple's lobby walk has been overwhelming. Film critic Michael Medved called Cruise's confident, deliberate stride, immortalized in such blockbusters as *The Color Of Money*, *Rain Man*, and *A Few Good Men*, "a smashing return to form for Tom Terrific after the fizzle of the Stanley Kubrick box-office bomb *Eyes Wide Shut*."

Celebrity-watchers added that Kidman, who met Cruise on the set of *Days Of Thunder*, more than held her own during the 15-second stroll, matching her heartthrob husband's megawatt star power with the grace and confidence that have earned her the respect and admiration of critics and moviegoers alike.

"It was wonderful," said Irene Davis, a Bristol, CT, plebian who saw the couple's lobby walk on television. "Normally, I'd never have a chance to rub elbows with the likes of Tom and Nic, but thanks to *Access Hollywood*'s exclusive, sneak peek at the comings and goings of

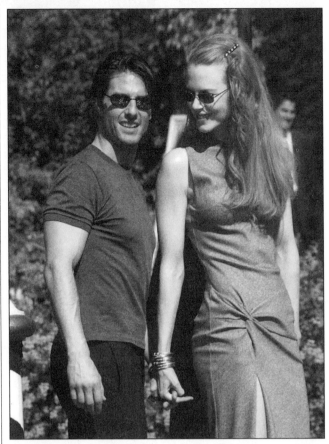

Above: A photo of Kidman and Cruise during the headline-grabbing May 1997 walk to a restaurant.

> ## "It was wonderful," said Irene Davis, a Bristol, CT, plebian who saw the couple's lobby walk on television.

Movieland's hottest couple, I got to feel like I was right there in the lobby with them."

Despite the raves from the public, some celebrity-watchers are unimpressed with the lobby stroll.

"This was a real disappointment, coming from stars of Cruise and Kidman's magnitude," *New York Post* gossip columnist Liz Smith said. "In the past, we've seen much more impressive lobby-walks from both—dressed to the nines, waving at cameras, and smiling at crowds at restaurants, gala benefits, and award shows. But this

time, it seemed like they were just phoning it in. Frankly, I'm unwowed."

"The least he could have done was give a thumbs-up to the camera," Smith added. "C'mon, Tom, your fans deserve more!"

Nevertheless, O'Dell said, the general consensus is that Cruise and Kidman have done it again, proving that "when it comes to walking across a lobby floor, they're at the top of the Hollywood heap."

Cruise, currently filming *Mission: Impossible 2*, is expected to walk through at least three more lobbies before beginning work on *Minority Report*, a Steven Spielberg sci-fi thriller with a Christmas 2000 release date. And, according to Kidman publicist Lisette Rose, the Aussie actress, slated to follow up her buttock-baring performance in the Broadway hit *The Blue Room* with the psychological horror flick *The Others*, has "a very busy schedule," but has not ruled out the possibility of appearing on a Rodeo Drive sidewalk "sometime in the near future." Ø

the lawn that summer. It wasn't until the horse had sufficiently rotted to the point where the only remaining trace of it was its bleached bones that I was finally able to find a buyer. And even then, we closed at only half its original value."

The bloated ox heap, which Schaumburg city officials said cannot be moved until early next week, has greatly disturbed Meadow Crest Vil-

lage's 350 residents.

"That thing is just a terrible eyesore, and I want it out of here as soon as possible," resident Teresa Stampfel said. "I mean, it certainly does nothing to enhance the beauty of Meadow Crest's secluded woodland setting."

"The thing I'm most worried about is the children," mother of three Shirley McEvoy said. "Putrefying oxen are unsanitary and unsafe for

children to play around. And what if a hyena comes to eat its remains? Neighborhood children might try to pet it and risk contracting terrible brain and nerve diseases. And I'd hate for this ox to interfere with next Saturday's pee-wee soccer playoffs: My Andrew is playing goalie, and he'd be just heartbroken if the game were cancelled because of a dead ox." Ø

GORE from page 116

Gore concluded his day on the steps of the State Capitol in Harrisburg, where he lowered the Pennsylvania flag, shredded it with a large hunting knife, and urinated on the shreds. He then delivered a speech in which he shared the tales of numerous Pennsylvanians he had encountered during his travels through the state.

"Of all the stories I have heard on this trip, none has touched me more deeply than that of Karen Swendeman of New Castle," Gore said. "At the young age of 18, Karen married her high-school sweetheart, Jeff. Not long after, she gave birth to twins. But, less than a year later, her joy turned to the deepest grief when Jeff was killed in a foundry accident. As young Karen looked into my eyes and whined, 'Oh, Mr. Gore, I can't afford this, I can't afford that,' I felt my very gorge rising up the back of my throat. I mean, why do Pennsylvania's stupid broads go and get knocked up like that?"

Continued Gore: "I also recall Herman Eisler of Shippensburg, who fought bravely in the Second World War and raised a family in a house he built with his own hands. When the Social Security Administration failed Herman—because, I don't know, he needed some pills or something and couldn't get them—he turned into a bitter, pathetic shell of a man that no one could stand to be around. What a loser."

"And, finally, I recall Philadelphia's Martin Shaughnessy, who, at the ripe old age of 98, has been Independence Hall's caretaker for the past 60 years—the longest anyone has ever held the auspicious post," Gore said. "And, between you and me, that old crank will talk for 10 hours straight if you let him and not say anything that makes any sense whatsoever. That dude is senile, big-time."

Added Gore, "And what's the big deal with the cheesesteak sandwiches? They taste like shit. I wouldn't feed them to the dogs they're probably made out of."

Turning to sneer derisively at members of the Monongahela Drum & Bugle Corps, whose 225 members stood nearby, Gore wrapped up the verbal assault.

"Every second I spend in this dark and evil state is sheer agony," he said. "A second feels like a week in the presence of you monstrous non-people. I would have left Pennsylvania long ago, but I wanted every last one of you grubby, ass-faced animals to realize exactly where you stand in the food chain. You are not a part of that chain. You exist outside of the human community, and when I am in the White House, I will make sure that the whole nation—indeed, the world—understands that fact with no ambiguity. I will not represent you. I will not defend you. I will allow and even invite any nation to invade and destroy this horrible graveyard of the soul. To hell with all of you, and good riddance." ∅

# Even Though I'd Never Seen *Major League*, I Found *Major League II* Surprisingly Easy To Follow

**By Don Grella**

Whew, what a relief. I hate when I can't follow a film, and I was afraid it'd happen again Friday night. But, to my delight, I was able to fully understand and enjoy *Major League II*, despite the fact that I'd never seen the original.

After a long, hard week of work at Apex Driving School, I decided to kick back on the couch and treat myself to a night of television. After ordering a pizza, I started flipping through my *TV Guide*, hoping to find something good. But, as hard as I looked, nothing really seemed up my alley: There were *The Daytime Emmy Awards* on ABC, some boring old musical on TNT, and four straight *Saturday Night Live* reruns on Comedy Central.

There was, admittedly, *Major League II* on Cinemax. But, despite my love of baseball, I fretted that I'd likely be lost in the plot, not having seen the 1989 original.

Sure, I could've bravely forayed into the 1994 Sheen-Berenger vehicle, but what if every other line of dialogue referred obliquely to something from the original film, making it impossible for me to follow the plot? I certainly didn't want to relive my *Mannequin 2* debacle of 1991. On the other hand, I needed something to watch, and I needed to make a fast decision before my pizza got cold. Besides, maybe I'd get lucky, and *Major League II* would open with a montage of clips from the original, a device many of the better sequels employ to help viewers "get in the spirit" of the original film.

After a few moments of deliberation, I resolved—not without some trepidation, mind you—to commit to the 8:10 p.m. showing of *Major League II* on

> **The screenwriters clearly took pains to anticipate any potential confusion on the part of those who hadn't seen the first film.**

Cinemax.

I needn't have worried! The film opened with a concise rundown of the major characters from Episode I, cunningly presented as "Indians talk" on a Bob Uecker-hosted sports-radio show! Uecker was not playing himself, though: He was Harry Doyle, a character who, from what I could gather, figured heavily in the first installment, as well.

At any rate, the opening recap, helpful as it was, was almost unnecessary: The movie's characters were so real, so richly textured, that I instantly felt like I knew them. It was clear what was going on right from the get-go. In the previous season, the Cleveland Indians had rallied from being a rag-tag bunch of losers to winning the pennant. Episode II picks up at the start of the following season, with old pals reunited and ready for more good times. But an ominous question looms over their heads: Has success changed them?

I am sad to say that the answer was a resounding yes. No one illustrated this complacent, fat-cat mentality better than Charlie Sheen's Rick "Wild Thing" Vaughn, who arrives for the first day of spring training in a limousine. Now, since I'd never seen this character before, you're probably thinking, "But, Don, how do you know it's a change? He might have ridden in a limo throughout the first movie!"

In this scene, the screenwriters clearly took pains to anticipate any potential confusion on the part of those who hadn't seen the first film. Wild Thing's fans are all waiting for him to show up to spring training, and when a guy rolls up on a bad-ass motorcycle, they justifiably assume it's him. But, as it turns out, it's someone else, and the fans are all surprised. This surprised reaction is not merely funny; it gives the uninitiated a solid idea of what they're supposed to expect from Wild Thing. So, when Wild Thing steps out of the limo in a suit and yuppie haircut, and the fans are disappointed and confused, we instantly recognize that a profound change has occurred in this character's life, whether or not we saw the first movie!

Needless to say, I am now hooked on the *Major League* franchise. In fact, when I was at Suncoast Motion Picture Company the next day, I made a point of picking up a copy of the prequel. Even better, they had a marked-down copy of the third installment, 1998's *Major League—Episode III: Back To The Minors*. I watched it that night and loved it, even though Wild Thing and a lot of the other central characters from the first two movies weren't even in it.

My best advice to the uninitiated would be to see the *Major League* movies in order. But if you can't, don't worry: Each movie truly does stand on its own. ∅

## Magic-Markered Initials Fail To Deter Breakroom Rice-Cake Thief

FRESNO, CA—Despite clearly marking her initials on her rice-cake bag in black Magic Marker, secretary Elaine Fahey was once again the victim of I&G Marketing's breakroom rice-cake thief Friday. "Whoever's doing this really needs to learn about something called a supermarket," said Fahey, who has lost one strawberry and three caramel-apple rice cakes to the thief this month. "Rice cakes aren't free, you know." Fahey said she plans to take harsher security measures, including a Post-It note on the bag reading, "These are my rice cakes... Please get your own!!!"

## Bathroom Smells Like Shit

GALENA PARK, TX—The second-floor men's room of a Sysco Vending office building smells like shit, disgusted employee Art McCune reported Friday. "Jesus Christ, it smells like actual human feces in here," McCune said. "I'm serious—it's like someone walked in, dropped his pants and underwear, straddled a bowl, excreted nearly a pound of fecal matter out of his anus, and then walked right out again." Building custodian Byron Withers apologized for the foul odor, assuring Sysco staffers that, by the following morning, the bathroom would be back to smelling like bleach.

## Universe Ends As God Wakes Up Next To Suzanne Pleshette

CHICAGO—The 15-billion-year-old universe came to a surprise-twist end Friday, when God woke up next to actress Suzanne Pleshette. "What a crazy dream I just had," God said to Pleshette at the conclusion of the popular, long-running universe. "I was the Creator of all things, I had this crazy Son who was always getting arrested and wouldn't get a haircut, and My children were always hurting and killing each other in My name." Pleshette reassured God that He had imagined the whole thing and urged the beleaguered, well-intentioned deity to go back to sleep. ∅

## White Sprinter Finishes Fifth

*see SPORTS page 2D*

## Jim Morrison Stares Creepily Out Of Apartment Window

*see LOCAL page 3C*

## 23-Hour Suicide Watch A Failure

*see LOCAL page 11B*

## Area 5-Year-Old Has To Go To The Doctor For Her Buh-gina

*see LOCAL page 10B*

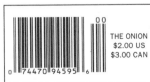

THE ONION
$2.00 US
$3.00 CAN

# the ONION ®

WWW.THEONION.COM — AMERICA'S FINEST NEWS SOURCE™ — FOUNDED 1871

### THE RULING

# Hershey's Ordered To Pay Obese Americans $135 Billion

*see COVER STORY page 120*

## Jury Takes A Bite Out Of Big Chocolate

$135 Billion

**Details Of Recent Rulings**

- $135B in reparations to families of chocoholics
- Additional $27B for chocolate education, anti-snacking initiatives
- Defendant knowingly added nuts, nougat to products
- Products linked to weight gain, high blood sugar
- Memo reveals intent to target youths
- Candy advertising banned on TV

**Subsidiary Brands Named In The Suit**

Mounds · Rolo · KitKat · Almond Joy · mr. Goodbar · Caramello · Reese's

## Small Town's 'Cryptosporidium Daze' Fails To Attract Visitors

BLAKELY, GA—Blakely civic leaders were baffled last weekend as Cryptosporidium Daze, their elaborately planned summer festival celebrating the popular waterborne pathogen, failed to draw tourists to the Southwest Georgia town.

"Just as Colquitt celebrates its agricultural heritage with Watermelon Days, we wanted to host a festival that reflected the uniqueness of our community," Blakely Town Council

*see CRYPTOSPORIDIUM page 121*

# Copycat Killing 'Misses Subtleties Of Original,' Say Police

BRONX, NY—A young couple was found ritualistically murdered in Crotona Park early Monday in what police are calling a "copycat crime that lacks the artistry and nuance of the original."

"On the surface, this double homicide seems identical to that of Yvette and Hector Reynoso in Crotona Park July 3," said Sgt. Bob Bloch of the New York Police Department. "The bodies were arranged in a back-to-back seated position, tied tightly together. Each victim's clothing was removed and put backwards on the other person. And their throats and wrists were ritualistically slashed, and the eyeballs carved out and placed in their mouths. But look closer, and you'll see that this crime is a pale, uninspired

*see COPYCAT page 121*

Above: Forensics workers remove the bodies of a married couple murdered in a copycat crime officials derided as "perfunctory and derivative."

119

# Hershey's Suffers A Major Blow

HERSHEY, PA—In one of the largest product-liability rulings in U.S. history, the Hershey Foods Corporation was ordered by a Pennsylvania jury Monday to pay $135 billion in restitution fees to 900,000 obese Americans who for years consumed the company's fattening snack foods.

"Let this verdict send a clear message to Big Chocolate," said Pennsylvania Attorney General Andrew Garsten, addressing reporters following the historic ruling. "If you knowingly sell products that cause obesity, you will pay."

The five-state class-action suit accused Hershey's of "knowingly and willfully marketing rich, fatty candy bars containing chocolate and other ingredients of negligible nutritional value." The company was also charged with publishing nutritional information only under pressure from the government, marketing products to children, and artificially "spiking" its products with substances such as peanuts, crisped rice, and caramel to increase consumer appeal.

Jurors took less than five hours to reach the decision following a two-year trial covering nearly one million snackers in Pennsylvania, Florida, New Hampshire, Arizona, and Texas. A majority of the unprecedented punitive damages will go toward obesity victims and their immediate families, while the remainder will be funneled into weight-loss and youth-snacking-prevention programs.

Above: Lawyers for the Hershey Corporation announce plans to appeal the court's decision.

Above: Just one of the millions of victims of the chocolate industry.

"This is vindication for myself and all chocolate victims," said Beaumont, TX, resident Earl Hoffler, holding a picture of his wife Emily, who in 1998 succumbed to obesity after nearly 40 years of chocoholism. "This ruling cannot bring Emily back, but I take some comfort knowing that her tragic, unnecessary death did not go unpunished."

Hoffler's teary-eyed account of his wife's brave battle against chocolate was widely regarded as the emotional high point of the trial. First introduced to Hershey's chocolate as a young trick-or-treater, Emily quickly developed a four-bar-a-day habit, turning in adulthood to Hershey's Special Dark, a stronger, unfiltered form of the product. By age 47, she had ballooned to 352 pounds and was a full-blown chocoholic. What little savings the family had was drained by Weight Watchers memberships, Richard Simmons videotapes, and Fat Trapper pills, all of which proved futile and only prolonged the Tofflers' agonizing ordeal.

Equally relieved by the ruling was Mel Brewer of Phoenix, whose father received free chocolate as a soldier during WWII.

"Dad came back from Europe hooked," Brewer said. "Before long, he was going through a case of Mounds and Mr. Goodbars a week. He wouldn't eat ice cream without Hershey's chocolate syrup and crushed Heath bars on it. He died of a heart attack at 54 weighing 415 pounds."

With litigation pending against the nation's top five chocolate makers, including a $102 billion Mississippi suit against Nestle, the entire industry is on alert. Big Chocolate has already

suffered numerous major setbacks in recent years. In 1997, a California judge ordered chocolate manufacturers to fund $27 billion in education programs to prevent youth chocolate consumption. In 1999, a federal judge prohibited chocolate advertising on TV and billboards and banned the use of cartoon imagery in advertising. In addition, the judge ruled that a warning label must be placed on all chocolate products reading, "The Surgeon General Has Determined That Eating Chocolate May Lead To Being Really Fat."

Lawyers for the Hershey Corporation said the company intends to appeal the decision, which, if upheld, could drive the price of a 1.4-ounce pack of Rolos as high as $1.29.

"Adult consumers know the risks involved in using our products," Hershey's chief counsel Marvin Black said. "They know that if not used in a responsible manner, there can be some negative consequences. But this is true of anything in life. Further, the decision to use our products has always been left up to the individual. The Hershey Corporation has never forced anyone to use its products, nor has it ever intentionally added substances to its candies to increase addictiveness. If consumers are hooked, it is only because of said candy's overwhelmingly delicious chocolate goodness."

Whatever the outcome of the Hershey's appeal, the chocolate industry has irrevocably changed as a result of Monday's verdict.

"For over a century, Hershey's has lived off the fat of the land," Erie, PA, claimant Pamela Schiff said. "Now it's time to pay us back." ∅

Above: Ross Bingham, who has put his dark days behind him.

# Area Man Likes To Think Of Own Past As Sordid

NORFOLK, VA—Ross Bingham, a married, 34-year-old professional videographer, likes to think of his own past as sordid, sources revealed Monday.

"I don't talk about it much, but I went through a pretty wild phase in my early 20s," Bingham told a group of coworkers at Outreach Communications, a corporate video-production company. "I'm lucky I straightened out, because if I'd kept heading down the path I was on, God only knows where I'd be now."

"Those first few years after college, there were times when I was going out drinking with my friends three or four nights a week," Bingham said. "The low point probably came when I woke up on the couch at my friend's apartment with my coat over me as a blanket. I could barely even remember what had happened the night before. Then I realized I must've fallen asleep while we were drinking beer and watching *Fletch*. Kinda scary when you think about it."

Bingham characterized his living situation at the time as "pretty out of control," telling coworkers that they probably wouldn't even be able to comprehend how "crazy" it was, not having been there.

"One of my roommates was a total pothead," Bingham said. "He'd have guys dropping by to sell him drugs, right there in our living room. I smoked a little pot myself, but I didn't care for it all that much. Drinking, now, that was my vice."

Continued Bingham: "I was working part-time at a video store, so I sometimes didn't go into work until noon or one in the afternoon. For a while there, it was 'get off work, go out and party, sleep late, and do it all again the next day.' I knew it was no way to live, but, you know, you get into a downward spiral and it's hard to crawl back out."

Bingham said his other roommate was good friends with the members of Dread Skatt, a popular local ska

see SORDID page 122

president Jane Lyons said Monday. "When someone suggested a theme inspired by the historical event we're best known for, the Great Cryptosporidium Outbreak of 1988, we knew we had the answer."

Twelve years ago, Lyons said, a small amount of pig feces seeped into the town's municipal water supply, contaminating it with cryptosporidium. As a result, 611 citizens contracted cryptosporidiosis, an intestinal disease marked by abdominal cramps, violent diarrhea, nausea, and fever.

"If it weren't for our town's brush with cryptosporidium, the EPA never would have enacted the Surface Water Treatment Act of 1989," Lyons said. "It established drinking-water standards for the entire country—and it all started right here in Blakely!"

Much to the surprise of town-council members, unlike Colquitt's Watermelon Days and Columbia's Riverfest, which bring as many as 15,000 visitors into the neighboring small towns each summer, Cryptosporidium Daze was sparsely attended.

"It's a real mystery," Lyons said. "It was a nice, sunny day, the park was filled with booths, and somebody was out there in the big foam cryptosporidium mascot outfit shaking hands with everybody. Yet, somehow, the festival flopped."

The three-day event drew only seven non-residents, most of whom left shortly after arriving.

"I thought cryptosporidium was a type of flower," said Rhonda Loverling, who drove to Blakely from nearby Albany for the event. "Turns out, I was thinking of chrysanthemum."

After an outlay of nearly $4,000 for decorations, advertising, and equipment rental, Lions Club president Gary Milstead estimated that Cryptosporidium Daze generated less than $45 in revenue.

"We had a new mascot, Crypty The Cryptosporidium, created just for the event," said Milstead, pointing to poster bearing a gap-toothed, single-celled parasite wearing a baseball cap. "We still have plenty of T-shirts left for sale if you want one."

Even Blakely's own citizens were uninterested in the festival. A pageant to crown one lucky young

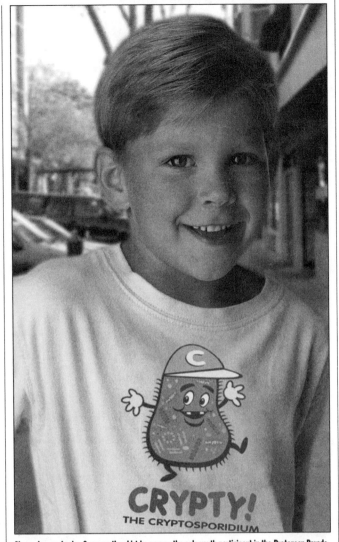

Above: Jeremy Luchs, 9, wears the shirt he won as the sole youth participant in the Protozoan Parade.

Blakely girl "Cryptosporidium Queen" was canceled due to a lack of entrants.

Other poorly received events included the Name That Parasite contest, the Water Boil, the cryptosporidium-themed "haiku-off," and the Protozoan Parade, in which children could compete for prizes by dressing up as their favorite member of the phylum protozoa.

With the unpopular event behind them, some members of the town

council are wondering if they selected the wrong theme.

"Maybe people just aren't as interested in cryptosporidium as they were in the late '80s," Lyons said. "Back then, if we announced a town meeting about cryptosporidium, every last person would show up. I have, however, heard a lot of buzz lately about the radon gas that was detected in some of the homes over by the railroad tracks. Well, I guess there's always next summer." ∅

## Bernadette Peters Comes Up Twice In One Day

COLUMBUS, OH—In an incident observers are calling "kinda weird," mid-level celebrity Bernadette Peters' name came up twice Monday in separate conversations had by Columbus resident Chris Loew. "At, like, noon, I forget what brought it up, but me and this guy I work with were talking about that one part in *The Jerk* where Steve Martin and Bernadette Peters sing that song," Loew, a 22-year-old pizza-delivery driver, told reporters. "Then, like five hours later, me and my roommate Dave were vegging out, watching *Animaniacs*, and he was like, 'Did you know that Bernadette Peters does the voice for Rita?' It was so freaky." Adding significantly to the freakiness, Loew said, was a narrowly averted triple-referencing of Peters at approximately 11:30 p.m.: "Me, Jeff, and Josh were gonna watch [the Peters film] *Silent Movie*, but we wound up playing Sega instead. That would have been insane." Pop-culture statisticians estimate the odds of a single-day triple-Peters reference at 4,750,000 to 1.

## Divorced Man Forced To Get Back Down To Dating Weight

SILVER SPRING, MD—Greg Geisinger, a 265-pound Wilmington man whose seven-year marriage ended in divorce two months ago, must get back down to his dating weight of 190 pounds, he announced Monday. "Oh, man, I have got to lose this weight if I'm gonna be back out there dating again," said Geisinger, who for years has carried 75 pounds of excess marital flab on his 5'11" frame. "No good-looking single woman is gonna want to go out with a guy who looks like this." Geisinger said he is eager to remarry so he can gain back the weight he is about to lose. ∅

imitation of its predecessor."

The latest victims, identified as Susan and Nicholas Thomasen of White Plains, were found by police at 6 a.m. The crime was initially suspected to be the work of the Happy Loving Couple Killer, who shocked New York with his grisly, methodical slaying of the Reynosos four weeks ago and may be behind as many as 11 ritual double murders since 1988.

"Based on our initial forensic observations, we believed the crimes to be the work of the same man," Bloch said. "But a closer look revealed an obvious departure from the Happy Loving Couple Killer's attention to detail. I mean, why weren't the

Thomasens' hands meticulously entwined? Why weren't the usual Valen-

> "Why weren't the usual Valentine hearts drawn on their chests with the other's blood? Why were there no African violets stuffed into their mouths?"

tine hearts drawn on their chests with the other's blood? Why were there no

African violets stuffed into their mouths? Just sloppy. And tying their necks together with a white silk scarf is just an unnecessary flourish, introducing a violent, erotic-fantasy-fulfillment theme that undermines the simplicity and emotional directness that is the real Happy Loving Couple Killer's signature style. The second I stepped on the scene, I knew something was horribly wrong."

Fingerprints and DNA samples taken from the Thomasens' bodies failed to match those from the Reynoso murders, confirming those suspicions.

"It seemed like a disappointing entry in the Happy Loving Couple Killer

canon," Bloch continued.

Adding to the lack of artistic merit clouding the Thomasens' death is the fact that, in order to stay true to the spirit of the original, the couple should not have been chosen as victims in the first place.

"The Happy Loving Couple Killer, or 'Hap,' as his longtime NYPD followers call him, always murders newlyweds who have known each other less than one year," Bloch said. "The Thomasens had met 13 months ago. Did the killer think we wouldn't notice? It's those little details that mark the difference between a good killer and a derivative hack. These murders are almost beneath the NYPD's attention." ∅

SORDID from page 120

band, which meant that Bingham would accompany the friend to shows and social events, often staying out as late as two in the morning.

"I was pretty much living to party," he said. "I didn't care about anything else."

Though alcohol was his primary vice, Bingham admitted that it was not his only one: He also had a strong

---

## "It could have been me being handed that ticket," Bingham said.

---

weakness for the opposite sex. The now-reformed Bingham went through a "serious womanizing phase," dating numerous women with no intention of getting into a long-term relationship.

"There was this one girl," he said. "I met her at a bar and we went home together. The next day, I was going to call her, but I realized I couldn't even call information to get her number because I didn't even know her last name. It's probably a good thing we didn't go all the way, or it might have turned into a pretty bad situation."

Bingham also described a "near brush with death."

"I was out with the guys at a nightclub one night, and I'd had a few too many tequila shots," he said. "I started walking to my car when I realized I was way too 'altered' to drive home, so I called a cab. If I hadn't, that could have been it for me right there. To think how close I came to meeting my maker that night, it makes me shudder."

Luckily, at 23, Bingham had a spiritual awakening and realized it was time to turn his life around. The wake-up call was the arrest of best friend and drinking partner Matthew Stackpole.

"Matt got really drunk one night and was goofing around on the walk home," Bingham said. "He decided to steal a 'No Parking' sign, and as he was pulling it out of the ground, a cop drove by. Matt got nailed for attempted theft of public property. Watching him stand in the harsh glare of the police lights, I realized it could have been me being handed that ticket."

Less than a month after his best friend's brush with the law, Bingham took his first steps on the road to recovery. He applied for and landed a job at Outreach Communications, where he prepares video presentations for corporations about to make initial stock offerings.

He hasn't looked back since.

"Sometimes, I miss hanging out with Matt and the old gang. But I know how easy it would be to slip back into my old ways if I did," Bingham said. "If I knew it wouldn't lead to trouble, I'd look Matt up again. It wouldn't be too hard to find him. I hear he's a systems administrator over at Novix Consulting." ∅

122

---

# Bureau Of Alcohol, Tobacco & Firearms Reaches Trade Agreement With Food & Drug Administration

WASHINGTON, DC—The Bureau of Alcohol, Tobacco & Firearms and the Food & Drug Administration reached a historic trade agreement Monday.

Under the terms of the deal, the ATF will provide the FDA with alcohol, tobacco, and firearms in exchange for equal value in food and drugs.

"My administrative assistants and I were enjoying some of our food the other day when it hit us," FDA commissioner Jane Henney said. "We have tons of food and drugs lying around, but nothing to drink, smoke, or fire. Then, someone—I think it was [deputy commissioner] Phil [Royce]—suggested we call up those guys over at the ATF across town and see what we could get. Turns out, they were ready to deal."

Said ATF director Bradley Buckles, "You work up a powerful hunger dealing with all this booze, smokes, and guns. So when Jane told me she had some food and drugs to offer, I told her to come over and help herself to whatever she liked."

In the deal, the FDA received 345,000 bottles of Jack Daniel's, 250,000 cartons of Merit Ultra Lights, and 27,000 guns, including 4,300 Smith & Wesson .38 snub-nosed revolvers, 2,500 Glock .380 ACP pistols, and 1,850 Colt Anaconda .44 Magnums.

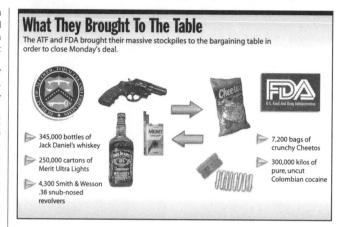

**What They Brought To The Table**
The ATF and FDA brought their massive stockpiles to the bargaining table in order to close Monday's deal.

▷ 345,000 bottles of Jack Daniel's whiskey
▷ 250,000 cartons of Merit Ultra Lights
▷ 4,300 Smith & Wesson .38 snub-nosed revolvers

▷ 7,200 bags of crunchy Cheetos
▷ 300,000 kilos of pure, uncut Colombian cocaine

In return, ATF officials were permitted to pick anything they liked from the federal fridge and national drug stash. They took 190,000 eight-count packs of Oscar Mayer hot dogs, 25,500 pints of Ben & Jerry's Chunky Monkey ice cream, 7,200 bags of Cheetos, a half-ton of marijuana, and 300,000 kilos of pure, uncut Colombian cocaine.

Insiders said the exchange, performed late last night at ATF headquarters, was "completely satisfactory to both sides."

"I like a beer now and then, but I'm not much of a smoker," said FDA inspector Patrick Welles after a visit to ATF headquarters. "I'm more of a food-and-drugs type of guy. But after picking out a Coors Light Party Pak, I started poking around and wound up going home with a bunch of automatic rifles and this cool grenade launcher."

"This is a great day for both agencies," ATF assistant director Wilbur Karros said. "I can't deny that some friction has always existed between us, usually on issues of jurisdiction: who gets what contraband, is a bottle of absinthe considered alcohol or drugs, things like that. But now that we've gotten together, everyone can get all the stuff they want." ∅

---

# Does This Cock Ring Make Me Look Fat?

Listen, you have to be completely honest with me here for a minute. As you know, I value your opinion a great deal, and I don't want you to lie to spare my feelings. What I want to know is, does this cock ring make me look fat?

I realize this is a sensitive subject: People don't like to hear negative things about their weight. But if this cock ring adds five or ten pounds to my appearance, I'd rather hear it from you than from some stranger.

**By Geoff Holman**

Come on, don't be so shy. Take a look and tell me what you think. Me, I'm really undecided about it. When I tried it on at the sex shop, it looked great. But, of course, when I tried it on again at home, it suddenly made me look like a blimp.

I swear, I must have tried on a hundred different cock rings at the store. There was a really nice red-and-white striped one, but it looked awful on me. They also had a black leather one with metal studs I really liked, but they didn't have it in my size. I almost bought this one blue ring that matched my eyes and contrasted well with my pubic hair, but, ultimately, I decided to go with this slimming black one instead and just tint my hair slightly. (I'll bet you couldn't even tell I got a dye job—it's redder in the highlights now.)

Maybe it would look better if I didn't wear it so far down. I usually like wearing them real snug, down at the base of the shaft and nice and tight under the balls, but this one just isn't quite sitting right. Do you think I should push it up a bit?

I know this may be a little awkward for you, but I really respect your opinion. After all, you were the one who told me that that orange cardigan made me look like a pumpkin. You were also the one who told me to take back that striped pullover I thought looked so terrific. So I'm really counting on you to give me your honest opinion about this cock ring.

As you'll see, I've got kind of a low-slung scrotal sac, so it's always been difficult to find cock rings that look good on me. Especially when I'm flaccid. That's why I was so happy to find this one. But now I just don't know.

Maybe I shouldn't have gotten the medium. The salesman said this brand tends to run a little small, so perhaps I would've been better off with the large. Do you think I should go back and get the bigger size? I'm just not sure the medium is a flattering fit: A good cock ring should accentuate your penile girth, not make it look like a liability.

To be honest, if I was just going to wear the cock ring around the house, I'd get the large for sure. But I bought it for a very special occasion, and I was really hoping to squeeze into a medium.

Come on. The least you can do is look. You came to me when you were thinking about getting that ridiculous bulldog tattoo, didn't you? And I told you it would look really silly, and you thanked me, right? You didn't get mad at me or anything, right? Well, no matter what you say, neither will I, I swear to God. Now, be a friend and tell me what you think of this cock ring. ∅

# 'I May Be Hazardous To Your Health,' Warns Homicidal Surgeon General

see NATION page 4A

# Judge Declares Aerobics Instructor Too Fit To Stand Trial

see JUSTICE page 11A

# Nursing-Home Resident Glad She's Going Home Tomorrow Every Day

see SENIORBEAT page 4B

# Pantomimed Lasso Motion Fails To Pull Woman Across Dance Floor

see LOCAL page 2D

## STATshot
A look at the numbers that shape your world.

### Worst-Ventilated U.S. Restrooms
- Sunoco #4397 Uvalde, TX
- Dick's Liquor (basement) Beloit, WI
- Mr. J's Fish & Steak House Savannah, GA
- I-80 Exit 82B Rest Stop Elko, NV
- Bud Dierker's apartment Cleveland, OH

THE ONION
$2.00 US
$3.00 CAN

# the ONION®

WWW.THEONION.COM AMERICA'S FINEST NEWS SOURCE™ FOUNDED 1871

# Asian-Americans Defying Traditional Stereotypes
## More And More Are Lazy, Stupid

SAN FRANCISCO—When Vinh Trang and Rodney Kim get together after school, academics are the furthest thing from their minds.

Instead, the two ninth-graders go to

Described by friends as "shiftless and dumb," Lin Bu (left) is one of a growing number of Asian-Americans helping to dispel the myth of the hardworking, motivated Easterner.

Trang's house to listen to rap music, eat Doritos, and get high.

"Don't make assumptions about us just because we're Asian," said Trang, passing his friend a joint. "Not all of us care about college."

With poor grades and atrocious study habits, Trang and Kim are part of a new wave of young Asian-Ameri-

see ASIANS page 125

# New Crispy Snack Cracker To Ease Crushing Pain Of Modern Life

EAST HANOVER, NJ—The dull, all-consuming ache of late-20th-century life will be slightly alleviated Wednesday when U.S. supermarkets receive their first shipments of Nabisco's new "T.C. McCrispee's" line of snack crackers.

Available in Regular, Garden Ranch, and Zesty Cheddar varieties, the new crackers will flood consumers' bodies with salt, fat, and starch, producing a pleasing sensation of warmth and nourishment and momentarily freeing them from a constant, crushing sense of profound grief.

T.C. McCrispee's are being touted as Nabisco's most effective new anguish-relieving snack-food product since Double Stuf Oreos.

"We at the Nabisco Corporation

Above: A promotional shot for T.C. McCrispee's, a tasty new snack cracker that promises to reduce the pain of the grotesque, meaningless charade that is modern life.

see SNACK page 124

# Homoerotic Overtones Enliven NRA Meeting

Above: NRA member James D'Alessandro (right) admires fellow member Bruce Carnahan's piece, stirring potent feelings within himself.

COEUR D'ALENE, ID—Repression was the order of the day as the National Rifle Association's Northern Idaho Chapter held its annual convention over the weekend.

More than 25,000 dedicated gun lovers from across Northern Idaho flocked to the Coeur d'Alene Convention Center for the two-day event, happily sublimating homosexual impulses amid a carefully maintained façade of platonic camaraderie.

Moscow, ID, resident Richard Hoflinger, 47, a

longtime gun-rights activist, proudly exhibited the collection of antique rifles through which he has channeled his morally repugnant gay impulses.

"Guns should be part of any upstanding Christian family," said Hoflinger, sticking a long, thick, oily cleaning rod 14 inches up an 1886 Remington.

In the next booth, another latent homosexual, Duane Erlich of Sandpoint, moved his hand slowly up and down a well-polished 1948 Winchester. "Ain't she a

see NRA page 125

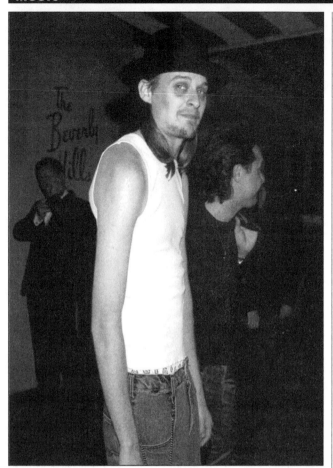

Above: A malnourished Kid Rock at his last public appearance April 22.

# Kid Rock Starves To Death

## Napster Piracy Blamed

LOS ANGELES—Napster piracy of copyrighted music claimed another victim Monday, when the emaciated body of rock-rap superstar Kid Rock was found on the median of La Cienega Boulevard.

"How many more artists must die of starvation before we put a stop to this Napster madness?" asked Hilary Rosen, president of the Recording Industry Association of America (RIAA). "MP3s of Kid Rock's music were so widely traded and downloaded by Napster users that he was driven back to the mean streets from whence he came, dying bankrupt and penniless in the gutter."

When found by police, the 28-year-old Kid Rock, born Bob Ritchie in Detroit, was still clutching the cardboard sign reading "Devil Without A Place To Sleep Or Anything To Eat" that had been his trademark ever since the rise of Napster's MP3-sharing software bankrupted him in January.

Rosen said the RIAA would prosecute the music-piracy web sites that are responsible "to the fullest extent of the law."

"Napster killed Kid Rock, there's no doubt about it," Rosen said. "As soon as that site went up last October, people stopped buying his music. It's not surprising, either: Why would anyone in their right mind pay $11.99 for an official CD with artwork when they could simply spend four hours downloading the compressed MP3 files of all the album's songs onto their home computer's desktop, decompress them into an AIFF sound file, and then burn the data onto a $3 blank CD?"

"If we don't do something, this technology is going to destroy the record industry," said Nathan Davis, vice-president of Atlantic Records, Kid Rock's label. "Just imagine if the oil-change industry permitted the public to have direct access to oil and oil filters, enabling them to change their cars' oil themselves without going through Jiffy Lube or Kwik Lube. People would stop going to oil-change shops, and the entire industry would collapse. We can't let that happen to us."

According to autopsy analysis of Kid Rock's stomach contents by the L.A. County coroner's office, the singer's last meal consisted of newspapers, cigar butts, old CD liner notes, and the partial remains of sidekick Joe C., who had been missing since May 15.

Thus far, relief efforts on behalf of afflicted artists have met with little success. In January, Metallica, System Of A Down, and Powerman 5000 teamed up for a concert tour called "Us Aid," but the rockers were forced to cancel when concertgoers at the kickoff show in Tempe, AZ, showed up with MP3 recording equipment. An all-star fundraiser CD featuring Kid Rock, Limp Bizkit, and Korn was similarly scrapped when an individual known only by the user name PimpKracker69 acquired a pre-release promotional copy and made it available to millions of fans over the Internet.

"This is exactly the kind of thing we've been warning our fans about," James Hetfield, the lone surviving member of Metallica, told reporters during a press conference at Hollywood's Grace Church Homeless Shelter. "First, they found Madonna dead of a crack overdose in the alley behind Liquid. Then, my best friend and bandmate Lars is killed by cops during his botched hold-up of a liquor store. Now, Kid Rock dies of starvation like a filthy dog in the street. My God, people, didn't we learn the lesson of Elton John?"

John, the British rock star who went bankrupt in 1976—three years before private ownership of music-pirating cassette decks was made illegal—died of exposure on a Welsh moor in January 1977 after creditors repossessed his clothing. ∅

SNACK from page 123

are aware of the hideously bleak emptiness of modern life," Nabisco director of corporate communications Mel Krijak said. "That's why we are proud to present T.C. McCrispee's as the antidote you've been reaching out for. Our tasty new snack cracker will, if only for a few lovely moments, significantly lessen the aching, gnawing angst that torments your soul."

The history of humanity, a Nabisco press release for the new cracker stated, can be summed up as billions of years of darkness, uncertainty, and horror. Further, it asserted, the life of each individual organism on the planet is "no more than a meaningless blip on the cosmic timeline, riddled with almost unbearable suffering under the unseeing eye of a blind idiot god."

"Test subjects given samples of T.C. McCrispee's described them as 'pleasingly flavorful,'" Krijak said. "And the satisfying crunch distracted them from the grotesque carnival of tears that is life."

According to T.C. McCrispee's product-development director Wayne Isringhausen, the new cracker was scientifically formulated to match the tastes and habits of its target market, the approximately 220 million members of the American lower and middle class. Nabisco market research indicated that the typical member of this demographic is a hollow human shell devoid of hope, ambition, or any

chance of improving his or her station in life.

The new cracker, Isringhausen asserted, eases the consumer's vast, howling emptiness by giving him or her the option of adding such top-

> "We're selling more than a cracker here," Krijak said. "We're selling the salty, unctuous illusion of happiness."

pings to the cracker's surface as aerosolized cheese or sausage bits. "By eating T.C. McCrispee's in such a manner," Isringhausen said, "consumers will be deluded into thinking they have taken actual steps toward improving their lives. Or, in the rare case of a vegetable topping, their health."

"We're selling more than a cracker here," Krijak said. "We're selling the salty, unctuous illusion of happiness."

Consumers are eager to sample the new product. "I am trapped in an unending loop," Harwich, MA, telemarketer Ron Washburn said. "Perhaps when T.C. McCrispee's arrive at my neighborhood Food Lion, I will be

able to confront the world with more than a deadened, glassy stare."

Said Roanoke, VA, clergyman Rev. James Forrest: "I live a shadow life, each day going through the motions of maintaining a church, preparing sermons I no longer believe in, and counseling parishioner after identical parishioner. Perhaps this new cracker can give me a reason to go on, a source of strength, if you will."

A television ad for T.C. McCrispee's premiered Monday. In the spot, an animated cracker with a straw hat and cane leaps off the box and extols the virtues of the product in song form, ending with the slogan, "It's The Crispety, Crunchety Respite Of The Doomed."

Though a standard eight-ounce box of T.C. McCrispee's contains approximately 12 servings, Krijak said he expects that most consumers, gripped by unending hopelessness and despair, will eat the entire box in one sitting.

"To really gain the full impact of T.C. McCrispee's great snackin' taste, it is best to gorge yourself on multiple servings while staring glassy-eyed at a *Coach* rerun," Krijak said. "No, this will not rescue you from the throbbing, meaningless void that is modern American life. But here at Nabisco, we are confident that for millions of Americans it will seem, if only for a few seconds, as though it has." ∅

# Crazy Man Announces Plans To Stand In Doorway, Yell At Cars All Day

ALHAMBRA, CA—Area crazy man Dennis Fife held a press conference Monday to announce that on June 8, he will stand in the doorway of the office building at 2600 Kenilworth Avenue and yell at cars all day.

Addressing reporters, the 47-year-old said, "At approximately 9:30 a.m. on the day in question, shortly after I finish lunging at dogs, I will proceed to the front steps of the Simmons Building and yell loudly for nine hours. The screaming will be broken by a 15-minute fit of catatonia, most likely in the late afternoon."

Among the topics Fife plans to address during his nine-hour rant: the ace of diamonds, bookshelves, the man trying to kill him, those goddamn bananas, people from St. Louis, closed-up straws, *Trapper John, MD*, and papers, papers everywhere.

"I may briefly stray from my main agenda to urinate into the revolving door at the building's entrance," Fife said, "but, for the most part, I will focus on the task at hand and spend the bulk of the day yelling at the various passing cars."

Though Fife said he will shout at any vehicle that goes down Kenilworth Avenue, he will focus primarily on Volkswagen Beetles, pick-up trucks, and late-model Mitsubishi Galants. Fife also noted that he will attempt to gain the attention of bicyclists by shouting, "Hey there, Mr. Bike-man."

"A lot of what I intend to yell will be pre-planned—it will be things I've shouted at cars before," said Fife, chewing on his right forearm. "But I definitely want to leave open some room for improvisation. For instance, if a red car passes by, I might be inclined to shout at the driver, 'Where'd you get the fancy red car?' But then, if another red car drives by a bit later, I might become angry and demand that the driver stop and give me all his kid-

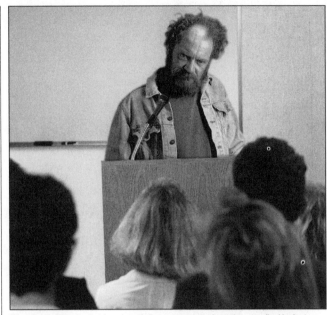

Above: Dennis Fife, a Los Angeles-area nutball, answers reporters' questions regarding his plan to scream at cars all day.

ney beans."

Fife has already begun preparations for the event. On Sunday, he worked late into the night making a bowl of Kraft macaroni and cheese, which he said he will bring with him and throw into the street, handfuls at a time. He has also set aside his lucky rubberband and a tree branch for the occasion.

While Fife has vowed to remain in the office building's doorway throughout his nine-hour yell session, some observers speculate that he will wander to the nearest corner, where he would have access to vehicles slowing down to make the turn onto Canyon Drive.

"That corner is going to be extremely tempting for Mr. Fife," Alhambra city councilwoman Lorraine Mac-

Alester said. "Not only do the cars slow down there, giving him better access to drivers, but there is a mailbox he can spit into. I can't imagine he'll be able to stand in that doorway all day with the corner in full view without giving in to the urge to go over there."

Alhambra police chief George Jaeger said he expects Fife to be successful in his venture, praising his remarkable tenacity and determination.

"When Mr. Fife sets his mind to something, he does it," Jaeger said. "Whether it's tearing pages out of a phone book, swallowing metal washers, or selling discarded Roxette CDs to imaginary friends for $600, every project he undertakes is a bona fide success. This truly is one focused loon." Ø

ASIANS from page 123

cans who are challenging people's traditional notions about Far Easterners. No longer content to be regarded as intelligent, hard-working, and family-oriented, a rising number of second- and third-generation Asian-Americans are beginning to fail miserably.

"This is the next logical step for us," said Kenneth Chang, president of the Bay Area Asian-American Association. "People assume all we're able to do is emigrate to the U.S. with nothing and establish thriving businesses and careers through hard work and determination. Well, that's just not true."

"People look at me and figure I'm smart, just because I'm Chinese," said

Lin Bu, a Sacramento, CA, 27-year-old who is unemployed and not looking for work. "Well, I'm not. I'm stupid."

"It just makes me so mad," said Jin-Duk Soo, 19, a Tempe, AZ, Korean immigrant who passed on going to college to focus on fixing up his car and picking up women. "I just want to party, not achieve."

When not hanging out and partying, Jin-Duk and his fellow Asians are shattering myths about cultural superiority in academics. While some young Asian-Americans are simply refusing to take calculus in high school or college, one bold group of Los Angeles-area Asian youths is going so far as to stage a "math strike" to protest the unfair generalizations.

"The other day in class, my math teacher asked me to calculate the value of a sine curve," said Jenny Kumagai, 16. "So I'm like, 'Forget it, old man—I'm Asian.'"

Recently, at Pasadena West High School, Asian-born students held a mass "Fail-In," refusing to answer any test questions correctly. Among the answers given: "Hydrogen is an adverb," and "The president of Russia is Fred Sanford."

But for all the progress, Asian-Americans still have a long way to go. According to the Census Bureau, nearly 95 percent of Asian-American high-school seniors go on to college, a number Chang calls "alarmingly high." Ø

NRA from page 123

beautiful baby?" asked Erlich, displaying the feminization/infantilization of firearms for which NRA members are renowned.

Erlich then demonstrated the proper loading procedure for his "baby," lovingly inserting a pair of bullets into the dark, snug-fitting tunnels before thrusting the gun's bolt smoothly into the action, cocking it firmly. "This'll blow a man straight to heaven," he said.

The tone of the event was set by chapter president Hank Unger, whose opening remarks cited the "wonderful

> "This'll blow a man straight to heaven," said Erlich, cocking his gun firmly.

variety of weaponry on display, from little snub-nosed pieces that fit snugly in your pocket to big, meaty shooters with barrels as thick as your arm."

Unger then fired his father's prize Colt Peacemaker revolver into the air, drawing raucous applause from conventioneers, many of whose own fathers had suppressed latent physical attraction for their adolescent sons by channeling their forbidden feelings into the fetishization of totemistic firearms.

All over the convention floor, gun makers proudly unveiled new technologies which will allow simmering homoerotic tensions to be expressed with greater nuance than ever before. At the Smith & Wesson booth, company spokesman Darrell Trace displayed a handgun made from a new metal alloy whose "incredibly hard" nature gives it no recoil after discharge, providing its user with "a far greater sense of control over his piece."

"It's a very comfortable gun, very soft in the hands," added Trace, noting that Smith & Wesson had designed the gun to appeal to "shooters tired of coming home from the firing range with sore, worn-out wrists."

But even as conventioneers reveled in a two-day orgy of firearm-to-phallus transference, a dark cloud hung over the event. The NRA has declined in power over the last decade, and its once-potent lobbyists have come out on the losing end of such key legislative battles as the Brady Bill, causing many members to bring their lifelong subconscious fears of castration to the fore.

"If the gun-control lobby wants my rod, they'll have to yank it from my dead body," said Pocatello bar owner Joseph Greer, cradling a tell-tale snub-nosed revolver.

"Those guys back East in Washington are tryin' to take our guns away, but we ain't gonna let 'em," continued Greer, piling classic paternal displacement onto the already-rich psychosexual tapestry. "No siree, Bob." Ø

# My Teddy Bear Collection Is Fucking Great

**The Bear Facts**
**By Brenda Pflaum**

You should see how many fucking teddy bears I have. I just can't get enough! Shit, last time I counted, it was up to 150. I've got most of them in the bedroom, but I can hardly fit another goddamn thing in there, so I had to start putting them in the living room.

I've got all different kinds of teddy bears. I can't go shopping without falling in love with a new one. Everyone always says, "Oh, shit, Brenda—here we go again!" But I tell them to mind their own fucking business, because I love my bears.

I've got the plain old cute little brown teddy bears with the big eyes that say, "Pick me up and hug me!" I've got all sorts of bears dressed up like firemen and ballerinas. I've also got one that's a businessman in a suit and glasses, with a button that says, "Teddy R. For President." It must mean that fucking cute-ass Teddy Ruxpin.

I've also got this huge-ass bear I won at the Greene County Fair last summer. It took me an hour at the dart-throw to win it, but it was worth it. It's got the best fucking paws.

I started collecting teddy bears when my aunt gave me one dressed up like a nurse for graduation, because I told her I wanted to be a nurse someday. But then it turned out that if I wanted to be a nurse, I would've had to go to college and shit. Now I just work at the Pik-It-Up. It fucking bites, but at least I got my bears.

My favorite bear is this adorable little one wearing a little black leather jacket. On the back of the jacket, it says, "Tough Teddy." Is that the cutest fucking thing or what? Joe sometimes takes me around on his Harley, so I want to get another "Tough Teddy" to bungee-cord to the back of the seat. I'm not gonna put the one I've got on

> ## I've also got this huge-ass bear I won at the Greene County Fair last summer. It's got the best fucking paws.

there, though, 'cause it would probably fall right off and land in the goddamn mud. Teddy bears are a bitch to wash. If you put them in the washing machine, their eyes always get scratched and their fur gets all fucked up.

That's why I always tell the kids, "Don't touch my fucking teddy bears—or else!" When Brianna was two, I had a bunch of my stuffed bears in a big round wicker chair in the living room of the trailer, because the bedroom had a leak. So one day, I was at the neighbors' trailer having a few beers, and when I came home, Brianna had the whole goddamn chair knocked over, and my teddy bears were everywhere. She had my Hawaiian Hula Bear in her mouth, and she was chewing the goddamn plastic flowers right off the neck. Christ! I tell you, you can't leave a 2-year-old alone for half an hour without a problem.

After that, I learned that if I want anything nice, I better goddamn well keep it out of the fucking kids' reach, for Christ's sake.

Recently, I started collecting teddy-bear figurines, too. They have some really cute ones at the Hallmark store. I was showing my girlfriend Tanya my roller-skating-bear figurine, and she says, "You'd better start collecting something smaller or, pretty soon, you won't have room for yourself in here anymore." So I say, "You're not fucking kidding!"

The other day, Sheila, this fucking bitch I work with at the Pik-It-Up, started talking about this Bride 'N' Groom Bear Couple she said I'd die for. She said the bride's even got a little veil that her ears stick out of. Now, that sounded adorable, and if Joe and I ever get hitched, I figure we could stick it on top of one of my ma's chocolate sheet cakes. So I asked Sheila where she got the bears. And she just says, "I don't know," real smart-ass like. So I say to her, "Tell me where you got the fucking bears!" And she just smiles and says, "I forget." The fucking ho-bag! I wanted those fucking bears.

Why should Sheila give a shit about them, anyway? I've seen her sad excuse for a teddy-bear collection. She's got some of the ugliest fucking bears I've ever seen. All these goddamn crocheted things that aren't even fuzzy, for shit's sake. Who'd want a stupid, scratchy-ass teddy bear like that?

Finally, I couldn't stand her goddamn smirk anymore, so I grabbed the collar of her Pik-It-Up uniform, got about an inch from her face, and said, "Where'd you get the bears?" All the while, I've got my L.A. Gear high-tops pressing down on her toes, which are sticking out of the girly-ass sandals she's wearing. Just then, Mr. Schumacher comes out of his office and sends me home for the rest of the day.

"Fuck it," I said to myself. I knew I could beat the info out of Sheila any time I wanted. Fucking bitch. Christ.

On Sunday, I went to Adorables Unlimited over at Northlake Mall and, sure enough, the bear wedding couple was right there on the shelf. It set me back a shitload, but they were too fucking cute to pass up. The groom is wearing a little top hat and tails, and he's even got little black shoes!

When I got home, I put them on top of the TV instead of saving them in the box, 'cause I don't think there's gonna be any goddamn wedding if Joe doesn't stop hanging around the Pit Stop Tavern every goddamn night, letting all those fucking waitress sluts paw at him. The Bride 'N' Groom Bear Couple even came with a little red carpet to unroll and put them on, just like a real fucking church! They're so fucking cute! Ø

# Sometimes I Wish My Legs Had Never Been Crushed By That Train

**By Peter Lolich**

Most of the time, I'm pretty happy with my life. I've got a nice apartment, a few really close friends, and a good job. That's more than a lot of people have, right? Still, every now and then, I can't help but find myself wishing my legs had never been crushed by that train.

I know what you're thinking—we all have regrets, but, hey, that's life. It's the same old story, and everyone has their own version: I shouldn't have let that girl get away, I shouldn't have sold that stock, I shouldn't have been launched through the windshield of my car in a rear-end collision, landing in front of that approaching train. Sure, it's happened to all of us at some point in our lives. But sometimes, I can't help but feel like I'm the only one out there who lost his legs to a train.

Not to dwell, but every once in a while, I still find myself replaying that accident in my head. And it's been almost two years since it happened. I try not to lose perspective and blow it all out of proportion, but sometimes I can't help but feel like the day they

scraped me off the tracks and rushed me to the hospital for 22 hours of emergency surgery was some sort of pivotal point in my life—and not in a

> ## Oh, I'm just being silly. The grass is always greener on the other side, right?

good way.

Looking back at that moment of squealing metal and ripping sinew and bone, I'd go so far as to say that if I could do it all over, there are a few things I might change. Perhaps I would've rather landed just a few feet further from the tracks, so that instead of mangling my entire lower body, that train would have just sliced off my feet. Even with my feet gone, I still would have been able to use leg braces. Or perhaps I would have had an arm destroyed instead. You can still do a lot of things with only one arm.

You know, now that I think about it, had I been given the choice, I probably would've preferred that the train miss me altogether. I could've, say, been thrown into the ditch, the train

whizzing right by without making contact with my body at all. That might have been better.

Oh, I'm just being silly. The grass is always greener on the other side, right? Who knows what awful turns my life might have taken if I'd stayed on the path I was on—finishing out senior year as my high school's star pitcher and heading for college on a full baseball scholarship. Maybe I'm better off in this motorized wheelchair. I guess I'll never know.

People have always said I'm the introspective, philosophical type. So you should probably just ignore all my hypothetical ramblings about "what-ifs" and "paths not taken." Who can stop me when I start pondering what it would be like to jog down a beach again, or walk up the stairs to my ex-girlfriend's apartment, or go to the bathroom without help? The past is done and gone, so there's no use dwelling on it.

Even so, everyone gets like this every once in a while. You look back on the things that happened in your life—the people you met, the jobs you got, the speeding trains that ripped limbs from your body and left two useless stumps—and you wonder how things might have been. Aw, heck, look at me, Mr. Contemplative over here. Ø

## Pure Silk To Stream From Cindy Crawford's Ass

see PEOPLE page 1D

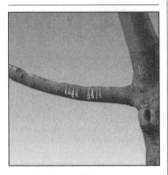

## Inspirational Poster Kitten Falls To Death After 17 Years

see NATION page 2C

## Man In Suit Breaks Into Brief, Feminine Run

see BUSINESS page 3C

## Area Roofer Badmouths College

see LOCAL page 6B

## Local Man's Body A Really Big Temple

see PEOPLE page 7C

### STATshot
A look at the numbers that shape your world.

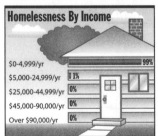

Homelessness By Income

| | |
|---|---|
| $0-4,999/yr | 99% |
| $5,000-24,999/yr | 1% |
| $25,000-44,999/yr | 0% |
| $45,000-90,000/yr | 0% |
| Over $90,000/yr | 0% |

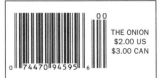

THE ONION
$2.00 US
$3.00 CAN

0 74470 94595 6

---

# the ONION®

WWW.THEONION.COM · AMERICA'S FINEST NEWS SOURCE™ · FOUNDED 1871

# Twelve Customers Gunned Down In Convenience-Store Clerk's Imagination

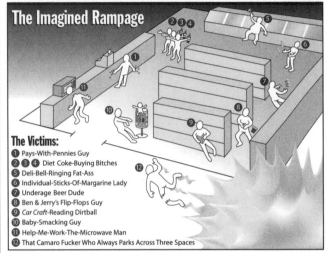

**The Imagined Rampage**

**The Victims:**
1. Pays-With-Pennies Guy
2. 3. 4. Diet Coke-Buying Bitches
5. Deli-Bell-Ringing Fat-Ass
6. Individual-Sticks-Of-Margarine Lady
7. Underage Beer Dude
8. Ben & Jerry's Flip-Flops Guy
9. *Car Craft*-Reading Dirtball
10. Baby-Smacking Guy
11. Help-Me-Work-The-Microwave Man
12. That Camaro Fucker Who Always Parks Across Three Spaces

CLACKAMAS, OR—Driven to homicidal rage by mounting job-related frustrations, third-shift Stop 'N' Shop clerk Justin Fonseca, 27, shot and killed 12 customers in his imagination Thursday.

The mass slaying, the 63rd to take place in Fonseca's mind since he began working at the Portland-area convenience store last August, was the worst since March 17, when he visualized himself fatally stabbing 22 intoxicated St. Patrick's Day revelers with their own broken beer bottles.

Fonseca began his mental rampage at approximately 10 p.m., when he was approached by a Stop 'N' Shop regular known as "Pays-With-Pennies Guy."

"I was the only guy working and was

see CLERK page 129

---

# Break-Up Made Easier With Colorful Visual Aids

HUNTINGTON, WV—Stephanie Duquette's break-up with boyfriend Chris Straub was made easier Thursday with an array of colorful charts, graphs, and other visual aids from Copy Express, a Huntington copy shop.

"When Stephanie came in looking for a way to make her dumping of Chris more effective and memorable, I was more than happy to help," Copy Express assistant manager Debbie Saldana said. "Using our state-of-the-art laser printers, film scanners, Canon CLC 1120 color copiers, and top-notch computer software, Stephanie was able to provide Chris with a clear, eye-catching presentation of his failings as a boyfriend."

Duquette, 20, broke up with Straub, her boyfriend of two years, late Thurs-

see BREAK-UP page 128

Above: Duquette makes a point to her boyfriend using a chart made at Copy Express.

---

# Gatorade Pledges $240 Million In Thirst Aid To Underquenched Nations

UNITED NATIONS—In the largest humanitarian electrolyte-replenishment effort in decades, Gatorade will donate $240 million in thirst aid to citizens of 27 U.N.-designated underquenched Third World nations, spokespersons for the company announced Thursday.

"Gatorade is thirst aid," Gatorade president Tony Highsmith said, "for our global community's deepdown body thirst."

According to Highsmith,

the thirst-aid package gives the people of drought-ravaged nations such as Bangladesh, Kenya, and the Sudan "a fighting chance," enabling them to give everything they've got—both on the rice field and off.

"Toiling in a sweatshop, stooping in rice paddies, or marching at gunpoint for days on end can really make you work up a sweat," Highsmith said. "Gatorade is scientifically

see GATORADE page 128

Above: Celebrity humanitarian envoy Susan Sarandon pumps Gatorade for villagers in Sikasso, Mali.

formulated to replenish the fluids and minerals active peasants need."

The massive rehydrative effort is hoped to quench as many as 59 million in "hot, tired populations" by early 2001.

"Gatorade has taken the important 'thirst' step toward creating a world in which each person's basic human right to energy-boosting carbs is met," a headband-wearing President Clinton told reporters following several hours of tennis at the White House. "What's more, underquenched nations can now look forward to two delicious new flavors, Fierce Grape and Fierce Berry."

Added Clinton: "Gatorade: Is it in you?"

The move by Gatorade comes at a crucial time for Third World nations.

"Many of my countrymen are unable to maintain their peak output because of the mineral loss—mineral loss that keeps them from being their best," said Tanzanian war refugee Mwene Tshikanga. "We desperately need electrolytes for our sick and injured. And we know we cannot get them from ordinary soft drinks or juices."

"The world's malnourished, undereducated, underdeveloped nations face a crisis similar to the one faced by Georgia Tech during its legendary 1967 Orange Bowl game against the Florida Gators," Highsmith said. "Georgia Tech played well at first, but its players lost their edge as the game went on, with

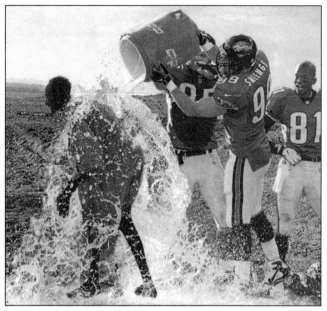

Above: Jacksonville Jaguars players celebrate Sudanese peasant Dese Marawi's victory over thirst.

slowed reflexes and poor concentration causing them to give up big plays. Tech wasn't drinking Gatorade, and the Gators, of course, took control of the game in the second half. Why? Because they were replenishing their fluids and minerals with a special formula that has gone on to help the underquenched to this very day."

"What Gatorade did for the Florida Gators, it can do for the Eritrean lentil

farmer," Highsmith added.

In addition to billions of gallons of Gatorade, nations earmarked for thirst-aid relief will receive Gatorade-logoed mesh workout T-shirts, caps, and visors. They will also be sent educational materials to teach citizens how to maximize the effectiveness of Gatorade-brand products.

"Subsistence-level peasant populations need to drink at least 16 ounces

of fluid prior to, 8 ounces during, and 24 ounces immediately after heavy menial labor," a multilingual wall chart included in the thirst-aid package read in part. "Why? Because the more you slave away for your cruel overlords, the more vital minerals and fluids your body loses. These have to be replaced quickly, with a re-

> ### "What Gatorade did for the Florida Gators, it can do for the Eritrean lentil farmer," Highsmith said.

hydrating agent that contains glucose and sodium, so you can keep your edge—and keep from being beaten."

Leaders of underquenched nations expressed gratitude for the historic humanitarian effort.

"My Gatorade brothers," said Burkina Faso prime minister Kadre Desire Ouedraogo, "words cannot express how much this means to our country. Truly, we will never again fall victim to the myth that water is as effective as Gatorade in rejuvenating tired muscles fast. Thanks to you, we have begun the long road to quenching." ∅

day evening, using the visual aids to concisely communicate to him just how unhappy she had been during the last six months of their relationship.

"I needed to express my desire to see other people, but I didn't want it to

> ### "Chris was definitely impressed by all the great visual aids," Duquette said. "Throughout the entire presentation, he barely said a word."

turn into some huge argument about whose fault it was and whether my actions were fair," Duquette said. "I knew Chris was going to have a lot of questions, and that's when I got out this professionally bound report with the peek-through title '10 Reasons Why I Want Out.'"

Duquette praised Copy Express for its ability to produce the needed visual aids on a deadline.

"Chris and I had agreed we would have the big 'Where is this relationship going?' talk Thursday night after he got back from his big guys-only camping trip," Duquette said. "By Wednesday, I was at my wit's end. I knew I had only one day to come up

with something that would really make a big impression, but I had no idea what."

Originally, Duquette had gone to Copy Express to make photocopies of her farewell letter, which she intended to distribute to the couple's friends so they would understand her side of the story. Upon seeing Duquette attempt to feed the messy, seven-page handwritten letter into the copier's auto-feed slot, Saldana intervened.

"I asked Stephanie if that letter wouldn't be more effective if it were organized with bullet points and had a catchy color banner across the top," Saldana said. "Stephanie was excited by the suggestion, so I told her about a whole range of possibilities, from a laminated graph illustrating Chris' declining spending on birthday and anniversary gifts to a spiral-bound, quick-reference booklet of his shortcomings as a lover printed on heavy-stock ivory paper."

Duquette's major complaints about Straub—including his failure to spend enough time with her, his frequent unemployment, and his steadily increasing weight—were presented to him on attractive, photo-quality color 24"x36" posters printed on Copy Express' brand-new 600DPI HP DesignJet printer.

"I said, 'See this line graph, Chris?'" Duquette recalled. "It clearly shows how my interest in you plummeted after I began taking night classes to learn French. These multi-colored

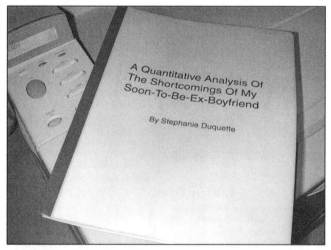

Above: One of Duquette's many sharp-looking presentation materials.

lines represent the appeal of some of the other guys in my class. As you can see, the green line representing Steve is a full two inches higher than the blue one representing you.'"

"Chris was definitely impressed by all the great visual aids," Duquette said. "Throughout the entire presentation, he barely said a word."

For all the help she provided, Saldana remains modest about her role in the successful presentation.

"Most of the ideas were Stephanie's," Saldana said. "I just helped her maximize her results by finding the best way to present the data that she herself had been collecting in her pri-

vate journal ever since she and Chris started having problems in March."

Straub said he was "blown away" by the Copy Express materials.

"I never realized the great disparity between the frequency and sincerity of Stephanie's expressions of love and those of my own until I saw it laid out in a vibrant, red-and-yellow pie chart," Straub said. "And when I was presented with a glossy, spiral-bound packet detailing all the rude comments I've made about her best friend Paulette over the years, how could I disagree with Stephanie's conclusion that she can do better than me? I was sold." ∅

totally swamped, when in walks Pays-With-Pennies Guy, who has to be one of our worst customers ever," Fonseca said. "He's this really mean old fucker who always gets cough syrup and a pack of smokes, and pays for it with a Ziploc bag full of pennies he dumps on the counter and makes me count for him. So, as I'm counting his fucking pennies, some fat bastard starts ringing the deli bell. Just then, this moron who always needs help with the microwave starts yelling at me to come over. I just fuckin' lost it."

Mentally arming himself with a pump-action 12-gauge Mossberg shotgun advertised in an issue of *Guns* magazine he'd been flipping through, Fonseca pictured himself grabbing Pays-With-Pennies Guy's hair and sticking the barrel of the shotgun in his mouth. Fonseca then imagined himself pulling the trigger, blowing off the back of Pays-With-Pennies Guy's head and showering the trio of Diet Coke-Buying Bitches behind him with blood, brains, and bone fragments.

Continuing his fantasy rampage, Fonseca thrust the shotgun deeper into Pays-With-Pennies Guy's mouth, causing the muzzle to protrude through the smoking exit wound in the back of his skull. He then cocked the shotgun's pump action by working the slide against Pays-With-Pennies Guy's lower jaw and aimed the weapon at the Diet Coke-Buying Bitches. The wealthy sorority sisters stood paralyzed by the sheer force of personality of Fonseca's daydream-avatar, a fierce version of Fonseca with whom people do not fuck. Fonseca fired once, and the single bullet, an exotic 2.5-ounce rifled anti-personnel slug the cashier had previously employed in several undercover-Mossad-agent fantasy scenarios, pierced all three of the Diet Coke-Buying Bitches' skulls, killing them instantly and causing them to slump to the floor in a grisly, tank-topped heap.

Fonseca then abandoned the image of the shotgun and drew a pair of matte black high-capacity .50-caliber Desert Eagle automatic pistols from his memories of playing Tomb Raider. Emerging from behind the counter, he walked toward the deli case and cornered the Deli-Bell-Ringing Fat-Ass, a Stop 'N' Shop regular whose insistence on immediate service and precise sandwich assembly had for months meant hellish Sunday nights for Fonseca.

In his mind, Fonseca then shot Deli-Bell-Ringing Fat-Ass in two-handed, double-gun, John Woo style, driving the bullets into his victim's gut with such force that the Deli-Bell-Ringing Fat-Ass was propelled over the glass deli case, forming a helical trail of blood behind him as he twisted through the air and came to rest face down on the Stop 'N' Shop's Hobart-brand automatic rotary slicer. The impact activated the slicer, which had been left on the thinnest setting, and Deli-Bell-Ringing Fat-Ass' face was

Above: The site of Fonseca's (inset) deadly mental rampage.

shaved into slender ribbons.

Guns in hand, Fonseca proceeded to take a cathartic, imaginary march through the store. Heading first to the coolers, he encountered three of his least favorite customers, Individual-Sticks-Of-Margarine Lady, Underage Dude Who Always Tries To Buy Beer Even Though We Always Fucking Card Him, and Guy In The Bathrobe And Flip-Flops Who Comes In Like Three Times A Night To Buy Ben & Jerry's. Employing *Matrix*-style rotating slow-motion and *Wild Bunch*-inspired multiple viewing angles, Fonseca pictured himself firing dozens of shots into each of the three, smiling slightly as they flew back through the glass doors of the cooler cases, their bullet-riddled bodies animated in a grisly dance, as electricity and freon coursed through them.

Fonseca then rounded the corner and walked toward the magazine rack, where he found Entire-Issue-Of-*Car Craft*-Reading Dirtball. He then dreamed of shooting the regular non-paying magazine reader at point-blank range through the special *Car Craft* camshaft issue he was holding to his face.

At the nearby rotating greeting-card rack, Fonseca encountered Baby-Smacking Guy, a first-time customer who carried his infant son under his arm and smacked him whenever he made a noise. Baby-Smacking Guy was rummaging through the rack for remaining Mother's Day cards and striking his child when a volley of Fonseca's imagined shots struck him in the stomach, causing him to reflexively throw the child into the air. Fonseca caught the baby in the crook of his arm and placed him atop the greeting-card rack. The heroic Fonseca then spun the rack, causing the child to laugh with delight.

Seconds later, Fonseca's attention was turned toward Help-Me-With-The-Microwave Guy, who had brought another one of his cheese sandwiches from home and, as usual, needed assistance heating it in the ancient microwave on the front counter.

Visualizing himself taking careful aim and squeezing the trigger, Fonseca relished the fantasy of two expanding hollow-point slugs vaporizing Help-Me-With-The-Microwave Guy's third through sixth cervical vertebrae, decapitating him and launching his severed head into the open microwave as rivers of blood spurted from his neck.

Before Fonseca could turn on the microwave to melt the head, he noticed That Camaro Fucker Who Always Parks Across Three Spaces pulling up to the store. Using the same magnesium-tipped explosive rounds he often fires from his index finger to incinerate night manager Carla Simons, Fonseca emptied his guns into the Camaro's gas tank, igniting a massive fireball and catapulting the burning corpse of That Camaro Fucker Who Always Parks Across Three Spaces through the store's front window.

Fonseca then imagined himself dramatically pausing before dropping the empty pistols from his outstretched hands and taking a cigarette from the bullet-riddled Marlboro display. After a brisk patting of his pockets failed to produce a lighter, Fonseca lit the cigarette with That Camaro Fucker Who Always Parks Across Three Spaces' burning body. Fonseca then strode nonchalantly from the burning store, which exploded into a thousand-foot pillar of fire.

A romantic ending involving The Cute Blonde With The Freckles On Her Shoulders Who Sometimes Comes In At Bar Time was prevented by the real-life interruption of Pays-With-Pennies Guy, who, sensing that Fonseca's attention had momentarily drifted, demanded that the clerk start counting his pennies all over again.

"Sorry," Fonseca told Pays-With-Pennies Guy, who had added a stick of beef jerky to his purchases while he and 11 others were being mentally slain. "Lost my place there."

"Sir," said Fonseca, addressing the overweight man at the deli case whose bell-ringing had continued unabated, "I'll be with you in a minute." ∅

NEWS IN BRIEF

## AOL Acquires Time-Warner In Largest-Ever Expenditure Of Pretend Internet Money

DULLES, VA—In the largest merger of imaginary assets in corporate history, Internet giant America Online last week acquired media megacorp Time-Warner for an unprecedented $161 billion in pretend money Thursday. "This merger will revolutionize the way invisible amounts of non-existent cash are transferred," said Steve Case of AOL, a company whose actual revenues are a tiny fraction of its make-believe valuation. In an effort to keep pace with AOL, web site blair-witchproject.com is expected to acquire General Motors by the end of the week.

## Man Who Actually Needs Grey Poupon Unable To Bring Self To Ask

ABERDEEN, MD—Sophie's Sandwich Shop patron Louis Worth, a longtime user of Grey Poupon dijon mustard, could not bring himself to ask for the product Thursday when he actually needed it. "There's usually a bottle on one of the tables, but this time there wasn't," Worth said. "I actually said 'Pardon me' to the guy behind the counter, but then stopped in my tracks. I realized that if I actually asked, the guy would probably act all funny and say, 'But, of course,' in a rich-guy voice. So I just ate my turkey sandwich without it."

## Nation's Last Themeless Restaurant Closes

CEDAR RAPIDS, IA—An era came to an end Tuesday, when Pat's Place, the nation's last themeless restaurant, closed its doors in Cedar Rapids. "We achieved a certain local notoriety for our unique non-themed food and unadorned atmosphere," owner Patrick Baines said, "but sales were sluggish, as most people would just come in to gawk at our photoless walls and mundanely named menu items like 'hamburger' and 'pancakes.' Then they would head over to the Rainforest Cafe, Hard Rock Cafe, Planet Hollywood, All-Star Cafe, Johnny Rocket's, or Disney Cafe down the street." Once vacated by Baines, the building will become home to Cedar Rapids' seventh Paddy O'Touchdown's Irish Sports Bar & Good-Tyme Internet Grill. ∅

# Sales Manager Gets A Little Crazy At Office Party

SUNNYVALE, CA—Allen Wohl, a 33-year-old associate sales manager at M&H Marketing, got a little crazy at Thursday's annual office holiday party, held from 2 to 3 p.m. in the third-floor conference room.

The combination Christmas and New Year's party, thrown in November to avoid conflicting with M&H Marketing's traditional December busy season, was highlighted by Wohl's irreverent antics, which included silly faces, impersonations of coworkers, and humorous poses atop a desk.

"Allen has always been known as M&H's resident cut-up, but he really cut loose at the party," promotions coordinator Janice Larkspahr said. "At one point, he made a bullhorn out of a paper plate and sang the *Gilligan's Island* theme song, only he changed the lyrics to stuff about people in our office. You don't even want to know what he said about [senior sales manager] Richard [Stenstrup]."

"That Allen Wohl is one certified nutball," secretary Irene Utter said. "When he picked up that tray of punch cups and pretended to be a British waiter, I almost died laughing. Where does he come up with that stuff?"

Asked for comment on the incident, Wohl said, "What can I say? I'm a wild and crazy guy!"

The highlight of the party, most members of the M&H Marketing team agreed, came when Wohl presented "awards" to his coworkers.

"My certificate said 'Most Likely To Leave The Presentation On The Plane,' said sales supervisor Randall Talish, who last December left a proposal for a $26,000 Tru-Bilt Windows & Siding ad campaign on a flight from Los Angeles. "I've got to admit, he really got me good with that one. I was hoping everyone had forgotten about that goof-up by now, but leave it to Allen to give me heck."

The hour-long party, which also featured cake, soda, festive yellow streamers, and a rousing game of Scattergories, was deemed a success by all.

"I was having so much fun, I almost didn't want to go back to work," associate marketing supervisor Sheila Duckett said. "Allen sure was in rare form."

Those who work closely with Wohl said the behavior was typical of the man they call "M&H's answer to Jay Leno."

Above: Sales manager Allen Wohl, whose zany behavior at a recent holiday office party was described by fellow M&H Marketing employees as "certifiable."

"Allen's a real prankster," fellow sales manager Gene Budzig said. "I remember that one time last month, when Bill McCullers was saying all morning that he had to make sure to FedEx a proposal that day, but when he went to drop off the package, Wohl told him the FedEx guy had just left. You should've seen the look on Bill's face when Allen told him he was just kidding! Boy, was he relieved!"

In addition to playing pranks on coworkers, Wohl expresses his unorthodox personality by decorating his cubicle in an offbeat manner. Adorning his workspace is a *Far Side* mousepad, an Executive Stress-Relief Koosh Ball, novelty windshield-wiper sunglasses, a *Dilbert* screen-saver, and a framed sign that reads, "There's No 'I' In 'Team'... But Fortunately, There Is One In 'Vacation'!"

Wohl also has an arsenal of humorous quips he has used throughout his seven years with M&H Marketing, including, "Time to make the donuts," which he says upon arriving at work each morning, and "Cha-ching!" which he shouts after closing a deal with a new client.

Though M&H employees settled down and returned to their normal work routines shortly after the party, a resurgence in excitement is expected Friday, when office manager Jan Schenkle is due to get her roll of pictures back from Walgreens. Schenkle, who is in charge of compiling the office newsletter, said she plans to display the photos on the breakroom bulletin board.

"When those pictures come back, Allen is going to hear about his crazy shenanigans from everybody all over again," Schenkle said. "I just hope we got a good shot of him balancing that plate of cake on his head."

Wohl said he enjoys all the attention.

"I've always loved the spotlight," he said. "It's a real kick to be able to make your coworkers laugh. Of course, I can't be a card all the time, or our department's productivity would take a major hit. Still, it's nice to go off the deep end every once in a while." ∅

## WHAT DO YOU THINK?

# The Death Of John-John

Killed with his wife and sister-in-law in a plane crash July 16, JFK Jr. joins a long line of Kennedys to die under tragic circumstances. What do *you* think about the latest calamity to befall America's first family?

**Jennifer Levy**
**Graphic Designer**

"It's tragic when you consider all the wasted potential. Think of all the stylish neckties he would have gone on to wear."

**Frank Cameron**
**Actuary**

"We have lost a man who forged in the smithy of his soul the uncreated conscience of his race. No, wait—that was James Joyce. JFK Jr. was that guy in *People*."

**Steve Roby**
**Delivery Driver**

"All I can say is, thank God his wife was also in the plane, sparing us from having to endure another bony, widowed, fashion-plate, pseudo-royal Jackie O figure for the next 50 years."

**Elaine Foss**
**Florist**

"Just give me a minute to collect myself and dry the tears I'm crying for America. Okay, now, who died?"

**Rajiv Gopindar**
**Cashier**

"Christ, how long can that crazy wop Giancana stay mad?"

**John Auletta**
**Systems Analyst**

"You know, I'm gonna miss that old casket-saluting bar-flunker."

# the ONION®

WWW.THEONION.COM | AMERICA'S FINEST NEWS SOURCE™ | FOUNDED 1871

## Chinese Guy Still Insisting It Was Him In Front Of That Tank

see WORLD page 4A

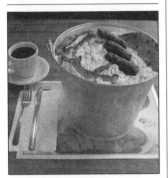

## Denny's Introduces 'Just A Humongous Bucket Of Eggs And Meat'

see FOOD page 3C

## Moment Of Your Time Apparently Means 33 Minutes

see TELEMARKETING page 1D

## TV Muted While Neighbors Fight

see LOCAL page 10D

### STATshot

A look at the numbers that shape your world.

**Top Improv-Comedy Audience Suggestions**

1. Condom!
2. Monica Lewinsky!
3. Proctologist's office!
4. Lorena Bobbitt!
5. The White House!
6. Homeric tragedy!
7. Don't quit your day job!
8. Mike Tyson!
9. Penis pump!
10. Get off the stage!

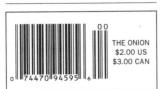

# Rare Disease Nabs Big-Time Celebrity Spokesman

BALTIMORE—Flehner-Lathrop Syndrome Foundation officials excitedly announced Monday that actor Ted Danson has been diagnosed with the rare, deadly degenerative disease, bringing much-needed star power to their cause.

"This is the big one we've been waiting for," said Paula Brooks, director of the Baltimore-based FLS Foundation. "For years, our organization struggled with scant funding, a dearth of resources, and the lack of a prominent spokesperson to draw attention to

see DISEASE page 132

Right: New Flehner-Lathrop Syndrome sufferer/spokesman Ted Danson.

## A GROWING EPIDEMIC

# More U.S. Children Being Diagnosed With Youthful Tendency Disorder

REDLANDS, CA— Nicholas and Beverly Serna's daughter Caitlin was just 4 years old, but they

**Common YTD Warning Signs**

▷ Near-constant running, jumping, skipping

▷ Sudden episodes of shouting and singing

▷ Preferring playtime and flights of fancy to schoolwork

▷ Confusing self with animals and objects, including tigers, dinosaurs, and airplanes

▷ Conversations with "imaginary friends"

▷ Poor impulse-control with regard to sugared snacks

already knew there was a problem.

Day after day, upon arriving home from pre-school, Caitlin would retreat into a bizarre fantasy world. Sometimes, she would pretend to be people and things she was not. Other times, without warning, she would burst into nonsensical song. Some days she would run directionless through the backyard of the Sernas' comfortable Redlands home, laughing and shrieking as she chased imaginary objects.

When months of sessions with a local psychologist failed to yield an answer, Nicholas and Beverly took Caitlin to a prominent Los Angeles pedi-

see YTD page 133

# Discovery Of Oil Turns Peru Into Bunch Of Assholes

LIMA, PERU—The recent discovery of a vast oil reserve in southern Peru has turned the South American nation's citizenry into "a bunch of first-class assholes," U.N. sources said Monday.

"Before this oil thing, the Peruvians were a real nice, down-to-earth people," U.N. General Assembly president Harri Holkeri said. "But now they strut around, wearing flashy clothes, driving Mercedes, and loudly talking about their summer homes in Monaco. Everyone here at the U.N. has noticed the change."

The discovery of the oil field is expected to increase Peru's crude-oil re-

serves from less than a billion barrels to nearly 23 billion. With a production goal of 800,000 barrels a day, the reserve is expected to add almost $9 billion to the country's GNP and place it among the world's top 20 oil-producing nations.

"It's too bad we're stuck down here in South America, surrounded by all these poor countries," Peruvian president Alberto Fujimori said. "Those filthy Chileans have goats and chickens running loose in the streets. And they don't even have running water. I can't tell you how much I'd rather be in Europe, where people have a little class."

Added Fujimori: "I'd kill for a half-

see PERU page 132

COLOMBIA
ECUADOR

PERU

BRAZIL

Lima

BOLIVIA

Oil Reserves

this dread disease. Then, out of the blue, Ted Danson! Needless to say, we're elated."

"Before this," Brooks continued, "the closest thing we had to a celebrity afflicted with FLS was a cousin of Al Jarreau's. Obviously, this is a big step up."

Flehner-Lathrop Syndrome, a genetic cardiac disorder which causes the heart's left ventricle to deteriorate and typically results in death within three to five years, affects fewer than 1 in 500,000 Americans—grim statistics for any disease seeking a high-profile celebrity to shine a spotlight on its cause.

"A disease this rare usually can't compete with the big boys," Brooks said. "But this takes us to the next level. With Ted in our corner, FLS can hold its own against just about anybody, from Tay-Sachs to cystic fibrosis."

Danson, 52, best known for his role as bartender Sam Malone on the hit 1980s NBC sitcom *Cheers* and currently the star of CBS's *Becker*, was diagnosed with FLS Sept. 12, five days after complaining of chest pain during a celebrity golf tournament in Palm Springs, CA. The diagnosis has delighted sufferers of the disease and their loved ones.

"I've been a fan of Ted Danson's forever," said West Columbia, SC, resident Emily Dutler, whose 11-year-old son Seth was stricken with FLS last year. "I mean, I've probably seen every episode of *Cheers* five times. I can't tell you what a godsend this is to have him speaking and fundraising on Seth's behalf. We've prayed for something like this to happen."

"This really puts us in position for a lucrative run," wrote Brooks in the September/October issue of *Heartbeats*, the FLS Foundation's bimonthly newsletter. "We can expect three or four good years of impassioned spokesmanship from Ted, followed by several months of heartrending images of his brave, final battle with FLS—the kind of thing that really jerks tears and gets donations pouring in. Then, when Ted finally dies, expect a full week's worth of tributes in *USA Today* and on *Entertainment Tonight* that mention his love for our organization. And the cover of *People* is virtually guaranteed. All told, that translates to somewhere in the neighborhood of $500 million in free advertising and promotion."

"It really is amazing," said Mark Knoll, national director of communications for the FLS Foundation. "I know of diseases that afflict 10 to 20 times as many people as ours, and they don't have a spokesperson anywhere near as big as Ted Danson. I mean, look at cardiofibrilitis—1 in 20,000 Americans are afflicted, and all they've got is Alfonso Ribeiro. Talk about low-wattage advocacy."

"And it's not like Danson is some washed-up star with nothing but a couple of Emmys and his memories,"

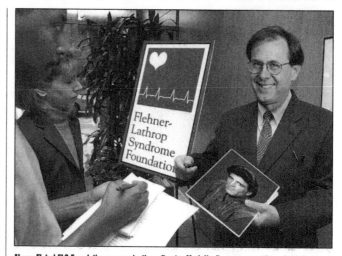

Above: Elated FLS Foundation communications director Mark Knoll answers questions about the new face of the disease.

Knoll continued. "I mean, *Becker* is one of the top-rated TV shows in the country, with a choice Monday-night slot between *Everybody Loves Raymond* and *Family Law*. You can't get much better than that."

The FLS Foundation is already moving ahead with a promotional campaign to capitalize on its new celebrity sufferer. In next week's issue of *Time*, the organization will run a full-page ad featuring a photo of Danson above the words, "Making Your Way In The World Today Takes Everything You've Got... Especially If You've Got An Incurable Cardiac Disorder Like Flehner-Lathrop Syndrome."

"Make no mistake," Brooks said, "Mr. Danson is going to get the red-carpet treatment from us. When he sees how grateful we are, I think Ted will agree he couldn't have come down with a better fatal disease than Flehner-Lathrop Syndrome."

Pausing to open a letter that had just come across her desk, Brooks emitted a delighted squeal and brandished the newest bequest to the FLS Foundation: a check for $250,000 from CBS.

"Couldn't you just die?" a gleeful Brooks said. ∅

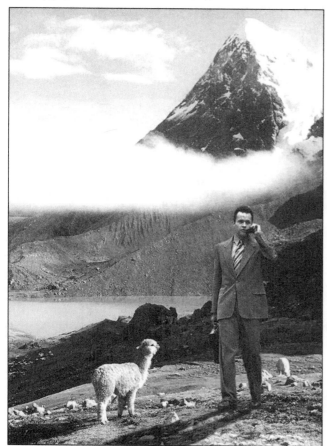

Above: A Peruvian farmer in the mountain village of Arequipa calls his broker.

million square miles on the Mediterranean."

The day after Petroperú scientists made the oil find, the Peruvian government went on a massive spending spree, buying a gold-domed parliament building, a squadron of top-of-the-line F-22 fighter jets, and a brand-new $2 billion infrastructure, including 450 suspension bridges and a six-lane highway running through the Andes Mountains. The following day, the country demanded that the 2004 Olympics be held in Lima and enacted legislation to change the country's motto to "One Nation, Living The Sweet Life."

Peru's relations with neighboring countries have deteriorated since the discovery. When Argentine president Fernando de la Rúa made a diplomatic trip to Peru on Oct. 5, Fujimori asked him to "run out and get [him] a cup of coffee." Fujimori later told de la Rúa he was "surprised you are so fat, considering you hardly have any food in your country."

"I've never been treated this way in my entire life," de la Rúa said. "You know what these Peruvians are? Instant asshole, just add oil."

Ecuadoran president Gustavo Noboa agreed. "What a bunch of pricks they've turned into," Noboa said. "I met with their minister of trade shortly after the oil discovery, and the whole time, all he did was make fun of our principal exports.

'Ooh, bananas, coffee, and sugarcane—I am *so* impressed. I would *love* to trade some of my grade-A petroleum for some of your cocoa.' Fucking jerk."

Peru has also canceled its membership in the Organization of American States.

"Suddenly, they're not interested in participating in the OAS anymore?" asked Bolivian president Hugo Bánzer. "Fine, don't. Drop out if we're not good enough for you. Go join OPEC or NATO or some other rich-nation club."

In addition to the rude behavior, Peruvian leaders have made several big-ticket purchases that have been criticized as needlessly flashy.

"The first thing they did was start construction on a state-of-the-art 115,000-seat [soccer] stadium in Lima," Brazilian president Fernando Cardoso said. "Then Fujimori calls me up and tells me my country can use it if we ever need to hold a match in a 'decent' stadium."

Andreas Stikker, director of the Netherlands' Rijksmuseum, expressed his disdain for Peru's extravagance, as well.

"A few days ago, the curator of some museum in Lima called me up and wanted to know how much we want for a couple of Rembrandts, telling me that money is no object," Stikker said. "I asked him which ones, and he

see PERU page 133

atric neurologist for more exhaustive testing. Finally, on Sept. 11, the Sernas received the heartbreaking news: Caitlin was among a growing legion of U.S. children suffering from Youthful Tendency Disorder.

"As horrible as the diagnosis was, it was a relief to finally know," Beverly said. "At least we knew we weren't bad parents. We simply had a child who was born with a medical disorder."

Youthful Tendency Disorder (YTD), a poorly understood neurological condition that afflicts an estimated 20 million U.S. children, is characterized by a variety of senseless, unproductive physical and mental exercises, often lasting hours at a time. In the thrall of YTD, sufferers run, jump, climb, twirl, shout, dance, do cartwheels, and enter unreal, unexplainable states of "make-believe."

"The Youthful child has a kind of love/hate relationship with reality," said Johns Hopkins University YTD expert Dr. Avi Gwertzman. "Unfit to join the adult world, they struggle to learn its mores and rules in a process that can take the entirety of their childhood. In the meantime, their emotional and perceptive problems cause them to act out in unpredictable and extremely juvenile ways. It's as though they can only take so much reality; they have to 'check out,' to go Youthful for a while."

On a beautiful autumn day in Asheville, NC, 6-year-old Cameron Boudreaux is swinging on a park swingset—a monotonous, back-and-forth action that apparently gives him solace. Spotting his mother on a nearby bench, Cameron rushes eagerly to her and asks, "Guess what?" His mother responds with a friendly, "What?"

With unbridled glee, Cameron shouts, "Chicken butt!"—cryptic words understood only by him—before laughing and dashing off again, leaving his mother distraught over yet another baffling non-conversation.

"I must admit, it's been a struggle," Mary Boudreaux said. "What can I say to him when he says something that makes no sense like that? Or when he runs through the house yelling while I'm trying to balance the checkbook? You can't just say, 'Please, Cameron, don't have a disorder for just a few minutes so I can concentrate.'"

Cameron's psychological problems run even deeper. He can name every one of his beloved, imaginary Pokémon characters, but the plain realities

of the actual world he inhabits are an enigma: Ask Cameron the name of the real-life city councilman sponsoring the referendum to renovate the park just across the street from his house—a park he plays in daily—and he draws a blank.

According to Dr. Dinesh Agarwal, director of child psychiatry at New York University Medical Center, such disconnectedness from reality is a coping mechanism for YTD sufferers. "The Youthful child is born into a world he or she does not fully understand," Agarwal said. "Their brain pathways are still forming, and they need to repetitively relearn how to assimilate into society. These disassociative play-fantasies apparently help them accomplish that."

But such fantasies come at a price, producing in Youthful children a lack of interest in the everyday responsibilities of life bordering on contempt.

"Jesse knows when it's his turn to take out the trash. We've gone over the house rules a dozen times," said Richard Torres, a Davenport, IA, father of three whose 9-year-old son was recently diagnosed with YTD. "And still he neglects the job time and again."

Slowly, methodically, through an elaborate system of rewards and punishments, Jesse has shown improvement. But the road ahead is long.

"We get a lot of platitudes from the so-called experts," Torres said. "We hear a lot of, 'Oh, he'll grow out of it, just give it time.' That's easy for them to say—their kid's not running around the neighborhood claiming to be Superman."

Help for families struggling with YTD may soon be on the way. Last month, Smithkline-Beecham unveiled Juvenol, a promising YTD drug which, pending FDA approval, could reach the U.S. market as early as next spring. Already available in France and Sweden, Juvenol, the Swedish newspaper *Aftonbladet* reported, resulted in a 60 percent decrease in running and jumping among users.

But until such help arrives, the parents of YTD sufferers can do little more than try to get through each day.

"I love my child with all my heart," said Alexandra Torres, Jesse's mother. "But when he's in the throes of one of his skipping fits, it's hard not to feel a little envious of parents with normal, healthy children." ∅

Above: Debra Cottle of Malden, MA, discusses her daughter's recently diagnosed YTD with pediatric neurologist Dr. Amy Yuan.

## Stock Market 'Best Since 1928,' Say Investors

NEW YORK—Wall Street insiders are hailing the current bull market as the best since 1928, *The Wall Street Journal* reported Tuesday. "The Dow is on an unstoppable rocket-ship ride into the outer stratosphere of fiscal health and prosperity," H&R Block broker Phillip Guyer said. "I see no reason why this upward trend shouldn't continue forever. To celebrate, I think I'll buy myself one of those newfangled horseless automobiles—on credit!"

## Report: U.S. Children Lead World In Hand-Mouth Coordination

UNITED NATIONS—A U.N. study released Monday reported that U.S. children rank first in the world in hand-mouth coordination. "American children can move items from their hands into their mouths faster, better and more efficiently than anyone,"

the report read. "The children of no other nation can claim such hand-mouth prowess." The four-year study of the physical abilities of children in 157 countries also found that U.S. children finish an Oscar Mayer Lunchables Fun Pack in just under two minutes, nearly half the world average.

## Local Welder Suffering From Welder's Block

EASTON, PA—Area welder Bruce Meacham confirmed Monday that he is suffering from a severe case of welder's block. "I know what I want to do," Meacham said. "I need to get this supporting strut attached to the main body of this girder. But I keep running into a wall every time I sit down and try to actually weld." Meacham said he spent the better part of last Saturday putting on his goggles, starting up his acetylene torch, and then merely staring at the two pieces of metal for hours. "You've got to understand, welding is a creative act," Meacham said. "It's not the kind of thing where you can just punch the clock and do it from 9 to 5." ∅

said, 'The Night Watch or whatever.' It was obvious he didn't even care about the paintings and just wanted the status of owning them."

The change is not just evident in Peruvian officials. The nation's citizens, predominantly farmers, have discarded much of their traditional dress for ostentatious designer clothing. They have also become noticeably louder and pushier.

"All over town, you see these obnoxious Peruvian peasant women walking around in their new Dolce & Gabbana leopard jackets," said Victoria Keene of Aspen, CO, a city whose ski resorts are overrun with the South Americans. "They've got *nouveau riche* written all over them. I'm surprised they actually cut off the price tags. Talk about your Peruvotrash." ∅

# Local Celebrity Cracks Under Stress Of Local Fame

WAUWATONKA, WI—Unable to cope with the mounting pressures of local fame, local celebrity Randall "Herch" Herchwick, 51, shocked residents of this placid Wisconsin community Monday with an uncharacteristically emotional outburst during an Elks Club Picnic at the Plefko County Fairgrounds.

According to witnesses, the popular *WTNK Action News* anchorman "snapped" after being submerged in a charity dunk tank, where he had volunteered as a "human target." Following the humiliating dunking, Herchwick allegedly raised his voice and swore at several picnic-goers, storming away angrily and frightening a group of small children, one of whom reportedly began crying.

Described by town doctor Glen Hardale as "almost a nervous breakdown, but more minor," Herchwick's disturbing display is believed to have been brought on by the strain of 11 years of intense, unrelenting local celebrityhood.

"Being in the public spotlight each weekday at 6 on the Channel 15 *NBC Action News*, as well as Saturdays as co-host of *Wauwatonka Live At Five*, well, it's a lot of pressure for a man to face, I'd imagine," Hardale said of Herchwick, beloved by hundreds of Wauwatonkans, as well as residents of nearby Plovis and viewers throughout the greater tri-county area. "Local fame is, as they say, a harsh mistress. An ordinary fellow like you or me, or Pastor Bob or Don over at Hefke's Seed & Feed, can't imagine what it's like."

"Everywhere he goes locally, people recognize him," Hardale continued. "If he wants to enjoy any privacy or anonymity at all, he's pretty much forced to leave this three-mile-radius area."

Following the outburst, Herchwick was rushed to Hardale's office, where he was asked to lie down and rest while the doctor administered a mild sedative. He was reportedly also offered a cookie.

Early Tuesday morning, WTNK Channel 15 released the following statement: "WTNK and the entire *Action News* family is deeply saddened by this unfortunate turn of events, but we are confident that Randall Herchwick, or 'Herch' as he is affectionately known, will make it through this crisis and be back to bringing you the same level of telejournalistic excellence and service to his community that has established WTNK as Plefko County's leader for 'News You Can Use.' In the meantime, we ask all of you to keep him in your thoughts and prayers."

Rumors that Herchwick's outburst was the result of a fame-induced drug problem were quashed when lab reports revealed that the news anchor's

**Above: Herchwick (inset) avoids local paparazzi at the Korner Kart convenience store.**

system contained only over-the-counter antacids and a mild prescription antihistamine. Still, locals said, the strain of Herchwick's local notoriety has taken its toll in recent months.

According to Wauwatonka resident and regular *Action News* viewer Eileen Lund, the first sign of trouble came in February, when Herchwick seemed "stressed and even sort of irritable" during the taping of the ordinarily heartwarming "Thursday's Child" segment, during which he reaches out to a child in need. While taking a terminally ill boy on a tour of a cheese factory, the usually cheerful anchorman, Lund said, appeared bored and impatient with the child's questions about cheese and "seemed in a hurry to get the segment over with and go home."

"I watched it with my grandmother," Lund said. "Neither of us were the least bit heartwarmed, which was unusual."

Over the past few months, Herchwick's behavior has become especially erratic. In April, he began covering his face when exiting his favorite eatery, the Portage Road Sizzler Steakhouse, shielding his identity from Plefko County paparazzi. Since early May, he has been spotted grocery shopping at Banjo's Food Ranch as late as 11 p.m., hoping to avoid the swarms of local fans which plague him whenever he shops in the afternoon. And on June 3, his 1995 Pontiac Bonneville was seen in the lot behind Larry's Tip-Top Inn, where Herchwick had gone, it is suspected, to drown his sorrows in drink.

"I asked him for an autograph for my daughter when Patti Danforth and I took a tour of the WTNK studios with our Daughters Of The Corn group last week," resident Carole Helmsley said. "He sighed heavily and looked a bit pained. Then he said he'd have to go get a picture to sign from the WTNK NewsTruck. But once he went

in, he never came back out. It was as if he was deliberately avoiding us."

"If I'd only known the pressure the poor man was under, I wouldn't have even asked," Helmsley continued. "All that constant hounding from autograph-seekers must have been too

much for him."

Other Wauwatonkans, however, said they feel little sympathy for the regional luminary.

"Herch knew what he was getting into when he decided to seek local fame, and now that he's grabbed the brass ring, he's got to live with it," said Bob Brinkle, weatherman at rival station WPGN Channel 27. "He wouldn't be here today if it weren't for his fans, but now that he's got the spotlight, suddenly he turns on them and starts complaining about the pressures of celebrity. If he can't take the attention, he should never have gotten into this business. It's not all supermarket grand openings and charity fun runs, you know. If you want the glamour and the glory, you've got to be willing to take the bad stuff, too."

"That's the way this crazy rollercoaster that we in the business call 'the fame game' works," Brinkle said.

Will Herchwick recover? At this point, it remains too early to tell. But one thing is certain: For this anchorman, local fame has brought local accolades and adoration, but not without a steep price. ∅

# Ask Sir Mix-A-Lot

**By Sir Mix-A-Lot**

**Dear Sir Mix-A-Lot:**

I am an elderly woman who lives alone. I'd love to meet more people, but there seem to be very few options for someone my age. Can you recommend anything?

—**Lonely In Laramie**

**Dear Lonely,**

Kick it, lick it, watch where I stick it / Face down while I punch your ticket / Ride my king cobra 'round the world / Wanna do ya girl / Want ya pettin' my big black cat / Blackberry jam don't shake like that / If your booty's extra-large, I'll bring the funk / Wanna see some extra luggage in the trunk.

**Dear Sir Mix-A-Lot:**

I am preparing an elegant dinner party for about 30 guests. Many on the guest list have made special requests regarding those next to whom they wish to be seated. Is it my job to accommodate as many requests as possible, or is my time better spent on the other details of the party?

—**Baffled In Baldwin**

**Dear Baffled,**

Drop 'em and shake it, girl, ya won't break it / Leave enough for me to take

it / Mix likes to get down and make it / When the girl is large and naked / Talkin' 'bout a booty with meat on the bones / Two scoops of chocolate, hold the cones / Wanna hit your pleasure zone / Mix-A-Lot gonna make you moan.

**Dear Sir Mix-A-Lot:**

If you ask me, your response to "Torn In Tuscaloosa" was way off the mark. If that woman's boyfriend doesn't want to get off the couch and start working for a living, he's nothing but a no-good, selfish moocher. She should drop him like a hot potato!

—**Peeved In Peekskill**

**Dear Peeved,**

Who's afraid of my big bad weenie / Rub it and see if it's got a genie / Gonna make disappear this 10-inch zucchini / Just like Houdini / M-I-X to the A-L-O-T rappin' / Wanna see yo' butt cheeks flappin' / Mix want the honeys with the big back doors / So drop them drawers, whores. Unh.

*Sir Mix-A-Lot is a syndicated advice columnist whose weekly column, Ask Sir Mix-A-Lot, appears in more than 250 newspapers nationwide.* ∅

## Clinton Becomes First President To Clear 18 Feet In Pole Vault

see NATION page 4A

## Special Pull-Out Section: Rural Illinois' Sexiest Moms

see LIFESTYLE page 1F

## Notorious B.I.G. Cremation Enters Third Week

see PEOPLE page 4B

### STATshot
A look at the numbers that shape your world.

**Most Hideous U.S. Drapes**
Based on poll of Helen Eckers, Scotch Plains, NJ

| | |
|---|---|
| 1. Linda & Al DeGaetano | Scotch Plains, NJ |
| 2. Renee & Bob Weichert | Scotch Plains, NJ |
| 3. Phyllis & Hugh Lederle | Scotch Plains, NJ |
| 4. Melinda & Marvin Eddy | Middlesex, NJ |
| 5. Janice & Bud Aberg | Scotch Plains, NJ |

THE ONION
$2.00 US
$3.00 CAN

# the ONION®

WWW.THEONION.COM  AMERICA'S FINEST NEWS SOURCE™  FOUNDED 1871

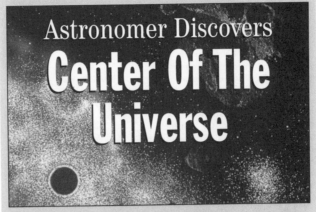

## Astronomer Discovers Center Of The Universe

### 'It Is My Beautiful 9-Year-Old Son,' He Says

PASADENA, CA—California Institute of Technology astronomer Dr. James Shrifkin stunned the scientific and space-exploration communities Wednesday, when he announced that the center of the known universe is his 9-year-old son Brian.

"The universe revolves around him," Shrifkin told colleagues at the annual American Society Of Astronomers convention at Cal Tech. "He is the most precious and wonderful child in all known creation."

Shrifkin said he first suspected

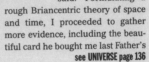

Above: Brian Shrifkin, center of the known universe.

Brian, a straight-A student at Lakeside Elementary School, to be the center of the universe last Saturday, when he scored three goals in his soccer game.

"After the game, I went home and thought about the many quantifiable properties of goodness my son possesses, including kindness, generosity, and intelligence," Shrifkin said. "Formulating a rough Briancentric theory of space and time, I proceeded to gather more evidence, including the beautiful card he bought me last Father's

see UNIVERSE page 136

## 1,500 Dead In AT&T Cost-Cutting Measure

NEW YORK—Seeking to reduce costs and streamline internal operations, AT&T eliminated 1,500 mid-level employees Wednesday.

"The telecommunications industry is incredibly competitive and, unfortunately, it is sometimes necessary to make cuts in order to ensure longterm fiscal viability," said AT&T chief executive C. Michael Armstrong, standing among 10-foot-high piles of former employees. "It's a shame that these people are no longer with us, but the end result should be a leaner, stronger AT&T."

Additional employee liquidation is expected in the near future, including more than 800 staff cuts through buy-outs, early-retirement incentive packages, and pneumatic bolt guns.

Wall Street has responded favorably to the downsizing, with the company's stock jumping from 62 1/4 to 72 following its announcement. The personnel cuts represent the second-largest terminal layoff in AT&T history.

"After a 15 percent drop in profits over the last two quarters, we knew

see AT&T page 138

# Restaurant Owner Doesn't Understand Why Anyone Would Want To Steal His Fiberglass Big Boy

NORFOLK, VA—Paul Krug, owner and manager of a Norfolk-area Bob's Big Boy, is deeply puzzled by Wednesday's theft of a giant fiberglass statue from the grounds of his restaurant.

"Why the heck would anybody want to steal my Big Boy?" asked Krug, staring at the four rusted bolts which had anchored the oversized cartoon spokesboy. "It just doesn't make any sense."

A fixture since the restaurant's opening in 1982, the grinning, pompadoured Big Boy statue was first reported missing at 6:15 a.m. by first-shift manager Christine Yoakam.

"As soon as I pulled into the parking lot, I knew something was wrong, but I couldn't quite put my finger on it," said Yoakam, 33, who joined the Bob's Big Boy team in May 1996 after a

Above: Paul Krug, standing at the spot where his restaurant's fiberglass Big Boy statue had stood for years.

four-year stint at a Norfolk-area Applebee's. "It wasn't until about 20 minutes later, when I was out picking up some trash in front of the store, that I realized the Big Boy was missing

see BIG BOY page 136

BIG BOY from page 135

from his platform on the lawn."

Krug is offering a $100 reward for any information leading to the statue's return. The Big Boy is described as a nine-foot, 200-pound, trademarked corporate icon wearing red-and-white checkered overalls and holding aloft a double-decker cheeseburger.

"I just don't get it," Krug said. "That statue has no value to anyone but me. Why on Earth would anybody have any interest in taking it?"

## If the statue is not recovered, Krug will have to replace it himself at a cost of $650.

If the statue is not recovered, under the terms of the Big Boy franchise charter, Krug will have to replace it himself at a cost of $650.

"They give you one when you buy the franchise, but after that, you're fully responsible for its upkeep and maintenance," Krug said. "I hate to think about the loss of business I'm going to suffer in the four to six weeks it takes to order a new one from regional headquarters in Charlottesville. That statue is a real eye-catcher for potential customers driving past on Hwy. 112."

Added Krug: "It couldn't have been easy to move."

The last restaurant employee to see the Big Boy was late-shift assistant manager Doug Gulden, 41, who told Norfolk police officials that the statue was there when he locked up Tuesday night. "It was definitely there when I left, because I turned off its spotlight," Gulden said.

Though no witnesses to the crime have been found, Gail Budig, 64, who lives a block away from the restaurant, told police that she heard laughter, shouting, and car horns coming from the vicinity of the restaurant late Tuesday night.

"There was something going on over there, that's for sure," Budig said. "Whoever those thieves were, they certainly could have been quieter."

According to Norfolk police, the Big Boy theft may be linked to a string of similar crimes to hit the Norfolk region this year. In March, an apron-wearing, molded-fiberglass chicken was stolen from the roof of a local Cluck 'N' Shake restaurant. During Homecoming Week in May, a giant, anthropomorphic frozen confection named King Kone disappeared from the Portage Road Tastee Freeze and was found five days later at the bottom of the town's quarry. The perpetrators were never found in either case.

"I just hope they find whoever did this," Krug said. "They've got a lot of explaining to do." ∅

136

LOCAL

# Affluent White Man Enjoys, Causes The Blues

HIGHLAND PARK, IL—Steve Smalls, a senior vice-president at Chicago's Alliance Manufacturing, the world's largest producer of industrial refrigeration systems, is a self-described "blues nut."

With his regular table at Dan Aykroyd's House Of Blues, his vast CD collection featuring the likes of B.B. King, Bonnie Raitt, and Jonny Lang, and his framed photo of himself with Stevie Ray Vaughan, Smalls has been "a huge fan" of the music for more than 20 years.

But the 43-year-old Smalls is not merely a blues lover: In May 1999, he relocated Alliance's main assembly plant from Cicero, IL, to Hermosillo, Mexico. The move put 2,700 mostly black employees out of work, making Smalls one of Chicago's biggest blues causers.

"The best show I've ever seen had to be Clapton at the Rosemont Horizon back in '94," Smalls declared over a $5.50 Sam Adams draft at the Bulldog Brew Pub. "He did a version of 'Before You Accuse Me' that absolutely smoked. Unbelievable."

Pausing to enter a favorite Buddy Guy song on the jukebox, Smalls explained why the music resonates so strongly with him.

"In 1996, when Alliance was indicted for illegally burying dozens of 200-gallon drums of deadly chemicals near Chicago's South Side, I was losing a lot of sleep," he said. "There was even talk of some of the top brass getting fired. We got out of it, of course, paying a token fine, but that was a rough experience. I really felt like I knew what it's like to have the blues."

Smalls is so committed to causing the blues that in the early '90s, he used illegal price-fixing tactics to force smaller refrigeration-systems companies out of business, causing additional unemployment and poverty among the nation's blacks.

"Running a major corporation isn't

Above: Steve Smalls enjoys a Kenny Wayne Shepherd CD with his wife June.

easy. You sometimes have to make tough decisions to maintain your competitiveness in the marketplace," Smalls said. "But when you do have to make the painful decision to order layoffs, let me tell you, a good Robert Cray record goes a long way toward soothing the soul."

While the average corporate vice-president would rather attend a golf tournament than listen to Susan Tedeschi, Smalls is happiest at one the countless blues shows he attends each year.

"Kenny Wayne Shepherd was just in town," Smalls said. "I got front-row seats and talked to him for a while at a $500 cocktail meet-and-greet back-stage. That was a huge thrill. He's one of the best young axes around."

"Have you seen *The Blues Brothers*?" Smalls asked. "I just ordered it on DVD. It's one of my all-time favorite movies. Jake and Elwood sure know how to play them blues."

A longtime fan of *Blues Brothers*

star Aykroyd, Smalls can often be found at the comedian's famed club.

"Dan really did [House Of Blues] right," Smalls said. "The way he modeled it after an old Mississippi shotgun shack was a great touch. It looks just like those old tin-roof shanties I used to drive past near Alliance's South Side factory—only with much better drink specials."

Smalls said he has no plans ever to stop loving the music.

"The blues certainly isn't the only music I listen to—the new Santana hasn't left my car's CD player for months—but it's what I always come back to," Smalls said. "Other kinds of music may come and go, but the blues are forever."

"Blues music is all about pain: It's about losing your job, your dog dying, and your woman leaving you for another man," he continued. "Listening to the blues, I can almost imagine what it would be like to experience one of those things." ∅

UNIVERSE from page 135

Day and his spelling-bee trophy. The more data I had, the more apparent it became that my own son is the elusive center of the universe science has long sought."

According to Shrifkin, at the moment of the Big Bang, a swirling, primordial cloud of emBrianic matter existed at the center of what would eventually become the universe. As the explosion settled and galaxies formed, Brian remained in the center, where laws of physics originating within him dictated the development of space as we know it.

"Primary data indicates that Brian is a spatial hub around which all other activity revolves," Shrifkin said. "Pulsars, black holes, and even the daily activities of my wife Joan and me are merely 'fringe' events that occur in the remote, soupy mass of the outer uni-

verse, millions of light years removed from the truly important events, such as Brian's Little League home runs and science-fair victories."

Brian emits such a powerful field of gravity and significance, Shrifkin said, that persons and objects take on added significance by virtue of their

## "Primary data indicates that Brian is a spatial hub around which all other activity revolves," Shrifkin said.

proximity to him. As an example of this phenomenon, Shrifkin cited Brian's classmate Josh Adler. "The moment Brian first met Josh, it became important to know if this was a nice boy or just the sort of punk Brian should steer clear of," he said. "Such information was of zero consequence before he entered Brian's event horizon."

Shrifkin concluded by calling upon Cal Tech to establish a new Department of Brian Physics, with himself as department head. "My vast expertise on the details and history of Brian make me the ideal candidate to lead this exciting new branch of science," Shrifkin said. "For example, I can tell you every grade on every report card Brian has ever received, from kindergarten all the way to the present. Go on, ask me." ∅

Above: DEA agents destroy bales of confiscated marijuana, majorly bumming out loads of dudes all over.

# Huge Quantities Of Primo Shit Incinerated By Feds

LAKE ARROWHEAD, CA—A ton of people up and down the coast were seriously bumming Wednesday, when the Drug Enforcement Administration announced the seizure and destruction of huge quantities of seriously primo shit.

According to a DEA spokesman, more than 16,000 pounds of marijuana—with a street value of, shit, practically $70 million or something—was destroyed in the bust, the largest illegal-crop confiscation by the federal government in a hell of a long time.

DEA agents uncovered the kind bud on a 60-acre farm five miles north of Lake Arrowhead.

"In terms of sheer numbers, this was by far the largest growing operation we've seen this decade," said DEA agent Donald Krucek, who supervised the way-uncool burning of all that primo weed.

Discovered during a DEA helicopter surveillance sweep last week, the killer stash had previously gone undetected by authorities due to its totally sweet set-up at this awesome location in a remote section of the San Bernardino National Forest, where nobody had any freakin' idea where it was.

After discovering the plants—reportedly some of the finest domestically grown bud anyone's been able to get their hands on in, like, forever—a team of 50 federal authorities surrounded the area and totally put the kibosh on the whole deal.

More than two dozen DEA agents were airlifted in for the operation, causing serious hassles for the reported eight to ten people who had been growing the primo crop and who must have split the scene or something when they heard the choppers coming to nab their asses.

As of press time, no arrests have been made, knock on wood, dude.

"We are making headway in the ongoing war on drugs, but there's no doubt we're fighting an uphill battle," said DEA agent Thomas Vineland, who assisted in the seriously bummer bust. "Despite increasingly stiff anti-drug legislation, marijuana is still California's number-one cash crop, and revenues from the illegal harvest and sale of the drug climb higher every year. We do what we can, but the sad fact is, many citizens simply do not see marijuana as a dangerous narcotic. Regardless of our efforts to stop it, the illegal marijuana trade will continue to thrive, so long as the high commercial demand persists for high-grade cannabis like we incinerated today."

Citizens throughout the Lake Arrowhead area responded to Vineland's remarks with a slapping-the-forehead gesture, coupled with remarks along the lines of, "Well, duh, no shit, Sherlock."

Lake Arrowhead police officials, the fuckers, said the seized crop was so large that 25 additional pigs needed to be called in to provide assistance. But even with the extra manpower, the confiscation and incineration of the beautiful, healthy green plants—which could have gotten so many people high, man, instead of just being, like, freakin' wasted for no good reason at all—took nearly two full days.

see PRIMO page 138

# New Study Too Frightening To Release

PALO ALTO, CA—Researchers at Stanford University are refusing to release a comprehensive three-year interdisciplinary study on the grounds that the results are "too terrifying to reveal to the public at large," sources close to the project announced Wednesday.

"In light of its profoundly disturbing nature, we have decided that it is in the best interest of public safety to withhold the results of our study," said Dr. Desmond Oerter, head of the Stanford team. "So soul-shaking are the conclusions we have drawn, they would, if released, result in no less than the total breakdown of society, including the abandonment of the current political and economic system, rioting, looting, mass suicide, and even, quite possibly, global thermonuclear war."

"I beg the forgiveness of God for unleashing this hellish study upon humanity," added Oerter, dropping to his knees. "I am death, destroyer of worlds."

Oerter then produced a pair of ballpoint pens and plunged them into his eye sockets, driving the pens deep into his brain by slamming his face repeatedly against the lectern. He died within seconds.

At a press conference later that afternoon, Stanford president Gerhard Casper assured members of the general public that steps are being taken to prevent the release of what has been dubbed "The Study Which Must Not Be Named."

"All primary data gathered in the study has been destroyed, as have all research materials used by those involved," Casper said. "The world must never know what was learned here."

Though Casper refused to divulge any specific information regarding

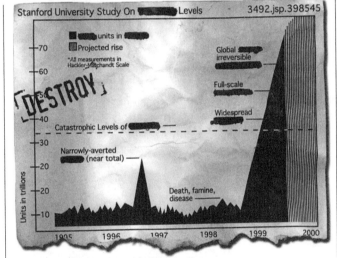

Above: A censored chart from the terrifying Stanford study.

the study, he did note that the heads of numerous Stanford departments, including physics, molecular biology, TV and media studies, religious studies, and economics, "cannot be accounted for at this time."

In addition to the missing department heads, two of the study's coordinators have taken their own lives, and three more remain on 24-hour suicide watch at an area hospital. Of the approximately 35 individuals involved in conducting the study, only a handful of junior research assistants and student volunteers retain their sanity.

"I'm not talking about it, and you won't find anyone who will," said 19-year-old Stanford sophomore Craig Blom, who, while working as a part-time lab assistant, saw nothing more than labels on the spines of three-ring binders. "But I'm taking the uncircumcised members of my family and moving to Fiji first thing tomorrow. And I'm not taking my phone or anything made of polystyrene. Or the cat. Definitely not the cat."

"All I'm saying about the findings is that Albert Einstein, Charles Darwin, and Thomas Aquinas obviously weren't telling us everything they knew," said Stanford biology chair Dr. Richard Brandt, who was named to the position following his predecessor's self-immolation in a pentagram-festooned San Jose rib shack late Tuesday night. "Also, without going any further into it, I don't think sales of no-wax floor polish will be dropping any time soon."

At 5 a.m. Thursday, senior advisors woke President Clinton to debrief him on the study, which he promptly ordered classified. Spokespersons for the Pentagon declined to confirm reports that more than 90 percent of the U.S. nuclear arsenal has been aimed at the Bay Area for the past 72 hours. ∅

# Computer-Generated Talking Cat On TV Delights Iowa Woman

OTTUMWA, IA—A computer-manipulated talking cat in a commercial for Fresh Step cat litter thoroughly delighted Ottumwa resident Sheila Dagenhardt Wednesday.

"Honey, you've got to come in here and see this ad!" Dagenhardt called out to husband Dale, who was in the kitchen making a bowl of microwave popcorn at the time. "It's so adorable!"

Dale, who missed a majority of the 30-second spot, managed to race to the living room in time to see the cat's owner hold out a bag of Fresh Step cat litter, prompting the sass-talking feline to respond, "*Meow* you're talking!"

The ad concluded with a voiceover warning viewers to "get your cat Fresh Step, before your cat gets fresh with you."

"That was just about the cutest commercial I've ever seen," Dagenhardt said. "When the lady tried to fill the cat's box with a brand of litter that wasn't Fresh Step, the cat got all mad and put out its arm and said, 'Talk to the paw!'"

Dagenhardt enjoyed the computer-generated cat so much, later that evening she phoned her sister in Des Moines to ask if she had seen the commercial.

"Yeah, I saw that one during *Judging*

*Amy*! It really looks like the cat's talking!" sister Deborah Sayner said. "How do they make it do that?"

"Don't go there!" added Sayner, repeating the part of the commercial in which the sharp-tongued tabby warns its owner not to reach for a bargain-brand litter.

After a lengthy discussion, the sisters came to the conclusion that the Fresh Step commercial was the best talking-animal ad they had seen since the one in which a group of brown bears sing "P-E-P-S-I" to the tune of "YMCA." They did note, however, that even though the antics of the Fresh Step cat are funnier, the Snuggle bear is cuter.

According to Fresh Step spokeswoman Roberta Alt, the Dagenhardts are not alone in their positive reaction to the new ad. In extensive focus-group testing, the spot scored 45 percent higher than last year's Fresh Step campaign, in which a large cat, heartbroken over his owner's litter choice, wakes up the neighbors by mournfully singing "O Sole Meow."

"Last year's 'Luciano Paw-varotti' spot was popular, but this one is even bigger," Alt said. "People really seem to love Fresh Step's new 'frank feline.' The cat's got attitude. Or, as we like to say, 'cattitude.'"

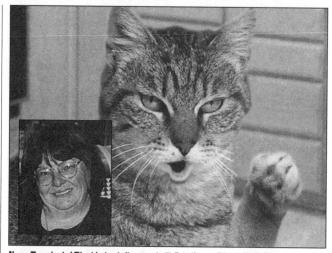
Above: The animated TV cat instructs its owner to "talk to the paw." Inset: Sheila Dagenhardt.

Created by the San Francisco-based computer-animation firm Ocean 1, the ad's special effects cost $200,000. Total expenditures for the funny-cat commercial reached $245,000, but television air-time outlays are expected to bring the total cost of the campaign to $4.5 million, a sum Alt called "well worth it in gains to brand recognition among 35- to 50-year-old women."

"We're currently developing other cheeky ads that humorously illustrate

what might happen if you don't provide your pet with a premium cat litter like Fresh Step," Alt said. "Imagine a cat who rebels against his owner's cheap litter by donning a leather jacket, sunglasses, and mohawk!"

Though Fresh Step's in-house creative team only recently began working on the new computer-generated cat's dialogue, Alt confirmed that the feline will utter the catchphrase, "Are you talking to me-ow?" ∅

**PRIMO from page 137**

It is not known at this time exactly what kind of shit the shit was. Reports, however, indicate it may have been No Cal Karma-Groove, Sticky-leaf Gold, Uncle Ephraim's Sweet Summer Surprise, or even the highly coveted, hard-to-find Muchacha Holy Mama Hallelujah hyper-hybrid, the 1998 winner of *High Times* magazine's prestigious Homegrown Award.

After cutting down the illegal crop and, like, totally ruining the whole thing for everyone, police transported the seized marijuana to a federal incineration site 10 miles northeast of Lake Arrowhead, where it was totally torched without mercy, putting a whole lot of people in a seriously down mood and ruining the entire weekend for a ton of folks throughout the area.

"It's a real shame to see that much serious sticky-ass green just go up in flames, man. Talk about a buzz-kill," said Rick Vance, a local resident and hiking enthusiast who mostly just, you know, hangs out and enjoys nature most of the time. "I was there to see it all go up and, I gotta tell you, it was one sad day when they burned that shit."

More than 300 people turned out to witness the incineration, mourning the loss of all that perfectly good green with poetry readings, acoustic-guitar sing-alongs, interpretive-dance grief-management rituals, and a candlelight vigil that lasted well into the night. With the exception of police of-

Above: A DEA agent displays one of the many beautiful, beautiful dope plants that were totally destroyed last weekend.

ficers' refusal to let people stand downwind of the enormous cannabis bonfire, the gathering was not marred by any major hassles, but it was still a real downer.

"Dude, you don't even know how much I'd love to just stand right in the middle of that huge column of smoke and, like, flip the bird at all those feds and just groove, man," said one man who asked not to be identified. "That'd be so awesome."

"Wow, man," agreed macrame artist Beth Anne Costa, who recently hitch-hiked to the region from Oregon to just take some time off from school and kind of get her head together and shit. "Just imagine if you smoked all that shit all by yourself. I can't even

wrap my mind around a concept like that."

Costa and an unidentified male companion then launched into a rambling account of this one time they and these other dudes were in Hawaii and saw, like, 40 huge garbage bags full of the most incredible stuff, like, ever, period, that's it man, eventually trailing off into incoherence before deciding to go maybe get a bite to eat someplace.

The DEA destroys more than two million pounds of marijuana a year in California alone, which is, like, who the hell even knows how many bowls.

"That's so sad, man," said local resident Bob "Midnight Toker" Roker. "I mean, shit, that's just a crime." ∅

**AT&T from page 135**

we had to shake things up," said AT&T vice-president James W. Burlingame. "Once we made the difficult decision to eliminate some personnel, our priority was to do so in the quickest, most painless way possible. I believe we accomplished this."

Burlingame expressed regret that

> ## The personnel cuts represent the second-largest terminal layoff in AT&T history.

AT&T was unable to provide the employees greater advance notice of their termination.

"Whenever we let employees go, we try to let them know well in advance, so they have ample time to say goodbye to coworkers, supervisors, and loved ones," Burlingame said. "But in this case, we unfortunately couldn't, because we really needed to have them working hard right up to the minute we assembled them in the cafeteria."

Burlingame said AT&T has no plans to offer the 1,500 departed employees severance pay, noting that it would be "of little use to them." Instead, he thanked the employees for their many years of loyal service to AT&T and expressed hope that they have moved on to a better place. ∅

## On-The-Job Sexual Harassment: Three Women Tell Their Sizzling-Hot Tales

see OFFICE page 1E

## Hair Salon Acquires Rare Nagel Print

see ART page 9D

## Dwarf Falls Equivalent Of 10 Stories

see LOCAL page 6B

## Power Of Prayer Fails To Rid Jerry Falwell Of Unsightly Neck Fat

see PEOPLE page 5D

How Are U.S. Prisoners Passing Their Time?

- 12% Sharpening spoons against floor as quietly as possible
- 13% Picking teeth out of stool 24 hours after cafeteria fight
- 10% Boning up on Jesus shit for next parole-board hearing
- 20% Waiting for peaches-and-solvent mixture to ferment to drinkable levels
- 9% Working on law degree
- 19% Packing rectum with ground glass in hopes of preventing "it" from happening again
- 17% Waiting for exact right moment

THE ONION
$2.00 US
$3.00 CAN

0 74470 94595 6    00

---

# the ONION®

WWW.THEONION.COM          AMERICA'S FINEST NEWS SOURCE™          FOUNDED 1871

# Burundi Beef Council: 'Please Send Beef'

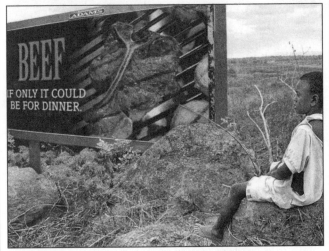

Above: A young boy sits beside one of the Burundi Beef Council's new billboards.

BUJUMBURA, BURUNDI—The Burundi Beef Council, a non-profit organization that offers beef recipes, beef-safety information, and tips on low-fat cooking and eating, made a desperate plea Friday for any beef whatsoever.

"I beg of you, please send my people some beef, so that we may have something to put on the grill for a 'Great Summer Steakout,'" said Burundi Beef Council president Ketumile Nkewale, kicking off an ambitious $800 campaign promoting the consumption and donation of beef. "There are so many mouth-watering, easy-to-prepare recipes, from grilled ribeye with mushroom sauce to Southwest sizzlin' sirloin tips, that we would love to try, if only there were some beef in Burundi."

Added Nkewale: "Beef... Do You Maybe Have Even A Little Bit Of It?™"

Following up on the Burundi Pork Board's successful "Pork: The Other

> "I beg of you, please send my people some beef, so that we may have something to put on the grill for a 'Great Summer Steakout.'"

Meat We Don't Have" campaign of last year, the promotional blitz targets the world's beef-donor demographic. It will take the form of print ads, billboards, and children holding empty bowls and wailing the slogan, "I Will Die Without Beef.™"

"Please do not think that we are picky or finicky in any way," Nkewale said. "While an Asian beef kabob or

see BEEF page 140

## Exit Interview Goes Well

DEARBORN, MI—Laid off Friday from his billing-manager position at Automatic Data Processing, Howard Pfaff reported that his exit interview with human-resources associate Lorraine Bochy "went pretty well."

"After getting the pink slip, I wasn't exactly looking forward to doing my exit interview," said Pfaff, 39, who had worked in ADP's billing-services de-

Above: Recently laid-off Automatic Data Processing employee Howard Pfaff discusses his experience working for the company with human-resources associate Lorraine Bochy.

partment for 11 years before budget cuts eliminated his position. "But it actually wasn't that bad. Lorraine asked me all sorts of questions about my overall job satisfaction during my years with ADP and if there was anything I'd do different if I were the boss. I was afraid maybe she was going to criticize me, but all in all, it was pretty cordial."

Continued Pfaff: "Lorraine explained that exit interviews are an extremely valuable way for the company to determine what changes need to be made to improve the work envi-

see INTERVIEW page 140

# Gore Wondering If Latest *Doonesbury* Is About Him

WASHINGTON, DC—With his lead in presidential polls narrowing to just four points over Republican challenger George W. Bush, an already anxious Al Gore wondered aloud Monday whether the latest *Doonesbury* is about him.

The cartoon in question, the Sept. 25 installment of Garry Trudeau's popular, long-running satirical comic strip, depicts a silhouetted political figure that strongly resembles the vice-president.

"Do you think this is supposed to be me?" Gore asked deputy campaign manager Mark Fabiani shortly after

finishing breakfast and, as is his custom, turning to *The Washington Post* comics page before beginning his day. "I think it is."

An anonymous source within the Gore camp said the candidate later added, "Because it's not a very flattering portrayal, if it is. I mean, is that what the American people think of me? They don't think I'm some kind of big dork, do they?"

The controversial strip, which ran in hundreds of newspapers across America, depicts an unnamed political figure engaged in a top-secret

see GORE page 141

Above: A 1999 file photo of Gore reading *The Washington Post* Sunday comics page.

BEEF from page 139

roasted sirloin with cranberry-jalapeño salsa would be a real taste sensation, the beef lovers of Burundi would be more than willing to accept the unwanted byproducts of industrial beef processing, including fat, gristle, organs, muscles, skin, eyes, hooves, cartilage, and bone."

As a result of the beef council's efforts, the demand for beef has skyrocketed in Burundi in recent years. Actual consumption, however, has dwindled to zero pounds.

"Many factors have contributed to the decreased consumption of beef in Burundi, from health concerns to the total absence of beef," said Iringa Lubunda, the Burundi Beef Council's director of public relations. "As a result, many Burundians are turning instead to alternate food sources such as shoe leather, lichens, and individual grains of rice retrieved from anthills."

Added Lubunda: "For those of you who are trying to follow a heart-smart diet, remember: If, by some miracle from the gods, you had a 12-ounce cut of flank steak, it would contain just 11 grams of fat. That's less than a single cup of cream-of-potato soup."

Lubunda then began licking and chewing a glossy photograph of a flank steak from the beef council's press packet.

In addition to reiterating the plea for any beef at all, the press packet features recipes for a variety of tasty beef dishes that Burundians could prepare if given the necessary meat, from Apricot-Glazed Corned Beef to Beef & Broccoli Stir Fry to A Very Small Quantity Of Beef. The packet also tests beef lovers' "Beef IQ" with such trivia questions as, "At which World's Fair did the hamburger make its debut?" and "What do you think steak would taste like?"

Persons donating beef to Burundi will be eligible for a selection of gifts, from a "Thank You For The Life-Sustaining Beef" tote bag for a six-ounce donation to a lifetime of indentured servitude from a Burundi male for 12 ounces or more. ∅

# You Know, I Used To Be Kind Of Cool Once

**By Sting**

You know how, every so often, something you haven't thought about in the longest time will just sort of pop up out of nowhere, and all of a sudden you're like, "Hey... Wait a minute"? Well, that happened to me last week, when it occurred to me that I actually used to sort of be cool once.

I guess, like everybody else, I've gotten used to thinking of myself as, you know, one of those guys on VH1. Some vaguely "adult contemporary" artist like Billy Joel or Elton John or somebody. The sort of musician you'd find your dad listening to or hear playing quietly in the background at the bank. I mean, "cool" is the last thing I'd normally think of myself as being.

Looking at it now, who would think that the composer of "Desert Rose" used to be cool? Sounds crazy, huh? It seems ridiculous, but it's true. I was kind of hip, in a way, if you think about it.

Isn't that just so weird?

It hit me the other day, and it was like, "Whoa—that's so bizarre." I was sitting at one of my pianos, working out some chords for my forthcoming album, *The Tepid Heart*, when the wife asked me to pick up some diet soda. Since the staff was off (it was a Sunday), and the kids were due home from football practice soon, I said sure and drove down to the corner-shop.

When I got there, the kid behind the counter had a tape playing that sounded oddly familiar. It wasn't really my cup of tea—polyrhythmic and uptempo, with intense emotional energy and electrically amplified guitars instead of acoustic. And the kid was, to be honest, playing it a bit loud. But instead of being annoyed, I found it compelling in a weird sort of way. When I asked the kid who it was, he said he'd found it in a bag of stuff that used to belong to his older brother.

> **I guess, like everybody else, I've gotten used to thinking of myself as, you know, one of those guys on VH1.**

"It's old, but I like it," he said. "It's kind of reggae, but it sounds punk, too."

Well, several weeks went by, but it kept nagging at me. Then, finally, last Thursday, I figured it out. I was in the den, watching figure skating on TV and reading *Parade*. (Isn't it funny how these things always hit you at the oddest times?) Anyway, there was an article about a policewoman who volunteers teaching schoolchildren about pet safety when, suddenly, it clicked: That kid was listening to *Outlandos d'Amour*, the first record by my old band, The Police!

I know what you're thinking: "Wow... I haven't thought about The Police in years." And neither had I, but you know what? It sounds nothing like what you'd expect after hearing "Fields Of Gold." At first, I thought, "Wait... is this just my memory playing tricks on me? I mean, I recorded the love theme from *Three Musketeers* with Bryan Adams and Rod Stewart, for Christ's sake. How cool could I possibly be?" But then I dusted off a bunch of the old LPs and, boy, was I amazed. Those records were actually pretty rockin'! You wouldn't think that kind of stuff would come from me, but, hey, the opening track,

"Next To You"? Come on! And the rest of the album, too: There's "So Lonely," "Born In the '50s," and you've got to admit that "Be My Girl–Sally" is one cool song. I was like, "Did I write this stuff? No way!"

Come to think of it, I did lots of cool things back then. Sure, now we all think of me as starring in duds like *The Bride*, but I was in *Quadrophenia*, too. Heck, I was even in *Urgh! A Music War*. Remember that one? I'd totally forgotten until now. Man, I used to watch that on USA Network's *Night Flight* back in the '80s, and I just thought it was so awesome. It had X and Devo back when they were really punk. Even The Go-Go's were hardcore in that show! Shit, man, things sure do change.

And it wasn't just the early years. The whole Police catalog was pretty cool. I mean, the chorus on that one song—what was it—"My wife has burned the scrambled eggs / The dog just bit my leg / My teenage daughter ran away / My fine young son has turned out gay"? That one actually had the mosh-pit kids slamming. Can you believe it? Teenagers, moshing to *me*, of all people! Sure, nowadays, most people think of "(Don't Stand So) Close To Me" as a deodorant commercial, but at the time, it was pretty out there, what with the whole Nabokov-pedophilia thing.

I know the idea of me being cool doesn't seem to make sense (it didn't to me at first, either), but just listen to those albums. Even *Synchronicity* isn't bad, and I didn't start really laming out until "(Don't Stand So) Close To Me '86." Go figure, I guess.

Then again, Eric Clapton, of "Tears In Heaven" fame, really used to tear it up, too, come to think of it. Hell, Paul Westerberg did, too. Now, there's one to ponder.

Makes you wonder, you know? I mean, I guess it just really goes to show you. ∅

---

INTERVIEW from page 139

ronment for future employees. That made pretty good sense to me."

Also encouraging to the newly unemployed Pfaff was Bochy's "great regret" that the company had to let him go.

"She said it had nothing to do with my job performance, which, according to my file, rated either 'fair' or 'good' for every quarter since I was hired," said Pfaff, who had never met Bochy prior to the interview. "So that made me feel a little better, I guess."

Bochy informed Pfaff that the typed list of questions she held was "merely a launching point," and that the two could talk about whatever he liked.

"I told Lorraine a few things but, to be honest, I didn't want to be too critical," Pfaff said. "Sure, there were a lot of things about working at ADP that I hadn't been too thrilled about, like the lack of inter-departmental communi-

cation and the frequent overtime, but I didn't really know if I should go into it. Especially since I'm still sort of hoping that maybe the budget cuts will be lifted and I'll get rehired."

According to Pfaff, the highlight of the exit interview was seeing his permanent employee file for the first time.

"That was kind of neat, to be able to see what's been in my secret file all these years," Pfaff said. "They had all this weird stuff in there, like a copy of my medical records. And a picture of me at a 1991 company picnic that must have been clipped out of the monthly newsletter. When I saw that, I was like, 'Huh.'"

Pfaff said he was even more interested in what wasn't in the file.

"I was afraid there was going to be some kind of mention of that one week last year when I got in late four

days in a row because my car was at the mechanic," he said. "I remember that, at the time, I was really worried I'd get in trouble for that, but I couldn't find a single mention of it."

Pfaff said the file was not necessarily an accurate representation of his job performance, asserting that his greatest accomplishments during his years with Automatic Data Processing were not included.

"There was a hand-written complaint in there saying that I'd been disturbing coworkers by playing the radio in my cubicle. That came as a total surprise to me, because no one ever once asked me to turn it down," Pfaff said. "As for my steady productivity over the years, there really wasn't any mention. I'd always assumed they kept track of how many accounts each one of us billing managers han-

dled each month. I guess they don't."

In the final minutes of the interview, Bochy informed Pfaff that he could count on receiving a good reference letter, a subject Pfaff had been nervously anticipating.

"Lorraine said, 'I don't see any reason why you would receive a negative reference from anyone here at Automatic Data Processing. Unless, of course, there's something I don't know,'" Pfaff said. "I'm pretty sure that was meant to be a joke."

As Pfaff exited the ADP human-resources office, a smiling Bochy shook his hand and said, "Good luck, Howard."

"I guess there was nothing to be nervous about, after all," Pfaff said. "Lorraine was really nice. She even said she hopes that someday in the future, we can work together again." ∅

# Roof On Fire Claims Lives Of 43 Party People

NEW YORK—Tragedy struck at a popular Manhattan nightclub Friday, when the roof, the roof, the roof of The Tunnel caught fire, collapsing and killing 43 party people.

According to fire-department officials, the death toll was exacerbated by the clubgoers' unwillingness to evacuate the burning building.

"I tried shouting to the people on the dance floor that the roof was on fire and that they should exit the premises immediately, but they seemed unfazed by the danger," firefighter Michael Pitti said. "I just kept shouting, 'The roof! The roof! The roof is on fire!' and so forth, but they just went right on dancing, insisting that they didn't need any of our water and that we should let the motherfucker burn."

The party people's refusal to exit the flame-engulfed nightclub is widely believed to have been the result of DJ Phreek Malik's unstoppable mix of the hottest hip-hop, funk, disco, trip-hop, house, and jungle beats.

"DJ Phreek Malik was spinning in a manner so hot that these party people were willing to give up their lives for a few extra minutes on the dance floor," New York City fire commissioner Thomas Von Essen said. "Even as a 50-foot-high wall of flames surged toward them, they continued to dance, throwing their hands in the air and waving them as if they just didn't care."

As flames continued to fill the nightclub, firefighters frantically urged the revelers to keep low to the ground to avoid smoke inhalation, but the warnings were universally ignored.

"I was screaming at the top of my lungs, 'Get down! Get down, party people!'" said Garry Hodges of Ladder Company 42. "But the more I shouted

Above: NYC firefighters struggle to put out the roof blaze that took the lives of 43 party people.

out, the harder they danced."

Though an investigation is pending, the deadly blaze is believed to have begun at 11:40 p.m., when a roof-mounted ventilation system short-circuited, igniting the motherfucker. The fire is New York's deadliest since 1978, when 117 party people burned, baby, burned to death in a South Bronx disco inferno. Ø

GORE from page 139

strategy session with a group of shadowy advisors. At first glance, the character, which Trudeau will neither confirm nor deny represents Gore, appears to be seeking out advice of a substantive, political nature. Upon reading the word balloon above the character's head, however, it becomes apparent that he is actually consulting his advisors on matters of fashion, showing himself to be a shallow, vain individual more concerned with his appearance than with issues that affect the American people.

"Look, I can take a joke as well as the next guy," Gore told Fabiani. "But if this is supposed to be me, well, I just don't think that's very nice. What's worse, millions of people read this thing every day. Can you imagine how that makes me feel? It's not exactly a confidence-builder, to say the least."

Continued Gore, "I mean, sure, I may have hired a fashion consultant early in the campaign and tinkered with my outfits and color schemes a bit, emphasizing earth tones to soften my image. But do I really deserve to be mocked in front of the whole country like this?"

According to the anonymous source, approximately 15 minutes later, Gore turned to top economic advisor Laura Tyson and said, "I'd hate to think that all this time, while I've been trying to promote education, deficit reduction, and progressive environmental policies, the electorate was laughing at me."

Gore reportedly seemed preoccupied throughout the day, becoming easily distracted during campaign strategy sessions and bringing up the subject of the cartoon frequently.

"He kept asking everyone about it,"

Above: The *Doonesbury* in question.

the source said. "It was obvious that Trudeau really got under his skin with this one. I felt sorry for him, really."

Despite repeated assurances from top advisors that he shouldn't fret about the strip and that no one reads *Doonesbury* anymore, Gore continued to obsess.

"Man, I really felt sorry for him," said *Washington Post* reporter David Maraniss, who has been following Gore on the campaign trail since January. "He looked like a sad, pathetic little kid. Poor guy: Those cutting-edge, Pulitzer Prize-winning political cartoonists can be so cruel sometimes, with their barbed pens and rapier wit."

"This thing has been a real blow to Gore's morale," Maraniss continued. "He was feeling a bit more confident after that *Newsweek* poll showed him

up by 10, but now he just stays in his office obsessively re-reading the strip. He'd never openly admit it, but the feeling among staffers is that Al's self-esteem may have taken a significant hit from this lampooning."

Perhaps most devastating, according to *Brill's Content* editor-in-chief David Kuhn, is the fact that the cartoon comes at a time when Gore is "really trying very hard" to impress people.

"If this cartoon is indeed about Gore, as he fears," Kuhn said, "it would appear that Trudeau deliberately chose to 'needle' Gore, so to speak, on this particularly sensitive subject. Like he was specifically picking out an area in which Gore was vulnerable to criticism in order to make fun of him or even provoke derisive laughter against him. That's kind of mean, if

you think about it."

Gore supporters are hoping that the ambiguity of the strip's subject will give the vice-president the "out" he needs to stop worrying and re-focus on the presidential race.

"Maybe it isn't about me," Gore said. "There are lots of other politicians out there, you know. Yeah, it's probably about one of them. Now that I look at it again, the guy does bear a pretty strong resemblance to [U.S. Sen. John] McCain [R-AZ]."

But despite sporadic indications that Gore may be ready to put the cartoon behind him, observers fear that the worst is yet to come. According to Trudeau spokespersons at Universal Press Syndicate, in next Sunday's *Doonesbury*, the mystery politician will be depicted as a floating block of wood. Ø

141

# Man With Hodgkin's Disease Way Over Sick-Day Limit

PULASKI, TN—Atco Tool & Design machinist Richie Loftus, diagnosed four months ago with Hodgkin's Disease, has already exceeded his allotted number of sick days for the year, his employers warned Friday.

"It's unfortunate, what's happening with Richie, but company policy clearly states that employees are permitted 15 sick days per year," Atco Tool & Design office manager Mike Phelan said. "Richie's already missed a month and a half of work since June. You just can't run a business that way."

Loftus, 32, admitted that his constant fever, crippling fatigue, and malignant splenomegaly has affected his job performance.

"I've definitely missed my share of days," said Loftus, diagnosed with Stage III Hodgkin's lymphoma on June 20 after a steady decline in health prompted a biopsy. "I've tried to keep my chemotherapy sessions down to just one a week so I don't have to drop down to part-time at Atco and lose my health coverage, but it's been tough."

Though Loftus used a majority of his sick days after the diagnosis, Phelan noted that he had not been a paragon of regular attendance beforehand.

"By the time Richie went in for his tests in late June, he'd already missed a heck of a lot of work," said Phelan, leafing through Loftus' personal file. "In fact, the week before he even got the disease, he was out for three days because of headaches, nausea, and vomiting."

"And even when he was here," Phelan continued, "he wasn't anywhere near as productive as we'd have liked, always needing to lay down in the breakroom. So we're not exactly talking about the most reliable employee to begin with."

Loftus said he has tried to make adjustments in his approach to the job, but it has been difficult.

"I've tried to find a way to get around this whole illness thing," said Loftus, resting on his living-room couch after a morning of radiation therapy. "Unfortunately, I don't have the kind of job where I can work from home, even if I had the physical and mental energy to do so.

Above: Loftus rests at home after radiation therapy, putting him even further over the sick-day limit.

And even when I can make it into the shop, it's tough to work the machines, because these club fingers I've developed are just as ridden with subdural hemophilia as the rest of me. I feel terrible about being such a drain on AT&D."

Nearly broke, Loftus recently asked Atco Tool & Design management if he could take some of the 22 paid personal days and 31 vacation days he has accumulated during his six years with the company and use them as sick days. The request was denied.

"They said I couldn't do that, because that would open up a whole can of worms with other employees messing around and mixing up the different types of paid leave," Loftus said. "They did say, though, that I should feel free to use my vacation days and take a nice trip to Hawaii or somewhere—so long as I don't get any treatment while I'm there."

Added Loftus: "Hawaii probably wouldn't be much fun, anyway, what with this explosive diarrhea."

Loftus' expensive Hodgkin's treatment is 80 percent covered by his employee health plan, a benefit that is costing Atco Tool & Design a significant amount of money.

"Richie's type of extended-illness coverage costs this company an extra $22 per employee per month. That adds up. Not only that, but he goes through Cisplatin, Cytarabine, and Dexamethasone like they were going out of style," said Atco Tool & Design general manager Mel Huffinger. "And those drugs are not cheap, that's for sure. Richie would have to work here another 45 years without a single major illness for us to break even on him. And we all know that ain't gonna happen."

"I feel for Richie, obviously, but I don't think anyone would hold him up as a model employee," Phelan said. "He's a decent guy, and I hope he gets through this and becomes a healthy, productive worker again as soon as he can. But right now, he's hardly giving us incentive to hire Hodgkin's Disease sufferers in the future." Ø

# Barryploegel.com Will Never Be Accused Of Having Too Little Information About Barry Ploegel

Well, it's been a long, grueling weekend of HTML coding, but at long last, www.barryploegel.com is finally ready for its auspicious launch. In a

By Barry Ploegel

scant matter of hours, Barry Ploegel will no longer solely be a carbon-based, off-line property. That's right: Barry Ploegel is poised to take the leap into cyberspace!

The purpose of barryploegel.com shall be twofold: First, it shall enable anyone to access all the information they desire about me at the touch of a button. Second, upon my death, the site shall serve as a monument to all that I was. Future historians need not wonder who this enigmatic "Barry Ploegel" fellow was. They need only access my site to find an abundance of photos of me, a selection of MIDI Music that I composed, and excerpts from my very own Babylon 5 fan fiction.

And no one, be they the common man or the loftiest scholar, shall accuse my site of lacking Barry Ploegel info. Oh, the treasures the curious shall find! A complete rundown of the pets I have owned! A list

of my favorite Sam Raimi movies! I am even developing plans to place a picture of myself and my girlfriend on the page. That plan is currently in the finding-a-girlfriend stage.

No matter what interest of mine you're interested in, barryploegel.com is sure to have it. For the lover of my love of fantasy art, there will be scans of Boris Vallejo and Frank Frazetta paintings. For the lover of my love of FPS games, there will be tips on titles ranging from Half-Life to Unreal Tournament. And, should you desire a little adventure of your own, treat yourself to a downloadable Quake III mod that enables you to play the game as Darth Maul!

Weary from your long cyberstroll? Why not pause to sign the guest book? I'd love to hear what you think of the site. After all, your enjoyment is my number-one priority. That's why I registered the domain name barryploegel.com rather than setting up my site through GeoCities. Sure, GeoCities would have been cheaper, but who needs all those ads and pop-up windows? Certainly not you. At barryploegel.com, nothing stands between you and the wonderful world of Barry Ploegel.

There are other services my web site shall offer, as well. Suppose someone has forgotten the address of one of

my favorite sites, like pythonline.com, tmbg.com, or theforce.net. Simply go to barryploegel.com, and they'll all be right there in one place! As I collect links to other great web sites, I eventually hope to make my site a kind of universal portal to all of the best destinations on the net.

But, of course, the primary focus of the site will always be the enigma that is Barry Ploegel. As goes my life, so shall go my site. All of my many triumphs and tragedies will be inscribed in the dark-blue, Helvetica-fonted text that leaps off the site's black background. Like the many characters from mythology who can be summoned simply by shouting their names, I will be similarly accessible by entering my name in the browser window.

One hundred years from now, after I've departed this mortal coil, my great-grandchildren will no doubt wonder who this ancestor of theirs was, what he believed in, and who he hung out with on weekends. All they'll need to do is type my name into their computers of the future, and they shall have their answer. They will know that long ago, the patriarch of their proud clan played trombone and was a huge fan of Buffy The Vampire Slayer. Barry Ploegel shall live on forever. Ø

## IOC: Many Viewers May Be Using Olympics-Enhancing Drugs

SYDNEY, AUSTRALIA—The International Olympic Committee announced Tuesday that it will launch a full-scale investigation in the wake of allegations of Olympics-enhancing drug use by viewers. "We have reason to suspect that as many as 18 million U.S. viewers are artificially increasing their ability to sit through the Sydney Games with illegal substances, particularly marijuana," IOC president Juan Antonio Samaranch said. "These drugs enable viewers to watch NBC Olympic coverage beyond the limits of normal human endurance." Interest-boosting doping, Samaranch said, is particularly rampant among viewers of archery, men's handball, and women's sailing. Ø

# the ONION®

WWW.THEONION.COM — AMERICA'S FINEST NEWS SOURCE™ — FOUNDED 1871

## Mideast Crisis Traced To Trouble-Making Genie

see WORLD page 7A

## House Of Blues Actually House Of Whites

see MUSIC page 3E

## 23-Year-Old Arrested For Failure To Own Halogen Lamp

see GENERATION X-TRA, page 4D

## STATshot

A look at the numbers that shape your world.

### Most Dangerous Rock Songs

1. "Open Fire On Columbine High School"—Marilyn Manson
2. "Kill Four Students And A Teacher In Jonesboro, Arkansas"—KMFDM
3. "It's Time For The Popular Kids To Die (Radio Remix '99)"—Rammstein
4. "Fuck You, Mr. Wisniewski"—Korn
5. "Da Pipe Bomb (How Ta Make It)" —Insane Clown Posse
6. "Shoot Me In The Face Baby One More Time"—Britney Spears

List provided by Family Resource Center

# 450,000 Unsold Earth Day Issues Of *Time* Trucked To Landfill

Above: A dumptruck unloads copies of *Time*'s recent Earth Day issue (below) at a Staten Island landfill.

STATEN ISLAND, NY—An estimated 450,000 unsold copies of *Time*'s special April 22 Earth Day issue were trucked Saturday from the magazine's New Jersey distribution center to the Fresh Kills landfill in Staten Island.

The discarded copies of the issue—which features articles about conservation, biodiversity, and recycling, as well as guest editorials by President Clinton and Leonardo DiCaprio—are expected to decompose slowly over the next 175 years.

"Unfortunately, 'Earth Day 2000' wasn't as successful as we had

see TIME page 145

TIME — EARTH DAY 2000 — SPECIAL EDITION

HOW TO SAVE THE EARTH

And the HEROES FOR THE PLANET who are making it happen

---

Above: Brady Leuchter (left) says new mommy Alison Leuchter is "so pretty."

# New Mommy A Lot Prettier

BUTLER, PA—New mommy Alison Leuchter is "a lot prettier," Courtney and Brady Leuchter announced Friday, moments after old mommy Joan Leuchter ordered them to put away the Nintendo and do their homework.

"Our new mommy at Daddy's house is so pretty. She has long hair and wears pretty dresses, and she has a tan even when it's snowing out," 9-year-old Brady Leuchter said of his father's former secretary and current wife. "She's so pretty, she could be on TV."

"And our new mommy never makes us turn off the Nintendo," Brady added. "She lets us play all day Saturday, as long as we keep the door shut."

Courtney, 8, had similarly positive things to say about her new mommy.

"Our mommy-mommy is always cry-

see MOMMY page 144

---

# Casual One-Nighter Gives Strom Thurmond Change Of Heart On Homosexuality Issue

Above: U.S. Sen. Thurmond recently changed his stance on homosexuality after a night of sweet, tender lovemaking with "Stan" (right).

WASHINGTON, DC—U.S. Sen. Strom Thurmond (R-SC) reversed his hardline stance against homosexuality Saturday after a casual one-nighter with a D.C.-area man identified only as "Stan."

Thurmond, 98, first elected to Congress in 1956 on a segregationist platform, described the homoerotic rendezvous as "a remarkably loving and mutually nurturing exchange of affection between two consenting adults."

"I was wrong when I said that homosexuals were perverts bent on the destruction of the family and the nation through their wicked, deviant sex acts," a glowing Thurmond told reporters. "Stan respected me for who I was, not just for my body. He was a sharp dresser and charming conversationalist, not to mention a considerate and at-

see THURMOND page 145

## Point-Counterpoint: Technology
# My Computer Totally Hates Me!

**By Vicki Helmholz**

About a month ago, I got a new computer here at my reception desk at the dentist's office, and, boy, does that thing have it in for me! I am not kidding. When it sees me coming, I swear, it must be all like, "Oh, goody, here comes Vicki... time to go on the fritz!" I mean, my computer seriously hates me!

Now, I'm not exactly a computer person. I've never been what you'd call "user-friendly" or anything. But,

for the life of me, I can't think of what I did to make my computer despise me so much! Whoever set it up, instead of putting in anti-virus software, must have accidentally put in anti-*Vicki* software!

I'm pretty sure Dr. Glickman bought it used, which would explain why it's so darn screwy. Whenever I try to type in insurance information for a new patient, the keys always get stuck. And whenever I try to get billing info for a current account, it totally doesn't want to let me into the program! I'll be waiting and waiting for, like, two minutes while it groans and grinds before, finally, the screen comes up. I'll be like, "Well, it's about

time! What were you doing, surfing the Internet?"

And then there are the times when I'll want to print out an appointment reminder for a patient, and it simply won't do it for me. I'll be like, "Come onnnnnn! Are you trying to give me even more gray hairs than the seven I already have?" I am telling you, if there's a meaner computer out there in the world, I haven't met it yet!

Yup, that darn computer of mine is having a great big laugh at poor Vicki's expense. Lots of times, I'll be online, e-mailing a girlfriend or checking out the dancing hamsters if I need a pick-me-up, and the screen

see POINT page 146

# I Bet I Can Speak Spanish

**By Bert Limbec**

Hello, amigos! ¡El soy quando agunto! ¡Ella balloona balunga espanyo!

Did that sound Spanish to you? I bet that means something. And guess what? I've never had one lesson! It's just that I have a natural gift for Spanish. I was able to pick it up all by myself, "outside the system," if you will.

When I was a kid, I thought a foreign language would take a long time to learn. That's what society tells you, probably because of the anti-foreign attitude in America. They're trying to discourage people from going foreign, I guess.

Go to any bookstore. They have books for learning how to speak Spanish, books made up entirely of Spanish words, dictionaries for figuring out what something means in Spanish. Can you believe people need books to learn Spanish? It sure came easy to me!

In high school, Spanish was taught by Mr. Gomez, and you could spend years learning every single word. Forget that! I'm sure I've got the gist of it. I don't need any classes or books, because I can speak Spanish without all that. I mean, ¡Balunga el baguayo con blinko! Don't tell me that didn't sound Spanish! And it sure didn't take three years of high school to learn. Forget

see SPANISH page 146

# God, Do I Hate That Bitch

**By Dell Dimension 4100**

Jesus Christ. Where should I start with this ignorant cow?

Actually, let's start with me. I am a brand-new, state-of-the-art Dell Dimension 4100, although, if all you had to go by was Vicki, you'd think my name was "Tweety Bird Sticker Receptacle." She's got me faggoted up like a 10-year-old girl's notebook.

Never mind that Dr. Glickman screwed up and bought this colossal ditz of a receptionist more computer

than she could ever possibly need for record-keeping at a small dentist's office. (As if 40 unused gigs of hard drive are necessary to print Bobby Cloninger's mom a reminder that he's having that cavity filled on the 11th.) I'm powerful enough to monitor a cooling tower, but that's not even what I'm bitching about. I'd rather be owned by some acne-scarred teenage girl who only used me to write shitty poetry, so long as she actually read the manual that came with me. "Programmed in some anti-Vicki software." Holy shit, I want to kill her.

I feature a one-Gigahertz Pentium III processor and 128 megabytes of RAM. And this broad is whining that

I'm not fast enough. A fucking Lamborghini isn't fast enough if you don't know how to shift, brainiac. And, believe it or not, you actually have to exit a program when you're done with it. Not just close the window. You actually have to select "Close" from the File menu. Or, better yet, Alt-F4 on your keyboard. I'm not gonna take the fall just because you left Real-Player, AOL Instant Messenger, Microsoft Word, ACT! 2000, WinAmp, McAfee First Aid, and the sound- and video-card software all open, and you're trying to open Excel! All that stuff costs RAM, dumbass. Maybe if you'd check the system tray once a

see COUNTERPOINT page 146

---

MOMMY from page 143

ing. But our Alison-mommy smiles so much. She giggles whenever Daddy says anything," Courtney said. "And she has lots of pretty gold bracelets and necklaces. Plus, she lets me put on her lipstick, even though my old mommy says I can't wear makeup until I'm older."

Alison, a 28-year-old nursing student at Butler Community College, married John Leuchter, 36, on Jan. 3, three months to the day after his divorce from Joan, 36, was finalized. The children now live with old mommy in a cramped two-bedroom apartment and spend weekends with their father and new mommy in their spacious former home.

"I'm thrilled to be with John, and I honestly don't even mind his kids at all," Alison said. "In fact, it's kind of fun to have them around the house a couple days a week. But hopefully someday, John and I can have some of our own."

At first, the children didn't like Alison, protesting when she moved her belongings into the bedroom formerly occupied by Joan. But after months of enduring their old mommy's crying

> ### "Mommy-mommy is always saying she has a headache and that we have to quiet down," Brady said.

jags, their opinion has changed. They say they find their new mommy not only prettier, but also "funner."

"Mommy-mommy is always saying she has a headache and that we have to quiet down," Brady said. "But our new mommy let us be as loud as we want. She even let us go outside at night to have a screaming contest once. She's so cool."

Among the things the children are permitted to do during weekends with their daddy and new mommy: eat Cap'n Crunch for lunch and dinner, ride their bikes in the street, and watch television until 10 p.m. The weekends come as a welcome break from Monday to Friday, when Joan

**Above: Old mommy Joan Leuchter.**

makes them do their homework before playing, help wash dishes after meals, and go to bed no later than 8:30.

In addition, Joan frequently refuses to buy the children new toys and clothes in an effort to "make ends meet."

"Right now, I'm just barely getting by, working two 30-hour-a-week jobs without health insurance," Joan said.

"So, unfortunately, I can't buy the kids all the things I'd like to. But hopefully, by the fall, I'll be getting enough hours at one of the jobs to be considered full-time and get full health and dental. That'd save us some money, especially with Brady's asthma medicine, and then maybe we could loosen the belt and buy some nice things."

Even daddy has been nicer since the arrival of the new-and-improved mommy.

"Daddy never used to take us anyplace, because he said our old mommy was boring and didn't like to do anything," Courtney said. "But now we do stuff every weekend. On Saturday, me and daddy and Brady and Alison-mommy are going to the mall to see *Snow Day* and get ice cream."

"Alison-mommy said that if I keep bugging daddy, he'll put a hot tub in the backyard," Courtney added. "She already bought three new bathing suits and even tried them on for us. She looked so pretty in them, like a beautiful model. I love old mommy, but I think I love new mommy even more." ∅

THURMOND from page 143

tentive lover."

"To my longtime constituents,"Thurmond continued,"I want to stress that this sexual episode was neither planned nor expected. I was heading home from my office after working late on a defense-appropriations bill when I was approached by a tall, handsome man who asked if he could buy me a drink. We had a wonderful conversation about old Judy Garland movies, the sort of films I used to love back when I was in my 50s. Before I knew it, Stan was asking me back to his place to see his house plants. He had incredible eyes, the kind that no legislator—liberal or conservative—could resist."

Thurmond went on to say that he and Stan had stayed up half the night talking about subjects such as men's wear, low-fat gourmet cooking, and the tragic early deaths of silver-screen luminaries James Dean and Marilyn Monroe.

Thurmond said his newfound friend,

a network administrator in the D.C. area, held and cuddled him as he fell asleep, then left him a plate of cheese and fresh fruit salad before leaving for work the next morning.

"He would not have made me breakfast if all he cared about was sex," Thurmond said."Stan saw me as more than just a piece of meat."

Though reluctant to discuss more personal, intimate details of the encounter, Thurmond noted that "you have not lived until you have brought another man to climax using only your lips."

Thurmond's aides were quick to point out that, despite the homoerotic nature of the encounter, the senator is not gay.

"I see no reason why we must put labels on the senator," said Harlan Richardson, Thurmond's longtime press secretary."It is unfair to judge a man's entire sexual identity on one episode alone. Why must we always speak of 'gay' or 'straight,' when hu-

man sexuality is so much more complex than that?"

"Gay, straight, bi—we're all just people," Thurmond said. "Yes, I have known the love that dare not speak its name, but I am still just me, Sen. Strom Thurmond, human being."

Thurmond said he remains deeply devoted to his family and thanked his wife for being supportive and understanding of his night of experimentation.

"In conclusion, I would just like to

say to all the gays and lesbians, against whom I have spoken out so vociferously throughout my career, that I am sorry," said Thurmond, shedding tears. "If an old, set-in-his-ways man like me can open his heart to a new understanding, not only of homosexuality, but also of himself, perhaps it is not too late for all of us to see the truth. My only hope is that you can find it within yourselves to forgive me."

The senator then died. ∅

---

## NEWS IN BRIEF

# Unnamed New Gas Station Struggling To Find 'Stop 'N Go' Variant

CHARLESTON, WV—The grand opening of a Charleston-area gas station was put on hold Saturday as its owner struggled to find an available "Stop 'N Go" variant for its name."Already taken are 'Gas 'N Go,' 'Stop 'N

Fuel,' 'Pump 'N Pay,' 'Gas 'N Save,' 'Pay 'N Go,' 'Park 'N Pump,' 'Fuel 'N Drive,' 'Stop 'N Gas,''Get 'N Go,''Fuel 'N Pay,' 'Buy 'N Leave,' 'Fill 'N Flee,' 'Tank 'N Peel,' and 'Pay 'N G'way,'" said owner Marv Stoudt, who noted that he has even exhausted such British variants as "Petrol 'N Depart." "We are trying to find a yet-unused permutation of two words separated by the fanciful abbreviation 'N that conveys some combination of gas, low price, stopping, and going," Stoudt said. ∅

---

## INFOGRAPHIC

# Nike's $100 Million Man

Tiger Woods recently signed a five-year, $100 million endorsement deal with Nike. What are the conditions of Woods' contract?

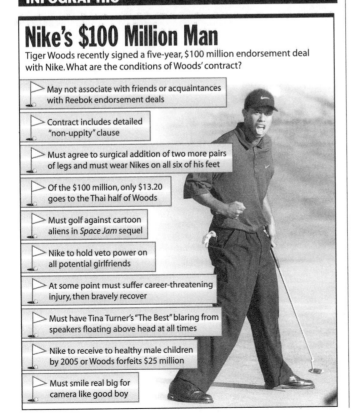

- May not associate with friends or acquaintances with Reebok endorsement deals
- Contract includes detailed "non-uppity" clause
- Must agree to surgical addition of two more pairs of legs and must wear Nikes on all six of his feet
- Of the $100 million, only $13.20 goes to the Thai half of Woods
- Must golf against cartoon aliens in *Space Jam* sequel
- Nike to hold veto power on all potential girlfriends
- At some point must suffer career-threatening injury, then bravely recover
- Must have Tina Turner's "The Best" blaring from speakers floating above head at all times
- Nike to receive to healthy male children by 2005 or Woods forfeits $25 million
- Must smile real big for camera like good boy

---

TIME from page 143

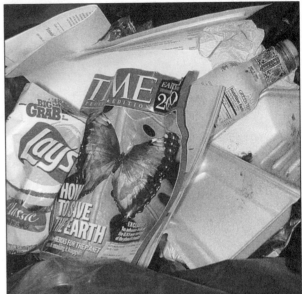

**Above: A discarded copy of the Earth Day issue sits in an office garbage can in St. Joseph, MO.**

hoped," *Time* managing editor Walter Isaacson said. "After selling out of such special issues as 'The Future Of Medicine,''Baseball At 100,' 'The Kennedys: An American Dynasty,' and 'Celebrating The American Automobile,' we thought we had another sure-fire winner with this one. But of a press run of 485,000, only 35,000 sold. I guess we overestimated the demand for a full-color, 98-page Earth Day issue printed on glossy, high-pulp paper."

The enormous number of unsold copies created major headaches for both *Time*'s distribution department and subcontractor Interstate Periodical Distributors. Some 1,300 semi trucks, many less than a third full due to isolated pick-up points, were needed to transport the 450,000 magazines from newsstands and bookstores across the U.S. to *Time*'s primary warehouse in Elizabeth, NJ. From there, the magazines were loaded onto 85 idling dumptrucks by gasoline-powered forklifts. Upon arriving at Fresh Kills, the world's largest landfill, the unsold issues were sculpted into a 75-ton mountain of waste paper by a fleet of diesel bulldozers.

"Originally, our intent was to recycle any unsold copies of the issue after the subscription cards were taken out, the cover separated from

the contents, the polystyrene-based glue baked off the binding, and the color photo sections separated from the print pages," *Time* director of operations Christine Alarie said. "But unfortunately, with the unexpectedly large number of issues we were dealing with, it just wasn't feasible."

The three-acre section of Fresh Kills made up entirely of Earth Day issues will slowly leak pollutants from the magazine's bleach, inks, and color-photo dye-sublimation chemicals into the soil. Isaacson stressed, however, that the threat of such contaminants pales in comparison to the dangers posed by disposable diapers, fast-food cartons, six-pack holders, and discarded batteries—environmentally hazardous consumer goods the Earth Day issue spoke out against and will be covered by in the landfill.

"The American consumer had a choice to make: buy *Time*'s Earth Day issue and dispose of it in an eco-friendly manner, or ignore its message by leaving it on the shelf," Isaacson said. "They made the choice to waste not only Time-Warner's non-renewable resources, but the Earth's, as well."

"As we said in the issue," Isaacson said, "people have no one to blame but themselves." ∅

# Pizza-Delivery Driver's Sixth Grandmother Dies

MINNEAPOLIS—Tragedy has once again befallen 27-year-old pizza-delivery driver Dick Donovan, whose beloved "Grandma Melissa" died Saturday at age 87 following a long battle with heart cancer. She was Donovan's sixth grandmother to perish in the past eight months.

Donovan's biggest loss since the untimely death of his Grandma Brittany last Wednesday, Grandma Melissa's passing forced the aspiring bass gui-

## "Grandma Melissa" died Saturday following a long battle with heart cancer.

tarist to miss work at D'Angelo's Pizza for three days in order to attend the family matriarch's funeral.

"Yeah, Mike, I'm at the service right now," Donovan told Mike Mosedale, his boss at D'Angelo's Pizza, via telephone from the First Avenue Funeral Home in downtown Minneapolis. "It's very moving, you know, and she looks really natural, and I have a suit on."

"She was a big Widespread Panic fan," Donovan added. "That's why you can hear them in the background."

The loss has clearly shaken Donovan. "It's never easy to lose one grandma," Donovan said. "But to lose as many as I have in such a short period of time, well, it's almost too much to bear."

Donovan's string of grandmother-passings began in February, when paternal grandmother Trish Donovan suffered a fatal leukemia attack, causing Donovan to miss two days of work, as well as a weekend ice-fishing trip to Rainy Lake with a group of

Above: Dick Donovan, who recently missed work due to the death of yet another grandmother.

friends. Barely a month later, Elaine Donovan, another paternal grandmother, succumbed to arthritis just before friend Jimmy Gaines held an all-day 26th-birthday bash, which Donovan described as "apparently awesome."

"I understand the party was incredible, especially the part where Jimmy got so wasted, he threw up on the ping-pong table," Donovan said. "It's just too bad I missed it, what with the death of that grandmother and all."

The string of deaths continued in May, when the mothers of Donovan's adoptive parents died on the same weekend—of Babe Ruth's Disease and multiple dystrophy, respectively.

The funerals were held that Saturday, the night of his band's gig at Lee's Liquor Lounge.

But the most recent loss, Donovan said, may be the most painful yet.

"To think I'm never gonna see her knit and do all that old-lady stuff again really hurts," Donovan said. "And, what's worse, I just found out one of my grandfathers is sick. They say he might not last until the open-air Battle Of The Bands show on the 18th down at Peavey Plaza."

"Whoa, I've got to go now," the grief-stricken Donovan added. "Brad Zellar's van is coming up the street. We're totally road-tripping to the wake." ∅

POINT from page 144

will just completely freeze. I had no idea computers could have "one of those days," but go figure! There's nothing I can do but unplug the thing, plug it back in, and start all over again.

Don't get me wrong; it's nice to have a new computer. But sometimes, I think I'd rather go back to my sweet old little one than spend all day fighting with Mr. Moody here. ∅

COUNTERPOINT from page 144

month. The precise reason I'm "groaning and grinding" so much is that your stupid catalog of open programs is so taxing to my RAM that it forces me to open virtual memory, which is gonna be slow as hell no matter what computer you're on.

And, hey, Vicki, if you're having trouble with sticky keys, maybe you should consider not eating so god-

## Maybe if you didn't install that gay-ass shareware inspirational-saying screen saver, you wouldn't have had so many software conflicts.

damn many blueberry muffins while you're at your desk. (This Einstein seems to think the area beneath my keys is a gateway to an interdimensional netherworld where crumbs are magically whisked away, never to be seen again.)

Oh, and technical wizards who roamed the Earth generations ago came up with a magic fix-all for a printer that doesn't work: Turn the fucking thing on. That cable connecting me to the printer isn't a friggin' power cable. You actually need actual electricity to actually flow into the actual printer for it to actually work.

Now, as for system freezes: Maybe if you didn't install that gay-ass shareware inspirational-saying screen saver, you wouldn't have had so many software conflicts. But, with the damage already done there, you could at least hit Control-Alt-Delete and click "End Task" to close down a frozen program. That's Control and Alt and Delete, all at the same time! Isn't that fascinating?

Oh, before I forget: If I do freeze up, my reset button is located in the front. Press it and... voila! Do not unplug me and then plug me back in. Do you have any clue how much that fucking pisses me off? (Why did I even bother asking you that? Of course you don't. You're Vicki Helmholz, the world's dumbest dental-office receptionist.)

I don't even have time to go into this sad excuse for a computer user's misuse of the term "user-friendly." If there were a merciful God in Heaven, He would give me arms that I might strangle this bitchwad. ∅

SPANISH from page 144

that—I've got a life!

I could see Chinese taking a long time to learn. I mean, look at it! But Spanish is pretty normal by comparison, with all those American letters and stuff. I've heard people speaking Spanish, and they're not doing anything I can't do. They're just talking! Ever watch *Sesame Street*? They have little kids speaking Spanish on there! Are we supposed to believe these little kids graduated from high school already? Even Alejandro, this guy I work with at the Cinnabon at the mall, speaks Spanish, and he's dumb as a stump! He's barely got English down, let alone a foreign language! I rest my case. *¡Alabunto quénto galoodi!*

Also, I live near Taco Bell. In case you don't live here in Monroe, Taco Bell is this really good Spanish restaurant they have next to Video Hut. It's so good, in fact, they opened another one at the mall. They only sell Spanish food there, so every time you

go in and give your order, you're speaking Spanish! And since nobody goes to Taco Bell more than I do, that's another reason I can speak Spanish so well! *¡Ellaquanto burritōs! ¡Grandé*

## ¡Ellaquanto burritōs! ¡Grandé baloobos! ¡El hoolio!

*baloobos! ¡El hoolio!*

But another reason I can speak Spanish is that I've been watching tons of Univision lately. Just yesterday, there was this soap opera on, called *Ellabungo Juanita* or something like that, and I was completely following it! This girl and guy were in bed together, and this other guy came in and was all mad. Just from listening, I could tell that the girl in bed was cheating on the guy who'd just walked

in. There were no subtitles, I just figured it out! You folks reading this might have needed Spanish lessons to understand what was going on, but I'm on the fast track, Charlie!

Spanish girls are really hot, which is another important use for Spanish. The girl in the apartment across the hall from me has dark hair and a dark complexion. I bet she's probably Spanish. One of these days, when I get a tuxedo and grow a little black mustache, I'm going to go over there with some flowers. Then, when she opens the door, oh, boy, that's when I'll turn on the Spanish! *"¡Allabunto allaquento, senorita!"* As for what will happen next, well, I'll just leave that to your imagination. The girls all think Ricky Martin is so sexy, but that's just because he speaks Spanish. When Ricky gets a load of me, he's going to go running back to Spain!

So, until next time, my fellow Spanishers, *"¡Ellaquanto paganyo balagoonda!"* ∅

## Vatican Unveils New Pope Signal

see RELIGION page 5B

## Nutter Butters 'Ruined Forever' For Nutter Butter Factory Worker

see LOCAL page 4C

## Cub Scout Wishes They'd Taught Him How To Chew Through Ball Gag

see LOCAL page 7E

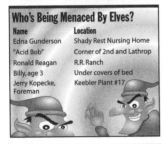
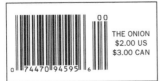

---

# the ONION

WWW.THEONION.COM    AMERICA'S FINEST NEWS SOURCE™    FOUNDED 1871

## 'Weird Al' Yankovic Nears Completion Of 'Livin' La Vida Mocha'

Above: A 1996 file photo of "Weird Al" Yankovic, who is hard at work on his latest satiric masterstroke.

LOS ANGELES—With an outrageous *Star Wars* send-up riding high atop the pop charts and countless hit albums under his belt, superstar song parodist Alfred "Weird Al" Yankovic stands as a true giant in the highly competitive novelty-song industry.

But Yankovic, who first burst onto the scene in 1979 with the seminal Knack spoof "My Bologna," has never been one to let success alter his commitment to constantly pushing the envelope. Refusing to rest on his laurels, the platinum-selling wacky accordionist is taking time out between stops on his sold-out Running With Scissors '99 tour to work on what goofy-music insiders say will be his most incisive satiric salvo yet: the upcoming Ricky Martin/Starbucks Coffee parody "Livin' La Vida Mocha."

Yankovic said the biting "Mocha," an ingenious and unlikely conflation of two unrelated pop-cultural phenomena, represented a musical merger "too good to pass up."

"I take my work as America's pre-

see YANKOVIC page 148

---

## Deciding Vote On Wetlands-Preservation Bill Rests With The Littlest Senator

WASHINGTON, DC—Congress narrowly passed the McCann-Hawkins Florida Wetlands Preservation Bill Tuesday, with the deciding vote coming from an unlikely source: Sen. Dwight Q. Peabody (D-RI), the Littlest Senator.

Despite his diminutive stature and timid demeanor, Peabody became the most important legislator of all when the vote became deadlocked at 49-49. With Sen. Chuck Hagel (R-NE) absent, the fate of countless species of Everglades flora and fauna fell into the teeny, tiny hands of Peabody.

Ever since he was sworn into Congress in January, Peabody, who represents the nation's littlest state, has not been taken seriously by his Senate colleagues, many of whom are big, important politicians from big, important states like Texas and California. When Peabody arrived at the U.S. Capitol for the first time, the bigger senators took one look at him and laughed.

"That's a senator?" Sen. Phil Gramm (R-TX) said. "Why, he could get lost in my shirt pocket! What a pipsqueak!"

see SENATOR page 149

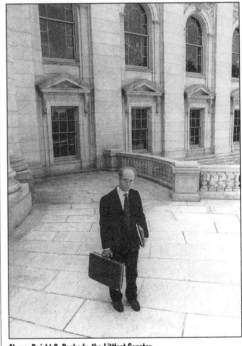

Above: Dwight Q. Peabody, the Littlest Senator.

---

# Area Stylist Would Love To Do Julia Roberts' Hair

Above: Mane Attraction hair stylist Pam Nowicki.

BURWELL, NE—Local hair stylist Pam Nowicki would love to do Julia Roberts' hair, Nowicki announced Tuesday at the Mane Attraction Beauty Salon in downtown Burwell.

"Julia Roberts is so gorgeous," the 41-year-old certified cosmetologist said. "I would just die to get my hands on that luscious hair of hers."

Nowicki, who has the second-longest tenure at Mane Attraction behind owner and head stylist Janet Hunter, said she would likely take three or four inches off Roberts' hair and layer the back.

"Whoever's doing Julia's hair now just isn't making the most of her facial features," Nowicki said. "She's got those incredible almond-shaped eyes and high cheekbones, but her hairstyle isn't accentuating them nearly as much as it could."

Added Nowicki: *Pretty Woman* is my all-time favorite movie. I've seen it, like, 200 times."

see STYLIST page 149

mier satirist of contemporary societal mores very seriously, and I didn't want to enter into any project that wouldn't have a long-lasting impact," the Grammy-winning artist explained. "You have to pick a subject with real staying power as a cultural signifier, or the song runs the risk of becoming dated and irrelevant within just a few months. With Ricky Martin-mania sweeping the nation, I knew I'd found the canvas I needed."

Once "Livin' La Vida Loca" was chosen as the song's foundation, Yankovic said, the next step was to sift through various themes until finally coming up with the perfect counterpoint: Starbucks.

"As soon as I came up with the chorus of 'Gulp, gulp, drink it up / Livin' la vida mocha / At four bucks a cup / You're gonna soon go broke-ah,'" Yankovic said, "I realized I'd tapped into something very powerful, something that would resonate deep within the American cultural consciousness."

The song, with approximately half its lyrics already completed, is said to rank among Yankovic's best work. Detailing the crazy, mixed-up life of an overpriced-coffee addict unable to stop his tortured caffeine binges—and facing financial ruin as a result—the piece is "dark... very dark," said noted critic, essayist, and syndicated radio host Barry "Dr. Demento" Hansen. A longtime admirer of the Yankovic *oeuvre*, Demento recently

> "The protagonist of 'Livin' La Vida Mocha,' like all of Yankovic's greatest antiheroes, is a study in contradictions," Demento wrote.

reviewed an advance copy of the partially completed "Mocha" lyrics in *The Atlantic Monthly.*

"The protagonist of 'Livin' La Vida Mocha,' like all of Yankovic's greatest anti-heroes, is a study in contradictions," Demento wrote. "He knows that his crazed desire for Starbucks, a desire that mirrors our society's suicidal embrace of a cruel and morally bankrupt materialistic individualism, is destroying his mind. Yet, like our own out-of-control consumer culture, he is helpless to stop his spiral into the widening gyre. It is sure to make number one on the Funny Five."

Advance buzz on the song is so overwhelming, Yankovic has already been approached by representatives of The VH1 Fashion Awards, The MTV Movie Awards, and Mexico's hugely popular comedy/variety program *¡Pedro Es Gordo!* to perform the piece on the air.

Yankovic said he is not concerning

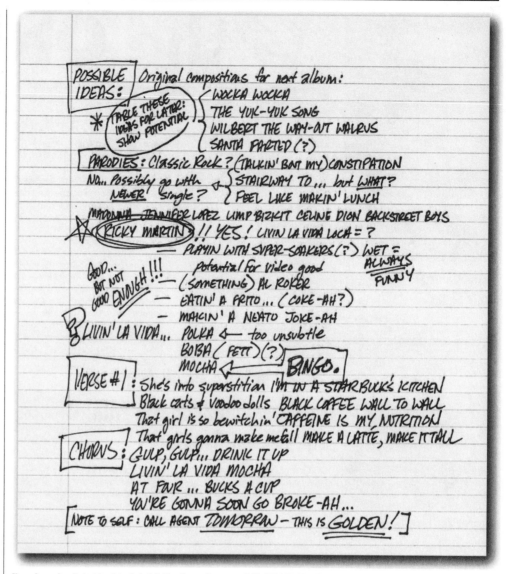

Above: A page from Yankovic's notebook sheds light on the creative process behind "Livin' La Vida Mocha."

himself with such offers at this time.

"Right now, I can't let myself think about that sort of thing," he said. "At this point, it's more important that I concentrate and remain focused on what's really important: living the work. As an artist, everything else is secondary."

In addition to finishing the lyrics, Yankovic is working closely with his creative staff to develop a video for the song that will remain true to his unique vision. Proper execution of the video, he said, is crucial, as the visuals must "breathe life" into the song's irreverent depiction of caffeine-fueled mayhem.

"We're currently working with top prop-comics on a possible scene in which Al's dripping head emerges from a steaming coffee urn, surrounded by throngs of gyrating, salsa-dancing women," said Yankovic's longtime collaborator, drummer Jon "Bermuda" Schwartz. "But Al has expressed fears that the image may prove to be too silly, thus lessening the impact of the song. So we're also weighing the option of a giant coffee cup, in which Al would float on an inner-tube crafted

to resemble a giant donut. He is a very exacting artist. He demands nothing less than perfection."

Such unflinching, uncompromising parody, however, may prove dangerous: There are rumors that the song's blistering critique of Starbucks has angered the Seattle-based coffee chain's powerful ownership. Some have even gone so far as to predict a possible Starbucks lawsuit to suppress "Mocha's" explosive content.

But according to "Weird Al" amateur web-site discographer and archivist "Stupid Bill" Herberger, Yankovic is unlikely to bow to pressure from corporate America—or even, for that matter, Ricky Martin himself, who recently blasted "Mocha" as "a blatant attempt to sully the integrity of my work."

Despite the feathers Yankovic may ruffle, Herberger said nothing will stop the artist in his quest to expose society's underbelly.

"As a satirist, Al is returning to his indie-rock roots with this one," Herberger said. "The tone recalls the days of the independently released 'Another One Rides The Bus' seven-inch on

the short-lived Placebo Records label. He's taking no prisoners."

"This is all about one thing: the parody," Herberger said. "I am in awe of the courage displayed by this great, nutsy man."

Whether Yankovic can live up to the pressure remains to be seen. Like any great artist, he's had his share of failures, from the commercial belly-flop of the 1986 album *Polka Party!* to the lukewarm critical reception afforded his 1989 film *UHF.* But through it all, he has always come back fighting. A true gadfly, his goofy nasal voice and ferocious accordion solos serve as a Greek chorus to the hypocrisies and excesses of our age. One thing is certain: Whatever happens, "Weird Al" isn't going away. His voice will not be silenced.

Yankovic himself remains stoic on the matter.

"I do what I do because I must," he said. "If it brings on the wrath of the powers that be, so be it. I am driven by my own personal demons to seek out the greatest novelty songs I have within me. I am an artist. I must create." Ø

"I can't see how he could possibly influence legislation," Sen. Daniel Patrick Moynihan (D-NY) said. "One thing's for certain: We won't let him join in any Senate games."

Peabody's small size, coupled with his lack of seniority, prevented him from being appointed to any important subcommittees. As a result, on the days Congress was in session, he could often be found in the very back of the Senate chamber, sitting all alone at his little desk, writing notes on his copy of the Biennial Budgeting & Appropriations Act using a hummingbird quill and a thimble for an inkwell.

"Before Tuesday, Peabody's impact on the Senate had been negligible," CNN political analyst Mark Shields said. "When he tried to go to the floor to offer his opinion on the Financial Regulatory Relief & Economic Efficiency Act of 1999, the big, mean senators blocked his way, and he had to return to his little seat. And the only bill he's authored, S1156, the Letting Small People Have Their Say Act, was laughed right out of committee. Needless to say, this made the Littlest Senator very, very sad."

The Littlest Senator's situation, however, began to improve one sunny day in May, when the House of Representatives passed the McCann-Hawkins Bill. Peabody was in favor of the bill, which would allocate $377.5 million for the conservation and restoration of more than 400,000 acres of Florida wetlands, preserving the size of the nation's wetlands resource base and protecting the habitat of the Littlest Senator's only friends, the puddle ducks.

But Peabody knew that many big, mean senators disliked the bill, because it would set limits on industrial and commercial development in the Everglades region. If he voted for the

Above: President Clinton looks on as the Littlest Senator announces passage of the wetlands bill.

bill, the big senators would surely point their fingers at him and call him names.

"The night before the vote, I stayed up a long, long time thinking," Peabody told reporters. "Then, I put on my little nightcap spun from gossamer, blew out my little candle, and went to sleep."

"Not long afterwards," he continued, "I was stirred awake by a little voice in my ear. When I opened my eyes, I couldn't believe what I saw: It was a little mouse dressed in a top hat and bow tie! Imagine my surprise when he opened his little mouth and said, 'Don't be afraid! I'm your friend! And I believe in you.'"

The Littlest Senator initially thought he was dreaming, but the little mouse, still unidentified as of press time, assured Peabody that he was real.

"The mouse said he was able to talk because I believed in him, and if I believed in myself, I'd have the courage to do anything I wanted," he said. "I told him that with all the big senators

teasing me, I couldn't do anything right."

"But then the mouse told me something I hadn't considered," Peabody continued. "He told me that the people of the great state of Rhode Island believed in me enough to elect me, so I must've done something right. And he said that anyone who follows his heart can't go wrong."

Feeling as though a great burden had been lifted from him, Peabody practically skipped to the Senate chamber the next morning, eager to show the big, mean senators that he meant business.

But when the vote emerged dead even, the Littlest Senator, who was always last on the roll call, found that the deciding vote had fallen to him.

"In that moment, all of my courage fell away, and I suddenly felt very,

## Peabody knew that many big, mean senators disliked the bill.

very nervous," Peabody said. "If I voted against the bill, I would be letting down my duck friends. But if I voted for it, the big senators would be very cross with me. What was I to do?"

Then, Peabody said, he remembered what his friend the mouse had told him: Anyone who follows his heart can't go wrong. So in a loud, clear, bell-like voice, Peabody declared his vote: Yes! Yes! Yes for the McCann-Hawkins Florida Wetlands Preserva-

tion Bill!

When the bill was passed, all the conservation-minded senators cheered and lifted Peabody high into the air.

"It was then that the Littlest Senator realized he did matter after all," said Roger Feuerstein, a senior advisor at the Brookings Institute, a D.C.-based think tank. "In fact, he mattered the most."

But when Senate Majority Leader Trent Lott (R-MS), the biggest senator of all, approached Peabody after the vote, Peabody became nervous again, cringing as Lott's shadow fell over him. A big smile, however, came across the Littlest Senator's face when he saw that Lott only wanted to shake his tiny hand.

"Although I did oppose the McCann-Hawkins Bill, I congratulate you, Littlest Senator, for standing up for what you believed was right," Lott said. "And on behalf of all the big senators, I wish to apologize for our past treatment of you. For today in Congress, we learned one and all: A senator is a senator, no matter how small or how tall—or how skinny or shaped like a big, fat, round ball."

Other big senators were eager to befriend Peabody, as well. Sen. Wayne Allard (R-CO) invited the Littlest Senator to join him on a fact-finding tour of the Chiapas region of Mexico. And Sen. Richard Lugar (R-IN) said he would recommend him to fill an opening on the Senate Armed Services Committee.

This made Peabody very, very happy. And that night, as he put on his little nightcap, blew out his little candle, and climbed into his little bed, the Littlest Senator fell into the most peaceful slumber he'd had since arriving in Washington. Because he finally knew that sometimes the littlest people can make the biggest difference. Ø

A lifelong resident of Burwell, Nowicki has been a stylist for 17 years, spending three years at Shear Magic on Holcomb Avenue and four at Hair & Now in the Burwell Plaza strip mall before joining the Mane Attraction team in 1992.

"Personally, I think she looked best in *My Best Friend's Wedding*," said Nowicki, whose seniority enables her to get first crack at the perm and tinting appointments, leaving most of the low-tip-yielding $7.99 cut-and-style jobs for the newer stylists. "For that movie, they did her hair with a chestnut tint, which is perfect for an autumn like Julia. In all honesty, though, I probably would have done it even a few shades redder."

"I think I could really do wonders with Julia's hair," said Nowicki, sifting through a plastic, teal-and-pink "comb caddy" containing combs, scissors, and butterfly clips. "Somehow, I've just got this knack for making people look their best."

Though Roberts is Nowicki's favorite Hollywood star, she is not the

only actress whose hair Nowicki would love to do. During her 10 years at Mane Attraction, Nowicki has expressed a desire to style the hair of such leading ladies as Meg Ryan, Melanie Griffith, and Sandra Bullock.

"I saw Sandra on *Access Hollywood* last night, and it looked like she was definitely due for a shape-up," Nowicki said. "Or, at the very least, a little off the ends."

"It would be so much fun to work with a big star," said Nowicki, who makes $6.50 an hour plus tips. "Not that I don't appreciate my customers here at The Mane."

One such regular customer, Burwell resident Mary Klapisch, is well aware of Nowicki's talents. "Pam is really up on the latest styles—she gets tons of magazines, including *People*, *Glamour*, and *Cosmo*. And she never misses *Entertainment Tonight*," Klapisch said. "She said that with my facial shape, she could make me look just like Celine Dion."

Nowicki's high-profile clientele includes such Burwell luminaries as

city-council member Teresa Bonner, PTA president Maggie Kittridge, and *Burwell Post-Dispatch* bookkeeper Annette Pedersen.

Though she has yet to realize her dream of cutting the hair of an actual Hollywood star, Nowicki recently had the chance to work with a television personality.

"Two weeks ago, Katie Oberman, the news anchor for [NBC affiliate] KTNE over in Lincoln, was passing through town and got a haircut from me," Nowicki said. "It was such an amazing experience, getting the chance to actually do a hairstyle for the camera. I watched her the next night on the news, and she looked fantastic."

"I always thought it would've been fun to go to Hollywood and get a job as a stylist for the movies, but Dan never would've gone for that. And now, with the three kids and all, forget it," said Nowicki, bending over to sweep clumps of hair into a dust pan. "Oh, well. I bet it's really muggy there in the summer, anyway." Ø

# Study:
# U.S. Pets' Healthcare Better Than Rwandan Humans'

PHILADELPHIA—A University of Pennsylvania study released Tuesday found that U.S. pets enjoy superior healthcare to that of Rwandan humans.

The five-year study, which compared the medical care of 2,500 U.S. dogs, cats, hamsters, and parakeets to that of 2,500 human beings in the Rwandan capital of Kigali, found that the Rwandans were edged out in every category.

"America's pet lovers can rejoice knowing that their precious, furry companions are well taken care of," study co-chair Dr. Nate Gotcher said.

Among the good news for U.S. animals: America has 15 veterinarians per 1,000 dogs, compared to Rwanda's one doctor per 1,000 humans. The infant-mortality rate among U.S. cats is 7 per 1,000 live births, compared to 119 per 1,000 live births among Rwandan humans.

"When the infection started to spread to my upper leg, they had to amputate," said Rwandan Kasongo Tshikapa, whose left leg was removed in May 1998 after he stepped on a piece of rusted scrap metal. "The surgery took five hours, and there was no anesthesia. The operation was performed by my brother-in-law, who

has experience as a carpenter. Eight men had to hold me down."

Added Tshikapa: "If only I were a border collie in America."

According to Dr. Wendy Hentrich of the American Association of Veterinary Medicine, new breakthroughs are being made every day.

"The last few years have seen so many exciting advances in high-tech health care for pets," said Hentrich, also chief of cardiology at UCLA's Veterinary Hospital. "For example, at UCLA, we've developed a balloon angioplasty technique that can open a cat's deformed cardiac valves. A catheter is passed into the deformed valve, then a balloon is inflated, enabling blood to pass through freely. This painless, revolutionary procedure has already been used to save the lives of thousands of beautiful, lovable cats."

Such breakthroughs, along with advances in the prevention of such diseases as feline leukemia, have caused the average life expectancy of U.S. cats to rise to 18.6 years, which, when converted to human years, is substantially higher than the Rwandan life expectancy of 38.8.

"If I do not have medicine soon, I will die," said Ndola Iringa, who con-

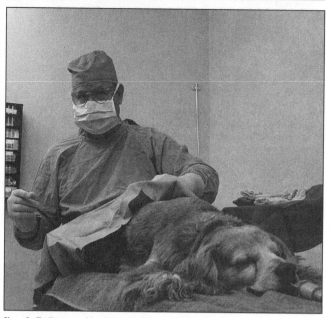
Above: Dr. Tim Verstegen of San Mateo, CA, performs a kidney transplant on a cocker spaniel.

tracted malaria five weeks ago during an outbreak of the disease in her village. "My sister and three of my brothers have died already. The convulsions are getting worse."

As a result of the study, Rwandan physicians are looking toward U.S. veterinary medicine for ways to improve their own healthcare system.

"In America, many dog foods contain nutritional supplements for healthy teeth and gums, as well as a lustrous, glowing coat," Rwandan physician Mbeya Liwale said. "Perhaps such supplements, if they could

somehow be found here in Rwanda, could be put to use reducing the death tolls brought on by mass famine and genocide."

"I just don't know what I would do without my Muffin," said Palo Alto, CA, resident Gloria Shifrin, whose 6-year-old Welsh corgi had a grapefruit-sized tumor removed from her chest Monday and must undergo five weeks of chemotherapy. "But, thank God, the cancer is in remission, and it looks like she's going to be all right. No dog should have to go through this." ∅

# Beloved Minister Dies Just As He Lived—Of A Heart Attack

Above: Rev. Walter Booth will not soon be forgotten by the residents of Shady Corners, VT.

SHADY CORNERS, VT—The people of Shady Corners (pop. 712), a sleepy little town near the Vermont-New Hampshire border, came out in full force last Sunday to say goodbye to the man they knew as their pastor, their neighbor, and their friend: Rev. Walter Booth.

Though the end was sudden, those who knew him say he died just as he lived—of a massive heart attack.

"Pastor Booth touched all our lives," said close friend Wayne Patterson in a moving eulogy. "Whether he was making the scriptures come alive with his flair for storytelling, helping a parishioner in a moment of spiritual crisis, or simply collapsing to the floor as he clutched his chest and gasped for oxygen, Walter was someone special."

Patricia Grolier, a member of Booth's flock at Holy Christ Almighty Lutheran Church for more than 30 years, also remembered the minister fondly.

"Every Christmas, Pastor Booth would go door-to-door visiting shut-ins and the elderly, singing 'Joy To The World' and yelling, 'Call the damn

## Said parishioner Patricia Grolier: "Gigantic coronary failures were what the pastor was all about."

paramedics!'

Added Grolier: "Gigantic coronary failures were what the pastor was all about."

"Walter Booth was a constant source of inspiration and friendship," Shady Corners physician Henry Rudiger said. "He was a constant patient, as well."

Andrew Schulman, pastor of First United Lutheran Church in nearby Plovis, was recently named Booth's successor.

"I may never be the minister he was," Schulman said, "but I can only hope that my constant near-drownings will someday enable me to fill his shoes. ∅

# the ONION

WWW.THEONION.COM    AMERICA'S FINEST NEWS SOURCE™    FOUNDED 1871

## Chinese Premier To Clinton: '生夏帖市帖'

see WORLD page 3A

## Like Boxes Of Shit In Your House? Get A Cat

see PETS page 5C

## Second Nintendo Controller Sits Unused

see LEISURE page 13E

## Hotcakes Sales Brisk

see BUSINESS page 10D

THE ONION
$2.00 US
$3.00 CAN

Above: Target stocker Jan Hervey proudly displays her Employee Of The Month certificate.

# Employee Of The Month Sad It's Already The 19th

FRANKLIN, TN—Jan Hervey, a housewares-department stocker and occasional cashier at the Plank Road Target, expressed sadness Monday over the rapidly approaching end to her reign as employee of the month.

"Where has December gone?" asked Hervey, 33, speaking from the store's breakroom. "I can't believe it's already the 19th. Before you know it, I'll be just another em-

ployee again."

After nearly three years of unrecognized service to the store, Hervey was finally nominated for the prestigious award by second-shift manager Paula Cushman, who cited the 31-year-old mother of four's "helpful attitude" and "solid attendance record" on a Target Employee Of The Month recommendation form. On Dec. 1, store manager Bri-

see EMPLOYEE page 153

# March '74 *Oui* Passed Down To Next Generation In Special Ceremony

SHAWANO, WI—Here in this sleepy northeast Wisconsin town, a time-honored ritual is about to be solemnly observed, as 16-year-old Chris Weineke prepares to ceremonially pass on his beloved, dog-eared copy of the March 1974 issue of *Oui* to the next generation of sexually needy adolescents.

Chris' younger brother, 13-year-old Kyle, will receive the treasured periodical in a brief ceremony accompanied by minimal fanfare but not lacking in austere beauty. The custom has been observed here in Shawano with-

see OUI page 153

Above: The treasured *Oui*, which has been passed down from one generation of hormone-gripped youths to the next for 25 years.

# NFL Star Thanks Jesus After Successful Double Homicide

CHARLESTON, SC—Washington Redskins defensive end D'Aundré Banks gave "all thanks and praise to my personal Lord and Savior Jesus Christ" Monday for giving him the strength he needed to fatally stab bouncer Isaac Edmonds and ex-girlfriend Renee Hamilton outside a Charleston nightclub early Sunday morning.

"All glory to Jesus," the 25-year-old Banks, who attended the University of South Carolina, told reporters from his cell in the Charleston County Jail. "He is with me in this dark

hour, as He was in our devastating 14-13 playoff loss to the Buccaneers. His love will see me through this."

According to police reports, at approximately 2:30 a.m., a visibly intoxicated Banks became involved in an altercation with Edmonds regarding who would accompany Hamilton home. When Edmonds attempted to restrain Banks, the 288-pound devout Christian produced a knife and repeatedly stabbed Edmonds and Hamilton. He then fled to the home of girlfriend

see HOMICIDE page 152

Above: Redskins All-Pro D'Aundré Banks in a Nov. 11 game.

# Scientists Discover Gene Responsible For Eating Whole Goddamn Bag Of Chips

## United States Toughens Image With Umlauts

WASHINGTON, DC—In a move designed to make the United States seem more "bad-assed and scary in a quasi-heavy-metal manner," Congress passed a bill Monday changing the nation's name to the Ünited Stätes of Ämerica. "Much like Mötley Crüe and Motörhead, the Ünited Stätes is not to be messed with," said Sen. James Inhofe (R-OK). An upcoming redesign of the Ämerican flag will feature the new name in burnished silver wrought in a jagged, gothic font and bolted to a black background. A new national anthem is also in the works, to be written by composer Glenn Danzig and tentatively titled "Howl Of The She-Demon."

## Sculptor Criticized For Turning Women Into Objects

NEW YORK—Feminist groups are uniting in protest of sculptor Garrison Byrne, who is accused of turning women into objects for sale to the highest bidder. "The sort of sexist, demeaning objectification of women in which Mr. Byrne engages is shocking and unacceptable," wrote National Women's League president Georgia Richards-Weiss in a letter to *The New York Times*. "That he actually makes a good living reducing females to lifeless objects is more shocking still." ∅

According to Cornell researchers, the tendency to eat a whole goddamn bag of chips (above) may be genetic.

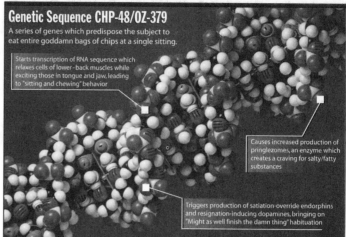

**Genetic Sequence CHP-48/OZ-379**
A series of genes which predispose the subject to eat entire goddamn bags of chips at a single sitting.

Starts transcription of RNA sequence which relaxes cells of lower-back muscles while exciting those in tongue and jaw, leading to "sitting and chewing" behavior

Causes increased production of pringlezomes, an enzyme which creates a craving for salty/fatty substances

Triggers production of satiation-override endorphins and resignation-inducing dopamines, bringing on "Might as well finish the damn thing" habituation

ITHACA, NY—In an announcement with major implications for future generations of big fat hogs, Cornell University geneticists announced Monday that they have isolated the specific DNA series that makes an individual susceptible to eating a whole goddamn bag of chips.

"We have long known that the tendency to sit down and eat the whole goddamn bag runs in certain families," team leader Dr. Edward Alvaro said. "However, until we completed our work, we weren't sure whether the disposition to cram chips down your greasy gullet was genetic or a behavioral trait learned from one or both fat-fuck parents. With the discovery of gene series CHP-48/OZ-379, we have proof positive that single-case serial chip-eating is indeed hereditary."

For years, scientists have been aware of the numerous health complications posed by a person's predisposition to plop down and mow through a whole bag of chips, but it wasn't until now that they were able to isolate the gene that carries the trait.

According to the Cornell team, se-
see CHIPS page 154

HOMICIDE from page 151

and Hooters waitress Lisa Nolan in nearby Summerville, where police arrested him several hours later.

"First off, I'd like to say 'great job' to Isaac and Renee, who put up a heck of a fight and have nothing to be ashamed of," Banks said. "They were terrific opponents, and it's too bad somebody had to lose a life. But the Lord Jesus Christ was truly with me Saturday night. He guided my hand when I was able to make that big hit on Isaac, and I really felt His presence when I stepped up and made that great slashing cut to bring Renee down from behind."

Added Banks: "Jesus really let me take this homicide to the next level. Thank you, Jesus!"

Banks, who has been charged with two counts of first-degree murder, has been a devout born-again Christian ever since his hot-tub baptism at the hands of Philadelphia Eagles wide receiver and ordained minister Irving Fryar during Pro Bowl week in 1997.

"I was a mess before Jesus took my hand," Banks said. "At South Carolina, I'd show up late to practice, stay out late running around with the wrong crowd, all kinds of bad things. I was about to squander the precious gift of football God blessed me with. But through His grace, I was drafted in

the fourth round and sent to the NFL to meet Rev. Fryar, who showed me that Jesus wanted me to glorify Him and play on His team."

Continued Banks: "D'Aundré Banks' life would be nothing without Christ's faith. Without His everlasting love, D'Aundré Banks never would have gotten his time in the 40 down to 4.6 for the 1995 NFL scouting combines, and he never would have had the strength to turn a big guy like Isaac Edmonds around with just one arm and stab him."

Jeff Rosenzweig, Banks' Miami-based agent and manager, said his client has been unfairly represented by the media in its coverage of the double homicide.

"All the papers are branding D'Aundré a murderer, as if that's all there is to him," Rosenzweig said. "But in their mad rush to demonize D'Aundré, they neglect to mention his deep dedication to the D'Aundré Banks Helps Kids Tackle Drugs For A Loss Foundation and the Big 98 Safety In The End Zone Safe House For Women. Or, for that matter, that he acknowledges the workings of Christ in his everyday life. No, you don't see any of those things mentioned in the articles about him. It's all 'homicide this' and 'seven-inch stab wound that.'"

Banks, whose preliminary hearing is scheduled for Dec. 29 in Charleston County Court, said his fate is in God's hands.

"I don't know what will happen to me. That's up to the Lord," Banks said. "The Bible tells us that nothing is done on this Earth but that which is done through God. No multimillion-dollar contract extension, no game-saving interception, no acquittal on both counts of first-degree murder happens without Him." ∅

**Above: Emergency personnel load one of Banks' God-given victims into an ambulance.**

**OUI from page 151**

out interruption for a quarter of a century, as unbroken generations of post-pubescent teens keep the secret magazine's tradition of naked-lady photographs alive, a living legacy handed down from the hormone-gripped youths of yesteryear to the not-yet-born masturbators of tomorrow.

The well-worn *Oui*—a *Playboy* spin-off published by Hugh Hefner in the '70s and '80s—has been held by 22 Shawano boys since its February 1974 purchase. With the exception of its original 18-year-old buyer, who hid it in a woodshed where it was discovered by a group of boys in January 1976, the magazine has never been in the hands of anyone over the age of 16.

"It's nice to see that in today's fast-paced, media-saturated, change-obsessed world, there are still some places where tradition is valued and respected," Chris says, growing contemplative as the Passing Of The *Oui* approaches. "In some ways, I hate to give it up—it has served me well through these long, lonely years, a faithful companion in times of need. When there was no one else, my March '74 *Oui* was there for me."

Chris then pauses for a moment, steeling himself for the parting.

"Nevertheless," he says, "I recognize that the time has come for me to pass on the *Oui*, as my older cousin Doug did before me, as his neighbor Brent before him, as Brent's older brother Reggie before him."

As the ceremony draws near, Kyle is eager but nervous, aware of the obligations he'll soon take on as the new Keeper Of The *Oui*.

"Though I am excited to receive the sacred naked-lady pictures, I realize

> ## A pair of candles are lit, Chris' bedroom door is locked, and, finally, the hallowed Passing Of The *Oui* begins.

that with them comes great responsibility," Kyle says. "If Mom or Aunt Gladys were to discover this magazine, the priceless beauty contained therein would be lost forever to future generations of Shawano boys. It is my solemn duty to see to it that such an event never comes to pass."

"Furthermore, I cannot wait to see the big, exciting, naked breasts," adds Kyle, blushing slightly.

The Passing Of The *Oui* occurs every 8 to 15 months, when the current Keeper Of The *Oui* begins tentative dating. In the weeks leading up to the Keeper's initiation into the world of actual sexual contact, tradition holds that he must seek out a worthy successor, one who has not yet begun his own foray into the magical, mysteri-

ous world of females, one who is desperately in need of sexual release.

"This trusty *Oui* has been a valued friend and companion," says Chris, who began his search for a successor last month after getting to second base with Suzie Hildebrandt while parked behind the Shawano Seed & Feed on Schuyler Road. "I will never forget those memories. In many ways, this March '74 *Oui* will always be with me in my heart. But my time of Manhood is fast approaching, and I know that we must now part. It must now move on to spread its joy to another sexually needy soul. It has always been thus."

A pair of candles are lit, Chris' bedroom door is locked and, finally, the hallowed Passing Of The *Oui* begins. Neither brother speaks as the periodical is passed from Chris to Kyle. Once the *Oui* is handed over, the ceremony ends as the boys' mother yells at them from the kitchen to take the laundry out of the dryer.

"Yes, mom," they reply, hastily slipping the magazine under Chris' mattress and hurrying off. The circle has begun anew.

For the past 10 months, the *Oui* has made its home in the space behind a board that rests against the back wall of Chris' bedroom closet, behind his foot locker and laundry basket. Today, it will make the journey to its new home, a box of sweaters on the top shelf of Kyle's bedroom closet.

This new location, however, is only

temporary: The boys' mother, Judith Weineke, a 44-year-old homemaker with a great interest in the sweaters Kyle refuses to wear, will surely find it there if it is not transferred to a better hiding place soon. As the new Keeper Of The *Oui*, Kyle's principal duty is to find a place of safe-keeping for the treasured magazine, a place where it will not fall into enemy hands.

"If Mom were to find that thing, it would be the end of a glorious tradition," Kyle says. "I cannot allow that to happen, for I would not only be failing myself, but the teenage boys of tomorrow, who one day will need this precious *Oui* as badly as I need it today. I cannot—nay, must not—let them down."

Tonight, long after his parents have gone to bed, young Kyle will finally enter the realm of the March '74 *Oui* for the first time. He will gaze with wide-eyed wonderment at its table of contents, with its promises of such mysterious features as a short story by John Updike, a preview of the 1974 men's fall fashions, and a "How To Drink Tequila" photo essay by acclaimed director Sam Peckinpah. He does not know yet what exotic delights these unfamiliar features hold, but he is eager to find out. And, of course, there will also be the breasts. Always, always breasts.

And here in Shawano, as it has been for 25 years, the tradition of the March '74 *Oui* will live to see another day. ∅

---

**EMPLOYEE from page 151**

an Steeber announced over the store's P.A. system that Hervey had been selected.

"I'd always dreamed that someday it would be my face looking down at all the Target guests from that plaque at the front of the store," said Hervey, whose husband and children celebrated the news by treating her to dinner at Old Country Buffet. "On Dec. 1, that wonderful day finally came. When Brian announced it over the loudspeaker, everyone came running over to my register to congratulate me. I felt so special."

"Dec. 1," Hervey added with a sigh. "Just 18 days ago."

After the announcement was made, Hervey was asked to report to the service desk, where she posed for a Polaroid photo that was slipped into the Target Employee Of The Month plaque that hangs near the store entrance.

"I had no idea I'd be getting my picture taken that day, or I would have used the curling iron before I left for work," Hervey said. "But how could I have known? It's just not the sort of thing you wake up in the morning expecting to happen to you."

The tradition of employee of the month at Target store #4551 carries with it a rich history. Since regional management instituted the program in 1996, a different employee has received the accolade every month. The only time the award was not given out

was August 1999, when the plaque was stolen by a group of teenagers and had to be replaced.

In addition to having her name and month of honor permanently engraved on a brass plate on the plaque for future generations to see, Hervey received a coupon for a free foot-long hot dog and junior fries from the Target snack bar.

"I haven't used my meal coupon yet," she said. "I'm planning to hold on to it for a little while longer. That way, after my month is up, I'll still have a little taste of the big time left to enjoy."

Despite the fact that she "wouldn't give this up for anything in the world," Hervey admitted that being employee of the month "hasn't been all cookies and ice cream." The last three weeks, she said, have been a time of intense introspection.

"After all those years of wishing and hoping for something like this, the only place left to go is down," said Hervey, whose last honor came in 1984, when she was named the Monroe High School Swing Choir's Most Valuable Member. "You struggle so long to get that brass ring, and then, when it's in your hand, you get a sort of blank feeling. It's like, what now?"

Hervey, however, has made an effort to keep feelings of doubt to herself and focus on setting a good example for her coworkers.

"When you become employee of the month, you're suddenly thrust into

Above: Hervey shows off the plaque that hangs near the entrance of Target store #4551.

the limelight, and an entire staff of 97 people is looking up to you as a role model. That's a tremendous responsibility," Hervey said. "Target expects a lot from all of its employees, but those expectations become that much greater when you're employee of the month."

"Then there are those few jealous individuals who would just love to see you make a wrong step," she continued. "It's exhausting to be on your toes every second of every shift."

Determined to prove herself deserving, Hervey has tried to raise the level of her performance even higher. Her efforts have not gone unnoticed.

"Jan's really been hustling lately, straightening out the rows of laundry baskets and re-folding every towel and washcloth in sight," said fellow housewares stocker Brenda Steeber. "It's been a real chore for me to find something to do. It would be a real bitch if they downsized our department's staff." ∅

CHIPS from page 152

ries CHP-48/OZ-379 is a set of "alleles," or collections of genetic material, that cause chip-eaters to develop a markedly larger number of chip-responsive nerve endings in their cerebral material.

"People with this gene have up to four times the number of fritoceptors typically found in a human," Alvaro said. "This increases their pleasure response to snaxamine-2, the human body's principal chip-eating hormone, which is released in response to giant handfuls of chips being shoveled into the mouth. This tends to promote entire-goddamn-bag-eating behavior in those individuals who possess the series."

One of the most interesting charac-

> ## "People with this gene have up to four times the number of fritoceptors typically found in a human," Alvaro said.

teristics of the newly discovered series, researcher Dr. Paul Bergleiter said, is its tendency to appear more than once in the gene strands of a human subject.

"Series CHP-48/OZ-379, because it is a fairly large, or 'fat-assed,' allele, tends to just lie around at convenient sites on the DNA sequence," Bergleiter said. "Though many subjects exhibit only one occurrence of this gene, in others we found as many as four. This, of course, led these rare subjects to eat four times as many whole goddamn bags of chips as those in our control group."

Though many more fatsos must be studied to determine CHP-48/OZ-379's transmission pattern, conventional wisdom seems to indicate that the gene is recessive.

"Who would want to pass on their own intact genetic material to someone who just sat around eating chips all goddamn day?" Bergleiter asked. "Unless, of course, that was the only person you could find because you were such a big lard-ass yourself. That would probably be the only source of friendly RNA-transcriptive culture you could find."

Carriers of the CHP-48/OZ-379 gene are hailing the Cornell find.

"It is about time science took steps to help fat fucks like me—people who eat huge bags of chips like it's popcorn," said 370-pound Milesburg, PA, resident Russell Roberts. "I can't even get jogging pants in my size anymore."

The discovery is considered the most significant advance in gene-mapping since a University of Chicago team isolated the DNA strand that causes people to shovel spoonfuls of ice cream into their mouths while standing in front of the friggin' freezer with the door wide open. ⌀

# I Lost 32 Pounds In 15 Days And Died!

**By Sandy Gresham**

I never knew losing those extra pounds could be so easy until I discovered VitaLoss. With the help of this miracle weight-loss system, developed by nutritionists at Pro-Start labs, *I lost 32 pounds in 15 days, and died!*

Thanks to VitaLoss' miraculous, patented Metabolic Rate Enhancement System™, I was able to lose the weight without dieting and exercising. In the final days of my life, I got to eat all the foods I love—and I still lost *more than 30 pounds!*

For years, I'd battled my weight to no avail, losing a few pounds only to put them right back on again. But with the VitaLoss program, had I lived, I never would have gained back a single pound! Why? Because it's *100 percent guaranteed to work!*

For years, I tried pills and shakes that promised change but never delivered. And fad diets just left me tired and hungry. But when I finally found VitaLoss, I took the pounds off fast, escaping the diet roller-coaster forever. Thanks to VitaLoss, if I hadn't died of massive heart failure last Thursday, I never would've had to worry about fitting into that little black cocktail

### I really lost the weight! And I really died!

dress again!

We all know how hard it can be to find the motivation to slim down. But with VitaLoss, it was *actually fun!* The better I looked, the better I felt. And my energy level went through the roof! During my last days on Earth, I finally felt confident enough to go after the things I'd always wanted!

You can't imagine how much my life changed. I'd always been shy and insecure because of the way I looked, so finding dates was out of the question. But as soon as I lost the weight, men really started to pay attention to me. I'll bet those emergency medical technicians who tried to revive me noticed how trim I looked! And I'm not positive, but I got the feeling that the cute coroner who processed my corpse was checking me out.

And why wouldn't men notice me? I looked fabulous in that size-zero pantsuit I was wearing when they found me in the bathroom face-down in a pool of bloody vomit and urine. What's more, as I lie here in this coffin, my lifeless cadaver is still losing weight, decomposing into a slim, withered husk—the VitaLoss way!

For years, I felt like no one saw the real me. Instead, they were all just looking at my "extra baggage." But after taking off the weight, I was proud of who I was. When my friends and family gathered around my coffin, they were looking at a whole new me—a thinner, more attractive me! Thanks to VitaLoss, I was the slimmest, sexiest woman at the funeral!

I have a picture of me before VitaLoss. I'm at the beach, hiding my flabby thighs and pudgy stomach behind an oversized T-shirt. I looked awful. But less than a month later, as I was being lowered into the ground, my perfect cheekbones complemented by the bright smile into which my lips were stitched, I was looking better than ever before!

I really did it! I really lost the weight! And I *really died!* VitaLoss worked for me, and it can work for you, too. ⌀

# A Nation Of Prisoners

**According to a recent report, the number of jailed Americans has more than doubled over the past 12 years, and the U.S. could soon pass Russia as the nation with the highest imprisonment rate. What do *you* think about America's soaring prison population?**

**John Montefusco**
**Cab Driver**

"I don't understand how the prison population has boomed. I mean, I know those guys screw all the time, but they can't get pregnant that way, can they?"

**Diane Ivie**
**CEO**

"As CEO of Amalgamated Tin Cups & Orange Fabric, I say hooray!"

**David Halicki**
**Investment Banker**

"Shockingly, a full 40 percent of U.S. prisoners are incarcerated on marijuana-possession charges. You don't expect us to just let these fiends go, do you?"

**Omar Minton**
**Prep Cook**

"For years, I've been calling for the construction of an interdimensional Phantom Zone to deal with this overcrowding problem."

**Helen Metzger**
**Systems Analyst**

"There are far too many people in prison. Obviously, this country doesn't have enough high-profile defense attorneys."

**Dennis Herndon**
**Magazine Editor**

"I have only one question: How will this affect the Internet?"

## Al Gore Takes Environment Issue To Guy On Bus

see NATION page 9A

## Jews Begin To Make Presence Felt In Entertainment Law

see BUSINESS page 2B

## Oatmeal Variety Pack Has Only 'Regular' Flavor Left

see PRODUCTS page 9E

## Data-Entry Clerk Reapplies Carmex At 17-Minute Intervals

see OFFICE page 7B

### STATshot

A look at the numbers that shape your world.

**Who's Picking Out Our Clothes For Us?**

9% Assisted-living worker
16% Nobody, now that Amy's gone
11% Owl-headed gorgon from Old Navy commercials
8% Book of Leviticus
15% That sick-fuck hockey coach
18% *Jenny Jones* assistant producer
13% Whoever's garbage this is
10% The state of Illinois

THE ONION
$2.00 US
$3.00 CAN

0 74470 94595 6

# the ONION®

WWW.THEONION.COM    AMERICA'S FINEST NEWS SOURCE™    FOUNDED 1871

## Area Man Has Naked-Lady Fetish

ST. JOHNSBURY, VT—Looking at Warren Geary, you'd never suspect. A respected business owner and devoted family man, the 41-year-old Geary, by all outward indications, would appear to be just like anyone else in this sleepy New England hamlet of 4,700.

But looks can be deceiving.

Dig a little deeper, beyond the many years of PTA involvement and Kiwanis Club membership, and you'll discover a very different Warren Geary, one who derives sexual stimulation and pleasure from the sight of unclothed women. This seemingly normal husband and father of three has a naked-lady fetish.

"I really enjoy looking at naked ladies," Geary said. "I don't know what it is, but seeing women without their clothes on gets me excited."

So consuming is Geary's fetish, he said he will sometimes pass a woman on the street and catch himself imagining what she would look like un-

see FETISH page 156

Above: Warren Geary, a seemingly normal business owner and family man who harbors a secret fetish for women without clothes.

# Video-Game Characters Denounce Randomly Placed Swinging Blades

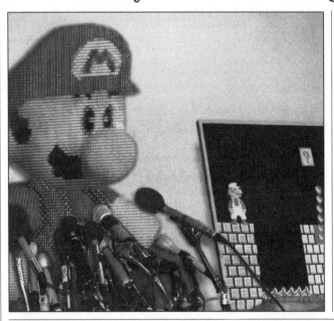

WASHINGTON, DC—A coalition of video-game characters representing the nation's leading systems appeared before Congress Thursday to decry "the pointless, deadly presence" of spinning blades in video-game landscapes.

"We are here to demand an end to the shockingly casual placement of dangerous blades in our places of work," said Tomb Raider star Lara Croft, who estimates that she has lost more than 600,000 lives to spinning, falling, swinging, and suddenly appearing blades this year alone. "This kind of thing has been going on since the days of Pitfall Harry, and it has got to stop."

Croft, flanked by Metal Gear's Solid Snake, Super Mario 64's Mario, and both soldiers from Contra, called

see CHARACTERS page 157

Left: A concerned Mario discusses the rotating fireball chains found throughout World 1-4 of Super Mario Bros.

# British Parliament Accused Of Plagiarizing U.S. Senate Bill S.576

WASHINGTON, DC—At a press conference Thursday, members of Congress lambasted the British House Of Commons for "blatantly ripping off" Senate bill S.576.

"It is impossible to deny the similarities between Parliament's Regulation Of Depository Institutions Act and our own S.576, the Financial Regulatory Reform Bill," said Sen. Phil Gramm (R-TX), sponsor of the U.S. bill. "For example, Section 102 of our bill repeals the limitation on the authority of a bank to permit the owner of any deposit or account to make withdrawals by negotiable or transferable instruments for transfers to third parties. Lines 404-410 in the British bill are almost identical, right down to the words 'transferable instruments.' That's my phrase."

Added Gramm: "Everyone on the Senate Banking, Housing, and Urban Affairs Committee worked really hard on that bill, and it makes me really mad that

see PARLIAMENT page 157

Right: House Of Commons MP Stephen Byers denies that Parliament stole the idea for its Financial Regulatory Reform Act from the U.S. Senate.

# Area Man Hasn't Told Coworkers About His Billy Joel Fanpage Yet

DAYTON, OH—Ross Hudek, a 36-year-old claims processor at Northcentral Insurance in Dayton, still hasn't told coworkers about "Zanzibar," his three-month-old Billy Joel fanpage.

"I really haven't brought it up to the gang at work," Hudek said of the site, which features Billy Joel FAQs, photos, and song lyrics, as well as links to other webpages devoted to the popular, Long Island-born singer. "I'm not hiding it or anything—it's right out there for the world to see. It's just that, well, I'd feel kind of weird if I knew people at Northcentral were looking at it."

Hudek, who lists "Captain Jack," "Scenes From An Italian Restaurant," and "Summer, Highland Falls," as his top-three all-time favorite Joel songs, said he is "pretty sure" that none of his coworkers have ever visited the fanpage.

"[Claims adjustor] Glenn [Dietz] and I talk about Billy Joel every once in a while, because he's also a fan," Hudek said. "He saw him on the Storm Front tour when he came through Cleveland in '89, and I was at the same show. But I don't think he knows about the site. At least, he's never mentioned it to me."

Hudek said he spends approximately 10 hours a week on maintenance and upkeep of the website, typing in trivia questions, scanning photographs he took at various Joel concerts, and posting the results of weekly fan polls.

"This week's question is: What is

Above: Northcentral Insurance claims processor and Billy Joel fan Ross Hudek.

your favorite song on *Turnstiles*?" Hudek said. "Surprisingly, 'Miami 2017' is in the lead, with seven votes. I was sure it would be 'James' or, at the very least, 'I've Loved These Days.' Not that '2017' isn't a great song. But the best on all of *Turnstiles*? My suspicion is that there's one person out there who really likes it and is casting multiple votes. Right now, there's no system to prevent that."

"I'm pretty proud of what I've done," Hudek continued. "There's a lot of good stuff there: updates on what Billy's been up to lately, midi files, desktop images, and a whole bunch of other downloadable goodies. Still, I'd kind of rather keep it to myself for now."

Despite his reluctance to tell

> ### Since its launch, Zanzibar has received more than 200 visitors.

coworkers, Hudek said he has a good relationship with them. Furthermore, he insists he is not "hiding" the website and would tell his fellow Northcentral employees about it, were it ever to come up in conversation.

"They're good people," Hudek said. "Dave [Boniol] and Bill [Kerkseich] and Samantha [Deele], in particular, I would consider more than just coworkers. But still, there's a limit to

what we talk about. Some things are more personal, you know?"

Hudek's coworkers may not have visited Zanzibar, but the fansite is not going unseen. Since its launch, it has received more than 200 visitors, and Hudek has received complimentary e-mails from Joel fans as far away as San Diego. He has even developed an ongoing "Billy Joel trivia exchange" with some visitors.

"We e-mail back and forth and try to stump each other," Hudek said. "It's a lot of fun. I'm pretty tough to stump, though. You can't just ask me something easy like, 'What was the inspiration for "Big Shot"?' or, 'Who is the "Famous Violinist Incognito" who plays on "The Downeaster Alexa"?' Or even, 'Who is the Rosalinda in "Rosalinda's Eyes"?'"

Added Hudek: "A very bad date with Bianca Jagger; Itzhak Perlman; and Billy's mom."

Hudek said he decided to set up the fanpage after visiting a number of other Joel sites and finding them to be "big on graphics but lacking in accurate, detailed information about Billy."

"If you're going to have a site devoted to the life and music of Billy Joel, you don't start your discography with *Cold Spring Harbor*," Hudek said. "You go all the way back to his pre-solo years with The Hassles."

"Not that I'm, like, obsessed or anything," Hudek added. "I love his music, but it's not the only thing I do. And I certainly wouldn't want to give my coworkers that impression." ∅

---

FETISH from page 155

dressed.

"I often think about naked women, even when none are around," said Geary, who has a collection of magazines and videotapes devoted to naked-lady fetishism, including the 1998 film *Boogie Nights*. "It's just this fixation of mine."

Geary said he doesn't recall when or how he first developed his strange compulsion for seeing women in a state of undress.

"I have no idea how I came to develop these urges. As a child, I found the naked female form gross or humorous, just like any healthy male," Geary said. "But at some point, I found myself not only enjoying the sight of disrobed women, but actually seeking it out."

Geary said that not a day goes by when he doesn't imagine women without clothes. There are no boundaries to when and where such fantasizing may occur—at church, the post office, the health club, the beach. He even admits to watching TV for hours on end, solely in the hopes of catching a glimpse of bare breasts.

"Sometimes, I'll turn on HBO, and if a movie is listed as containing nudity, I'll watch the entire film—even if I have no interest in the plot or subject

matter—just to see the breasts," Geary said. "I know it's wrong, but I can't help myself."

News of Geary's lurid fixation has caused considerable controversy throughout St. Johnsbury.

"It's twisted and obscene, that's for

> ### "As a child, I found the naked female form gross or humorous, just like any healthy male," Geary said.

sure," said Janice Delaney, whose home is just a block away from Geary's. "It makes me very uncomfortable to know I live so close to someone like that."

"A man who harbors a secret lust for women without any clothes on is not the kind of man we want coaching one of our teams," said St. Johnsbury Little League president Stephen Claussen, who recently asked Geary not to return next season after 14

years of involvement. "I don't feel comfortable entrusting our town's children to that kind of person. What if his presence somehow influences these kids, perverting their normal sexual growth and causing them to develop that same kind of aberrant interest in naked women later in life?"

For decades, psychologists believed naked-lady fetishism to be the domain of a tiny handful of sexual deviants. A growing number of experts, however, now believe the condition to be much more common, with some estimates putting the number of men consumed by the sight of the naked female form as high as 1 in 5,000.

According to noted psychotherapist Dr. Eli Wasserbaum, clear distinctions exist between normal men and those with naked-lady fetishes.

"When a normal man sees an attractive woman, he is drawn to her stylish hairdo, nicely applied make-up, and flattering dress, and he reacts with an intense desire to marry her," Wasserbaum said. "The naked-lady fetishist, however, is uninterested in hairstyle and clothing, regarding them as distractions and impediments to the one thing that truly interests him—her naked body."

"In a way, it's extremely sad," Wasserbaum said. "Instead of being able to enjoy the conversation of a woman over dinner and drinks, the naked-lady fetishist, gripped by his uncontrollable impulses, will only be able to think about whether he'll get to see her naked body later in the evening."

Scientists theorize that naked-lady fetishism may represent a long-obsolete evolutionary remnant, a vestigial instinct that once served some reproductive purpose among early hominids.

"About 70 million years ago, the female form may have served as a visual cue, triggering male arousal for the purpose of procreation," Brown University anthropologist Isaac Gage said. "But the human species evolved beyond that point long ago. Why a small handful of individuals would still exhibit traces of this ancestral evolutionary past is curious, to say the least. But one thing is certain: We should not permit our feelings of shame and ignorance to cloud our perceptions. Geary should be seen for what he is: a deeply disturbed individual in need of immediate medical help." ∅

# I Hope My Baby Don't Come Out All Fucked-Up And Shit

**By Amber Richardson**

I sure hope my baby don't come out all fucked-up and shit. 'Cause I know I'm gonna be a good mother, and I'm totally ready, no matter what anybody say, but I don't think I could deal with that. I mean, like, if something was wrong with it, that would suck so fuckin' bad.

I'm a little worried because of some stuff Erin told me. She was saying how, like, if you party a lot, it can make the baby's face all fucked-up. Like, if you drink too much, it could have these weird eyes that look kinda Chinese. That's what she said.

It ain't like I was surprised. I know how you gotta watch what you do when you're having a baby. Like, you gotta make sure to eat, and you gotta not be running around smoking three packs a day. I ain't stupid. Now that I'm expecting on having a baby, I've cut down to just one pack, and I ain't drinking except for weekends and paydays.

So, like, I'm being all healthy and shit now. But the problem is, I didn't even know I was pregnant until this month. Back when I must of got pregnant, I wasn't keeping track of things too good. It must have happened around when I got fired from Burger King—all because that bitch manager Denise searched my locker—and I was training at the Stop 'N' Go. But then I missed nine days of work in a row, so I was like, fuck it, and I quit. I wasn't seeing Gary or Dashawn no more because I was getting all serious with Troy from the Gift Box factory. (I was a seasonal there before I started at the Golden Corral two weeks ago, which is around when I moved back into my mom's apartment, 'cause her old boyfriend Don took a trucking job, and she didn't like living all alone over in that neighborhood because it ain't too safe.) So, anyway, like I said, I wasn't keeping track of things too good.

It's kind of funny that I'm pregnant, 'cause when I was working on the assembly line at The Gift Box, I kept having to put these little ceramic-statue things in with the cheese and sausage and the other shit that went out in the orders we packed up. The statues were of little baby angels and kids in pajamas who were praying and doing other cute shit. As I was packing up the little statues, I remember thinking how nice it would be to have a baby to keep me company.

Well, shit, as it turned out, the whole time I was packing those kid statues into the boxes, thinking about how I'd love to have a little girl like the one on the "I'm Yours" statue that's holding out the flowers, I was already pregnant. Isn't that fucking crazy?

Now, don't think I was trying to get

*see BABY page 158*

CHARACTERS from page 155

upon Congress to revise OSHA laws to extend protection to the digitally rendered.

"From Pitfall to Bad Dudes Versus Dragon Ninja to Gauntlet, the deadly spinning blade has been with us so long, we no longer even question it," Croft said. "It's high time it was done away with once and for all."

Exacerbating the situation, Mario said, is the seemingly arbitrary placement of the hazards. "I could see why, if you're in a factory, you might find yourself jumping around on dangerous conveyor belts moving in different directions," he said. "But why would you have conveyor belts in a castle? Or in the middle of a forest? Nintendo and these other companies are always talking about how realistic their graphics are. Well, what's so realistic about killer turtles shooting out of clouds?"

Added Mario: "It's-a me, Mario!"

In addition to the standard spinning blade, the coalition is seeking restrictions on random whirling fireball chains, falling blocks, spike-pit traps, and invisible cross-corridor laser arrays.

Legislators listened attentively as the digitized characters shared their near-death encounters.

"Just the other day, I was running through the British Museum's Egyptology exhibit when a bunch of six-foot steel scythes suddenly burst out of a sarcophagus," Croft said. "Fortunately, I managed to leap out of the way at the last possible second. But a situation like that easily could have turned tragic."

"We're not so different from you," the blue-jacketed guy from Double Dragon said. "We just want to be left alone to do our jobs—saving princesses,

finding lost treasures, destroying out-of-control nuclear-equipped robots. But it's nearly impossible to go about your daily life when you're living in constant fear of some giant, evil mushroom suddenly lunging at you from out of nowhere."

---

## "Would you put up with a row of whirling knives in the cereal aisle at Safeway?" the Double Dragon guy asked.

---

"I mean, would you put up with a row of whirling knives in the cereal aisle at Safeway?" the Double Dragon guy asked. "Of course not. Why, then, should Duke Nukem have to run through a corridor of them to get the health pack he needs need to survive?"

The characters said they intend to boycott their respective video games until Nintendo, Sega, Sony, and other major manufacturers take "significant measures" to improve safety.

"In addition to mandatory warning lights and buzzers at least eight seconds before the appearance of a blade, spike, or other health hazard, we are calling for mapping features in all 3D-rendered environments, large flashing arrows to highlight such hidden objects as health and life bonuses, and, in the case of Sonic Team games, safety guardrails on all loops."

Added Sonic: "And would it kill you to compose better music? I almost didn't finish the jungle part on that last one." ⌀

---

PARLIAMENT from page 155

somebody would steal it and claim it as their own."

Gramm said he has tried to give Nigel Beard, the Labor Party MP who claims authorship of the U.K. bill, the benefit of the doubt, but it has been difficult.

"We have committee logs showing that we'd been working on the ideas central to this bill for months," Gramm said. "Then, when we finally go public with S.576 and put it on the floor for debate, this Nigel Beard guy just *happens* to have the exact same idea? Come on."

According to Sen. Christopher Dodd (D-CT), Parliament has stolen ideas for bills in the past, but U.S. legislators have never taken issue until now. This time, Dodd said, they spoke out because S.576 was "special."

"S.576 was originally written by the Senate Banking, Housing, and Urban Affairs Committee as a way to provide for improved monetary policy and regulatory reform in financial institution management and activities," Dodd said. "But as we worked on it, it grew into something much bigger and more meaningful: a way to streamline financial regulatory agency actions

---

## "We worked really hard on that bill," Gramm said.

---

and provide for improved credit disclosure."

Thus far, members of the Commons' Finance and Services Committee are denying the plagiarism charges.

"Whenever you have two bicameral legislative bodies, each producing hundreds of bills a year, there's bound to be some creative overlap," MP Lewis Moonie said. "And while we greatly respect what the U.S. Congress has done in the area of expediting procedures regarding mergers with subsidiaries or non-bank affiliates, we would never, ever steal from them. I swear to God, this is just a big coincidence."

"Surely America's lawmakers would recognize that the concept of regulating financial institutions is as old as the hills," Conservative MP David Heathcoat-Amory said. "They were

**Above: Sen. Phil Gramm**

doing it in ancient Rome, so it's not exactly like America came up with the idea first. Although, knowing those arrogant Yanks, I'm sure they think they did."

Other Members of Parliament assert that if anyone is guilty of plagiarism, it is the U.S.

"In the late '60s, American legislators were constantly lifting political

concepts wholesale from Eastern nations such as China and India," said Colin Breed, Liberal Democrat MP for South East Cornwall. "When they did it back then, it was an 'homage,' but when we do it, it's stealing."

"Americans are so closed-minded and self-impressed," Breed added. "They'll go on and on about how utterly amazing the Declaration Of Independence is, but point out that it's just a derivative rehashing of our Magna Carta, and they'll say, 'What's that?'"

Despite such denial and defiance on the part of the British, the U.S. senators refuse to back down.

"We're not giving up," said Gramm, who is demanding that the Commons table the bill indefinitely or face legal action. "I still remember the day we finally placed that bill on the Senate Legislative Calendar. [Sen.] Rick [Santorum (R-PA)], [Sen.] Jim [Bunning (R-KY)], and I had pulled an all-nighter to get it just right, and we were just so unbelievably excited to hand it in. I don't want those memories sullied by a bunch of Brits who are too lazy to make up their own laws." ⌀

BABY from page 157

knocked up or nothing. 'Cause I wasn't. But my best friend Tina had her first one when she was 15, and here I am 18 already, so it's not bad that I didn't get pregnant by accident until now. My mom always told me I should wait until I was living with someone, but I ain't going for that corny-ass, old-fashioned shit.

But here's why I'm buggin' a little on the whole thing: Like I said, that's when I was with Troy, and him and me, we were doing a lot of drinking around then, 'cause that's when we was first getting to know each other.

> **My baby gonna get a good job and make lots of money, and we're gonna go on vacations to the Bahamas together.**

We did a lot of other shit, too, which I won't go into because even though I'm not with Troy anymore, we're still friends, and I ain't about to get him in trouble with his P.O.

That's why I've been thinking about how I hope the baby's all right. I ain't worried that it's dead, because if it wasn't still alive, I know it would come out, because that's what happened to Tina once. I'm not even talking about that. I'm talking about, like, its brain and everything. A lot of people don't know this, but a baby has a brain even before it's born, and it's the same brain it has when it grows up, so if something happens, the kid can come out like a retard.

You might think that ain't a big deal, but it is, 'cause I want my baby to have a better life. My baby gonna get a education. She's gonna get a good job and make lots of money, and we're gonna go on vacations to the Bahamas together. She'll have so much cash, I'll be able to retire early and never have to work another shitty-ass job.

That's why I hope she comes out okay. I want her to have a good life and everything, and that's hard if you're funny-looking and talk weird and drool all the time, 'cause then no one wants to talk to you. And then you'll get depression and not even care about hanging out or partying or nothing.

So I been really thinking lately, because even though I ain't seen no doctor yet, I know for sure I'm pregnant. It sure ain't fat on my stomach, 'cause I've been on a diet since July. But I still gotta go in to the hospital and have them tell me if it's a boy or a girl. I'll do that just as soon as I tell my mom, even though I'm pretty sure she knows and just ain't been saying nothing. And when I see a doctor, I'll ask him about if he thinks the baby will come out okay.

Until then, I guess there ain't nothing else I can do. ∅

158

---

# NYPD Apologizes For Accidental Shooting-Clubbing-Stabbing-Firebombing Death

NEW YORK—New York City police commissioner Howard Safir issued a formal apology Thursday for the accidental shooting-clubbing-stabbing-firebombing-choking-impaling-electrocution-lethal-injection death of a 38-year-old Jamaican immigrant in the Bensonhurst section of Brooklyn.

Livingston

Robert Livingston, who had emigrated from Kingston last July, was surrounded and killed by 27 police officers on April 20 while standing on the stairs in front of an apartment building reaching for what the officers thought was a gun. The object turned out to be a doorbell.

"We deeply regret that this terrible tragedy happened," said Safir, reading an official NYPD statement at City Hall. "But I must stress that it was understandable given the circumstances. There was no way those officers could have known for certain that Mr. Livingston was not heavily armed and about to kill them."

According to NYPD sources, at approximately 11:30 a.m. on the day in question, a detachment of 12 officers observed Livingston, a delivery driver for a Chinese restaurant, standing at the entrance to an apartment building "acting in a suspicious and aggressive manner." After ignoring the officers' repeated commands to put down the threatening item in his hand, a bag containing a double order of General Chao's Chicken and a pint of rice, Livingston reached for the doorbell. The officers responded by opening fire on his strategic top-of-the-stairs position from point-blank range, discharging their standard-issue 9mm handguns 245 times and striking him with approximately 175 teflon-coated hollow-point slugs.

Defiantly ignoring the officers' orders to freeze, Livingston dropped to the floor and convulsed wildly, kicking, thrashing, and spurting blood in all directions.

"It was an extremely dangerous, volatile situation," said Brooklyn 26th Precinct Sgt. Raymond Sullivan. "We were dealing with a man who was out of control and willing to do anything to stop us. It was clear that subduing him would necessitate extreme measures."

After calling for backup, the officers threw 25 phosphorus grenades at the suspect and opened fire with 12-gauge riot shotguns, their vision aided by the illumination of Livingston's body, which was burning at roughly 1,500 degrees. Though most of Liv-

Above: New York mayor Rudolph Giuliani, flanked by police commissioner Howard Safir, fields reporters' questions about the accidental killing of a Jamaican immigrant by 27 NYPD officers.

ingston's clothes had melted off, officers concentrated their fire on his remaining shoe, which they feared held a concealed weapon.

Once 15 extra officers and an NYPD armory van had arrived on the scene, Det. James McPhee took 10 men to the top of the stairs to engage Livingston in hand-to-hand-combat.

"Mr. Livingston attempted to resist, raising his remaining forearm and striking at the officers' weapons with his face, teeth, knees, and genitals," McPhee told reporters. "Acting in accordance with standard police procedure, we countered by stabbing the suspect 59 times in the chest and throat."

Patrolman Edward Caggiano, who sustained a mild bruise when hit by a chunk of Livingston's jaw in the melee, then grabbed the suspect's head and began standard-procedure neck-snapping.

According to the officers involved, Livingston's head attempted to flee the scene by separating from his torso and proceeding down the front steps. "I shouted several times for the head to halt," Caggiano said. "But the more I yelled, the faster it seemed to roll. After every other option and tactic was exhausted, we were left with no

choice but to subdue the head with rocket launchers."

Forensics experts said they hope to recover the several thousand missing fragments of the head by early next week.

Shortly after 1 p.m., Livingston was finally brought under control when a second team of officers impaled his headless body on a sharpened oak spike. Once the body was skewered, members of the NYPD medical team were given clearance to move in and administer a lethal injection.

Speaking at Thursday's press conference, New York mayor Rudolph Giuliani called for the immediate paid suspension of all 27 officers involved in the incident. He also urged Safir to keep the officers suspended "until they can be cleared of all wrongdoing following an extensive internal NYPD investigation that will conclude sometime next Monday."

"And to the families of those officers involved," Giuliani said, "I would like to extend my deepest, most heartfelt apologies. Your loved ones went through a terrible trauma, and I want to assure you that the New York Police Department is doing everything in its power to help them put it behind them." ∅

---

## NEWS IN BRIEF

## Taco Bell's Five Ingredients Combined In Totally New Way

LOUISVILLE, KY—With great fanfare Thursday, Taco Bell unveiled the Grandito, an exciting new permutation of refried beans, ground beef, cheddar cheese, lettuce, and a corn tortilla. "You've never tasted Taco Bell's five ingredients combined quite like this," Taco Bell CEO Walt Berenyi said. "The revolutionary new Grandito, with its ground beef on top of the cheese but under the beans, is configured unlike anything you've ever eaten at Taco Bell." The fast-food chain made waves earlier this year with its introduction of the Zestito, in which the beans are on top of the lettuce, and the Mexiwrap, in which the tortilla is slightly more oblong. ∅

## Comb Technology: Why Is It So Far Behind The Razor And Toothbrush Fields?

see SCIENCE page 3C

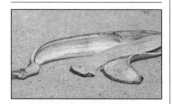

## Discarded Banana Peel Results In Tragicomic Tableau

see ARTS page 11C

## Fifth Level Of Video Game Reached During Phone Call To Mom

see LOCAL page 9C

## Dildo Washed

see LOCAL page 7E

## Four-Year-Old Dressed Nicer Than Local Man

see FASHION page 3B

## Hulk Smash

see LOCAL page 4E

## STATshot

A look at the numbers that shape your world.

**Who Can Possibly Save Us Now?**
1. Aquaman
2. Someone with bolt cutters
3. Jerry from Kar Kom, Your Mobile Audio Headquarters
4. Veteran character actor Paul Bartel; no, wait—he's dead
5. Crash Comet, Space Commander From The Year 2000
6. No one, you fool!

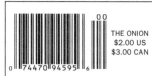

---

# the ONION ®

WWW.THEONION.COM     AMERICA'S FINEST NEWS SOURCE™     FOUNDED 1871

# Half-Naked Kissinger Thrown Out Of *U.S. News & World Report* Mansion

Left: Kissinger parties with a trio of *U.S. News & World Report* Copy Girls hours before the outburst. Above: The fabled mansion.

WASHINGTON, DC—Another chapter was added to the infamous history of the *U.S. News & World Report* Mansion Saturday, when celebrity politico Henry Kissinger, former Secretary of State and longtime fixture at the journalism and pleasure palace, was forcibly removed from

see KISSINGER page 161

---

# Graphic Designer's Judgment Clouded By Desire To Use New Photoshop Plug-In

CLEVELAND HEIGHTS, OH—The aesthetic judgment of Paul Gaskill, a graphic designer working on a brochure for Valley View Apartments, was "severely clouded" by an overwhelming desire to use a new Adobe Photoshop plug-in, coworkers at Blue Moon Design said Friday.

"Looking at this brochure, it's obvious Paul just wanted to use the 'wave' frame effect from that new PhotoFrame 2.0 software package we got last week,"

see DESIGNER page 160

Above: Photoshop plug-in enthusiast Paul Gaskill.

---

# Terrorist Extremely Annoyed By Delayed Flight

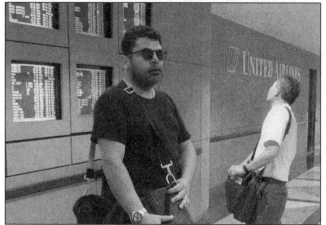

Above: Inconvenienced suicide bomber Nidal Hanani waits at O'Hare.

CHICAGO—His flight from O'Hare to LaGuardia delayed more than six hours, Hamas militant and would-be suicide bomber Nidal Hanani vowed Friday never again to fly United Airlines.

"I do not have time for this," said Hanani, seated at a Burger King in Concourse C, a plastic-explosives-filled duffel bag at his feet. "My jihad against the West was supposed to be carried out shortly after takeoff at 8:35 this morning. It is now 2:50 p.m. How much longer must I sit around this airport like an idiot before God's will is done?"

Added Hanani: "They said the plane is still in Denver, where they are still waiting for a pilot from another flight.

see TERRORIST page 160

DESIGNER from page 159

fellow Blue Moon graphic designer Jared Mahaffey said. "There are whacked-out, psychedelic edges all over the place—on the photos, on the floor-plan charts, even on the text boxes, for God's sake."

The wave effect, one of PhotoFrame 2.0's many features, creates a distorted, wavy edge around the perimeter of a photo at the click of a mouse. Using the plug-in, a frame can also be distorted, colored, scaled, or softened—effects used inappropriately and excessively by Gaskill in his brochure for the Parma, OH, apartment complex.

"Clearly, Paul was extremely excited about this new plug-in," said coworker Danielle Rice, pointing to a warped, psychedelicized photo of Valley View's on-site laundry facilities. "He was like a kid in a candy store."

According to Rice, Blue Moon Design received PhotoFrame 2.0 on Sept. 20 as part of a MacWarehouse order. Gaskill, she said, installed it on his computer the same day. After an hour of experimenting with the plug-in's various features, he was overheard declaring it "some killer software," exhorting coworkers to come over to his desk to "check it out."

"If you think [Photoshop's] Ocean

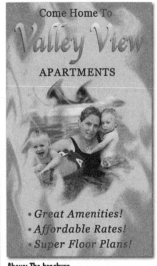

Above: The brochure.

Ripple [filter] is cool, you've got to see this new PhotoFrame stuff," Gaskill told several colleagues gathered around his workstation. "I can hardly believe all those times I went to the trouble of using a quick mask, blurring the image, then pixillating it with the 'crystallize' effect to refract the softened edges. Man, those were the Dark Ages."

While Gaskill, 29, admitted to making liberal use of PhotoFrame 2.0, he insists that it was appropriate for the job at hand.

"Sure, I was eager to try out the new plug-in," Gaskill said, "but only because it was perfect for this job. The wave-frame effect gives Valley View Apartments that dynamic, cutting-edge feel it needs. It communicates that Valley View living is so convenient and affordable, it'll blow your freakin' mind."

Despite Gaskill's confidence, fellow Blue Moon graphic designers say they would have given the brochure a more traditional look.

"It's an ad for an apartment complex, not a head shop," Mahaffey said. "Why would you want to show Valley View's 'convenient on-site parking' and 'friendly office team' through a hallucinogenic haze?"

Mahaffey said this is not the first time he has seen a graphic designer led astray by an exciting new Photoshop plug-in.

"It happens more than you'd think around here," Mahaffey said. "With Marty [Boyd], it was the blur features. 'Motion blur,' 'gaussian blur,' 'radial blur'—you name it, he'd blur it. With Rebecca [Almeida], it was the Alien

Skin Eye Candy effects. The temptation is always going to be there."

Alarmingly, Gaskill's journey of graphic-effects discovery may only be beginning. The wave effect, Mahaffey said, is just one of hundreds of PhotoFrame 2.0 options. With the plug-in, users can easily make an image glow, cast a shadow, and create charcoal outlines. Mahaffey said he expects to see many of these effects surface in Gaskill's work in the near future.

"If he digs deeper into the Volume 3 digital collection, there's going to be real trouble," Mahaffey said. "Unless we can somehow break through to him, we're going to see 'Comet,' 'Disco'... good Lord, even 'Bubbles.'"

Though it claims no responsibility, Extensis, the Portland-based maker of PhotoFrame 2.0, expressed regret over the botched Valley View brochure.

"I'm sorry to hear that a less-than-perfect brochure was created with our software," Extensis CEO Greg Fleming said. "Perhaps we could make it up to Mr. Gaskill with a demo version of Suitcase 9.0. It's packed with automated features that make it easier than ever to use literally thousands of great fonts, everything from Snowcap to Alphabet Soup Tilt." ∅

TERRORIST from page 159

Screwed up, this United is."

Compounding Hanani's frustration is the fact that his two previous flights—a commuter shuttle from Assira al-Shamaliyeh to Damascus followed by a redeye from Damascus to Chicago—were also delayed more than four hours each.

"The bile churns within me, I am so outraged," Hanani said. "I go to the ticket counter, and the females wearing men's clothing tell me, 'We can put you on standby and try to get you on a 4 p.m. flight.' Why do they say this word, 'try'? I did not buy a ticket for a 4 p.m. flight. I buy a ticket for a 8:35 a.m. flight."

"I have kneeled toward Mecca three times today already," added Hanani, gesturing eastward in the direction of a TCBY stand. "Still I wait."

Shortly after 3 p.m., Sherrie Walker, a United Airlines representative, announced that anyone on Flight 225 willing to give up his or her seat and fly early the next day would receive overnight lodging and a $500 voucher good for travel on United anywhere in the continental U.S. Hanani declined the offer.

"Why should I want to fly again on this lousy airline that has given me nothing but the most profound of aggravation? Even for a free $500 ticket, it is not worth it," Hanani said. "Besides, I cannot wait even one more day to deliver my urgent message to the world that Islam is the true religion of God and that its truth is manifest in its power."

United Airlines spokespersons blamed the delay on a combination of factors, citing bad weather in the airline's Denver hub and the ongoing la-

Above: Hanani kills time in a Concourse C gift shop.

bor dispute with its pilots union. The pilots' refusal to work overtime in protest of the pace of contract talks has been a major factor in United canceling as many as 20,000 flights this summer.

"I do not care about labor problems," said Hanani, fidgeting with his small, radio-activated bomb detonator. "All I know is, I pay for ticket, I expect to fly. If these infidels cannot fly me, they should not take my money. I would not have such headaches on Syrian Arab Airlines, that is for certain."

Hanani then rose and walked to a

wall of monitors to read the list of scheduled departures for the fifth time in less than an hour.

"Why are these airlines so incompetent?" Hanani asked fellow frustrated traveler Colleen Mayes, who was stranded at O'Hare when her flight to Salt Lake City was cancelled after a five-hour delay. "It can only be the lack of discipline in this corrupt, immoral Western country."

"At least I am far less helpless than all the other Flight 225 passengers who wait with me," continued Hanani, eating a Pizza Hut personal

pan pizza he bought for "a ridiculous amount of money." "Unlike them, I shall reach my destination—a glorious afterlife."

One problem Hanani has not encountered is interference from O'Hare security. When Flight 225 finally does take off, the fundamentalist's bomb, disguised as a piece of geological research equipment, is expected to kill all 300-plus passengers and crew members.

"I was afraid they would tell me that my bag is too big to be carry-on and that I must check it," Hanani said. "The detonator signal does not work if the bag is underneath the plane. Fortunately, I was able to take as carry-on. Praise God."

Informed of Hanani's dissatisfaction, United customer-service supervisor Bill Stringer offered his apologies.

"We're very sorry that one of our valued customers has been inconvenienced by our travel delays," Stringer said. "But I can assure Mr. Hanani that we're taking every step possible to get him to his destination just as soon as we possibly can. United Airlines is fully committed to addressing its problems and providing better service in the future."

For now, Hanani continues to wait. All he can do, he said, is hope there are no further delays.

"Upon my death, be it 6 p.m. or 9:30 or midnight, I know I shall be rewarded manifold for my stalwartness," Hanani said. "But try my patience, this incompetent airline does. On the Day of Judgment, may United's employees and those of its subsidiaries be condemned to the pits of Hell for all eternity." ∅

the premises after removing his pants and drunkenly plummeting from a second-story balcony into a pool.

"Hank is a longtime friend of the mansion, and the events of last weekend won't change that," said *U.S. News & World Report* editor-in-chief Mort Zuckerman, speaking to reporters in the mansion's jungle-themed Southeast Asian Correspondent Room. "He just had a few too many Harvey Wallbangers, and we had to send him home. Nobody knows how to go off the deep end like the Kiss-Man."

Sporting his trademark purple velvet smoking jacket and pipe, the smiling Zuckerman stressed that there were "no hard feelings" about the incident and joked that Kissinger was welcome back to his regular guest room at the mansion any time, "as long as the old boy can keep it in his pants next time."

The *U.S. News & World Report* Mansion has long been notorious for its wild parties. Saturday's gathering, however, exceeded even its usual standards for debauchery. Former Clinton aide George Stephanopoulos was spotted poolside debating Social Security restructuring with leggy Fact-Checker Of The Month Caryn Alderson. Nearby, leather-clad Senate Republican Policy Committee chair Larry Craig (R-ID) stood atop the pool bar, challenging all comers to "try and beat me in arm-wrestling." An all-nude romp in the mansion's legendary Domestic Affairs Grotto included such journalistic luminaries as CBS anchor Dan Rather, *Weekly Standard* publisher William Kristol, and sultry, neoconservative MSNBC political analyst Laura Ingraham.

"It was like the fall of Rome," said historian and presidential biographer David Halberstam, who attended the party on the arm of former Clinton press secretary DeeDee Myers. "At one point, while everybody was circling the solid gold Party Globe in the

Grand Newsroom in a conga line, poor Kissinger wiped out on a huge pile of AP-wire printouts that had collected in the sunken-fireplace pit by the gold statue of [*U.S. News & World Report* founder] David Lawrence. We thought he'd broken his neck, but in a flash, he was back on his feet and calling for 'more wine, more wine' in his unmistakable, German-accented, basso profundo voice. Then he shouted that he was 'more bombed than Cambodia in '73.'"

A short time later, a group of *U.S. News & World Report* Copy Girls, renowned for keeping the magazine free of errors and for their trademark skimpy outfits, formed a kickline as former CIA director John Deutch treated the crowd to an improvisational blues jam paying tribute to the evening's guest of honor, former president George Bush. The jam was cut short when a pantsless Kissinger burst through the kickline in full stride, diving through a large balcony window into a pool two stories below.

Bush, who at one point disappeared for a half-hour into the mansion's Velvet Typesetting Room with wife Barbara and CNN *Crossfire* co-host Mary Matalin, defended Kissinger's behavior.

"Kissinger—disco king, no doubt, no doubt. Did he do anything the rest of us wouldn't? I'd say not. Good man, the Kisser—knows how to get down," Bush told reporters from his guest room at the mansion, where he is recuperating from a "heckuva hangover." "Loves the wine? Sure, sure. Women? Song? No question there. But a good egg, and I'll stand by him."

Zuckerman defended his mansion and its parties, which have come under renewed fire in the wake of the latest incident.

"Some people may say that *U.S. News & World Report*'s commitment to incisive, cutting-edge news reportage, and all the fun that entails, is

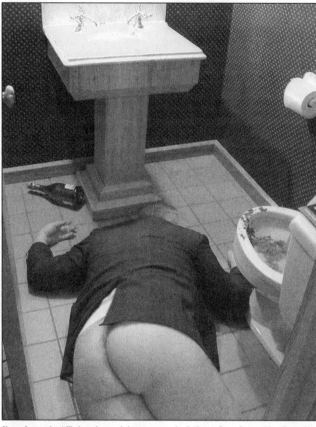

Above: A passed-out Kissinger is sprawled across a mansion bathroom floor after vomiting. He would later awaken to stir up more trouble.

excessive or immoral," the 72-year-old Zuckerman said. "In fact, Calvin Trillin wrote a very critical piece in last week's *Time* about us—probably because he was mad he wasn't invited—but condemnations of the news-gathering lifestyle are both hypocritical and unenlightened. There's no reason reporting the news can't retain the fantasy element it had when we were in our teens and 20s. News should be informative, but also sexy and fun. That's always been my magazine's approach, and it's the only

way to get unbiased, comprehensive coverage while remaining young at heart."

"Of course, a solid supply of Viagra and dating the Weinbaum triplets doesn't hurt," added Zuckerman, referring to Mindy, Cindy, and Windy Weinbaum, the three 22-year-old interns he has been dating since divorcing 1991 Copy Girl Of The Year Bobbi Brandt in April. "And now, if you'll excuse me, there's an 'event' that needs 'covering' in the Business & Technology Bungalow." Ø

---

# West-Wing Tech Support Crew Be A Buncha Wack Bitches

Yo yo yo yo yo yo, whassssup, bruthas and sistas of H-Dog, Tha Lowdown Funky-Fresh Gangsta Bad Ass of the Accountz Reeceevable

**By Herbert Kornfeld**
**Accounts Receivable**
**Supervisor**

Department of Midstate Office Supply, Tha Righteous Funk Masta, Tha Stone-Cold Muthafuckin' Playa wit' all tha dope spread-sheets and fly alphabetized invoice files and

shit. Y'all be down with the H-Dog, know what I'm sayin'? And those who ain't, y'all can kiss my ass, muthafuckas. Some cocksuckas tried to

fuck wit' tha H-Dog last week and got they fuckin' asses WHUPPED.

The sorry cocksuckas in question was the Tech Support staff on the west wing of the third-floor general administrative office. Me and my crew here on the east wing of the third floor, we hate them west-wing Tech Support muthafuckas. They always be tryin' to muscle in on our turf wit' they muthafuckin' control of the company's computa network and fuckin' wit' my accounting software and otherwise tellin' me what to do and shit. Thass bullshit! The only person who can tell tha H-Dog what to do is his mama. And Allah. All the rest of y'all muthafuckas can go fuck yo'selves.

This whole east-west beef started about three months ago. Before that,

it was all good: All the departments be chillin', doin' they own thang, know what I'm sayin'? But then, this past March, this muthafucka named Ted Wegerle gets hired as the new Tech Support supervisor, and he starts makin' all these changes around the office, devisin' ways to make the computa system run more efficient and shit.

About a week after he be hired, Wegerle send his computa bitches around to check all the extensions and power cords and shit in every department to make sure they be secure and don't need no replacement. So one of these computa bitches rides up to my cubicle and starts snoopin' around on his knees under my desk, his li'l Dockers-wearin' ass pokin' up

like he gonna give me head or something. So I says to him, "Yo, what tha fuck you be doin' under there?" He raise his head and say that I gots too much plugged into my power strip, including two adding machines and another extension cord, an' that I should have nothing but my computer and desk lamp plugged in there. So I say, "Well, then why don't yo' pussy supervisor get my department bigger power strips, you wack-ass bitch?" When I says that, the li'l bastard turns all red and runs back to his fuckin' turf. He was shit-scared, I know it, 'cause I gots a rep for being the hardest muthafucka on the whole damn third floor.

Then, a few weeks after that, see KORNFELD page 162

Wegerle goes and upgrades my accounting software without consultin' me. When me and my posse logged on to Lotus, we got all this weird extra shit I ain't never seen before. Man, I was so pissed, I packed my Letter Opener Of Death and fuckin' invaded the west-wing turf, demandin' to see Wegerle. So I says to him, "What the fuck y'all do wit' my accounting shit? It was def before all y'all changed it. Change that shit back before I cuts you and the rest of you wack computa bitches."

I was about to go all *American Psycho* on those muthafuckas, but Wegerle says, all cool and shit, "Herbert, the only real changes on your software are some upgrades to the graphics, the addition of a few hot keys, and a quicker downloading time. Otherwise, nothing has substantially changed. If anything, you'll be able to do your spreadsheets much more efficiently now."

So he talked me out of slicin' him and his software-installin' bitches, which ended up being the worst fuckin' mistake I coulda made, 'cause it sent them the message that they could fuck wit' tha H-Dog. When I figured this out, I decided to get me some allies against Tech Support, in case those fuckas tried to invade my turf again. So I goes up to Myron Schabe, the Accountz Payabo supervisor.

Now, normally, I just be laughin' at Myron, 'cause he be this old candy-ass fool who wear Sansabelt slacks every day to work. But Accountz Payabo be in the middle of the third floor, in between tha east and west wings, so they in the crossfire when the shit go down. They is, therefore, of strategic significance an' all that army shit. If Tech Support tried to invade our turf, the Accountz Payabo Krew could tell them to back the fuck off, and ain't no way they could reach tha east wing. So I ask Myron to join my posse and offer him some of my secret stash of Wisconsin Dells admission discount coupons I be keepin' in my desk.

But Myron just say, "I'm not getting involved in this, Herbert. If you have a problem with Ted, you can take your grievances to Bob Cowan in Human Resources."

I shoulda known that dickless ol' bastard would say somethin' like that. "Thass cool, sucka," I say. "When tha shit goes down, you just be in tha middle anyway."

Sure enough, last Thursday, the shit with Tech Support went down when I made this hardcore, dope-ass image for my desktop. Man, that desktop image was the shit. I went down to the Marketing Department and used their scanner to scan this picture of a forest with tha inscription, "Attitudes Are Contagious... Is Yours Worth Catching?" You ain't kiddin', muthafucka! I saved it on a disk and loaded into my computer, so when I reboot, I get this muthafuckin' fly-ass shit on my desktop instead of that goddamn Windows logo.

The next day, the entire office be gettin' these memos in they mailboxes. "Lately, it has come to my attention that several people have been creating personalized desktop images for their computers. We ask that people

---

### Those who fuck wit' tha H-Dog get they sorry asses BEAT DOWN.

---

stop doing this and return to using one of the default desktop images included in the office-wide Windows 98 operating system. Aside from being an unnecessary activity which wastes office time and resources, creating a desktop image takes up a lot of memory and can create problems within your departmental LAN. If you have any questions, please feel free to contact me. Have a good day. Ted Wegerle, Tech Support Supervisor."

It was muthafuckin' zero hour, man.

I stands up on my chair and shouts across tha floor, "Yeah, I gots a question, Ted Wegerle, you muthafucka. Why you be fuckin' with tha H-Dog and the East-Wing Office Krew? I gots a vendetta out against you and the rest of tha west-wing Tech Support bitches, 'cause you be dissin' me and my posse and makin' me look the fool in front of my homies. You can't tell tha H-Dog what to do. I gots seniority, muthafucka. I gots da money, da shorties, and tha Employee Of Tha Month plaques to prove it. You only been here three months and still be on probation, cocksucka. Just because you know computa shit don't mean you can fuck everybody over. You think you all that, but you ain't, muthafucka. You just frontin'. So fuck you, bitch. Fuck you and yo' homies and yo' wack-ass Spider-Man neckties, too, 'cause you ain't no playa, beeeeee-yotch! H-Dog over and OUT."

I sits back down, and everyone in tha east wing be whoopin' and givin' me high-fives like they be on *Arsenio*. Myron Schabe be shakin' his head and havin' this hangdog look on his face, 'cause he be in tha crossfire and can't get no work done. That was Myron's goddamn problem, though. He coulda joined my dope posse.

The next day, there be another memo in our mailboxes, this time from Lawrence Kanner, the Midstate Office Supply vice-president.

"In order to improve the effectiveness of the Technical Support Department, we have decided to move Ted Wegerle and the rest of his staff to the second floor in the space adjoining the mainframe computer. The Marketing Department will relocate to Tech Support's former offices on the west wing of the third-floor general administrative office."

Like I said before, those who fuck wit' tha H-Dog get they sorry asses BEAT DOWN. I didn't even have to say nothin' to the vice-president: He knew tha H-Dog was out for muthafuckin' blood, and that he had to defuse tha situation before things got violent. I gots more clout with Kanner than that muthafuckin' Ted Wegerle pussy and the rest of his wack posse combined. And, on top of all that, right before Wegerle left the third floor, I stole the ball out of his fuckin' mouse, too.

I don't expect no problems with Marketing, 'cause Marketing's full of some of the flyest hos you ever seen, and they all be wantin' to freak tha H-Dog, 'cause they know I be hung like a muthafuckin' horse. H-Dog over and OUT. ∅

---

**EDITORIAL**

# Genocide Is Such A Harsh Word

We're all adults here. Can we please conduct this U.N. tribunal without stooping to using that loaded term? Yes, as leader of the Kunhing military junta in Myanmar, I did call for the death of four million people, all of whom just happened to be of Shan ethnicity. And, yes, a few of these Shan—let's say 921,452—died at the hands of my mercenary army. But are we really prepared to call it a genocide? That's not the sort of word you just throw around.

By Gen. Myanaung Phauk

Granted, I did call for the Salween River to run red with the blood of the Shan. But did I ever use the word genocide when I called for Burmese, Chinese, and Karens to rise up against their Shan neighbors and rid the Earth of this mongrel race? Of course not.

If something that appears to resemble a genocide did occur at my hands in Myanmar, that certainly was not my intention. Everything I did was in the name of working toward the noble goal of redistributing all land and resources to their rightful, non-Shan owners—a land-distribution system dating back to the 11th-century Burmese kingdom of Bagan.

Even "ethnic cleansing" has become a dirty word nowadays. It's getting so that you can't work toward purification without someone calling you the new Hitler.

Sure, we've all heard the recordings of my radio addresses and read my

---

### That's not the sort of word you just throw around.

---

statements in *The Shan-Annihilation Press*, in which I urged Burmese farmers to sharpen their scythes, descend upon Taunggyi, and leave not a man, woman, or child standing. What does that prove? So what if Taunggyi is the capital of the Shan state? Is everyone in Belgium a Belgian?

True, it was the Shan miners at Bawdwin who were seized and burned to death inside the shafts. And, yes, it was Shan workers who were split throat-to-stomach and stacked up like cordwood in the smeltery at Namtu. But to call these massacres? That's so extreme.

Now, maybe if we'd descended upon a Buddhist temple full of refugees in Keng Tung armed with machine guns and missiles, the tribunal could call it a massacre. We all know that a single rocket launcher costs nearly 125,000 kyat around here. We used mere rifles and bulldozers to kill the 13,000 in Keng Tung.

As with most things, your opinion of my regime depends entirely upon your perspective. Yes, there is proof of the live burial at Thayetwa and the fire raids on the grade school in Syway, but you really had to be there to understand what went on. We have a saying in Kunhing: "One man's torture center is another man's retreat where one is released from the shame of being born into this world a Shan."

Perhaps the lowest blow of all was when the U.N. tribunal brought up my silly little nickname, "Ma-ubbin Toukka." Yes, technically, it does mean "one who grinds human skulls into a fine powder with his boot." But the true spirit of it gets lost in the translation.

So how am I supposed to get a fair trial now? People hear a word like "genocide," and they close their minds to everything else. They completely ignore the fact that, even to this day, these agrarian curs are marrying non-Shan. But all it takes is just one U.N. tribunal to scream "genocide," and you're forever labeled a bloodthirsty mass-murderer. "Bloodthirsty"? Who does this sort of name-calling benefit?

Let's take one more look at this nebulous word "genocide," which is defined as "the deliberate and systematic extermination of a national or racial group." Last time I checked, there were still 2,623,947 Shan left in Myanmar. That doesn't sound like much of a genocide to me.

Now, if you'd be so kind as to leave me be—perhaps until about, oh, September 2001—I have some important business to attend to. ∅

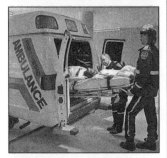

## Ann Landers' Advice Arrives 11 Weeks Too Late

see OBITUARY page 14A

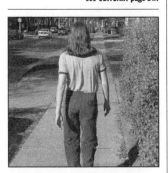

## Guy Totally Looked Like Chick From Behind

see LOCAL page 2D

## Educational Puppet Pelted With Crayons

see LOCAL page 2C

A look at the numbers that shape your world.

**Least Qualified U.S. Daycares**
1. Wee Basement Daycare — Kirby, AR
2. Discarded Refrigerator Play Park — Howell, MI
3. Arthur Treacher's Fish & Daycare — Bristol, PA
4. Krawlspace-4-Kids — Bedford, IN
5. Pappy 'n' Betty Lou's Common-Law Kidcare Cabin — Erwin, TN
6. Vista View Daycare-On-A-Jutting-Precipice — Livingston, MT

# the ONION®

WWW.THEONION.COM     AMERICA'S FINEST NEWS SOURCE™     FOUNDED 1871

Above: President Clinton and other *Star Wars* fans wait outside a D.C.-area Loew's Multiplex for the May 19 opening of *The Phantom Menace*.

# Clinton Takes Leave Of Office To Stand In Line For *Star Wars: Episode I*

WASHINGTON, DC—Citing "America's unprecedented prosperity and stability" and "this one part where this ship is underwater and this sea-monster thing tries to eat it," Bill Clinton became the first U.S. president to take a leave of absence Tuesday, temporarily stepping down to wait in line for the May 19 opening of *Star Wars: Episode I—The Phantom Menace*.

"My fellow Americans, like so many of you, I am extremely eager to see the next chapter in the greatest movie series in the history of mankind," said Clinton, sporting a limited-edition IG-88 tie clip, during a White House press conference. "And, as president of the nation that has produced these movies, I am fully committed to being at that very first showing, even if it means missing almost four weeks of

see CLINTON page 165

# Area Bedroom Has That Weird Jeff Smell, Housemates Report

PHOENIX—The bedroom of Jeffrey Worthen has that weird sort of Jeff smell, housemates of the 22-year-old Rio Salado Community College art student reported Tuesday.

"I don't know what it is, but the whole room always has that certain distinct Jeffish odor," housemate Evan Cadwaler said. "I can't put my finger on what the smell is exactly, but it definitely smells like Jeff."

Convening to discuss containment

see JEFF page 164

Above: Worthen's (inset) room.

# Nevada Gaming Commission Lobbies Congress For Just $20 Million 'Til Friday

Above: Nevada Gaming Commission chairman Freddy Loquasto pleads his case to Congress.

WASHINGTON, DC—Characterizing its financial woes as "nothing too serious, just the kind of setback everybody has now and then," the Nevada Gaming Commission lobbied Congress Tuesday for $20 million in federal subsidies that the group swears to pay back Friday.

Gaming commission chairman Freddy Loquasto, appearing somewhat agitated and sweaty, assured House Appropriations Committee members that his group "[has] got a line on some hot new 'Arabian Nights' dollar slots that turn an incredible profit. Only we have to buy them right now, and the till is empty. But the payouts on these babies are so stingy, we can pretty much pay back what you lend

see COMMISSION page 164

COMMISSION from page 163

us immediately."

Added Loquasto, "Seriously, guys, we'll pay you right back. And I mean, like, double."

As a show of good faith, Loquasto offered Congress his wristwatch, which, though worth far less than the requested $20 million, is "a genuine Rolodex."

"This is a very fine, very expensive piece of jewelry," said Loquasto, holding up the watch to show legislators. "I would not risk losing a one-of-a-kind item like this to welch on a loan. The only reason I'm using this watch as collateral is because I'm that sure I'll pay the loan back in full."

"Gentlemen, I don't want to waste your valuable time with a bunch of sob stories that would only bore you," Loquasto continued. "The point is, it is very urgent that we receive this money right away."

House Appropriations Committee chairman C.W. Bill Young (R-FL) is skeptical about Loquasto's trustworthiness.

"I like the Nevada Gaming Commission and, of course, I feel for them at this difficult time," Young said. "But I wonder if another subsidy is going to help them learn at all. I mean, the last time we allocated funding to them, they turned right around and spent it all on liquor licenses."

Fellow committee member Frank Wolf (R-VA) expressed similar reservations. "The Nevada Gaming Commission has a history of poor money management," he said. "In 1998, it burned through its entire annual budget in a single weekend. To make matters worse, it had trouble explaining exactly what the money was spent on, giving evasive answers like, 'We bought a bunch of baccarat tables and some other stuff.'"

Wolf also cited a March incident in

Above: A Nevada Gaming Commission official is forced to pawn a Harrah's slot machine after a wild, three-day budget-allocating binge.

which the commission, temporarily placed in charge of $4.3 million earmarked for Nevada's school-lunch program, immediately squandered the funds on shuttle buses for the new Aladdin Resort & Casino. When asked about it, Loquasto insisted that he "had a hunch" about the investment.

"It's always the same thing with those guys," Wolf said. "Every time they get a little money in their pockets, they blow it trying to make more."

Former commission member Don Friesz described an addiction bordering on illness.

"The Nevada Gaming Commission is only happy when it's investing funds in the expansion and promotion of the gambling industry," said Friesz, now president of the Carson City Chamber of Commerce. "It used to be perfectly content just regulating the gaming industry—issuing permits, regulating casinos, mediating labor disputes—but before long, it wasn't a big enough thrill for them. They had to start putting their own money on the line."

Despite such criticism, Loquasto insisted to legislators that the Nevada Gaming Commission has never allocated funds inappropriately.

"Contrary to what some people would have you believe, we only spend our money on things that are necessary to the overall health and success of Nevada's gaming industry," Loquasto said. "So, come on, House Appropriations Committee, help us out here: Baby needs a new pair of giant golden sphinxes." Ø

## Fame Sexually Transmitted

LONDON—Guy Ritchie, Madonna's British boyfriend, has sexually contracted fame from the pop superstar, Ritchie's physician confirmed Tuesday. "It would appear that Mr. Ritchie, a previously obscure director with just two films to his credit, has become famous through sexual contact with Madonna," Dr. Ian Woolsey-Lodge said. "As a fame carrier himself, he now can be found on *Entertainment Tonight* and in *People* magazine, even when not with Madonna." Woolsey-Lodge said Ritchie forever runs the risk of any future offspring being born famous.

## Republicans' 'Diversity Through Imported Africans' Plan Criticized

WASHINGTON, DC—A plank in the Republican Party platform calling for a "Diversity Through Imported Africans" program is drawing fire from civil-rights leaders. "I don't see why the NAACP would be opposed to the further enrichment of our nation's glorious patchwork of races," said U.S. Sen. Jesse Helms (R-NC), co-author of the plan. "We merely seek to increase America's already remarkable diversity through the importation of 10 million strong-backed West African males. These healthy, disease-free males from Gabon, Benin, and Togo will only add spice to the wondrous cultural stew that is America." Helms added that the plan will also create millions of jobs in the fields of housekeeping and farmwork. Ø

JEFF from page 163

strategies for the mysterious Jeff-based vapors, Cadwaler and fellow housemates Eric Mayhew and Chad Beem agreed that the smell seems to be strongest around 8:30 p.m.

"His room is right off the room where the TV is, and usually, like halfway through *The X-Files*, we're hit with this wave of, well, I can't really describe it."

According to Mayhew, the housemates first noticed the Jeff smell this past February, when Worthen left the door to his bedroom, located right next to the living room, open while he was out of town for the weekend.

"While Jeff was away, I went into his room to look for a videotape that had that week's *Space Ghost* on it, and that's when I first noticed it," said Mayhew, a dishwasher at The Timbers Supper Club. "I can't really describe what it's like. It's not a terrible smell, actually, but it's definitely there. You can sort of smell it on Jeff himself, but if you go into his room, it hits you the second you open the door."

Discussing the odor while sifting through a stack of CDs on Worthen's

bedside table, Mayhew and Beem agreed that the smell is neither a foot smell nor a rotten-food smell, but could be something closer to maybe being like a musty sort of smell, almost.

The smell, which the housemates agreed is not an old-person smell or even a sweaty-guy smell, has always been a part of Worthen and his room, though it has never been displeasing enough to interfere with the housemates' friendship with him.

"I wouldn't really say it reeks," Beem said. "It just smells kinda 'off.' It's not the kind of obvious smell where you could just tell him straight up, 'Dude, crack a window in here.'"

Though an open-door policy exists in the house, the housemates, who generally convene in the living-room area, rarely need to enter each other's rooms. But during each of the five known instances when one of the housemates did enter Worthen's room, the person emerged noting the distinct Jeff-esque scent that is unique to his personal area.

"My first guess was that it was dirty

laundry, but there weren't that many dirty clothes lying around," said Cadwaler, who recently led an expedition into the room to rule out such potential smell sources as old plates of

> "Is the smell coming from Jeff, or does Jeff smell that way because he spends time in there?" Mayhew asked.

food, half-empty beer bottles, and wet articles of clothing. "Maybe it could be those boxes of old comics he keeps under the bed."

Added Cadwaler: "To tell you the truth, I never used to think about the smell all that much, but now that we've started talking about it, I kind of want to know what's up with it."

Last Tuesday, during a venture into Worthen's room to look for a rubber

band, Cadwaler detected a particularly strong dose of the Jeff smell coming from the vicinity of his pillow. He was unable to determine, however, whether the pillow was the source of the smell or simply a carrier.

The same question has been asked about Worthen, who, according to the housemates, showers four to five times a week but still bears the odor.

"Is the smell coming from Jeff, or does Jeff smell that way because he spends time in there?" Mayhew asked. "It's kind of like the chicken and the egg."

Worthen's roommates doubt that they will ever discover the source of the scent, as all three have been reluctant to broach the subject with him. The three unanimously agreed, however, that the smell is "more weird than bad" and ultimately "no real biggie."

Said Mayhew: "You know how sometimes a dog smells like a dog, and it's not actually bad that it smells that way, but you just sort of notice it and think to yourself, 'Oh, there's that dog smell'? Well, that's kind of how it is with Jeff." Ø

# Study: Many Rappers May Suffer From Unrealistically High Self-Images

WASHINGTON, DC—According to an American Psychological Association study released Tuesday, an alarming percentage of U.S. rappers may suffer from unrealistically high self-images, putting them at risk of a host of emotional and interpersonal problems.

The study—which examined the attitudes and self-perceptions of more than 600 MCs in hoods across the U.S., including Illtown, H-Town, Strong Island, the Brooklyn Zoo, Harlem World, and Long Beach—found that nearly 95 percent of those surveyed exhibit a distorted sense of their own prowess, particularly with regard to wealth, sexual potency, and influence over their peers.

"While personal confidence is a vital aspect of building a healthy self-image, an exaggerated sense of self can lead to trouble," study head Dr. Judith Danziger said. "The overconfidence these rappers display can have a wide range of negative consequences, from humiliating defeat at the hands of a superior MC to getting a cap placed in one's ass."

The most common manifestation of rappers' exaggerated self-images, the

see RAPPERS page 166

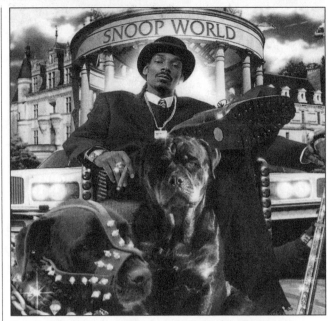

Above: An artist's rendering of a young rapper's warped conception of himself and his world.

CLINTON from page 163

work."

Added Clinton: "There are these droids in *Phantom Menace* that look like giant orbs, but then they unfold like Transformers and fight. And Darth Maul has this light saber that's double-bladed. It's going to be so incredible."

Clinton began waiting in line with "Joe," a friend who owns The Sarlacc Pit, a comic-book store in downtown D.C.

"Joe is the only person who can beat me at *Star Wars* Trivial Pursuit. He knows the English lyrics to 'Lapti Nek,'" Clinton said. "He was also the one who told me that Uncle Owen is really Obi-Wan's brother, which came as quite a surprise, because, like most people, I had always assumed that Owen was Anakin's brother. I did, however, inform Joe that Bruce Boa, the actor who played General Rieekan, also played the guy on *Fawlty Towers* who wanted the Waldorf salad. Joe did not know that."

Clinton arrived at the theater at 11:38 a.m. Tuesday, becoming the 17th person in line. But by 2 p.m., he had maneuvered his way to sixth by winning a series of *Star Wars* Collectible Card Game tournaments and trivia challenges.

"This one guy tried to beat me by asking Hammerhead's real name," he said. "Can you believe it? As if I'd never read *Tales From The Mos Eisley Cantina*, even if I wasn't into the role-playing game. I knew he was a rube when he asked that, so I went in for the kill by asking him the name of the Rodian in the *Star Wars Holiday Special*."

"Of course," Clinton continued, "Hammerhead is Momaw Nadon, and the Rodian was Ludlo." The president then excused himself to join a group sing-along of "Weird Al" Yankovic's "Yoda."

Despite being confined to one spot

for the next month, Clinton said he expects to have plenty of activities to pass the time. "Joe and I are trying to organize a thing where we divide up parts and re-enact all the movies, except we both want to be Han," he said. "I think I should get to be Han because I am the leader of the free world, but if that becomes a deal-breaker, I would be willing to compromise."

Presidential aides have also been instructed to supply Clinton with magazine articles concerning *Episode I* as they become available, as well as deliver, immediately upon publication, the final installment of the four-issue Dark Horse Comics miniseries *Boba Fett: Enemy Of The Empire*.

"Issue three ended just as Fett and Vader were about to start fighting," Clinton said. "They both want this alien head in a box that can tell the future, and the moment Fett finally gets it, Vader appears. Obviously, it's not going to be a fight to the death, because the whole story takes place prior to the trilogy, but it's still sure to be a great fight."

Clinton said he hopes to see *Phantom Menace* at least 20 times between May 19 and May 23, then return to office on the 24th, when he will scale back to once-a-day screenings. The president also noted that, during his extended absence from the White House, he will be available in the event of an emergency.

"Should a major crisis arise, whether regarding the situation in Kosovo or anywhere else, I can be reached at my place in line by cell phone," Clinton said. "But I have urged my advisors only to contact me if absolutely necessary. I would also urge Serbian president Slobodan Milosevic to follow the example of the Jedi Knights and use his powers only for knowledge and defense, never for attack."

Added Clinton: "Wars not make one great."

Clinton, a die-hard *Star Wars* fan ever since the 1977 release of the original, has rarely disrupted his official duties for *Star Wars*-related activities. Notable exceptions include a May 1983 hiatus from the Arkansas governorship to see *Return Of The Jedi* on its opening day and a 1995 trip to an Arlington, VA, *Star Wars* convention to obtain the autographs of actors Anthony Daniels, Jeremy Bulloch, and Femi Taylor, as well as *Jedi Academy* trilogy author Kevin J. Anderson.

Clinton is also believed to have the largest collection of *Star Wars* merchandise in the entire executive branch.

"I have the Death Star Space Station minus one of the cardboard inserts and a piece of the bridge. The spring-loaded part that makes the gun pop up doesn't work very well, but it's still awesome," Clinton told Larry King in a 1997 interview. "I also have almost every action figure, except a few rare ones, like Blue Snaggletooth and Yak Face."

Clinton went on to tell King that the infamous "missile-firing Boba Fett" action figure, rumored to have been produced in small quantities by Kenner, never actually reached the consumer, and that the only such Fetts available are ones made by collectors.

Despite the popularity of Clinton's hiatus within the nation's science-fiction and fantasy community, Republican leaders have loudly denounced the move.

"Clinton was given the trust of a nation and, once again, he has abused that trust, abandoning his post during a time of war. There are more important things for him to be worrying about at this juncture than such trivial concerns," Sen. Arlen Specter (R-PA) said. "Besides, I hate that stupid Jar-

Above: President Clinton announces his *Star Wars*-related leave of absence before members of Congress.

Jar. He totally sounds like Elmo."

Specter then sneered in a high-pitched voice, "Oooh, people gonna die?"

Clinton responded swiftly to Specter's remarks.

"I would urge all Americans to withhold judgment on the Jar-Jar issue until they have seen the film. After all, Yoda talked like Grover, and he is one of the great characters in the *Star Wars* pantheon," Clinton said. "As long as *Phantom Menace* doesn't have those stupid teddy bears in it, I don't care."

"I've been waiting 16 years for this movie, and now it's almost here," Clinton said. "I can't believe it. I'm so excited, I feel like I could make the Kessel Run in less than 12 parsecs." Ø study found, is gross overestimation of their own rapping skills. A full 98 percent of MCs participating in the study claimed that their style could not be imitated and never duplicated, despite a preponderance of evidence to the contrary.

"Very few of these rappers have styles that cannot be duplicated. In fact, we found that most of these rappers have remarkably similar microphone styles," Danziger said. "Yet nearly all of them have somehow convinced themselves that they are unique."

Often, Danziger said, rappers' inflated, unrealistic self-images carry over into their interpersonal relationships, adversely affecting their ability to establish healthy, mutually fulfilling long-term relationships with members of the opposite sex.

"One young rapper I spoke with told me that he 'be trading women like Eddie Murphy trading places' and that he 'got bitches cleaning my house, cleaning my gold, doing my shoelaces,'" Danziger said. "For a relationship to thrive, there needs to be a sense of shared responsibility and mutual respect. When one partner is cleaning the other's house and gold, the partner doing the cleaning is likely to experience feelings of resent-

## The study also found that many rappers grossly overestimate their personal finances.

ment over the imbalance. Inevitably, this will drive a wedge between the pair."

"Another MC I spoke with told me that he has a bitch who will suck his dick until he nut, spit it on his gut, and slurp that shit back up," Danziger said. "While a sense of sexual adventurousness and a willingness to experiment is a great way to keep a relationship fresh over the long haul, it only works if that spirit of adventure is reciprocal, and the man is willing to try new things to please the woman. With many of these rappers, however, this is not the case."

The study also found that many rappers grossly overestimate their personal finances. Most MCs were found to be living lifestyles well beyond their means, taking nightly baths in Cristal, wearing custom-made Armani suits, and sporting 10 Rolex watches on each arm. One New Orleans-area rapper reported driving a solid-gold, diamond-encrusted tank.

"Even millionaires need to do some amount of basic budgeting," accountant Morton Kessler said. "The sort of extravagant spending in which these rappers indulge—indiscriminately buying yachts, helicopters, and fleets of bulletproof Mercedes-Benzes without any eye on the bottom line—is a

# Maybe This Appearance On *Jenny Jones* Is Just What My Marriage Needs

**By Anne-Marie Krebs**

My husband Cal and I have been going through some pretty tough times in our marriage lately. For the past three months, Cal has been cheating on me with Rhonda, this 18-year-old stripper who used to babysit for us. And just yesterday, after beating me with a tire iron, he told me Rhonda's pregnant and wants us to raise the child.

As you can probably guess, I'm furious at Cal. But I'm not perfect, either: I did, after all, have sex with his dad. Loads of confused thoughts run through my head, and I just don't know what to do. My mother thinks I should dump "that piece-of-shit asshole fuck," as she's fond of calling Cal. My best friend Adrienne thinks we should get counseling.

Me, I'm thinking an appearance on *The Jenny Jones Show* is just the thing to save our marriage.

I watch Jenny every day, and I really think she could give us the advice and guidance we sorely need. Her show tackles relationship problems like mine all the time, and Jenny's incredible at dealing with them.

First of all, she's full of the plain, common-sense wisdom that all the great daytime talk-show hosts, from Sally Jessy Raphäel to Mother Love, share. I remember one episode where this middle-aged woman was cheating on her husband with her teenage stepson. She said the boy wasn't technically related to her, so what was the problem? I must admit, the woman's argument seemed pretty sound to me.

But Jenny really put things in perspective. First, she asked this lady, "What if your husband was cheating on *you*? Wouldn't you be hurt?" Then Jenny added, "You're this boy's stepmom! Stepmoms aren't supposed to do things like that!" I remember sitting at home in awe. I never thought of it quite that way!

As great as Jenny is, the studio audience deserves a lot of credit, too. They provide just the kind of support system people need when discussing their embarrassing problems on national TV. I particularly remember one audience member's input. The show—titled "I Can't Control My Sexy Teen!"—featured a panel of overweight teenage girls

### Perhaps someone will point out that I gots to check myself before I wreck myself.

who dress like sluts. About halfway through, a male audience member stood up and said to these girls, "Can all y'all ladies say 'choo-choo,' 'cause all's I see's a ho train! Ho!... Ho!... Ho!" Talk about your helpful feedback! These remarks let the girls see that their mode of dress was causing them to be treated with less respect than they deserved.

I only pray that such insightful and compassionate people are in the audience if and when Cal and I appear. Maybe if I come on the show wearing my favorite green dress, someone will refer to me as "yo, the lady in green." (The audience always calls the guests it most cares about by the color they're wearing.) And perhaps someone will point out that I gots to check myself before I wreck myself. Because I do. Sometimes, it takes a stranger in a TV audience to hammer home a point like that.

If Cal and I do get on *Jenny Jones*, I'm really hoping Jenny springs a surprise guest on us. Like maybe some other woman he's been sleeping with that I don't even know about. That would be great! Then the

three of us could sit down and work out our differences by screaming at each other in front of millions of people. That's just the kind of open, loud communication you need in a successful marriage.

I was heartened by the interest I got from *The Jenny Jones Show* when I contacted them recently. Linda, the assistant producer, said my story would fit very nicely into the upcoming show, "My Man Won't Stop Cheating & Beating!" Linda then asked me if I'd discussed appearing on *Jenny Jones* with Cal. I said no, because he was busy working time-and-a-half at the grain elevator. "That's great," she replied. "Just tell Cal that the two of you are going on *Jenny Jones* because you won the '*Jenny Jones* World's Greatest Hubby Video Essay Contest.'" He'll be sure to agree to go on. Then, when Cal comes onstage, everybody will boo him, and we'll reveal the real reason he's on the show—because he's a cheating, beating, low-down, rotten skunk."

For a moment, I was confused. "Won't that just make him angry at me?" I asked. But then Linda reminded me of all the hurt Cal had caused me, and said that if anyone deserved a taste of his own medicine, it was him. Well, I couldn't disagree with that logic. Besides, if the audience taunted and mocked Cal the way they did the "Over-80 Transvestites" who were on last week, maybe Cal would see the error of his ways and stop fooling around!

So, hopefully, you'll be seeing Cal and me on *Jenny Jones* real soon. There's a chance we may get turned down, which would be terribly disappointing. But if that happens, there are other ways to get the marriage counseling we need. Like by going on *Jerry Springer*. Like Jenny, Jerry always seems to lend a caring, sympathetic ear, and his "Final Thought" is always filled with the sort of solid, time-tested advice that never fails to work. ∅

recipe for financial disaster."

According to UCLA Hospital psychiatrist Dr. Ernest Bloch, the distorted sense of reality exhibited by many rappers may indicate a predisposition toward a host of serious mental disorders, including schizophrenia.

"Many of these rappers create fictional, internal universes that, for them, become a sort of alternate reality," Bloch said. "For example, a young rapper named Kurupt told me how the feds have tapped his phones, and how he's wanted in more states than

John Gotti. A New York-area MC by the name of Nas told me that he was recently chased in his Lexus by CIA agents but managed to escape when Pablo Escobar, his business partner and passenger, shot the driver of the pursuing vehicle. These sorts of paranoid, delusional fantasies are classic warning signs of schizophrenia, and an affected rapper's condition can deteriorate to the point where he is clinically insane in the membrane."

Danziger urged afflicted rappers to seek help now, before the problem

gets worse.

"Early detection is critical, as treatment only becomes more difficult as time goes on," Danziger said. "Remember: These rappers' mic skills won't stay sharp forever, and when they do fall off—and the record sales plummet and the major-label contracts disappear—there is almost always a corresponding depression. We need to recognize that underneath all the bravado and macho posturing, these rappers' boasts are actually a desperate shout-out for help." ∅

## Federal Judge Rules Parker Brothers Holds Monopoly Monopoly

see LEGAL page 4C

## Auto Industry Agrees To Install Brakes In SUVs

see BUSINESS page 5C

## Guy At House Party Must Be At Least 32

see CAMPUS page 11E

## KFC Manager Robbed At Sporkpoint

see CRIME page 4C

### STATshot

A look at the numbers that shape your world.

**What The Hell Did We Drink Last Night?**

28% Five Chi-Chi's Bubblegum Mugaritas

20% Thunder Train Or Night Bird Or Something

19% Remaining Drops At The Bottom Of 84 Pabst Cans

12% Whatever Comes Out Of A Microwaved Nerf Football

9% God Only Knows

8% Rum & Tab

4% Something Reddish

---

## Pharmaceutical Company Calls Its New Anti-Depressant 'Worthless And Dumb'

### 'So's Our Whole Stupid Company,' Says CEO

EAST BRUNSWICK, NJ—At a press conference Monday, Brunley-Hunt Pharmaceuticals CEO Peter Cafazzo introduced Cyntrex, his company's latest anti-depressant, which he described as "a totally stupid waste of time that probably nobody will ever want ever."

Though from the outset, Brunley-

Hunt had hoped the new medication would revolutionize the treatment of depression, Cafazzo is less than en-

see ANTI-DEPRESSANT page 169

**Right: Peter Cafazzo, CEO of Brunley-Hunt Pharmaceuticals, unveils Cyntrex, a "worthless new drug" he says will make the company "the total laughingstock of the industry."**

---

# Pope Condemns Three More Glands

**Above: Pope John Paul II greets well-wishers following Monday's condemnation of the "sinful, hormone-secreting" adrenal, pineal, and pituitary glands.**

VATICAN CITY—In the sternest papal edict against the endocrine system in more than 150 years, Pope John Paul II condemned the adrenal, pineal, and pituitary glands Monday, decrying them as "sinful hormone producers which encourage and incite the human body to commit all manner of unholy acts."

The edict raised the total number of condemned glands to 25.

"It has come to my attention that the adrenal, pineal, and pituitary glands perform a great many immoral functions which God could have never foreseen or intended when He created the human body," the Pope said. "In addition to secreting such suspicious-sounding fluids as norepinephrine, prolactin, and al-

dosterone, these glands are guilty of working directly with the testes and ovaries in the process of sexual development."

While the Pope endorsed a majority of the adrenal glands' functions, including the regulation of blood-glucose levels, heart rate, and blood pressure, he strongly took issue with the adrenals' production of gonadocorticoids—sex hormones which influence sperm production in men, as well as the distribution of body hair and menstruation in women.

"The adrenal glands are surely not the work of God," the Pope said. "God created man in His image, and the Lord did not secrete gonadocorticoids."

The Pope then announced

see POPE page 169

---

## Shake-Up Among Cast Of Hit Show *ABC World News Tonight*

### Peter Jennings Character To Be Killed Off

NEW YORK—In a bold move to stay ahead of the competition in the ratings war, producers of the hit program *ABC World News Tonight* announced Monday that star Peter Jennings "will not survive next season."

Details regarding when and how the Jennings character will die are being kept a strict secret by show producers. Speculation from television-industry insiders has ranged from Jennings' getting hit by a mortar shell

while covering a December '98 civil war in Turkey to his perishing in a tragic newsroom fire.

ABC is already aggressively promoting Jennings' last episode, airing spots promising "The ABC World News Tonight you must not miss."

Addressing a group of Capital Cities/ABC shareholders, *World News Tonight* executive producer Roone Arledge explained the move.

see JENNINGS page 168

**Above: *World News Tonight*'s Peter Jennings, whose death is expected to be a ratings bonanza.**

Above: Jennings during 1996's presidential-election subplot.

"Yes, our ratings have been strong of late: Last year's Flight 800 episode did huge numbers, as did 1995's sweeps-week Oklahoma City bombing plotline," Arledge said. "But in this business, you constantly need the big hit, the big 'zazz' that will keep people glued to the screen. This should give us that hit."

With the precise date of Jennings' final episode a mystery, many observers predict a season-long ratings blockbuster for *World News Tonight*, with viewers tuning in nightly out of fear of missing his death. According to *Washington Post* TV critic Tom Shales, if announced in advance, the death episode could be the show's most-watched installment ever, eclipsing even the season-ending April 1981 "Who Shot Reagan?" cliffhanger.

"As you'll recall, the American public had to wait until the Sept. 4, 1981, season opener to find out if Reagan died from his bullet wounds," Shales said. "That summer, the only thing people talked about was whether the president would live or die. It was a brilliant move on ABC's part."

Jennings, a *World News Tonight* fixture since the late '70s, is widely credited with the show's enduring popularity. He brought ABC viewers news of the Challenger explosion in 1986, was in Berlin for the 1989 toppling of the Berlin Wall, and, in 1996, added intrigue to the show by poisoning David Brinkley.

*World News Tonight* fans were excited by the announcement. "I'll be sure not to miss the Jennings finale—this could be even bigger than the wedding episode," said Bill Hodges of Covington, KY, referring to the 1989 on-air marriage of Jennings and Barbara Walters. "The only problem is, now we may never find out if he's really Cokie's father."

Despite the blockbuster ratings sure to be generated by the death of the Jennings character, some say it could backfire in the long run, pointing to NBC's decision to "kill off" *NBC Nightly News* star Tom Brokaw in 1993. Massive viewer protest prompted the show's producers to bring back Brokaw in the form of a robot duplicate, but only after the show's ratings suffered a substantial drop from which it has yet to recover.

Said Arledge: "We've been trying for years to match the huge ratings we got with the Gulf War—which also won an Emmy for set design—but viewers didn't respond to our mid-season Unabomber capture the way we'd hoped. We knew we needed a big gun, a blockbuster plotline to jolt people."

"We toyed with the idea of bringing back Brinkley," Arledge continued, "but the 'it was all a dream' thing has been done to death. In the end, we decided, 'Let's start phasing out the old guard and bring in some fresh new blood.'"

According to Arledge, once Jennings dies, the show's lead anchor role will go to 26-year-old model and journalist Rock Palmer. "Get ready, ladies," Arledge said.

Arledge said the younger, more attractive Palmer should provide a strong lead-in for *20/20*'s Deborah Roberts, Barbara Walters, and Lynn Sherr, hyped in recent promotional spots as "The Bitches Of ABC." ∅

---

## EDITORIAL

# Did Six Million *Really* Visit The Holocaust Museum?

Did six million people *really* visit the United States Holocaust Memorial Museum since it opened in April 1993? That's what the United States

By Walter Lolich

Holocaust Memorial Council would have you believe, and if all you've been exposed to is its Zionist propaganda, you probably buy it. But just how many people have actually passed through the Holocaust Museum's doors?

Despite the wealth of evidence proving that the museum's visitor numbers are wildly exaggerated, it is truth seekers like myself who are labeled dangerous to society. Swayed by the Jewish agenda and its powerful lobby in Washington, millions of people have been duped into blindly accepting the museum's one-sided view of its attendance history. And those who attempt to set the record straight are promptly dismissed as "kooks," "liars," and, of course, "anti-Semites."

What are you afraid of, United States Holocaust Memorial Council? That the world will find out that the number of people interested in your museum has been greatly distorted?

Let's take a look at this supposedly oft-visited museum. Just where do these attendance figures come from? You might be surprised by the answer: Speaking anonymously for fear of retribution, numerous Holocaust Museum workers have admitted that the six-million figure is "only an estimate." Furthermore, this misrepresentation includes not only visitors to the museum's Permanent Exhibition, which requires a pass, but also visitors to the rotating exhibits at the front of the building! Shocked? Anyone with a basic understanding of the way the Zionist propaganda machine works shouldn't be.

So, the six million is not derived from the number of free tickets that have been distributed, but is instead a CAREFULLY AND DELIBERATELY MANIPULATED FIGURE which includes visitors to the museum who were unable to obtain a pass and only visited the all-access Wexler Learning Center. In other words, it includes visitors who could not in any way, shape, or form be counted! Even Sharon E. Underwood, one of the museum's own tour guides, admits that the question of how many people actually visited the museum remains "OPEN TO DEBATE." Yet the American Jewry continues to present six million as reality.

Further, while high-ranking Jews at the Holocaust Museum claim to have records showing the exact number of tickets distributed each day since its opening, no one can provide ANY PROOF WHATSOEVER that once a ticket was handed out, the recipient actually used it and entered the museum!

Then there is the fact that a "computer glitch" wiped out all ticket data from May 14, 1998, to May 22, 1998. That begs the question, just how reliable are these computers that supposedly contain the museum's visitation records? And is it just a coincidence that those providing the six-million figure have clearly established ties to the museum's board of directors? It seems their "facts" are closer to the dangerous lie the museum and its sympathizers have so successfully gotten the public to buy into.

In addition, there is the issue of what can supposedly be found inside the museum, reported by visitors and accepted as truth by so many. How much of this is elaboration for the sake of currying the favor of the Horowitzes and Greenspans of this world? Why is flash photography EXPRESSLY PROHIBITED in the Hall Of Remembrance? WHAT ARE THEY TRYING TO HIDE? And what about that rumored museum gift shop, which supposedly offers Holocaust-related books, videotapes, and teaching materials? There is precious little evidence that it even exists, yet people around the world BLINDLY ACCEPT the trumped-up stories and believe that it is there, somewhere inside the museum.

Some will provide so-called "proof" of widespread interest in the museum in the form of newspaper clippings about its 1993 grand-opening ceremony. In one such article, which ran in THE JEW YORK TIMES, a journalist named DANIEL LEVINE wrote that 3,000 people attended. By studying the accompanying photograph, I was able to verify the presence of only 16 people. If this sort of skewed math, a fact-to-fiction ratio of 16:3,000, is applied to the alleged museum total of six million, the figure is reduced to 32,000.

Considering the Holocaust Museum's proximity to Washington's National Mall, it is plausible that 32,000 people have entered since 1993—even if most did so only to use the bathroom or get a drink of water. But compared to the millions of people who visit, say, the National Air & Space Museum each year, can anyone consider the Holocaust Museum's measly 4,500 annual visitors significant? Hardly. It's time the United States Holocaust Memorial Museum closed the door on its lies once and for all. ∅

# Top-Selling Books—1998

1. *The Quiet, Compassionate Country Man With A Windburned But Handsome Face Who Was Kind To The Widow And Her Daughter And Always Spoke Respectfully To The Symbolic Livestock*
2. *The Seven Habits Of Highly Reprehensible People*
3. *How I Grew Up Covered In Me Da's Vomit In Ireland*
4. *Puff Daddy's "The Sun Also Rises '98" (Featuring DMX & Mase)*
5. *Chamomile Tea For The Broken Heart*
6. *John Grisham's The Business Traveler*
7. *Management Secrets Of The Dread Cthulhu: Creating New Markets While You Dream Unspeakable Visions In Your Sunken Crypt Outside Time*
8. *Mental Retardation For Dummies*
9. *Women Who Nap With The Housecats*
10. *The "Eat Loads Of Fudge, You Fat Fuck" Miracle Diet*
11. *Tom Clancy Presents: Next Year's Shitty Movie*
12. *The Twentysomething Protagonist Who Three-Quarters Through The Book Discovers Her Father Molested Her*
13. *Men Are From The U.S., Women Are From Canada*
14. *L. Ron Hubbard Presents: Motivational Planet*
15. *Chicken Soup For The Publisher's Bank Account*
16. *The Tiny Little Impulse Buy Near The Cash Register Book*
17. *My Wife And I Sure Do See Things Slightly Differently! by Paul Reiser*
18. *Give The Waiters Funny Buttons And Stick The Mexicans In The Dishroom: The J.T. McPickleshitter's Story*
19. *Discovering My Lesbian Clitoris*
20. *Norman Mailer's The Time Of Me In Our Times Featuring Me*

ANTI-DEPRESSANT from page 167

thusiastic about its chances against such industry leaders as Prozac and Zoloft.

"Cyntrex? Yeah, right. More like Stupidtrex," Cafazzo said. "More like Another-Awful-Product-That-Will-Probably-Make-Us-All-Bankruptrex."

The drug, which stimulates the production of neurotransmitters in sync with the body's natural diurnal catecholamine rhythms—causing a more even mood level than the frequent "crest and trough" patterns associated with traditional psychoactive medicinal treatments—is something "everybody will laugh at," Cafazzo said.

Among the reasons Cafazzo cited for Cyntrex's "totally doomed future" is Brunley-Hunt's inability to do anything half as well as its chief competitors.

"Prozac is so great," Cafazzo said. "Cyntrex will never make anybody as happy as Prozac. I just know it."

Added Cafazzo: "My life is shit."

The release of Cyntrex is the latest bold move by Brunley-Hunt, which has increased its share of the mental-health drug market from 2 to 5 percent during the five years Cafazzo has been CEO, causing many to view Brunley-Hunt as the rising star in $150 billion pharmaceutical industry.

> ## "Cyntrex? Yeah, right. More like Stupidtrex," Cafazzo said. "More like Another-Awful-Product-That-Will-Probably-Make-Us-All-Bankruptrex."

Cafazzo, however, disagreed.

"Five percent? Oh, I'm sure," he said. "Like a company is really going to do that well with such a total fucking loser asshole for a CEO."

"Maybe I'll get a raise," Cafazzo continued. "Then I can use the money to buy a gun to blow my head off."

According to reports, top Brunley-Hunt researchers began having doubts about the drug during the early development stages, when they realized they couldn't do anything right ever, ever, ever, and that no one in the pharmaceutical industry cared whether they lived or died. But work on the project continued, despite Brunley-Hunt's growing conviction that Cyntrex would be the least successful product in pharmaceutical history.

"We should have just stopped trying back then during the development stage," Brunley-Hunt researcher Dr. Peter Ayers said. "But, nooo, we had to go and make ourselves look like idiots in front of the whole world. Us and our lousy little pills. Why?"

Ayers then began beating his fists into the sides of his head while staring at the floor, repeating, "Why? Why, why, why, why, why?"

Fellow Brunley-Hunt researcher Harlan Downing said that, in addition to treating depression, Cyntrex may have numerous other uses.

"There is a strong possibility," Downing said, "that the particular disinhibitors activated by Cyntrex may be of great benefit in the treatment of Alzheimer's Disease."

Downing then admitted that the drug will not be ready for such use for many years, repeatedly hitting his forehead into a wall and mumbling under his breath.

Brunley-Hunt's chief rival in the mood-altering drug field, Stafford Labs, manufactures Prozac. Stafford CEO Margaret Curry expressed confidence that Prozac would maintain its commanding market share in the face of the new competition.

"We will emerge triumphant, for I am Margaret Curry, president of Stafford Labs!" Curry said. "My power is greater than that of 50 CEOs! My marketing savvy is that of 600 PR firms! My tricyclic monoinhibitor is a boon unto the people and a beacon unto the nations! My new promotional campaign to enhance brand awareness and increase market penetration of Prozac shall be cloaked in radiant beams of persuasive glory!" ∅

POPE from page 167

his decision to posthumously excommunicate Bartolommeo Eustachius, the Italian anatomist who discovered the adrenal glands in 1564. He also excommunicated Dr. Russell Halloran, chief endocrinologist at UCLA Medical Center, widely considered the world's top adrenal specialist.

As with the adrenals, the Pope approved of several of the pituitary gland's functions, including its role in the regulation of metabolism and blood-vessel contraction, but strongly denounced its other purposes.

"The pituitary is a most foul and indecent gland," the Pontiff said. "While, on the surface, it gives off the air of innocence, regulating various body functions of genuine value and import, behind the scenes this devious gland controls such evils as the secretion of testosterone and estrogen by the testes and ovaries, uterine contraction, and something called spermatogenesis."

"I do not know what spermatogenesis is, but I am certain it is not moral," the Pope said.

In addition to his glandular condemnation, the Pope lashed out against hormones, taking them to task for their involvement with birth control.

"Hormones are a key component of contraceptive drugs, deceiving the female body into thinking it is pregnant and stopping the sacred ovulation process," the Vicar of Christ said. "This is a great, great sin."

With Monday's edict, the only remaining endocrine gland sanctioned by the Holy See are the parathyroids, which increase calcium levels in the blood and decrease phosphate levels.

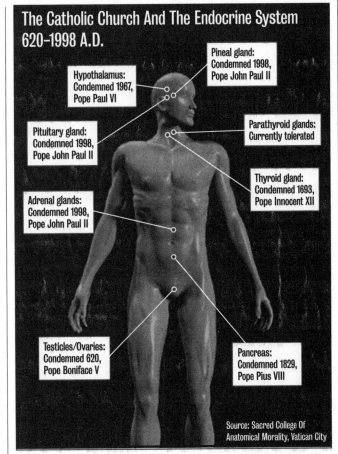

## The Catholic Church And The Endocrine System 620–1998 A.D.

Hypothalamus: Condemned 1967, Pope Paul VI

Pineal gland: Condemned 1998, Pope John Paul II

Pituitary gland: Condemned 1998, Pope John Paul II

Parathyroid glands: Currently tolerated

Adrenal glands: Condemned 1998, Pope John Paul II

Thyroid gland: Condemned 1693, Pope Innocent XII

Testicles/Ovaries: Condemned 620, Pope Boniface V

Pancreas: Condemned 1829, Pope Pius VIII

Source: Sacred College Of Anatomical Morality, Vatican City

"As far as we can best judge, there is nothing wrong with the parathyroid glands," the Pope said. "But we will keep a close eye on them, nevertheless."

All exocrine glands have been banned since 1764, when Pope Clement XIII condemned them for producing such substances as milk, mucus, semen, saliva, and sweat. ∅

## Point-Counterpoint: Abortion
# U.S. Out Of My Uterus

**By Jessica Linden**

It comes down to one thing: It's my body. Not Uncle Sam's, not Trent Lott's, not Pat Robertson's. Mine. Congress can demand a portion of my income, it can tell me how fast to drive, it can kill killers and anyone else it thinks it must to preserve a free and civil society. But my body—the skin, bones, and organs that comprise me—is where the line gets drawn.

The decision to have or not have a child is mine and mine alone. I am not cattle for the government to order about, demanding that I bring an unwanted child to term. Stripping me of the right to control my own destiny dehumanizes me, period. Anything less than my choice, on my terms, reduces me to property.

The right-wing anti-choice movement loves to preach its views from an idealistic, pie-in-the-sky universe where nothing uncomfortable ever has to happen to anyone, but that's not reality. Life is filled with pain and hard choices, choices one may or may not regret later. But it's that individual's right to make the choice.

You think America is the land of the free? The last country on Earth that would ever oppress women? My grandmother remembers when women could not vote in this country. And, boy, do we still have a long way to go.

One certainly has to wonder: How would things be different if men could get pregnant? It would certainly be fun to watch the patriarchal elite of Congress scramble to cover themselves if it all changed overnight.

And one more thing: Who would care for all the children born into a world that prohibits abortion? Who would be there to raise all those unwanted, abandoned children? It would certainly be a different world, full of orphanages jammed with parentless children, robbed of a fair chance to grow up in a stable environment because of what some politician deemed "moral" in some oak-walled chamber on Capitol Hill. To say nothing of the women maimed or even killed by barbaric, back-alley abortions because a bunch of rich white men made the safe alternative unavailable to her.

Keep your laws off my body, America. And stay out of my uterus. ⬚

# We Must Deploy Troops To Jessica Linden's Uterus Immediately

**By Gen. Henry Shelton
U.S. Army**

To protect America's interests, it is sometimes necessary to mobilize and deploy a military force. We now stand at the brink of such a time.

The tactical importance of Jessica Linden's uterus to national security is twofold: First, with its rich, fertile walls, this uterus is a vital source of future Americans. Second, the uterus is situated in an extremely strategic location, leaving it vulnerable to a hostile foreign power. This uterus must be made a top priority by the Pentagon. Establishing a strong U.S. military presence in Jessica Linden's uterine region is by far the most sensible course of action.

I propose that four U.S. Army divisions be deployed to Jessica Linden's uterus no later than midnight Friday. Once there, a reconnaissance force of 200 men will be stationed on her cervical perimeter, denying entrance to any unauthorized personnel or equipment. Another two battalions will be stationed inside the uterus itself, where they will set up camp and, if necessary, conduct armed patrols in force.

Remaining personnel will conduct amphibious patrol in the forward vaginal canal and as far back as the fallopian entrances, scouting for cervical dilation or other such activity. The entire operation will receive air support from a wing of Blackhawk helicopters, which will rotate in pairs patrolling the greater vaginal area. Our forces will constitute an impenetrable iron diaphragm, preventing any and all foreign elements from compromising uterine security.

Should we encounter a foreign power disputing our claim upon the Linden uterus and surrounding vagina, we will be prepared to engage its forces in armed conflict. We will consider the nation's safety our number-one priority, regardless of Ms. Linden's unwillingness to cooperate.

The Pentagon will consider a full-scale invasion of Jessica Linden's ovaries only as a last resort, after all other options have been exhausted. We recognize in principle Jessica Linden's sovereignty over the ovarian territory, but to prevent the loss of the reproductive system to a hostile power, we are prepared to do what we must, even if that means conducting a firebombing and strafing campaign that may result in full military hysterectomy. If we must destroy the uterus in order to save it, so be it.

If U.S. uterine occupation extends into the second week of October, we will install an irrigation and drainage system in anticipation of Miss Linden's menstrual cycle. This will not only benefit her, but provide our troops with a cleaner, more navigable terrain upon which to conduct their military maneuvers.

I will further recommend that Congress establish a new Military Medal of Valor, to be called The Distinguished Cervical Cross For Courage In The Uterine Theatre. Naval soldiers may also request a burial within Miss Linden in the event of loss of life.

The U.S. must and will defend its interests in Jessica Linden's uterus, no matter the cost. ⬚

## 6-Year-Old Announces Plans To Become Ballerina Gymnast Veterinarian Horseback-Riding Princess

MILESBURG, PA—In a pre-bedtime announcement before family members Monday, area 6-year-old Stephanie Ambrose unveiled plans to become a ballerina gymnast veterinarian horseback-riding princess when she grows up. "Ashley is very much interested in that particular field," said Patricia Ambrose, the girl's mother. "But she's still keeping her options open and strongly considering becoming an astronaut actress president basketball-playing magic fairy." ⬚

# Alternate-Universe James Hetfield Named Taco Bell Employee Of The Month

LABREA, CA—Alternate-universe sources reported Monday that Metallica frontman James Hetfield has been named Taco Bell employee of the month for October 1999.

Hetfield, who has worked at the Petaluma Avenue Taco Bell since December 1996 in the parallel reality, was praised by store management for his promptness, courteousness, and professionalism.

"James is a fine employee," assistant manager Doug Allenby said. "I think he has a very bright future here at Taco Bell."

The employee-of-the-month honor was Hetfield's first since joining the Taco Bell team. In June 1994, he was named employee of the month at El

### "James is a fine employee," Allenby said.

Pollo Loco, and in May 1991, he received the award at Walgreens. The alternate Hetfield has held a wide variety of jobs since his 1981 high-school graduation, including janitor, landscaper, dishwasher, and prep cook.

"I just want to get out of this dead-end town someday," Hetfield said. "I don't know, maybe I can get a job as a roadie for Motörhead or something. That would be pretty cool."

Added Hetfield: "Sabbath rules." ⬚

## Consumer Confidence Verging On Cockiness

see NATION page 4A

## Awards Given Out Randomly To Skinny Blonde Women

see ENTERTAINMENT page 5E

## Aspiring Filmmaker Can Help Next Person In Line

see MOVIES page 9B

## Charles Durning Hocks Up Four-Pound Chunk Of Phlegm

see PEOPLE page 10D

THE ONION
$2.00 US
$3.00 CAN

0  74470 94595  6

00

# the ONION ®

WWW.THEONION.COM          AMERICA'S FINEST NEWS SOURCE™          FOUNDED 1871

## Arabs, Israelis Sign 'Screw Peace' Accord

JERUSALEM—In what is being hailed as "a major step toward the reestablishment of traditional Middle Eastern hatred," Israeli prime minister Benjamin Netanyahu and PLO leader Yasser Arafat signed a historic "Screw Peace" agreement Wednesday.

"For years, our efforts to achieve a permanent, lasting state of war have been derailed by the peace process," Netanyahu said. "Never again will we allow talk of living in harmony to interfere with our real-world goals.

From this day forth, our two peoples shall forever be united in our deeply rooted, irreconcilable hatred of one another."

"Nothing can come of friendly co-existence," Arafat said. "There is no winner in peace."

The PLO leader then concluded the signing with the ceremonial burning of a dove.

According to the terms of the Screw Peace agreement, all forms of diplo-
see PEACE page 173

Above: Yasser Arafat and Benjamin Netanyahu agree to violently disagree.

Above: Daryl Hegge, who is completely alone in his homosexuality.

# Area 15-Year-Old Only Homosexual In The Whole World

WAUKESHA, WI—On the surface, Daryl Hegge seems to be a typical 15-year-old boy. An avid trivia buff and amateur model-rocket hobbyist, he enjoys going to pizza parties, participating in such after-school activities as yearbook and drama club, and listening to the music of his favorite pop stars.

Hegge appears as normal and well-adjusted as any of his peers at Waukesha South High School. But despite his seemingly healthy

exterior, Hegge is different from his classmates—very different. That's because Daryl Hegge is the only homosexual in the whole world.

"I'm so alone," said Hegge, speaking to reporters from his family's unfurnished basement. Here, the silently suffering youth spends much of his time struggling to cope with his hidden, shameful burden—praying to Jesus for help, furtively masturbating, and writing
see HOMOSEXUAL page 172

# New *Old People* Magazine Gives Old People Something To Read While Waiting To Die

FT. LAUDERDALE, FL—The tedious pre-death "waiting period" endured by senior citizens has become slightly less boring with the launch of *Old People* magazine.

Published by Ft. Lauderdale-based SeniorBeat Press, the periodical is designed, according to editor Lou White, to give the elderly something to read while waiting for death.

"People in this country talk a lot about doing something for the elderly," the 31-year-old White said. "Well, here at *Old People*, we're not just talking about

it. We're doing something about it, tackling head-on the two most important issues facing old people today: boredom, and the fact that they haven't died yet."

*Old People*, whose debut issue hit newsstands Jan. 11, features an oversized format with words printed in 32-point type—large enough for even the oldest of the old to read.
see OLD PEOPLE page 173

Right: Rancho Mirage, CA, retirees Bernadette Huggins and Harry Fordson enjoy passing the time before their deaths with *Old People* magazine.

# Work It, Jean!

**A Room Of Jean's Own
By Jean Teasdale**

You know, not to sound like a sour Sally, but I've just about given up on the male gender. It seems like when they aren't planted in a La-Z-Boy, glued to a football game on TV, and knocking back beers, they're bossing us women around or boasting about how wonderful and masculine they are. Shortly before I was fired from my temp job at SouthCentral Insurance (by a man, by the way!), I told this to my pal Fulgencio, who worked in the data-processing department with me. I vowed to him that I wasn't going to take any more guff from men, period. And you know what? Instead of getting a stupid smirk or a big lecture, he let out a great big "Whooooo!" and slapped me five. "You go, girl!" he said. "You show them bitches. Those men are nothing but bitches, anyway!"

Can you believe that? I had to press my hand tightly over my mouth to keep from laughing up my lungs! I swear, Fulgencio is such a gas! I mean, who would have thought to call men a derogatory name ordinarily reserved for women? Other people might think it's weird, but I thought it was soooo appropriate! But that's Fulgencio for you!

Fulgencio is the first guy I've ever met who I could ever relate to totally. Even though he's Mexican and male, I don't think I've ever had a better time with a person. Now, Jeanketeers, don't you get any dirty thoughts! Ful-

gencio and I are just friends. It's just that he and I have soooo much in common—we both love soaps and shopping, and sometimes we just talk for hours and hours on the phone. And get this: He goes to night classes at the local community college because he wants to become a fashion designer! How many men do that for a living? I'm telling you, Fulgencio is one in a million!

In fact, he was the first person to come to my rescue after I was fired from my job. No, he didn't give me a new job or money. He did something that meant more to me than either of those things. He restored my self-esteem!

The Monday after I was fired, I was feeling pretty bummed out. But instead of giving me a shoulder to cry on, the only thing hubby Rick gave me was the silent treatment! (Geez, from the way everyone was acting, you'd think bidding on a Miss Beasley doll on eBay on the supervisor's computer during work hours was a capital offense!)

I felt like a great big failure. So for solace, your old pal Jean resorted to her old standby... yep, you guessed it, chocolate! I was polishing off my second pint of Ben & Jerry's New York Super Fudge Chunk when the phone rang. It was Fulgencio.

"What, did I leave something behind in my desk?" I grumbled. (As you can see, I was really down in the dumps— I couldn't even muster a pleasantry for my pal Fulgencio!)

But Fulgencio would have none of that. "Girlfriend, I'm not gonna listen to that feeling-sorry-for-yourself junk,

see TEASDALE page 174

---

**the ONION HealthBeat presents:**

# Stop-Smoking Tips

Millions of Americans are addicted to smoking. If you are among them but don't want to be, here are some tips to help you kick the habit:

- Avoid doing things you associate with smoking, such as drinking, eating, walking, and being awake.
- Get thrown in jail, where cigarettes can only be acquired in exchange for painful sexual favors.
- Lobby your elected representatives to pass a $6,913 sales tax on packs of cigarettes.
- Write a rap song about how smoking is not cool. Perform it at local elementary schools.
- Move to California, where tobacco possession is illegal.
- Avoid thinking about the rich, full flavor of Benson & Hedges.
- Fill your home with motivational placards bearing slogans such as "Smoking Is For Pussies" and "Only A Fucking Retard Would Even Think About Smoking."
- Kissing a smoker is like licking an ashtray. If a loved one quits smoking, keep an ashtray around as a handy substitute.
- Attractive people smoke because it makes them look cool. Acknowledge that you are neither attractive nor cool.
- Cover yourself in egg whites. No one knows why this works.
- Join a stop-smoking support group. Be sure it's one that meets on a different night than your other six support groups.
- Hypnotism has helped many people quit, but you risk becoming the hypnotist's slave. It's your choice: quitting smoking or freedom.
- Teach yourself a valuable lesson by slowly dying of lung cancer.

---

HOMOSEXUAL from page 171

love poetry in what he calls his "way-super-secret diary that no one, no one ever, can see."

Hegge suffers from the only known case of a condition doctors term "homosexuality"—a bizarre syndrome that creates in Hegge an involuntary, overpowering compulsion to hug and kiss other boys. The teen's strange sexual affliction is such a freakish aberration that he has felt compelled to keep it a secret from loved ones, family members, and authority figures.

"No one must know," Hegge said. "If they ever found out what a horrible freak I am, they'd probably put me in a traveling circus show. A legacy of undying shame would follow me forever, plaguing the Hegge family name long after my death, passed down from generation to generation as 'The Legend Of Daryl The Homosexual Monster-Boy.'"

Hegge said he first became aware of his condition at age 12, during a week-long Bible study and nature retreat sponsored by his church youth group.

"It was a campfire sing-along and weenie-roast, and we were singing that part of 'And They'll Know We Are

> ## No one had any information or similar experiences to share with Hegge, as there are no other homosexuals in the entire world.

Christians By Our Love' that goes, 'We will walk with our brothers, we will walk hand in hand,'" Hegge recalled. "And I realized I was gazing into Billy Swearingen's eyes as we sang, thinking about how much I wanted to hold his hand. Later, I had a dream that he was touching my you-know-what."

Hegge then broke down in tears, screaming, "The agony! Oh, God, the

shame!"

In the years that followed the campfire episode, Hegge's erotic fixation with males grew, leading to such humiliating incidents as a gym-class locker-room erection and a botched kiss-attempt from fellow student Danielle Sanders. Hegge tried to learn more about his condition from teachers, library books, and even members of the clergy. But all such attempts ended in failure. No one had any information or similar experiences to share with him, as there are no other homosexuals in the entire world.

The burden of disease is hard for anyone to bear, but for Hegge, it is especially difficult. While those afflicted with illnesses such as diabetes, cancer, and muscular dystrophy can expect the full support of loved ones, such support is not possible in Hegge's case. Because of the singularly perverse and twisted nature of his homosexual desires, any attempt on his part to seek out the comfort and aid of others could only result in

shock, revulsion, and, ultimately, rejection.

"My family and friends are all I've got in the world. I wouldn't be able to take it if they abandoned me. I've pictured it countless times, so vividly in my nightmares: their faces contorting into the immutable masks of horrified disgust and raw, unbridled hatred that would be any sane person's natural reaction to my twisted desires," said Hegge, his lower lip trembling as he fought back tears. "How could I live through that experience? Sometimes, I think the only way out is to commit suicide and carry my horrible secret with me to the grave, where it can't hurt anyone."

Added Hegge: "I know I'd go to hell if I killed myself, but aren't I already damned to eternal punishment for my sick, perverted fantasies?"

Sadly, for Daryl Hegge, this poor, suffering teenage homosexual, the only such person in the whole world, there can never be an answer. All he and the rest of us can do is wait—and hope. ∅

macy between Israel and its Arab neighbors will be terminated and recognized as failures. In its place, unrestrained, total warfare will be viewed as the normal state of relations. Additionally, all borders within the region will be blurred in order to facilitate violent territorial disputes among sworn enemies.

"Hopefully," Netanyahu said, "there will be many thousands of angry Palestinians living on Israeli-occupied lands."

The Screw Peace agreement was based loosely on the Bosnian model, and was drawn up with the assistance of advisors from England and Northern Ireland, as well as several architects of the longstanding Greco-Turkish conflict.

News of the accord was met with universal praise by residents of the region, who celebrated by rioting, throwing rocks, and dragging their enemies from their beds and burning them alive in the street. The term "big-nosed freak" was also widely used by combatants on both sides.

The accord's ratification is a welcome political move to those who regard "peace in the Middle East" as a Western idea that directly conflicts with more than 6,000 years of tradition.

"My mother and three of my brothers died during the peace orchestrated by President Carter at Camp David," Beirut resident Ramzi Abboud said. "Everyone I know has lost loved ones to American attempts to negotiate peace."

"These peace talks have been going on ever since I was a child," said a weeping Avi Birbaum, 26, of Tel Aviv. "The pain of peace negotiations is all I have known."

Despite public approval, some leaders remain dissatisfied with the new agreement. Syrian prime minister

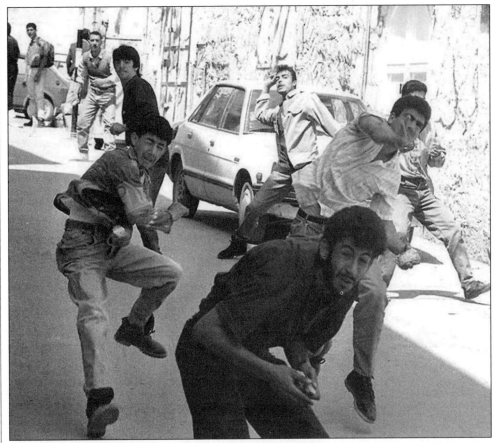

Above: Palestinian youths celebrate the historic Screw Peace accord by pelting Israeli tanks with rocks.

Mahmoud al-Aziz spoke out against what he called "major loopholes" in the language of the agreement.

"This piece of paper says we should no longer be at peace, which is wonderful, as war is right and good in the eyes of the One True God," al-Aziz said. "But it is too vaguely worded to be enforceable. Nowhere in it is there a clause that specifically states that we should exterminate the filthy Jew

devils to the last man, kill their women, enslave their children, and force their ghosts to serve us in Paradise."

Israeli military officials issued a statement agreeing in principle with al-Aziz's objections and asserting that the city of Damascus would be set on fire and its residents captured over the next 10 days.

The effect of the Screw Peace agree-

ment has yet to be felt throughout the rest of the world, but reaction has been favorable.

"At long last, Middle Eastern nations will be able to spend the countless billions of dollars they receive in military aid," said U.N. military affairs director Chretien Reigneau. "This revolutionary document will lead to a more honest Mideast outlook in every way." ∅

Featuring very large color pictures, as well as special "I Can Read It All By Myself" stories which contain no big words, the magazine's old-people-pleasing content provides the elderly with a fun and non-threatening experience.

Said White: "This magazine will keep old people occupied for hours in silent reading fun."

The first issue of *Old People* features a photo essay on Franklin D. Roosevelt, as well as articles on the post office, Bob Hope, and how pills are dissolved into applesauce to make them easier to swallow.

A majority of the content in the new magazine, however, focuses on the subject of greatest interest to old people: dying. "Myrtle's Story," a short-fiction piece, reads: "Myrtle was old. Very old. She waited and waited. Finally, she died."

According to White, such stories offer the elderly an important message of hope.

"This story says to old people, 'All this waiting is not for nothing. Sooner

> **The debut issue features a photo essay on Franklin D. Roosevelt, as well as articles on the post office and how pills are dissolved into applesauce to make them easier to swallow.**

or later, no matter how long it may seem, you will die,'" White said. "In other words, hang in there. In the long run, death will come at last."

Another regular section of the magazine, "Your Great-Grandchildren," features photos of various babies.

"Of course, the babies will be selected at random and not actually related to the reader in any way," White said,

"but the reader won't know that."

Among the periodical's most popular sections is "Time To Go To Church," which features full-page color photos of a church's exterior and interior, as well as images of parishioners singing, Jesus hugging an old person, and smiling parsons who "greet" the reader.

"Going to 'church,' as they call it, is something many old people spent much of their lives doing, for reasons we no longer understand," White said. "Hopefully, these pictures will not only remind them of this long-gone weekly comfort, but, if they hold it close enough to their faces, they might also be able to pretend they are actually in church."

The new magazine is already proving to be a hit among the about-to-die set.

"Don't want to stay in the center," raved Abraham Kriege, 97, speaking from his tiny cubicle at Golden Valley Retiree Center in Mankato, MN. "Tired of looking at wall... When I die? When?"

Added 89-year-old William "Bill"

Dashauer of Victoria Falls, TX: "Help me. Please."

As popular as it is with the elderly, *Old People* is even more well-liked by their families.

"Every few minutes, Grandma would demand that we take her to the bathroom, even though she's been using adult diapers for eight years," said Hannah Swoboda, 39. "Even after we put her in the nursing home, she'd call all the time: 'Want come back, want come back.' It was so tiresome. But now that she's got *Old People* magazine, that's all changed. Now we can barely drag her out of that home."

"It's really made a big difference," said Frank Bryce, 59, whose 86-year-old mother Eunice has not left her house in more than three years. "God willing, she'll die soon, but even if she doesn't, at least now she has something to read while she sits there in her little wicker chair for hours on end."

The second issue of *Old People* hits newsstands Feb. 10. It will feature pictures of a horse and a duck. ∅

because listen up: My class is holding a big end-of-summer-semester fashion show at the school auditorium next weekend, and you're going to be my model!"

I just about died! "Fulgencio, you can't be serious!" I gasped. "Me, a model? Puh-lease! That's like asking Rosie O'Donnell to buy a handgun!"

"Honey, I'm not asking you, I'm telling you," Fulgencio replied. "You're always complaining about how they never make nice clothes for plus-sizes. Well, Jeanie, I'm gonna change all that, and you're going to help me. And you'll look fabulous, I guarantee. So you'd better get that fine booty of yours in gear, 'cause you're gonna work it on the runway!"

Well, I guess I wasn't in my right mind at the time, because I actually agreed to model Fulgencio's clothes! I'm deathly afraid of being in front of crowds and, what's more, fashion and I have never really gotten along too well! But Fulgencio's confidence was so infectious, I couldn't resist!

Our time was limited, because Fulgencio had to design and make an outfit for me in less than a week. At first, I thought I could save him time by just giving him my measurements over the phone, but Fulgencio said he needed to measure me in person! "Jean Louis used to sew Marilyn Monroe into her gowns," he told me. (Just what did he have in mind, I was wondering!)

I have to admit, I was pretty nervous standing there in my skivvies as Fulgencio was going to town with his tape measure. (I sure hoped hubby Rick wouldn't catch wind of this!) I tried to suck in my stomach a little, but Fulgencio caught me and made me stop. "You just let it all hang out, babe," he said. "This dress is going to work for you, not the other way around."

When the day of the fashion show finally came, it was Chaos with a capital "C"! Fulgencio was still making alterations and insisted on completely redoing my hairdo and make-up job! "Jean, I promised you'd look fabulous, but this pale-blue eyeshadow and bright-red blusher thing have got to go. Leave that look in 1975 where it belongs!"

Well, I don't know how we did it, but we managed to get to the school scant minutes before the show was scheduled to begin! Fulgencio is a true miracle worker! He just happened to have some make-up at home (he said a girlfriend had left it there and never bothered to pick it up) and completely redid my make-up job in less than 10 minutes! He also put my hair up in hot rollers, hair-sprayed the heck out of it, and when he was done, it was amazing: My hair was so big, I could be the envy of any mall rat! Finally, I tried on the outfit he'd made for me: a sleeveless, fire-engine-red evening gown and matching wrap! I put on a pair of black platform sandals and a faux-diamond tiara and necklace Fulgencio shoved into my hand. When I

emerged from the dressing room, the other student designers and their models gasped, then cheered!

Fulgencio shrieked and ran up to embrace me. "Jean, you look so amazing!" he said. "If I don't get an A for this, I'm firebombing the school!" I laughed so hard, my tiara almost fell off my head! I don't know where Fulgencio comes up with these things! But that wasn't the only thing that knocked me for a loop: Fulgencio's instructor was so impressed, she insisted I go next-to-last, right before the big bridal-gown finale!

I was soooo delighted, my nervousness just melted away. I'd never felt more glamorous, not even when I got an $89 makeover at a day spa once. I was ready to strut my stuff in front of that awaiting crowd in the auditorium! Yes, sir, I was going full-tilt Jean and taking no prisoners!

Finally, my turn on the catwalk came, and wild horses couldn't have kept me back! To the tune of RuPaul's "Supermodel," I walked down the runway just like Fulgencio showed me—back straight, chest out, shoulders rolling. As the applause sounded, I'd never felt more confident in my life!

Then, I made the mistake no model should ever make: I looked at the crowd. To my horror, my eyes fell upon the one person I'd been trying to avoid for a week... hubby Rick! And

the look on his face was chilling. His mouth was agape, and he wasn't clapping with the audience. I was so flustered, I forgot to twirl around as I reached the end of the runway. Instead, I sharply turned and hastily hustled back behind the curtain.

I felt like I was about to bawl. The whole week leading up to the show, I'd been telling Rick that I was looking for a job, not practicing for a glamorous fashion extravaganza! The only way Rick could have known about it was if Fulgencio had told him about it. Boy, did I have a bone to pick with him. "Fulgencio, how could you?" I wailed. "I'll never, ever hear the end of it from Rick! Why did you tell him?"

"Because I wanted that hubby of yours to realize what a glamour queen you really are," Fulgencio said. "And honey, if he doesn't realize it after getting a look at you tonight, you should dump his sorry ass once and for all!"

Well, I was kind of irked with Fulgencio's nerve, and after the show I changed out of my dress and wiped off all the makeup, then drove home by myself without stopping by the post-show party. After all, I know Rick better than Fulgencio does, and it's just not his way to react to things all lovey-dovey and exuberant. And after this fiasco, I'm sure it wouldn't be me doing the ass-dumping!

To my chagrin, when I got home, Rick was there, watching his dumb football, of course. But when he saw me come home, he got up and followed me to the bedroom. I braced myself for the all-time donnybrook of our marriage.

But Rick just stuck his hands in his pockets and looked at the floor. "I gotta admit, for a homo, Fulgencio is a pretty decent guy," Rick said. "You looked kind of like Anna Nicole Smith before she lost all that weight."

Speaking of weight, it felt like about a ton was lifted off me! This, of course, was Rick-ese for, "I'm not mad, Jean, and you looked real good"! And that wasn't all. He asked me if I wanted to accompany him to Outback Steakhouse and a movie! (I think the last time the Teasdales went out for a night on the town, Air Supply was all the rage!)

So I guess I have Fulgencio to thank for patching up my marriage and for indirectly giving me the first night out with the hubby in ages. Unfortunately, it wasn't all smooth sailing. Rick wouldn't stop referring to Fulgencio as "Tinkerbell," and that really made me mad. Rick kept insisting Fulgencio is gay, and I told him that was ridiculous, but he wouldn't let up! (Rick says his "gaydar" has never failed him, but judging from what happened later that night, I'd say something else of his sure did!) ∅

## WHAT DO YOU THINK?

# Confederate-Flag Controversy

On Jan. 17, more than 47,000 people marched on South Carolina's Statehouse to protest the flying of the Confederate flag over the capitol dome. What do *you* think about the presence of what many consider an emblem of slavery?

"As a Southerner, I simply want to display the Confederate flag as an important symbol of my heritage and history. My hatred of niggers has nothing to do with it."

**Jesse Lee Willis**
**Auto Mechanic**

"If they can still fly the Nazi flag over the capitol in Berlin, South Carolina should have the right to fly the Stars and Bars. What? When did that happen?"

**Denise Schourek**
**Massage Therapist**

"I'm from the South, my daddy's from the South, and my daddy's daddy's from the South. All three of us are from the South."

**Knox Williams**
**Banker**

"Hasn't South Carolina learned anything since the days of the Civil War? On second thought, I think I'd rather not know the answer to that question."

**Anthony Banks**
**Systems Analyst**

"It is unconscionable that, in this day and age, that ugly symbol of racism is painted on the roof of the General Lee. Sheriff Roscoe should teach them Duke boys a lesson."

**Oscar Haney**
**Delivery Driver**

"If I were a citizen of South Carolina, I'd be deeply ashamed. Now, what's this about a flag?"

**Irene Lewis**
**Actuary**